… The Complete Book of
Modern Asian

Editorial director Susan Tomnay
Creative director Hieu Chi Nguyen
Editor Stephanie Kistner
Feature writers Karen Hammial, Sarah Schwikkard
Designer Caryl Wiggins
Food director Pamela Clark
Food editor Cathie Lonnie
Nutritional information Belinda Farlow

Sales director Brian Cearnes
Marketing manager Bridget Cody
Business analyst Ashley Davies

Chief executive officer Ian Law
Group publisher Pat Ingram
General manager Christine Whiston
Editorial director (AWW) Deborah Thomas

The publishers would like to thank the following for props used in photography:
Moa & More, Surry Hills;
Beautiful on the inside, Surry Hills.

Photographers Alan Benson, Steve Brown, Luke Burgess, Scott Cameron, Chris Chen, Gerry Colley, Joshua Dasey, Ben Dearnley, Sue Ferris, Joe Filshie, Adrian Lander, Louise Lister, Andre Martin, Rob Palmer, Prue Ruscoe, Stuart Scott, George Seper, Brett Stevens, John Paul Urizar, Ian Wallace, Andrew Young, Tanya Zouev
Stylists Wendy Berecry, Julz Beresford, Janelle Bloom, Margot Braddon, Kate Brown, Kirsty Cassidy, Marie-Helene Clauzon, Kay Francis, Yale Grinham, Jane Hann, Mary Harris, Trish Heagerty, Opel Khan, Amber Keller, Michaela Le Compte, Vicki Liley, David Morgan, Kate Murdoch, Michelle Noerianto, Sarah O'Brien, Justine Osborne, Louise Pickford, Christine Rooke, Stephanie Souvlis, Linda Venturoni-Wilson

Cover and chapter opener photography
Photographer Joshua Dasey
Stylist Margot Braddon
Home economist Amanda Lennon

Produced by ACP Books, published by ACP Books, a division of ACP Magazines Ltd.
54 Park St, Sydney NSW Australia 2000. GPO Box 4088, Sydney, NSW 2001.
Phone +61 2 9282 8618 Fax +61 2 9267 9438
acpbooks@acpmagazines.com.au www.acpbooks.com.au
To order books, phone 136 116. Send recipe enquiries to recipeenquiries@acpmagazines.com.au
Printed by C&C Offset Printing, 4/F C&C Building, 36 Ting Lai Road, Tai Po, Hong Kong.

Rights enquiries Laura Bamford, Director ACP Books. lbamford@acpuk.com

Australia Distributed by Network Services, GPO Box 4088, Sydney, NSW 2001.
Phone +61 2 9282 8777 Fax +61 2 9264 3278 networkweb@networkservicescompany.com.au
United Kingdom Distributed by Australian Consolidated Press (UK), 10 Scirocco Close, Moulton Park Office Village, Northampton NN3 6AP.
Phone +44 1604 642 200 Fax +44 1604 642 300 books@acpuk.com www.acpuk.com
New Zealand Distributed by Netlink Distribution Company, ACP Media Centre, Cnr Fanshawe and Beaumont Streets, Westhaven, Auckland. PO Box 47906, Ponsonby, Auckland, NZ.
Phone +64 9 366 9966 Fax 0800 277 412 ask@ndc.co.nz
South Africa Distributed by PSD Promotions, 30 Diesel Road Isando, Gauteng Johannesburg. PO Box 1175, Isando 1600, Gauteng Johannesburg.
Phone +27 11 392 6065/6/7 Fax +27 11 392 6079/80 orders@psdprom.co.za

Clark, Pamela.
The Australian women's weekly: the complete book of modern asian.

ISBN 978-1-86396-593-4

1. Cookery, Asian. I. Clark, Pamela. II. Title. III. Title: Complete book of modern Asian.
IV. Title: Australian women's weekly.

641.595

© ACP Magazines Ltd 2007
ABN 18 053 273 546

This publication is copyright. No part of it may be reproduced or transmitted in any form without the written permission of the publishers.

The Australian Women's Weekly

The Complete Book of Modern Asian

China • Thailand • Vietnam • Malaysia • Japan

acp books

contents

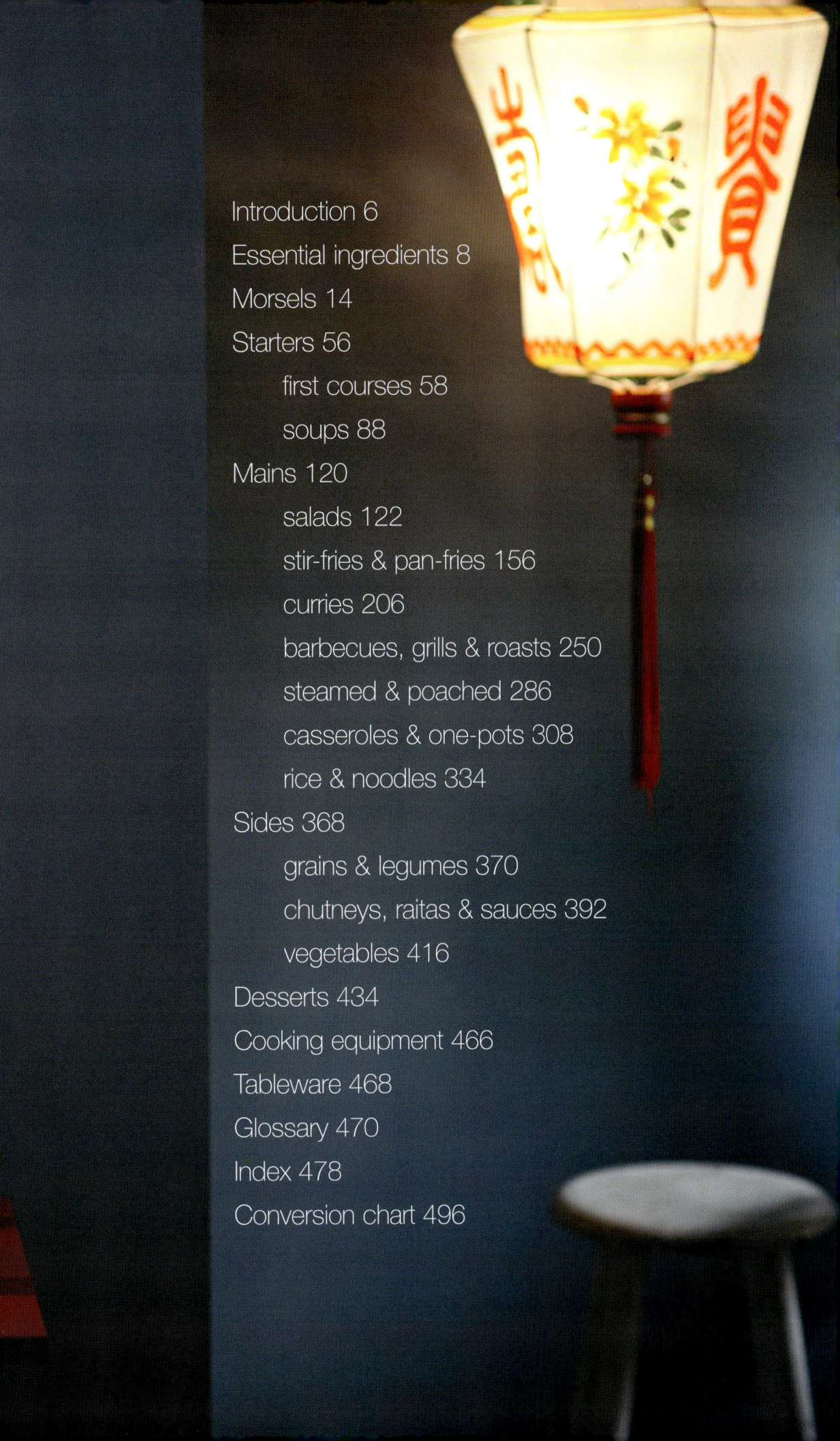

Introduction 6
Essential ingredients 8
Morsels 14
Starters 56
    first courses 58
    soups 88
Mains 120
    salads 122
    stir-fries & pan-fries 156
    curries 206
    barbecues, grills & roasts 250
    steamed & poached 286
    casseroles & one-pots 308
    rice & noodles 334
Sides 368
    grains & legumes 370
    chutneys, raitas & sauces 392
    vegetables 416
Desserts 434
Cooking equipment 466
Tableware 468
Glossary 470
Index 478
Conversion chart 496

introduction

We've come round to regarding the wonderful food of Asia, particularly Southeast Asia, as if it were our own – both on our neighbourhood takeaway menus and our domestic shopping lists. Green curry, spring rolls, sushi and laksa nestle compatibly with pizza, fish and chips, tomatoes and chops. Simple to prepare, quick to cook and wide-ranging in appeal, this immensely varied and healthy food comfortably fits the way we live today. The recipes inside will both widen your repertoire and excite your passions as you discover the infinite possibilities of the food of Asia.

Essential ingredients

daikon

betel leaves

BETEL LEAVES Grown and consumed in India and throughout South-East Asia, betel leaves are used raw as a wrap, cooked as a vegetable, or chopped and used as both a herb and a medicine. They are available at some greengrocers and most Asian food stores, especially those specialising in Vietnamese produce.
BUK CHOY Also known as bok choy, pak choi, chinese white cabbage or chinese chard; has a fresh, mild mustard taste. Use both stems and leaves, stir-fried or braised. Baby buk choy, also known as pak kat farang or shanghai bok choy, is much smaller and more tender than buk choy.

CHOY SUM Also known as pakaukeio or flowering cabbage, choy sum is a member of the buk choy family. Easy to identfy with its long stems, pale green leaves and yellow flowers, it's eaten, stems and all, steamed or sitr-fried.
DAIKON Popular in Japan, this long, white radish has a wonderful, sweet flavour. After peeling, eat it raw in salads or shredded as a garnish; it is also great when sliced or cubed and cooked in stir-fries and casseroles.
The flesh is white, but the skin can be either white or black; buy those that are firm and unwrinkled from Asian food stores.

kaffir lime leaves

choy sum

Essential Ingredients

galangal

gai lan

GAI LAN Is a member of the cabbage family, and is also known as chinese kale and chinese broccoli; this green vegetable is appreciated more for its stems than its coarse leaves. It is similar in texture to regular broccoli, but milder in taste. Gai lan can be served steamed and stir-fried, in soups and noodle dishes.

GALANGAL Also called ka or lengkaus if fresh and laos if dried and powdered. A rhizome with a hot ginger-citrusy flavour; looks like ginger but is dense, fibrous and harder to cut. Used similarly to ginger and garlic as a seasoning and an ingredient. Fresh ginger can be used for fresh galangal, but the flavour of the dish will not be the same.

HOKKIEN NOODLES Also known as stir-fry noodles; are fresh wheat noodles resembling thick, yellow-brown spaghetti needing no pre-cooking before being used.

KAFFIR LIME LEAVES Also known as bai magrood; look like two glossy dark-green leaves joined end to end, forming a rounded hourglass shape. Used fresh or dried, like bay leaves or curry leaves, in many Asian dishes. Sold fresh, dried or frozen, the dried leaves are less potent so double the number called for in a recipe if you substitute them for fresh leaves. A strip of fresh lime peel may be substituted for each kaffir lime leaf.

buk choy

hokkien noodles

baby buk choy

lemon grass

palm sugar

LEMON GRASS Also known as takrai, serai or serah. A tall, clumping, lemon-smelling and tasting, sharp-edged aromatic tropical grass; the white lower part of the stem is used, finely chopped, in much of the cooking of South-East Asia. Can be found, fresh, dried, powdered and frozen, in supermarkets and greengrocers, as well as Asian food stores.
NORI Is a type of dried seaweed used in Japanese cooking. Sold in thin sheets, plain or toasted (yaki-nori) and used for making sushi. The thin, dark sheets are usually a dark purplish-black, but they turn green and acquire a pleasant, nutty flavour when toasted. Also available shredded (ao-nori), for use as a flavouring or a garnish. It is available from Asian food stores and most supermarkets.
PALM SUGAR Also known as jaggery, jawa melaka and gula melaka; from the coconut palm. Dark brown to black in colour; usually sold in rock-hard cakes.
RICE NOODLES Are a common form of noodle used throughout South East Asia. Chewy and pure white, they do not need pre-cooking before use.
SICHUAN PEPPERCORNS Also known as szechuan or chinese pepper, a mildly hot spice that comes from the prickly ash tree. Although it is not related

thai basil

sichuan peppercorns

Essential Ingredients

wasabi paste

nori: shredded & toasted sheets

to the peppercorn family, small, red-brown aromatic sichuan berries look like black peppercorns and have a distinctive peppery-lemon flavour and aroma. Available from Asian food stores and specialty spice stores.
SOBA NOODLES Also known as buckwheat noodles, are made from various proportions of buckwheat flour. Usually available dried, but can be purchased fresh from local noodle makers.
STAR ANISE The dried, star-shaped seed pod can be used whole as a flavouring and the seeds used alone as a spice; both can be used ground. While it does have a slight liquorice-like taste, it should not be compared to or confused with anise, being far more spicily pungent, with overtones of clove and cinnamon. Available from supermarkets and Asian food stores.
TAMARIND Is the product of a native tropical African tree. Dried tamarind is reconstituted in a hot liquid which gives a sweet-sour, astringent taste to food.
TAT SOI Also known as pak choy and chinese flat cabbage, tat soi is a variety of bok choy. Its dark green leaves are cut into sections rather than separated and used in soups, braises and stir-fries. Available from some supermarkets and greengrocers.

star anise

soba noodles

water chestnuts

tamarind

THAI BASIL Is also known as horapa; it's different from holy basil and sweet basil in both look and taste, having smaller leaves and purplish stems. It has a slight aniseed taste and is one of the identifying flavours of Thai food. This basil is available from Asian food stores, some specialist fruit and vegetable shops and supermarkets.

TOFU Also known as bean curd, tofu is an off-white, custard-like product made from the milk of crushed soy beans. Available fresh as soft or firm, and processed as fried or pressed dried sheets. Silken tofu refers to the method by which it is made – where it is strained through silk. Available from supermarkets and Asian food stores.

TURMERIC Also known as kamin; is a rhizome related to galangal and ginger, must be grated or pounded to release its somewhat acrid aroma and pungent flavour. Known for the golden colour it imparts to dishes. Fresh turmeric can be substituted with the more common dried powder (use 2 teaspoons of ground turmeric plus a teaspoon of sugar for every 20g of fresh turmeric called for in a recipe).

VIETNAMESE MINT Is not a mint at all, but a pungent and peppery narrow-leafed member of the

vietnamese mint

tofu (firm)

Essential Ingredients

rice noodles

tat soi

buckwheat family. Not confined to Vietnam, it is also known as cambodian mint, pak pai (Thailand), laksa leaf (Indonesia), daun kesom (Singapore), and rau ram in Vietnam. It is a common ingredient in Asian foods, particularly soups, salads and stir-fries.
WASABI An Asian horseradish used to make the pungent, green-coloured paste traditionally served with Japanese raw fish dishes. Available, in powdered or paste form, wasabi can be found in supermarkets and Asian food stores.
WATER CHESTNUTS Resemble chestnuts in appearance, hence the English name. They are small brown tubers with a crisp, white, nutty-tasting flesh. Their crunchy texture is best experienced fresh, however, canned water chestnuts are more easily obtained and can be kept about a month, once opened, under refrigeration.
WOMBOK Also known as chinese cabbage, peking cabbage, wong bok or petsai. Elongated in shape with pale green, crinkly leaves, this is the most common cabbage in South-East Asia; forms the basis of the pickled Korean condiment, kim chi, and provides the crunch in Vietnamese rice paper rolls. Shredded or chopped, it's eaten raw or braised, steamed or stir-fried.

wombok

turmeric

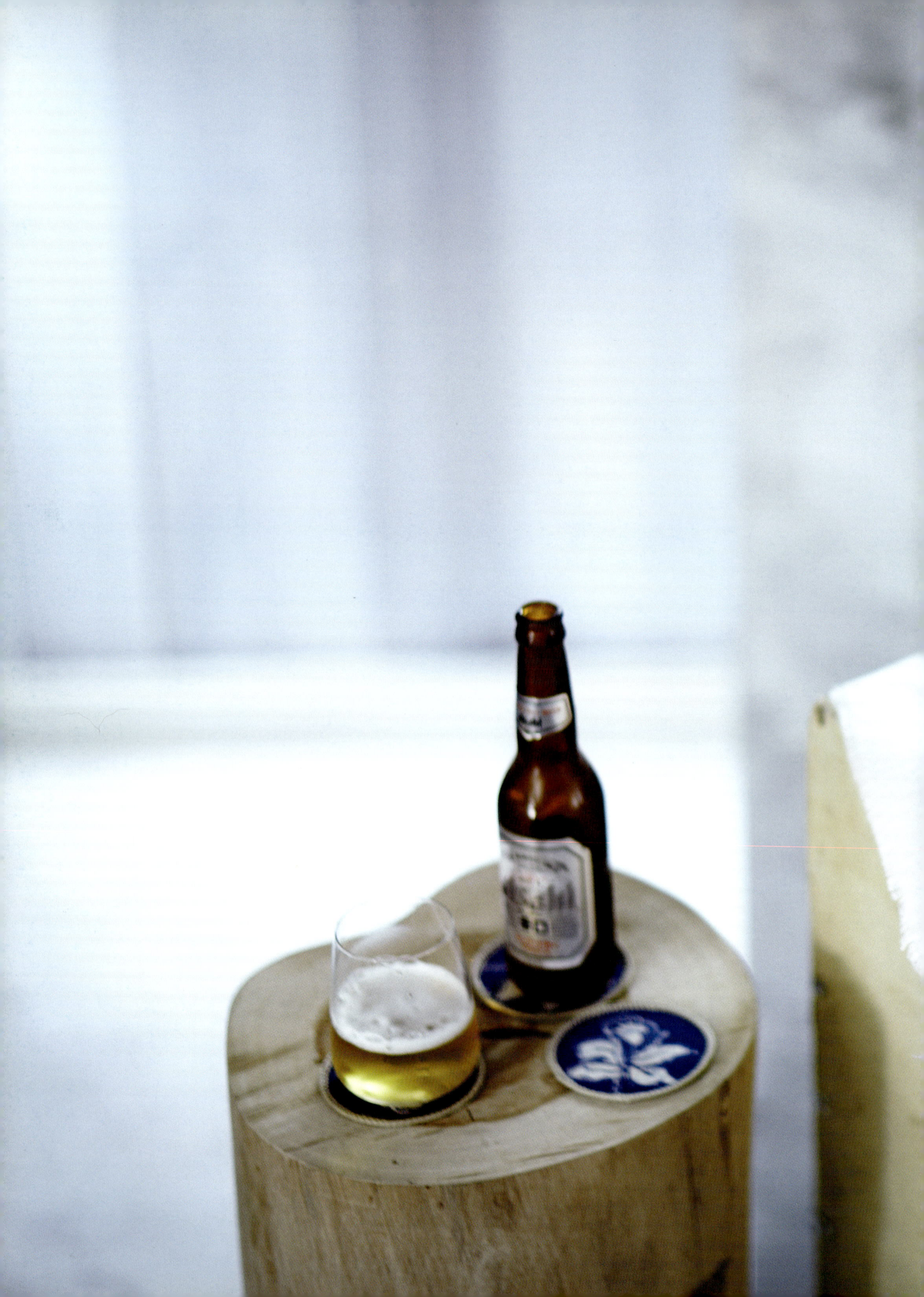

Morsels

Many Asian snacks, dips and street-foods easily translate into simple and simply delicious savoury finger foods and appetisers which welcome everyone to the table and excite the collective palate. This inventive selection, with its emphasis on fresh ingredients, ease of preparation and visual appeal, sets the tone for the meal that lies ahead.

spicy teriyaki tuna *page 37*

lime and coconut prawns *page 41*

mini scallop and lime kebabs *page 45*

thai-style oysters *page 37*

crisp potato and peanut cakes

preparation time 20 minutes
cooking time 50 minutes makes 36

3 medium potatoes (600g)
250g tapioca
2 tablespoons finely chopped peanuts
½ cup finely chopped fresh coriander
2 long green chillies, chopped finely
4cm piece fresh ginger (20g), grated
1 tablespoon sunflower oil
1 teaspoon cumin seeds
¼ teaspoon ground tumeric
sunflower oil, for shallow-frying, extra

TOMATO AND ONION RAITA
1 teaspoon black mustard seeds
500g yogurt
2 medium ripe tomatoes (300g), seeded, chopped finely
2 spring onions, chopped finely
½ cup finely chopped fresh coriander

1 Boil, steam or microwave potatoes until soft; drain. Cool slightly; mash in medium bowl until smooth.
2 Place tapioca in large heatproof bowl; cover with boiling water. Stand 10 minutes; drain.
3 Add tapioca to the potato with peanuts, coriander, chilli and ginger.
4 Heat oil in small frying pan; cook cumin seeds, stirring until fragrant. Stir in tumeric. Add seed mixture to potato mixture; mix well.
5 Form heaped tablespoons of the potato mixture into patties. Heat extra oil in large frying pan; shallow-fry patties, in batches, until browned both sides. Drain on absorbent paper.
6 Make tomato and onion raita; serve with patties.
TOMATO AND ONION RAITA
Dry-fry mustard seeds in small frying pan until seeds begin to pop; transfer to medium bowl. Stir in yogurt, tomatoes, onion and coriander.
per cake 2.2g total fat (0.5g saturated fat); 263kJ (63 cal); 9.1g carbohydrate; 1.3g protein; 0.6g fibre

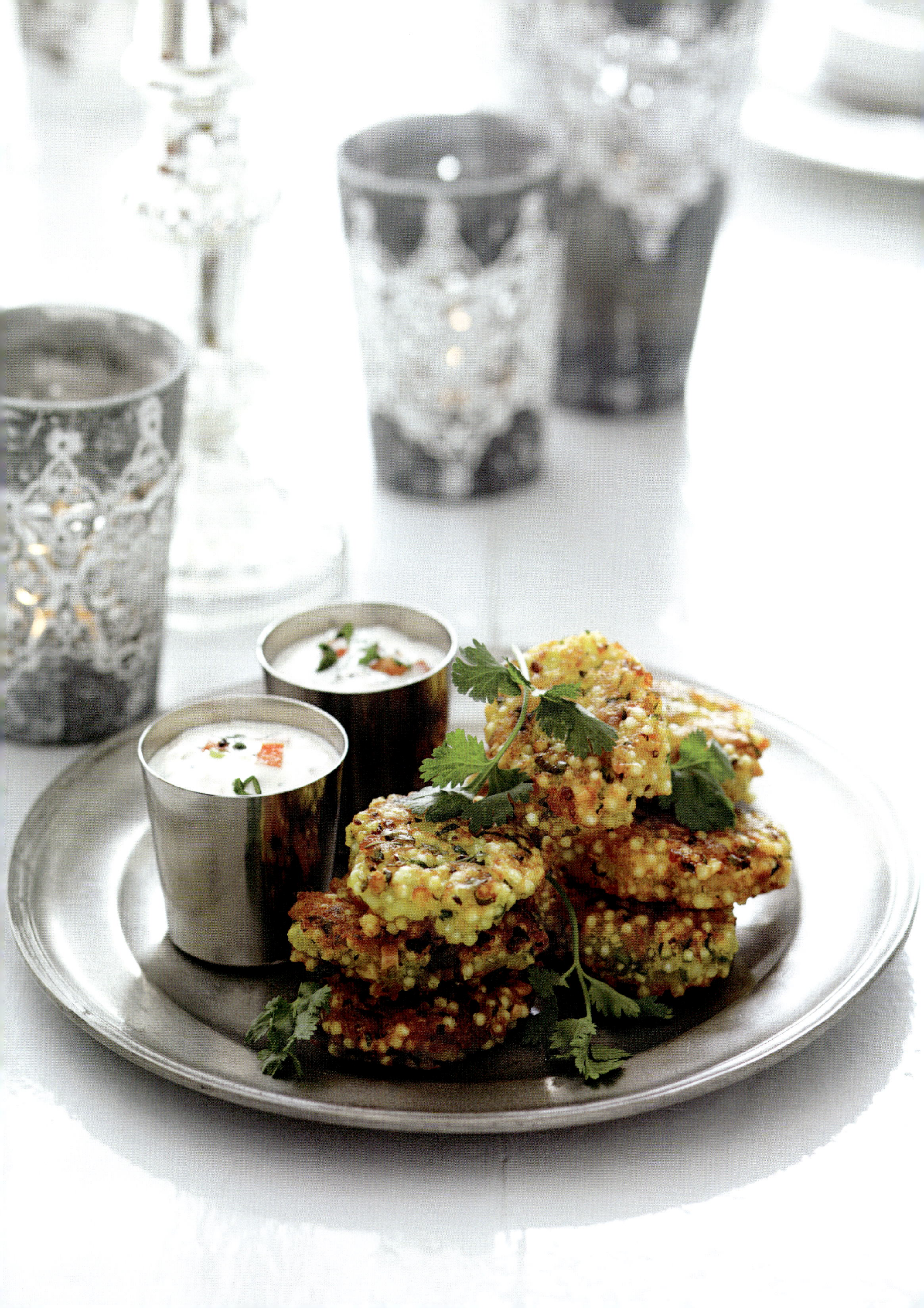

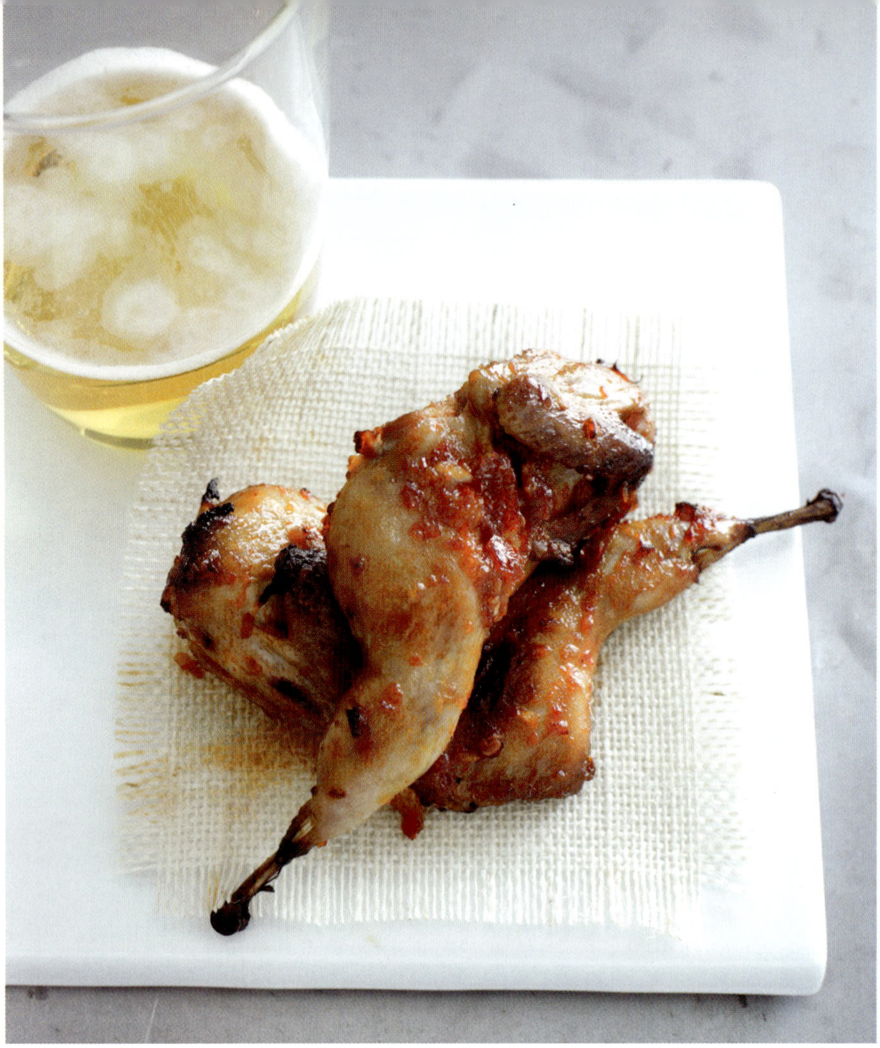

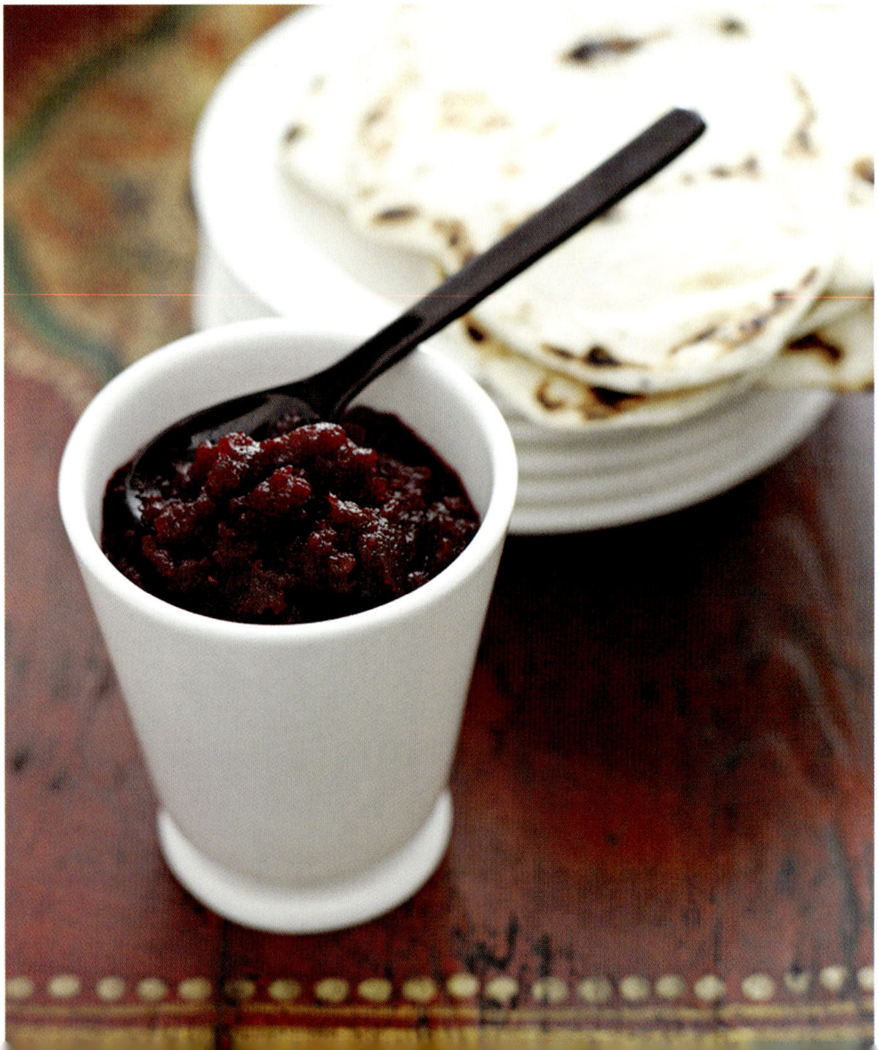

baked garlic and chilli quail

preparation time 15 minutes (plus refrigeration time)
cooking time 25 minutes serves 4

4 quails (640g)
4 cloves garlic, crushed
¼ cup (75g) sambal oelek
2 tablespoons honey
2 tablespoons light soy sauce
2 teaspoons brown sugar
2 tablespoons peanut oil

1 Cut quails in half through centre of breast bones and either side of backbone; discard backbone.
2 Combine quail, garlic, sambal oelek, honey, sauce, sugar and oil in medium bowl. Cover; refrigerate overnight.
3 Preheat oven to 180°C/160°C fan-forced.
4 Place quail on rack over baking dish; roast 15 minutes. Increase oven temperature to 220°C/200°C fan-forced; roast further 10 minutes or until quail are crisp and tender.
per serving 18.2g total fat (4.0g saturated fat); 1254kJ (300 cal); 18.2g carbohydrate; 15.9g protein; 0.5g fibre

beetroot dip

preparation time 10 minutes
cooking time 45 minutes makes 2½ cups

4 medium beetroot (700g)
1 teaspoon cumin seeds
2 teaspoons grated fresh ginger
1 tablespoon grated palm sugar

1 Wash beetroot, leaving skin on. Trim stem to about 3cm long. Cook beetroot, covered, in medium saucepan of salted water about 45 minutes or until tender; drain. Cool slightly.
2 Peel beetroot; chop coarsely. Blend or process beetroot until smooth; transfer to medium bowl.
3 Meanwhile, dry-fry cumin seeds in small frying pan until fragrant. Cool; crush seeds coarsely using a mortar and pestle.
4 Add cumin to beetroot with ginger and sugar; mix well.
5 Serve dip at room temperature with naan or pappadums, if desired.
per tablespoon 0g total fat (0g saturated fat); 42kJ (10 cal); 1.9g carbohydrate; 0.4g protein; 0.6g fibre

thai spring rolls

preparation time 20 minutes
cooking time 20 minutes (plus refrigeration time)
serves 4

20g rice vermicelli noodles
2 teaspoons peanut oil
100g pork mince
1 clove garlic, crushed
1 fresh small red thai chilli, chopped finely
1 green onion, chopped finely
1 small carrot (70g), grated finely
1 teaspoon finely chopped coriander root and stem mixture
1 teaspoon fish sauce
50g cooked small prawns, shelled, chopped finely
1 teaspoon cornflour
2 teaspoons water
12 x 12cm-square spring roll wrappers
vegetable oil, for deep-frying

CUCUMBER DIPPING SAUCE
1 lebanese cucumber (130g), seeded, sliced thinly
½ cup (110g) white sugar
¾ cup (180ml) water
⅓ cup (80ml) white vinegar
4cm piece fresh ginger (20g), grated finely
½ teaspoon salt
2 fresh small red thai chillies, sliced thinly
3 green onions, sliced thinly
1 tablespoon coarsely chopped fresh coriander

1 Place noodles in medium heatproof bowl; cover with boiling water. Stand until just tender; drain. Using kitchen scissors, cut noodles into random lengths.
2 Heat peanut oil in wok; stir-fry pork, garlic and chilli until pork is changed in colour. Add onion, carrot, coriander mixture, sauce and prawns; stir-fry until vegetables just soften. Place in small bowl with noodles; cool.
3 Blend cornflour with the water in another small bowl. Place 1 level tablespoon of the filling near one corner of each wrapper. Lightly brush edges of each wrapper with cornflour mixture; roll to enclose filling, folding in ends.
4 Make cucumber dipping sauce.
5 Heat vegetable oil in wok; deep-fry spring rolls, in batches, until browned lightly. Drain on absorbent paper
6 Serve spring rolls with dipping sauce.
CUCUMBER DIPPING SAUCE
Place cucumber in heatproof serving bowl. Place sugar, the water, vinegar, ginger and salt in small saucepan, stir over heat, without boiling until sugar is dissolved; pour over cucumber. Sprinkle with chilli, onion and coriander. Cover; refrigerate until cold.
per serving 11g total fat (2g saturated fat); 932kJ (223 cal); 19.3g carbohydrate; 10.7g protein; 2.1g fibre

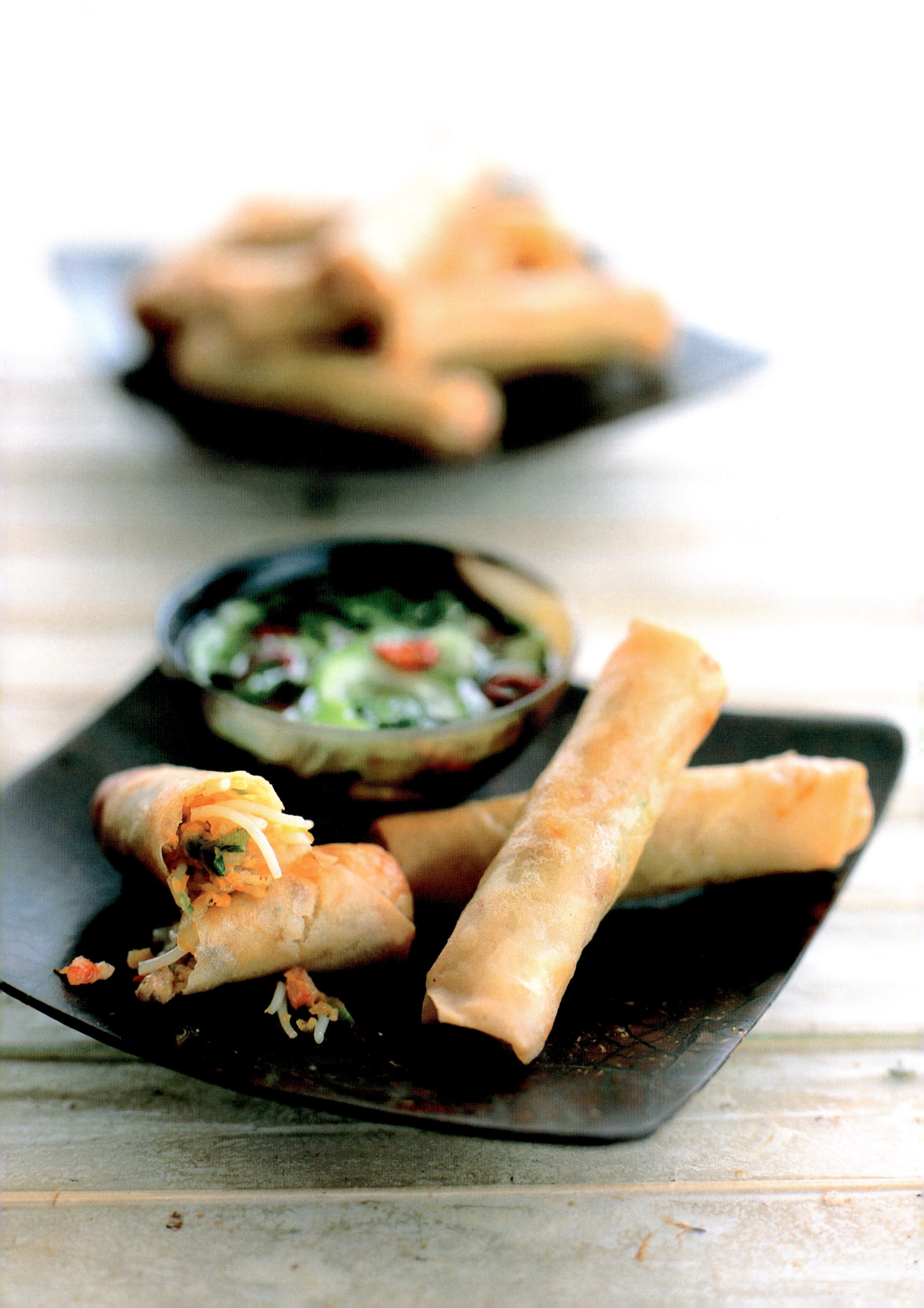

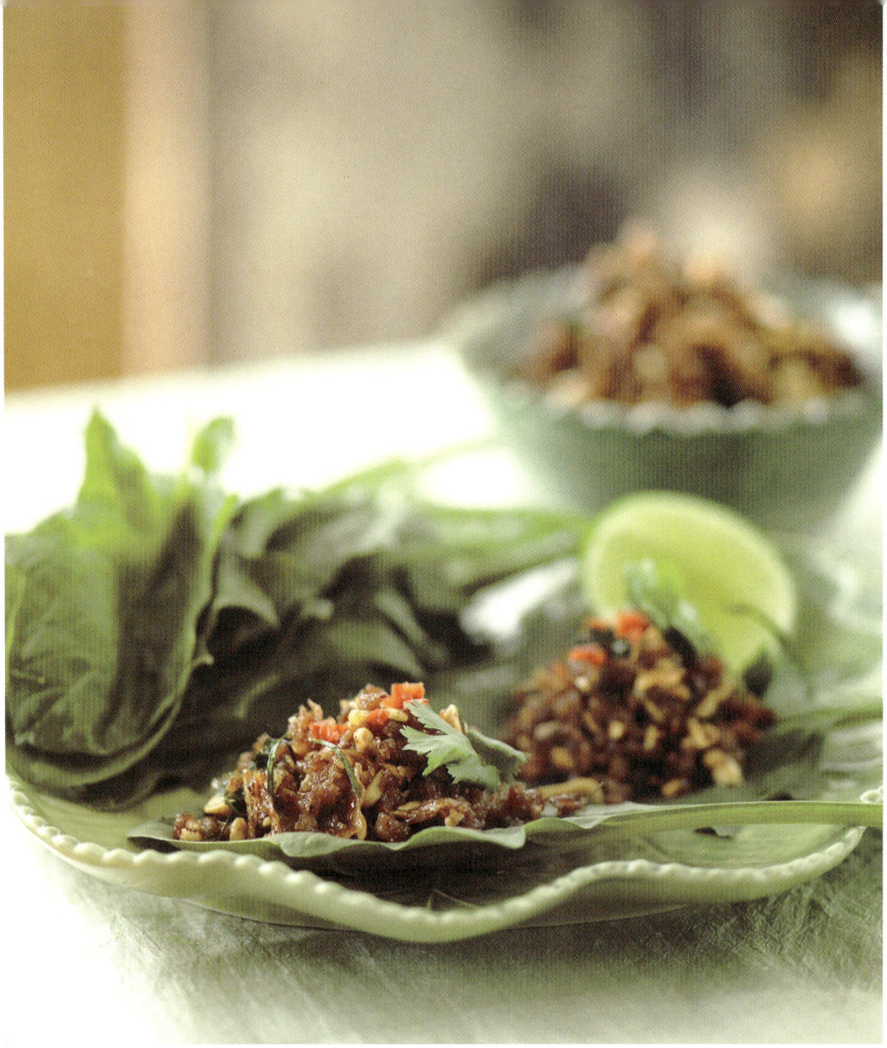

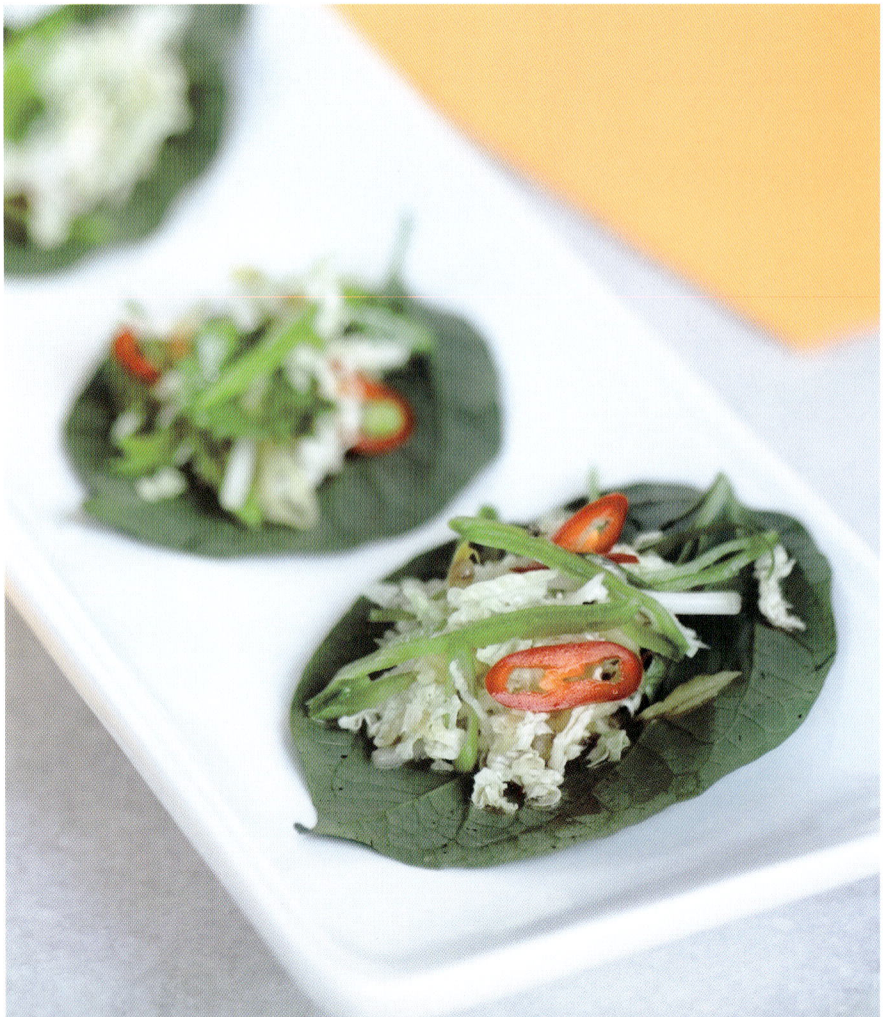

sticky pork with kaffir lime leaves

preparation time 20 minutes
cooking time 20 minutes serves 8

2 tablespoons peanut oil
300g minced pork
¾ cup (195g) grated palm sugar
⅓ cup (80ml) fish sauce
4 kaffir lime leaves, shredded thinly
½ cup (50g) deep-fried shallots
½ cup (50g) deep-fried garlic
½ cup (70g) coarsely chopped roasted unsalted peanuts
1½ cups lightly packed fresh coriander leaves
4 kaffir lime leaves, shredded thinly, extra
1 fresh long red chilli, sliced thinly
600g baby spinach leaves, trimmed
1 lime (60g), cut into wedges

CORIANDER PASTE
4 coriander roots
5 cloves garlic, chopped
12 white peppercorns

1 Heat half of the oil in large frying pan; cook pork, stirring, about 5 minutes or until browned lightly. Drain on absorbent paper; cool.
2 Meanwhile, make coriander paste.
3 Heat remaining oil in large frying pan; cook paste about 1 minute or until fragrant. Add sugar, sauce and lime leaves; simmer, uncovered, about 7 minutes or until mixture thickens.
4 Return pork to pan with half of the shallots, half of the garlic and half of the peanuts; cook, uncovered, about 5 minutes or until mixture is sticky.
5 Add remaining shallots, garlic and peanuts to mixture. Stir in 1 cup of the coriander and extra lime leaves.
6 Top pork mixture with chilli and remaining coriander; serve with spinach leaves and lime wedges.

CORIANDER PASTE
Wash coriander roots thoroughly; chop coarsely. Using a mortar and pestle or food mill, crush the coriander roots, garlic and peppercorns to form a smooth paste.
per serving 12.8g total fat (2.5g saturated fat); 1175kJ (281 cal); 26.4g carbohydrate; 13.3g protein; 3.6g fibre

green mango salad on betel leaves

preparation time 25 minutes
makes 24

½ small green mango (150g), grated coarsely
2 green onions, sliced thinly
1 fresh long red chilli, sliced thinly
½ cup (40g) bean sprouts
½ cup loosely packed fresh coriander leaves
50g snow peas, trimmed, sliced thinly
1 cup (80g) shredded wombok
3cm piece fresh ginger (15g), grated
2 tablespoons rice vinegar
1 tablespoon peanut oil
2 teaspoons mirin
2 teaspoons light soy sauce
24 large betel leaves

1 Place mango, onion, chilli, sprouts, coriander, snow peas and wombok in medium bowl with combined ginger, vinegar, oil, mirin and sauce; toss gently to combine.
2 Place one level tablespoon of the mango mixture on each leaf.
per leaf 0.8g total fat (0.1g saturated fat); 50kJ (12 cal); 0.8g carbohydrate; 0.3g protein; 0.3g fibre

curry puffs

preparation time 30 minutes (plus cooling time)
cooking time 35 minutes serves 4

2 teaspoons peanut oil
2 teaspoons finely chopped coriander root
2 green onions, chopped finely
1 clove garlic, crushed
100g beef mince
½ teaspoon ground turmeric
½ teaspoon ground cumin
¼ teaspoon ground coriander
2 teaspoons fish sauce
1 tablespoon water
½ cup (110g) mashed potato
2 sheets ready-rolled frozen puff pastry
1 egg, beaten lightly
vegetable oil, for deep frying

1 Heat peanut oil in wok; stir-fry coriander root, onion, garlic and beef until beef is changed in colour. Add turmeric, cumin and ground coriander; stir-fry until fragrant. Add sauce and the water; simmer, uncovered, until mixture thickens. Stir in potato; cool.
2 Using 9cm cutter, cut four rounds from each pastry sheet. Place 1 level tablespoon of the filling in centre of each round; brush around edge lightly with egg. Fold pastry over to enclose filling, pressing edges together to seal.
3 Just before serving, heat vegetable oil in large saucepan. Deep-fry curry puffs, in batches, until crisp and browned lightly; drain on absorbent paper.
4 Serve hot curry puffs with sweet chilli dipping sauce (see page 414).
per serving 33.6g total fat (4.2g saturated fat); 2040kJ (488 cal); 33.9g carbohydrate; 12.5g protein; 1.8g fibre
TIP *You need to cook 150g potatoes for ½ cup mash.*

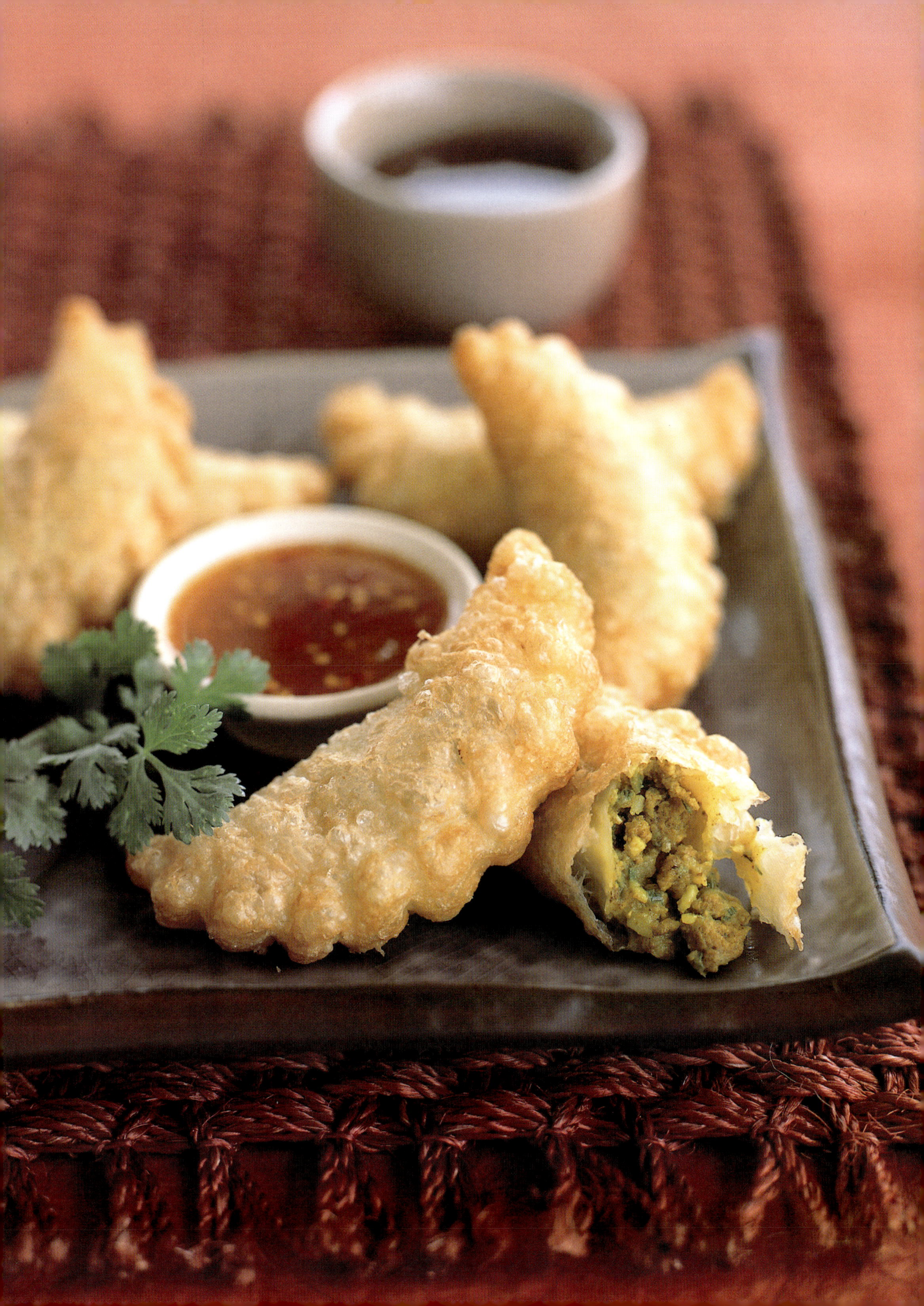

The Complete Book of Modern Asian

spicy butterflied prawns on crisp wontons

preparation time 25 minutes
cooking time 15 minutes serves 4

4 x 9cm-square wonton wrappers
1kg uncooked medium king prawns
vegetable oil, for shallow-frying
1 tablespoon peanut oil
2 cloves garlic, crushed
1 fresh small red thai chilli, sliced thinly
1 tablespoon lime juice
2 tablespoons sweet chilli sauce
3 green onions, sliced thinly
2 teaspoons roasted sesame seeds

SEASONING
½ teaspoon black peppercorns
¼ teaspoon coriander seeds
¾ teaspoon sea salt flakes
¼ teaspoon lemon pepper

1 Cut wrappers in half diagonally. Shell and devein prawns, leaving tails intact. Cut along back of prawns, taking care not to cut all the way through; flatten slightly.
2 Heat vegetable oil in wok; shallow-fry wrappers, in batches, until browned lightly, drain on absorbent paper. Reheat oil; shallow-fry prawns, in batches, about 30 seconds or until prawns are almost tender and just changed in colour. Drain on absorbent paper.
3 Meanwhile, make seasoning.
4 Heat peanut oil in same cleaned wok; stir-fry garlic and chilli until fragrant. Add prawns, juice, sauce and seasoning; stir-fry until heated through. Stir in onion.
5 Serve prawns on wontons wrappers; sprinkle with sesame seeds.

SEASONING
Lightly crush peppercorns and seeds using mortar and pestle; stir in salt and lemon pepper.

per serving 19.8g total fat (2.8g saturated fat); 1321kJ (316 cal); 7.0g carbohydrate; 27.1g protein; 1.0g fibre

sticky-glazed pork with pineapple

preparation time 10 minutes (plus refrigeration time)
cooking time 15 minutes makes 32

2 pork fillets (600g)
2 tablespoons char sui sauce
1 tablespoon light soy sauce
½ small pineapple (450g), sliced thinly
½ cup (25g) snow pea sprouts, trimmed

1 Combine pork and sauces in large bowl. Cover; refrigerate 1 hour.
2 Cook pineapple on heated oiled grill plate (or grill or barbecue) until browned lightly. Remove from grill, cover to keep warm. Halve slices.
3 Cook pork over low heat on same grill plate, covered, about 10 minutes or until cooked. Cover; stand 5 minutes, slice thinly.
4 Top pineapple with 2 slices of pork then sprouts.

per piece 0.5g total fat (0.2g saturated fat); 117kJ (28 cal); 1.3g carbohydrate; 4.3g protein; 0.3g fibre

samosas with tamarind sauce

preparation time 40 minutes (plus cooling time)
cooking time 30 minutes makes 48

1 small brown onion (80g), chopped finely
1 clove garlic, crushed
2 teaspoons ground cumin
1 tablespoon medium curry paste
300g lamb mince
2 tablespoons finely chopped fresh coriander
1 small kumara (250g), chopped finely
¼ cup (60ml) chicken stock
1 tablespoon lime juice
¼ cup (30g) frozen peas
3 sheets ready-rolled shortcrust pastry
1 egg, beaten lightly

TAMARIND SAUCE
2 tablespoons tamarind paste
2 tablespoons finely chopped fresh lemon grass
2 tablespoons finely grated palm sugar
⅓ cup (80ml) orange juice

1 Cook onion, garlic, cumin and curry paste in medium frying pan, stirring, until onion softens. Add lamb; cook, stirring, until lamb changes colour. Stir in coriander, kumara, stock and lime juice; bring to a boil. Reduce heat, simmer, uncovered, until kumara softens. Stir in peas; simmer, uncovered, until most of the liquid has evaporated. Cool.
2 Preheat oven to 200°C/180°C fan-forced. Oil two oven trays.
3 Cut each pastry sheet into 16 squares. Divide lamb mixture among squares, brushing edges with a little egg. Bring four corners of each square together in centre, pressing together to enclose filling.
4 Place samosas on trays; brush tops with remaining egg. Bake, uncovered, about 15 minutes or until browned lightly.
5 Meanwhile, make tamarind sauce.
6 Serve hot samosas with sauce.
TAMARIND SAUCE
Cook ingredients in small saucepan, stirring, over low heat until smooth.

per samosa 3.6g total fat (1.8g saturated fat); 268kJ (64 cal); 5.4g carbohydrate; 2.3g protein; 0.4g fibre
per teaspoon tamarind sauce 0g total fat (0g saturated fat); 21kJ (5 cal); 1.1g carbohydrate; 0g protein; 0g fibre

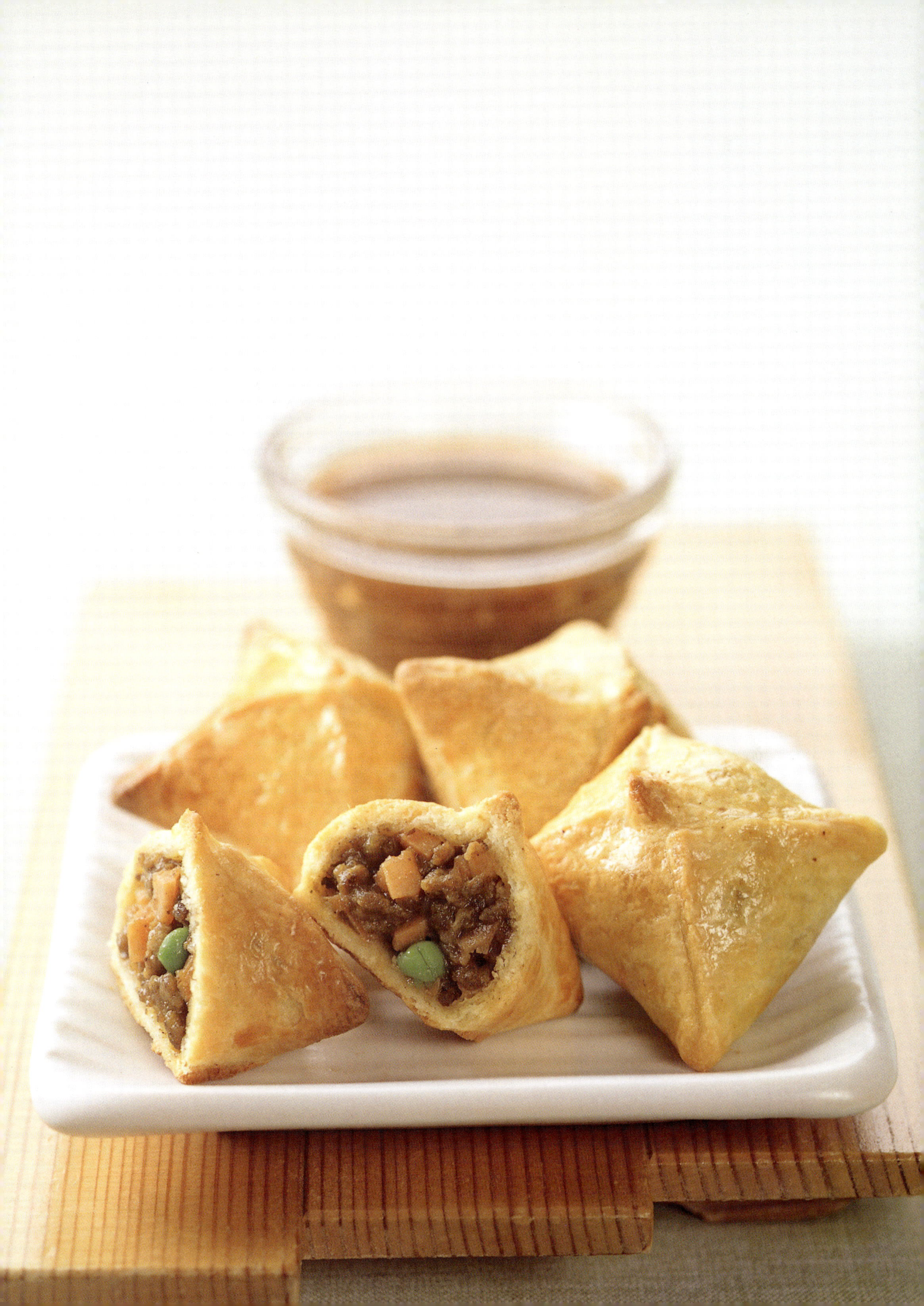

The Complete Book of Modern Asian

sushi rice

preparation time 10 minutes (plus standing time)
cooking time 15 minutes makes 2 cups

1 cup (200g) koshihikari rice
1 cup (250ml) water
SUSHI VINEGAR
2 tablespoons rice vinegar
1 tablespoon sugar
¼ teaspoon salt

1 Place rice in large bowl, fill with cold water, stir with one hand; drain. Repeat process two or three times until water is almost clear. Drain rice in strainer 30 minutes.
2 Meanwhile, prepare sushi vinegar.
3 Place drained rice and the water in medium saucepan, cover tightly; bring to a boil. Reduce heat, simmer, covered tightly, over low heat about 12 minutes or until water is absorbed. Remove from heat; stand, covered, 10 minutes.
4 Spread rice in large non-metallic bowl. Using large flat wooden spoon or plastic spatula, repeatedly slice through rice at a sharp angle to break up lumps and separate grains, gradually pouring in sushi vinegar. Not all of the vinegar may be required; the rice shouldn't become wet.
5 Continue to lift and turn rice with spoon, from outside to centre of bowl, about 5 minutes or until rice is almost cool. Cover rice with damp cloth while making sushi variations of your choice.
SUSHI VINEGAR
Stir ingredients in small bowl until sugar dissolves.
per ¼ cup 0.1g total fat (0g saturated fat); 414kJ (99 cal); 22.3g carbohydrate; 1.7g protein; 0.2g fibre
TIP *Sushi rice can be made up to 4 hours ahead. Cover; refrigerate until required.*

tuna and cucumber mini maki

preparation time 30 minutes
makes 48

4 sheets toasted seaweed (yaki-nori)
2 cups prepared sushi rice (see above)
2 teaspoons wasabi paste
120g piece sashimi tuna, cut into 5mm strips
1 lebanese cucumber (130g), seeded, cut into thin strips
¼ cup (60ml) japanese soy sauce

1 Fold one sheet of seaweed in half parallel with lines marked on rough side of sheet; cut along fold. Place a half sheet, shiny-side down, lengthways across bamboo mat about 2cm from edge closest to you.
2 Dip fingers in bowl of vinegared water; shake off excess. Mould ¼ cup of the rice into oblong shape; place across centre half of seaweed. Wet fingers again; gently rake rice evenly over seaweed, leaving 2cm strip at far end of seaweed uncovered.
3 Swipe a dab of wasabi across centre of rice. Place tuna strips, end to end, in a row over wasabi across centre of rice; repeat with cucumber.
4 Starting with edge closest to you, pick up mat with thumb and index finger of both hands; use remaining fingers to hold filling in place as you roll mat. Roll forward, pressing gently but tightly, wrapping seaweed around rice and filling. When roll is complete, the strip of uncovered seaweed will stick to the roll to form a join.
5 Unroll mat; place sushi roll, join-down, on board. Cut roll into six pieces with sharp knife. Repeat process with remaining seaweed, rice, wasabi, tuna and cucumber.
6 Serve immediately with soy sauce and more wasabi, if desired.
per mini maki 0.2g total fat (0.1g saturated fat); 88kJ (21 cal); 3.7g carbohydrate; 1g protein; 0.2g fibre

asian star
money bags

preparation time 30 minutes
cooking time 20 minutes
makes 12 money bags & 1½ cups dipping sauce

1 tablespoon peanut oil
1 small brown onion (80g), chopped finely
1 clove garlic, crushed
1 tablespoon grated fresh ginger
100g chicken mince
1 tablespoon finely grated palm sugar
1 tablespoon finely chopped roasted unsalted peanuts
2 teaspoons finely chopped fresh coriander
3 green onions
24 x 8cm-square wonton wrappers
vegetable oil, for deep-frying

PEANUT DIPPING SAUCE
1 tablespoon peanut oil
2 cloves garlic, crushed
1 small brown onion (80g), chopped finely
2 fresh small red chillies, chopped coarsely
10cm stick fresh lemon grass (20g), chopped finely
¾ cup (180ml) coconut milk
2 tablespoons fish sauce
¼ cup (55g) dark brown sugar
½ cup (140g) crunchy peanut butter
½ teaspoon curry powder
1 tablespoon lime juice

1 Heat peanut oil in wok; stir-fry onion, garlic and ginger until onion softens. Add chicken; stir-fry until chicken is changed in colour. Add sugar; stir-fry about 3 minutes or until sugar dissolves. Stir nuts and coriander into filling mixture.
2 Cut upper green half of each onion into four long slices; discard remaining onion half. Submerge onion strips in hot water for a few seconds to make pliable.
3 Place 12 wrappers on chopping board; cover each wrapper with another, placed on the diagonal to form star shape. Place rounded teaspoons of the filling mixture in centre of each star; gather corners to form pouch shape. Tie green onion slice around neck of each pouch to hold closed; secure with toothpick.
4 Make dipping sauce (freeze excess for a future use).
5 Just before serving, heat vegetable oil in wok; deep-fry money bags, in batches, until crisp and browned lightly. Drain on absorbent paper; serve with dipping sauce.
PEANUT DIPPING SAUCE
Heat oil in small saucepan; cook garlic and onion until softened. Stir in remaining ingredients; bring to a boil. Reduce heat, simmer, stirring, about 2 minutes or until sauce thickens.
per money bag 5.1g total fat (0.9g saturated fat); 435kJ (104 cal); 10.8g carbohydrate; 3.8g protein; 0.6g fibre
per tablespoon dipping sauce 4.7g total fat (1.7g saturated fat); 251kJ (60 cal); 2.5g carbohydrate; 2.2g protein; 0.8g fibre

Stack pairs of the wrappers with the top one on a diagonal to form star shape.

Wrap the strips of onion around the neck of the pouches and secure them with toothpicks.

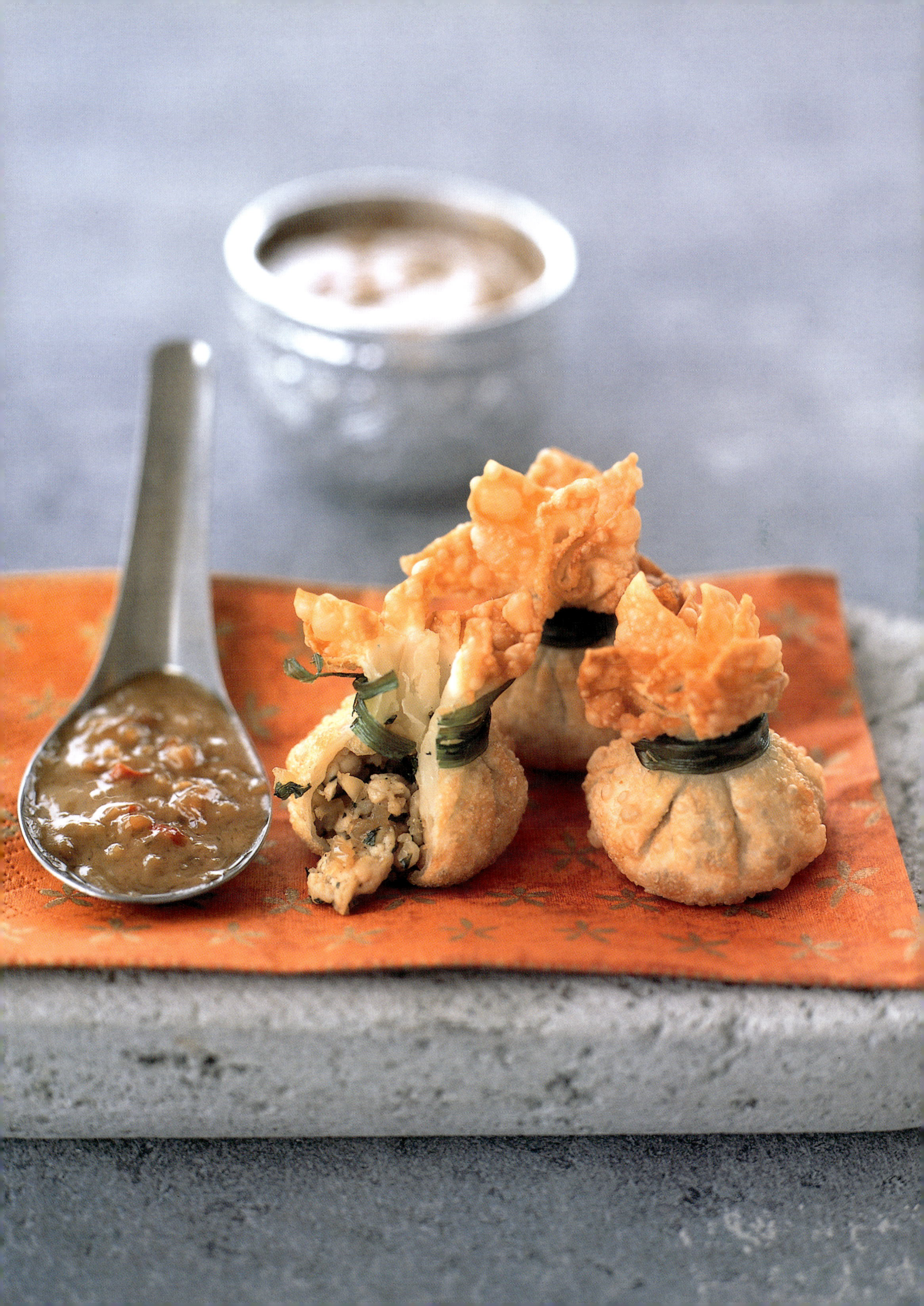

The Complete Book of Modern Asian

spicy teriyaki tuna

preparation time 30 minutes (plus refrigeration time)
cooking time 15 minutes makes 24

¾ cup (180ml) japanese soy sauce
2 tablespoons honey
¼ cup (60ml) mirin
1 tablespoon wasabi paste
1 teaspoon sesame oil
300g sashimi tuna steak
2 tablespoons thinly sliced drained pickled ginger

1 Combine sauce, honey, mirin, wasabi and oil in medium bowl; reserve ½ cup of marinade in small jug. Place tuna in bowl with remaining marinade; turn tuna to coat in marinade. Cover; refrigerate 3 hours or overnight. Drain tuna; discard marinade.
2 Cook tuna in heated oiled medium frying pan until browned both sides and cooked as desired (do not overcook as tuna has a tendency to dry out).
3 Cut tuna into 24 similar-sized pieces (approximately 2cm each).
4 Place chinese spoons on serving platter. Place one piece of tuna on each spoon; top with 1 teaspoon of the reserved marinade and a little ginger.
per spoon 0.9g total fat (0.3g saturated fat); 138kJ (33 cal); 2.2g carbohydrate; 3.6g protein; 0.1g fibre

thai-style oysters

preparation time 30 minutes (plus refrigeration time)
makes 24

24 oysters, on the half shell
¼ cup (60ml) lime juice
1 tablespoon fish sauce
2 teaspoons white sugar
2 tablespoons coconut cream
1 baby onion (25g), sliced thinly
1 fresh long red chilli, sliced thinly
2 tablespoons finely chopped fresh coriander
2 tablespoons finely chopped fresh mint

1 Remove oysters from shells; discard shells.
2 Combine oysters in medium bowl with juice, sauce and sugar, cover; refrigerate 1 hour. Stir in coconut cream.
3 Combine onion, chilli and herbs in small bowl.
4 Place chinese spoons on serving platter. Place one undrained oyster on each spoon; top with herb mixture.
per spoon 0.6g total fat (0.4g saturated fat); 59kJ (14 cal); 0.6g carbohydrate; 1.4g protein; 0.1g fibre

pork and garlic chive-wrapped prawns

preparation time 30 minutes
cooking time 15 minutes serves 4

250g pork mince
2 tablespoons finely chopped fresh garlic chives
1 fresh small red thai chilli, chopped finely
2cm piece fresh ginger (10g), grated
12 uncooked large king prawns (840g)
12 x 12cm-square spring roll wrappers
2 tablespoons cornflour
¼ cup (60ml) water
peanut oil, for deep-frying

1 Combine mince, chives, chilli and ginger in medium bowl.
2 Shell and devein prawns, leaving tails intact. Cut along back of each prawn, without cutting all the way through; flatten prawns slightly.
3 Place spring roll wrapper on board; fold one corner up to meet centre. Place one flattened prawn onto wrapper; top prawn with 1 level tablespoon pork mixture. Brush around edges with blended cornflour and the water. Fold wrapper around filling, leaving tail exposed; press edges together to seal. Repeat with remaining prawns, pork mixture and wrappers.
4 Heat oil in wok; deep-fry prawns, in batches, until cooked. Drain on absorbent paper.
5 Serve prawns with sweet chilli or soy sauce, if desired.
per serving 15.7g total fat (3.7g saturated); 1359kJ (325 cal); 10.6g carbohydrate; 35.1g protein; 0.4g fibre

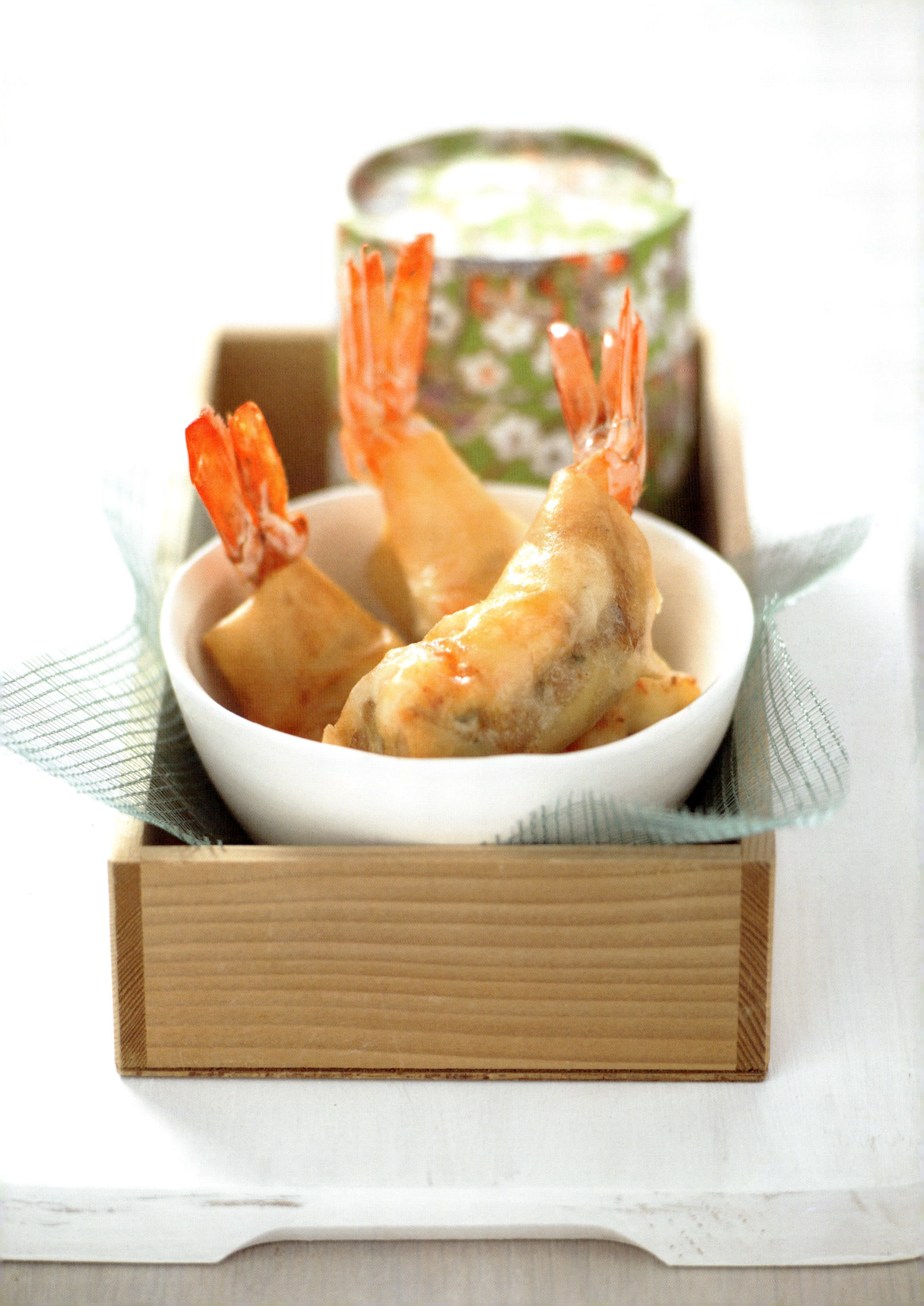

The Complete Book of Modern Asian

lime and coconut prawns

preparation time 15 minutes (plus refrigeration time)
cooking time 15 minutes makes 24

24 uncooked medium king prawns (1kg)
⅓ cup (80ml) lime juice
½ cup (125ml) coconut milk
½ cup (75g) plain flour
1½ cups (100g) shredded coconut
peanut oil, for deep-frying
PEANUT DIPPING SAUCE
⅓ cup (50g) toasted unsalted peanuts
⅓ cup (80ml) lime juice
¼ cup (60ml) chicken stock
¼ cup (60ml) coconut milk
2 tablespoons smooth peanut butter
1 tablespoon sweet chilli sauce

1 Shell and devein prawns, leaving tails intact. Combine prawns, juice and coconut milk in medium bowl. Cover; refrigerate 1 hour.
2 Meanwhile, make peanut dipping sauce.
3 Drain prawns; reserve marinade. Holding prawns by tail, coat in flour then reserved marinade, then in coconut. Heat oil in wok; deep-fry prawns, in batches, until brown. Drain.
4 Serve prawns with warm dipping sauce.
PEANUT DIPPING SAUCE
Combine nuts, juice, stock and coconut milk in small saucepan; bring to a boil. Reduce heat, simmer, uncovered, 5 minutes. Blend or process with peanut butter and sauce until smooth.
per prawn 8.6g total fat (4.5g saturated fat); 485kJ (116 cal); 3.6g carbohydrate; 6.2g protein; 1.3g fibre

gyoza with soy vinegar sauce

preparation time 40 minutes (plus refrigeration time)
cooking time 15 minutes makes 40

300g pork mince
2 tablespoons kecap manis
1 teaspoon sugar
1 tablespoon sake
1 egg, beaten lightly
2 teaspoons sesame oil
3 cups (240g) finely shredded wombok
4 green onions, sliced thinly
40 gyoza or gow gee wrappers
1 tablespoon vegetable oil
SOY VINEGAR SAUCE
½ cup (125ml) light soy sauce
¼ cup (60ml) red vinegar
2 tablespoons white vinegar
2 tablespoons sweet chilli sauce

1 Combine pork, kecap manis, sugar, sake, egg, sesame oil, cabbage and onion in large bowl. Cover; refrigerate 1 hour.
2 Place 1 heaped teaspoon of the pork mixture in centre of one wrapper; brush one edge of wrapper with a little water. Pleat damp side of wrapper only; pinch both sides together to seal. Repeat with remaining pork mixture and wrappers.
3 Cover base of large frying pan with water; bring to a boil. Add dumplings, in batches; reduce heat, simmer, covered, 3 minutes. Using slotted spoon, remove dumplings from pan. Drain pan; dry thoroughly.
4 Heat vegetable oil in same pan; cook dumplings, in batches, unpleated side and base only, until golden brown.
5 Make soy vinegar sauce; serve with hot gyozas.
SOY VINEGAR SAUCE
Combine ingredients in small bowl.
per gyoza 1.5g total fat (0.4g saturated fat); 176kJ (42 cal); 5.1g carbohydrate; 2g protein; 0.1g fibre

vietnamese chicken spring rolls

preparation time 1 hour
cooking time 25 minutes makes 40

1 medium red capsicum (200g)
1 tablespoon peanut oil
700g chicken breast fillets
4cm piece fresh ginger (20g), grated
2 cloves garlic, crushed
4 green onions, chopped finely
100g bean thread noodles
1 medium carrot (120g), cut into matchsticks
1 tablespoon coarsely chopped vietnamese mint
500g buk choy, sliced finely
¼ cup (60ml) sweet chilli sauce
1 tablespoon light soy sauce
40 spring roll wrappers
peanut oil, for deep-frying

1 Halve capsicum, discard seeds and membrane; slice into very thin strips.
2 Heat half of the oil in medium saucepan; cook chicken, in batches, until browned and cooked. Cool 10 minutes; shred finely.
3 Heat remaining oil in same pan; cook ginger, garlic and onion, stirring, about 2 minutes or until onion is soft.
4 Meanwhile, place noodles in medium heatproof bowl, cover with boiling water; stand until just tender, drain. Coarsely chop noodles.
5 Combine capsicum, carrot, chicken, onion mixture and noodles in large bowl with mint, buk choy and sauces.
6 Place 1 rounded tablespoon of the mixture across edge of one wrapper; roll to enclose filling, folding in ends. Place on tray, seam-side down. Repeat with remaining mixture and wrappers; place on tray in single layer.
7 Heat oil in wok; deep-fry spring rolls, in batches, until browned lightly and cooked through. Drain on absorbent paper.
8 Serve spring rolls with sweet chilli dipping sauce (see page 414), if desired.

per roll 3.8g total fat (0.7g saturated fat); 305kJ (73 cal); 4.6g carbohydrate; 4.8g protein; 0.6g fibre

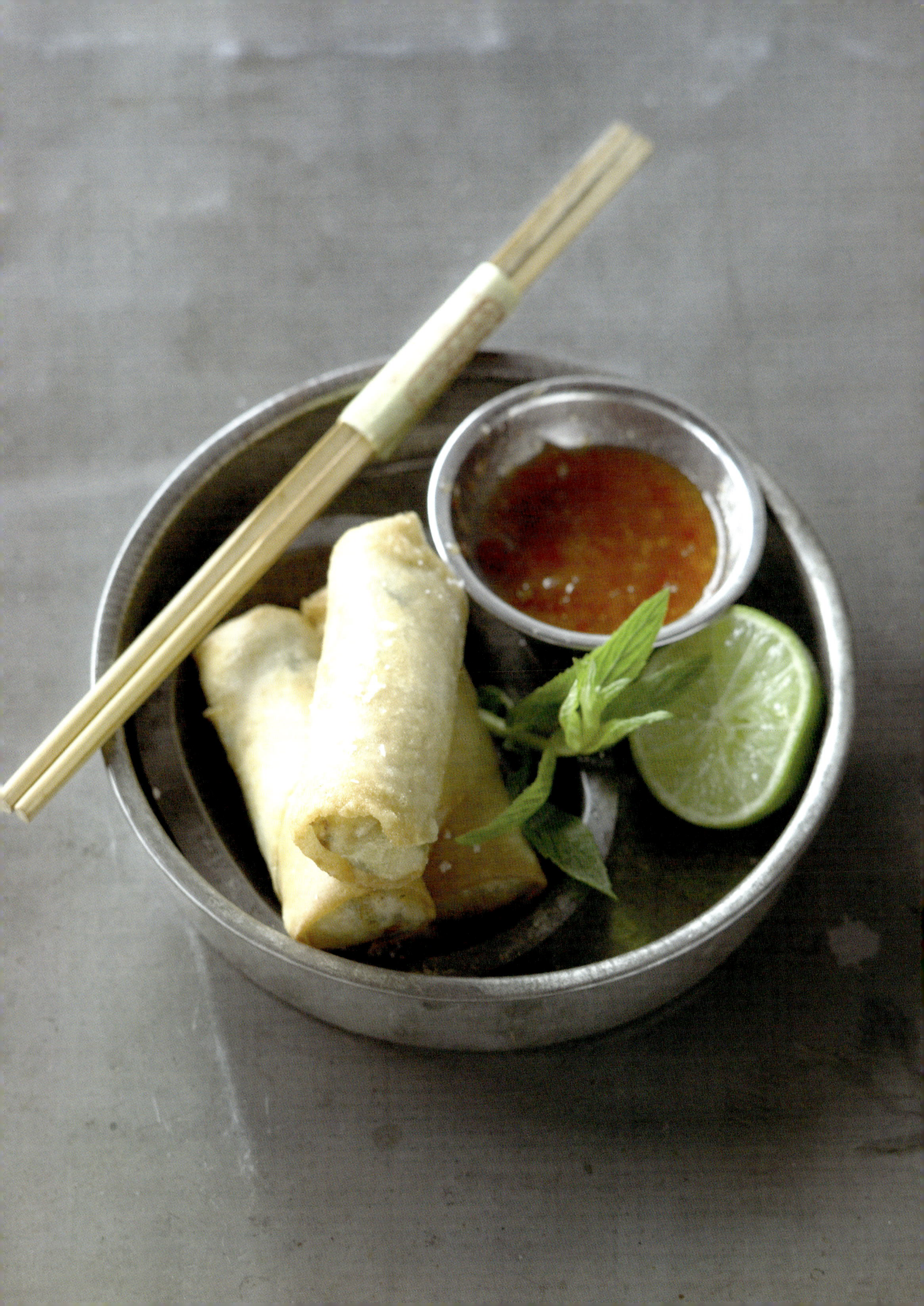

The Complete Book of Modern Asian

prawn dumplings

preparation time 40 minutes
cooking time 10 minutes makes 24

1kg uncooked prawns
¼ cup (50g) bamboo shoots, chopped finely
1 tablespoon finely chopped fresh chives
2 teaspoons sesame oil
2 teaspoons cornflour
24 gow gee wrappers

1 Shell and devein prawns; chop finely. Combine prawns in large bowl with bamboo shoots, chives, oil and cornflour. Blend or process half of the prawn mixture until just smooth. Return to large bowl with remaining prawn mixture; stir to combine.
2 Place one wrapper on your hand; place 1 heaped teaspoon of the prawn mixture into centre of wrapper. Gently cup your hand and gather sides of wrapper to form pleats, leaving top open. Press base of wrapper on bench to flatten. Repeat with remaining wrappers and prawn mixture.
3 Place dumplings, in single layer, about 1cm apart in baking-paper-lined steamer fitted over wok of boiling water; steam, covered, about 10 minutes or until dumplings are cooked through.
4 Serve dumplings hot with light soy sauce, if desired.
per dumpling 0.6g total fat (0.1g saturated fat); 180kJ (43 cal); 4.8g carbohydrate; 4.3g protein; 0.1g fibre

mini scallop and lime kebabs

preparation time 15 minutes (plus refrigeration time)
cooking time 5 minutes makes 24

24 scallops (600g), roe removed
2 tablespoons vegetable oil
4cm piece fresh ginger (20g), grated
3 cloves garlic, crushed
3 limes
12 fresh kaffir lime leaves, halved lengthways
24 sturdy toothpicks

1 Place scallops in medium bowl with combined oil, ginger and garlic in medium bowl. Cover; refrigerate 30 minutes.
2 Meanwhile, cut each lime into eight wedges. Thread one piece of lime leaf and one lime wedge on each toothpick.
3 Cook scallops on heated oiled grill plate (or grill or barbecue) until cooked as desired. Stand 5 minutes; thread one onto each toothpick.
per kebab 1.7g total fat (0.2g saturated fat); 121kJ (29 cal); 0.3g carbohydrate; 3.6g protein; 0.3g fibre

vegetable gow gees with miso dipping sauce

preparation time 40 minutes
cooking time 30 minutes makes 28

2 teaspoons peanut oil
2 cloves garlic, crushed
5cm piece fresh ginger (25g), grated
1 fresh small red thai chilli, chopped finely
150g oyster mushrooms, chopped finely
2 small carrots (140g), chopped finely
3 green onions, sliced thinly
½ cup (40g) bean sprouts
100g soft tofu, chopped finely
227g can water chestnuts, drained, chopped finely
¼ cup finely chopped fresh coriander
28 gow gee wrappers

MISO DIPPING SAUCE
1 tablespoon white miso paste
1 tablespoon japanese soy sauce
1 tablespoon lime juice
1 green onion, sliced thinly
2 tablespoons water

1 Heat oil in large frying pan; cook garlic, ginger and chilli until fragrant. Add mushrooms, carrot, onion, sprouts, tofu and chestnuts; cook, stirring occasionally, about 5 minutes or until vegetables soften. Remove from heat; stir in coriander. Cool 10 minutes.
2 Place 1 level tablespoon of the mixture in the centre of each wrapper. Brush edges with a little water; fold wrapper over to completely enclose filling, pressing edges together to seal.
3 Place gow gees, in single layer, about 1cm apart in baking-paper-lined steamer fitted over wok of boiling water; steam, covered, about 10 minutes or until gow gees are heated through.
4 Meanwhile, combine ingredients for miso dipping sauce in small bowl.
5 Serve gow gees with dipping sauce.
per gow gee 0.5g total fat (0.1g saturated fat); 159kJ (38 cal); 6g carbohydrate; 0.9g protein; 0.8g fibre

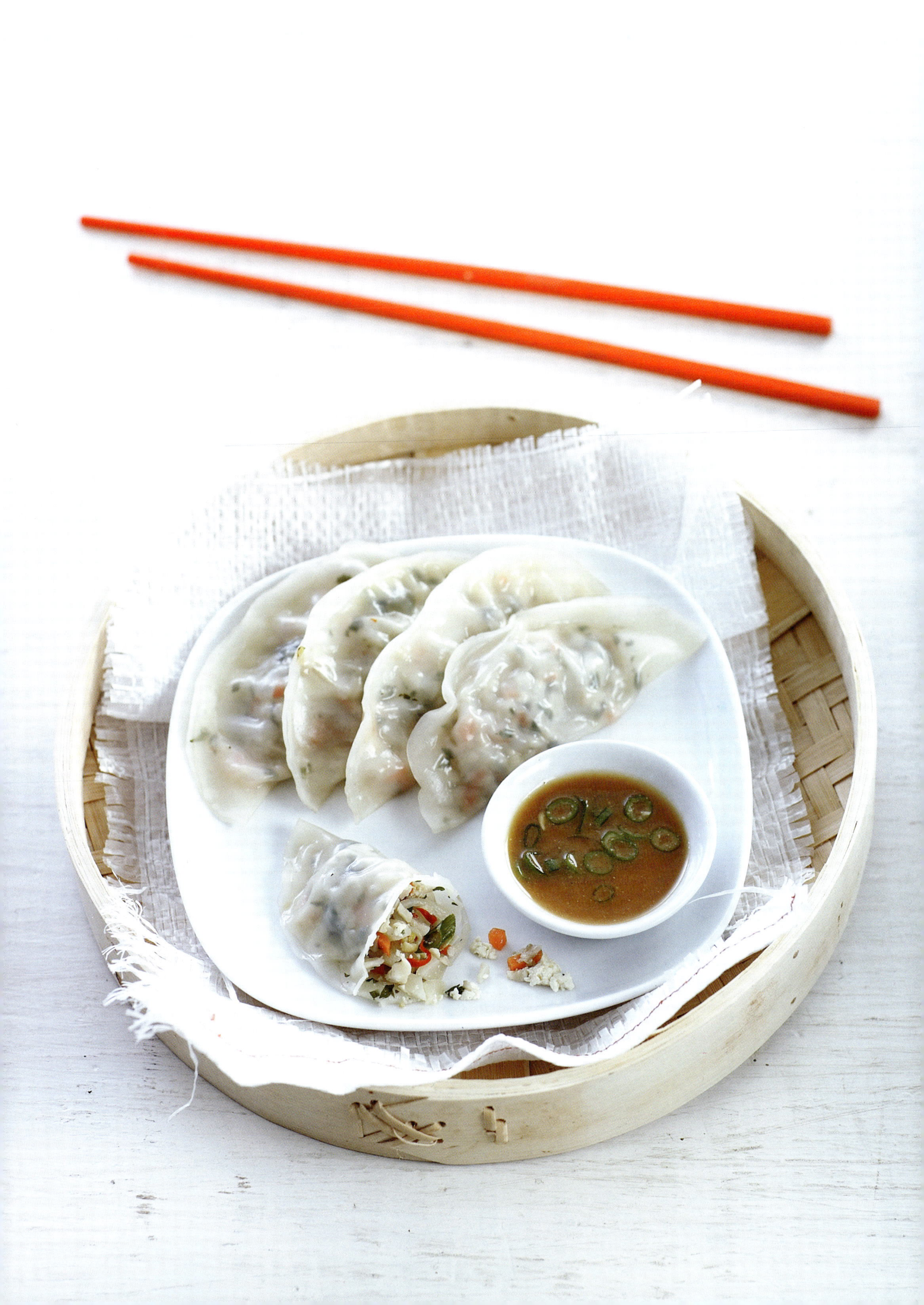

The Complete Book of Modern Asian

coconut chicken salad in crisp wonton cups

preparation time 25 minutes
cooking time 25 minutes (plus cooling time) makes 40

350g chicken breast fillets
¾ cup (180ml) chicken stock
1 cup (250ml) coconut cream
4 fresh kaffir lime leaves, shredded finely
1 tablespoon brown sugar
1 tablespoon fish sauce
1 clove garlic, crushed
1 fresh small red thai chilli, chopped finely
40 square wonton wrappers
cooking-oil spray
100g snow peas, trimmed, sliced thinly
½ cup finely chopped fresh coriander

1 Preheat oven to 200°C/180°C fan-forced. Oil 12-hole mini (1-tablespoon/20ml) muffin pan.
2 Place chicken, stock, coconut cream and lime leaves in medium saucepan; bring to a boil. Reduce heat, simmer, uncovered, about 10 minutes or until chicken is cooked through. Cool chicken in coconut mixture 10 minutes.
3 Remove chicken from coconut mixture; chop chicken finely. Bring coconut mixture to a boil. Reduce heat, simmer, uncovered, until mixture reduces by half. Strain into medium bowl; stir in sugar, fish sauce, garlic and chilli. Cool to room temperature.
4 Meanwhile, push wonton wrappers into pan holes; coat lightly with oil. Bake, uncovered, about 7 minutes or until wonton cups are browned lightly. Stand in pans 2 minutes; turn onto wire racks to cool.
5 Place chicken, snow peas and coriander in medium bowl with coconut dressing; toss gently to combine. Divide chicken mixture among wonton cups.
per cup 1.8g total fat (1.3g saturated fat); 209kJ (50 cal); 5.2g carbohydrate; 3g protein; 0.2g fibre

sashimi stacks

preparation time 30 minutes
makes 16

½ lebanese cucumber (65g), seeded
½ medium avocado (125g)
400g piece sashimi salmon
1 teaspoon wasabi paste
4 green onions, quartered lengthways
½ sheet toasted seaweed (yaki-nori), cut into 1cm strips
2 teaspoons toasted sesame seeds
2 tablespoons japanese soy sauce

1 Cut cucumber and avocado into long thin strips.
2 Cut salmon into 32 thin slices.
3 Place 16 slices of the salmon on serving platter; spread each with a little wasabi then divide cucumber, avocado and onion among slices. Top each stack with one remaining salmon slice.
4 Wrap seaweed strip around each stack; sprinkle each with sesame seeds.
5 Serve sashimi stacks with soy sauce.
per stack 3g total fat (0.6g saturated fat); 205kJ (49 cal); 0.3g carbohydrate; 5.2g protein; 0.2g fibre

pork and prawn vietnamese summer rolls

preparation time 35 minutes
cooking time 50 minutes makes 12

200g pork belly
650g cooked medium king prawns
1⅓ cups (80g) finely shredded iceberg lettuce
1 cup (80g) bean sprouts
½ cup loosely packed fresh mint leaves
12 x 17cm-square rice paper sheets

1 Cover pork with water in medium saucepan; bring to a boil, covered. Reduce heat, simmer, uncovered, about 45 minutes or until pork is tender. Drain; when cool enough to handle, slice thinly.
2 Meanwhile, shell and devein prawns; chop prawn meat finely.
3 Combine lettuce, sprouts and mint in medium bowl.
4 To assemble rolls, place 1 sheet of rice paper in medium bowl of warm water until just softened. Lift sheet from water carefully; place, with one point of the square sheet facing you, on board covered with tea towel. Place a little of the prawn meat vertically along centre of sheet; top with a little of the pork then a little of the lettuce filling. Fold top and bottom corners over filling then roll sheet from side to side to enclose filling. Repeat with remaining rice paper sheets, prawn meat, pork and lettuce filling.
5 Serve summer rolls with hoisin and peanut dipping sauce (see page 414), if desired.

per roll 4.2g total fat (1.3g saturated fat); 431kJ (103 cal); 6.1g carbohydrate; 9.4g protein; 1.3g fibre

coconut chicken vietnamese summer rolls

preparation time 20 minutes
cooking time 10 minutes makes 12

300g chicken tenderloins
½ cup (125ml) coconut cream
½ cup (125ml) chicken stock
10cm stick fresh lemon grass (20g), chopped coarsely
5cm piece fresh ginger (25g), grated
1 tablespoon coarsely chopped coriander root and stem mixture
100g snow peas, trimmed, sliced thinly
½ cup coarsely chopped fresh coriander
12 x 17cm-square rice paper sheets

1 Place chicken, coconut cream, stock, lemon grass, ginger and coriander root and stem mixture in medium saucepan; bring to a boil. Reduce heat, simmer, uncovered, about 5 minutes or until chicken is cooked through. Cool chicken in poaching liquid 10 minutes. Remove chicken from pan; reserve ¼ cup of the poaching liquid, discard remainder.
2 Chop chicken finely. Place chicken in medium bowl with snow peas, coriander and poaching liquid; toss gently to combine.
3 To assemble rolls, place 1 sheet of rice paper in medium bowl of warm water until just softened. Lift sheet from water carefully; place, with one point of the square sheet facing you, on board covered with tea towel. Place a little of the chicken filling vertically along centre of sheet; fold top and bottom corners over filling then roll sheet from side to side to enclose filling. Repeat with remaining rice paper sheets and chicken filling.
4 Serve summer rolls with sweet chilli dipping sauce (see page 414), if desired.

per roll 3.4g total fat (2.2g saturated fat); 309kJ (74 cal); 4.1g carbohydrate; 6.4g protein; 0.6g fibre

Morsels

The Complete Book of Modern Asian

deep-fried prawn balls

preparation time 25 minutes (plus refrigeration time)
cooking time 10 minutes   serves 4

1kg cooked large prawns
5 green onions, chopped finely
2 cloves garlic, crushed
4 fresh small red thai chillies, chopped finely
1cm piece fresh ginger (5g), grated finely
1 tablespoon cornflour
2 teaspoons fish sauce
¼ cup coarsely chopped fresh coriander
¼ cup (25g) packaged breadcrumbs
½ cup (35g) stale breadcrumbs
vegetable oil, for deep-frying

1 Shell and devein prawns; cut in half. Blend or process prawn halves, pulsing, until chopped coarsely. Place in large bowl with onion, garlic, chilli, ginger, cornflour, sauce and coriander; mix well.
2 Roll rounded tablespoons of prawn mixture into balls with wet hands. Roll prawn balls in combined breadcrumbs; place, in single layer, on plastic-wrap-lined tray. Cover; refrigerate 30 minutes.
3 Heat oil in wok; deep-fry prawn balls, in batches, until browned lightly and cooked through.
4 Serve prawn balls with sweet chilli sauce, if desired.
per serving 10.9g total fat (1.5g saturated fat); 1196kJ (286 cal); 17.1g carbohydrate; 28.5g protein; 2.2g fibre

salt and lemon-pepper squid

preparation time 15 minutes
cooking time 15 minutes   serves 4

600g squid hoods
½ cup (75g) plain flour
2 teaspoons coarse cooking salt
1 tablespoon lemon pepper
peanut oil, for deep-frying

1 Halve squid hoods lengthways, score insides in crosshatch pattern; cut each half lengthways into five pieces. Toss squid in medium bowl with combined flour, salt and lemon pepper until coated; shake off excess.
2 Heat oil in wok; deep-fry squid, in batches, until tender and browned lightly. Drain on absorbent paper.
per serving 10.3g total fat (2.1g saturated fat); 1053kJ (252 cal); 12.6g carbohydrate; 26.9g protein; 0.7g fibre

fish cakes

preparation time 15 minutes (plus refrigeration time)
cooking time 10 minutes makes 16

500g skinless redfish fillets, boned
2 tablespoons red curry paste (see page 249)
2 fresh kaffir lime leaves, torn
2 green onions, chopped coarsely
1 tablespoon fish sauce
1 tablespoon lime juice
2 tablespoons finely chopped fresh coriander
3 snake beans (30g), chopped finely
2 fresh small red thai chillies, chopped finely
peanut oil, for deep-frying

1 Cut fish into small pieces. Blend or process fish with paste, lime leaves, onion, sauce and juice until mixture forms a smooth paste. Combine fish mixture in medium bowl with coriander, beans and chilli.
2 Roll heaped tablespoons of mixture into balls with wet hands; flatten balls into cake shape. Place on tray, cover, refrigerate at least 30 minutes.
3 Heat oil in wok; deep-fry fish cakes, in batches, until browned lightly and cooked through. Drain on absorbent paper; serve with cucumber dipping sauce (see page 22) and lime wedges, if desired.
per fish cake 3.7g total fat (0.7g saturated fat); 263kJ (63 cal); 0.4g carbohydrate; 6.7g protein; 0.4g fibre

stuffed chicken wings

preparation time 50 minutes
cooking time 15 minutes serves 6

12 large chicken wings (1.5kg)
500g chicken mince
2 green onions, chopped finely
2cm piece fresh ginger (10g), chopped finely
2 cloves garlic, crushed
1 fresh small red thai chilli, chopped finely
1 tablespoon cornflour
2 tablespoons cornflour, extra
1 egg, beaten lightly
1 cup (100g) packaged breadcrumbs
vegetable oil, for deep-frying

SWEET CHILLI PEANUT SAUCE
½ cup (110g) white sugar
2 tablespoons water
2 tablespoons white vinegar
1 tablespoon coarsely chopped roasted unsalted peanuts
1 fresh small red thai chilli, chopped coarsely

1 Holding end of large third joint of wing, trim around bone with knife. Cut, scrape and push meat down to middle joint, without cutting skin. Twist bone; remove and discard bone. Repeat with remaining wings.
2 Blend or process mince, onion, ginger, garlic, chilli and cornflour until combined. Using fingers, fill cavities of wings with mince mixture; secure ends with toothpicks.
3 Make sweet chilli peanut sauce.
4 Toss wings in extra cornflour, shake away excess. Dip into egg then breadcrumbs.
5 Heat oil in large saucepan; deep-fry wings, in batches, until well browned and cooked through. Drain on absorbent paper; remove toothpicks.
6 Serve chicken wings with sauce.
SWEET CHILLI PEANUT SAUCE
Stir sugar and the water in small saucepan over heat until sugar is dissolved; bring to a boil. Reduce heat, simmer, uncovered, 2 minutes; cool. Stir in vinegar, peanuts and chilli.
per serving 33.5g total fat (7.2g saturated fat); 2780kJ (665 cal); 34.3g carbohydrate; 56g protein; 1.2g fibre

Morsels

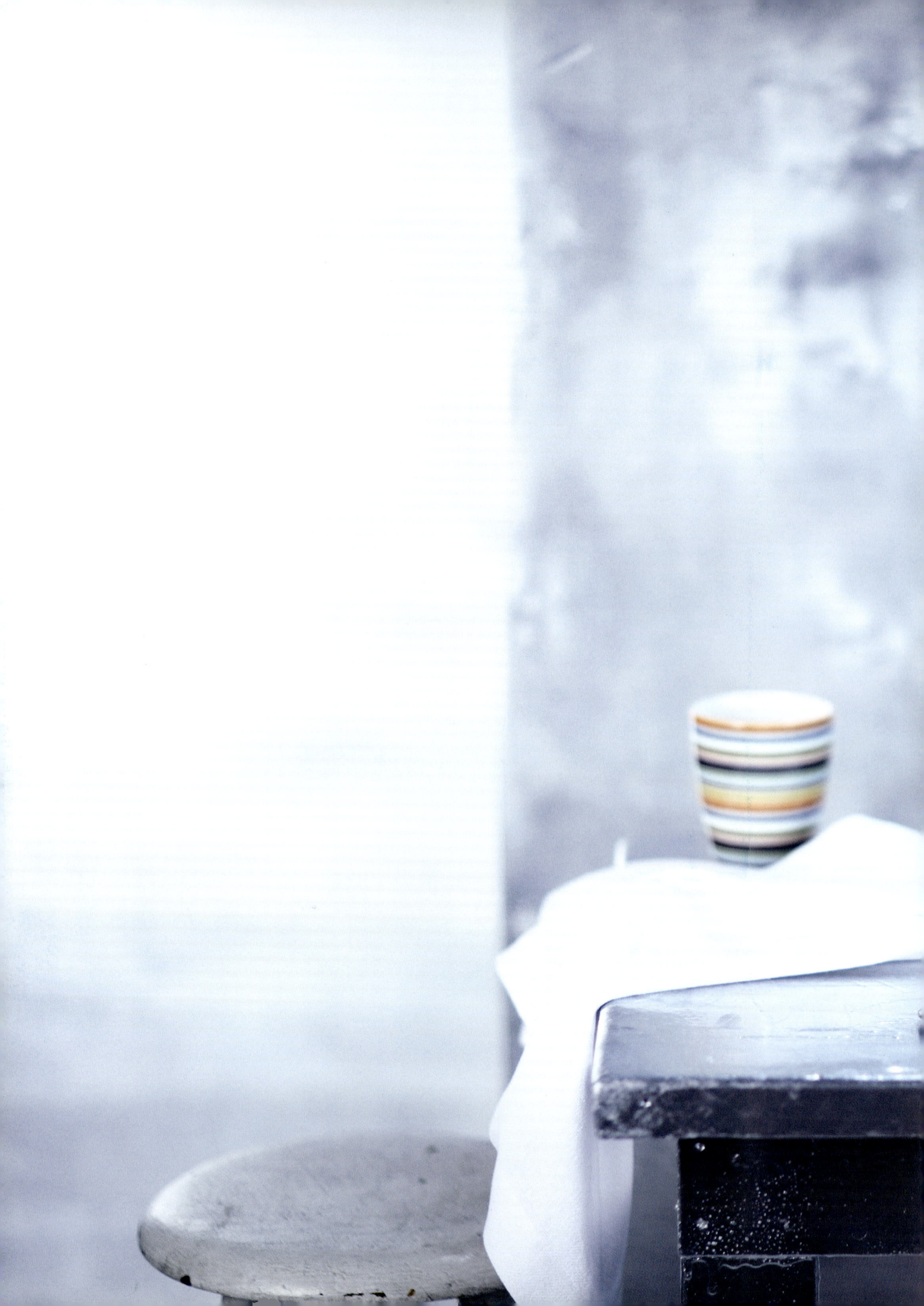

Starters

The first course in an Asian meal should have a connection with or be complementary to the main that is to follow, and our enticing assortment offers a diverse and adaptable choice of recipes to help you get "startered". Plus, down-sized, they are versatile enough to do double-duty and become a collection of yum cha ideas.

seafood wontons with sesame dressing *page 63*

barbecued pork and crunchy noodle salad *page 71*

first courses

japanese-style tuna with chilli-daikon *page 63*

deep-fried spicy quail *page 71*

chicken larb with thai pickle

preparation time 15 minutes
cooking time 15 minutes (plus standing time) serves 4

¼ cup (60ml) chicken stock
2 tablespoons lime juice
1 tablespoon fish sauce
1 tablespoon grated palm sugar
500g chicken mince
1 clove garlic, crushed
2 shallots (50g), sliced thinly
2 tablespoons finely chopped fresh coriander
1 tablespoon finely chopped fresh mint
1 fresh long red chilli, sliced thinly
1 medium iceberg lettuce, shredded coarsely

THAI PICKLE
½ cup (110g) white sugar
½ cup (125ml) white vinegar
1 tablespoon coarse cooking salt
½ cup (125ml) water
1 small red capsicum (150g), sliced thinly
½ cup (40g) bean sprouts
1 lebanese cucumber (130g), seeded, sliced thinly

1 Make thai pickle.
2 Meanwhile, place stock, juice, sauce and palm sugar in large saucepan; bring to a boil. Add chicken and garlic; reduce heat, simmer, stirring, about 5 minutes or until chicken is cooked through. Cool 10 minutes. Stir in shallot, herbs and chilli.
3 Serve larb with drained thai pickle on lettuce. Accompany with steamed jasmine rice, if desired.
THAI PICKLE
Place sugar, vinegar, salt and the water in small saucepan; bring to a boil. Cool 5 minutes. Place capsicum, sprouts and cucumber in medium bowl; pour vinegar mixture over capsicum mixture. Cover; stand 30 minutes.

per serving 10.5g total fat (3.1g saturated fat); 1438kJ (344 cal); 34.1g carbohydrate; 26.7g protein; 2.9g fibre

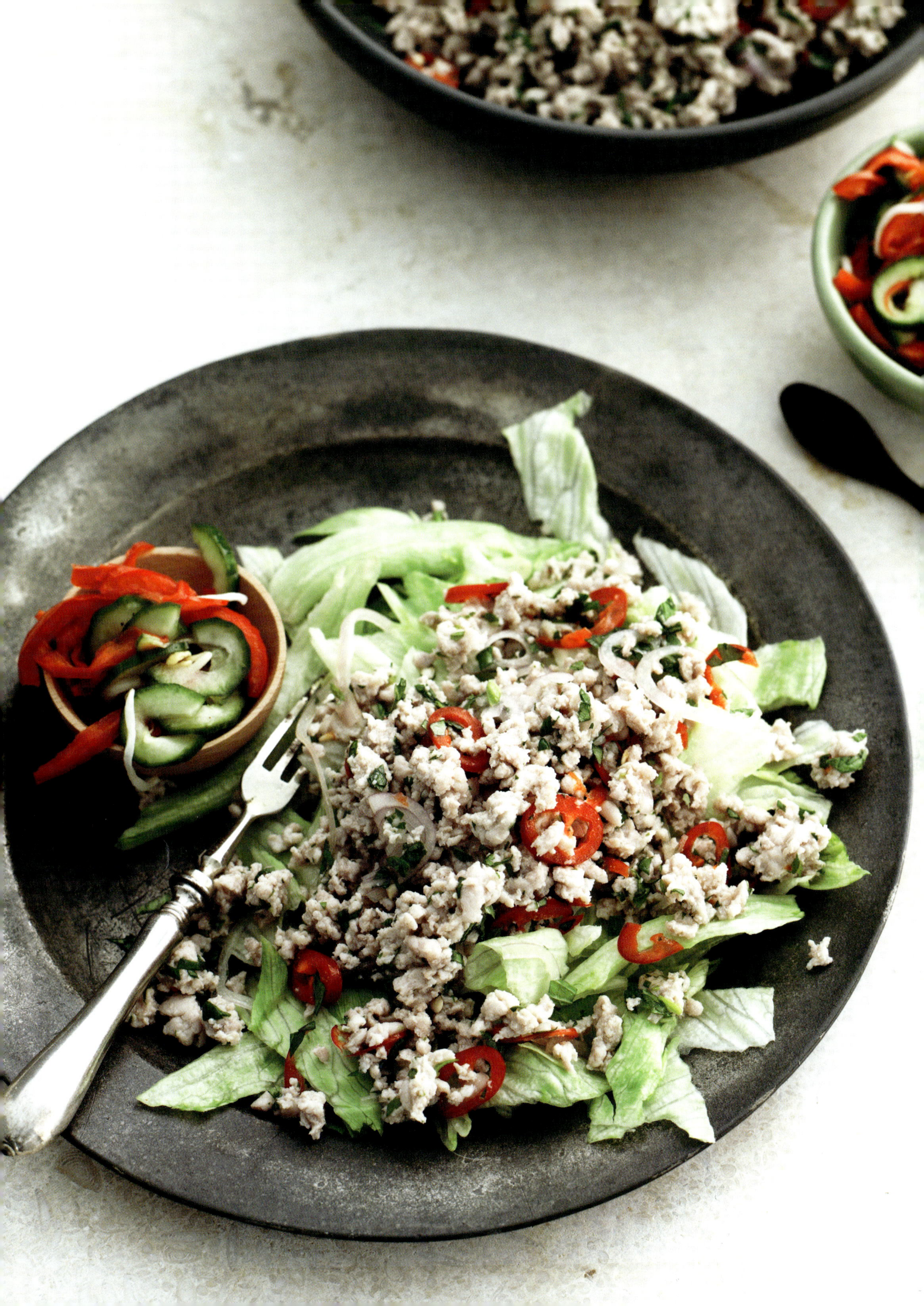

The Complete Book of Modern Asian

japanese-style tuna with chilli-daikon

preparation time 25 minutes
serves 4

600g piece sashimi tuna
⅓ cup (80ml) rice vinegar
½ small daikon (200g)
4 dried long red chillies, chopped finely
2 tablespoons mirin
1 teaspoon sesame oil
1 teaspoon black sesame seeds
1 sheet toasted seaweed (yaki-nori), shredded finely

1 Slice tuna as thinly as possible; place, in single layer, on large platter, drizzle with vinegar. Cover; refrigerate until required.
2 Meanwhile, grate peeled daikon finely. Place daikon and chilli in fine sieve set over small bowl; stir with small wooden spoon to combine then press with back of spoon to extract as much daikon liquid as possible.
3 Drain vinegar from tuna. Divide tuna among serving plates; drizzle with combined mirin and oil, sprinkle with seeds. Serve tuna with chilli-daikon and seaweed.

per serving 10.3g total fat (3.7g saturated fat); 1112kJ (266 cal); 2.5g carbohydrate; 38.5g protein; 1.4g fibre

seafood wontons with sesame dressing

preparation time 30 minutes
cooking time 10 minutes serves 4

6 medium uncooked king prawns (270g)
2 small red fish fillets (100g), chopped coarsely
2 cloves garlic, crushed
2cm piece fresh ginger (10g), grated
½ teaspoon sesame oil
24 wonton wrappers
12 scallops, without roe (300g)
1 egg white, beaten lightly
1 cup loosely packed coriander leaves
2 green onions, sliced thinly

SESAME DRESSING
2 tablespoons kecap manis
2 tablespoons rice wine vinegar
¼ teaspoon sesame oil
1 fresh long red chilli, sliced thinly

1 Shell and devein prawns; chop coarsely. Process prawns, fish, garlic, ginger and oil until almost smooth.
2 Place 1 heaped teaspoon of the prawn filling in the centre of 12 wonton wrappers, then one scallop on top of the filling. Lightly brush edges with egg white. Place another wrapper on top, pressing around edge of filling firmly to seal.
3 Using a 7cm cutter, cut the wontons into rounds; discard excess wonton pastry. Transfer to tray lined with a tea towel.
4 Place ingredients for sesame dressing in screw-top jar; shake well.
5 Cook wontons, in two batches, in a large saucepan of simmering water, uncovered, about 3 minutes or until seafood is just cooked through. Remove wontons from pan with a slotted spoon; drain on absorbent paper.
6 Divide wontons among serving plates, drizzle with dressing; top with combined coriander and onions.

per serving 2.8g total fat (0.6g saturated fat); 1066kJ (255 cal); 28.5g carbohydrate; 27.9g protein; 0.8g fibre

onion and spinach pakoras with cucumber raita

preparation time 20 minutes
cooking time 30 minutes makes 16

2 cups (300g) chickpea flour
2 large uncooked potatoes (600g), grated coarsely
2 large brown onions (400g), sliced thinly
100g baby spinach leaves, chopped coarsely
4 cloves garlic, crushed
1 teaspoon chilli powder
½ teaspoon ground cumin
1 teaspoon salt
¼ teaspoon ground turmeric
1 teaspoon garam masala
¼ teaspoon baking powder
¼ cup coarsely chopped fresh mint
¼ cup (60ml) water
2 tablespoons olive oil

CUCUMBER RAITA
1 lebanese cucumber (130g), grated coarsely
200g low-fat yogurt
¼ cup (60ml) lemon juice
¼ cup coarsely chopped fresh mint

1 Using hand, combine all ingredients except the oil, in medium bowl. Shape ¼ cups of the potato mixture into patties.
2 Heat oil in large frying pan; cook pakoras, in batches, about 10 minutes or until browned lightly both sides.
3 Meanwhile, make cucumber raita.
4 Serve pakoras with raita.
CUCUMBER RAITA
Combine ingredients in small bowl.
per pakora 2.8g total fat (0.4g saturated fat); 489kJ (117 cal); 17.9g carbohydrate; 4.4g protein; 3.4g fibre

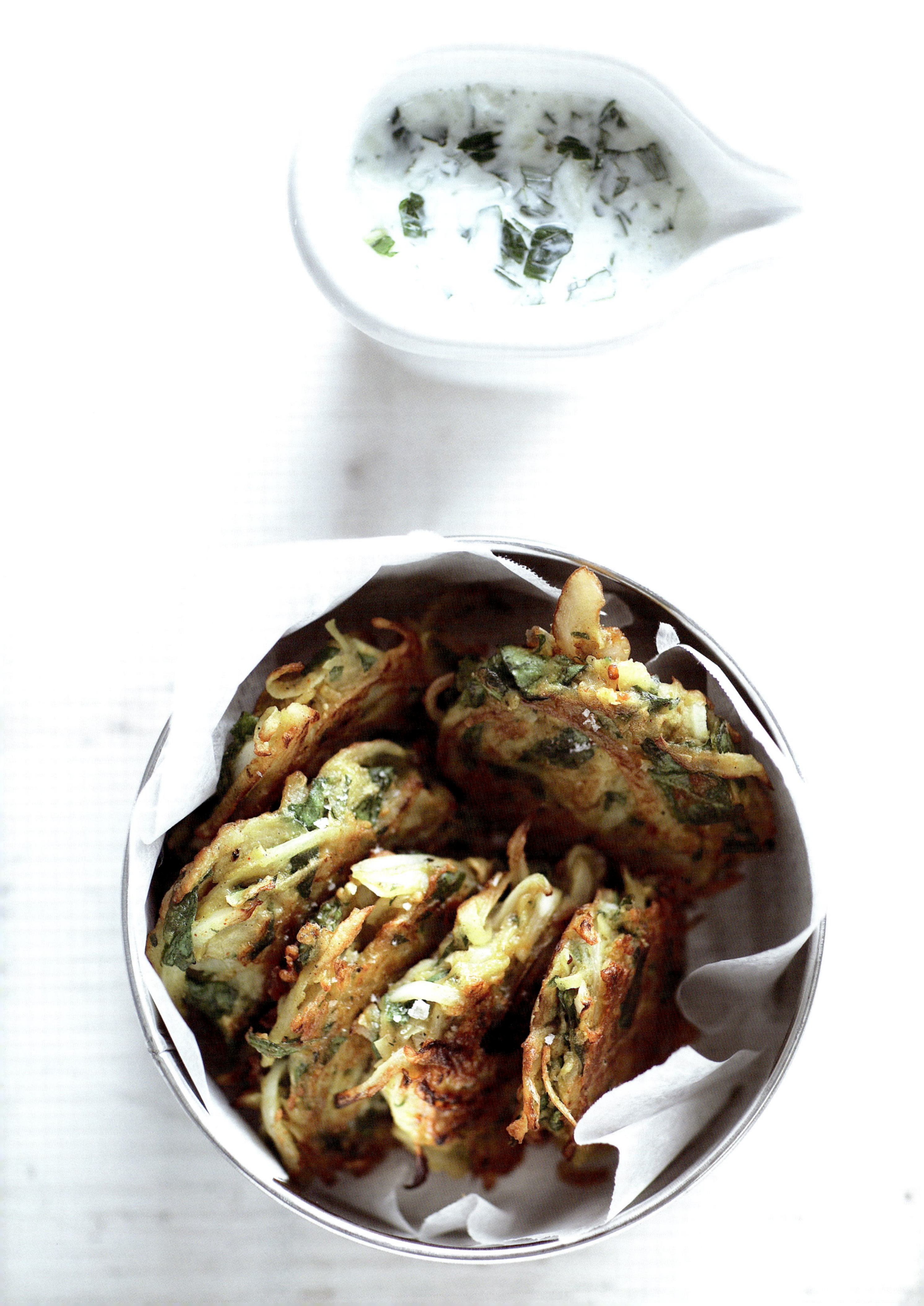

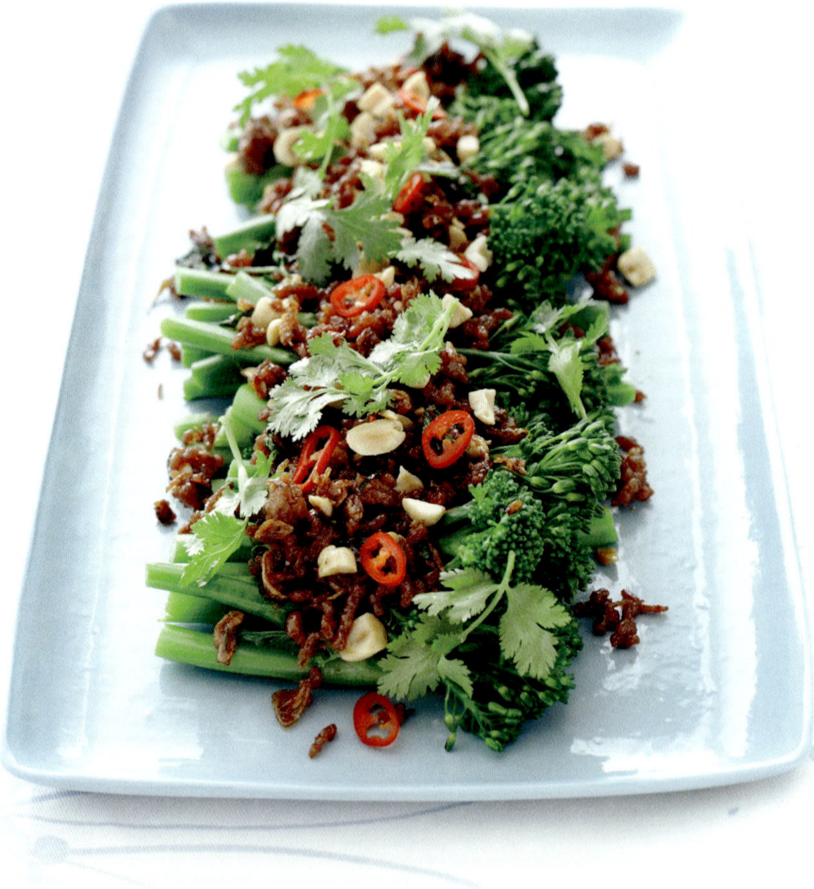

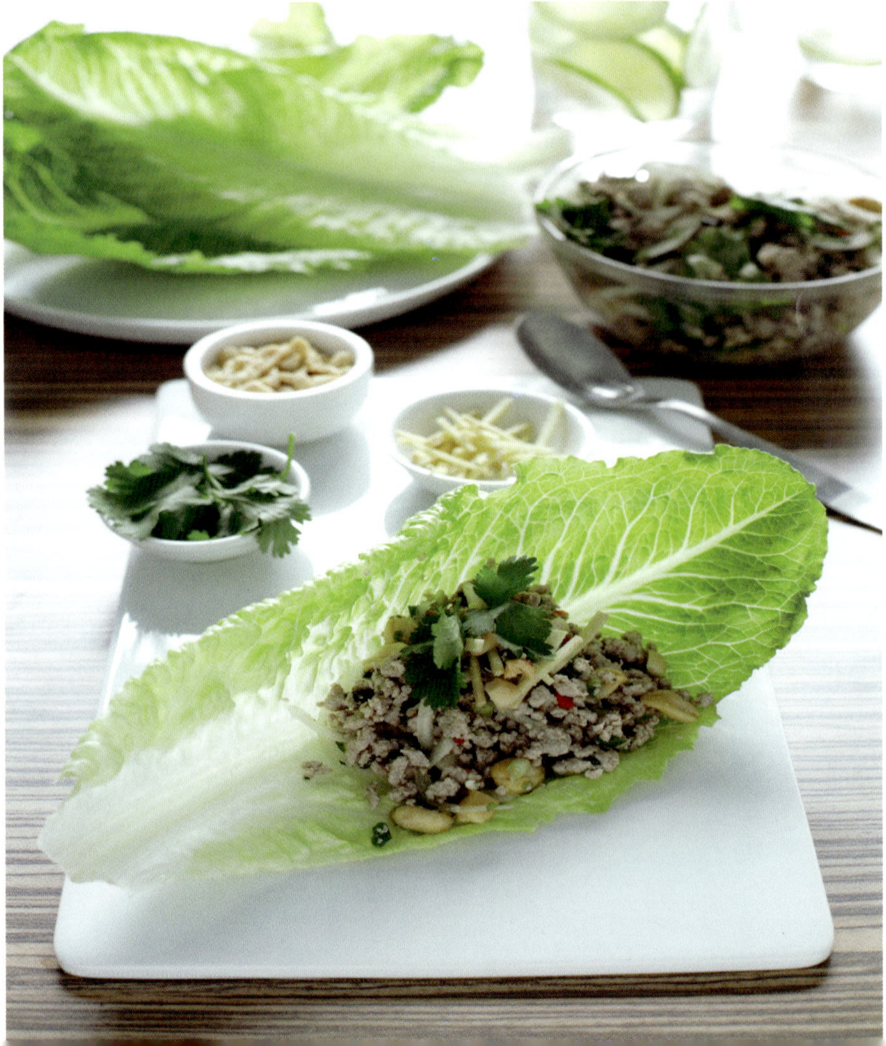

thai-style sticky pork on broccolini

preparation time 15 minutes
cooking time 10 minutes serves 4

1 tablespoon peanut oil
300g minced pork
2 cloves garlic, sliced thinly
½ cup (80g) grated palm sugar
2 tablespoons fish sauce
4 kaffir lime leaves, shredded
½ cup (50g) fried shallots
½ cup (75g) chopped toasted peanuts
350g broccolini, halved crossways
1¼ cups lightly packed coriander leaves
1 tablespoon lime juice
1 fresh long red chilli, sliced thinly

1 Heat oil in wok; stir-fry pork until browned lightly. Add garlic; stir-fry about 1 minute. Remove from wok.
2 Add sugar, sauce and lime leaves to wok; bring to a boil. Reduce heat, simmer, uncovered, about 2 minutes or until thick. Return pork to wok with half of the shallots and half of the peanuts; cook, uncovered, about 2 minutes or until mixture is sticky.
3 Meanwhile, boil, steam or microwave broccolini until just tender; drain.
4 Stir 1 cup of the coriander leaves into pork mixture with juice, remaining shallots and peanuts.
5 Place broccolini on serving platter, top with pork mixture, remaining coriander and chilli. Serve with lime wedges, if desired.
per serving 19.8g total fat (3.9g saturated fat); 1605kJ (384 cal); 23.3g carbohydrate; 25.4g protein; 6.1g fibre

pork, ginger and mint larb

preparation time 20 minutes
cooking time 10 minutes serves 4

500g pork fillet, chopped coarsely
1 tablespoon peanut oil
1 tablespoon water
¼ cup (60ml) lime juice
2 tablespoons fish sauce
2 fresh small red thai chillies, chopped finely
1 small brown onion (80g), sliced thinly
4 green onions, chopped finely
¼ cup (35g) peanuts
4cm piece fresh ginger (20g), grated
2 tablespoons finely chopped fresh mint
2 tablespoons fresh coriander leaves
8 cos lettuce leaves
1 tablespoon coarsely chopped peanuts, extra
4cm piece fresh ginger (20g), cut into thin strips
2 tablespoons fresh coriander leaves, extra

1 Process pork until finely minced.
2 Heat oil in large frying pan; cook pork and water, stirring, until pork is tender. Remove pan from heat, stir in juice, sauce and chilli; cool.
3 Place pork mixture in large bowl with onions, nuts, grated ginger, mint and coriander; toss gently to combine.
4 Serve pork salad over lettuce; sprinkle with extra chopped nuts, ginger strips and extra coriander.
per serving 20.3g total fat (5g saturated fat); 1396kJ (334 cal); 4.8g carbohydrate; 31.7g protein; 3.1g fibre

salt and pepper quail with lemon pepper dipping sauce

preparation time 30 minutes
cooking time 20 minutes serves 4

6 quails (960g)
½ cup (75g) plain flour
1½ tablespoons sea salt flakes
2 teaspoons coarsely ground black pepper
vegetable oil, for deep-frying

LEMON PEPPER DIPPING SAUCE
¼ cup (60ml) vegetable oil
1 teaspoon finely grated lemon rind
⅓ cup (80ml) lemon juice
2 tablespoons grated palm sugar
1 teaspoon ground white pepper

HERB SALAD
½ cup loosely packed vietnamese mint leaves
½ cup loosely packed fresh coriander leaves
1 cup (80g) bean sprouts
1 fresh long red chilli, sliced thinly

1 Rinse quails under cold water; pat dry. Discard necks from quails. Using kitchen scissors, cut along sides of each quail's backbone; discard backbones. Halve each quail along breastbone.
2 Make lemon pepper dipping sauce. Make herb salad.
3 Combine flour, salt and pepper in large bowl. Add quail; coat quail in flour mixture. Shake off excess.
4 Heat oil in wok; deep-fry quail, in batches, 6 minutes or until cooked. Drain on absorbent paper.
5 Divide quail among serving plates; top with herb salad. Serve with remaining dipping sauce.
LEMON PEPPER DIPPING SAUCE
Place ingredients in screw-top jar; shake well.
HERB SALAD
Place ingredients in medium bowl with 1 tablespoon of the dipping sauce; toss gently until combined.
per serving 34.8g total fat (6.2g saturated); 2098kJ (502 cal); 21.4g carbohydrate; 25.5g protein; 2g fibre

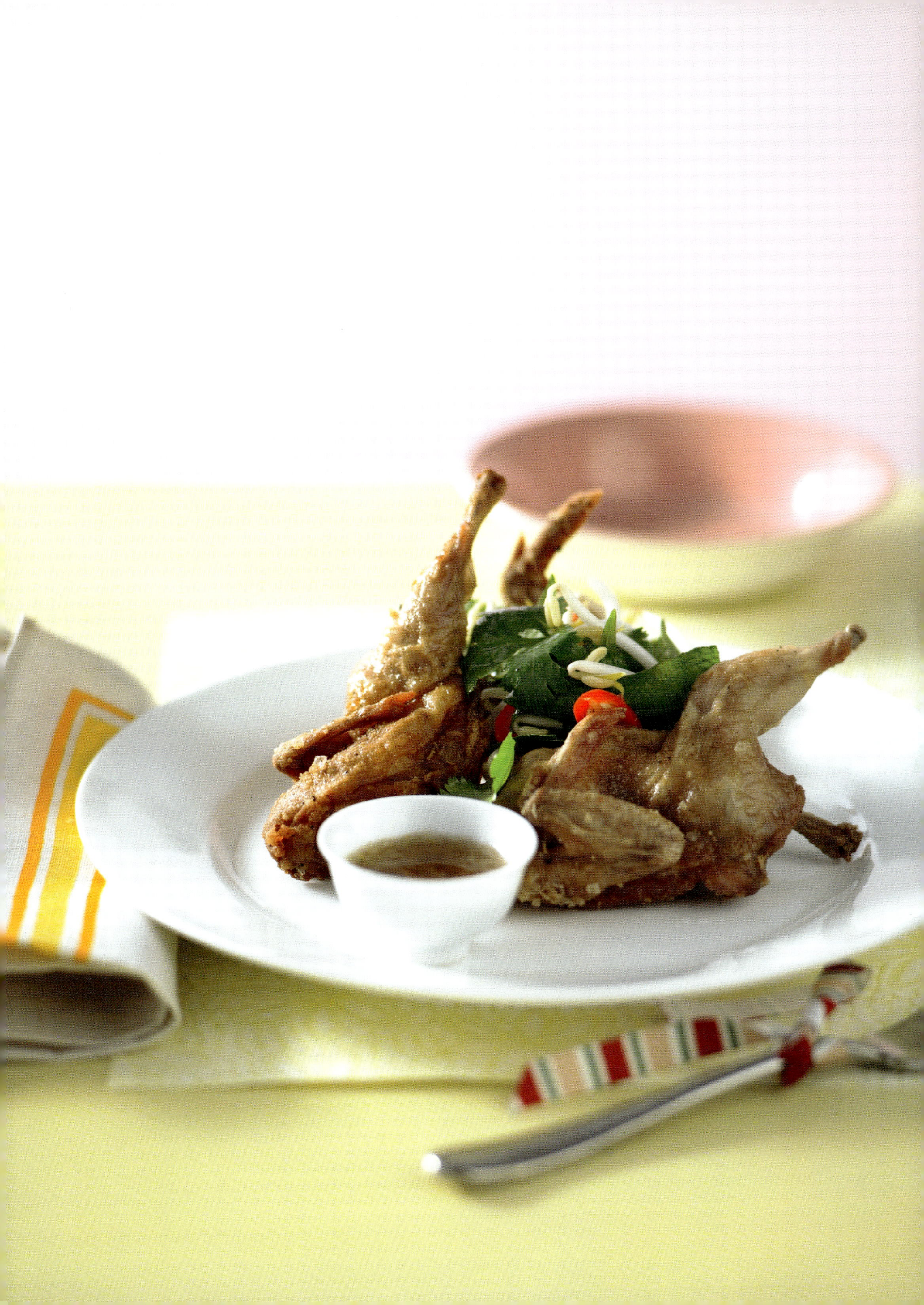

The Complete Book of Modern Asian

barbecued pork and crunchy noodle salad

preparation time 20 minutes
serves 6

10 trimmed red radishes (150g), sliced thinly, cut into matchsticks
1 large red capsicum (350g) sliced thinly
2 baby buk choy (300g), sliced thinly
6 green onions, sliced thinly
1 cup (80g) bean sprouts
½ cup (70g) roasted slivered almonds
2 x 100g packets fried noodles
400g chinese barbecued pork, sliced thinly

SWEET-SOUR DRESSING
¼ cup (60ml) peanut oil
2 tablespoons white vinegar
2 tablespoons brown sugar
2 tablespoons light soy sauce
1 teaspoon sesame oil
1 clove garlic, crushed

1 Make sweet-sour dressing.
2 Place radish, capsicum and buk choy in large bowl with remaining ingredients and dressing; toss gently to combine.
SWEET-SOUR DRESSING
Place ingredients in screw-top jar; shake well.
per serving 29.7g total fat (7.6g saturated fat); 1789kJ (428 cal); 17.6g carbohydrate; 20.4g protein; 6.1g fibre

deep-fried spicy quail

preparation time 25 minutes (plus refrigeration time)
cooking time 45 minutes serves 4

8 quails (1.3kg)
2 tablespoons kecap manis
2 tablespoons peanut oil
vegetable oil, for deep-frying
3cm piece fresh ginger (15g), chopped finely
4 cloves garlic, chopped finely
1 fresh long red chilli, chopped finely
¼ cup (60ml) kecap manis, extra
6 green onions, sliced thinly

1 Rinse quails under cold water; pat dry. Discard necks from quails. Using kitchen scissors, cut along each side of each quail's backbone; discard backbones. Halve each quail along breastbone.
2 Combine quail in large bowl with kecap manis and half the peanut oil. Cover; refrigerate 1 hour. Drain quail; pat dry.
3 Heat vegetable oil in wok; deep-fry quail, in batches, about 6 minutes or until skin is crisp and quails are cooked. Drain on absorbent paper.
4 Heat remaining peanut oil in cleaned wok; stir-fry ginger, garlic and chilli until fragrant. Return quail to wok with extra kecap manis; stir-fry until quail is hot. Remove from heat; sprinkle with onion.
per serving 36.1g total fat (7.5g saturated fat); 1923kJ (460 cal); 1.9g carbohydrate; 32.1g protein; 1g fibre

asian star

peking duck

preparation time 30 minutes (plus refrigeration time)
cooking time 1 hour serves 4

2kg duck
⅓ cup (80ml) water
1 tablespoon treacle
1 teaspoon rice vinegar
1 tablespoon dry sherry
1 teaspoon five-spice powder
4cm piece fresh ginger (20g), sliced thickly
2 star anise
1 lebanese cucumber (130g)
5 green onions

PANCAKES
2 cups (300g) plain flour
1 cup (250ml) boiling water
2 teaspoons peanut oil

PEANUT AND HOISIN SAUCE
1 tablespoon peanut butter
2 tablespoons hoisin sauce
1 tablespoon peanut oil
1 tablespoon sake

1 Wash duck under cold water; pat dry inside and out with absorbent paper. Tie string around neck of duck. Lower duck into large saucepan of boiling water for 30 seconds; remove from pan. Drain well; pat dry with absorbent paper. Tie string to refrigerator shelf and suspend duck, uncovered, over drip tray overnight.
2 Preheat oven to 240°C/220°C fan-forced.
3 Tuck wings under duck. Place duck, breast-side up, on wire rack in large baking dish; brush entire duck with combined water, treacle, vinegar, sherry and five-spice. Place ginger and star anise inside cavity of duck. Roast, uncovered, 10 minutes; turn duck breast-side down. Brush with marinade; roast, uncovered, 10 minutes. Turn duck breast-side up; brush with marinade.
4 Reduce oven temperature to 200°C/180°C fan-forced; roast, uncovered, brushing occasionally with remaining marinade, about 30 minutes or until duck is cooked as desired.
5 Increase oven temperature to 240°C/220°C fan-forced; roast, uncovered, about 10 minutes or until skin is crisp and browned.
6 Meanwhile, make pancakes.
7 Combine ingredients for peanut and hoisin sauce in small bowl.
8 Place duck on chopping board; remove skin. Slice skin and duck meat thickly.
9 Using teaspoon, remove seeds from cucumber. Cut cucumber and onions into 5cm strips. Serve warm pancakes with duck meat, crisp skin, cucumber, onion and sauce.

PANCAKES
Sift flour into large bowl; add the water, stirring quickly with a wooden spoon until ingredients cling together. Knead dough on floured surface about 10 minutes or until smooth. Divide dough into 20 pieces; roll pieces into balls, flatten slightly. Brush tops of dough with oil. Place one piece of dough on top of another, oiled surfaces together; roll out into an 18cm pancake. Repeat with remaining balls. Cook pancakes, one at a time, in small lightly oiled frying pan, over medium heat, about 30 seconds or until browned lightly. Turn pancake; brown other side. Pull pancakes apart with fingers to make two thin pancakes. Wrap pancakes in foil after each is cooked to prevent drying out.

per serving 27.2g total fat (6.6g saturated fat); 3219kJ (770 cal); 64.6g carbohydrate; 61.2g protein; 5.5g fibre

Stir dough ingredients in large bowl until ingredients cling together.

Place one piece of divided dough on top of another, oiled surfaces together. Roll out into an 18cm pancake.

Pull cooked pancakes apart with fingers to make two thin pancakes.

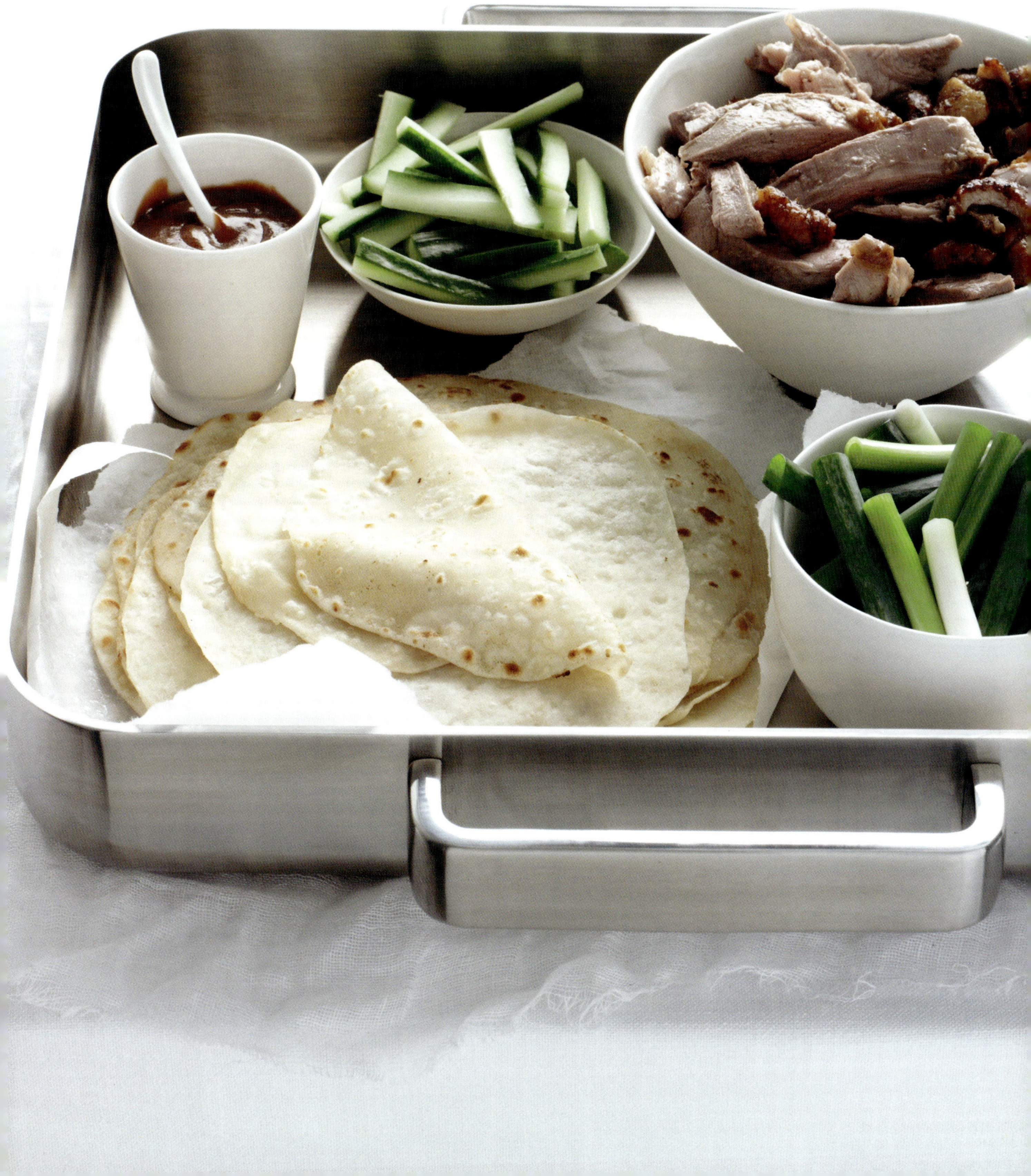

The Complete Book of Modern Asian

chicken yakitori with sesame dipping sauce

preparation time 20 minutes
cooking time 10 minutes serves 4

12 chicken tenderloins (1kg)

SESAME DIPPING SAUCE
¼ cup (60ml) light soy sauce
2 tablespoons mirin
3 teaspoons white sugar
½ teaspoon sesame oil
1 teaspoon sesame seeds

1 Make sesame dipping sauce.
2 Thread each tenderloin onto a skewer; brush skewers with half of the dipping sauce. Cook skewers, in batches, in heated oiled grill pan (or grill or barbecue) until chicken is cooked.
3 Serve skewers with remaining dipping sauce.
SESAME DIPPING SAUCE
Stir ingredients in small saucepan over medium heat until sugar dissolves.
per serving 20.4g total fat (6.4g saturated fat); 1643kJ (393 cal); 3.8g carbohydrate; 47.1g protein; 0.1g fibre

beef and rice noodle salad

preparation time 10 minutes
cooking time 10 minutes serves 4

400g beef rump steak
100g rice vermicelli noodles
150g snow peas
2 lebanese cucumbers (260g), sliced thickly
⅓ cup fresh coriander leaves

LIME AND CHILLI DRESSING
¼ cup (60ml) lime juice
2 tablespoons peanut oil
1 fresh small red thai chilli, sliced thinly

1 Cook beef on heated oiled grill plate (or grill or barbecue) until cooked as desired. Cover; stand 5 minutes. Slice thinly.
2 Place vermicelli in large heatproof bowl, cover with boiling water; stand until just tender. Drain.
3 Cut snow peas in half diagonally.
4 Make lime and chilli dressing.
5 Place beef, noodles, snow peas and cucumber in large bowl with dressing; toss gently to combine. Sprinkle with coriander.
LIME AND CHILLI DRESSING
Place ingredients in screw-top jar; shake well.
per serving 16.3g total fat (4.6g saturated fat); 1346kJ (322 cal); 17.3g carbohydrate; 25.4g protein; 1.7g fibre

crying tiger

*preparation time 20 minutes
(plus standing and refrigeration time)
cooking time 10 minutes serves 4*

50g dried tamarind
1 cup (250ml) boiling water
400g beef eye fillet
2 cloves garlic, crushed
2 teaspoons dried green peppercorns, crushed
1 tablespoon peanut oil
2 tablespoons fish sauce
2 tablespoons dark soy sauce
10cm stick (20g) fresh lemon grass, chopped finely
2 fresh small red thai chillies, chopped finely
1 large carrot (180g)
1 cup (80g) thinly sliced wombok

CRYING TIGER SAUCE
¼ cup (60ml) fish sauce
¼ cup (60ml) lime juice
2 teaspoons grated palm sugar
1 teaspoon finely chopped dried red thai chilli
1 green onion, sliced thinly
2 teaspoons finely chopped fresh coriander
½ cup reserved tamarind pulp (see step 1)

1 Soak tamarind in the water for 30 minutes. Pour tamarind into a fine strainer set over a small bowl; push as much tamarind pulp through the strainer as possible, scraping underside of strainer occasionally. Discard any tamarind solids left in strainer; reserve ½ cup of pulp for the crying tiger sauce.
2 Halve beef lengthways. Combine remaining tamarind pulp, garlic, peppercorns, oil, sauces, lemon grass and chilli in large bowl with beef. Cover; refrigerate 3 hours or overnight.
3 Make crying tiger sauce.
4 Cook beef on heated oiled grill plate (or grill or barbecue) about 10 minutes or until cooked as desired. Cover beef; stand 10 minutes, slice thinly.
5 Meanwhile, cut carrot into 10cm lengths; slice each length thinly, cut slices into thin matchsticks.
6 Place sliced beef on serving dish with carrot and wombok; serve crying tiger sauce separately.
CRYING TIGER SAUCE
Whisk ingredients in small bowl until sugar dissolves.
per serving 10.9g total fat (3.3g saturated fat); 991kJ (237 cal); 8.5g carbohydrate; 24.8g protein; 2.7g fibre

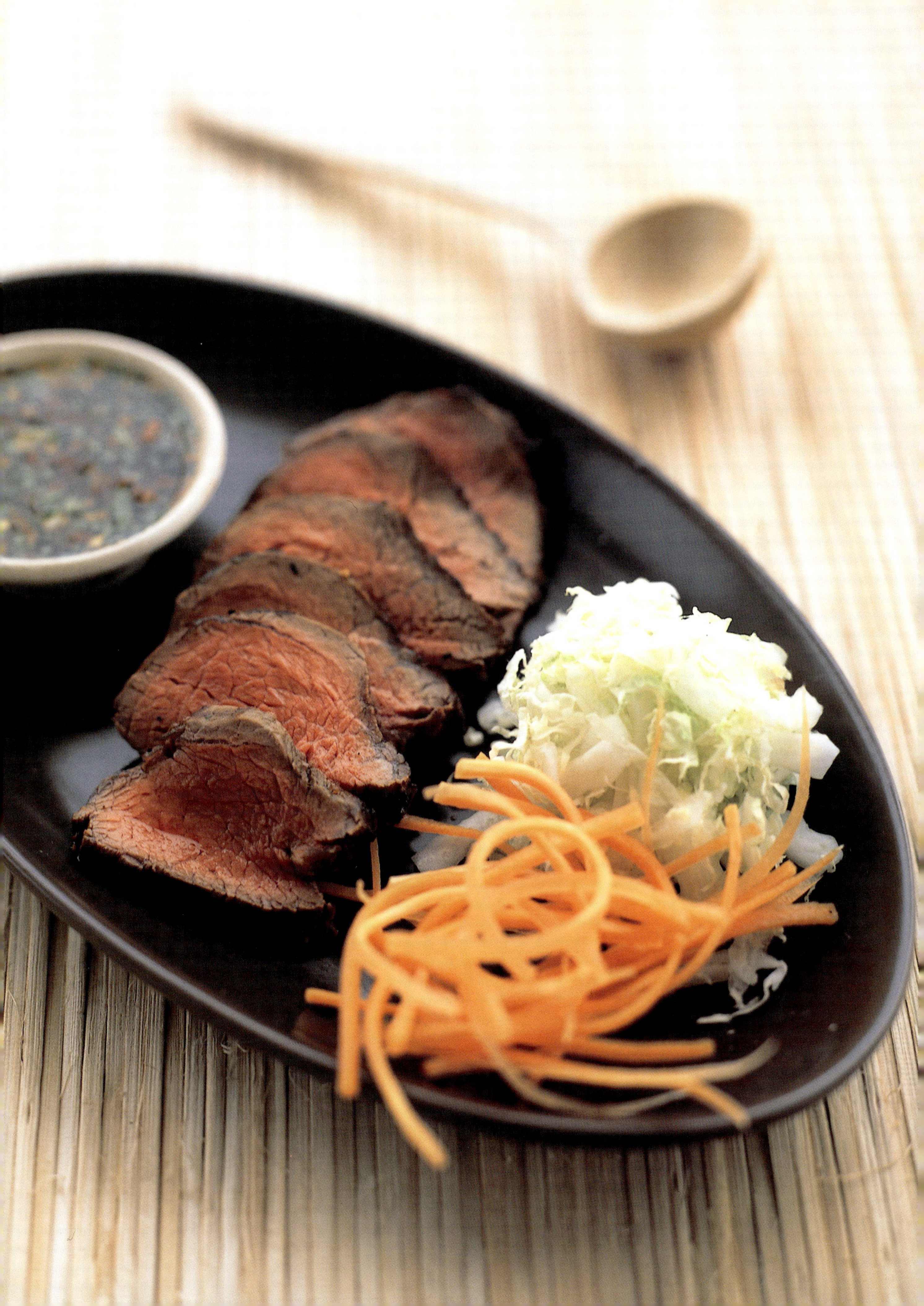

The Complete Book of Modern Asian

mixed sashimi

preparation time 45 minutes
serves 4

½ small daikon (200g)
300g piece sashimi tuna
300g piece sashimi salmon
300g piece sashimi kingfish
1 teaspoon wasabi paste
2 tablespoons japanese pink pickled ginger
⅓ cup (80ml) japanese soy sauce

1 Shred daikon finely; place in bowl of iced water. Reserve.
2 Place tuna on chopping board; using sharp knife, cut 6mm slices at right angles to the grain of the tuna, holding the piece of tuna with your fingers and slicing with the knife almost vertical to the board. Repeat with salmon and kingfish.
3 Divide drained daikon and fish among serving plates; serve with wasabi, ginger and soy sauce.
per serving 11.5g total fat (3.5g saturated fat); 1329kJ (318 cal); 2.5g carbohydrate; 50.3g protein; 1.1g fibre

thai crab and mango salad

preparation time 20 minutes
serves 4

500g fresh crab meat
1 firm medium mango (430g)
100g mizuna
1 cup loosely packed fresh mint leaves
LIME AND CHILLI DRESSING
⅓ cup (80ml) lime juice
2 fresh long red chillies, sliced thinly
5cm piece fresh ginger (25g), cut into matchsticks
2 shallots (50g), sliced thinly
1 tablespoon fish sauce
2 tablespoons grated palm sugar
2 teaspoons peanut oil

1 Make lime and chilli dressing.
2 Combine crab in medium bowl with half the dressing.
3 Using vegetable peeler; slice mango into thin strips. Place mango, mizuna and mint in large bowl with remaining dressing; toss gently to combine.
4 Divide salad among serving plates; top with crab.
LIME AND CHILLI DRESSING
Place ingredients in screw-top jar; shake well.
per serving 3.5g total fat (0.6g saturated fat); 790kJ (189 cal); 19.4g carbohydrate; 18g protein; 3g fibre
TIP You can use an equal weight of prawns or lobster instead of the crab meat in this salad. Make sure your mango is quite firm, otherwise it will not slice well.

lemon grass chicken with chilli dipping sauce

preparation time 20 minutes
cooking time 10 minutes serves 4

200g rice vermicelli noodles
2 tablespoons peanut oil
600g chicken thigh fillets, sliced thinly
2 x 10cm sticks fresh lemon grass (40g), chopped finely
1 clove garlic, crushed
1 tablespoon fish sauce
2 cups (120g) shredded iceberg lettuce
1 medium carrot (120g), grated coarsely
1 lebanese cucumber (130g), halved, seeded, sliced thinly
¼ cup (35g) toasted peanuts, chopped
1 red radish (35g), grated finely

CHILLI DIPPING SAUCE
⅓ cup (75g) sugar
½ cup (125ml) water
1 tablespoon white vinegar
1 fresh small red thai chilli, chopped finely

1 Place noodles in medium heatproof bowl, cover with boiling water. Stand until just tender; drain. Rinse under cold water; drain.
2 Meanwhile, make chilli dipping sauce.
3 Heat half of the oil in wok; stir-fry chicken, in batches, until browned and cooked through. Return all chicken to wok; make a well in the centre. Add remaining oil, lemon grass and garlic; cook about 1 minute or until fragrant and softened. Add sauce; stir-fry until chicken is coated in sauce.
4 Divide the noodles among serving bowls. Top with lettuce, carrot, cucumber and chicken. Sprinkle with peanuts and radish. Serve with dipping sauce.
CHILLI DIPPING SAUCE
Stir sugar and the water in small saucepan over low heat until sugar dissolves; bring to a boil. Reduce heat, simmer, uncovered, 2 minutes or until sauce thickens slightly. Remove from heat; add vinegar and chilli.
per serving 24.4g total fat (5.4g saturated fat); 1914kJ (458 cal); 33g carbohydrate; 32.3g protein; 2.9g fibre

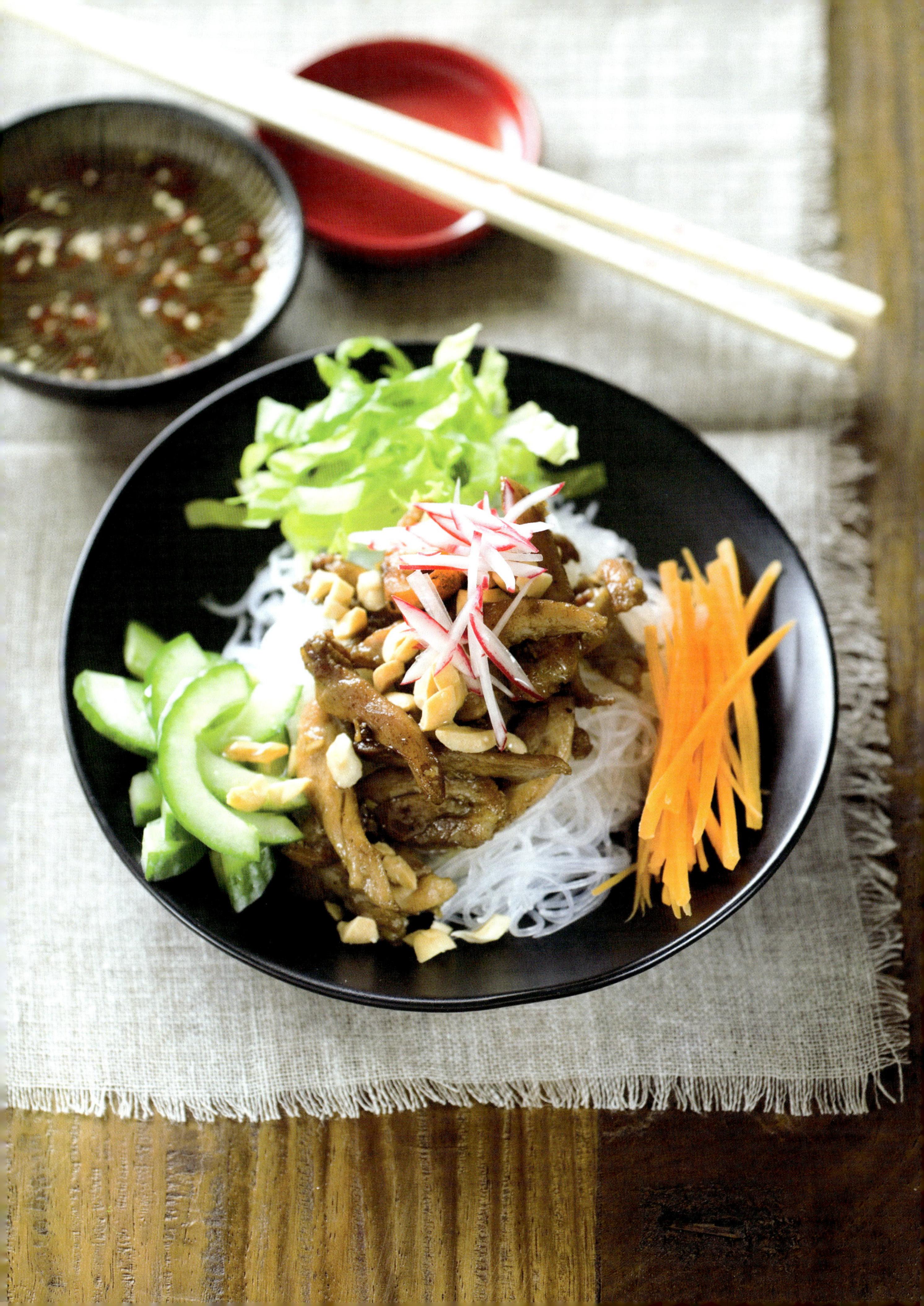

The Complete Book of Modern Asian

sang choy bow

preparation time 15 minutes
cooking time 10 minutes serves 4

1 tablespoon sesame oil
1 medium brown onion (150g), chopped finely
2 cloves garlic, crushed
600g pork mince
¼ cup (60ml) light soy sauce
¼ cup (60ml) oyster sauce
1 medium red capsicum (150g), chopped finely
3 cups (240g) bean sprouts
3 green onions, chopped coarsely
1 tablespoon toasted sesame seeds
8 large iceberg lettuce leaves

1 Heat oil in wok; stir-fry brown onion and garlic until onion softens. Add mince; stir-fry until cooked through. Add sauces and capsicum; reduce heat, simmer, uncovered, stirring occasionally, 3 minutes.
2 Just before serving, stir in sprouts, green onion and seeds. Divide lettuce leaves among serving plates; spoon sang choy bow into leaves.

per serving 19.9g total fat (5.3g saturated fat); 1856kJ (444 cal); 9.4g carbohydrate; 54.4g protein; 4.8g fibre

pickled green papaya salad

preparation time 20 minutes (plus standing time)
cooking time 5 minutes serves 4

1 cup (250ml) water
½ cup (125ml) rice vinegar
½ cup (110g) white sugar
1 teaspoon salt
1 fresh long red chilli, halved lengthways
1 small green papaya (650g)
150g sugar snap peas
100g bean thread noodles
½ small pineapple (450g), quartered, sliced thinly
1 small red onion (100g), sliced thinly
1 cup firmly packed fresh mint leaves
1 fresh long red chilli, sliced thinly

PALM SUGAR DRESSING
¼ cup (60ml) lime juice
2 tablespoons grated palm sugar

1 Combine the water, vinegar, sugar, salt and halved chilli in small saucepan; bring to a boil. Reduce heat, simmer, uncovered, 5 minutes. Strain into small jug; discard solids. Cool 10 minutes.
2 Meanwhile, peel papaya. Quarter lengthways, discard seeds. Grate papaya coarsely.
3 Place papaya in medium bowl with vinegar mixture. Cover; stand 1 hour.
4 Meanwhile, boil, steam or microwave peas until just tender; drain. Place noodles in medium heatproof bowl, cover with boiling water; stand until just tender, drain. Rinse under cold water; drain. Using kitchen scissors, cut noodles into random lengths.
5 Make palm sugar dressing.
6 Place drained papaya, peas and noodles in medium bowl with pineapple, onion, mint and dressing; toss gently to combine.
7 Divide salad among serving bowls; top with sliced chilli.
PALM SUGAR DRESSING
Place ingredients in screw-top jar; shake well.

per serving 0.4g total fat (0.0g saturated fat); 577kJ (138 cal); 29g carbohydrate; 3.1g protein; 6.4g fibre

mussels with basil and lemon grass

preparation time 20 minutes
cooking time 10 minutes serves 6

1kg large mussels
1 tablespoon peanut oil
1 medium brown onion (150g), chopped finely
2 cloves garlic, crushed
10cm stick fresh lemon grass (20g), chopped finely
1 fresh small red thai chilli, chopped finely
1 cup (250ml) dry white wine
2 tablespoons lime juice
2 tablespoons fish sauce
½ cup loosely packed fresh thai basil leaves
½ cup (125ml) coconut milk
1 fresh small red thai chilli, sliced thinly
2 green onions, sliced thinly

1 Scrub mussels under cold water; remove beards.
2 Heat oil in wok; stir-fry brown onion, garlic, lemon grass and chopped chilli until onion softens and mixture is fragrant.
3 Add wine, juice and sauce; bring to a boil. Add mussels; reduce heat, simmer, covered, 5 minutes or until mussels open (discard any that do not).
4 Meanwhile, shred half of the basil finely. Add shredded basil and coconut milk to wok; stir-fry until heated through.
5 Divide mussel mixture among serving bowls; sprinkle with sliced chilli, green onion and remaining basil.
per serving 12.1g total fat (6.8g saturated fat); 886kJ (212 cal); 6.9g carbohydrate; 8.4g protein; 1.7g fibre

crab fried rice in omelette

preparation time 15 minutes
cooking time 25 minutes serves 4

¼ cup (60ml) peanut oil
4 green onions, chopped finely
2 fresh small red thai chillies, chopped finely
1 tablespoon red curry paste
2 cups cooked jasmine rice
250g fresh crab meat
2 tablespoons lime juice
2 tablespoons fish sauce
8 eggs
2 tablespoons water
1 lime, cut into wedges

1 Heat 1 tablespoon of the oil in wok; stir-fry onion and chilli until onion softens. Add curry paste; stir-fry until mixture is fragrant.
2 Add rice; stir-fry until heated through. Remove from heat; place in large bowl. Add crab meat, juice and sauce; toss gently to combine.
3 Whisk eggs with the water in medium bowl. Heat about a quarter of the remaining oil in same cleaned wok; pour a quarter of the egg mixture into wok. Cook omelette, tilting pan, over low heat until egg is almost set. Spoon a quarter of the fried rice into centre of the omelette; using spatula, fold four sides of omelette over to enclose filling.
4 Press omelette firmly with spatula; turn carefully to brown other side. Remove omelette from wok; cover to keep warm. Repeat with remaining oil, egg mixture and fried rice until you have four omelettes. Place omelettes on serving plate; serve with lime wedges.
per serving 26.9g total fat (6g saturated fat); 2930kJ (701 cal); 83.7g carbohydrate; 29.4g protein; 1.9g fibre
TIP You will need to cook ⅔ cup (130g) jasmine rice.

First Courses

The Complete Book of Modern Asian

pomelo salad

preparation time 20 minutes
cooking time 15 minutes serves 4

1 small red onion (100g)
4 large pomelos (4kg)
2 green onions, sliced thinly
2 fresh small red thai chillies, sliced thinly
¼ cup coarsely chopped fresh coriander
½ cup (70g) coarsely chopped roasted unsalted peanuts
2 cloves garlic, crushed
1 tablespoon grated palm sugar
¼ cup (60ml) lime juice
1 tablespoon light soy sauce

1 Halve red onion; cut each half into paper-thin wedges.
2 Peel and carefully segment pomelos; discard membranes. Place segments in large bowl with onions, chilli, coriander and nuts.
3 Combine remaining ingredients in small jug; stir until sugar dissolves. Pour dressing over pomelo mixture; toss gently to combine.

per serving 9.7g total fat (1.2g saturated fat); 1241kJ (297 cal); 38.1g carbohydrate; 11.2g protein; 6.2g fibre

chilli salt squid

preparation time 20 minutes
cooking time 10 minutes serves 8

1kg small whole squid
peanut oil, for deep-frying
2 fresh long red chillies, sliced
1 cup loosely packed fresh coriander leaves
⅓ cup (50g) plain flour
2 fresh long red chillies, chopped finely, extra
2 teaspoons sea salt
1 teaspoon ground black pepper

1 Gently separate body and tentacles of squid by pulling on tentacles. Cut head from tentacles just below eyes and discard head. Trim the long tentacle of each squid.
2 Remove the clear quill from inside the body and discard. If you have broken the ink sac, wash the squid thoroughly.
3 Peel side flaps from body with salted fingers (the salt gives more grip), then peel away the dark skin. Wash squid well and pat dry with absorbent paper.
4 Cut along one side of the body and open out. Score the inside surface in a criss-cross pattern, using a small sharp knife. Cut the body into pieces.
5 Heat oil in wok; deep-fry chilli until softened. Drain on absorbent paper. Deep-fry coriander carefully (oil will spit) for 10 seconds or until changed in colour; drain on absorbent paper.
6 Toss squid in combined flour, extra chilli, salt and pepper. Shake away excess. Deep-fry squid, in batches, until tender; drain on absorbent paper. Sprinkle squid with coriander and chilli.

per serving 8.1g total fat (1.7g saturated fat); 807kJ (193 cal); 9.6g carbohydrate; 19.7g protein; 1g fibre

The Complete Book of Modern Asian

Soups are eaten 24/7 throughout Asia, offering sustenance for the workday ahead at breakfast, and succour as evening descends. From the tom yums of Thailand and phos of Vietnam to the subtle broths of China and misos of Japan, Asian cultures embrace the stockpot as much as they do the wok, and this rich collection offers something for every meal and mood.

coconut, chicken and kaffir lime soup *page 105*

pho bo *page 106*

soups

chilli crab laksa *page 98*

chicken pho *page 93*

chinese wonton soup

preparation time 40 minutes
cooking time 2 hours 10 minutes serves 4

1kg chicken bones
1 small brown onion (80g), quartered
1 medium carrot (120g), quartered
3 litres (12 cups) water
4cm piece fresh ginger (20g), grated
2 fresh small red thai chillies, halved lengthways
150g pork mince
1 clove garlic, crushed
1 green onion, chopped finely
2 tablespoons finely chopped water chestnuts
2 tablespoons finely chopped fresh coriander
1 teaspoon sesame oil
2 tablespoons chinese cooking wine
¼ cup (60ml) light soy sauce
2 teaspoons caster sugar
12 wonton wrappers
1 cup firmly packed watercress sprigs
4 fresh shiitake mushrooms, sliced thinly

1 Combine chicken bones, onion, carrot, the water, three-quarters of the ginger and half of the chilli in large saucepan; bring to a boil. Reduce heat, simmer, uncovered, about 2 hours or until reduced by half. Strain broth through muslin-lined sieve or colander into large bowl; discard solids.
2 Meanwhile, chop remaining chilli finely. Combine in small bowl with pork, garlic, onion, water chestnut, coriander, oil, 2 teaspoons of the wine, 1 teaspoon of the soy sauce, half of the sugar and remaining ginger.
3 Place 1 level tablespoon of pork filling on centre of each wonton wrapper; brush around edges with a little water, gather edges around filling, pinch together to seal. Repeat process with remaining pork filling and wonton wrappers.
4 Skim fat from surface of broth; return broth to large saucepan. Add remaining wine, remaining soy sauce and remaining sugar; bring to a boil. Add wontons to pan; cook, uncovered, about 5 minutes or until cooked through.
5 Meanwhile, divide watercress and mushrooms among serving bowls. Using slotted spoon, transfer wontons from pan to bowls then ladle broth into bowls.
per serving 4.4g total fat (1.3g saturated fat); 648kJ (155 cal); 16.2g carbohydrate; 11.2g protein; 2.7g fibre

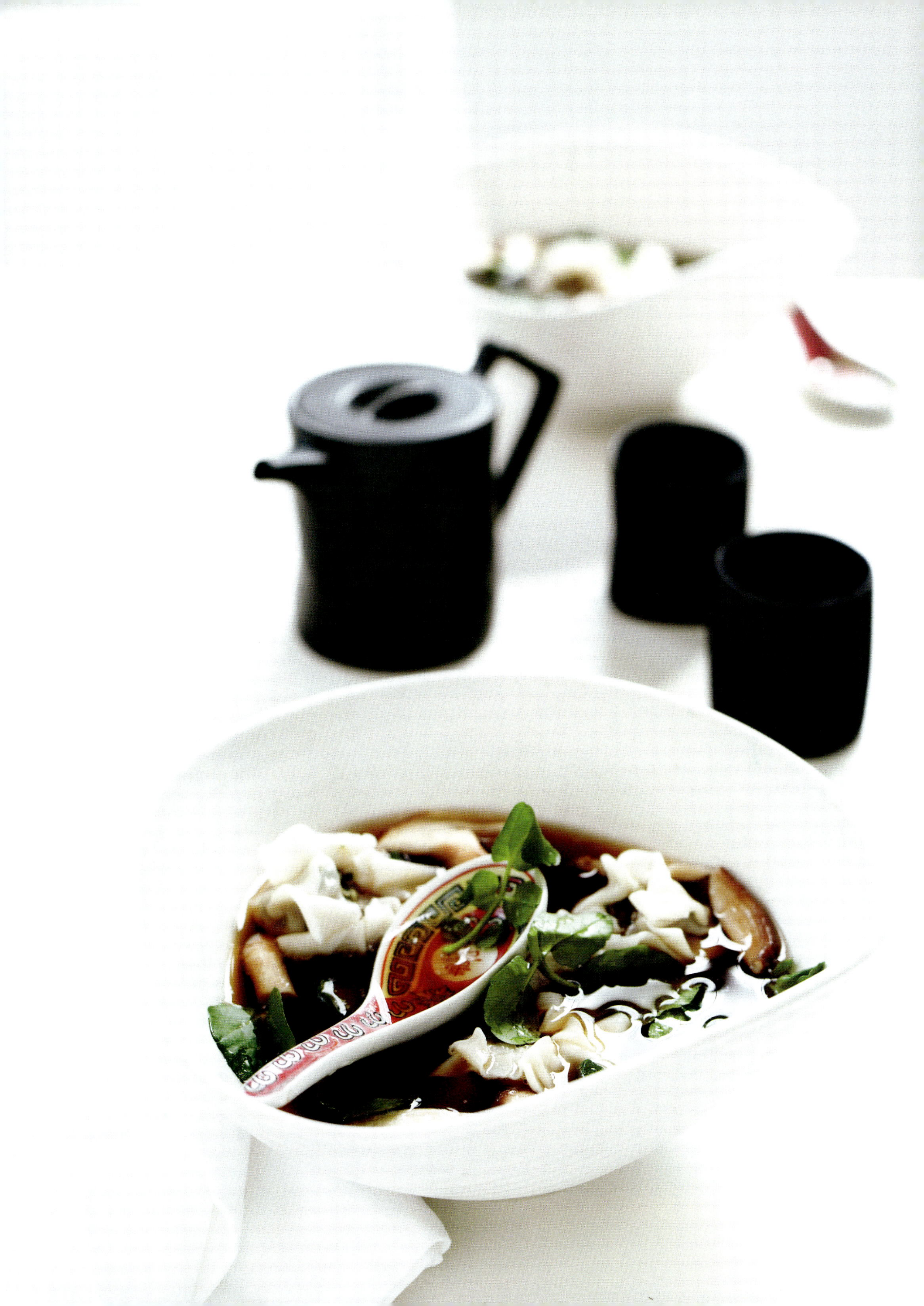

The Complete Book of Modern Asian

prawn soup

preparation time 30 minutes
cooking time 25 minutes serves 6

500g uncooked king prawns
2cm piece fresh ginger (10g), sliced thinly
1 teaspoon black peppercorns
2 cloves garlic, crushed
10cm stick fresh lemon grass (20g), chopped finely
3 litres (12 cups) water
2 fresh long red chillies, sliced thinly
400g fresh rice noodles
¼ cup (60ml) lemon juice
⅓ cup (80ml) fish sauce, approximately
2 green onions, sliced thinly
⅓ cup firmly packed fresh coriander leaves
¼ cup firmly packed fresh mint leaves

1 Peel and devein prawns, discard heads. Place prawn shells, ginger, peppercorns, garlic, lemon grass, the water and half of the chilli in large saucepan; bring to a boil. Reduce heat, simmer, uncovered, 20 minutes. Strain stock, discard solids; return liquid to cleaned pan.
2 Add prawns to stock; simmer, covered, 3 minutes or until prawns are changed in colour.
3 Place noodles in medium heatproof bowl, cover with boiling water; stand until just tender. Drain.
4 Add juice to stock, gradually add sauce to taste.
5 Divide prawns and noodles among serving bowls; top with stock, onion, herbs and remaining chilli.
per serving 0.7g total fat (0g saturated fat); 497kJ (119 cal); 15.8g carbohydrate; 11.3g protein; 1.1g fibre

chicken pho

preparation time 20 minutes (plus cooling time)
cooking time 30 minutes serves 6

3 litres (12 cups) chicken stock
8cm piece fresh ginger (40g), sliced thinly
2 tablespoons fish sauce
2 cloves garlic, quartered
½ cup coarsely chopped fresh coriander roots
1 star anise
400g chicken breast fillets, sliced thinly
400g rice stick noodles
12 green onions, sliced
3 cups (240g) bean sprouts
½ cup loosely packed vietnamese mint leaves
½ cup loosely packed fresh coriander leaves
sambal oelek, to serve
1 medium lemon (140g), cut into wedges

1 Combine stock, ginger, sauce, garlic, coriander roots and star anise in large saucepan; bring to a boil. Reduce heat, simmer, uncovered, 10 minutes. Strain into bowl; discard ginger, coriander roots, garlic and star anise.
2 Return stock to pan, add chicken; simmer, uncovered, about 5 minutes or until chicken is cooked through.
3 Meanwhile, place noodles in large heatproof bowl, cover with boiling water; stand until just softened. Drain.
4 Divide noodles, onion and bean sprouts among serving bowls; top with soup, mint and coriander. Serve with sambal and lemon.
per serving 4.1g total fat (1.4g saturated fat); 936kJ (224 cal); 20.7g carbohydrate; 24.6g protein; 3.2g fibre

chicken laksa

preparation time 30 minutes (plus cooling time)
cooking time 45 minutes serves 4

1 litre (4 cups) water
12 fresh kaffir lime leaves
2 cloves garlic, quartered
800g chicken thigh fillets
½ cup (150g) laksa paste (see page 114)
3¼ cups (800ml) coconut milk
2 fresh red thai chillies, chopped finely
150g dried rice stick noodles
175g singapore noodles
2 tablespoons grated palm sugar
⅓ cup (80ml) lime juice
2 tablespoons fish sauce
80g fried tofu puffs, halved
1½ cups (120g) bean sprouts
½ cup loosely packed fresh coriander leaves
½ cup loosely packed vietnamese mint leaves

1 Place the water in large saucepan; bring to a boil. Add 4 lime leaves, garlic and chicken; reduce heat, simmer, covered, about 15 minutes or until chicken is cooked through. Cool chicken in liquid 15 minutes. Slice chicken thinly; reserve. Strain stock through muslin-lined sieve or colander into large bowl; discard solids. Allow stock to cool; skim fat from surface.
2 Cook laksa paste in large saucepan, stirring, until fragrant. Stir in stock, coconut milk, chilli and remaining torn lime leaves; bring to a boil. Reduce heat, simmer, uncovered, 20 minutes.
3 Meanwhile, place rice stick noodles in large heatproof bowl, cover with boiling water, stand until just tender; drain. Place singapore noodles in separate large heatproof bowl; cover with boiling water, separate with fork, drain. Divide both noodles among serving bowls.
4 Stir sugar, juice, sauce, tofu and chicken into laksa. Ladle laksa over noodles; sprinkle with combined sprouts and herbs.

per serving 69.7g total fat (42.2g saturated fat); 4577kJ (1095 cal); 65g carbohydrate; 53.2g protein; 10.8g fibre

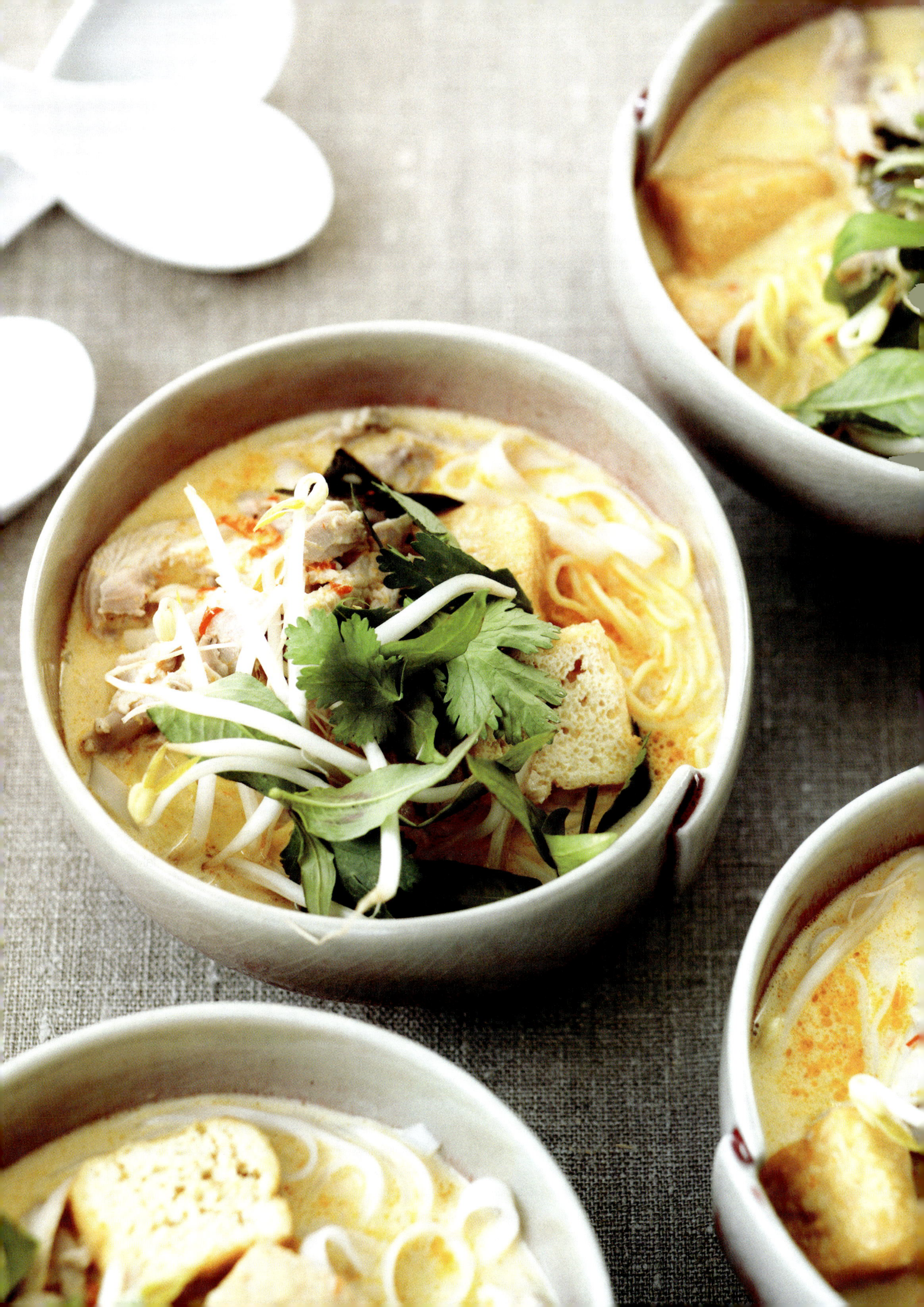

The Complete Book of Modern Asian

spicy seafood soup

preparation time 20 minutes
cooking time 15 minutes serves 4

1 uncooked medium blue swimmer crab (325g)
200g firm white fish fillets
8 medium black mussels (200g)
150g squid hoods
1.25 litres (5 cups) chicken stock
2 x 10cm sticks fresh lemon grass (40g), chopped finely
4cm piece fresh galangal (20g), sliced thinly
4 fresh kaffir lime leaves
6 small green thai chillies, chopped coarsely
4 dried long red thai chillies, chopped finely
8 uncooked large prawns (560g)
1 teaspoon grated palm sugar
2 tablespoons fish sauce
1 tablespoon lime juice
¼ cup loosely packed fresh thai basil leaves

1 Remove and discard back shell and gills of crab; rinse under cold water. Chop crab body into quarters, leaving claws intact. Cut fish into bite-sized portions; scrub mussels, remove beards. Score inside of squid hoods in a diagonal pattern; cut into 2cm slices.
2 Combine stock, lemon grass, galangal, lime leaves and the chillies in large saucepan; bring to a boil.
3 Add crab, fish, mussels, squid and unshelled prawns to boiling stock mixture; cook, uncovered, about 5 minutes or until seafood is just cooked through. Remove from heat (discard any mussels that do not open); stir in remaining ingredients. Serve hot.

per serving 3.7g total fat (1.3g saturated fat); 907kJ (217 cal); 5.9g carbohydrate; 39.2g protein; 0.9g fibre

curry and lime lentil soup

preparation time 15 minutes
cooking time 30 minutes serves 4

2 teaspoons vegetable oil
1 tablespoon hot curry paste
1 medium brown onion (150g), chopped finely
2 cloves garlic, crushed
2cm piece fresh ginger (10g), grated
1 teaspoon cumin seeds
1 cup (200g) red lentils
2 cups (500ml) vegetable stock
2½ cups (625ml) water
400g can diced tomatoes
1 teaspoon finely grated lime rind
¼ cup (60ml) lime juice
⅓ cup finely chopped fresh flat-leaf parsley

1 Heat oil in large saucepan; cook curry paste, stirring, until fragrant. Add onion, garlic, ginger and cumin; cook, stirring, until onion softens.
2 Add lentils, stock, the water and undrained tomatoes; bring to a boil. Reduce heat; simmer, uncovered, about 20 minutes or until lentils soften.
3 Stir in rind and juice; return to a boil. Stir in parsley off the heat.

per serving 6g total fat (1g saturated fat); 995kJ (238 cal); 25.4g carbohydrate; 15.5g protein; 10g fibre

chilli crab laksa

preparation time 40 minutes (plus standing time) cooking time 30 minutes serves 4

2 uncooked whole mud crabs (1.5kg)
2 tablespoons peanut oil
3 fresh long red chillies, chopped finely
2 cloves garlic, crushed
2cm piece fresh ginger (10g), grated
½ cup (125ml) fish stock
⅔ cup (180g) laksa paste (see page 114)
3¼ cups (800ml) coconut milk
1 litre (4 cups) chicken stock
3 fresh kaffir lime leaves, shredded finely
1 fresh long red chilli, chopped finely, extra
1 tablespoon lime juice
1 tablespoon fish sauce
1 tablespoon grated palm sugar
250g rice stick noodles
3 green onions, sliced thinly
3 cups (240g) bean sprouts
½ cup loosely packed fresh coriander leaves

1 Place crabs in large container filled with ice and water; stand 1 hour. Leaving flesh in claws and legs, prepare crab by lifting tail flap and, with a peeling motion, lift off back shell. Remove and discard whitish gills, liver and brain matter; crack claws with back of knife. Rinse crabs well. Using cleaver or heavy knife, chop each body into quarters.
2 Heat oil in wok; stir-fry chilli, garlic and ginger until fragrant. Add crab and fish stock to wok; bring to a boil. Reduce heat, simmer, covered, about 20 minutes or until crab is changed in colour. Discard liquid in wok.
3 Meanwhile, cook paste in large saucepan, stirring, until fragrant. Stir in coconut milk, chicken stock, lime leaf and extra chilli; bring to a boil. Reduce heat, simmer, covered, 20 minutes. Stir in juice, sauce and sugar.
4 Meanwhile, place noodles in large heatproof bowl; cover with boiling water. Stand until tender; drain.
5 Divide noodles and crab among serving bowls; ladle laksa into bowls, top with onion, sprouts and coriander.
per serving 68.2g total fat (40g saturated fat); 4096kJ (980 cal); 31.8g carbohydrate; 56.1g protein; 11g fibre

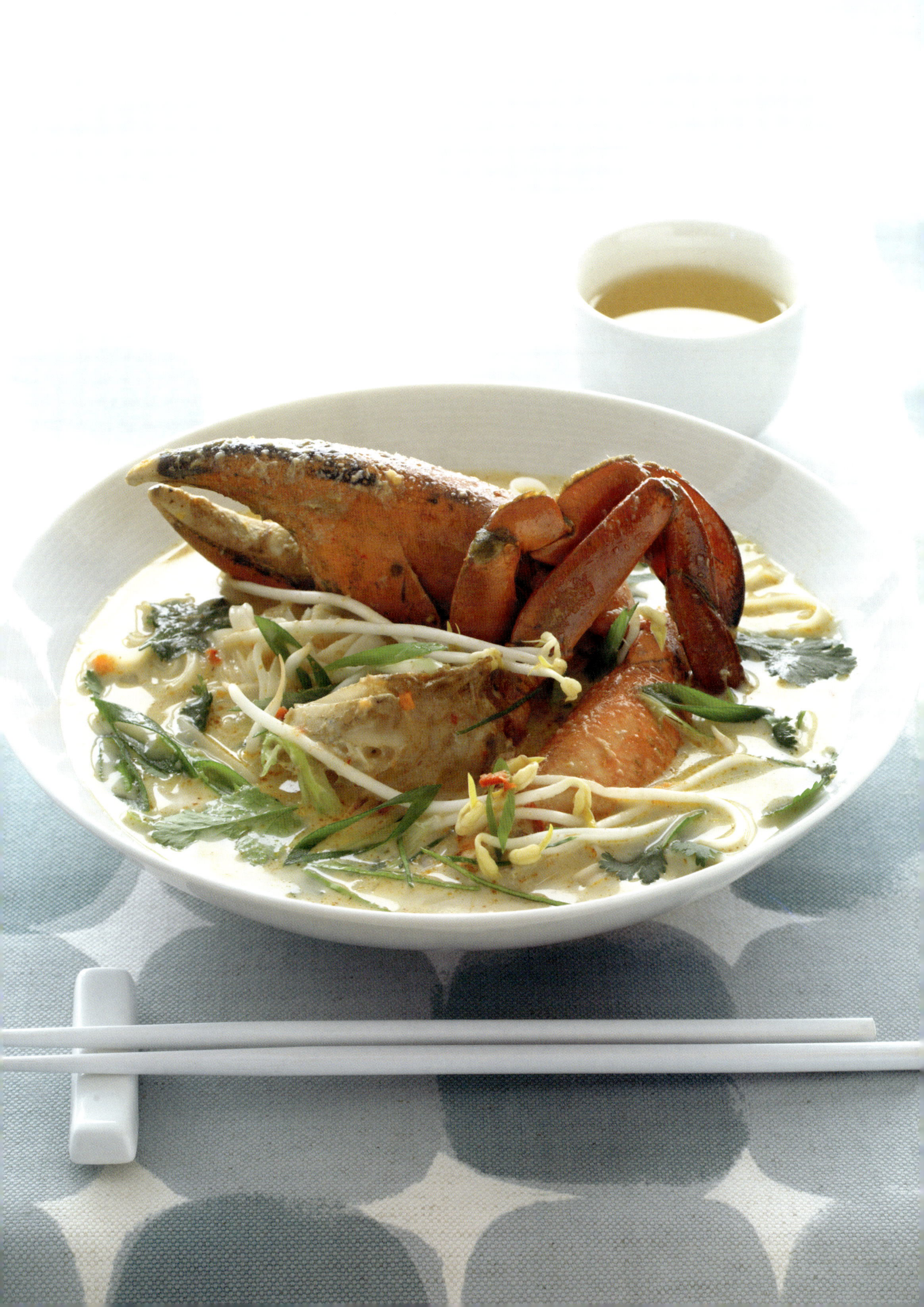

The Complete Book of Modern Asian

combination long soup

preparation time 10 minutes
cooking time 30 minutes serves 4

1 litre (4 cups) water
500g chicken breast fillets
2 litres (8 cups) chicken stock
1 tablespoon japanese soy sauce
2cm piece fresh ginger (10g), grated
225g fresh thin wheat noodles
100g cooked shelled small prawns
200g chinese barbecued pork, sliced thinly
4 green onions, sliced thinly
1 small red capsicum (150g), sliced thinly
100g mushrooms, sliced thinly
1¼ cups (100g) bean sprouts

1 Bring the water to a boil in large saucepan; add chicken, return to a boil. Reduce heat, simmer, covered, about 10 minutes or until chicken is cooked. Cool chicken in poaching liquid 10 minutes. Remove chicken from pan; discard poaching liquid. When cool enough to handle, slice chicken thinly.
2 Bring stock, sauce and ginger to a boil in same cleaned pan; add noodles, separating with a fork. Add chicken and remaining ingredients; reduce heat, simmer, uncovered, about 5 minutes or until soup is hot.
per serving 26.6g total fat (11.2g saturated fat); 2633kJ (630 cal); 37.9g carbohydrate; 56g protein; 7.8g fibre

malaysian chicken noodle soup

preparation time 15 minutes
cooking time 25 minutes serves 6

2 cloves garlic, crushed
3 teaspoons ground cumin
½ teaspoon ground turmeric
400g chicken breast fillets, sliced thickly
1.5 litres (6 cups) chicken stock
1 tablespoon white sugar
½ teaspoon shrimp paste
3 teaspoons sambal oelek
2cm piece fresh galangal (10g), grated finely
50g rice vermicelli noodles
1 cup (80g) bean sprouts
3 butter lettuce leaves, shredded
2 tablespoons coarsely chopped fresh coriander

1 Stir garlic, cumin and turmeric in large saucepan over heat about 1 minute or until fragrant.
2 Add chicken, stock, sugar, paste, sambal oelek and galangal to pan; stir until combined, bring to a boil. Reduce heat, simmer, uncovered, 10 minutes.
3 Add noodles to pan; simmer 10 minutes.
4 Stir in bean sprouts, lettuce and coriander.
per serving 4g total fat (1.3g saturated fat); 577kJ (138 cal); 7.4g carbohydrate; 17.6g protein; 1.2g fibre

asian star

tom yum goong

preparation time 50 minutes
cooking time 15 minutes serves 4

1.5 litres (6 cups) fish stock
1 tablespoon coarsely chopped coriander root and stem mixture
10cm stick fresh lemon grass (20g), chopped finely
8 fresh kaffir lime leaves, torn
8cm piece fresh ginger (40g), sliced thinly
2 fresh small red thai chillies, sliced thinly
1 tablespoon fish sauce
12 uncooked large king prawns (840g)
8 green onions, cut into 2cm lengths
⅓ cup (80ml) lime juice
⅔ cup loosely packed fresh coriander leaves
½ cup loosely packed fresh thai basil leaves, torn

1 Place stock, coriander root and stem mixture, lemon grass, lime leaves, ginger, chilli and sauce in large saucepan; bring to a boil. Reduce heat, simmer, uncovered, 10 minutes.
2 Meanwhile, shell and devein prawns, leaving tails intact. Add prawns, onion and juice to pan; simmer, uncovered, about 4 minutes or until prawns just change in colour. Remove from heat; stir in coriander and basil leaves.

per serving 1.6g total fat (0.5g saturated fat); 606kJ (145 cal); 4.5g carbohydrate; 27g protein; 1.2g fibre

To make your own fish stock, use prawn heads and shells.

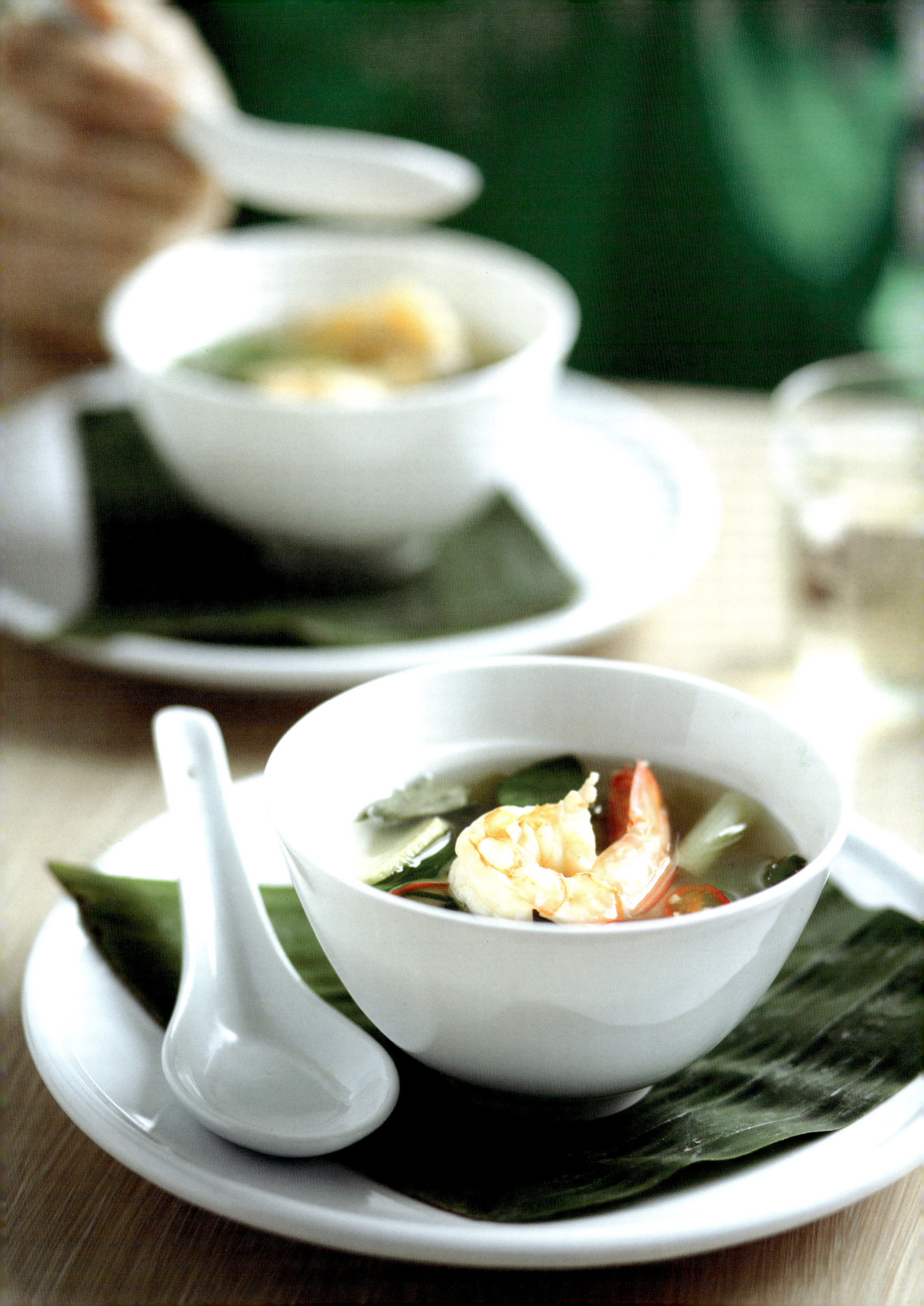

The Complete Book of Modern Asian

chicken in citrus wakame broth

preparation time 25 minutes
cooking time 25 minutes serves 4

5g wakame (dried seaweed)
3cm piece fresh ginger (15g), sliced thinly
1 fresh small red thai chilli, sliced thinly
2 cloves garlic, sliced thinly
2 kaffir lime leaves, torn
1 litre (4 cups) chicken stock
2 cups (500ml) water
2 chicken breast fillets (400g)
100g dried soba noodles
½ cup (40g) bean sprouts
2 tablespoons fish sauce
⅓ cup (80ml) lime juice
2 baby buk choy (300g), leaves separated

1 Place wakame in small bowl, cover with cold water; stand about 10 minutes or until softened. Drain then squeeze out excess water. Chop coarsely, removing any hard ribs or stems.
2 Combine ginger, chilli, garlic, lime leaves, stock, the water and chicken in large saucepan; bring to a boil. Reduce heat, simmer, uncovered, about 10 minutes or until cooked through. Cool chicken in broth 10 minutes; remove from pan. Strain broth through muslin-lined sieve over large bowl; discard solids, return broth to pan. Slice chicken thinly.
3 Meanwhile, cook soba in large saucepan of boiling water, uncovered, until just tender; drain. Divide soba, wakame and sprouts among serving bowls.
4 Bring broth to a boil; reduce heat and stir in sauce, juice and buk choy. Serve broth topped with chicken. Serve with lime wedges, if desired.
per serving 3.9g total fat (1.2g saturated fat); 1053kJ (252 cal); 20.9g carbohydrate; 30.7g protein; 3.3g fibre

coconut, chicken and kaffir lime soup

preparation time 15 minutes
cooking time 45 minutes serves 4

1 tablespoon peanut oil
600g chicken thigh fillets, cut into 1cm strips
¼ cup (75g) green curry paste
1 litre (4 cups) chicken stock
3¼ cups (800ml) coconut milk
1 long green chilli, chopped finely
8 fresh kaffir lime leaves, shredded
250g rice vermicelli noodles
2 tablespoons grated palm sugar
2 tablespoons lime juice
2 tablespoons fish sauce
1 cup (80g) bean sprouts
½ cup loosely packed vietnamese mint leaves

1 Heat oil in large saucepan; cook chicken, in batches, until browned lightly.
2 Place paste in same pan; cook, stirring, until fragrant. Return chicken to pan with stock, coconut milk, chilli and lime leaf; bring to a boil. Reduce heat, simmer, uncovered, 30 minutes, skimming fat from surface occasionally. Add noodles; cook, uncovered, until noodles are just tender. Stir in sugar, juice and sauce.
3 Serve bowls of soup sprinkled with sprouts and mint.
per serving 63.9g total fat (41.6g saturated fat); 3478kJ (832 cal); 25g carbohydrate; 38g protein; 6.8g fibre

pho bo

preparation time 40 minutes
cooking time 2 hours 30 minutes serves 6

1.5kg beef bones
2 medium brown onions (300g), chopped coarsely
2 medium carrots (240g), chopped coarsely
4 trimmed celery stalks (400g), chopped coarsely
2 cinnamon sticks
4 star anise
6 cardamom pods, bruised
10 black peppercorns
2 tablespoons fish sauce
6 cloves
12cm piece fresh ginger (60g), sliced thinly
6 cloves garlic, sliced thinly
500g piece gravy beef
4 litres (16 cups) water
2 tablespoons dark soy sauce
200g bean thread vermicelli noodles
½ cup loosely packed vietnamese mint leaves
4 fresh small red thai chillies, sliced thinly
1 medium brown onion (150g), sliced thinly, extra
½ cup loosely packed fresh coriander leaves
1¼ cups (100g) bean sprouts

1 Preheat oven to 220°C/200°C fan-forced.
2 Combine beef bones, onion, carrot and celery in large baking dish; roast, uncovered, about 45 minutes or until browned all over. Drain excess fat from dish.
3 Combine beef mixture, cinnamon, star anise, cardamom, peppercorns, fish sauce, cloves, ginger, garlic, gravy beef and the water in large saucepan. Bring to a boil; simmer, uncovered, 1½ hours, skimming occasionally. Strain through muslin-lined strainer into large bowl. Reserve broth and beef; discard bones and spices. When beef is cool enough to handle, shred finely; return to cleaned pan with soy sauce and broth.
4 Just before serving, place noodles in large heatproof bowl; cover with boiling water, stand until tender, drain.
5 Divide noodles among serving bowls; top with broth and beef mixture, mint, chilli, extra onion and coriander. Serve with sprouts.
per serving 4.7g total fat (1.9g saturated fat); 1074kJ (257 cal); 30.1g carbohydrate; 23g protein; 6.2g fibre

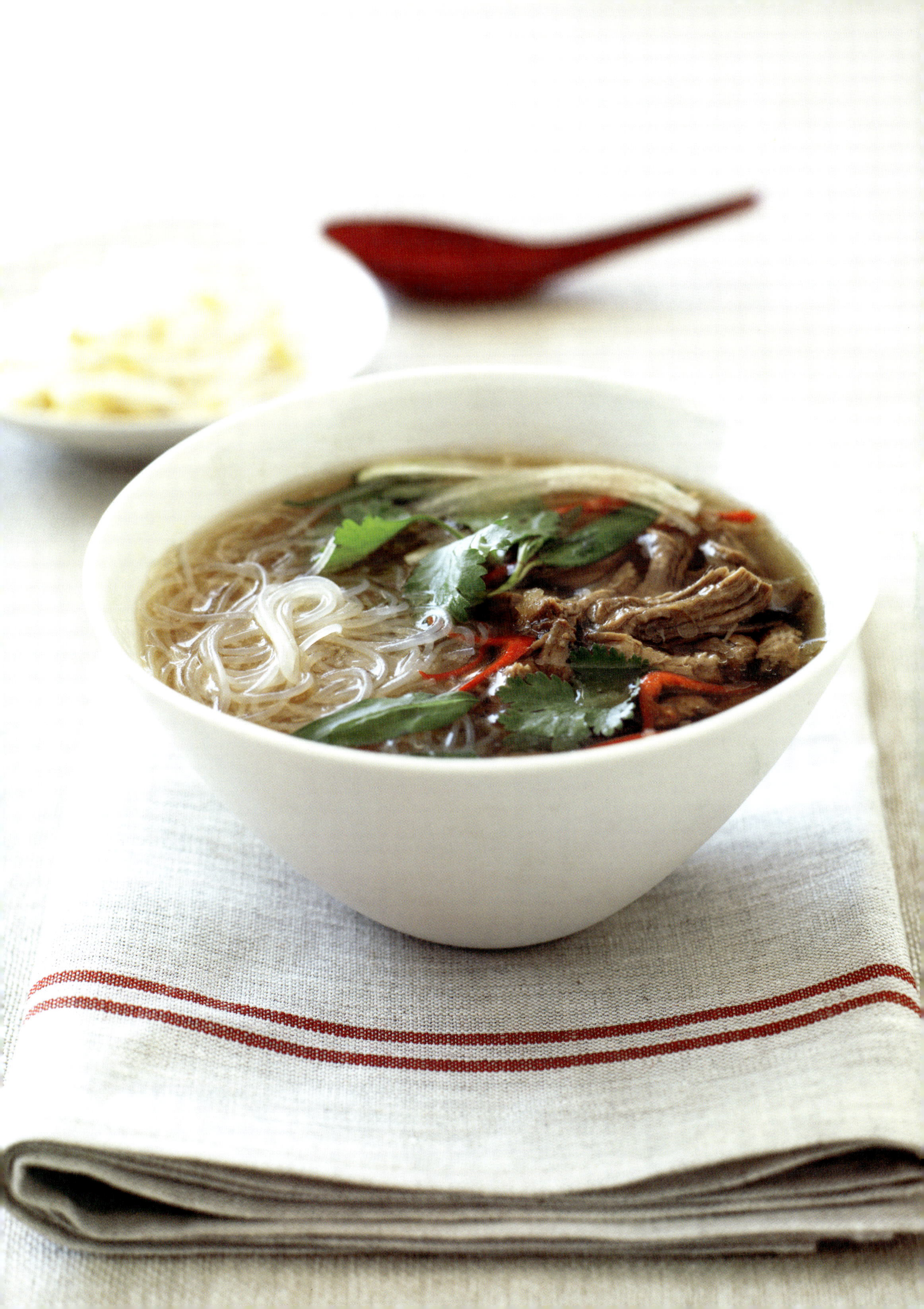

The Complete Book of Modern Asian

udon noodle soup

preparation time 10 minutes
cooking time 30 minutes serves 4

1.5 litres (6 cups) dashi
2 tablespoons japanese soy sauce
1 tablespoon mirin
2 teaspoons white sugar
2 chicken breast fillets (400g)
100g fresh shiitake mushrooms, sliced thinly
300g dried udon noodles
230g can sliced bamboo shoots, rinsed, drained
8 large spinach leaves
4 eggs
4 green onions, sliced thinly

1 Preheat oven to 220°C/200°C fan-forced.
2 Bring dashi, sauce, mirin and sugar to a boil in large saucepan; add chicken and mushrooms, return to a boil. Reduce heat, simmer, uncovered, about 10 minutes or until chicken is cooked through. Cool chicken and mushrooms in cooking liquid 10 minutes. Remove chicken from pan, slice thinly. Reserve mushrooms and dashi broth.
3 Meanwhile, cook noodles in large saucepan of boiling water, uncovered, until just tender; drain. Rinse under cold water; drain.
4 Return broth to a boil. Divide noodles, chicken, bamboo shoots, spinach and hot broth with mushrooms among four 3-cup (750ml) ovenproof dishes. Make small hollows among noodles in each dish; break 1 egg into each hollow. Cook, uncovered, about 10 minutes or until egg just sets.
5 Serve soup sprinkled with onion.
per serving 39g total fat (8.4g saturated fat); 4761kJ (1139 cal); 121.1g carbohydrate; 85.3g protein; 27.8g fibre

duck and mushroom soup

preparation time 30 minutes (plus standing time)
cooking time 30 minutes serves 6

20g dried shiitake mushrooms
15g dried black fungus
1kg chinese barbecued duck
1 litre (4 cups) water
1 litre (4 cups) chicken stock
2 teaspoons grated palm sugar
1 tablespoon mushroom soy sauce
230g can bamboo shoots, rinsed, drained
100g swiss brown mushrooms, sliced thinly
1 tablespoon cornflour
1 tablespoon water, extra
4 green onions, sliced thinly

1 Place shiitake and black fungus in small bowl, cover with cold water; stand 1 hour. Drain; slice thinly.
2 Remove and discard bones from duck; reserve skin, slice meat thinly. Preheat grill.
3 Combine the water and stock in large saucepan; bring to a boil. Add duck, shiitake, black fungus, sugar, sauce, bamboo shoots and mushrooms; return to a boil.
4 Place duck skin, in single layer, on oven tray; grill about 5 minutes or until crisp. Discard excess fat; chop skin coarsely.
5 Meanwhile, add blended cornflour and the water to soup; simmer, uncovered, about 2 minutes or until thickened slightly.
6 Serve bowls of soup sprinkled with crisp duck skin and onion.
per serving 22.4g total fat (6.8g saturated fat); 1246kJ (298 cal); 4.7g carbohydrate; 19.5g protein; 1.1g fibre

vegetable dumplings in asian broth

preparation time 45 minutes
cooking time 55 minutes serves 4

100g fresh shiitake mushrooms
2 green onions
1 medium brown onion (150g), chopped coarsely
1 medium carrot (120g), chopped coarsely
2 cloves garlic, chopped coarsely
2cm piece fresh ginger (10g), chopped coarsely
1 star anise
1 teaspoon sichuan peppercorns
¼ cup (60ml) light soy sauce
2 tablespoons chinese cooking wine
4 coriander roots
1 teaspoon white sugar
1.5 litres (6 cups) water
800g buk choy
1cm piece fresh ginger (5g), extra, grated
1 clove garlic, extra, crushed
227g can water chestnuts, drained, chopped finely
1 egg white, beaten lightly
¼ cup (15g) stale breadcrumbs
2 tablespoons finely chopped fresh coriander
1 tablespoon vegetarian mushroom oyster sauce
20 wonton wrappers
100g enoki mushrooms, trimmed

1 Separate stems from caps of the shiitake mushrooms; reserve stems. Finely chop a quarter of the shiitake caps; slice remaining shiitake caps thinly. Coarsely chop white section of green onion. Thinly slice green section; reserve green section in small bowl.
2 Combine shiitake mushroom stems, white section of green onion, brown onion, carrot, garlic, ginger, star anise, peppercorns, soy sauce, wine, coriander roots, sugar and the water in large saucepan; bring to a boil. Reduce heat, simmer, uncovered, 45 minutes. Strain stock through muslin-lined sieve or colander into large bowl; discard solids. Return stock to same cleaned pan; bring to a boil. Reduce heat, simmer, covered.
3 Meanwhile, separate bases and leaves of buk choy. Finely chop half of the bases; discard remaining bases. Combine chopped bases with finely chopped shiitake mushrooms, extra ginger, extra garlic, water chestnuts, egg white, breadcrumbs, coriander leaves and oyster sauce in large bowl. Make dumplings by placing 1 heaped teaspoon of the mushroom mixture in centre of a wonton wrapper; brush around edges with a little water. Fold wrapper in half diagonally; pinch edges together to seal. Repeat with remaining mushroom mixture and wrappers.
4 Add sliced shiitake and enoki mushrooms to simmering stock; cook, uncovered, 5 minutes. Add dumplings; cook, uncovered, about 5 minutes or until dumplings are cooked through. Stir in buk choy leaves.
5 Divide soup among serving bowls; top with reserved sliced green onion.
per serving 1.6g total fat (0.2g saturated fat); 978kJ (234 cal); 40g carbohydrate; 11.6g protein; 6.8g fibre

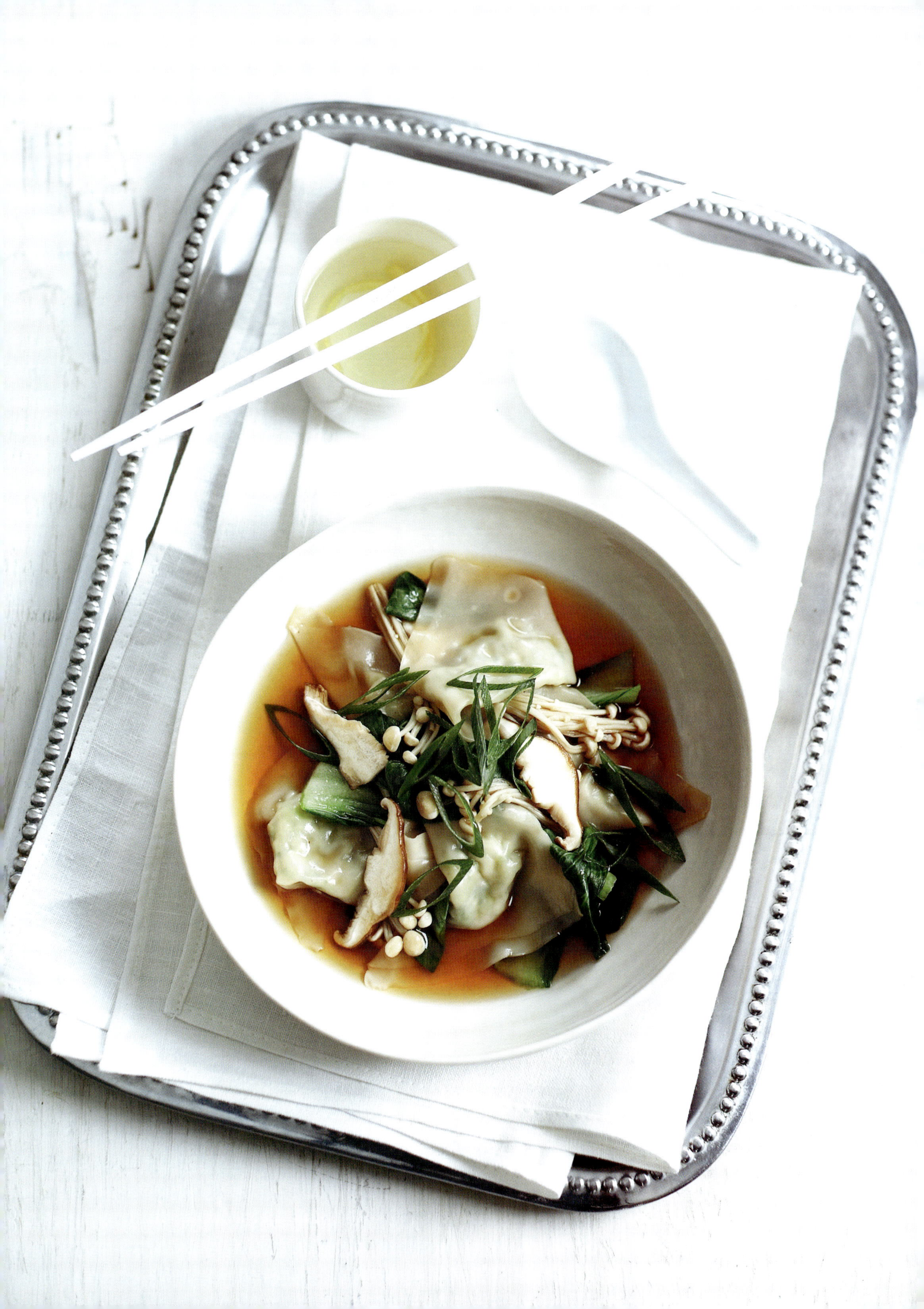

The Complete Book of Modern Asian

asian beef and rice noodle soup

preparation time 10 minutes
cooking time 15 minutes serves 4

1.5 litres (6 cups) water
2 cups (500ml) beef stock
5cm piece fresh ginger (25g), grated
2 cloves garlic, sliced thinly
1 tablespoon sambal oelek
2 tablespoons fish sauce
1 tablespoon brown sugar
450g fresh rice noodles
500g rump steak, sliced thinly
6 green onions, sliced thinly
1 cup (80g) bean sprouts
½ cup loosely packed fresh mint leaves

1 Combine the water, stock, ginger and garlic in large saucepan; bring to a boil. Add sambal oelek, fish sauce and sugar; simmer, uncovered, for 1 minute.
2 Meanwhile, place noodles in large heatproof bowl, cover with boiling water; separate with fork, drain. Divide noodles among serving bowls.
3 Place steak in simmering broth; bring to a boil. Pour broth and steak over noodles; top with onion. Serve with bean sprouts, mint and lemon wedges, if desired.
per serving 9.4g total fat (3.9g saturated fat); 1476kJ (353 cal); 31.1g carbohydrate; 33.9g protein; 2.5g fibre

chicken and galangal soup

preparation time 15 minutes
cooking time 35 minutes serves 4

3 cups (750ml) chicken stock
4cm piece fresh galangal (20g), sliced thickly
2 x 10cm sticks fresh lemon grass (40g),
    cut into 5cm pieces
4 fresh kaffir lime leaves
2 teaspoons coarsely chopped coriander root and
    stem mixture
500g chicken thigh fillets, sliced thinly
200g drained canned straw mushrooms, rinsed
1 cup (250ml) coconut milk
1 tablespoon lime juice
1 tablespoon fish sauce
1 teaspoon grated palm sugar
¼ cup loosely packed fresh coriander leaves
2 fresh small red thai chillies, sliced thinly
2 fresh kaffir lime leaves, shredded, extra
10cm stick fresh lemon grass (20g), sliced finely

1 Combine stock, galangal, lemon grass pieces, whole lime leaves and coriander mixture in large saucepan, bring to a boil; reduce heat, simmer, covered, 5 minutes. Remove from heat; stand 10 minutes. Strain stock through muslin into large heatproof bowl; discard solids.
2 Return stock to same cleaned pan. Add chicken and mushrooms; bring to a boil. Reduce heat, simmer, uncovered, about 5 minutes or until chicken is cooked through. Stir in coconut milk, juice, sauce and sugar; cook, stirring, until just heated through (do not allow to boil).
3 Remove from heat; stir in coriander leaves, chilli, shredded lime leaves and lemon grass slices.
per serving 19.2g total fat (13.2g saturated fat); 1359kJ (325 cal); 6.3g carbohydrate; 30.8g protein; 2.7g fibre

vegetable laksa

preparation time 45 minutes
cooking time 20 minutes serves 6

700g piece butternut pumpkin, diced into 2cm pieces
5 baby eggplants (300g), sliced thickly
3 cups (750ml) vegetable stock
1⅔ cups (400ml) coconut milk
250g rice stick noodles
500g buk choy, chopped coarsely
2 tablespoons lime juice
1¼ cups (100g) bean sprouts
6 green onions, sliced thinly
½ cup loosely packed fresh coriander leaves
½ cup loosely packed vietnamese mint leaves

LAKSA PASTE
7 dried medium red chillies
½ cup (125ml) boiling water
1 tablespoon peanut oil
3 cloves garlic, quartered
1 medium brown onion (150g), chopped coarsely
10cm stick fresh lemon grass (20g), chopped finely
4cm piece fresh ginger (20g), grated
1 tablespoon halved macadamias (10g)
1 tablespoon coarsely chopped coriander root and stem mixture
1 teaspoon ground turmeric
1 teaspoon ground coriander
2 teaspoons salt
¼ cup loosely packed vietnamese mint leaves

1 Make laksa paste.
2 Place ½ cup of the paste in large saucepan; cook, stirring, about 1 minute or until fragrant. Add pumpkin and eggplant; cook, stirring, 2 minutes. Add stock and coconut milk; bring to a boil. Reduce heat, simmer, covered, 10 minutes or until vegetables are just tender.
3 Meanwhile, place noodles in large heatproof bowl, cover with boiling water, stand until just tender; drain.
4 Stir buk choy into laksa; return to a boil. Stir juice into laksa off the heat. Divide noodles among serving bowls; ladle laksa over noodles, sprinkle with combined sprouts, onion and herbs.

LAKSA PASTE
Cover chillies with the boiling water in small heatproof bowl; stand 10 minutes, drain. Blend or process chillies with remaining ingredients until mixture forms a smooth paste. Measure ½ cup of the paste for this recipe and freeze remaining, covered, for future use.

per serving 20.2g total fat (13.4g saturated fat); 1689kJ (404 cal); 41.5g carbohydrate; 10.3g protein; 7.4g fibre

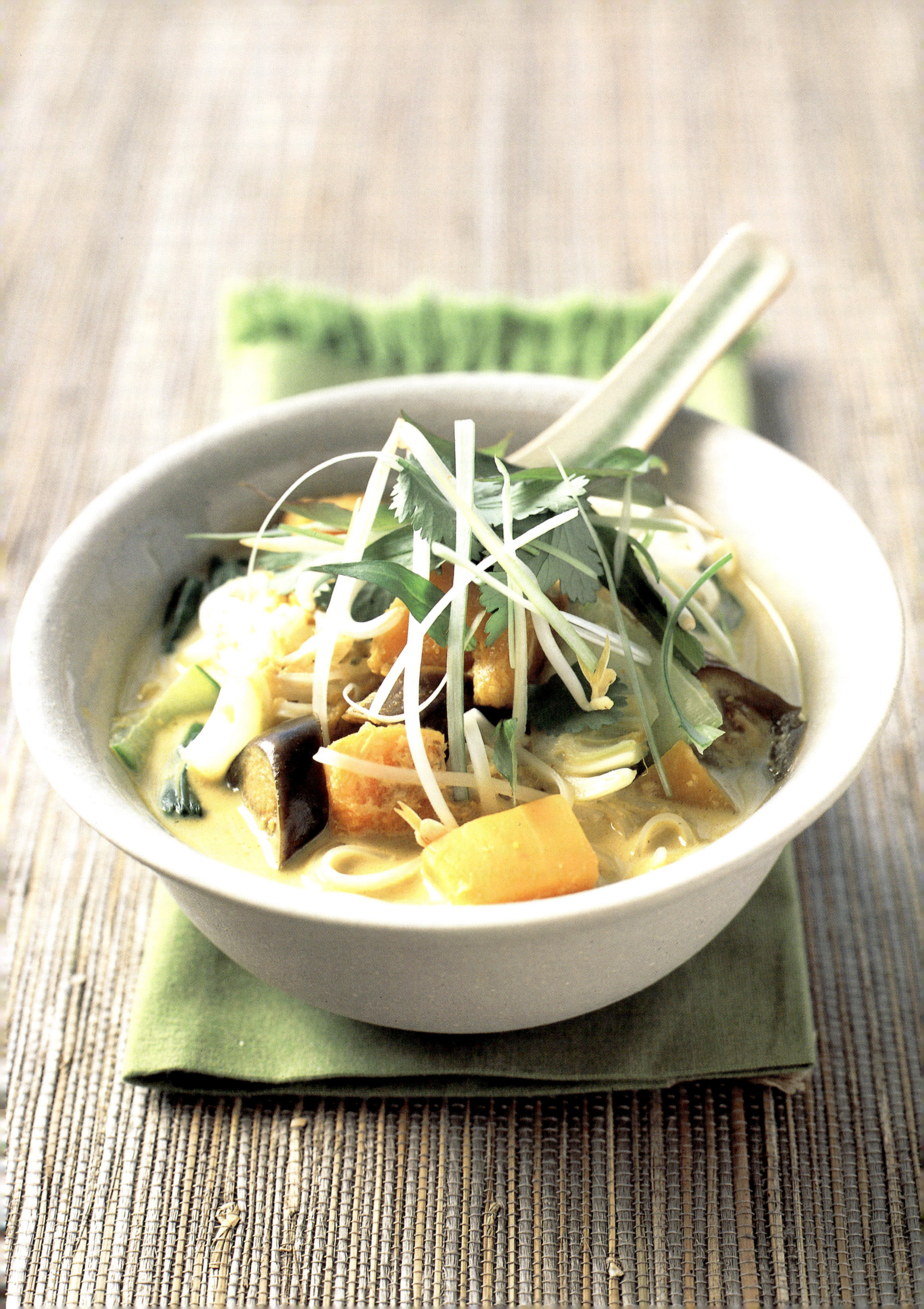

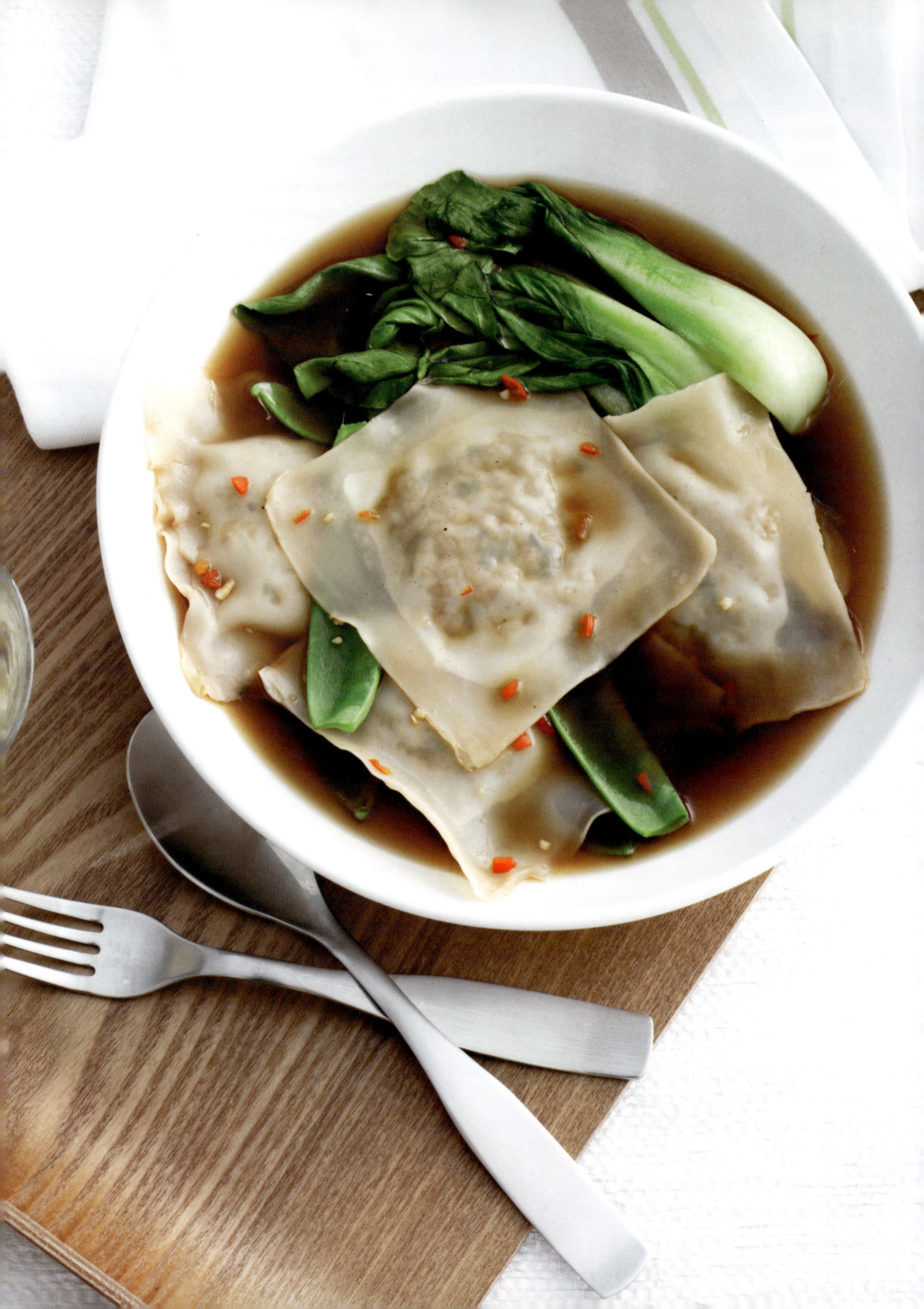

ravioli with asian greens

preparation time 40 minutes
cooking time 30 minutes serves 4

1 tablespoon sesame oil
4 green onions, chopped finely
4cm piece fresh ginger (20g), grated
4 cloves garlic, crushed
450g chicken mince
2 tablespoons light soy sauce
½ teaspoon five-spice powder
100g wombok, sliced thinly
¼ cup coarsely chopped fresh coriander
40 wonton wrappers
1½ cups (375ml) chicken stock
1½ cups (375ml) water
2 fresh small red thai chillies, chopped finely
2 tablespoons light soy sauce, extra
1 tablespoon char siu sauce
¼ cup (60ml) chinese cooking wine
500g baby buk choy, quartered lengthways
150g snow peas, trimmed, halved

1 Heat oil in wok; stir-fry onion, ginger and garlic until onion softens. Add mince; stir-fry until mince changes colour. Add soy sauce, five-spice and wombok; stir-fry until wombok is tender. Stir in coriander; cool 10 minutes.
2 Place 1 level tablespoon of the mince mixture in centre of one wrapper; brush around edges with water. Top with another wrapper; press edges together to seal. Repeat with remaining mince mixture and wrappers.
3 Add stock, the water, chilli, extra soy sauce, char siu sauce and wine to same cleaned wok; bring to a boil. Cook ravioli, in batches, uncovered, about 3 minutes or until ravioli float to surface. Remove ravioli with a slotted spoon; drain.
4 Cook buk choy and snow peas in stock mixture until vegetables are tender.
5 Divide ravioli and vegetables among serving bowls; ladle stock mixture over vegetables.
per serving 15.8g total fat (3.8g saturated fat); 2161kJ (517 cal); 52.9g carbohydrate; 35.9g protein; 4.3g fibre

asian broth with crisp pork belly

preparation time 20 minutes
(plus standing and refrigeration time)
cooking time 2 hours serves 4

½ cup (100g) dried soy beans
1kg boned pork belly, rind-on
1½ teaspoons cooking salt
1 teaspoon five-spice powder
2 cups (500ml) water
1 litre (4 cups) chicken stock
1 fresh small red thai chilli, chopped finely
2 star anise
5cm piece fresh ginger (25g), slivered
⅓ cup (80ml) hoisin sauce
500g choy sum, sliced thinly
3 green onions, sliced thinly

1 Place beans in small bowl, cover with cold water; stand overnight.
2 Place pork on chopping board, rind-side up; using sharp knife, score pork by making shallow cuts diagonally in both directions at 1cm intervals. Rub combined salt and half the five-spice into cuts; slice pork into 10 pieces. Place pork, rind-side up, on tray, cover loosely; refrigerate overnight.
3 Preheat oven to 240°C/220°C fan-forced.
4 Rinse beans under cold water; drain. Place beans in medium saucepan of boiling water; return to a boil. Reduce heat, simmer, uncovered, until tender. Drain.
5 Meanwhile, place pork on metal rack set over shallow baking dish; roast, uncovered, 30 minutes. Reduce oven temperature to 160°C/140°C fan-forced; roast pork, uncovered, further 45 minutes or until crackling is browned and crisp. Cut pork pieces in half.
6 Place beans in large saucepan with the water, stock, chilli, star anise, ginger, sauce and remaining five-spice; bring to a boil. Reduce heat, simmer, covered, 30 minutes. Stir in choy sum and onion.
7 Serve bowls of soup topped with pork.

per serving 59.4g total fat (20.2g saturated fat); 3670kJ (878 cal); 12.3g carbohydrate; 71.9g protein; 6g fibre

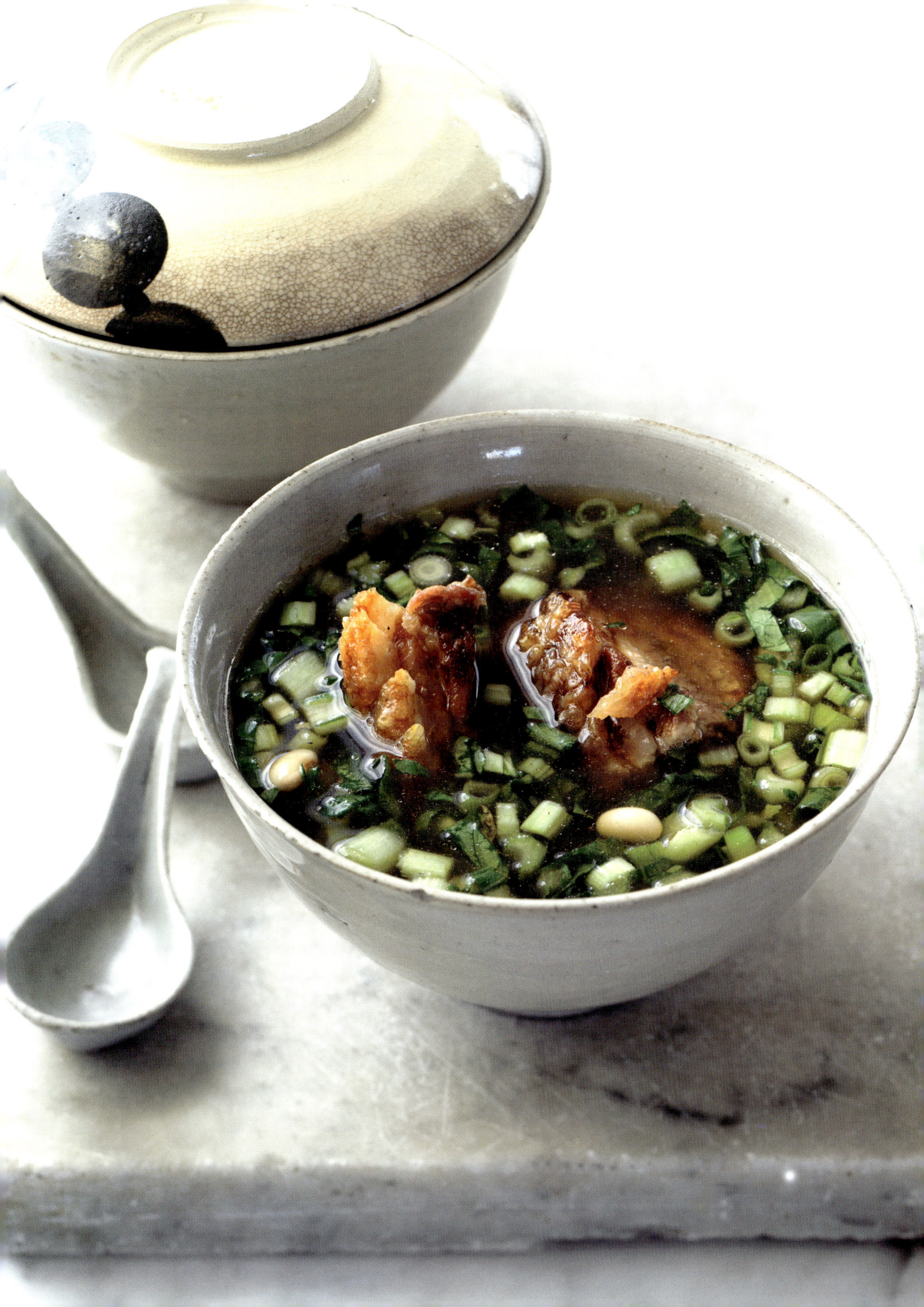

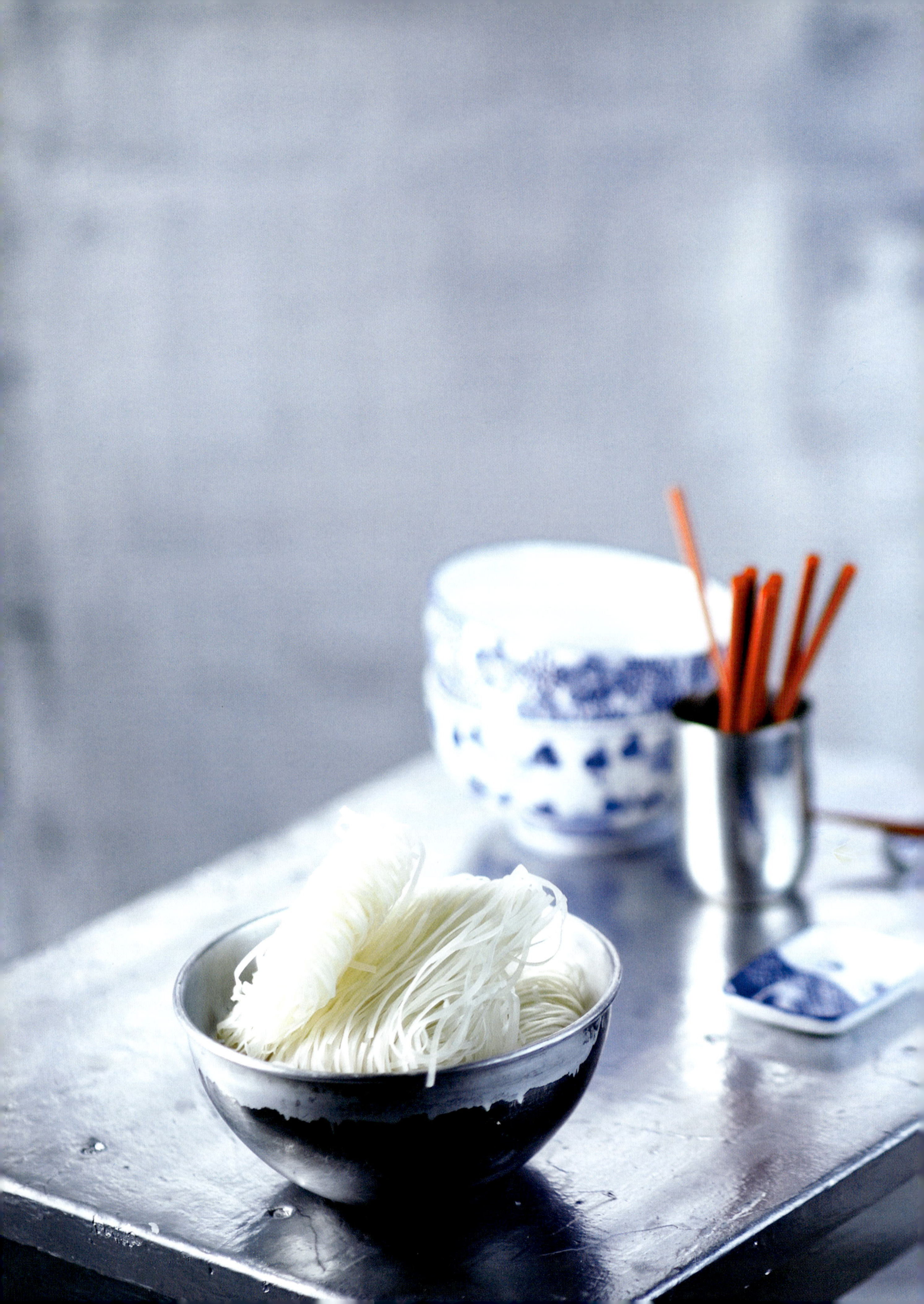

Mains

Served as a main course or as one of a large selection of dishes that make up a meal, the ubiquitous Asian salad can easily be eaten on its own, bulked up with masses of leaves and herbs, served on plain rice or even – bolstered with the tang of tamarind or the piquancy of lime-infused under-ripe fruits – presented after the main to signal the end of the meal.

gado gado *page 155*

crispy-fried duck and mango salad *page 131*

salads

five-spice pork and nashi salad with chilli plum dressing *page 127*

bang bang chicken salad *page 143*

lemon grass lamb with vietnamese vermicelli salad

preparation time 25 minutes
cooking time 20 minutes serves 4

3 lamb backstraps (600g)
10cm stick fresh lemon grass (20g), chopped finely
2 tablespoons light soy sauce
1 tablespoon brown sugar
2 tablespoons vegetable oil
70g rice vermicelli noodles
2 lebanese cucumbers (260g), seeded, sliced thinly
½ small pineapple (450g), chopped coarsely
1 cup (80g) bean sprouts
1 cup loosely packed fresh coriander leaves
1 cup loosely packed fresh mint leaves
1 large carrot (180g), grated coarsely
1 large butter lettuce, trimmed, leaves separated

SWEET AND SOUR DRESSING
¼ cup (60ml) hot water
2 tablespoons fish sauce
1 tablespoon brown sugar
2 tablespoons lime juice
2 fresh small red thai chillies, chopped finely
1 clove garlic, crushed

1 Place ingredients for sweet and sour dressing in screw-top jar; shake well.
2 Combine lamb, lemon grass, sauce, sugar and oil in medium bowl.
3 Place noodles in medium heatproof bowl; cover with boiling water. Stand until just tender; drain. Rinse under cold water; drain.
4 Place noodles in large bowl with cucumber, pineapple, sprouts, herbs, carrot and 2 tablespoons of the dressing; toss gently to combine.
5 Cook lamb, both sides, on heated oiled grill plate (or grill or barbecue) until cooked as desired. Cover; stand 5 minutes, slice thinly.
6 Top lettuce with salad; serve with lamb, drizzled with remaining dressing.

per serving 22.9g total fat (7.2g saturated fat); 1856kJ (444 cal); 20.6g carbohydrate; 35.9g protein; 6g fibre

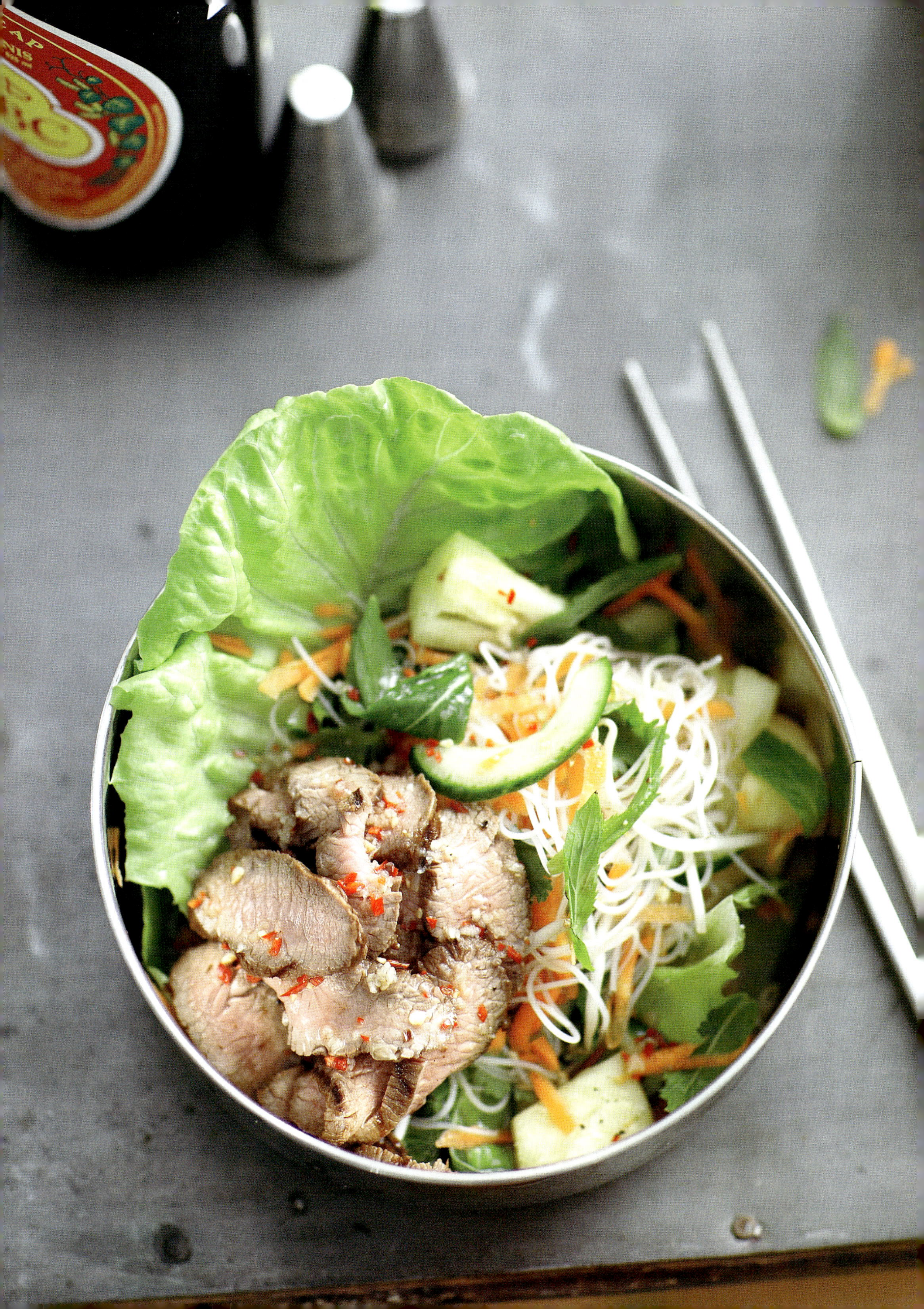

The Complete Book of Modern Asian

five-spice pork and nashi salad with chilli plum dressing

preparation time 10 minutes (plus refrigeration time)
cooking time 20 minutes   serves 4

600g pork fillets, trimmed
2 teaspoons vegetable oil
1 teaspoon five-spice powder
300g mizuna
2 green onions, sliced thinly
2 medium nashi (400g), sliced thinly

CHILLI PLUM DRESSING
¼ cup (60ml) plum sauce
1 tablespoon water
1 tablespoon lemon juice
1 fresh long red chilli, sliced thinly

1 Combine pork, oil and five-spice in large bowl. Cover; refrigerate 3 hours or overnight.
2 Cook pork on heated oiled grill plate (or grill or barbecue) about 20 minutes. Cover; stand 10 minutes then slice thickly.
3 Place ingredients for chilli plum dressing in screw-top jar; shake well.
4 Place mizuna, onion and nashi in large bowl with two-thirds of the dressing; toss gently to combine. Serve salad topped with pork slices, drizzled with remaining dressing.

per serving 14.8g total fat (4.3g saturated fat); 1522kJ (364 cal); 22.5g carbohydrate; 33.3g protein; 3.1g fibre

green mango and seared tuna salad

preparation time 20 minutes
cooking time 10 minutes   serves 4

1 green mango (350g)
2 teaspoons sesame oil
800g tuna steaks, cut into 3cm pieces
½ teaspoon dried chilli flakes
2 tablespoons roasted sesame seeds
2 cups (100g) snow pea sprouts
½ cup firmly packed fresh coriander leaves
½ cup firmly packed fresh mint leaves
½ small red onion (50g), sliced thinly

LIME AND GINGER DRESSING
¼ cup (60ml) lime juice
3cm piece fresh ginger (15g), grated
1 tablespoon fish sauce

1 Place ingredients for lime and ginger dressing in screw-top jar; shake well.
2 Using vegetable peeler, slice mango into thin ribbons.
3 Combine oil and fish in medium bowl. Cook fish on heated oiled grill plate (or grill or barbecue) until cooked as desired.
4 Return fish to same cleaned bowl with chilli and seeds; mix gently.
5 Place remaining ingredients in medium bowl with dressing; toss gently to combine. Serve salad topped with fish.

per serving 17.8g total fat (5.4g saturated fat); 1894kJ (453 cal); 15.5g carbohydrate; 55.5g protein; 3.7g fibre

sesame tofu salad

preparation time 25 minutes
cooking time 10 minutes serves 4

2 x 300g blocks firm silken tofu
2 tablespoons toasted sesame seeds
2 tablespoons kalonji
2 teaspoons dried chilli flakes
2 tablespoons cornflour
vegetable oil, for deep-frying
5 green onions, sliced thinly
1 large avocado (320g), chopped coarsely
100g red oak lettuce leaves, torn
100g mizuna
1 fresh long red chilli, sliced thinly

SESAME DRESSING
2 shallots (50g), chopped finely
2 tablespoons toasted sesame seeds
1 tablespoon sesame oil
1 tablespoon kecap manis
1cm piece fresh ginger (5g), grated
¼ cup (60ml) lemon juice

1 Place ingredients for sesame dressing in screw-top jar; shake well.
2 Cut each tofu block lengthways into four slices; dry gently with absorbent paper. Combine sesame, kalonji, chilli and cornflour in large shallow bowl; press seed mixture onto both sides of tofu slices.
3 Heat oil in wok; deep-fry tofu, in batches, until browned lightly. Drain on absorbent paper.
4 Place remaining ingredients in large bowl; toss gently to combine. Divide salad among serving plates; top with tofu, drizzle with dressing.

per serving 59.7g total fat (9.9g saturated fat); 2796kJ (699 cal); 9.2g carbohydrate; 22.8g protein; 6.2g fibre

sesame omelette and crisp mixed vegetable salad

preparation time 25 minutes
cooking time 10 minutes serves 4

8 eggs
½ cup (125ml) milk
½ cup coarsely chopped fresh garlic chives
2 tablespoons toasted sesame seeds
8 cups (640g) finely shredded wombok
2 fresh long red chillies, sliced thinly
1 large red capsicum (350g), sliced thinly
1 large green capsicum (350g), sliced thinly
1 tablespoon coarsely chopped fresh mint
1 tablespoon finely chopped fresh lemon grass

CHILLI SESAME DRESSING
2 teaspoons toasted sesame seeds
¼ cup (60ml) rice vinegar
¼ cup (60ml) peanut oil
1 teaspoon sesame oil
¼ cup (60ml) sweet chilli sauce

1 Whisk eggs in large jug with milk, chives and seeds until well combined. Pour a quarter of the egg mixture into heated lightly oiled wok; cook over medium heat, tilting pan, until omelette is just set. Remove from wok; repeat with remaining egg mixture to make four omelettes. Roll cooled omelettes tightly; cut into 3mm "wheels".
2 Place ingredients for chilli sesame dressing in screw-top jar; shake well.
3 Place three-quarters of the omelette in large bowl with wombok, chilli, capsicums, mint, lemon grass and dressing; toss gently to combine. Divide salad among serving plates; top with remaining omelette.

per serving 31.1g total fat (7.2g saturated fat); 1726kJ (413 cal); 11.4g carbohydrate; 20.2g protein; 5.3g fibre

Salads

The Complete Book of Modern Asian

crispy-fried duck and mango salad

preparation time 20 minutes
cooking time 10 minutes   serves 4

¼ cup (60ml) lime juice
1 tablespoon sweet chilli sauce
1kg chinese barbecued duck
2 teaspoons peanut oil
500g silverbeet, trimmed, chopped coarsely
1 cup loosely packed fresh coriander leaves
3 cups (240g) bean sprouts
1 medium mango (430g), sliced thinly
2 limes, cut into wedges

1 Combine juice and sauce in small jug.
2 Remove skin then meat from duck; discard bones, slice skin thinly.
3 Heat oil in wok; stir-fry skin until crisp. Drain. Slice duck meat thinly; stir-fry until hot.
4 Place duck meat and juice mixture in large bowl with silverbeet, coriander, sprouts and mango; toss gently to combine. Sprinkle salad with slivered duck skin; serve with lime wedges.

per serving 39.8g total fat (11.6g saturated fat); 2261kJ (541 cal); 12.5g carbohydrate; 31.8g protein; 4.7g fibre

hot and sour prawn vermicelli salad

preparation time 30 minutes (plus refrigeration time)
serves 4

1kg cooked medium king prawns
250g rice vermicelli noodles
1 lime
1 lemon
1 medium red capsicum (200g), sliced thinly
1 medium yellow capsicum (200g), sliced thinly
1 medium red onion (170g), sliced thinly
¼ cup (60ml) peanut oil
¼ cup (60ml) rice vinegar
1 tablespoon sambal oelek
1 tablespoon fish sauce
2 tablespoons grated palm sugar
1 cup firmly packed fresh coriander leaves

1 Shell and devein prawns, leaving tails intact.
2 Place noodles in large heatproof bowl of boiling water, stand until just tender; drain. Rinse under cold water; drain.
3 Meanwhile, halve lime and lemon lengthways; slice one unpeeled half of each thinly, place in large bowl. Squeeze remaining halves over bowl; add prawns, noodles and remaining ingredients, toss gently to combine. Cover; refrigerate 1 hour before serving.

per serving 15.4g total fat (2.6g saturated fat); 1960kJ (469 cal); 48.2g carbohydrate; 32.1g protein; 3.6g fibre

crisp pork belly with wombok salad

preparation time 50 minutes (plus refrigeration time) cooking time 2 hours 15 minutes serves 4

2 cups (500ml) salt-reduced chicken stock
⅓ cup (80ml) chinese cooking wine
½ cup (125ml) lime juice
¼ cup (60ml) japanese soy sauce
2 dried red chillies
2 star anise
1 tablespoon coarsely chopped coriander root and stem mixture
2cm piece fresh ginger (10g), sliced thinly
2 cloves garlic, halved
2 fresh kaffir lime leaves, torn
800g piece pork belly
¼ cup (60ml) oyster sauce
⅓ cup (90g) firmly packed grated palm sugar
2 tablespoons fish sauce
1 tablespoon peanut oil
2 fresh long red chillies, chopped finely
2cm piece fresh ginger (10g), grated
1 clove garlic, crushed
½ medium wombok (500g), shredded finely
1 medium red capsicum (200g), sliced thinly
1 large carrot (180g), sliced thinly
1 cup (80g) bean sprouts
2 green onions, sliced thinly
½ cup loosely packed fresh coriander leaves
½ cup loosely packed vietnamese mint leaves
½ cup (70g) roasted unsalted peanuts, chopped coarsely
¼ cup (20g) fried shallots

1 Combine stock, wine, half of the juice, soy sauce, dried chillies, star anise, coriander mixture, sliced ginger, halved garlic, lime leaves and pork in large deep flameproof dish; bring to a boil. Reduce heat, simmer, covered tightly, about 1½ hours or until pork is tender.
2 Remove pork from dish. Strain broth through muslin-lined sieve into medium saucepan; discard solids. Bring broth to a boil; boil, uncovered, 10 minutes.
3 Slice pork lengthways into 1cm-thick slices. Combine pork with half the broth and oyster sauce in large bowl. Cover; refrigerate 2 hours.
4 Meanwhile, to make dressing, stir sugar into remaining broth; bring to a boil, stirring until sugar dissolves. Reduce heat, simmer, uncovered, 5 minutes or until thickened slightly. Remove from heat; stir in remaining juice, fish sauce, oil, fresh chilli, grated ginger and crushed garlic. Cool.
5 Preheat oven to 240°C/220°C fan-forced. Oil two oven trays, line with baking paper.
6 Drain pork; discard marinade. Place pork, in single layer, on trays; cook, uncovered, turning occasionally, 20 minutes or until crisp. Cut pork slices into 2cm dice.
7 Meanwhile, place wombok, capsicum, carrot, sprouts, onion, coriander leaves, mint, nuts and dressing in large bowl. Add pork; toss gently to combine.
8 Divide salad among serving bowls, sprinkle with fried shallots.

per serving 58.7g total fat (17.6g saturated fat); 4009kJ (959 cal); 37.7g carbohydrate; 64.8g protein; 16.8g fibre
TIP This recipe can be prepared, up to step 5, the day before serving.

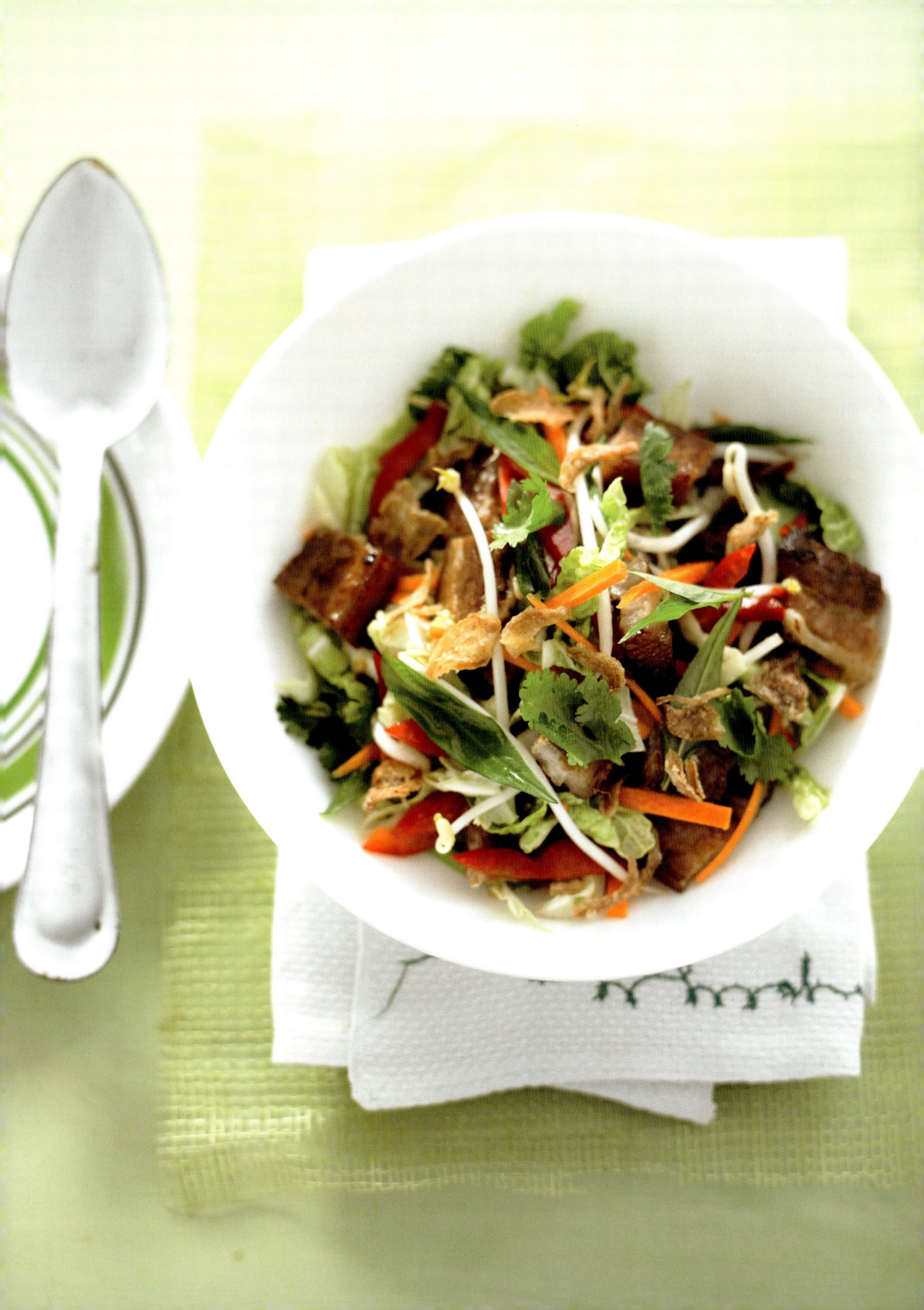

The Complete Book of Modern Asian

thai chicken and lychee salad

preparation time 20 minutes
serves 4

3 cups (480g) shredded cooked chicken
565g can lychees in syrup, drained, halved
1 small red onion (100g), sliced thinly
8 green onions, sliced thinly
2 cups (160g) bean sprouts
½ cup firmly packed fresh mint leaves
½ cup firmly packed fresh coriander leaves
1 teaspoon finely grated lime rind
1 teaspoon sambal oelek
¼ cup (60ml) lime juice
1 teaspoon sesame oil
1 tablespoon brown sugar
2 teaspoons fish sauce

1 Combine chicken, lychees, onions, sprouts, mint and coriander in large bowl.
2 Place remaining ingredients in screw-top jar; shake well. Drizzle dressing over salad; toss gently to combine.
per serving 7.6g total fat (1.9g saturated fat); 1162kJ (278 cal); 28g carbohydrate; 21.8g protein; 4.4g fibre

crisp fish salad with chilli lime dressing

preparation time 20 minutes
cooking time 30 minutes serves 4

250g firm white fish fillets
vegetable oil, for deep-frying
1 medium red onion (170g), sliced thinly
6 green onions, sliced thinly
2 lebanese cucumbers (260g), seeded, sliced thinly
1 cup firmly packed vietnamese mint leaves
1 cup firmly packed fresh coriander leaves
2 tablespoons coarsely chopped roasted unsalted peanuts
2 teaspoons finely grated lime rind

CHILLI DRESSING
4 small green thai chillies, chopped finely
2 tablespoons fish sauce
⅓ cup (80ml) lime juice
1 tablespoon brown sugar.

1 Preheat oven to 180°C/160°C fan-forced.
2 Place ingredients for chilli dressing in screw-top jar; shake well.
3 Place fish on wire rack over oven tray; roast, uncovered, 20 minutes. When cool enough to handle, cut fish into pieces, then blend or process, pulsing, until mixture resembles coarse breadcrumbs.
4 Heat oil in wok; deep-fry fish, in batches, until browned lightly and crisp. Drain on absorbent paper.
5 Place onions, cucumber and herbs in large bowl with dressing; toss gently to combine. Sprinkle salad with crisp fish, nuts and rind; serve immediately.
per serving 7.8g total fat (1.3g saturated fat); 761kJ (182 cal); 9.3g carbohydrate; 16.9g protein; 3.4g fibre

asian star

thai beef salad

preparation time 25 minutes (plus refrigeration time)
cooking time 10 minutes serves 4

500g beef rump steak
¼ cup (60ml) fish sauce
¼ cup (60ml) lime juice
3 lebanese cucumbers (390g), seeded, sliced thinly
4 fresh small red thai chillies, sliced thinly
4 green onions, sliced thinly
250g cherry tomatoes, halved
¼ cup firmly packed vietnamese mint leaves
½ cup firmly packed fresh coriander leaves
½ cup firmly packed fresh thai basil leaves
1 tablespoon grated palm sugar
2 teaspoons dark soy sauce
1 clove garlic, crushed

1 Combine beef, 2 tablespoons of the fish sauce and 1 tablespoon of the juice in medium bowl. Cover; refrigerate 3 hours or overnight.
2 Drain beef; discard marinade. Cook beef on heated oiled grill plate (or grill or barbecue) until cooked as desired. Cover beef; stand 5 minutes then slice thinly.
3 Meanwhile, combine cucumber, chilli, onion, tomato and herbs in large bowl.
4 Place sugar, soy sauce, garlic, remaining fish sauce and remaining juice in screw-top jar; shake well. Add beef and dressing to salad; toss gently to combine.
per serving 8.7g total fat (3.8g saturated fat); 999kJ (239 cal); 7.9g carbohydrate; 30.7g protein; 2.9g fibre

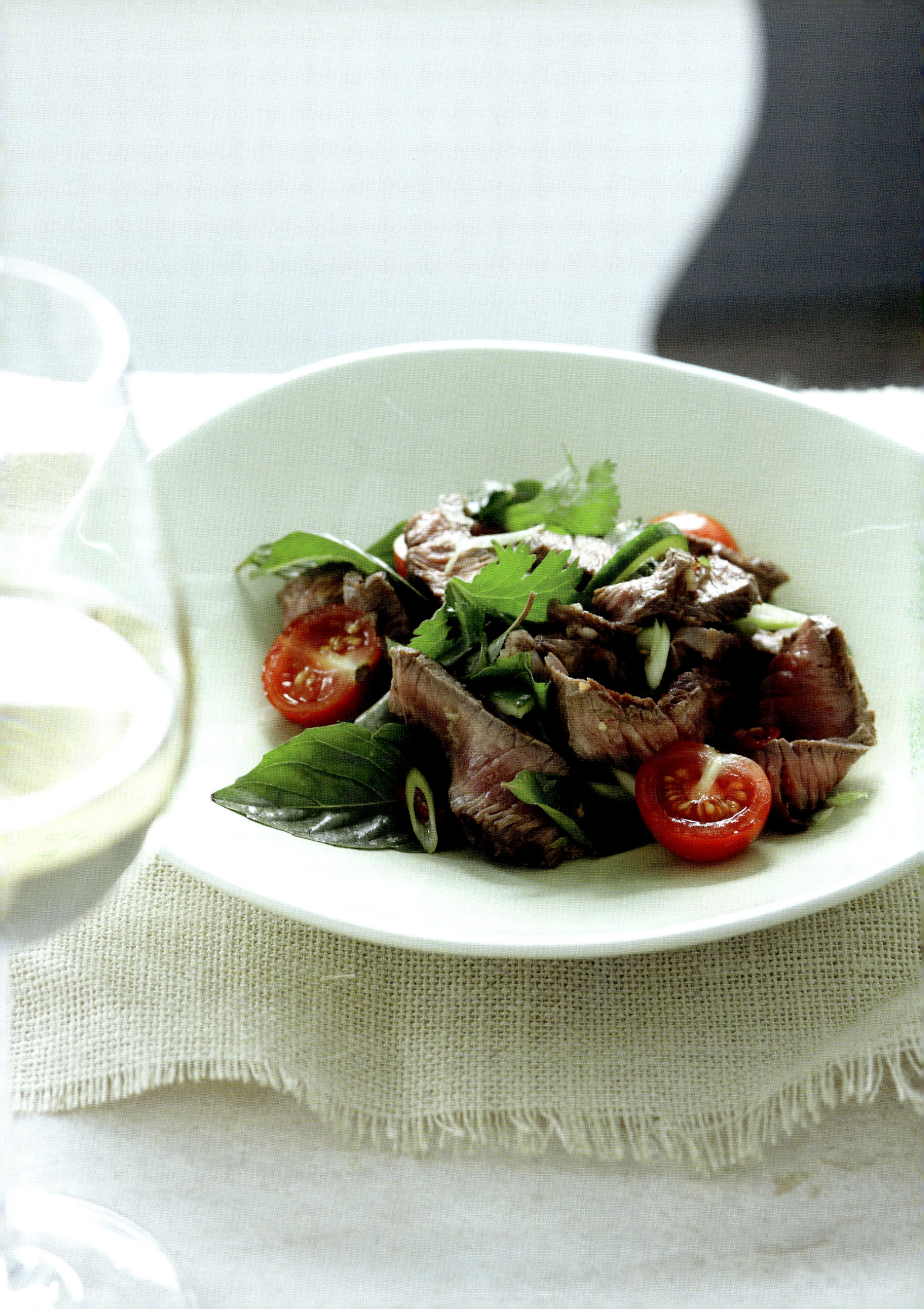

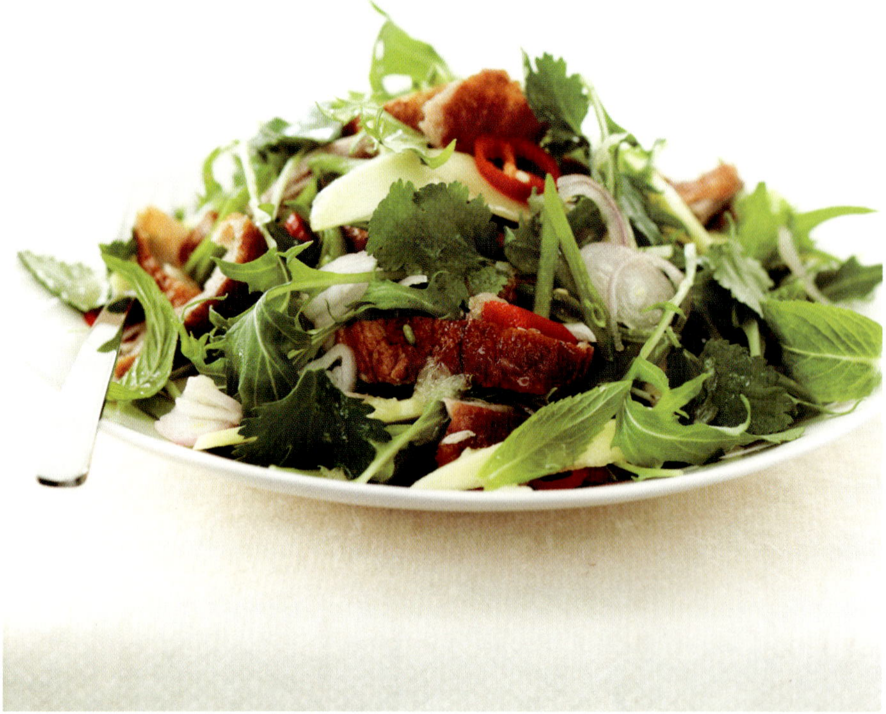

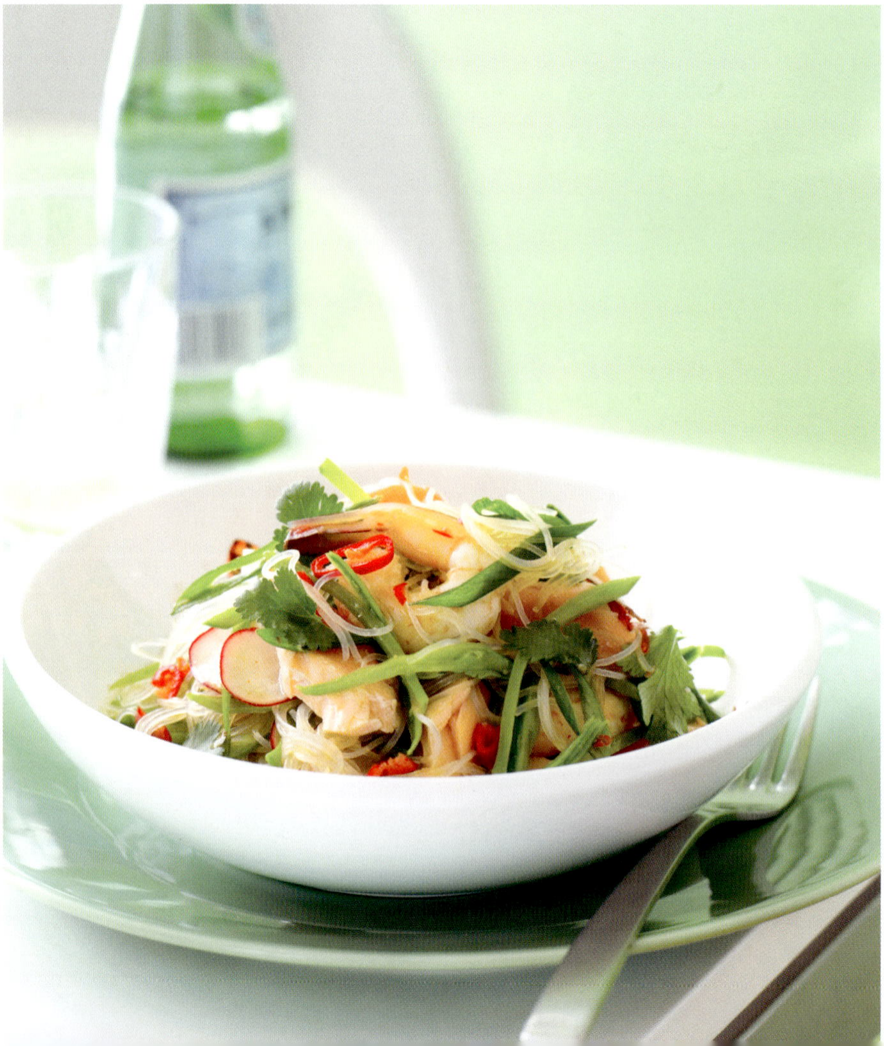

thai-style duck salad

preparation time 25 minutes
serves 4

1kg chinese barbecued duck
150g snow peas, trimmed, sliced thinly
1 green mango (350g), sliced thinly
3 shallots (75g), sliced thinly
125g mizuna
⅓ cup firmly packed fresh mint leaves
⅓ cup firmly packed fresh coriander leaves
1 fresh long red chilli, sliced thinly

THAI DRESSING
2 tablespoons fish sauce
2 tablespoons grated palm sugar
⅓ cup (80ml) lime juice
2 teaspoons peanut oil

1 Remove meat, leaving skin on, from duck; discard bones. Chop meat coarsely; place in large bowl with remaining ingredients.
2 Place ingredients for thai dressing in screw-top jar; shake well. Pour over salad; toss gently to combine.
per serving 35.2g total fat (10g saturated fat); 2082kJ (498 cal); 17.8g carbohydrate; 28.1g protein; 3.3g fibre

thai-style seafood and rice vermicelli salad

preparation time 15 minutes
cooking time 5 minutes serves 4

16 uncooked medium king prawns (720g)
125g rice vermicelli noodles
1 litre (4 cups) water
3cm piece fresh ginger (15g), sliced thinly
10cm stick fresh lemon grass (20g), coarsely chopped
2 cloves garlic, sliced thinly
400g salmon fillets, chopped coarsely
150g snow peas, trimmed, sliced thinly
250g radishes, trimmed, sliced thinly
½ cup coarsely chopped fresh coriander leaves
3 green onions, sliced thickly

DRESSING
2 tablespoons fish sauce
2 tablespoons sweet chilli sauce
⅓ cup (80ml) lime juice
1 fresh long red chilli, chopped finely
1 tablespoon coarsely grated palm sugar

1 Shell and devein prawns. Place noodles in large heatproof bowl; cover with boiling water. Stand until just tender; drain.
2 Combine ingredients for dressing in screw-top jar; shake well.
3 Place the water, ginger, lemon grass and garlic in medium frying pan; bring to a boil. Reduce heat; add prawns and salmon, simmer until prawns change colour and salmon is just cooked through. Drain well. Flake fish with fork.
4 Place noodles, dressing, prawns and salmon in medium bowl with remaining ingredients; toss gently to combine.
per serving 8.6g total fat (1.8g saturated fat); 1542kJ (369 cal); 29.4g carbohydrate; 42.7g protein; 2.8g fibre

sushi salad

preparation time 25 minutes
cooking time 15 minutes serves 4

2 cups (400g) koshihikari rice
2 cups (500ml) water
2 lebanese cucumbers (260g)
½ small daikon (200g)
1 lemon, unpeeled, quartered, sliced thinly
400g piece sashimi salmon, sliced thinly
¼ cup (35g) toasted sesame seeds
1 sheet toasted seaweed (yaki-nori), shredded finely

MIRIN AND WASABI DRESSING
4cm piece fresh ginger (20g), grated
2 tablespoons mirin
1 teaspoon wasabi paste
1 tablespoon light soy sauce
⅓ cup (80ml) water
¼ cup (60ml) rice wine vinegar

1 Rinse rice in strainer under cold water until water runs clear. Place drained rice and the water in medium saucepan, cover tightly; bring to a boil. Reduce heat, simmer, covered tightly, about 12 minutes or until water is absorbed and rice is just cooked. Remove from heat; stand rice, covered, 10 minutes.
2 Meanwhile, place ingredients for mirin and wasabi dressing in screw-top jar; shake well.
3 Using vegetable peeler, slice cucumbers into ribbons. Slice daikon thinly; cut slices into matchstick-sized pieces.
4 Place rice, cucumber and daikon in large bowl with lemon, fish, dressing and half of the seeds; toss gently to combine.
5 Divide salad among serving bowls; top with seaweed and remaining seeds.

per serving 12.7g total fat (2.3g saturated fat); 2445kJ (585 cal); 83g carbohydrate; 29.3g protein; 5.7g fibre

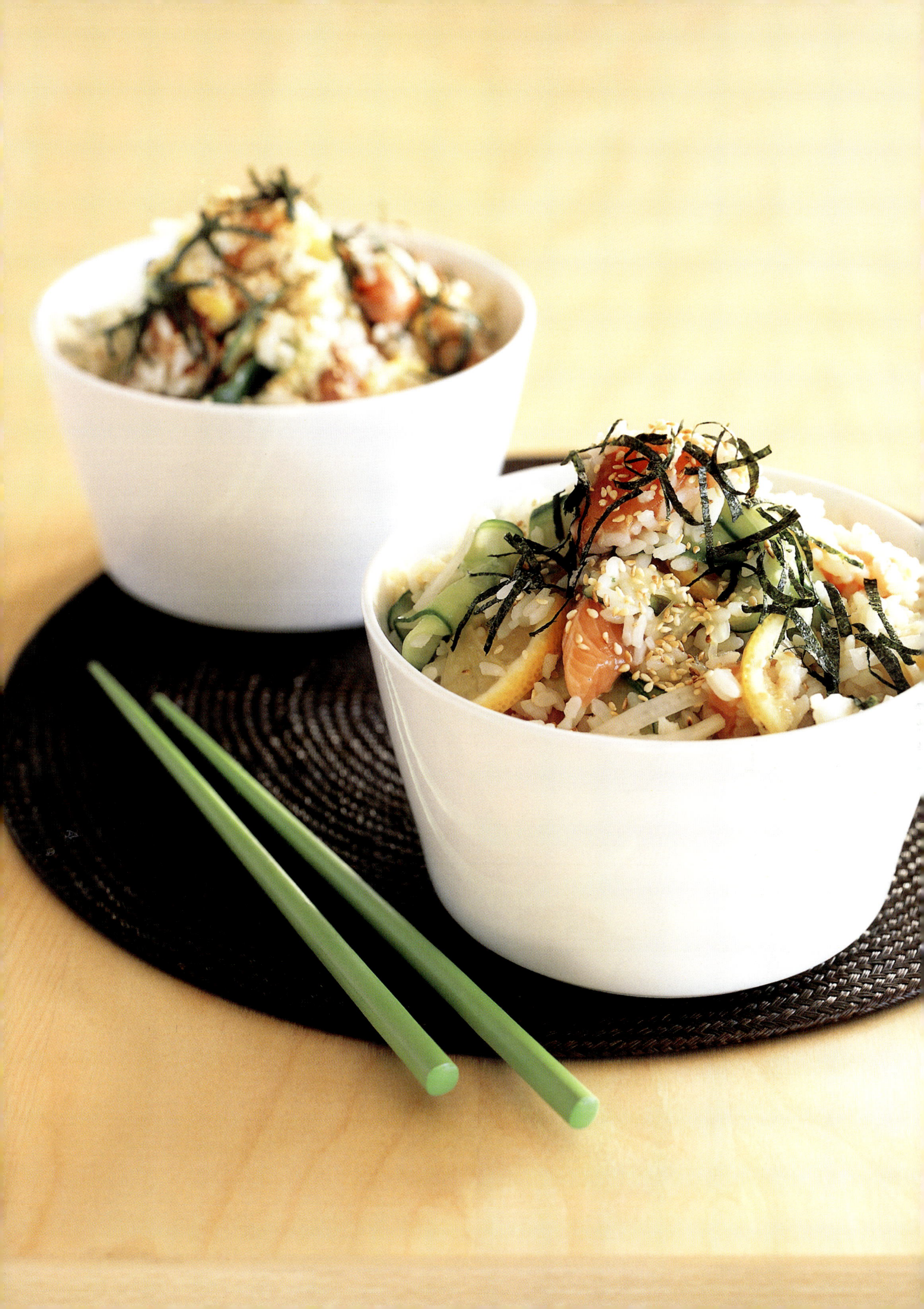

The Complete Book of Modern Asian

bang bang chicken salad

preparation time 20 minutes
cooking time 10 minutes serves 4

500g chicken thigh fillets
200g snake beans, cut into 5cm lengths
300g dried udon noodles
80g baby tat soi leaves
2 cups loosely packed fresh coriander leaves

SESAME AND PEANUT DRESSING
½ cup (75g) toasted sesame seeds
½ cup (75g) toasted unsalted peanuts
⅓ cup (125ml) mirin
⅓ cup (80ml) sake

1 Place chicken in medium saucepan of boiling water; return to a boil. Reduce heat, simmer, uncovered, about 10 minutes or until cooked through. Cool chicken in poaching liquid 10 minutes; discard liquid. Slice chicken thinly.
2 Meanwhile, boil, steam or microwave beans until tender; drain. Rinse under cold water; drain.
3 Blend or process ingredients for sesame and peanut dressing until combined.
4 Cook noodles in large saucepan of boiling water, uncovered, until just tender; drain. Rinse under cold water; drain.
5 Place chicken, beans and noodles in large bowl with tat soi, coriander and dressing; toss gently to combine.
per serving 29.3g total fat (5.2g saturated fat); 2976kJ (712 cal); 55.9g carbohydrate; 43g protein; 8.1g fibre

pork, lime and peanut salad

preparation time 25 minutes (plus refrigeration time)
cooking time 15 minutes serves 4

800g pork fillets, sliced thinly
¼ cup (60ml) lime juice
4cm piece fresh ginger (20g), grated
500g choy sum, chopped coarsely
2 tablespoons water
2 medium carrots (240g), cut into matchsticks
½ cup firmly packed fresh basil leaves
1 cup firmly packed fresh coriander leaves
4 green onions, sliced thinly
¼ cup (35g) coarsely chopped toasted
    unsalted peanuts

SWEET CHILLI DRESSING
1 tablespoon fish sauce
1 tablespoon sweet chilli sauce
2 tablespoons lime juice
1 fresh small red thai chilli, chopped finely

1 Combine pork, juice and ginger in large bowl. Cover; refrigerate 3 hours or overnight.
2 Place ingredients for sweet chilli dressing in screw-top jar; shake well.
3 Stir-fry pork, in batches, in heated lightly oiled wok until cooked as desired. Cover to keep warm. Stir-fry choy sum with the water in wok until just wilted.
4 Place pork, choy sum and dressing in large bowl with carrot, herbs and onion; toss gently to combine. Sprinkle with nuts.
per serving 10.4g total fat (2.2g saturated fat); 1344kJ (321 cal); 6.8g carbohydrate; 48.8g protein; 5g fibre

vietnamese chicken salad

preparation time 20 minutes
cooking time 15 minutes serves 4

500g chicken breast fillets
1 large carrot (180g)
½ cup (125ml) rice wine vinegar
2 teaspoons salt
2 tablespoons caster sugar
1 medium white onion (150g), sliced thinly
1½ cups (120g) bean sprouts
2 cups (160g) finely shredded savoy cabbage
¼ cup firmly packed vietnamese mint leaves
½ cup firmly packed fresh coriander leaves
1 tablespoon crushed toasted peanuts
2 tablespoons fried shallots

VIETNAMESE DRESSING
2 tablespoons fish sauce
¼ cup (60ml) water
2 tablespoons caster sugar
2 tablespoons lime juice
1 clove garlic, crushed

1 Place chicken in medium saucepan of boiling water; return to a boil. Reduce heat, simmer, uncovered, about 10 minutes or until cooked through. Cool chicken in poaching liquid 10 minutes; discard liquid (or reserve for another use). Shred chicken coarsely.

2 Meanwhile, cut carrot into matchstick-sized pieces. Combine carrot in large bowl with vinegar, salt and sugar, cover; stand 5 minutes. Add onion, cover; stand 5 minutes. Add sprouts, cover; stand 3 minutes. Drain pickled vegetables; discard liquid.

3 Place pickled vegetables in large bowl with chicken, cabbage, mint and coriander.

4 Place ingredients for vietnamese dressing in screw-top jar; shake well. Pour over salad; toss gently to combine. Sprinkle with nuts and shallots.

per serving 8.9g total fat (2.3g saturated fat); 1271kJ (304 cal); 24.3g carbohydrate; 31g protein; 5.1g fibre

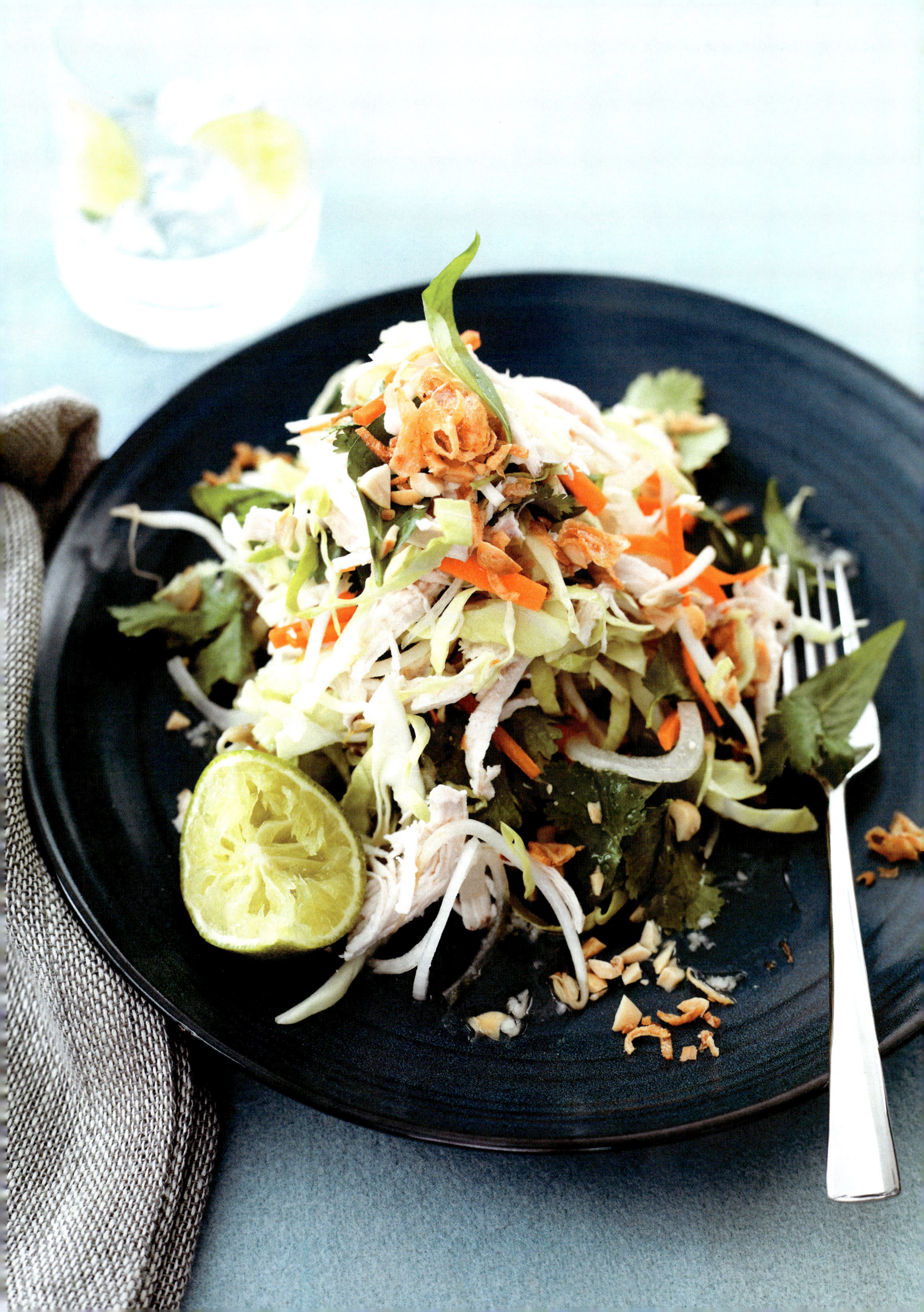

The Complete Book of Modern Asian

spicy citrus prawn and tat soi salad

preparation time 20 minutes (plus refrigeration time)
cooking time 10 minutes   serves 4

1kg uncooked medium king prawns
1 teaspoon finely grated orange rind
2 tablespoons orange juice
1 tablespoon sambal oelek
2 lebanese cucumbers (260g)
2cm piece fresh ginger (10g), grated
2 tablespoons peanut oil
¼ cup (60ml) rice vinegar
2 tablespoons orange juice
2 teaspoons fish sauce
1 tablespoon grated palm sugar
2 tat soi (300g), trimmed
½ cup firmly packed fresh mint leaves

1   Shell and devein prawns, leaving tails intact. Combine prawns in medium bowl with rind, juice and half the sambal. Cover; refrigerate 30 minutes.
2   Using vegetable peeler, slice cucumber into ribbons.
3   Cook prawns in large frying pan, in batches, until just changed in colour.
4   Place prawns in large bowl with cucumber, remaining sambal and remaining ingredients; toss gently to combine.
per serving 1.1g total fat (0.2g saturated fat); 665kJ (159 cal); 7.9g carbohydrate; 27.2g protein; 2.9g fibre

tandoori chicken, spinach and mint salad with spiced yogurt

preparation time 20 minutes (plus refrigeration time)
cooking time 15 minutes   serves 4

800g chicken tenderloins
⅓ cup (100g) tandoori paste
¼ cup (70g) yogurt
1 tablespoon vegetable oil
8 large uncooked pappadums
150g baby spinach leaves, trimmed
2 lebanese cucumbers (260g), sliced thickly
250g cherry tomatoes, halved
1 cup firmly packed fresh mint leaves

SPICED YOGURT
1 clove garlic, crushed
¾ cup (210g) yogurt
1 tablespoon lemon juice
1 teaspoon ground cumin
1 teaspoon ground coriander

1   Combine chicken, paste and yogurt in medium bowl. Cover; refrigerate 3 hours or overnight.
2   Combine ingredients for spiced yogurt in small jug.
3   Heat oil in large frying pan; cook chicken, in batches, until cooked through.
4   Microwave 2 pappadums at a time on HIGH (100%) about 30 seconds.
5   Place chicken in large serving bowl with spinach, cucumber, tomato and mint; toss gently to combine. Drizzle with spiced yogurt; serve with pappadums.
per serving 12.5g total fat (3.4g saturated fat); 1731kJ (414 cal); 16.4g carbohydrate; 55.1g protein; 6.7g fibre

chilli, lime and ginger octopus salad

preparation time 25 minutes (plus refrigeration time)
cooking time 10 minutes serves 4

1kg cleaned baby octopus, halved lengthways
2 tablespoons peanut oil
1 tablespoon finely grated lime rind
2 tablespoons lime juice
2 cloves garlic, crushed
3 fresh small red thai chillies, chopped finely
150g mizuna
100g snow peas, trimmed, halved
227g can water chestnuts, drained, rinsed, sliced thinly
1 medium red capsicum (200g), sliced thinly
1¼ cups (100g) bean sprouts
1 cup loosely packed fresh coriander leaves
1 fresh long red chilli, sliced thinly

LIME AND GINGER DRESSING
3cm piece fresh ginger (15g), grated
¼ cup (60ml) peanut oil
2 tablespoons lime juice
1 tablespoon white wine vinegar
2 teaspoons white sugar

1 Combine octopus, oil, rind, juice, garlic and chilli in large bowl. Cover; refrigerate 3 hours or overnight.
2 Place ingredients for lime and ginger dressing in screw-top jar; shake well.
3 Cook octopus on heated oiled grill plate (or grill or barbecue) about 10 minutes.
4 Place mizuna, peas, chestnuts, capsicum, sprouts and coriander in large bowl with dressing; toss gently to combine. Sprinkle salad with sliced chilli; serve salad accompanied with octopus.

per serving 25.2g total fat (4.1g saturated fat); 1894kJ (453 cal); 10.1g carbohydrate; 44.5g protein; 4.3g fibre

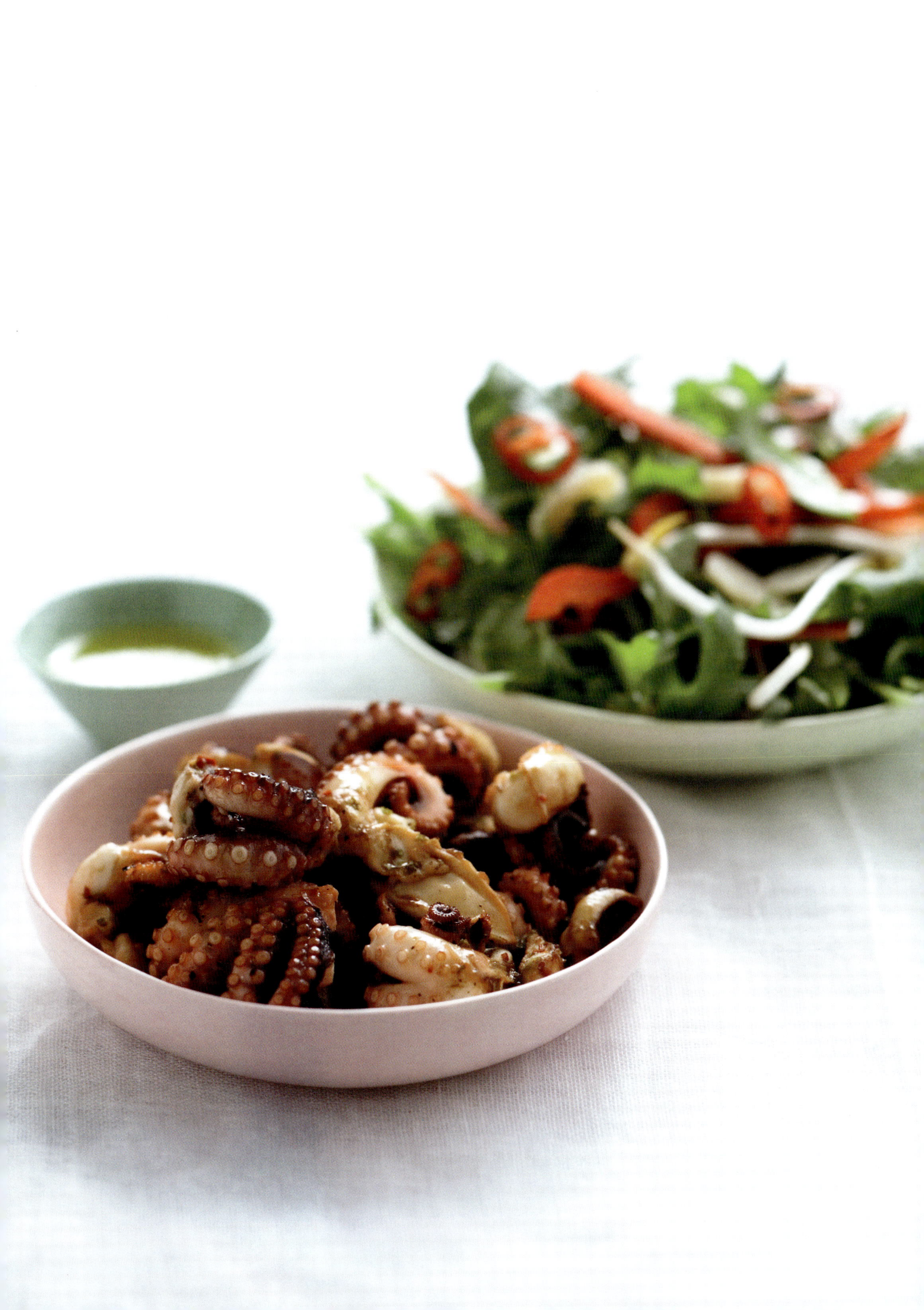

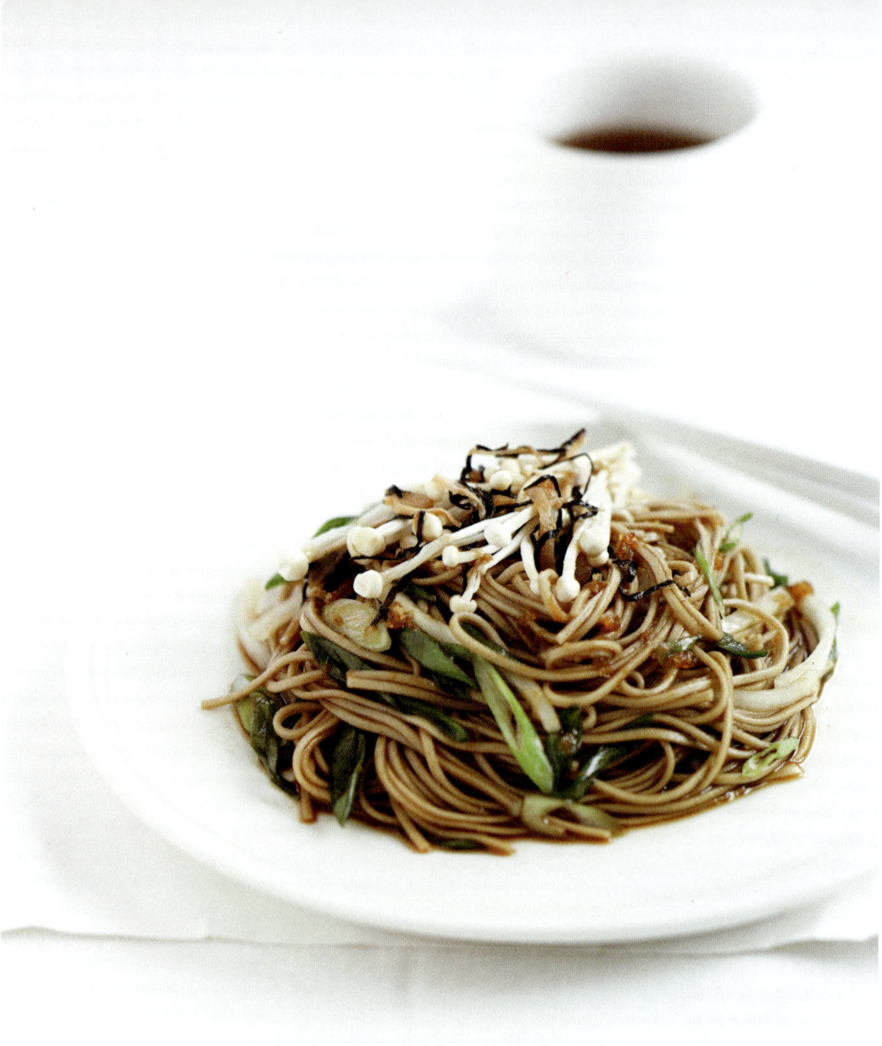

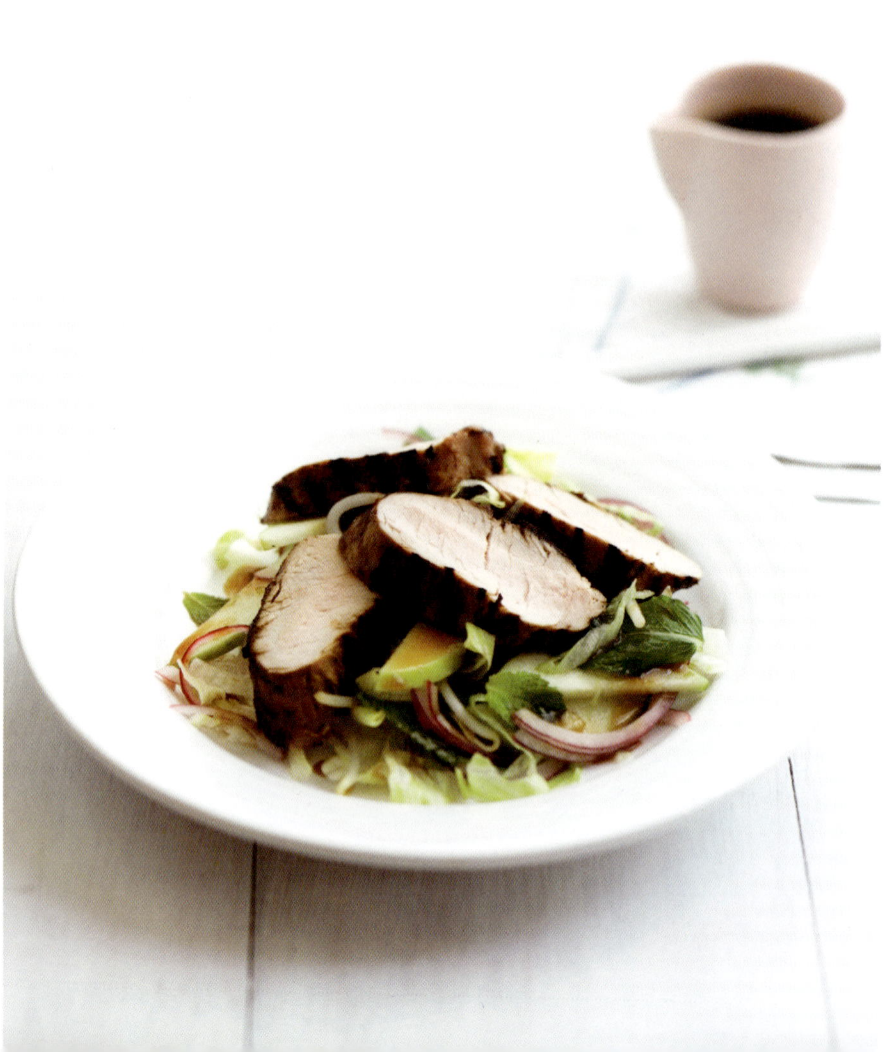

soba and daikon salad

preparation time 20 minutes
cooking time 15 minutes serves 4

300g dried soba noodles
1 small daikon (400g), cut into matchsticks
4 green onions, sliced thinly
1 teaspoon sesame oil
100g enoki mushrooms
2 tablespoons thinly sliced pickled ginger
1 toasted seaweed sheet (yaki-nori), sliced thinly

MIRIN DRESSING
¼ cup (60ml) mirin
2 tablespoons kecap manis
1 tablespoon sake
1 clove garlic, crushed
1cm piece fresh ginger (5g), grated
1 teaspoon white sugar

1 Cook soba in large saucepan of boiling water, uncovered, until just tender; drain. Rinse under cold water; drain.
2 Place ingredients for mirin dressing in screw-top jar; shake well.
3 Place soba in large bowl with daikon, onion and half of the dressing; toss gently to combine.
4 Heat oil in small frying pan; cook mushrooms, stirring, 2 minutes.
5 Divide soba salad among serving plates; top with combined mushrooms, ginger and seaweed. Drizzle with remaining dressing.

per serving 2.4g total fat (0.3g saturated fat); 1292kJ (309 cal); 56.6g carbohydrate; 10.9g protein; 5.3g fibre

chinese pork and apple salad

preparation time 20 minutes (plus refrigeration time)
cooking time 20 minutes serves 4

⅓ cup (80ml) hoisin sauce
1 tablespoon fish sauce
1 tablespoon light soy sauce
2 tablespoons rice vinegar
¼ cup (90g) honey
½ teaspoon five-spice powder
2 cloves garlic, crushed
2cm piece fresh ginger (10g), grated
750g pork fillets, halved
1 tablespoon water
½ medium iceberg lettuce, chopped coarsely
50g bean sprouts
1 small red onion (100g), sliced thinly
1 medium green apple (150g), unpeeled, sliced thinly
⅓ cup firmly packed fresh mint leaves

1 Combine sauces, vinegar, honey, five-spice, garlic and ginger in medium jug.
2 Combine pork and ½ cup (125ml) of the sauce mixture in medium bowl. Cover; refrigerate 3 hours or overnight.
3 Stir the water into remaining sauce mixture; refrigerate until required.
4 Drain pork; reserve marinade. Cook pork on heated oiled grill plate (or grill or barbecue), brushing occasionally with reserved marinade. Cover; stand 10 minutes then slice thickly.
5 Place lettuce, sprouts, onion, apple and mint in medium bowl; toss gently to combine. Top salad with pork; serve with refrigerated sauce mixture.

per serving 16.4g total fat (5.3g saturated fat); 1923kJ (460 cal); 32.4g carbohydrate; 42.6g protein; 5.4g fibre

char-grilled beef and noodle salad

preparation time 30 minutes
cooking time 30 minutes serves 4

600g piece beef fillet, trimmed
2 lebanese cucumbers (260g), seeded, sliced thinly
1 cup (80g) bean sprouts
1 medium red onion (170g), sliced thinly
1 cup loosely packed fresh coriander leaves
1 cup loosely packed fresh mint leaves
6 fresh kaffir lime leaves, sliced thinly
vegetable oil, for deep-frying
200g dried egg noodles

HOT AND SOUR DRESSING
⅓ cup (80ml) lime juice
2 tablespoons fish sauce
1 tablespoon brown sugar
1 tablespoon finely sliced fresh lemon grass
3 fresh small red thai chillies, sliced thinly
1 clove garlic, crushed

1 Place ingredients for hot and sour dressing in screw-top jar; shake well.
2 Cook beef on heated oiled grill plate (or grill or barbecue) until browned and cooked as desired. Cover; stand 10 minutes. Slice beef thinly.
3 Meanwhile, combine cucumber, sprouts, onion, coriander, mint and lime leaves in large bowl.
4 Heat oil in wok; deep-fry noodles, in batches, until puffed and browned lightly. Drain on absorbent paper.
5 Add beef and dressing to salad in bowl; toss gently to combine. Divide noodles among serving plates; top with beef salad.

per serving 12.9g total fat (4.3g saturated fat); 1969kJ (471 cal); 44.3g carbohydrate; 41.4g protein; 4.9g fibre

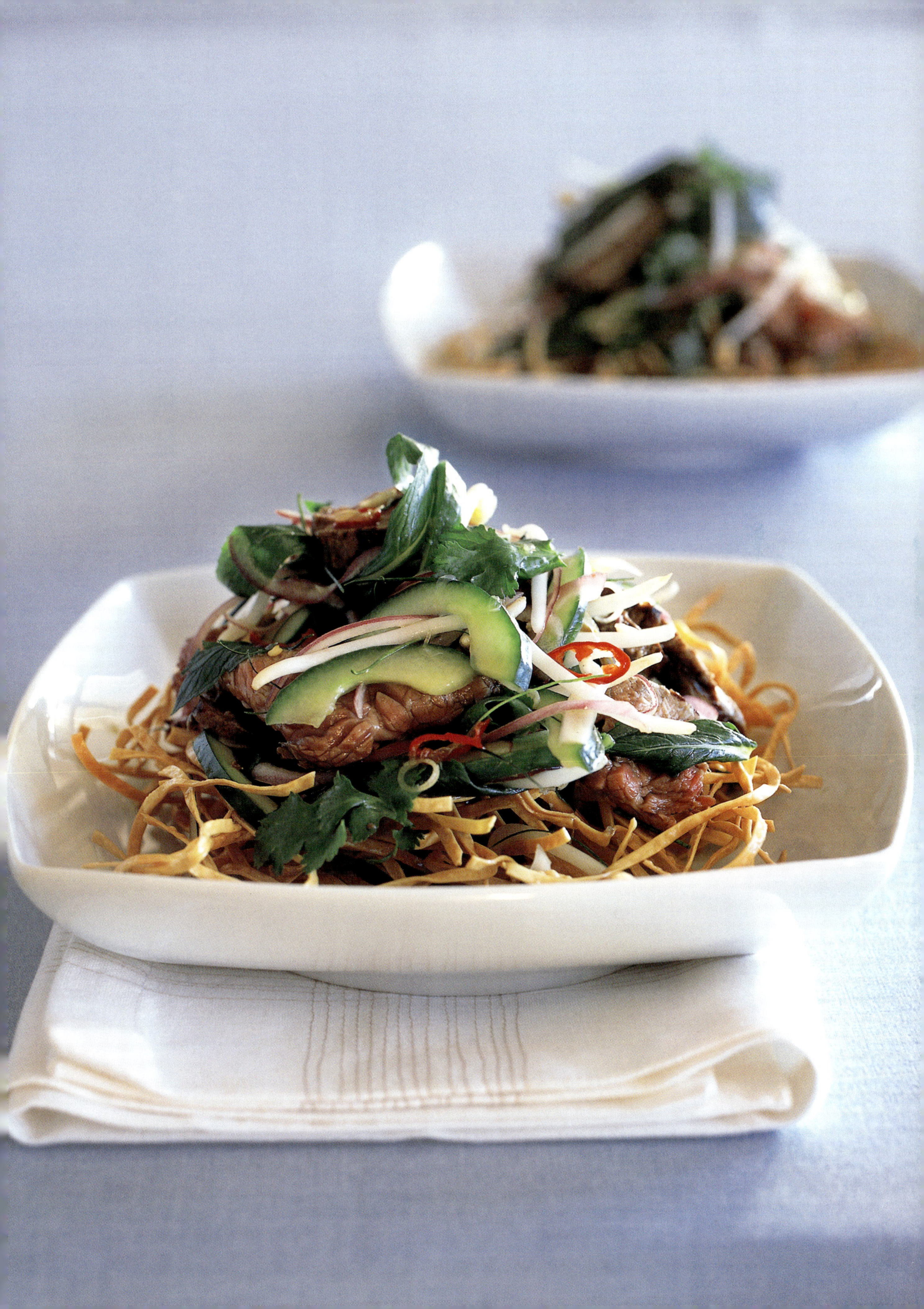

The Complete Book of Modern Asian

gado gado

preparation time 30 minutes
cooking time 15 minutes serves 4

4 medium carrots (480g), cut into batons
1 medium potato (200g), chopped coarsely
200g cauliflower, cut into florets
100g snow peas, trimmed, halved
1 lebanese cucumber (130g), cut into batons
1½ cups (100g) coarsely chopped iceberg lettuce
1½ cups (120g) bean sprouts
½ cup coarsely chopped fresh coriander

PEANUT SAUCE
½ cup (70g) toasted unsalted peanuts
2 cloves garlic, quartered
4 green onions, chopped coarsely
½ teaspoon brown sugar
1 tablespoon soy sauce
½ teaspoon chilli powder
1 tablespoon lemon juice
¾ cup (180ml) water
140ml can light coconut milk

1 Boil, steam or microwave carrot, potato, cauliflower and peas, separately, until just tender; drain. Rinse under cold water; drain.
2 Meanwhile, make peanut sauce.
3 Place carrot, potato, cauliflower and peas in large bowl with cucumber, lettuce, sprouts and coriander; toss gently to combine. Serve salad drizzled with sauce.
PEANUT SAUCE
Using mortar and pestle, grind nuts until crushed finely; transfer to small bowl. Using mortar and pestle, crush garlic and green onion into a coarse paste. Cook garlic mixture in medium oiled frying pan, stirring, 2 minutes. Add remaining ingredients; bring to a boil. Reduce heat, simmer, uncovered, 3 minutes. Add nuts; simmer, uncovered, 5 minutes.
per serving 9.8g total fat (8.8g saturated fat); 1208kJ (289 cal); 20.3g carbohydrate; 11.1g protein; 9.2g fibre
TIP The peanut sauce can be made in a blender or food processor instead of a mortar and pestle.

beef with green papaya, chilli and coriander salad

preparation time 20 minutes
cooking time 15 minutes serves 4

600g piece beef rump steak
800g green papaya
2 medium tomatoes (300g), seeded, sliced thinly
3 cups (180g) finely shredded iceberg lettuce
2 lebanese cucumbers (260g), seeded, sliced thinly
⅓ cup (80ml) lime juice
2 tablespoons fish sauce
1 tablespoon brown sugar
2 cloves garlic, crushed
3 small green chillies, chopped finely
¼ cup coarsely chopped fresh coriander

1 Cook beef on heated oiled grill plate (or grill or barbecue) until cooked as desired. Cover beef; stand 5 minutes, slice thinly.
2 Meanwhile, peel papaya. Quarter lengthways, discard seeds; grate papaya coarsely.
3 Place beef and papaya in large bowl with tomato, lettuce and cucumber. Place remaining ingredients in screw-top jar; shake well. Drizzle dressing over salad; toss gently to combine.
per serving 10.5g total fat (4.5g saturated fat); 1304kJ (312 cal); 13.9g carbohydrate; 37.7g protein; 4.7g fibre

The Complete Book of Modern Asian

Stir-frying brings out the culinary explorer in everyone: there are few things that can't be cooked – and cooked well – in a wok, and as the medium requires neither added fat nor a lot of time, it's as perfect for today's lifestyle as it was in centuries past. Shallow-frying, too, comes into its own in many Asian meat and seafood dishes.

capsicum, chilli and hoisin chicken *page 174*

chiang mai pork and eggplant *page 189*

stir-fries & pan-fries

orange-flavoured octopus and broccolini *page 197*

honey and five-spice beef with broccolini *page 189*

twice-cooked chicken with asian greens

preparation time 45 minutes (plus standing and refrigeration time)
cooking time 1 hour serves 4

2.5 litres (10 cups) water
1 litre (4 cups) chicken stock
2 cups (500ml) chinese cooking wine
8 cloves garlic, crushed
10cm piece fresh ginger (50g), sliced thinly
1 teaspoon sesame oil
1.6kg chicken
peanut oil, for deep-frying
1 tablespoon peanut oil
150g snow peas, trimmed
500g choy sum, chopped coarsely
350g gai lan, chopped coarsely
2 green onions, sliced thinly

CHAR SIU DRESSING
2 cloves garlic, crushed
5cm piece fresh ginger (25g), grated finely
¼ cup (60ml) char siu sauce
2 tablespoons soy sauce
1 teaspoon white sugar
1 tablespoon rice vinegar

1 Combine the water, stock, wine, garlic, ginger and sesame oil in large saucepan; bring to a boil. Boil, uncovered, 10 minutes. Add chicken; reduce heat, simmer, uncovered, 15 minutes. Remove from heat, cover; stand chicken in stock 3 hours. Remove chicken; pat dry with absorbent paper. Reserve stock for another use.
2 Using sharp knife, halve chicken lengthways; cut halves crossways through the centre. Cut breasts from wings and thighs from legs to give you eight chicken pieces in total. Cut wings in half; cut breast and thighs into thirds. Place chicken pieces on tray; refrigerate, uncovered, 3 hours or overnight.
3 Make char siu dressing.
4 Heat peanut oil for deep-frying in wok; deep-fry chicken pieces, in batches, until browned. Drain on absorbent paper.
5 Heat the 1 tablespoon of peanut oil in cleaned wok; stir-fry snow peas, choy sum and gai lan until just tender. Add 2 tablespoons of the dressing; stir-fry to combine.
6 Divide vegetables among serving plates; top with chicken, drizzle with remaining dressing and sprinkle with onion.

CHAR SIU DRESSING
Stir garlic, ginger, sauces and sugar over heat in small saucepan until mixture comes to a boil. Remove from heat; stir in vinegar.

per serving 47.4g total fat (12.5g saturated fat); 3081kJ (737 cal); 17.8g carbohydrate; 43.8g protein; 8.9g fibre

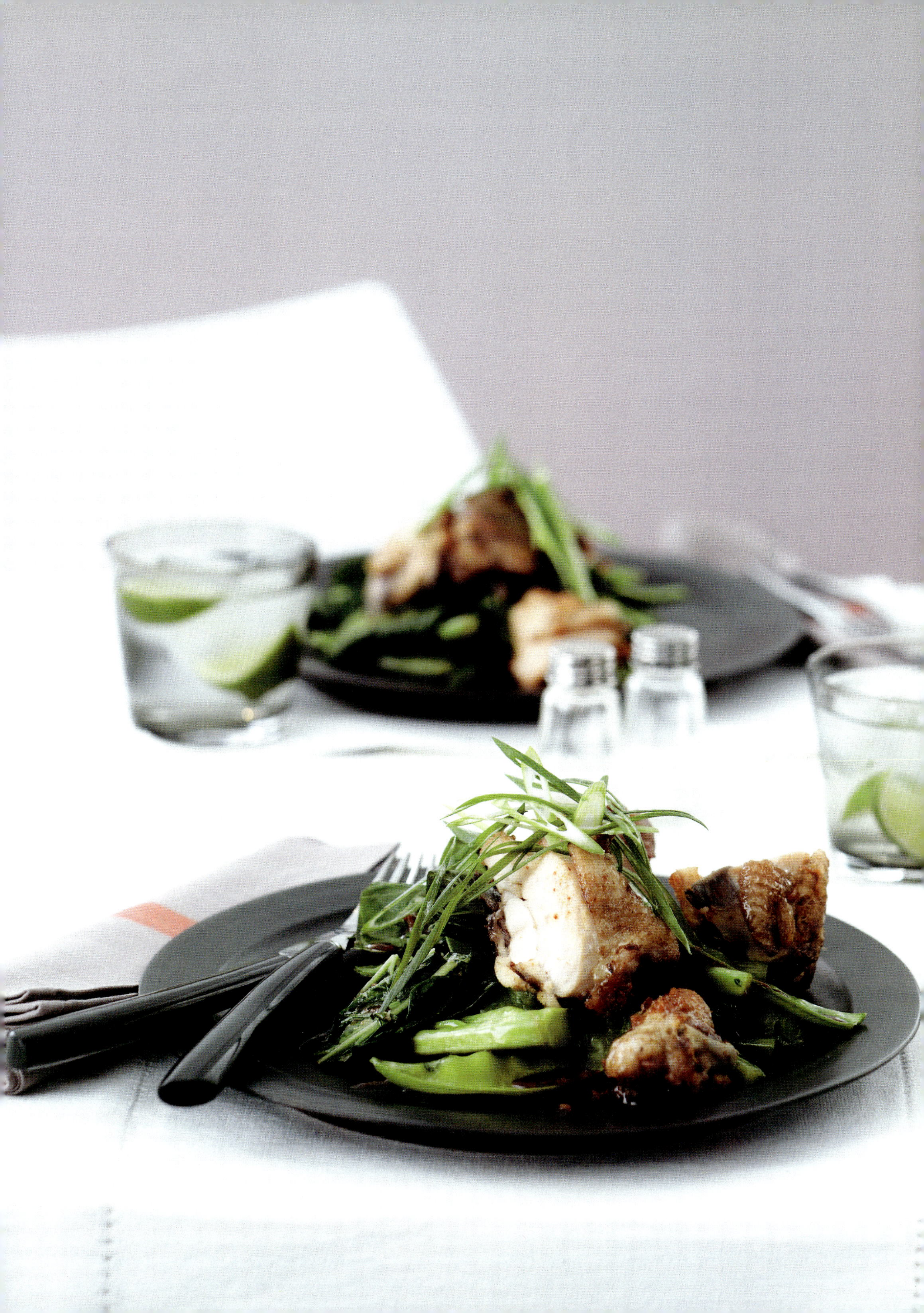

The Complete Book of Modern Asian

wok-seared mushroom omelettes

preparation time 15 minutes
cooking time 20 minutes serves 4

½ small red capsicum (75g), sliced thinly
2 green onions, sliced thinly
1 fresh small red thai chilli, chopped finely
1 cup (80g) bean sprouts
30g shiitake mushrooms, sliced thinly
50g oyster mushrooms, sliced thinly
½ cup firmly packed fresh coriander leaves
12 eggs
2 tablespoons fish sauce
2 teaspoons oyster sauce
⅓ cup (80ml) vegetable oil
2 tablespoons oyster sauce, extra
¼ teaspoon sesame oil
1 tablespoon chopped fresh chives

1 Combine capsicum, onion, chilli, sprouts, mushrooms and coriander in small bowl. Combine eggs and sauces in medium bowl; beat lightly. Add half the vegetable mixture to egg mixture.
2 Heat a quarter of the vegetable oil in wok. When oil is just smoking, add a quarter of the egg mixture then, working quickly using a slotted spoon, push cooked egg mixture in from sides of wok and the uncooked mixture to the outside.
3 When omelette is almost set, sprinkle a quarter of the remaining vegetables over one half of the omelette. Reduce heat to low; cook for 1 minute, folding omelette in half over top of vegetables after 30 seconds. Remove omelette from wok with two lifters; drain on absorbent paper. Keep warm. Repeat three times with remaining egg mixture and vegetables.
4 Serve omelettes drizzled with combined extra oyster sauce and sesame oil; top with chives, and extra coriander and green onion, if desired.
per serving 36.9g total fat (7.9g saturated fat); 1910kJ (457 cal); 5.7g carbohydrate; 25.6g protein; 1.9g fibre

crispy fish with asian greens

preparation time 10 minutes
cooking time 15 minutes serves 4

8 whiting fillets (600g)
¼ cup (35g) cornflour
vegetable oil, for deep-frying
500g gai lan, chopped coarsely
¼ cup (60ml) oyster sauce
2 teaspoons sesame oil
2 green onions, sliced thinly
½ cup firmly packed fresh coriander leaves
1 long fresh red chilli, sliced thinly

1 Toss fish in cornflour; shake away excess. Heat oil in wok; cook fish until browned lightly and cooked through. Drain on absorbent paper.
2 Boil, steam or microwave gai lan until just tender; drain.
3 Arrange gai lan on serving plates, drizzle with combined oyster sauce and sesame oil; top with fish, sprinkle with onions, coriander and chilli. Serve with steamed rice, if desired.
per serving 12g total fat (1.7g saturated fat); 1279kJ (306 cal); 13.6g carbohydrate; 33.5g protein; 5.9g fibre

mussels with asian flavours

preparation time 20 minutes
cooking time 15 minutes serves 4

1.5kg black mussels
1¼ cups (250g) jasmine rice
1 tablespoon sesame oil
4cm piece fresh ginger (20g), grated
1 tablespoon finely chopped fresh lemon grass
3 fresh small red thai chillies, chopped finely
⅓ cup (80ml) sweet sherry
2 teaspoons cornflour
½ cup (125ml) water
2 tablespoons mirin
1 tablespoon soy sauce
12 green onions, sliced thinly
¼ cup coarsely chopped fresh mint
¼ cup coarsely chopped fresh coriander

1 Scrub mussels under cold water; discard beards.
2 Cook rice in medium saucepan of boiling water, uncovered, until just tender. Drain; cover to keep warm.
3 Meanwhile, heat oil in wok; stir-fry ginger, lemon grass and chilli until fragrant. Add mussels and sherry; cook, covered, about 5 minutes or until mussels open (discard any that do not).
4 Blend cornflour with the water, mirin and soy sauce in small jug; add to wok, stir-fry until mixture boils and thickens slightly. Remove from heat; stir in onion and herbs. Serve mussels with rice.

per serving 6.4g total fat (1.1g saturated fat); 1593kJ (381 cal); 58.9g carbohydrate; 14.1g protein; 1.7g fibre

masala fish

preparation time 15 minutes (plus refrigeration time)
cooking time 8 minutes serves 4

600g piece swordfish
2 teaspoons chilli powder
½ teaspoon ground turmeric
1 teaspoon ground cumin
⅓ cup (80ml) lime juice
⅓ cup (65g) rice flour, for dusting
vegetable oil, for shallow-frying

1 Trim fish, removing skin; cut fish into 3cm-thick steaks, then cut steaks into 8 pieces.
2 Combine spices and lime juice in small bowl; pour spice mixture over fish in shallow dish, turn to coat. Cover; refrigerate 3 hours.
3 Remove fish from marinade; pat dry with absorbent paper. Toss fish pieces in rice flour; shake away excess. Heat oil in large frying pan; shallow-fry fish until cooked as desired. Drain on absorbent paper.
4 Stack fish high in the centre of a plate on banana leaf, if desired. Garnish with lime wedges, if desired.

per serving 16.8g total fat (2.8g saturated fat); 1396kJ (334 cal); 13.5g carbohydrate; 31.8g protein; 0.6g fibre

Stir-fries & Pan-fries

The Complete Book of Modern Asian

twice-cooked pork

preparation time 15 minutes
cooking time 1 hour 10 minutes
(plus cooling and standing time) serves 4

800g pork belly, skin removed
4cm piece fresh ginger (20g), grated
2 green onions, chopped coarsely
1 tablespoon vegetable oil
1 medium red capsicum (200g), sliced thinly
1 medium green capsicum (200g), sliced thinly
1 medium yellow capsicum (200g), sliced thinly
2 cloves garlic, crushed
¼ cup (60ml) hoisin sauce
2 tablespoons dark soy sauce
1 tablespoon lime juice
¼ teaspoon chilli flakes
3 green onions, sliced thinly

1 Place pork, ginger and chopped onion in wok; cover with cold water, bring to a boil. Simmer, uncovered, 30 minutes. Cool pork in water; drain.
2 Place pork on tray; stand about 20 minutes or until completely dried. Slice thinly.
3 Heat oil in cleaned wok; stir-fry pork, in batches, until crisp. Drain; cover to keep warm.
4 Reserve about 2 teaspoons of the oil in wok; discard remainder. Add capsicums and garlic; stir-fry until tender. Stir in sauces, juice and chilli. Serve capsicum topped with pork and sprinkled with sliced onion.
per serving 50.3g total fat (15.9g saturated fat); 2738kJ (655 cal); 11.1g carbohydrate; 39.3g protein; 3.6g fibre

mongolian lamb stir-fry

preparation time 15 minutes
cooking time 20 minutes serves 4

2 tablespoons peanut oil
600g lamb strips
2 cloves garlic, crushed
1cm piece fresh ginger (5g), grated
1 medium brown onion (150g), sliced thickly
1 medium red capsicum (200g), sliced thickly
230g can bamboo shoots, rinsed, drained
¼ cup (60ml) soy sauce
1 tablespoon black bean sauce
1 tablespoon cornflour
2 tablespoons rice wine vinegar
6 green onions, cut into 5cm lengths

1 Heat half of the oil in wok; stir-fry lamb, in batches, until browned all over.
2 Heat remaining oil in same wok; stir-fry garlic, ginger and brown onion until onion softens. Add capsicum and bamboo shoots; stir-fry until vegetables are just tender.
3 Return lamb to wok with sauces and blended cornflour and vinegar; stir-fry until sauce boils and thickens slightly. Remove from heat; stir in green onion. Serve stir-fry with steamed rice, if desired.
per serving 22.7g total fat (7.7g saturated fat); 1593kJ (381 cal); 9g carbohydrate; 34.3g protein; 2.5g fibre

pork with sticky asian glaze

preparation time 30 minutes (plus refrigeration time)
cooking time 2 hours 15 minutes serves 6

1 tablespoon vegetable oil
1.5kg piece pork neck
5 shallots (125g), sliced thinly
2cm piece fresh ginger (10g), sliced finely
5 cloves garlic, sliced thinly
½ cup (125ml) dark soy sauce
½ cup (100g) crushed yellow rock sugar
2 star anise
2 cups (500ml) chicken stock
2 cups (500ml) water
8 dried whole shiitake mushrooms
½ cup canned bamboo shoots, rinsed, drained
1kg fresh wide rice noodles
350 gai lan, chopped coarsely
3 green onions, sliced thinly

1 Heat oil in large saucepan; cook pork until browned all over. Add shallots, ginger and garlic to pan; cook, stirring, 1 minute. Add sauce, sugar, star anise, stock and the water; bring to a boil. Reduce heat, simmer, covered, over low heat 1½ hours, turning pork occasionally during cooking.
2 Meanwhile, soak mushrooms in small bowl of warm water 20 minutes. Remove stems, cut in half.
3 Add mushrooms and bamboo shoots to pork; simmer, uncovered, further 30 minutes, turning pork occasionally. Remove pork from saucepan; cover to keep warm. Strain cooking liquid into large jug, reserve mushroom mixture. You will need 2½ cups (625ml) cooking liquid.
4 Place reserved cooking liquid in medium saucepan; bring to a boil. Boil, uncovered, about 10 minutes or until reduced to ¾ cup (180ml).
5 Meanwhile, place noodles in heatproof bowl; cover with boiling water. Stand until just tender; drain. Boil, steam or microwave broccoli until just tender. Slice pork thickly.
6 Place noodles on serving plates, top with broccoli, sliced pork and mushroom mixture. Drizzle with reduced cooking liquid, top with green onions.
per serving 8.3g total fat (1.8g saturated fat); 2479kJ (593 cal); 60.9g carbohydrate; 64.6g protein; 5.1g fibre

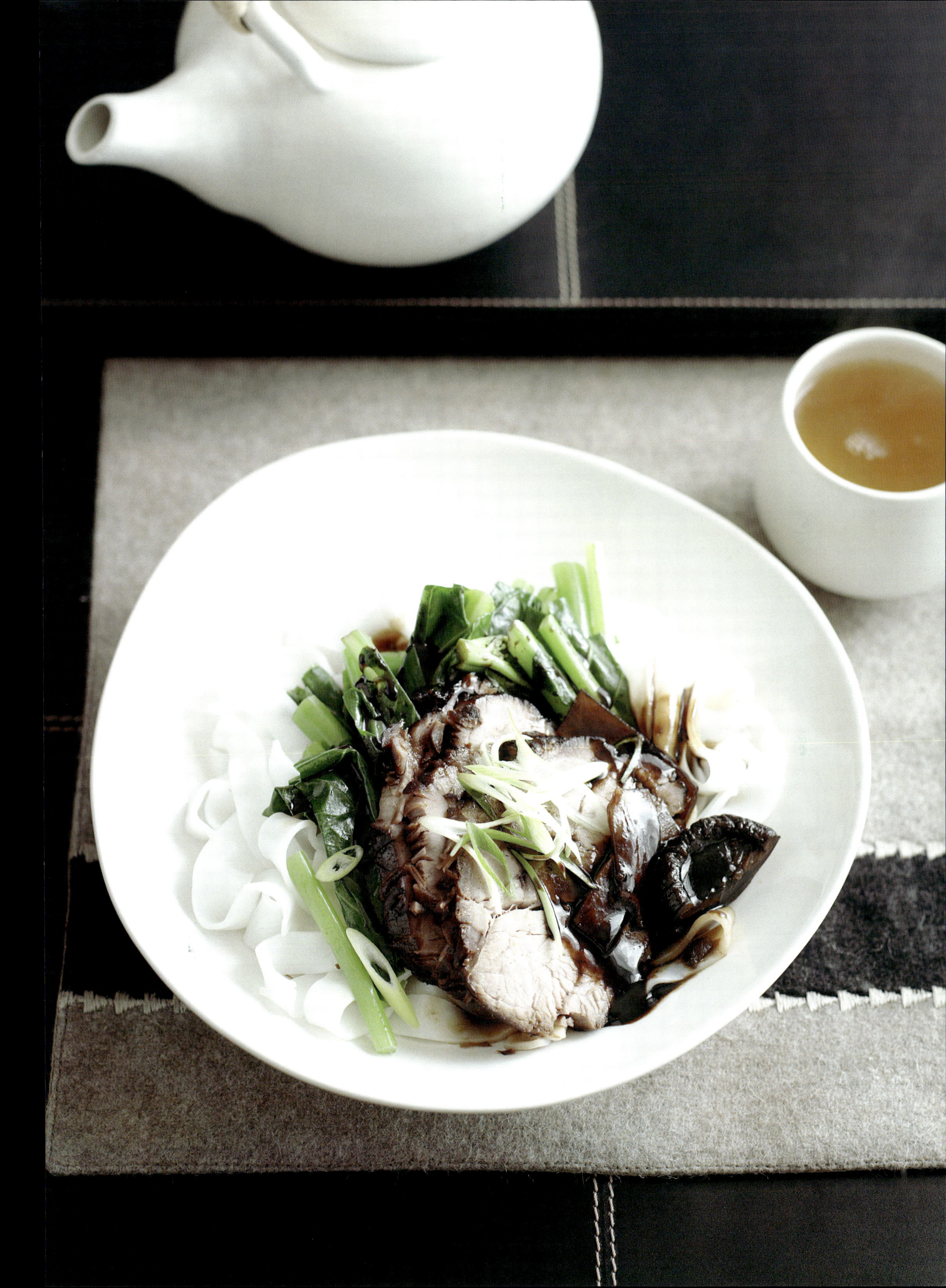

The Complete Book of Modern Asian

sukiyaki

preparation time 20 minutes
cooking time 10 minutes serves 4

400g fresh udon noodles
300g fresh firm silken tofu
4 eggs
¼ cup (60ml) vegetable oil
600g beef rump steak, trimmed, sliced thinly
8 oyster mushrooms
4 green onions, sliced thinly
300g spinach, trimmed, chopped coarsely
2 cups (160g) bean sprouts

BROTH
1 cup (250ml) japanese soy sauce
½ cup (125ml) sake
½ cup (125ml) mirin
½ cup (125ml) water
½ cup (110g) white sugar
2 cloves garlic, crushed

1 Place ingredients for broth in medium saucepan; cook over medium heat, stirring, until sugar dissolves. Remove from heat; cover to keep warm.
2 Place noodles in heatproof bowl, cover with boiling water; separate with fork, drain. Cut into random lengths.
3 Cut tofu into 2cm cubes; spread, in single layer, on absorbent-paper-lined-tray. Cover tofu with more absorbent paper, stand 10 minutes.
4 Break eggs into individual serving bowls; beat lightly.
5 Heat half the oil in wok; stir-fry beef, in batches, until browned.
6 Heat half the remaining oil in wok; stir-fry tofu, in batches, until browned.
7 Add remaining oil to wok; stir-fry mushrooms, onion, spinach and sprouts until vegetables are just tender.
8 Return beef and tofu to wok with noodles and broth; stir-fry until hot. Serve sukiyaki from wok, with each diner using chopsticks to pick up sukiyaki ingredients and dip in their individual bowl of egg and eat.
per serving 52g total fat (17.2g saturated fat); 4811kJ (1151 cal); 87.4g carbohydrate; 65.7g protein; 13.6g fibre

chicken and thai basil stir-fry

preparation time 20 minutes
cooking time 15 minutes serves 4

2 tablespoons peanut oil
600g chicken breast fillets, sliced thinly
2 cloves garlic, crushed
1cm piece fresh ginger (5g), grated finely
4 fresh small red thai chillies, sliced thinly
4 fresh kaffir lime leaves, shredded
1 medium brown onion (150g), sliced thinly
100g mushrooms, quartered
1 large carrot (180g), sliced thinly
¼ cup (60ml) oyster sauce
1 tablespoon soy sauce
1 tablespoon fish sauce
⅓ cup (80ml) chicken stock
1 cup (80g) bean sprouts
¾ cup loosely packed thai basil leaves

1 Heat half of the oil in wok; stir-fry chicken, in batches, until browned all over and cooked through.
2 Heat remaining oil in wok; stir-fry garlic, ginger, chilli, lime leaves and onion until onion softens and mixture is fragrant. Add mushrooms and carrot; stir-fry until carrot is just tender.
3 Return chicken to wok with sauces and stock; stir-fry until sauce thickens slightly. Remove from heat; stir through sprouts and basil.
per serving 15.9g total fat (3.5g saturated fat); 1367kJ (327 cal); 9.2g carbohydrate; 35g protein; 3.4g fibre

stir-fried lamb in black bean sauce

preparation time 15 minutes
cooking time 15 minutes serves 4

600g lamb strips
1 teaspoon five-spice powder
2 teaspoons sesame oil
2 tablespoons peanut oil
2 cloves garlic, crushed
1cm piece fresh ginger (5g), grated
1 medium brown onion (150g), sliced thinly
1 small red capsicum (150g), sliced thinly
1 small yellow capsicum (150g), sliced thinly
6 green onions, sliced thinly
1 teaspoon cornflour
½ cup (125ml) chicken stock
1 tablespoon soy sauce
2 tablespoons black bean sauce

1 Combine lamb, five-spice and sesame oil in medium bowl.
2 Heat half of the peanut oil in wok; stir-fry lamb, in batches, until browned lightly.
3 Heat remaining peanut oil in same wok; stir-fry garlic, ginger and brown onion until onion is soft. Add capsicums and green onion; stir-fry until capsicum is just tender.
4 Add blended cornflour, stock and sauces to wok with lamb; stir until sauce boils and thickens slightly and lamb is cooked as desired.

per serving 25.3g total fat (8.1g saturated fat); 1680kJ (402 cal); 8.5g carbohydrate; 34.4g protein; 2.1g fibre

chilli beef stir-fry

preparation time 10 minutes
cooking time 10 minutes serves 4

¼ cup (60ml) olive oil
700g beef rump steak, sliced thinly
300g green beans, cut into 5cm lengths
1 clove garlic, crushed
2 fresh long red chillies, sliced thinly
1/3 cup (90g) thai chilli jam
350g baby buk choy, quartered
450g hokkien noodles
¼ cup (60ml) beef stock
4 green onions, sliced thinly
⅓ cup firmly packed fresh mint leaves

1 Heat oil in wok; stir-fry beef, in batches, until browned and tender.
2 Add beans to wok; stir-fry until almost tender. Add garlic, chilli and jam; stir-fry until fragrant. Add buk choy, stir-fry until buk choy just wilts.
3 Meanwhile, place noodles in large bowl, cover with boiling water; separate noodles with a fork, drain.
4 Return beef to wok with stock, noodles, green onion and mint; stir-fry until hot.

per serving 28.9g total fat (7.9g saturated fat); 3177kJ (760 cal); 68.1g carbohydrate; 53.5g protein; 6g fibre

Stir-fries & Pan-fries

The Complete Book of Modern Asian

ginger beef stir-fry

preparation time 20 minutes
cooking time 10 minutes serves 4

6cm piece fresh ginger (30g), peeled
2 tablespoons peanut oil
600g beef rump steak, sliced thinly
2 cloves garlic, crushed
120g snake beans, cut into 5cm lengths
8 green onions, sliced thinly
2 teaspoons grated palm sugar
2 teaspoons oyster sauce
1 tablespoon fish sauce
1 tablespoon light soy sauce
½ cup loosely packed thai basil leaves

1 Slice ginger thinly; stack slices, then slice again into thin slivers.
2 Heat half of the oil in wok; stir-fry beef, in batches, until browned all over.
3 Heat remaining oil in wok; stir-fry ginger and garlic until fragrant. Add beans; stir-fry until just tender.
4 Return beef to wok with onion, sugar and sauces; stir-fry until sugar dissolves and beef is cooked as desired. Remove from heat; stir through basil.
per serving 19.4g total fat (6.2g saturated fat); 1421kJ (340 cal); 4.6g carbohydrate; 35.9g protein; 1.9g fibre

sweet and sour duck with broccolini

preparation time 25 minutes
cooking time 10 minutes serves 4

1kg chinese barbecued duck
2 small red onions (200g), cut into
  thin wedges
1 fresh small red thai chilli, chopped finely
250g broccolini, cut into 3cm pieces
¼ cup (60ml) chicken stock
¼ cup (90g) honey
¼ cup (60ml) rice vinegar
1 tablespoon light soy sauce
2 teaspoons pomegranate molasses
4 green onions, cut into 3cm lengths
1 tablespoon sesame seeds, roasted

1 Quarter duck; discard bones. Slice duck meat thickly, keeping skin intact. Heat oiled wok; stir-fry duck, in batches, until skin is crisp.
2 Heat oiled wok; stir-fry red onion and chilli until onion softens slightly. Add broccolini, stock, honey, vinegar, sauce and molasses; stir-fry until sauce thickens slightly.
3 Remove from heat; serve broccolini mixture with duck and green onion; sprinkle with seeds.
per serving 38.9g total fat (11.3g saturated fat); 2437kJ (583 cal); 24.7g carbohydrate; 33g protein; 3.7g fibre

capsicum, chilli and hoisin chicken

preparation time 15 minutes (plus refrigeration time)
cooking time 15 minutes serves 4

800g chicken breast fillets, sliced thinly
2 cloves garlic, crushed
1½ teaspoons five-spice powder
10cm stick fresh lemon grass (20g), chopped finely
2cm piece fresh ginger (10g), grated
2 tablespoons peanut oil
1 medium brown onion (150g), sliced thinly
1 fresh long red chilli, chopped finely
1 medium red capsicum (200g), sliced thickly
⅓ cup (80ml) hoisin sauce
2 teaspoons finely grated lemon rind
1 tablespoon lemon juice
½ cup coarsely chopped fresh coriander
2 tablespoons fried shallots
1 green onion, sliced thinly

1 Combine chicken with half the garlic, 1 teaspoon of the five-spice and all of the lemon grass and ginger in large bowl. Cover; refrigerate 1 hour.
2 Heat half the oil in wok; stir-fry brown onion, chilli, capsicum and remaining garlic, until onion softens. Remove from wok.
3 Heat remaining oil in wok; stir-fry chicken mixture, in batches, until cooked.
4 Return onion mixture and chicken to wok with sauce, rind, juice and remaining five-spice; stir-fry until sauce thickens slightly. Remove from heat; toss coriander into stir-fry, sprinkle with shallots and green onion.
per serving 15.4g total fat (3.1g saturated fat); 1601kJ (383 cal); 12.1g carbohydrate; 47.2g protein; 3.9g fibre

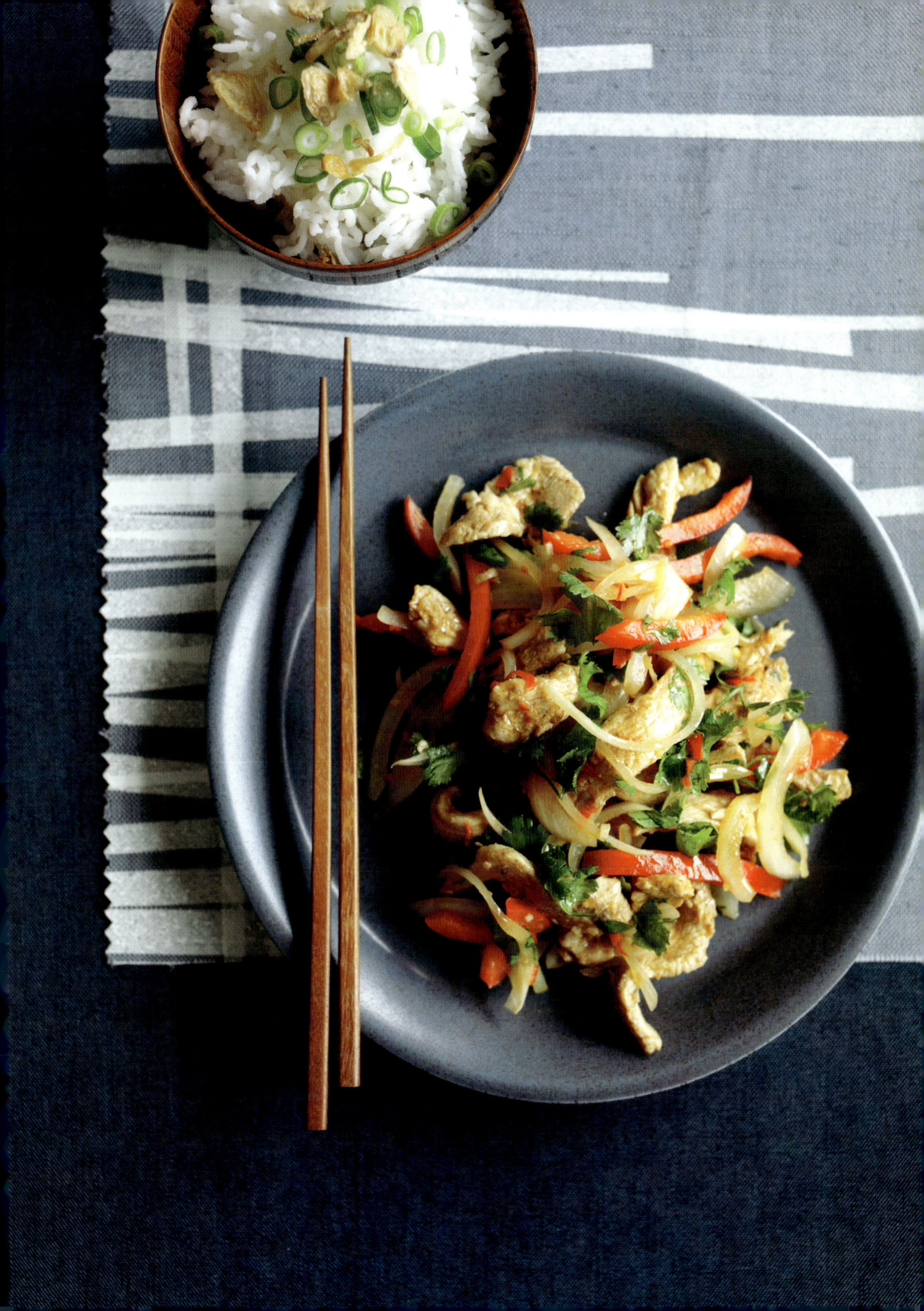

The Complete Book of Modern Asian

chicken with red nam jim

preparation time 15 minutes
cooking time 20 minutes   serves 4

4 x 200g chicken thigh cutlets, skin-on
3 fresh long red chillies, chopped coarsely
3 fresh small red chillies, chopped coarsely
1 shallot (25g), chopped coarsely
2 cloves garlic, crushed
2cm piece fresh ginger (10g), chopped coarsely
⅓ cup (80ml) lime juice
2 tablespoons fish sauce
1 tablespoon grated palm sugar
¼ cup (35g) finely chopped unsalted roasted peanuts

1 Cook chicken in heated oiled frying pan until cooked through.
2 Blend or process chillies, shallot, garlic, ginger, juice, sauce and sugar until smooth. Stir in nuts.
3 Serve chicken with red nam jim.

per serving 18.7g total fat (4.9g saturated fat); 1480kJ (354 cal); 5.4g carbohydrate; 40.6g protein; 1.4g fibre

crisp duck with tamarind soy sauce

preparation time 5 minutes
cooking time 10 minutes   serves 4

4 x 150g duck marylands
1 teaspoon peanut oil
1 clove garlic, crushed
2 tablespoons soy sauce
1 teaspoon brown sugar
2 tablespoons tamarind concentrate
2cm piece fresh ginger (10g), grated
⅓ cup (80ml) water
1 green onion, sliced thinly

1 Cook duck in heated oiled large frying pan until cooked through.
2 Heat oil in small saucepan; cook garlic, stirring, until fragrant. Add sauce, sugar, tamarind, ginger and the water; bring to a boil. Reduce heat, simmer, uncovered, about 2 minutes or until sauce thickens. Remove pan from heat; stir in onion.
3 Serve duck drizzled with tamarind soy sauce.

per serving 40.5g total fat (12g saturated fat); 1793kJ (429 cal); 2.7g carbohydrate; 14.6g protein; 0.4g fibre

kung pao prawns

preparation time 30 minutes
cooking time 15 minutes serves 4

28 uncooked large king prawns (2kg)
2 tablespoons peanut oil
2 cloves garlic, crushed
4 fresh red thai chillies, chopped finely
1 teaspoon sichuan peppercorns, crushed
500g choy sum, trimmed, chopped coarsely
¼ cup (60ml) light soy sauce
¼ cup (60ml) chinese cooking wine
1 teaspoon white sugar
227g can water chestnuts, rinsed, halved
4 green onions, chopped coarsely
½ cup (70g) roasted unsalted peanuts

1 Shell and devein prawns, leaving tails intact.
2 Heat half of the oil in wok; stir-fry prawns, in batches, until changed in colour. Drain.
3 Heat remaining oil in wok; stir-fry garlic, chilli and peppercorns until fragrant. Add choy sum; stir-fry until wilted. Return prawns to wok with sauce, wine, sugar and chestnuts; stir-fry 2 minutes. Remove from heat; stir in onion and nuts.

per serving 19.4g total fat (2.9g saturated fat); 1998kJ (478 cal); 8.5g carbohydrate; 8.5g protein; 7.5g fibre

crisp twice-fried lamb with thai basil

preparation time 15 minutes
cooking time 20 minutes serves 4

⅓ cup (80ml) sweet chilli sauce
¼ cup (60ml) oyster sauce
2 tablespoons light soy sauce
800g lamb strips
¾ cup (110g) plain flour
vegetable oil, for deep-frying
1 tablespoon vegetable oil, extra
1 small brown onion (80g), sliced thinly
2 cloves garlic, sliced thinly
250g sugar snap peas, trimmed
2 cups (160g) bean sprouts
1 cup loosely packed thai basil leaves

1 Combine sauces in small jug; pour two-thirds of the sauce mixture into medium bowl with lamb, mix well. Drain lamb, discard liquid.
2 Coat lamb in flour; shake off excess. Heat oil in wok; deep-fry lamb, in batches, until browned. Drain.
3 Heat extra oil in cleaned wok; stir-fry onion and garlic until onion softens. Add peas and remaining sauce mixture; stir-fry until peas are almost tender.
4 Return lamb to wok; stir-fry until hot. Remove from heat; stir in sprouts and basil.

per serving 34.5g total fat (10.2g saturated fat); 2713kJ (649 cal); 32.4g carbohydrate; 49.6g protein; 5.4g fibre

Stir-fries & Pan-fries

The Complete Book of Modern Asian

chengdu chicken

preparation time 20 minutes (plus refrigeration time)
cooking time 15 minutes   serves 4

800g chicken breast fillets, chopped coarsely
2 tablespoons light soy sauce
2 tablespoons chinese cooking wine
1 teaspoon sesame oil
¼ cup (60ml) peanut oil
300g spinach, trimmed, chopped coarsely
2 cloves garlic, crushed
2cm piece fresh ginger (10g), grated
4 green onions, sliced thinly
1 tablespoon rice vinegar
1 teaspoon white sugar
2 tablespoons finely grated orange rind
2 tablespoons sambal oelek
1 teaspoon sichuan peppercorns, crushed

1 Combine chicken, half of the sauce, half of the wine and half of the sesame oil in large bowl. Cover; refrigerate 20 minutes.
2 Heat 1 tablespoon of the peanut oil in wok; stir-fry spinach until just wilted. Remove from wok; cover to keep warm.
3 Heat half of the remaining peanut oil in wok; stir-fry chicken mixture, in batches, until browned.
4 Heat remaining peanut oil in wok; stir-fry garlic, ginger and onion until onion just softens.
5 Return chicken and remaining sauce, wine and sesame oil to wok with vinegar, sugar, rind and sambal; stir-fry until chicken is cooked. Serve spinach topped with chicken; sprinkle with pepper.
per serving   19.8g total fat (3.8g saturated fat); 1710kJ (409 cal); 5.7g carbohydrate; 48g protein; 2.1g fibre

peanut chilli beef with choy sum

preparation time 10 minutes
cooking time 15 minutes   serves 4

700g beef strips
½ cup (140g) crunchy peanut butter
¼ cup (75g) sambal oelek
¼ cup (60ml) kecap manis
2 tablespoons peanut oil
2 medium white onions (300g), cut into 8 wedges
½ small wombok (350g), shredded coarsely
400g choy sum, chopped coarsely

1 Combine beef, half of the peanut butter, 2 teaspoons of the sambal and 2 teaspoons of the kecap manis in medium bowl.
2 Combine remaining peanut butter, sambal and kecap manis in small jug.
3 Heat half of the oil in wok; stir-fry beef, in batches, until cooked as desired. Cover to keep warm.
4 Heat remaining oil in wok; stir-fry onion and wombok, in batches, until browned lightly. Return onion and wombok to wok with choy sum; stir-fry to combine, then pour reserved peanut butter mixture into wok. Stir-fry until choy sum just wilts and mixture is hot.
5 Serve vegetable mixture topped with beef.
per serving   37.7g total fat (9g saturated fat); 2541kJ (608 cal); 13.8g carbohydrate; 50.7g protein; 7.2g fibre

asian star

singapore chilli crab

preparation time 10 minutes
cooking time 20 minutes serves 4

4 uncooked medium blue swimmer crabs (1.5kg)
1 tablespoon peanut oil
1 small brown onion (80g), chopped finely
½ teaspoon cayenne pepper
400g can crushed tomatoes
1 tablespoon soy sauce
2 tablespoons brown sugar
2 cloves garlic, crushed
3cm piece fresh ginger (15g), grated
1 fresh small red thai chilli, sliced thinly
1 teaspoon cornflour
½ cup (125ml) water

1 Remove and discard back shell and gills of crab; rinse under cold water. Chop crab body into quarters, leaving claws intact.
2 Heat oil in wok; stir-fry onion until softened. Add pepper, undrained tomatoes, sauce, sugar, garlic, ginger and chilli; bring to a boil then reduce heat. Add crabs; simmer 15 minutes.
3 Add blended cornflour and the water to wok; stir until tomato mixture boils and thickens.
per serving 5.4g total fat (0.9g saturated fat); 650kJ (155 cal); 12.3g carbohydrate; 13.3g protein; 1.8g fibre

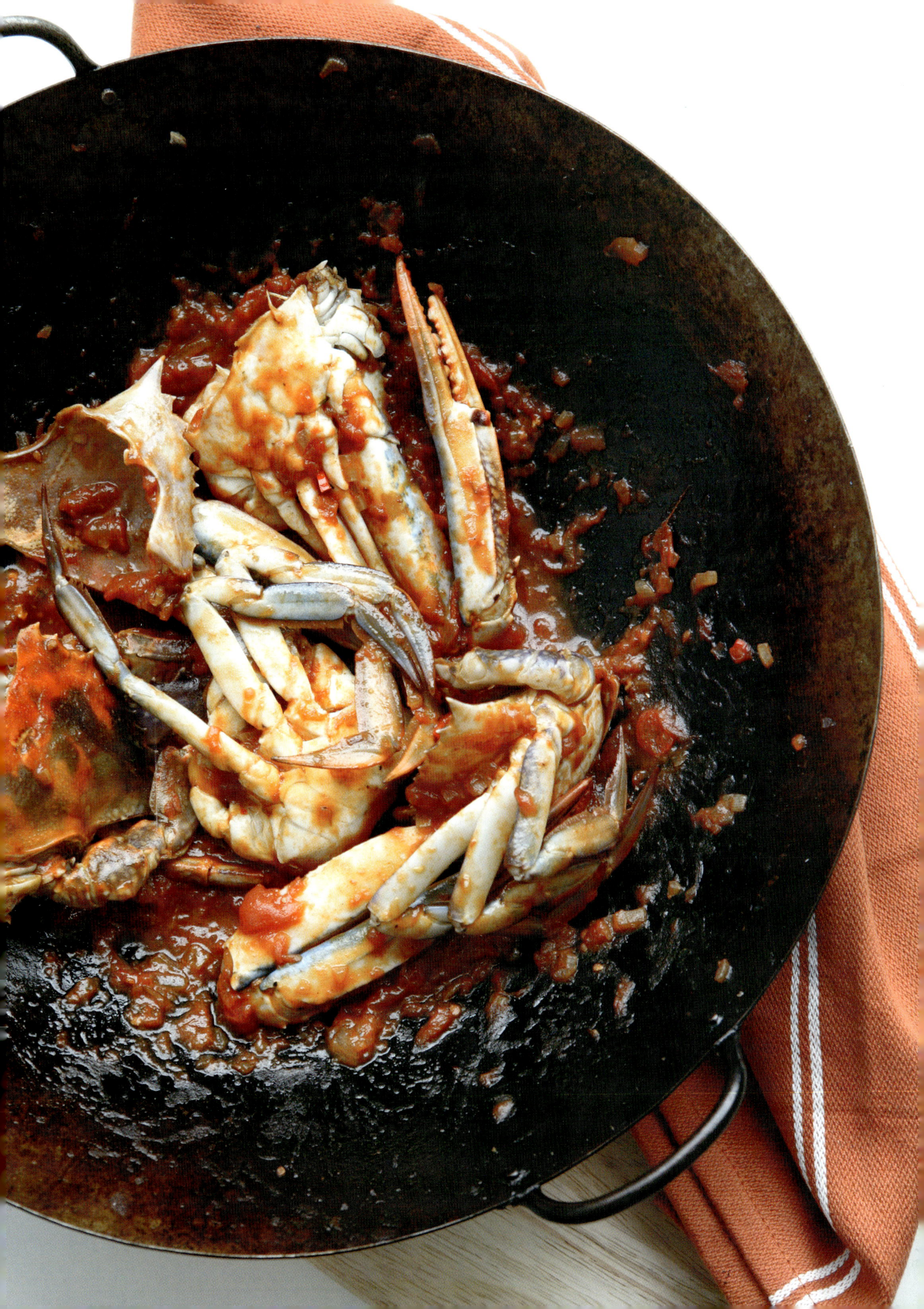

The Complete Book of Modern Asian

tamarind honey prawns with pineapple

preparation time 20 minutes
cooking time 15 minutes serves 4

1.2kg uncooked medium king prawns
1 tablespoon vegetable oil
3 cloves garlic, crushed
1 fresh long red chilli, sliced thinly
1 medium red capsicum (200g), sliced thinly
150g snow peas, trimmed
⅓ cup (100g) tamarind concentrate
2 tablespoons kecap manis
1 tablespoon honey
230g can bamboo shoots, rinsed, drained
½ small pineapple (450g), chopped coarsely
4 green onions, sliced thinly

1 Shell and devein prawns, leaving tails intact.
2 Heat oil in wok; stir-fry prawns, garlic, chilli, capsicum and peas until prawns are changed in colour. Add remaining ingredients; stir-fry until hot.
per serving 5.8g total fat (0.8g saturated fat); 1141kJ (273 cal); 18.5g carbohydrate; 34.6g protein; 4.3g fibre

mixed mushrooms and chicken with crispy noodles

preparation time 15 minutes
cooking time 20 minutes serves 4

1 tablespoon peanut oil
1kg chicken thigh fillets, sliced thinly
2 cloves garlic, crushed
8 green onions, chopped coarsely
200g fresh shiitake mushrooms, chopped coarsely
200g gai lan, chopped coarsely
100g oyster mushrooms, chopped coarsely
⅓ cup (80ml) vegetarian mushroom oyster sauce
100g enoki mushrooms
50g fried noodles

1 Heat oil in wok; stir-fry chicken, in batches, until cooked.
2 Return chicken to wok with garlic and onion; stir-fry until onion softens. Add shiitake mushrooms; stir-fry until tender. Add gai lan, oyster mushrooms and sauce; stir-fry until vegetables are tender.
3 Remove from heat; toss in enoki mushrooms and noodles.
per serving 24.3g total fat (7g saturated fat); 2065kJ (494 cal); 15.9g carbohydrate; 51.1g protein; 4.5g fibre

indian rice pilaf with spiced beef

preparation time 10 minutes
cooking time 30 minutes serves 4

2 tablespoons ghee
1 small brown onion (80g), sliced thinly
1 clove garlic, crushed
1 teaspoon cumin seeds
1 teaspoon caraway seeds
⅛ teaspoon ground turmeric
1 cup (200g) basmati rice
2 cups (500ml) chicken stock
2 tablespoons currants
500g beef mince
1½ teaspoons curry powder
⅓ cup (80ml) sweet chilli sauce
¼ cup (60ml) water
4 green onions, sliced thinly
⅔ cup (80g) frozen peas
¼ cup firmly packed fresh coriander leaves

1 Heat 1 tablespoon of the ghee in large frying pan; cook onion, garlic, seeds and turmeric, stirring, until onion softens.
2 Add rice to pan; stir over heat until coated in ghee. Stir in stock; bring to a boil. Reduce heat as low as possible; cook, covered, 12 minutes. Remove from heat; stand, covered, 5 minutes. Stir in currants.
3 Meanwhile, heat remaining ghee in large frying pan; cook beef, stirring, until browned. Add curry powder; cook until fragrant. Stir in sauce, water, green onions and peas; cook, stirring, until peas are soft and heated through.
4 Serve pilaf topped with spiced mince and coriander.
per serving 19.1g total fat (9.8g saturated fat); 2926kJ (700 cal); 93.2g carbohydrate; 35.7g protein; 4.1g fibre

beef with oyster sauce

preparation time 15 minutes
cooking time 10 minutes serves 4

400g buk choy
250g gai lan
2 tablespoons peanut oil
2 cloves garlic, crushed
500g beef rump steak, sliced thinly
50g snow peas
425g can baby corn, drained, chopped coarsely
6 green onions, chopped
2 tablespoons oyster sauce
1 tablespoon fish sauce
1 tablespoon brown sugar

1 Break buk choy and gai lan into large pieces; steam or microwave until just tender, drain well. Cover to keep warm.
2 Heat oil in wok; stir-fry garlic and beef, in batches, until cooked as desired.
3 Stir-fry peas, corn, onion, sauces and sugar in wok until peas are almost tender.
4 Return beef to wok; stir-fry until hot. Serve mixture over buk choy and gai lan.
per serving 18.1g total fat (5.4g saturated fat); 1463kJ (350 cal); 10.6g carbohydrate; 33g protein; 6.7g fibre

Stir-fries & Pan-fries

The Complete Book of Modern Asian

chiang mai pork and eggplant

preparation time 20 minutes
cooking time 25 minutes serves 4

3 fresh small red thai chillies, halved
6 cloves garlic, quartered
1 medium brown onion (150g), chopped coarsely
500g baby eggplants
¼ cup (60ml) peanut oil
700g pork leg steaks, sliced thinly
1 tablespoon fish sauce
1 tablespoon dark soy sauce
1 tablespoon grated palm sugar
4 purple thai shallots (100g), sliced thinly
150g snake beans, cut into 5cm lengths
1 cup loosely packed thai basil leaves

1 Blend or process chilli, garlic and onion until mixture forms a paste.
2 Quarter eggplants lengthways; slice each piece into 5cm lengths. Cook eggplant in large saucepan of boiling water until just tender; drain, pat dry.
3 Heat half the oil in wok; stir-fry eggplant, in batches, until browned lightly. Drain.
4 Heat remaining oil in wok; stir-fry pork, in batches, until cooked.
5 Stir-fry garlic paste in wok about 3 minutes or until fragrant and browned lightly. Add sauces and sugar; stir-fry until sugar dissolves.
6 Add shallot and beans; stir-fry until beans are tender. Return eggplant and pork to wok; stir-fry until hot. Remove from heat; sprinkle with basil.
per serving 19.3g total fat (4.1g saturated fat); 1672kJ (400 cal); 10.1g carbohydrate; 43.6g protein; 5.8g fibre

honey and five-spice beef with broccolini

preparation time 10 minutes (plus refrigeration time)
cooking time 15 minutes serves 4

750g beef strips
1 teaspoon five-spice powder
4cm fresh ginger (20g), grated
2 tablespoons peanut oil
¼ cup (60ml) dark soy sauce
2 tablespoons honey
2 teaspoons lemon juice
350g broccolini, chopped coarsely
⅓ cup (35g) walnuts, chopped coarsely
1 tablespoon roasted sesame seeds

1 Combine beef, five-spice, ginger and half of the oil in large bowl. Cover; refrigerate 1 hour.
2 Heat remaining oil in wok; stir-fry beef, in batches, until browned.
3 Add sauce, honey and juice to wok; bring to a boil. Simmer, 2 minutes.
4 Return beef to wok with broccolini; stir-fry until broccolini is tender. Remove from heat; sprinkle with nuts and seeds.
per serving 28.1g total fat (6.9g saturated fat); 2077kJ (497 cal); 12.8g carbohydrate; 46.7g protein; 4.6g fibre

twice-fried sichuan beef

preparation time 20 minutes (plus standing time)
cooking time 25 minutes serves 4

600g piece beef eye fillet, sliced thinly
2 tablespoons dry sherry
2 tablespoons light soy sauce
1 teaspoon brown sugar
½ cup (75g) cornflour
vegetable oil, for deep-frying
2 teaspoons sesame oil
1 clove garlic, crushed
1 fresh red thai chilli, chopped finely
1 medium brown onion (150g), sliced thickly
1 medium carrot (120g), halved, sliced thinly
1 small red capsicum (150g), sliced thinly
500g gai lan, chopped coarsely
1 tablespoon cracked sichuan peppercorns
2 tablespoons oyster sauce
¼ cup (60ml) light soy sauce, extra
½ cup (125ml) beef stock
2 teaspoons brown sugar, extra

1 Combine beef, sherry, soy sauce and sugar in medium bowl. Stand 10 minutes; drain. Toss beef in cornflour; shake off excess.
2 Heat vegetable oil in wok; deep-fry beef, in batches, until crisp. Drain on absorbent paper. Reserve oil for another use.
3 Heat sesame oil in cleaned wok; stir-fry garlic, chilli and onion until onion is soft. Add carrot and capsicum; stir-fry until just tender. Add gai lan; stir-fry until just wilted.
4 Add beef with peppercorns, oyster sauce, extra soy sauce, stock and extra sugar; stir-fry until heated through. Serve with steamed rice, if desired.
per serving 21.2g total fat (5.3g saturated fat); 1960kJ (469 cal); 28.9g carbohydrate; 36.4g protein; 3.4g fibre

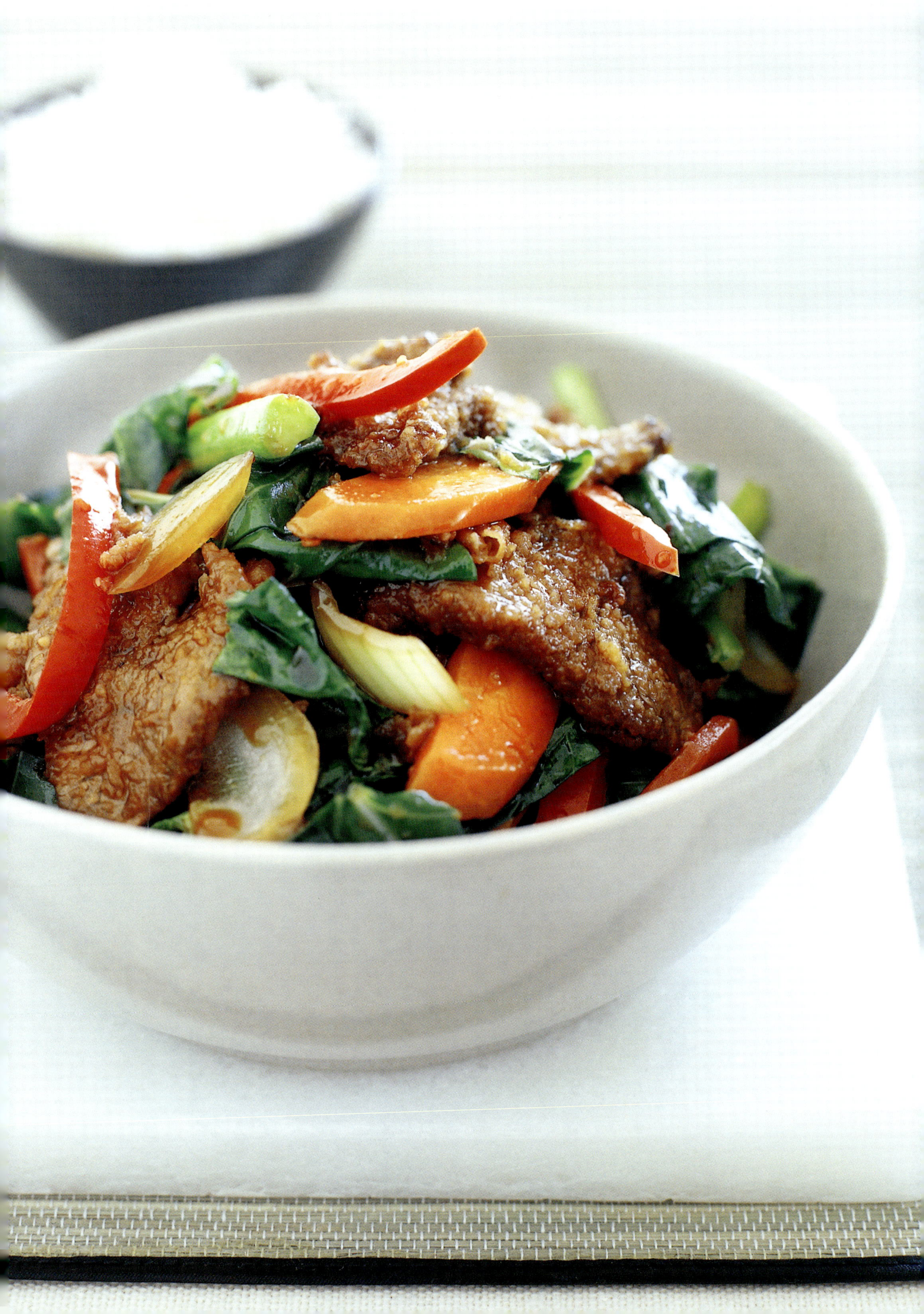

The Complete Book of Modern Asian

eggplant egg foo yung

preparation time 10 minutes
cooking time 20 minutes serves 4

1 cup (250ml) chicken stock
1 tablespoon oyster sauce
1 tablespoon dry sherry
1 tablespoon cornflour
¼ cup (60ml) water
10 eggs
4 cups (320g) bean sprouts, chopped coarsely
1 fresh small red thai chilli, chopped finely
2 baby eggplants (120g), chopped finely
4 green onions, sliced thinly
1 tablespoon peanut oil

1 Combine stock, sauce and sherry in small saucepan; bring to a boil. Stir in blended cornflour and water; return to a boil. Boil, stirring, until sauce thickens.
2 Combine eggs, sprouts, chilli, eggplant and three-quarters of the onion in large bowl.
3 Heat oil in large frying pan; add ½ cup of the egg mixture. Flatten egg mixture with spatula; cook, uncovered, until browned and set underneath. Turn, cook other side. Repeat with remaining egg mixture; you will get eight omelettes.
4 Divide omelettes among serving dishes; drizzle with sauce, top with remaining onion.
per serving 18.2g total fat (5g saturated fat); 1154kJ (276 cal); 6.8g carbohydrate; 20.5g protein; 3.3g fibre

ginger teriyaki beef

preparation time 10 minutes
cooking time 15 minutes serves 4

⅓ cup (80ml) teriyaki sauce
½ cup (125ml) hoisin sauce
2 tablespoons mirin
1 tablespoon peanut oil
750g beef strips
250g broccoli, cut into florets
250g sugar snap peas, trimmed
115g fresh baby corn, halved lengthways
4cm piece fresh ginger (20g), grated
1½ cups (120g) bean sprouts

1 Combine sauces and mirin in small jug.
2 Heat half of the oil in wok; stir-fry beef, in batches, until browned.
3 Heat remaining oil in wok; stir-fry broccoli until almost tender.
4 Return beef to wok with sauce mixture, peas, corn and ginger. Stir-fry until vegetables and beef are cooked. Remove from heat; sprinkle with sprouts.
per serving 20.7g total fat (7.2g saturated fat); 2073kJ (496 cal); 23.2g carbohydrate; 48g protein; 10.5g fibre

chilli chicken with broccoli and cashews

preparation time 10 minutes
cooking time 20 minutes serves 4

1 tablespoon peanut oil
600g chicken mince
1 clove garlic, crushed
1 small brown onion (80g), sliced thinly
300g broccoli, cut into florets
2 tablespoons fish sauce
1 tablespoon hot chilli sauce
8 green onions, sliced thinly
1¼ cups (100g) bean sprouts
⅓ cup (50g) roasted unsalted cashews
4 fresh kaffir lime leaves, sliced thinly
1 fresh long red chilli, sliced thinly

1 Heat half of the oil in wok; stir-fry chicken, in batches, until cooked.
2 Heat remaining oil in wok; stir-fry garlic and brown onion until onion softens. Add broccoli; stir-fry until almost tender.
3 Return chicken to wok with sauces, green onion, sprouts, nuts and leaves; stir-fry just until hot. Remove from heat; sprinkle with chilli.

per serving 23.4g total fat (5.6g saturated fat); 1643kJ (393 cal); 6.3g carbohydrate; 36.9g protein; 5.8g fibre

tamarind duck stir-fry

preparation time 20 minutes (plus soaking time)
cooking time 10 minutes serves 4

25g dried tamarind
½ cup (125ml) boiling water
6cm piece fresh ginger (30g), peeled
1 tablespoon peanut oil
2 cloves garlic, crushed
2 fresh long red chillies, chopped finely
1 large whole barbecued duck (1kg), cut into 12 pieces
1 medium red capsicum (200g), sliced thinly
¼ cup (60ml) chicken stock
2 tablespoons oyster sauce
1 tablespoon fish sauce
2 tablespoons grated palm sugar
200g baby buk choy, chopped coarsely
100g snow peas, sliced thinly
8 green onions, cut into 5cm lengths
⅓ cup firmly packed fresh coriander leaves

1 Soak tamarind in the boiling water for 30 minutes. Pour tamarind into a fine strainer over a small bowl; push as much pulp through the strainer as possible, scraping underside of strainer occasionally. Discard any tamarind solids left in strainer; reserve pulp liquid.
2 Slice ginger thinly; stack slices, then slice again into thin slivers.
3 Heat oil in wok; stir-fry ginger, garlic and chilli until fragrant. Add duck and capsicum; stir-fry until capsicum is tender and duck is heated through.
4 Add stock, sauces, sugar and reserved pulp liquid, bring to a boil; boil, 1 minute. Reduce heat, add buk choy; stir-fry until just wilted. Add snow peas and onion; stir-fry until both are just tender. Remove from heat; stir in coriander.

per serving 42.2g total fat (12g saturated fat); 2454kJ (587 cal); 19.3g carbohydrate; 32g protein; 3.4g fibre

Stir-fries & Pan-fries

The Complete Book of Modern Asian

peppercorn beef

preparation time 20 minutes (plus refrigeration time)
cooking time 20 minutes serves 4

800g beef rump steak, sliced thinly
2 tablespoons dark soy sauce
3cm piece fresh ginger (15g), grated
2 cloves garlic, crushed
2 teaspoons cornflour
1 teaspoon sesame oil
2 teaspoons pepper medley
¼ teaspoon sichuan peppercorns
2 tablespoons peanut oil
1 medium brown onion (150g), sliced thinly
150g snake beans, chopped coarsely
2 tablespoons chinese cooking wine
½ cup (125ml) water
2 tablespoons oyster sauce
4 green onions, sliced thickly

1 Combine beef, soy sauce, ginger, garlic, cornflour and sesame oil in large bowl. Cover; refrigerate 1 hour.
2 Meanwhile, using mortar and pestle, crush pepper medley and sichuan peppercorns finely.
3 Heat half of the peanut oil in wok; stir-fry beef, in batches, until browned.
4 Heat remaining oil in wok; stir-fry brown onion, beans and pepper mixture until onion is tender. Return beef to wok with wine, the water and oyster sauce; bring to a boil. Stir-fry until beans are cooked. Remove from heat; stir in green onion.
per serving 24g total fat (7.8g saturated fat); 1889kJ (452 cal); 7.6g carbohydrate; 47.8g protein; 2.1g fibre

orange-flavoured octopus and broccolini

preparation time 20 minutes (plus refrigeration time)
cooking time 15 minutes serves 4

1kg whole cleaned baby octopus, quartered
½ cup (150g) tamarind concentrate
¼ cup (60ml) japanese soy sauce
1 teaspoon finely grated orange rind
⅓ cup (80ml) orange juice
1 tablespoon honey
½ teaspoon ground cumin
2 cloves garlic, crushed
2cm piece fresh ginger (10g), grated
1 fresh long red chilli, chopped finely
⅓ cup (80ml) peanut oil
1 medium brown onion (150g), sliced thinly
350g broccolini, chopped coarsely
200g snow peas
¼ cup (40g) roasted unsalted cashews
1 fresh long red chilli, sliced thinly

1 Combine octopus, tamarind, sauce, rind, juice, honey, cumin, garlic, ginger, chopped chilli and half the oil in large bowl. Cover; refrigerate 1 hour.
2 Drain octopus over medium bowl; reserve ½ cup of the marinade.
3 Heat half of the remaining oil in wok; stir-fry octopus, in batches, until tender.
4 Heat remaining oil in cleaned wok; stir-fry onion until soft. Add broccolini and snow peas; stir-fry until tender.
5 Return octopus to wok with reserved marinade; bring to a boil, then remove from heat (do not overcook or octopus will toughen). Stir in nuts, sprinkle with thinly sliced chilli.
per serving 28.1g total fat (5.2g saturated fat); 2688kJ (643 cal); 21.7g carbohydrate; 72.9g protein; 6.9g fibre

crisp duck with mandarin, chilli and mint

preparation time 25 minutes
cooking time 30 minutes serves 4

2 small mandarins (200g)
½ cup (135g) firmly packed grated palm sugar
½ cup (125ml) water
⅓ cup (80ml) mandarin juice
1 tablespoon lime juice
2 teaspoons fish sauce
1 fresh long red chilli, chopped finely
1 star anise
2 tablespoons plain flour
2 teaspoons sea salt flakes
1 teaspoon dried chilli flakes
4 duck breast fillets (600g)
4 green onions, sliced thinly
½ cup loosely packed fresh mint leaves
1 fresh long red chilli, sliced thinly

1 Using vegetable peeler, cut four 5cm-strips of peel from mandarins. Remove remaining peel and pith; discard. Segment mandarins into small heatproof bowl.
2 Stir peel, sugar and the water in small saucepan over low heat until sugar dissolves; bring to a boil. Reduce heat, simmer, uncovered, without stirring, about 10 minutes or until syrup thickens slightly. Add juices, sauce, chopped chilli and star anise to pan; bring to a boil. Reduce heat, simmer, uncovered, about 5 minutes or until thickened slightly. Discard star anise; pour dressing into bowl with mandarin segments. Cool.
3 Meanwhile, combine flour, salt and dried chilli in medium bowl. Coat duck fillets, one at a time, in flour mixture; shake off excess. Cook duck, skin-side down, in heated oiled large frying pan, over medium heat, about 10 minutes or until crisp. Turn duck; cook about 5 minutes or until cooked as desired. Remove from heat; slice thickly.
4 Divide duck and mandarin segments among serving plates; top with onion, mint and sliced chilli, drizzle with dressing.
per serving 55.6g total fat (16.7g saturated fat); 3148kJ (753 cal); 42.3g carbohydrate; 21.2g protein; 1.7g fibre
TIP You need about six small mandarins in total for this recipe: two for the rind and segments, and four for the required amount of juice.

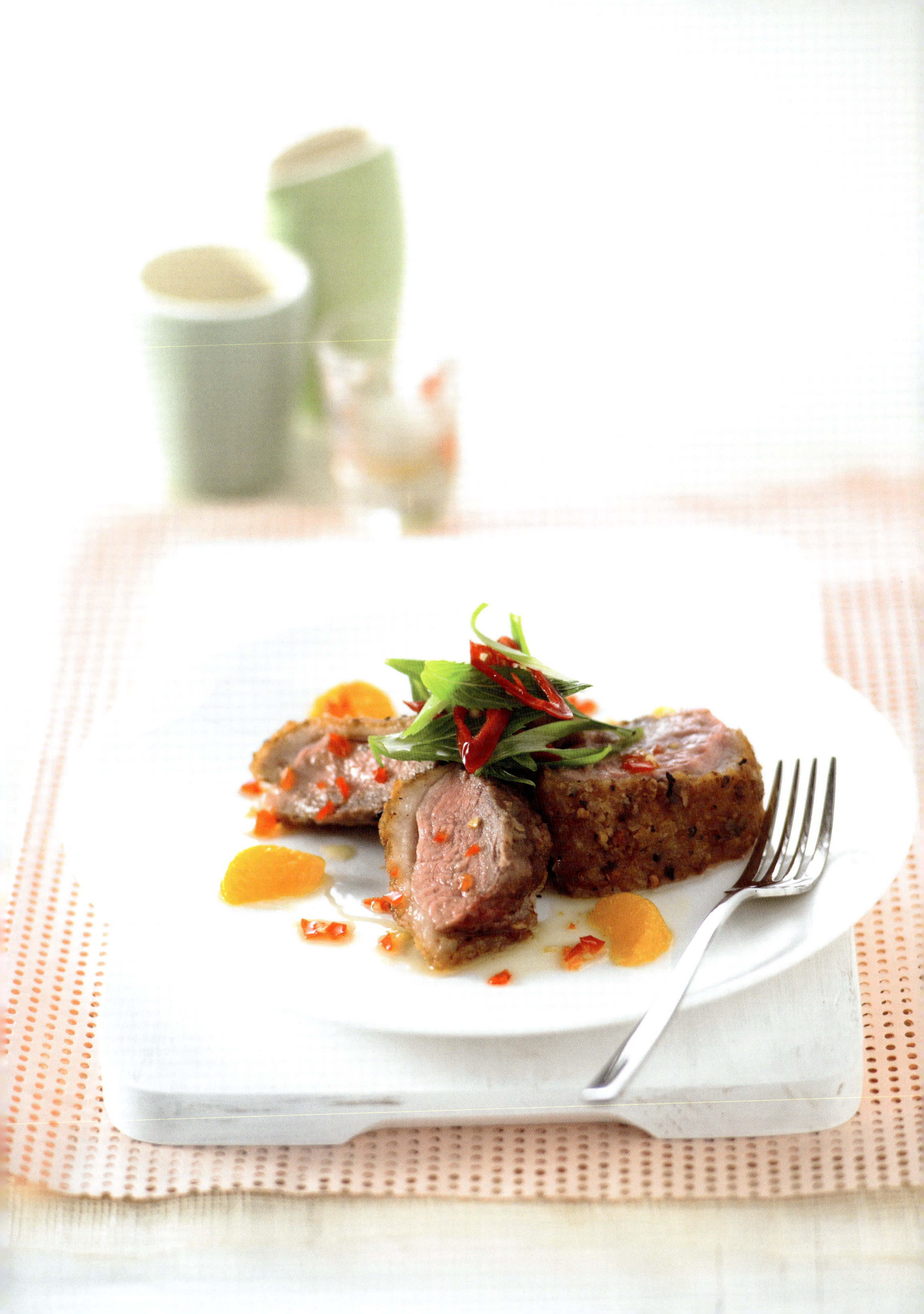

The Complete Book of Modern Asian

chilli beef and vegetables with noodles

preparation time 20 minutes (plus refrigeration time)
cooking time 15 minutes serves 4

500g piece beef fillet, thinly sliced
4 cloves garlic, crushed
¼ cup (60ml) fish sauce
1 tablespoon soy sauce
2 tablespoons oyster sauce
3 fresh small red thai chillies, chopped finely
2 teaspoons brown sugar
10cm stick fresh lemon grass (20g), chopped finely
¼ cup coarsely chopped fresh coriander
450g thick rice noodles
2 teaspoons peanut oil
6 spring onions (150g), trimmed, quartered
150g snow peas
340g baby buk choy, chopped coarsely
2 medium tomatoes (300g), cut into wedges

1 Combine beef, garlic, sauces, chilli, sugar, lemon grass and coriander in large bowl. Cover; refrigerate 3 hours or overnight.
2 Place noodles in medium heatproof bowl, cover with boiling water; stand until just tender, drain.
3 Heat oil in wok; stir-fry beef mixture, in batches, until browned all over.
4 Stir-fry onions in wok until browned lightly. Add snow peas, buk choy, tomatoes, noodles and beef mixture; cook, stirring, until heated through. Serve sprinkled with extra fresh coriander leaves, if desired.
per serving 10.9g total fat (3.6g saturated); 1626kJ (389 cal); 35.6g carbohydrate; 34.1g protein; 5.1g fibre

cantonese lobster

preparation time 20 minutes
cooking time 15 minutes serves 4

4 uncooked lobster tails in shell (680g)
2 tablespoons plain flour
peanut oil, for deep-frying
1 clove garlic, crushed
2cm piece fresh ginger (10g), grated
1 medium brown onion (150g), sliced thinly
2 fresh small red thai chillies, chopped finely
200g pork mince
1 cup (250ml) chicken stock
¼ cup (60ml) sweet sherry
2 tablespoons light soy sauce
1 tablespoon black bean sauce
1 tablespoon cornflour
1 tablespoon water
150g snow peas, trimmed
¼ cup firmly packed fresh coriander leaves
¼ cup firmly packed fresh mint leaves

1 Using kitchen scissors, cut soft shell from under lobster tails to expose meat. Cut lobster tails in half lengthways; cut each piece in half crossways. You will have 16 pieces.
2 Place plain flour in medium bowl; add lobster, toss to coat in flour.
3 Heat oil in wok; deep-fry lobster, in batches, until cooked through. Drain.
4 Reheat 1 tablespoon of the oil used for deep-frying lobster in wok. Stir-fry garlic, ginger, onion and chilli until onion softens. Add pork; stir-fry until just browned. Add stock, sherry, sauces and blended cornflour and the water; bring to a boil, stirring, until mixture boils and thickens.
5 Return lobster to wok; stir-fry 1 minute. Remove from heat; stir in peas and herbs.
per serving 13.2g total fat (3.2g saturated fat); 1547kJ (370 cal); 13.6g carbohydrate; 44.3g protein; 2.2g fibre

salt and pepper tofu with chilli lime dressing

preparation time 25 minutes (plus standing time)
cooking time 10 minutes serves 4

2 x 300g packets fresh firm tofu
1 small red capsicum (150g), sliced thinly
1 small yellow capsicum (150g), sliced thinly
100g snow peas, sliced thinly
1 small carrot (70g), sliced thinly
1 cup (80g) bean sprouts
½ cup loosely packed fresh coriander leaves
1 teaspoon coarsely ground black pepper
1 tablespoon sea salt
¼ teaspoon five-spice powder
⅓ cup (50g) plain flour
peanut oil, for deep-frying
CHILLI LIME DRESSING
2 tablespoons peanut oil
¼ cup (60ml) lime juice
2 tablespoons sweet chilli sauce

1 Dry tofu with absorbent paper. Cut each piece in half horizontally; cut each half into quarters (you will have 16 pieces). Place tofu pieces, in single layer, on absorbent paper. Cover with more absorbent paper; stand 15 minutes.
2 Meanwhile, combine capsicums, snow peas, carrot, sprouts and coriander in large bowl.
3 Whisk ingredients for chilli lime dressing together in small bowl.
4 Combine pepper, salt, five-spice and flour in medium bowl; coat tofu in mixture, shake away excess. Heat oil in wok; deep-fry tofu, in batches, until browned lightly. Drain on absorbent paper.
5 Serve tofu topped with salad; drizzle with dressing.
per serving 28.2g total fat (4.7g saturated fat); 1772kJ (424 cal); 17.8g carbohydrate; 22g protein; 6.1g fibre

prawn sambal

preparation time 20 minutes
cooking time 10 minutes serves 4

40 uncooked medium king prawns (1.8kg)
1 tablespoon peanut oil
1 large brown onion (200g), chopped finely
2 cloves garlic, crushed
2cm piece fresh ginger (10g), grated
10cm stick fresh lemon grass (20g), chopped finely
415g can whole peeled tomatoes
1 tablespoon sambal oelek
2 teaspoons lemon juice
1 teaspoon sugar
1 medium red capsicum (200g), chopped finely

1 Shell and devein prawns, leaving tails intact.
2 Heat oil in wok; stir-fry onion, garlic, ginger and lemon grass, stirring, until onion is soft.
3 Add undrained crushed tomatoes, sambal, juice, sugar and capsicum; bring to a boil. Reduce heat, simmer, uncovered, until sauce thickens.
4 Add prawns; stir-fry until prawns just change colour.
per serving 6.4g total fat (1.1g saturated fat); 1262kJ (302 cal); 10.5g carbohydrate; 48.6g protein; 2.9g fibre

Stir-fries & Pan-fries

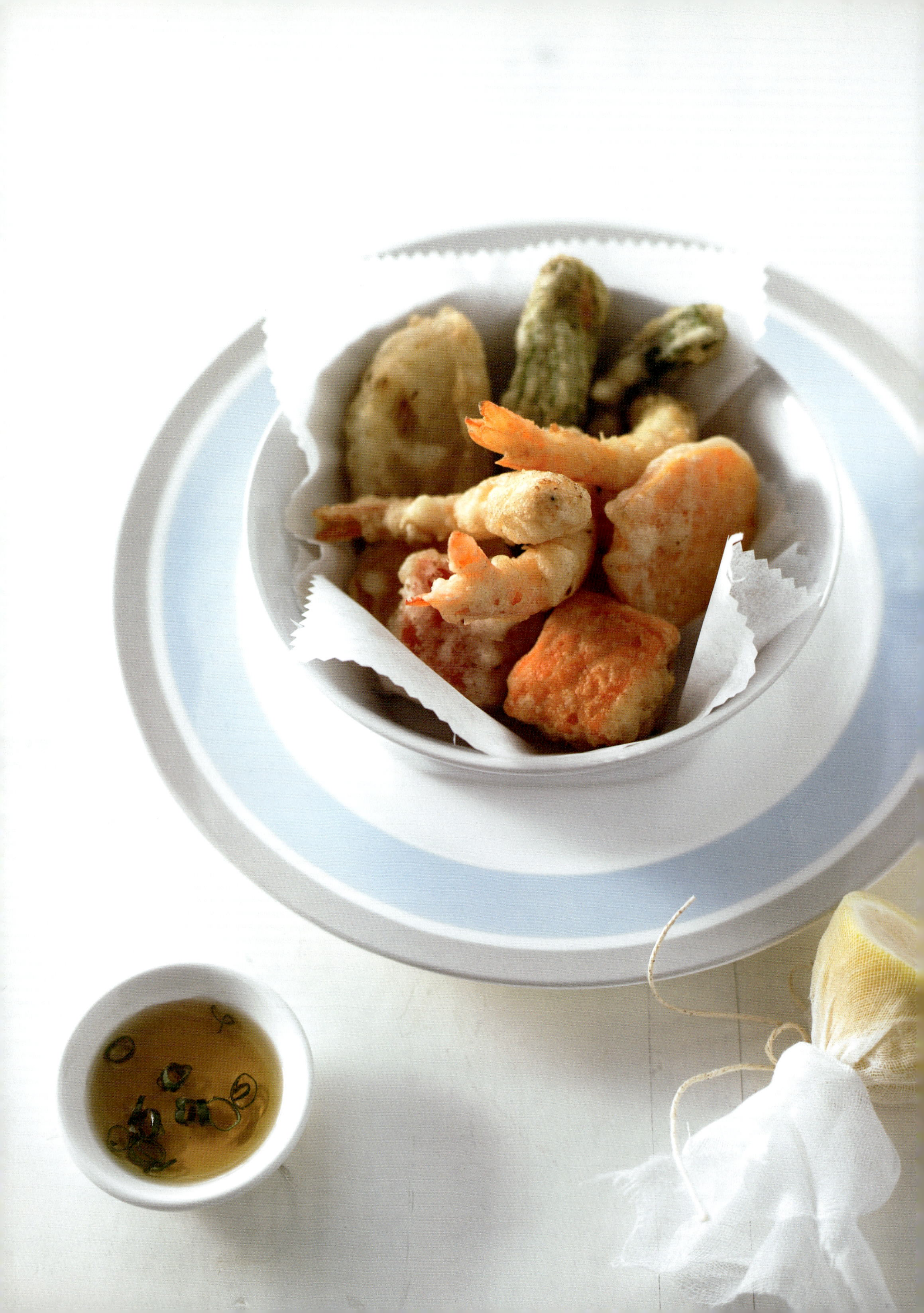

seafood and vegetable tempura

preparation time 35 minutes
cooking time 25 minutes serves 6

540g uncooked medium king prawns
1 medium brown onion (150g)
peanut oil, for deep-frying
450g ocean trout fillets, cut into 3cm pieces
1 large red capsicum (350g), cut into 3cm pieces
1 small kumara (250g), sliced thinly
8 baby zucchini with flowers attached (160g), stamens removed
1 cup (150g) plain flour
1 lemon, cut into wedges

TEMPURA BATTER
1 egg white
2 cups (500ml) cold soda water
1¼ cups (185g) plain flour
1¼ cups (185g) cornflour

LEMON DIPPING SAUCE
½ cup (125ml) rice vinegar
¼ cup (55g) caster sugar
1 teaspoon light soy sauce
¼ teaspoon finely grated lemon rind
1 green onion (green part only), sliced thinly

1 Shell and devein prawns, leaving tails intact. Make three small cuts on the underside of each prawn, halfway through flesh, to prevent curling when cooked.
2 Halve onion from root end. Push four toothpicks, at regular intervals, through each onion half to hold rings together; cut in between toothpicks.
3 Make tempura batter. Make lemon dipping sauce.
4 Heat oil in wok. Dust prawns, onion, fish, capsicum, kumara and zucchini in flour; shake off excess. Dip, piece by piece, in batter; deep-fry until crisp. Drain on absorbent paper.
5 Serve tempura with dipping sauce and lemon wedges, if you like.

TEMPURA BATTER
Whisk egg in large bowl until soft peaks form; add soda, whisk to combine. Add sifted flours, whisk to combine (batter should be lumpy).

LEMON DIPPING SAUCE
Heat vinegar, sugar and sauce in small saucepan, stirring, until sugar dissolves. Remove from heat, add rind; stand 10 minutes. Strain sauce into serving dish; discard rind. Sprinkle sauce with onion.

per serving 16.6g total fat (3.1g saturated fat); 1831kJ (438 cal); 40.2g carbohydrate; 16.6g protein; 3.5g fibre
TIP Only fry small batches of food at a time, making sure that the oil returns to correct temperature before adding next batch.

They may have originated in India, but curries are far too delicious to have been kept the province of a single region forever. Transported eastward by traders, they became "native" to Thailand, Burma, Vietnam, even Japan – and, as most of us know, continued their gastronomic journey to our shores, currying favour in many a family's best-loved recipe repertoire.

chicken green curry *page 223*

red chicken curry *page 215*

curries

bengali mushroom and lamb with mango chutney yogurt *page 223*

cauliflower, pea and paneer balti *page 215*

duck jungle curry

preparation time 40 minutes
cooking time 2 hours serves 4

2kg duck
¼ cup (60ml) peanut oil
1 medium brown onion (150g), chopped coarsely
1 medium carrot (120g), chopped coarsely
2 cloves garlic, halved
4cm piece fresh ginger (20g), sliced thickly
½ teaspoon black peppercorns
2 litres (8 cups) cold water
5 fresh kaffir lime leaves, torn
¼ cup (75g) red curry paste (page 249)
150g thai eggplants, halved
1 medium carrot (120g), sliced thinly
100g snake beans, cut into 4cm lengths
230g can bamboo shoots, rinsed, drained
2 x 5cm stems (10g) pickled green peppercorns
½ cup firmly packed fresh thai basil leaves
4 fresh small red thai chillies, chopped coarsely
2 tablespoons fish sauce

1 Discard neck then wash duck inside and out; pat dry with absorbent paper. Using sharp knife, separate drumstick and thigh sections from body; separate thighs from drumsticks. Remove and discard wings. Separate breast and backbone; cut breast from bone. You will have six pieces. Cut duck carcass into four pieces; discard any fat from carcass.
2 Heat 1 tablespoon of the oil in large saucepan; cook carcass pieces, stirring occasionally, about 5 minutes or until browned. Add onion, chopped carrot, garlic and ginger; cook, stirring, about 2 minutes or until onion softens. Add black peppercorns, the water and four of the lime leaves; simmer, uncovered, 1 hour 15 minutes, skimming fat from surface of mixture regularly.
3 Strain mixture through muslin-lined sieve into large heatproof jug. Reserve 3 cups of liquid; discard solids and remaining liquid.
4 Preheat oven to 200°C/180°C fan-forced.
5 Heat remaining oil in same cleaned pan; cook thighs, drumsticks and breasts, in batches, until browned. Remove skin from breasts and legs; slice skin thinly. Place sliced duck skin on oven tray; roast, uncovered, about 10 minutes or until crisp.
6 Discard excess oil from pan; reheat pan, cook curry paste, stirring, about 1 minute or until fragrant. Add eggplant, sliced carrot, beans, bamboo shoots, green peppercorns, half of the basil, remaining lime leaf and reserved liquid; simmer, uncovered, 5 minutes. Add duck pieces; simmer, uncovered, about 10 minutes or until vegetables are tender. Stir in chilli and sauce.
7 Place curry in serving bowls; sprinkle with remaining basil and crisped duck skin.

per serving 121.0g total fat (34.4g saturated fat); 5334kJ (1276 cal); 8.1g carbohydrate; 41.0g protein; 5.4g fibre

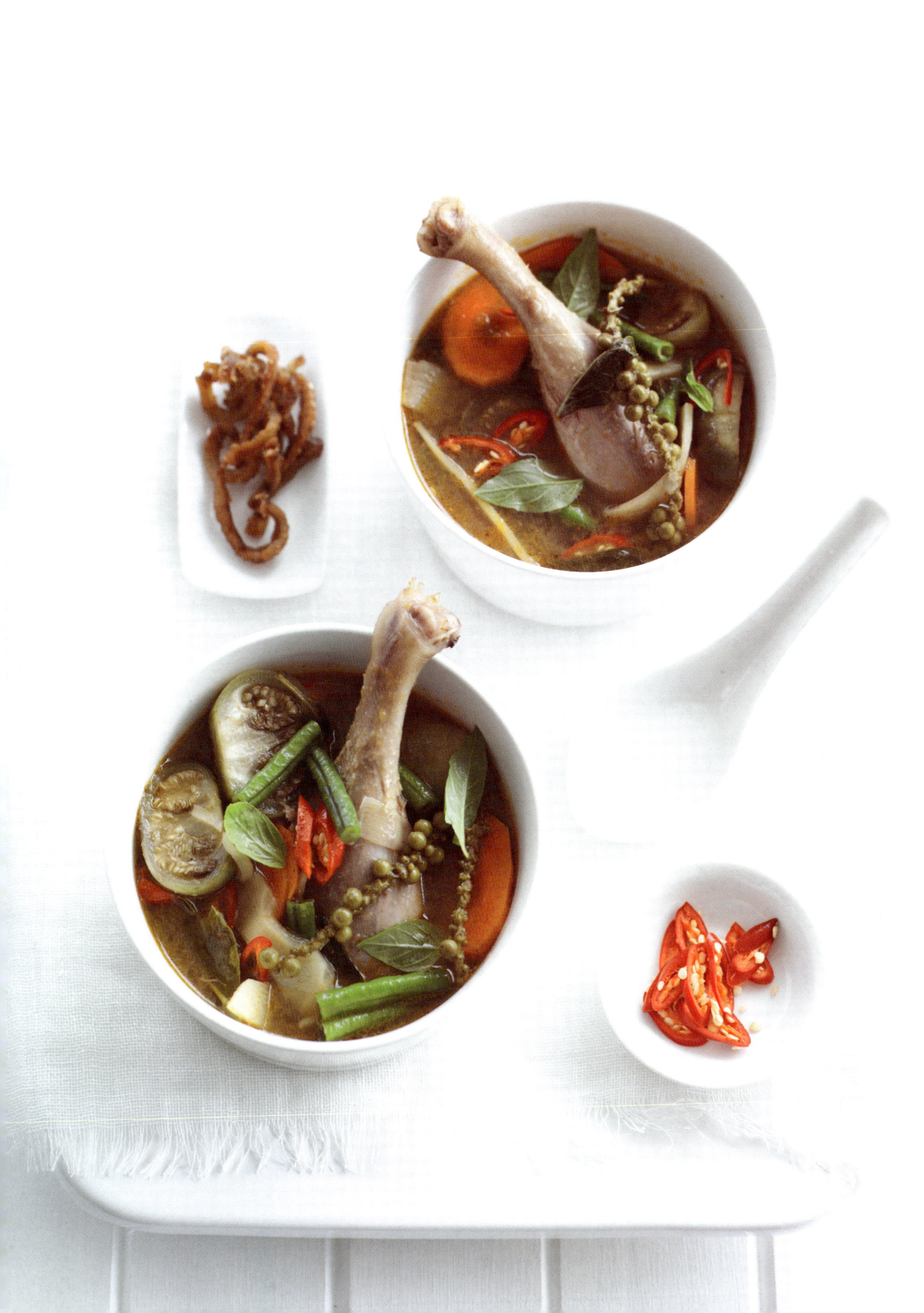

The Complete Book of Modern Asian

fish curry with coriander and snake beans

preparation time 15 minutes
cooking time 15 minutes serves 4

80g ghee
½ small brown onion (80g), chopped finely
3 cloves garlic, crushed
4cm piece fresh ginger (20g), grated
1 fresh long red chilli, sliced thinly
½ teaspoon ground turmeric
1½ teaspoons sweet paprika
2 teaspoons ground coriander
1 cup (250ml) coconut milk
½ cup (125ml) water
2 teaspoons tamarind puree
1 teaspoon salt
250g snake beans, cut into 5 cm lengths
700g blue-eye fillets, chopped coarsely
½ cup loosely packed fresh coriander leaves

1 Heat ghee in large saucepan; cook onion, garlic and ginger, stirring, until soft. Add chilli and spices; cook, stirring, until fragrant.
2 Add coconut milk, water, tamarind and salt; bring to a boil. Add beans and fish, simmer, uncovered, about 5 minutes or until fish is just cooked through.
3 Top curry with coriander and serve with steamed basmati rice and pappadums, if desired.
per serving 37g total fat (25.7g saturated fat); 2165kJ (518 cal); 5.5g carbohydrate; 39.6g protein; 3.7g fibre

dry beef curry with onions and peanuts

preparation time 30 minutes
cooking time 1 hour 15 minutes serves 6

1kg beef chuck steak, chopped coarsely
3 cups (750ml) coconut milk
1 cup (140g) finely ground roasted unsalted peanuts
1 tablespoon fish sauce
2 teaspoons tamarind concentrate
6 baby onions (150g), quartered
¼ teaspoon ground cloves
¼ teaspoon ground cardamom
¼ teaspoon ground cinnamon
1½ tablespoons lime juice
1 teaspoon grated palm sugar
CURRY PASTE
2 teaspoons dried chilli flakes
1 medium red onion (170g), chopped finely
3 cloves garlic, crushed
10cm stick fresh lemon grass (20g), chopped finely
1 teaspoon galangal powder
2 teaspoons finely chopped fresh coriander root
1 teaspoon grated lime rind
½ teaspoon shrimp paste
1 dried kaffir lime leaf
1 teaspoon paprika
½ teaspoon ground turmeric
½ teaspoon cumin seeds
2 teaspoons peanut oil

1 Blend or process ingredients for curry paste until well combined.
2 Combine beef, coconut milk and peanuts in large saucepan; bring to a boil. Reduce heat, simmer, covered, 1 hour, stirring occasionally.
3 Stir in curry paste, sauce, tamarind, onion, spices, juice and sugar; simmer, uncovered, 10 minutes.
per serving 46g total fat (27.8g saturated fat); 2642kJ (632 cal); 10.0g carbohydrate; 43.0g protein; 5.0g fibre

masala dosa with mint rasam

preparation time 20 minutes
cooking time 35 minutes serves 4

2 large potatoes (600g), diced into 1.5cm pieces
1 tablespoon dried chickpeas
2 teaspoons vegetable oil
2 medium brown onions (300g), sliced thinly
1 teaspoon black mustard seeds
1 teaspoon ground turmeric
½ teaspoon dried chilli flakes
10 dried curry leaves
¾ cup (180ml) buttermilk
2 tablespoons finely chopped fresh coriander
4 chapatis
¼ cup (80g) mango chutney

MINT RASAM
2 teaspoons red lentils
2 teaspoons coriander seeds
½ teaspoon cumin seeds
½ teaspoon dried chilli flakes
2 medium tomatoes (300g), chopped coarsely
1 long green chilli, chopped finely
1 cup coarsely chopped fresh mint
¼ cup (50g) red lentils, extra
1 tablespoon tamarind paste
1¼ cups (310ml) water

1 Boil, steam or microwave potato until tender; drain.
2 Meanwhile, using mortar and pestle, lightly crush chickpeas.
3 Heat oil in large frying pan; cook onion, stirring, until soft. Add seeds, turmeric, chilli, curry leaves and crushed chickpeas; cook, stirring occasionally, over medium heat 10 minutes. Add potato and buttermilk; cook, covered, over low heat 5 minutes. Stir coriander into the potato masala.
4 Meanwhile, make mint rasam.
5 Warm chapatis, one at a time, in large heated frying pan; place a quarter of the potato masala on each chapati then roll to make filled masala dosa. Serve with mint rasam and chutney.

MINT RASAM
Dry-fry lentils, seeds and chilli flakes in small frying pan, stirring, until fragrant. Using mortar and pestle, crush mixture finely. Place tomato, green chilli, mint and lentil mixture in medium saucepan; cook, stirring, 5 minutes. Add extra lentils, tamarind and the water; bring to a boil. Boil, uncovered, stirring occasionally, about 10 minutes or until lentils are soft and liquid has almost evaporated.

per serving 4.6g total fat (1.1g saturated fat); 1308kJ (313 cal); 53.4g carbohydrate; 14.0g protein; 10.2g fibre
TIP Chapatis are available from Indian food shops and on the bread shelf in most supermarkets. You can also make them at home (see recipe on page 379).

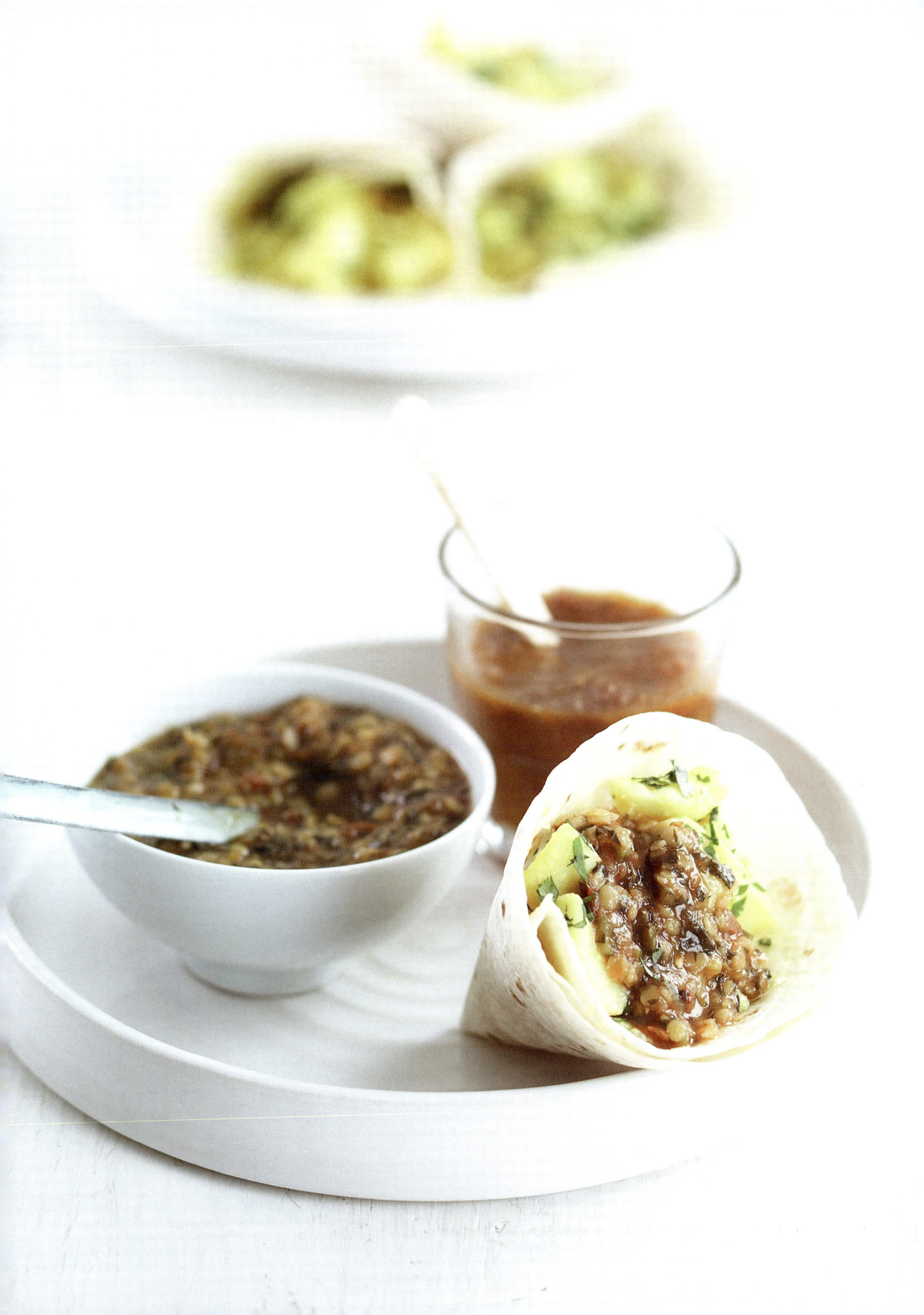

The Complete Book of Modern Asian

cauliflower, pea and paneer balti

preparation time 20 minutes
cooking time 25 minutes   serves 4

1 tablespoon sesame seeds
2 tablespoons vegetable oil
6 dried curry leaves
¼ teaspoon black mustard seeds
1 teaspoon ground coriander
1 teaspoon hot chilli powder
1 teaspoon ground cumin
2 cloves garlic, crushed
400g can diced tomatoes
1kg cauliflower, trimmed, cut into florets
½ cup (125ml) water
1 cup (120g) frozen peas
400g paneer cheese, cut into 2cm cubes
¼ cup coarsely chopped fresh coriander

1 Heat wok; roast sesame seeds until browned lightly. Remove from wok.
2 Heat oil in wok; stir-fry leaves and mustard seeds until seeds pop.
3 Add ground coriander, chilli, cumin and garlic to wok; stir-fry until fragrant. Add undrained tomatoes; simmer, stirring, about 2 minutes or until mixture thickens slightly.
4 Add cauliflower and the water; stir-fry until cauliflower is almost tender. Add peas, cheese and chopped coriander; stir-fry until hot. Remove from heat; sprinkle with sesame seeds.

per serving 34.9g total fat (16.7g saturated fat); 2002kJ (479 cal); 11.4g carbohydrate; 26.6g protein; 8.1g fibre

red chicken curry

preparation time 30 minutes
cooking time 25 minutes   serves 4

2 tablespoons peanut oil
750g chicken thigh fillets, chopped coarsely
⅓ cup (100g) red curry paste (see page 249)
4 green onions, sliced thinly
2 tablespoons fish sauce
1 cup (250ml) coconut milk
1 fresh small red thai chilli, sliced thinly

1 Heat oil in wok; cook chicken, in batches, until browned lightly.
2 Cook curry paste and onion in wok, stirring, about 2 minutes or until fragrant.
3 Return chicken to wok with sauce and coconut milk; bring to a boil. Reduce heat, simmer, uncovered, about 10 minutes or until chicken is cooked through. Serve topped with sliced chilli.

per serving 33.5g total fat (15.9g saturated fat); 2048kJ (490 cal); 5g carbohydrate; 41.6g protein; 2.2g fibre

seafood and thai eggplant yellow curry

preparation time 20 minutes (plus refrigeration time)
cooking time 20 minutes (plus cooling time) serves 4

500g squid hoods
400g firm white fish fillets
8 uncooked medium prawns (360g)
8 small black mussels (200g)
1 teaspoon shrimp paste
1 tablespoon peanut oil
2 tablespoons yellow curry paste (see page 248)
2 cloves garlic, crushed
2cm piece fresh ginger (10g), grated finely
1 medium brown onion (150g), sliced thickly
10cm stick fresh lemon grass (20g), chopped finely
1 fresh long red thai chilli, chopped coarsely
12 fresh thai eggplants (350g), quartered
1 cup (250ml) fish stock
400ml can coconut milk
3 fresh kaffir lime leaves, torn
1 tablespoon grated palm sugar
12 scallops (300g)
½ cup firmly packed fresh coriander leaves
2 tablespoons lime juice
2 fresh long red thai chillies, sliced thinly

1 Cut squid into 1.5cm slices. Cut fish into 3cm pieces. Shell and devein prawns, leaving tails intact. Scrub mussels; remove beards.
2 Wrap shrimp paste in foil, place in heated wok; roast, tossing, until fragrant. Discard foil, return shrimp paste to heated wok with oil and curry paste; stir until combined.
3 Add garlic, ginger, onion, lemon grass and chopped chilli to wok; cook, stirring, until onion softens. Add eggplant; cook, stirring, 2 minutes. Add stock, coconut milk, lime leaves and sugar; bring to a boil. Reduce heat, simmer, stirring occasionally, 10 minutes.
4 Add fish; cook, uncovered, 3 minutes. Add remaining seafood; cook, covered, about 5 minutes or until prawns change colour and mussels open (discard any that do not). Stir in coriander and juice.
5 Place curry in serving bowls; sprinkle with sliced chilli and extra coriander leaves, if desired.
per serving 34.3g total fat (20.9g saturated fat); 2830kJ (677 cal); 14.2g carbohydrate; 74.9g protein; 6.0g fibre

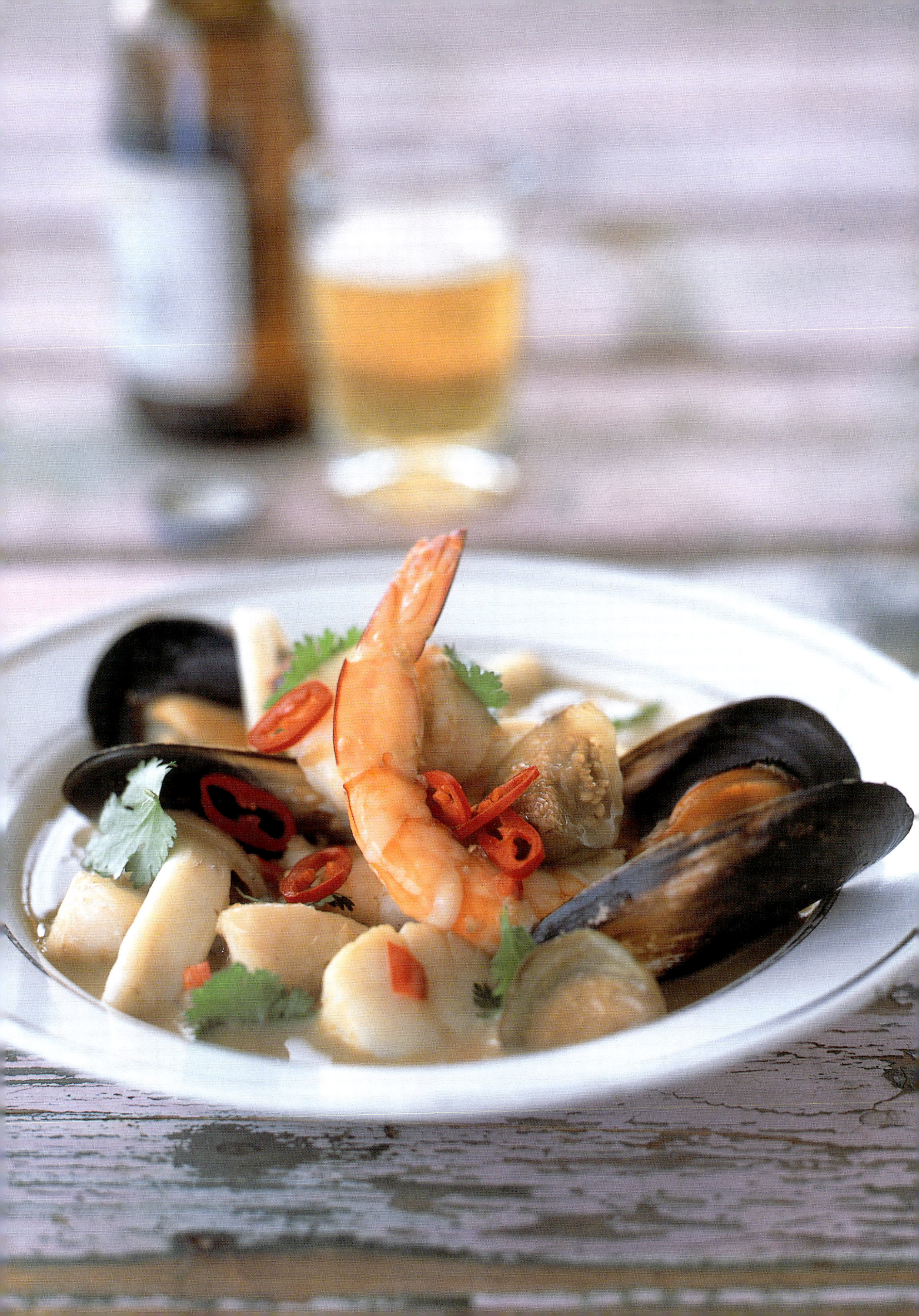

The Complete Book of Modern Asian

lamb korma

preparation time 25 minutes (plus refrigeration time)
cooking time 40 minutes serves 4

⅓ cup (55g) blanched almonds
3 tablespoons ghee
800g lamb strips
1 large brown onion (200g), sliced thinly
2 cloves garlic, crushed
4cm piece fresh ginger (20g), grated
2 teaspoons poppy seeds
½ cup (150g) prepared korma paste
½ cup (125ml) chicken stock
300ml cream
⅓ cup (95g) yogurt

1 Blend or process nuts until finely ground.
2 Heat 2 tablespoons of the ghee in large saucepan; cook lamb, in batches, until browned.
3 Heat remaining ghee in same pan; cook onion, garlic and ginger, stirring, until onion softens. Add ground nuts, seeds and paste; cook, stirring, until fragrant.
4 Return lamb to pan with stock and cream; simmer, uncovered, about 15 minutes or until sauce thickens slightly. Serve korma accompanied by yogurt.
per serving 84.1g total fat (40.3g saturated fat); 4172kJ (998 cal); 9.2g carbohydrate; 50.6g protein; 6.4g fibre

sri lankan fried pork curry

preparation time 20 minutes
cooking time 1 hour 20 minutes serves 4

2 tablespoons vegetable oil
20 fresh curry leaves
½ teaspoon fenugreek seeds
1 large brown onion (200g), chopped finely
4 cloves garlic, crushed
3cm piece fresh ginger (15g), grated
1 tablespoon curry powder
2 teaspoons cayenne pepper
1kg pork belly, chopped coarsely
1 tablespoon white wine vinegar
2 tablespoons tamarind concentrate
1 cinnamon stick
4 cardamom pods, bruised
1½ cups (375ml) water
400ml can coconut milk

1 Heat half of the oil in large saucepan; cook leaves and seeds until seeds pop and mixture is fragrant. Add onion, garlic and ginger; cook, stirring, until onion softens.
2 Add curry powder and cayenne to pan, then pork; stir well to combine. Add vinegar, tamarind, cinnamon, cardamom and the water; simmer, covered, 1 hour.
3 Heat remaining oil in large frying pan. Transfer pork to pan; cook, stirring, until pork is browned and crisp.
4 Meanwhile, add coconut milk to curry sauce; simmer, stirring, about 5 minutes or until curry thickens slightly. Return pork to curry; stir to combine.
per serving 78.2g total fat (35.7g saturated fat); 3766kJ (901 cal); 8.0g carbohydrate; 42.1g protein; 3.6g fibre

panang pork curry with pickled snake beans

preparation time 30 minutes
(plus cooling and refrigeration times)
cooking time 1 hour 30 minutes serves 6

2¾ cups (680ml) coconut milk
3⅓ cups (830ml) water
1.5kg pork shoulder, trimmed, cut into 2cm cubes
1⅔ cups (410ml) coconut cream
⅓ cup (100g) panang curry paste (see page 249)
¼ cup (65g) grated palm sugar
¼ cup (60ml) fish sauce
6 fresh kaffir lime leaves, sliced thinly
190g can sliced bamboo shoots, drained
⅓ cup coarsely chopped thai basil
¼ cup coarsely chopped fresh coriander
2 fresh long red chillies, sliced thinly

PICKLED SNAKE BEANS
350g snake beans, trimmed
1 cup (250ml) water
1 cup (250ml) white vinegar
1 tablespoon malt vinegar
1 cup (220g) sugar
2 tablespoons salt

1 Make pickled snake beans.
2 Combine half of the coconut milk and the water in medium saucepan; bring to a boil. Add pork; bring to a boil. Reduce heat, simmer, uncovered, about 1 hour or until tender. Remove pan from heat; cool pork in liquid 30 minutes.
3 Heat coconut cream in large saucepan over heat about 10 minutes or until fat separates from cream. Add curry paste; cook, stirring, 10 minutes. Stir palm sugar and fish sauce into mixture; after sugar dissolves, add 1 cup pork cooking liquid (discard any that remains). Stir in remaining coconut milk, lime leaves, bamboo shoots and drained pork; simmer, uncovered, until heated through.
4 Just before serving, stir basil and coriander through curry off the heat, sprinkle with chilli; serve with pickled snake beans and, if desired, steamed jasmine rice.

PICKLED SNAKE BEANS
Cut beans into 5cm lengths; place in medium heatproof bowl. Combine the water, vinegars, sugar and salt in small saucepan; stir over heat until sugar dissolves. Bring to a boil, then immediately remove from heat; cool pickling liquid 10 minutes, then pour over beans. Cover; refrigerate 3 hours or overnight before serving.

per serving 50.8g total fat (36.9g saturated fat); 3954kJ (946 cal); 56.7g carbohydrate; 62.9g protein; 6.1g fibre

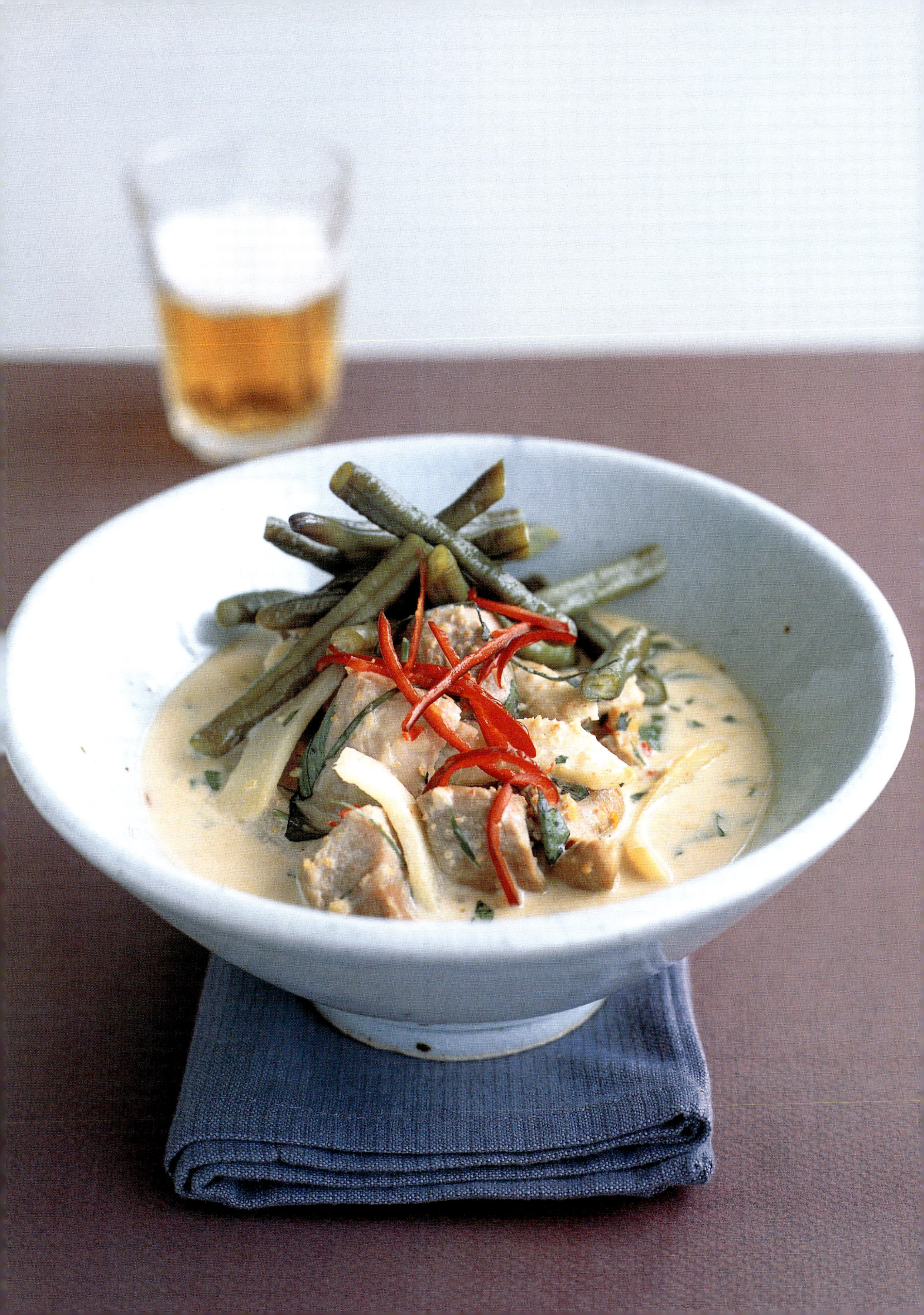

The Complete Book of Modern Asian

chicken green curry

preparation time 40 minutes
cooking time 25 minutes serves 4

¼ cup (70g) green curry paste (see page 249)
3¼ cups (800ml) coconut milk
2 fresh kaffir lime leaves, torn
1 tablespoon peanut oil
1kg chicken thigh fillets, quartered
2 tablespoons fish sauce
2 tablespoons lime juice
1 tablespoon grated palm sugar
100g green beans, trimmed, chopped coarsely
2 small zucchini (300g), chopped coarsely
⅓ cup loosely packed fresh thai basil leaves
¼ cup coarsely chopped fresh coriander
1 tablespoon fresh coriander leaves
1 long green chilli, sliced thinly
2 green onions, sliced thinly

1 Cook curry paste in large saucepan, stirring, until fragrant. Add coconut milk and lime leaves; bring to a boil. Reduce heat, simmer, stirring, 5 minutes.
2 Meanwhile, heat oil in large frying pan; cook chicken, in batches, until just browned. Drain on absorbent paper.
3 Place chicken in pan with curry paste mixture; stir in fish sauce, juice and sugar. Simmer, covered, about 5 minutes or until chicken is cooked through. Add beans, zucchini, basil and chopped coriander; cook, stirring, until vegetables are just tender.
4 Place curry in serving bowl; sprinkle with coriander leaves, chilli and onion. Serve with steamed jasmine rice and extra thinly sliced green chilli, if desired.
per serving 59.7g total fat (40.6g saturated fat); 3490kJ (835 cal); 14g carbohydrate; 58.7g protein; 6.3g fibre

bengali mushroom and lamb with mango chutney yogurt

preparation time 20 minutes
cooking time 25 minutes serves 4

2 tablespoons vegetable oil
2 medium potatoes (400g), cut into 2cm pieces
600g lamb backstraps, sliced thinly
1 medium red capsicum (200g), chopped coarsely
1 fresh long red chilli, sliced thinly
1 large brown onion (200g), chopped coarsely
150g mushrooms, sliced thinly
2 teaspoons curry powder
½ cup (160g) mango chutney
2 tablespoons water
½ cup firmly packed fresh coriander leaves
⅓ cup (50g) roasted unsalted cashews
8 roti wraps (320g)
2 tablespoons mango chutney, extra
⅓ cup (95g) yogurt

1 Heat 1 tablespoon of the oil in wok; stir-fry potato, in batches, until tender.
2 Heat 2 teaspoons of remaining oil in wok; stir-fry lamb, in batches, until browned.
3 Heat remaining oil in wok; stir-fry capsicum, chilli, onion and mushrooms until onion softens. Add curry powder; stir-fry until fragrant.
4 Return potato and lamb to wok with chutney and the water; stir-fry until hot. Remove from heat; sprinkle coriander and nuts over stir-fry.
5 Serve with roti, extra chutney and yogurt.
per serving 30.8g total fat (9g saturated fat); 3415kJ (817 cal); 81.8g carbohydrate; 48.6g protein; 9.6g fibre

curry kapitan

preparation time 30 minutes
cooking time 1 hour serves 6

2 tablespoons vegetable oil
2 medium brown onions (300g), sliced thinly
¼ cup (60ml) water
1.5kg chicken pieces
2¼ cups (560ml) coconut milk
1 cup (250ml) coconut cream

SPICE PASTE
10 fresh small red thai chillies
4 cloves garlic
3 teaspoons grated fresh turmeric
2 teaspoons grated fresh galangal
2 teaspoons finely chopped fresh lemon grass
10 candlenuts
1 tablespoon ground cumin

1 Blend or process ingredients for spice paste until smooth.
2 Heat oil in large saucepan; cook onion, stirring, until soft. Add spice paste and the water; cook, stirring, until fragrant.
3 Add chicken and coconut milk; bring to a boil. Reduce heat, simmer, covered, 20 minutes. Remove lid; simmer, uncovered, further 30 minutes, stirring occasionally, or until chicken is tender. Stir in coconut cream. Serve with roti (see page 383), if desired.
per serving 58.8g total fat (32.3g saturated fat); 2888kJ (691 cal); 8.3g carbohydrate; 32.1g protein; 3.6g fibre

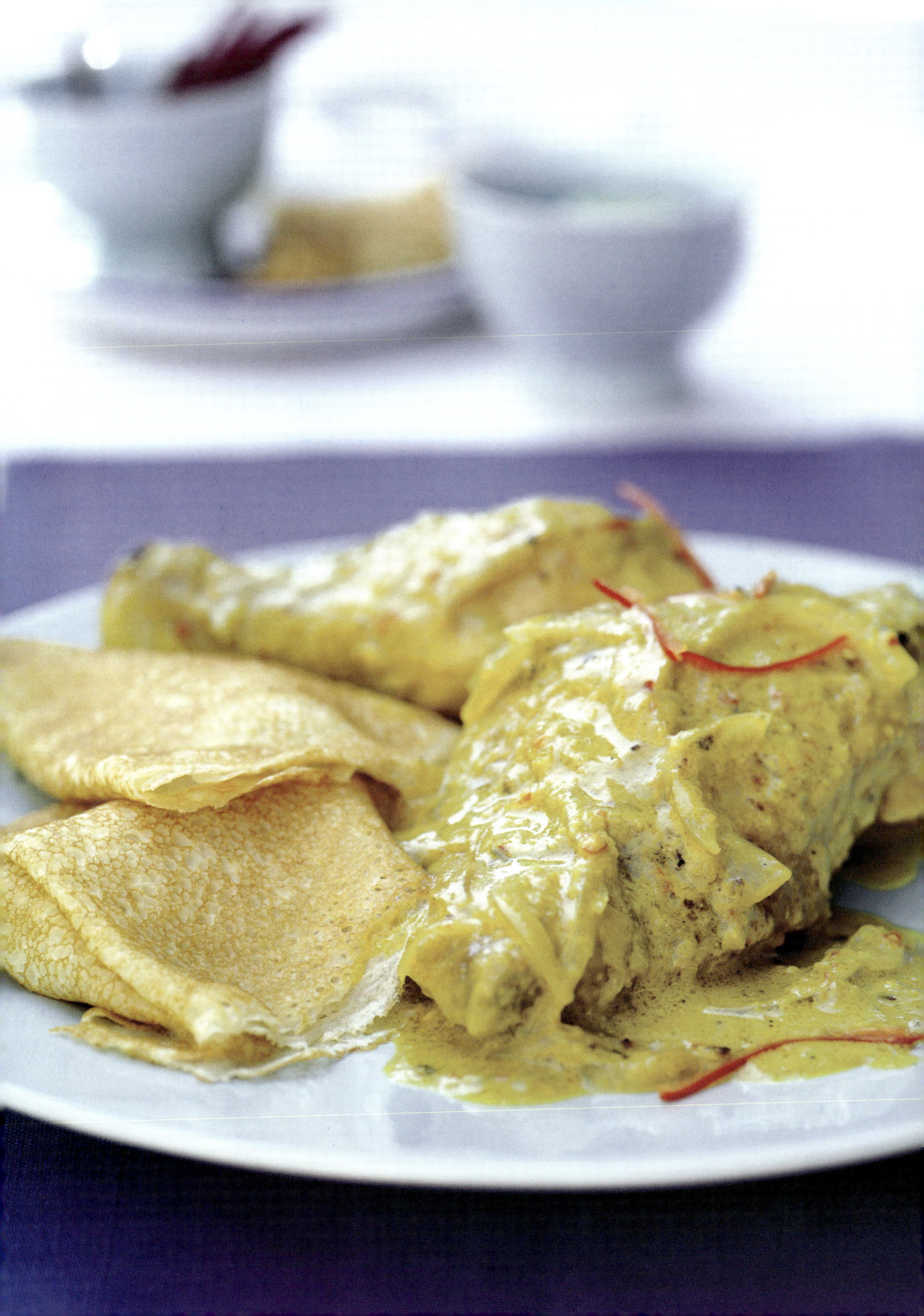

The Complete Book of Modern Asian

aromatic vietnamese beef curry

preparation time 15 minutes
cooking time 20 minutes serves 4

2 tablespoons peanut oil
800g beef strips
1 medium brown onion (150g), chopped finely
3 cloves garlic, crushed
1 fresh long red chilli, chopped finely
10cm stick fresh lemon grass (20g), chopped finely
1 star anise
1 cinnamon stick
4 cardamom pods, bruised
350g snake beans, cut in 4cm lengths
2 tablespoons ground bean sauce
2 tablespoons fish sauce
½ cup coarsely chopped fresh coriander
½ cup (40g) toasted almond flakes

1 Heat half of the oil in wok; stir-fry beef, in batches, until browned. Cover to keep warm.
2 Heat remaining oil in wok; stir-fry onion until soft. Add garlic, chilli, lemon grass, star anise, cinnamon, cardamom and beans; stir-fry until beans are tender. Discard star anise, cinnamon and cardamom.
3 Return beef to wok with sauces; stir-fry until heated through. Remove from heat, stir in coriander and nuts.
per serving 27.2g total fat (7.1g saturated fat); 2011kJ (481 cal); 7.4g carbohydrate; 49.6g protein; 4.9g fibre

pork curry with eggplant

preparation time 30 minutes
cooking time 20 minutes serves 6

750g pork fillets
¼ cup (60ml) coconut cream
2½ cups (625ml) coconut milk
1 medium eggplant (300g), chopped coarsely
1 tablespoon fish sauce
2cm piece fresh ginger (10g), grated finely
2 teaspoons grated palm sugar
3 small green thai chillies, sliced
3 fresh small red thai chillies, sliced
¼ cup firmly packed fresh basil leaves

CURRY PASTE
2 teaspoons dried chilli flakes
1 medium red onion (170g), chopped finely
3 cloves garlic, crushed
10cm stick fresh lemon grass (20g), chopped finely
1 teaspoon galangal powder
2 teaspoons chopped fresh coriander root
1 teaspoon grated lime rind
½ teaspoon shrimp paste
1 dried kaffir lime leaf
1 teaspoon paprika
½ teaspoon ground turmeric
½ teaspoon cumin seeds
2 teaspoons peanut oil

1 Blend or process ingredients for curry paste until well blended.
2 Cut pork into 2cm slices, then cut slices in half.
3 Place coconut cream and curry paste in large saucepan; cook, stirring, 1 minute or until fragrant. Add pork; cook 5 minutes.
4 Stir in coconut milk, eggplant, sauce, ginger, sugar and chillies; bring to a boil. Reduce heat, simmer, covered, until pork is tender. Stir in basil; serve with fresh lime wedges, if desired.
per serving 35.4g total fat (24.4g saturated fat); 1998kJ (478 cal); 8.7g carbohydrate; 30.2g protein; 3.9g fibre

asian star

beef massaman curry

preparation time 35 minutes
cooking time 2 hours 20 minutes serves 4

1kg beef skirt steak, cut into 3cm pieces
1½ cups (375ml) beef stock
5 cardamom pods, bruised
¼ teaspoon ground clove
2 star anise
1 tablespoon grated palm sugar
2 tablespoons fish sauce
1 tablespoon tamarind concentrate
2 x 400ml cans coconut milk
2 tablespoons massaman curry paste (see page 248)
2 teaspoons tamarind concentrate, extra
½ cup (125ml) beef stock, extra
8 baby brown onions (200g), halved
1 medium kumara (400g), chopped coarsely
¼ cup (35g) coarsely chopped roasted unsalted peanuts
2 green onions, sliced thinly

1 Place beef, stock, cardamom, clove, star anise, sugar, sauce, tamarind and half the coconut milk in large saucepan; bring to a boil. Reduce heat, simmer, uncovered, about 1 hour 30 minutes or until beef is almost tender.
2 Strain beef over large bowl; reserve spicy beef sauce, discard cardamom and star anise.
3 Place curry paste in same cleaned pan; stir over heat until fragrant. Add remaining coconut milk, extra tamarind and extra stock; bring to a boil, stirring, about 1 minute or until mixture is smooth. Add beef, brown onion, kumara and 1 cup of reserved spicy beef sauce; cook, uncovered, over medium heat, about 30 minutes or until vegetables and beef are tender.
4 Place curry in serving bowl; sprinkle with peanuts and green onion. Serve with steamed rice, if desired.
per serving 55.5g total fat (39.9g saturated fat); 3766kJ (901 cal); 29.6g carbohydrate; 67.7g protein; 7.9g fibre

Use the flat side of a heavy knife to bruise the cardamom pods and expose their seeds.

Strain beef over a large bowl and then discard cardamom pods and star anise.

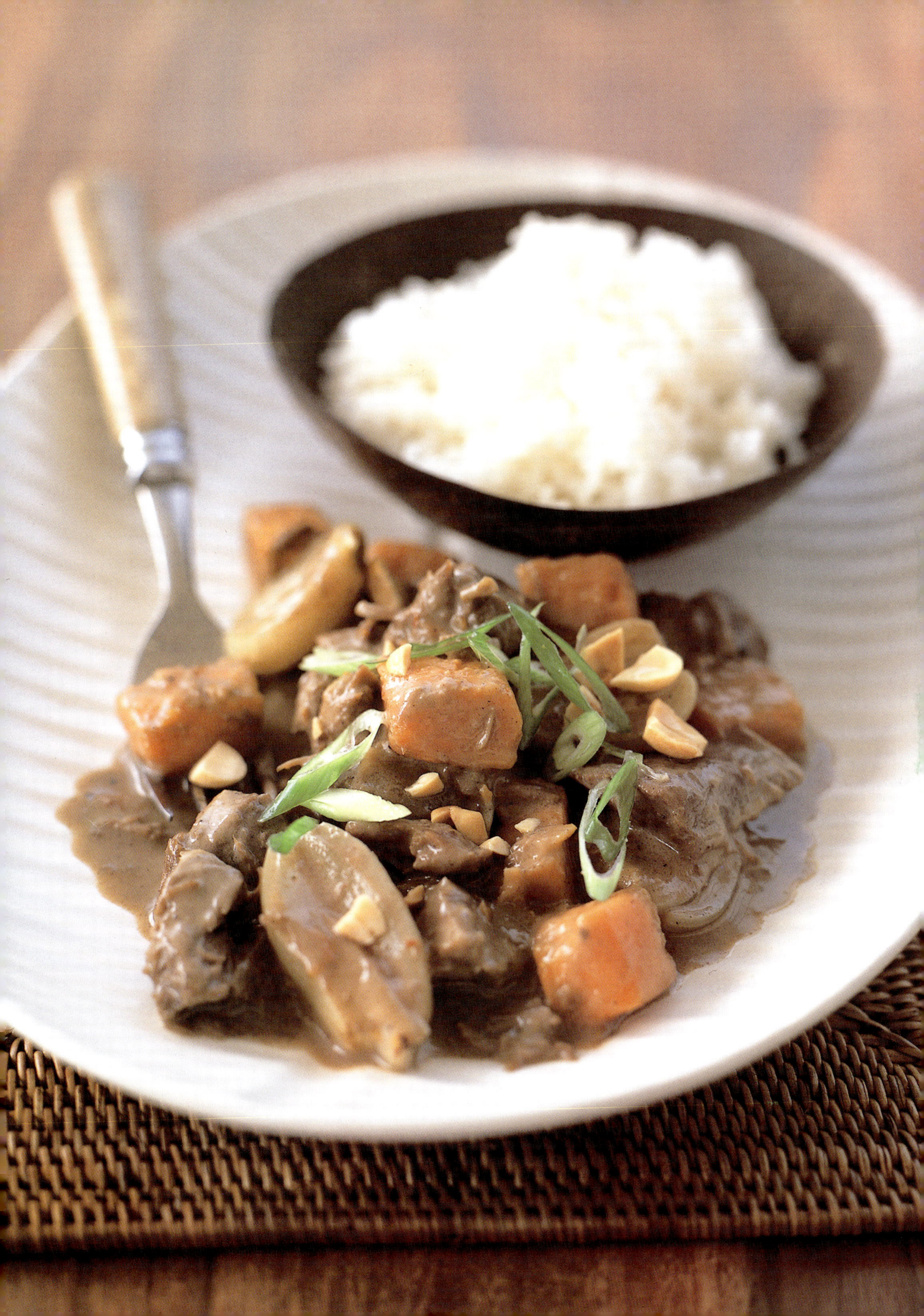

The Complete Book of Modern Asian

rogan josh

preparation time 20 minutes
cooking time 2 hours serves 4

1kg boned leg of lamb, trimmed, diced into 3cm pieces
2 teaspoons ground cardamom
2 teaspoons ground cumin
2 teaspoons ground coriander
20g butter
2 tablespoons vegetable oil
2 medium brown onions (300g), sliced thinly
4cm piece fresh ginger (20g), grated
4 cloves garlic, crushed
2 teaspoons sweet paprika
½ teaspoon cayenne pepper
½ cup (125ml) beef stock
425g can crushed tomatoes
2 bay leaves
2 cinnamon sticks
200g yogurt
¾ cup (110g) toasted slivered almonds
1 fresh long red chilli, sliced thinly

1 Combine lamb, cardamom, cumin and coriander in medium bowl.
2 Heat butter and half of the oil in large deep saucepan; cook lamb mixture, in batches, until browned all over.
3 Heat remaining oil in same pan; cook onion, ginger, garlic, paprika and cayenne over low heat, stirring, until onion softens.
4 Return lamb to pan with stock, undrained tomatoes, bay leaves and cinnamon. Add yogurt, 1 tablespoon at a time, stirring well between each addition; bring to a boil. Reduce heat, simmer, covered, about 1½ hours or until lamb is tender.
5 Remove from heat, sprinkle lamb with nuts and chilli; serve with cucumber raita (see page 397) and warmed naan bread (see page 379), if desired.
per serving 52.8g total fat (15.9g saturated fat); 3256kJ (779 cal); 11.6g carbohydrate; 62.8g protein; 5.4g fibre

chicken panang curry

preparation time 15 minutes
cooking time 20 minutes serves 4

2 x 400ml cans coconut milk
¼ cup (75g) panang curry paste (see page 249)
2 tablespoons grated palm sugar
2 tablespoons fish sauce
2 fresh kaffir lime leaves, torn
2 tablespoons peanut oil
1kg chicken thigh fillets, quartered
100g snake beans, chopped coarsely
½ cup firmly packed fresh thai basil leaves
½ cup (70g) coarsely chopped roasted unsalted peanuts
2 fresh long red thai chillies, sliced thinly

1 Place coconut milk, paste, sugar, sauce and lime leaves in wok; bring to a boil. Reduce heat, simmer, stirring, about 15 minutes or until mixture reduces by about a third.
2 Meanwhile, heat oil in large frying pan; cook chicken, in batches, until browned lightly. Drain on absorbent paper.
3 Add beans, chicken and half of the basil leaves to curry mixture; cook, uncovered, stirring occasionally, about 5 minutes or until beans are just tender and chicken is cooked through.
4 Place curry in serving bowl; sprinkle with peanuts, chilli and remaining basil.
per serving 75g total fat (42.8g saturated fat); 4197kJ (1004 cal); 17.8g carbohydrate; 62.6g protein; 7.7g fibre

malaysian fish curry

preparation time 15 minutes
cooking time 30 minutes serves 4

2 tablespoons vegetable oil
1⅔ cups (400ml) coconut milk
1 cup (250ml) coconut cream
2 cups (400g) jasmine rice
4 blue-eye fillets (800g), skinless
⅓ cup (15g) flaked coconut, toasted
4 fresh kaffir lime leaves, sliced thinly

SPICE PASTE
4 shallots (100g), quartered
50g piece galangal, quartered
½ teaspoon ground turmeric
½ teaspoon fennel seeds
1 teaspoon ground coriander
¼ cup (75g) prepared madras curry paste
2 tablespoons lime juice
2 cloves garlic, quartered
4 fresh small red thai chillies
1 teaspoon caster sugar

1 Blend or process ingredients for spice paste until smooth.
2 Heat half of the oil in large frying pan; cook paste, stirring, over medium heat until fragrant. Add coconut milk and cream; bring to a boil. Reduce heat, simmer, uncovered, about 15 minutes or until curry sauce thickens slightly.
3 Meanwhile, cook rice in large saucepan of boiling water, uncovered, until tender; drain. Cover to keep warm.
4 Heat remaining oil in large frying pan; cook fish, uncovered, about 10 minutes or until cooked as desired.
5 Divide fish among shallow serving bowls; top with curry sauce, sprinkle with coconut and lime leaves. Serve rice in separate bowl; sprinkle curry with sliced chilli, if desired.

per serving 56.2g total fat (34.9g saturated fat); 4468kJ (1069 cal); 89.0g carbohydrate; 52.4g protein; 6.7g fibre

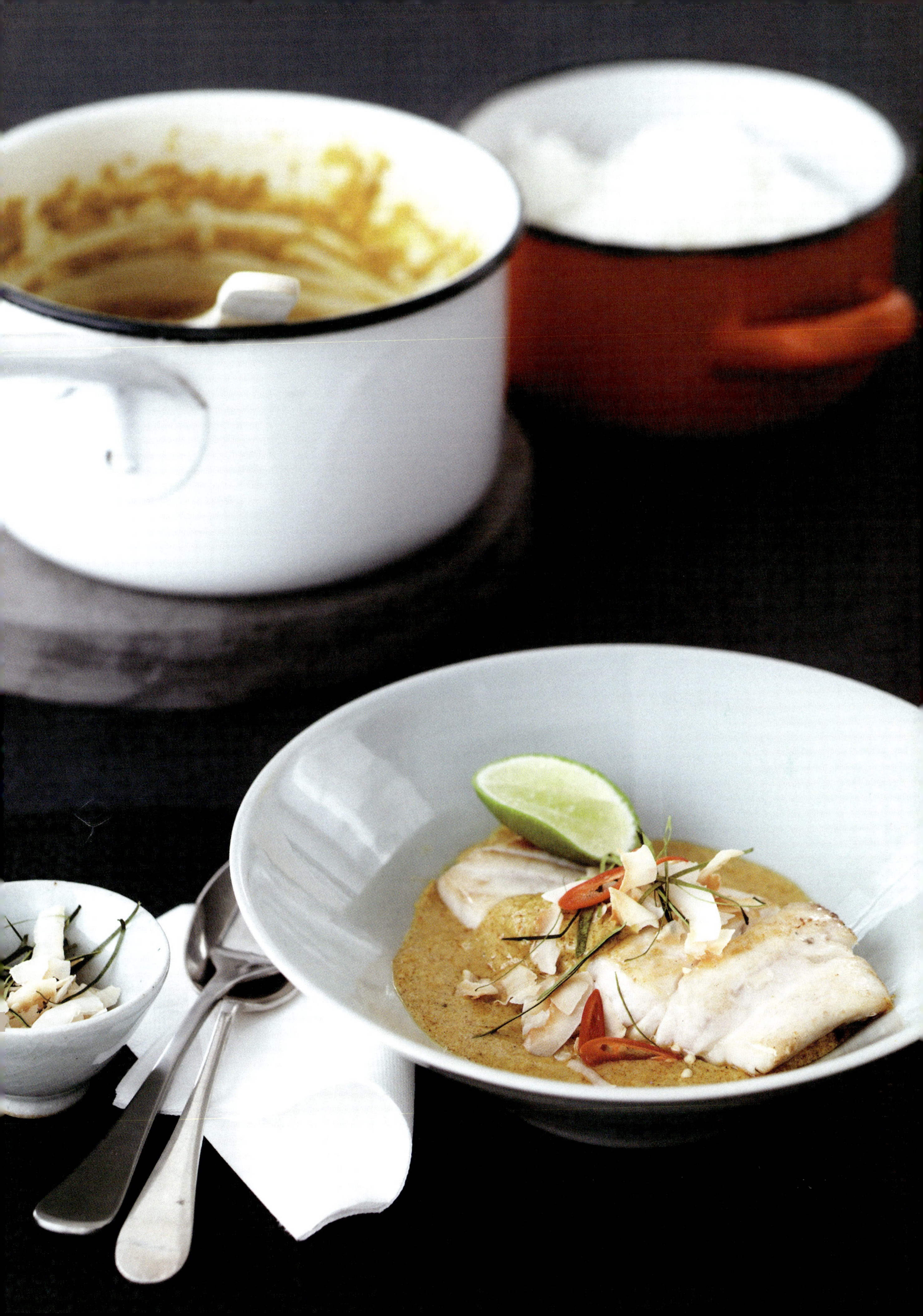

The Complete Book of Modern Asian

fish ball and eggplant red curry

preparation time 20 minutes
cooking time 15 minutes serves 4

500g firm white fish fillets, chopped coarsely
1 clove garlic, quartered
1 tablespoon finely chopped coriander root and stem mixture
1 tablespoon soy sauce
1 tablespoon cornflour
2 teaspoons peanut oil
2 tablespoons red curry paste (see page 249)
400ml can coconut milk
½ cup (60g) pea eggplants
2 teaspoons grated palm sugar
1 tablespoon lime juice
1 tablespoon fish sauce
2 green onions, sliced thinly
½ cup (40g) bean sprouts
2 fresh long red thai chillies, sliced thinly
¼ cup loosely packed fresh coriander leaves

1 Blend or process fish with garlic, coriander mixture, soy sauce and cornflour until mixture forms a smooth paste; roll heaped teaspoons of mixture into balls.
2 Place oil and curry paste in large saucepan; stir over heat until fragrant. Add coconut milk; bring to a boil, stirring, until combined. Add fish balls and eggplants; reduce heat, simmer, uncovered, about 5 minutes or until fish balls are cooked through. Add sugar, juice, fish sauce and onion; stir until sugar dissolves.
3 Place curry in serving bowl; sprinkle with sprouts, chilli and coriander leaves.
per serving 29.5g total fat (19.8g saturated fat); 1789kJ (428 cal); 10g carbohydrate; 29.5g protein; 4.0g fibre

spinach and mushroom korma

preparation time 15 minutes
cooking time 25 minutes serves 4

⅓ cup (50g) unsalted roasted cashews
1 tablespoon ghee
1 large brown onion (200g), sliced thinly
2 cloves garlic, crushed
4cm piece fresh ginger (20g), grated
2 teaspoons kalonji seeds
½ cup (160g) prepared korma paste
⅔ cup (160ml) cream
400g swiss brown mushrooms
500g spinach, trimmed, chopped coarsely
⅓ cup (95g) yogurt

1 Blend or process nuts until finely ground.
2 Heat ghee in large saucepan; cook onion, garlic and ginger, stirring, until onion softens. Add nuts, seeds and paste; cook, stirring, until fragrant.
3 Add cream and mushrooms; simmer, covered, 15 minutes. Add spinach; cook, stirring, until wilted. Serve curry with yogurt.
per serving 41.8g total fat (17.2g saturated fat); 2065kJ (495 cal); 11.6g carbohydrate; 13.6g protein; 11.8g fibre

chicken korma

preparation time 20 minutes (plus 1 hour standing time) cooking time 1 hour 5 minutes serves 8

1.5kg chicken thigh fillets, sliced thickly
¼ cup (70g) yogurt
¾ cup (60g) desiccated coconut
⅓ cup (50g) raw cashews
1 tablespoon vegetable oil
3 bay leaves
1 cinnamon stick
10 green cardamom pods
10 whole cloves
2 medium red onions (340g), sliced thinly
4cm piece fresh ginger (20g), grated
3 cloves garlic, crushed
1 teaspoon chilli powder
1 teaspoon ground turmeric
2 teaspoons ground coriander
1 teaspoon ground cumin
3 medium fresh tomatoes (450g), chopped
⅓ cup (80ml) water
3 cups (70ml) water, extra

1 Rub chicken fillets with beaten yogurt. Cover; refrigerate 1 hour.
2 Meanwhile, place coconut in heatproof bowl, cover with ½ cup (125ml) hot water; stand 1 hour. Drain. Blend or process coconut and cashews to a fine paste.
3 Heat oil in large saucepan; cook bay leaves, cinnamon, cardamom and cloves until fragrant. Add onion; cook, stirring, until browned lightly. Add ginger, garlic and spices, cook, stirring, until fragrant. Add chopped tomatoes and the water; cook, stirring, about 5 minutes or until mixture thickens and tomatoes break down. Add ground coconut paste and the extra water; simmer, uncovered, about 20 minutes.
4 Add chicken mixture; simmer, uncovered, a further 30 minutes or until chicken is tender. Serve garnished with fried fresh curry leaves, if desired.

per serving 24.2g total fat (9.5g saturated fat); 1655kJ (396 cal); 5.6g carbohydrate; 38.1g protein; 3g fibre

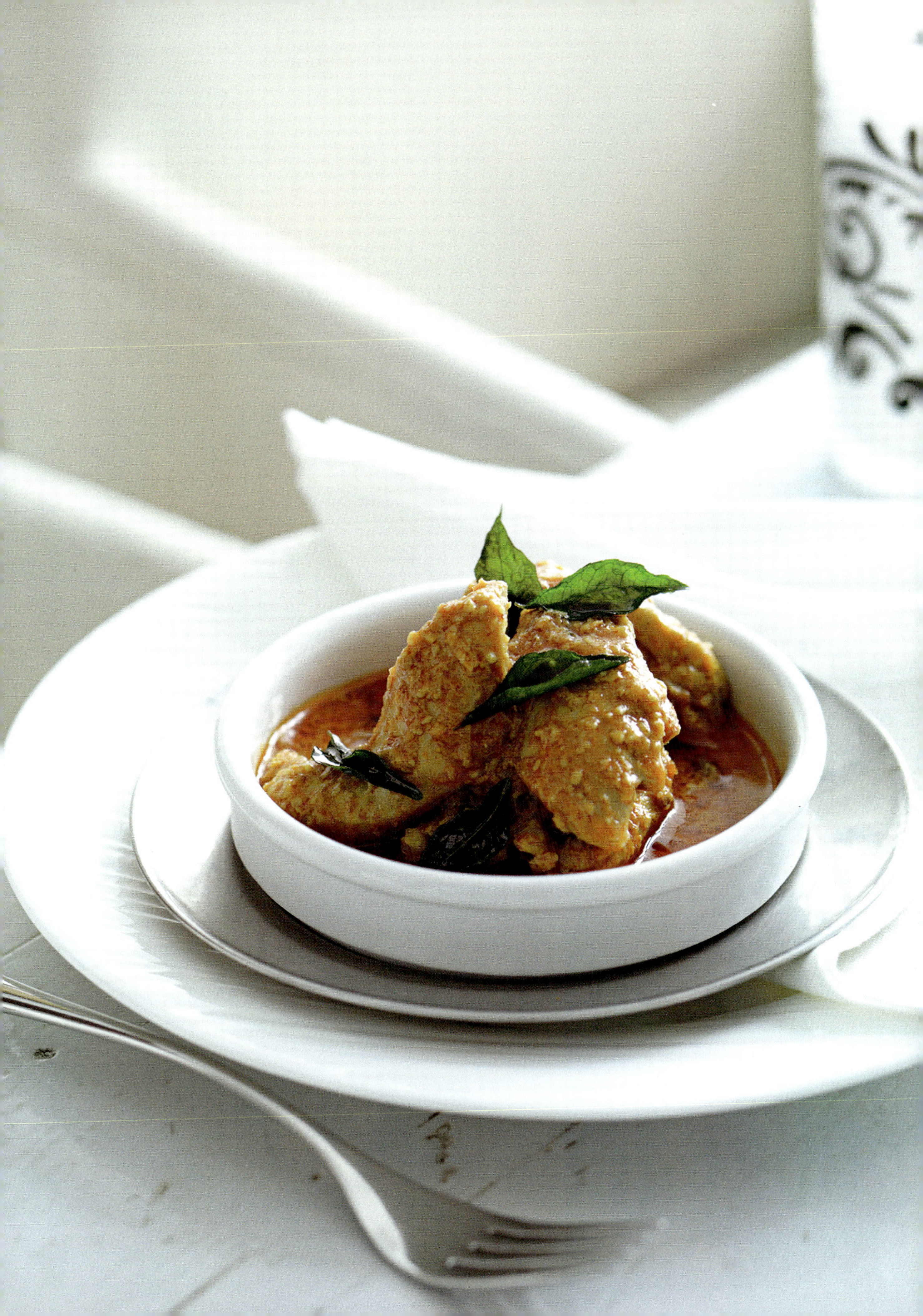

The Complete Book of Modern Asian

lamb rendang

preparation time 30 minutes
cooking time 3 hours 15 minutes serves 4

2 teaspoons coriander seeds
¼ teaspoon ground turmeric
2 large brown onions (400g), chopped coarsely
4 cloves garlic, quartered
2 x 10cm sticks fresh lemon grass (40g), chopped coarsely
2cm piece fresh galangal (10g), sliced thinly
4 fresh small red thai chillies, chopped coarsely
2 fresh long red chillies, chopped coarsely
2 tablespoons coarsely chopped coriander root and stem mixture
2 tablespoons peanut oil
1.5kg butterflied leg of lamb
400ml can coconut milk

1 Dry-fry spices in small frying pan, stirring, about 1 minute or until fragrant. Blend or process spices with onion, garlic, lemon grass, galangal, chillies and coriander mixture until mixture forms a paste.
2 Preheat oven to 150°C/130°C fan-forced.
3 Heat half of the oil in large flameproof baking dish; cook lamb, turning occasionally, until browned all over. Remove from dish.
4 Heat remaining oil in same dish; cook onion paste, stirring, until fragrant. Add coconut milk; bring to a boil.
5 Return lamb to dish; cook in oven, uncovered, turning occasionally, about 3 hours or until liquid has evaporated. Cover; stand 10 minutes before serving.
per serving 50.2g total fat (28.8g saturated fat); 3490kJ (835 cal); 8.1g carbohydrate; 86.5g protein; 3.7g fibre

tamarind and citrus pork curry

preparation time 20 minutes (plus standing time)
cooking time 50 minutes serves 4

70g dried tamarind, chopped coarsely
¾ cup (180ml) boiling water
1 tablespoon peanut oil
1 large red onion (300g), chopped finely
1 fresh long red chilli, sliced thinly
5cm piece fresh ginger (25g), grated
2 cloves garlic, crushed
10 fresh curry leaves
2 teaspoons fenugreek seeds
½ teaspoon ground turmeric
1 teaspoon ground coriander
1 teaspoon finely grated lime rind
1 tablespoon lime juice
400ml can coconut cream
6 baby eggplants (360g), chopped coarsely
1kg pork fillet, cut into 2cm dice

1 Soak tamarind in the boiling water 30 minutes. Place fine sieve over small bowl; push tamarind through sieve. Discard solids in sieve; reserve pulp in bowl.
2 Heat oil in large saucepan; cook onion, chilli, ginger, garlic, curry leaves, seeds and spices, stirring, until onion softens.
3 Add pulp, rind, juice, coconut cream and eggplant; simmer, covered, 20 minutes. Add pork; simmer, uncovered, about 20 minutes or until pork is cooked.
per serving 45.8g total fat (25.7g saturated fat); 3060kJ (732 cal); 19.7g carbohydrate; 57.7g protein; 6.8g fibre

pork vindaloo

preparation time 25 minutes
cooking time 1 hour 50 minutes serves 4

2 tablespoons ghee
1kg pork shoulder, cut into 3cm pieces
1 large red onion (300g), sliced thinly
½ cup (150g) prepared vindaloo paste
2 cloves garlic, crushed
2 cups (500ml) water
¼ cup (60ml) white vinegar
4 medium potatoes (800g), quartered
2 fresh small red thai chillies, chopped finely
2 fresh long red chillies, sliced thinly

1 Heat ghee in large saucepan; cook pork, in batches, until browned all over.
2 Cook onion in same pan, stirring, until soft. Add paste and garlic; cook, stirring, about 1 minute or until fragrant.
3 Return pork to pan with the water and vinegar; simmer, covered, 50 minutes.
4 Add potato; simmer, uncovered, about 45 minutes or until potato is tender. Stir in chopped chilli; serve curry sprinkled with thinly sliced chilli.
per serving 40.7g total fat (13.7g saturated fat); 3173kJ (759 cal); 33.3g carbohydrate; 61.0g protein; 8.3g fibre

vegetable yellow curry

preparation time 20 minutes
cooking time 30 minutes serves 4

1 tablespoon vegetable oil
2 tablespoons yellow curry paste (see page 248)
1⅔ cups (400ml) light coconut milk
1 cup (250ml) vegetable stock
1 large kumara (500g), chopped coarsely
200g green beans, trimmed
150g firm tofu, diced into 2cm cubes
2 tablespoons lime juice
¼ cup coarsely chopped fresh coriander

1 Heat oil in large saucepan; cook curry paste, stirring, until fragrant. Add coconut milk and stock; bring to a boil. Reduce heat, simmer, stirring, 5 minutes. Add kumara; simmer, covered, about 10 minutes or until kumara is tender.
2 Add beans, tofu and juice; cook, stirring, until beans are tender. Stir in coriander.
3 Serve curry with steamed rice and topped with fresh coriander, if desired.
per serving 8.2g total fat (11.1g saturated fat); 915kJ (219 cal); 23.8g carbohydrate; 10.3g protein; 4.2g fibre

Curries

The Complete Book of Modern Asian

beef panang curry

preparation time 40 minutes
cooking time 15 minutes serves 4

500g beef rump steak
1 tablespoon kecap manis
1 clove garlic, crushed
2 tablespoons peanut oil
⅓ cup (100g) panang curry paste (see page 249)
2 tablespoons fish sauce
2 tablespoons grated palm sugar
8 fresh kaffir lime leaves, torn
400ml can coconut milk
100g snake beans, cut into 8cm lengths
125g fresh baby corn
½ cup coarsely chopped fresh coriander
1 fresh long red chilli, sliced thinly

1 Combine beef with kecap manis, garlic and half the oil in a small bowl. Cover; refrigerate 1 hour.
2 Heat remaining oil in wok; cook curry paste, stirring, until fragrant. Add fish sauce, palm sugar and lime leaves; stir-fry 1 minute. Add coconut milk; bring to a boil. Reduce heat, simmer, uncovered, for 10 minutes or until thickened.
3 Meanwhile, cook beef on heated oiled grill pan (or grill or barbecue) until cooked as desired. Cover; stand for 5 minutes. Slice the beef thickly.
4 Add beans and corn to curry; simmer, uncovered, for about 5 minutes or until just tender.
5 Serve curry topped with beef, coriander and chilli.
per serving 45g total fat (24.5g saturated fat); 2608kJ (624 cal); 17.9g carbohydrate; 35.4g protein; 5.2g fibre

madras lamb curry

preparation time 10 minutes
cooking time 30 minutes serves 4

500g butternut pumpkin, diced into 2cm pieces
200g green beans, chopped coarsely
2 tablespoons vegetable oil
600g lamb backstrap, diced into 2cm pieces
1 medium brown onion (150g), chopped finely
2 cloves garlic, crushed
½ cup (150g) prepared madras curry paste
1 cup (250ml) beef stock
425g can crushed tomatoes, drained
1 cup (250ml) buttermilk
½ cup coarsely chopped fresh coriander

1 Boil, steam or microwave pumpkin and beans, separately, until just tender; drain. Rinse beans under cold water; drain.
2 Meanwhile, heat half of the oil in wok; stir-fry lamb, in batches, until just browned.
3 Heat remaining oil in same wok; stir-fry onion and garlic until onion softens. Add paste; stir-fry until fragrant. Return lamb to wok with stock and tomatoes; bring to a boil. Add pumpkin, reduce heat; simmer, covered, stirring occasionally, 10 minutes.
4 Add beans and buttermilk; stir over low heat until heated through. Remove from heat; stir in coriander.
5 Serve curry with steamed basmati rice and sprinkled with extra chopped fresh coriander, if desired.
per serving 36.9g total fat (9.7g saturated fat); 3829kJ (916 cal); 97.4g carbohydrate; 47.9g protein; 9.1g fibre

sour pork curry

preparation time 30 minutes
cooking time 2 hours 15 minutes serves 4

1 tablespoon vegetable oil
1kg pork neck
1 teaspoon shrimp paste
¼ cup coarsely chopped coriander root and stem mixture
2cm piece fresh galangal (10g), chopped finely
5 dried long red chillies, chopped finely
3 fresh long red chillies, chopped finely
2 tablespoons fish sauce
¾ cup (235g) tamarind concentrate
2 tablespoons caster sugar
2 cups (500ml) chicken stock
1 litre (4 cups) water
½ cup fresh thai basil leaves, chopped coarsely

1 Heat oil in large flameproof casserole dish; cook pork, uncovered, until browned. Remove from dish.
2 Preheat oven to 160°C/140°C fan-forced.
3 Add paste, coriander mixture, galangal and chillies to same dish; cook, stirring, until fragrant. Add sauce, tamarind, sugar, stock and the water; bring to a boil. Return pork to dish; cook, covered, in oven 1 hour. Uncover; cook 1 hour.
4 Remove pork from dish; cover, stand 10 minutes before slicing thickly. Remove curry sauce from heat, stir in basil.
per serving 9.3g total fat (2.1g saturated fat); 1680kJ (402 cal); 18.3g carbohydrate; 59.7g protein; 1.5g fibre

tofu and thai eggplant massaman curry

preparation time 30 minutes
cooking time 25 minutes serves 4

2 teaspoons peanut oil
2 tablespoons massaman curry paste (see page 248)
400ml can light coconut milk
¾ cup (375ml) vegetable stock
4 baby eggplants (240g), sliced thickly
350g thai eggplants, quartered
3 medium potatoes (600g), chopped coarsely
200g firm tofu, sliced thickly
1 tablespoon grated palm sugar
1 tablespoon lime juice
¼ cup loosely packed fresh coriander leaves

1 Heat oil in large saucepan; cook curry paste, stirring, until fragrant. Add milk, stock, eggplants and potato; bring to a boil. Reduce heat, simmer, uncovered, about 20 minutes or until potato is tender and sauce has thickened slightly.
2 Add tofu, sugar and juice to pan; stir until tofu is heated through.
3 Divide curry among serving plates; top with coriander. Serve with steamed jasmine rice, if desired.
per serving 19.3g total fat (12.1g saturated fat); 1605kJ (384 cal); 34.7g carbohydrate; 14.3g protein; 7.6g fibre

Curries

The Complete Book of Modern Asian

xacutti

preparation time 25 minutes
cooking time 1 hour 15 minutes serves 4

1 cup (80g) desiccated coconut
½ teaspoon ground cinnamon
4 whole cloves
8 dried long red chillies
1 teaspoon ground turmeric
1 tablespoon poppy seeds
1 tablespoon cumin seeds
1 tablespoon fennel seeds
2 tablespoons coriander seeds
2 teaspoons black peppercorns
2 star anise
6 cloves garlic, quartered
2 tablespoons ghee
1 large brown onion (200g), chopped finely
1kg diced rump
2 cups (500ml) water
2 cups (500ml) beef stock
2 tablespoons lime juice

1 Dry-fry coconut in large frying pan over medium heat, stirring, until browned lightly; remove coconut from pan. Dry-fry cinnamon, cloves, chillies, turmeric, seeds, peppercorns and star anise in same pan, stirring, about 1 minute or until fragrant.
2 Blend or process coconut, spice mixture and garlic until fine.
3 Heat ghee in large saucepan; cook onion, stirring, until onion softens. Add coconut spice mixture; cook, stirring, until fragrant. Add beef; cook, stirring, 2 minutes or until beef is coated with coconut spice mixture.
4 Add the water and stock; simmer, covered, 30 minutes, stirring occasionally. Uncover; cook 30 minutes or until beef is tender and sauce thickened slightly. Stir juice into curry off the heat; sprinkle with fresh sliced chilli if desired.
per serving 38.2g total fat (23.8g saturated fat); 2512kJ (600 cal); 5.0g carbohydrate; 57.5g protein; 5.2g fibre

cauliflower and green pea curry

preparation time 20 minutes
cooking time 30 minutes serves 4

600g cauliflower florets
2 tablespoons ghee
1 medium brown onion (150g), chopped finely
2 cloves garlic, crushed
2cm piece fresh ginger (10g), grated
¼ cup (75g) prepared hot curry paste
¾ cup (180ml) cream
2 large tomatoes (440g), chopped coarsely
1 cup (120g) frozen peas
1 cup (280g) yogurt
3 hard-boiled eggs, sliced thinly
¼ cup finely chopped fresh coriander

1 Boil, steam or microwave cauliflower until just tender; drain.
2 Meanwhile, heat ghee in large saucepan; cook onion, garlic and ginger, stirring, until onion softens. Add paste; cook, stirring, until mixture is fragrant.
3 Add cream; bring to a boil then reduce heat. Add cauliflower and tomato; simmer, uncovered, 5 minutes, stirring occasionally.
4 Add peas and yogurt; stir over low heat 5 minutes or until peas are just cooked. Serve curry sprinkled with egg and coriander.
per serving 40.9g total fat (21.9g saturated fat); 2132kJ (510 cal); 15.5g carbohydrate; 17.0g protein; 8.6g fibre

curry pastes

massaman curry paste

preparation time 15 minutes (plus standing time)
cooking time 20 minutes makes 1 cup

20 dried long red chillies
1 teaspoon ground coriander
2 teaspoons ground cumin
2 teaspoons ground cinnamon
½ teaspoon ground cardamom
½ teaspoon ground clove
5 cloves garlic, quartered
1 large brown onion (200g), chopped coarsely
2 x 10cm sticks fresh lemon grass (40g), sliced thinly
3 fresh kaffir lime leaves, sliced thinly
4cm piece fresh ginger (20g), chopped coarsely
2 teaspoons shrimp paste
1 tablespoon peanut oil

1 Preheat oven to 180°C/160°C fan-forced.
2 Place chillies in small heatproof jug, cover with boiling water; stand 15 minutes, drain.
3 Meanwhile, dry-fry coriander, cumin, cinnamon, cardamom and clove in small frying pan, stirring until fragrant.
4 Place chillies and spices in small shallow baking dish with remaining ingredients. Roast, uncovered, 15 minutes.
5 Blend or process roasted curry paste mixture, or crush using mortar and pestle, until smooth.

per tablespoon 1.7g total fat (0.3g saturated fat); 105kJ (25 cal); 1.5g carbohydrate; 0.5g protein; 0.4g fibre

yellow curry paste

preparation time 20 minutes (plus standing time)
cooking time 3 minutes makes 1 cup

2 dried long red chillies
1 teaspoon ground coriander
1 teaspoon ground cumin
½ teaspoon ground cinnamon
2 fresh yellow banana chillies (250g), chopped coarsely
1 teaspoon finely chopped fresh turmeric
2 cloves garlic, quartered
1 small brown onion (80g), chopped finely
10cm stick (20g) fresh lemon grass, chopped finely
2 teaspoons finely chopped fresh galangal
1 tablespoon coarsely chopped fresh coriander root and stem mixture
1 teaspoon shrimp paste
1 tablespoon peanut oil

1 Place chillies in small heatproof jug, cover with boiling water; stand 15 minutes, drain.
2 Meanwhile, dry-fry ground coriander, cumin and cinnamon in small frying pan, stirring until fragrant.
3 Blend or process spices and chillies with remaining ingredients until mixture is smooth.

per tablespoon 1.6g total fat (0.3g saturated fat); 84kJ (20 cal); 0.9g carbohydrate; 0.4g protein; 0.5g fibre

panang curry paste

preparation time 20 minutes (plus standing time)
cooking time 3 minutes   makes 1 cup

25 dried long red chillies
1 teaspoon ground coriander
2 teaspoons ground cumin
2 cloves garlic, quartered
8 green onions, chopped coarsely
2 x 10cm sticks fresh lemon grass (40g), sliced thinly
2cm piece fresh galangal (10g), chopped finely
2 teaspoons shrimp paste
½ cup (75g) roasted unsalted peanuts
2 tablespoons peanut oil

1 Place chillies in small heatproof jug, cover with boiling water; stand 15 minutes, drain.
2 Meanwhile, dry-fry coriander and cumin in small frying pan over medium heat, stirring until fragrant.
3 Blend or process chillies and spices with remaining ingredients until mixture forms a paste.
per tablespoon 6.1g total fat (0.9g saturated fat); 288kJ (69 cal); 1.3g carbohydrate; 1.9g protein; 0.9g fibre

red curry paste

preparation time 20 minutes (plus standing time)
cooking time 5 minutes   makes 1 cup

20 dried long red chillies
1 teaspoon ground coriander
2 teaspoons ground cumin
1 teaspoon hot paprika
2cm piece fresh ginger (10g), chopped finely
3 cloves garlic, quartered
1 medium red onion (170g), chopped coarsely
2 x 10cm sticks fresh lemon grass (40g), sliced thinly
2 tablespoons coarsely chopped fresh
    coriander root and stem mixture
2 teaspoons shrimp paste
1 tablespoon peanut oil

1 Place chillies in small heatproof jug, cover with boiling water; stand 15 minutes, drain.
2 Meanwhile, dry-fry ground coriander, cumin and paprika in small frying pan, stirring until fragrant.
3 Blend or process chillies and spices with ginger, garlic, onion, lemon grass, coriander mixture and paste until mixture forms a paste.
4 Add oil to paste; continue to blend until smooth.
per tablespoon 1.6g total fat (0.3g saturated fat); 92kJ (22 cal); 1.2g carbohydrate; 0.4g protein; 0.5g fibre

green curry paste

preparation time 20 minutes
cooking time 3 minutes   makes 1 cup

2 teaspoons ground coriander
2 teaspoons ground cumin
10 long green chillies, chopped coarsely
10 small green chillies, chopped coarsely
1 teaspoon shrimp paste
1 clove garlic, quartered
4 green onions, chopped coarsely
10cm stick fresh lemon grass (20g), chopped finely
1cm piece fresh galangal (5g), chopped finely
¼ cup coarsely chopped fresh coriander
    root and stem mixture
1 tablespoon peanut oil

1 Dry-fry ground coriander and cumin in small frying pan over medium heat, stirring until fragrant.
2 Blend or process spices with chillies, paste, garlic, onion, lemon grass, galangal and coriander mixture until mixture forms a paste.
3 Add oil to paste; continue to blend until smooth.
per tablespoon 1.6g total fat (0.3g saturated fat); 67kJ (16 cal); 0.3g carbohydrate; 0.2g protein; 0.2g fibre

Barbecuing, grilling and roasting are ancient styles of cooking indigenous to every Asian culture from the Bosporus to the Pacific: proof that there's no need to improve on perfect. From satay and teppanyaki to tandoori and tikka, high heat coupled with spiced or marinated meat, poultry and seafood are an incendiary marriage made in culinary heaven.

chinese barbecued spareribs *page 268*

sichuan duck with watercress and snow pea salad *page 283*

barbecues, grills & roasts

grilled tuna with japanese chilled soba salad *page 271*

seared salmon kerala-style with lime pickle yogurt *page 271*

raan with spiced yogurt

preparation time 35 minutes (plus refrigeration time)
cooking time 20 minutes serves 4

2 teaspoons coriander seeds
1 teaspoon cumin seeds
5 cardamom pods, bruised
1 teaspoon chilli powder
1 teaspoon ground turmeric
1 cinnamon stick
2 cloves
2 star anise
1 medium brown onion (150g), chopped coarsely
4 cloves garlic, quartered
2cm piece fresh ginger (10g), chopped coarsely
¼ cup (40g) blanched almonds
½ cup (140g) low-fat yogurt
2 tablespoons lemon juice
1.2kg butterflied leg of lamb, trimmed

SPICED YOGURT
1 cup (280g) low-fat yogurt
¼ cup finely chopped fresh mint
1 clove garlic, crushed
¼ teaspoon ground cumin
¼ teaspoon ground coriander

1 Dry-fry seeds, cardamom, chilli, turmeric, cinnamon, cloves and star anise in small heated frying pan, stirring, about 2 minutes or until fragrant. Blend or process spices with onion, garlic, ginger, nuts, yogurt and juice until mixture forms a paste.
2 Pierce lamb all over with sharp knife; place on metal rack in large shallow baking dish. Spread paste over lamb, pressing firmly into cuts. Cover; refrigerate 3 hours or overnight.
3 Cook lamb on heated oiled grill plate (or grill or barbecue), covered, about 20 minutes or until browned both sides and cooked as desired. Cover lamb; stand 10 minutes then slice thickly.
4 Meanwhile, combine ingredients for spiced yogurt in small bowl.
5 Serve lamb with yogurt and accompany with a green bean salad, if desired.
per serving 18g total fat (5.8g saturated fat); 1831kJ (438 cal); 9.4g carbohydrate; 58.3g protein; 2.3g fibre

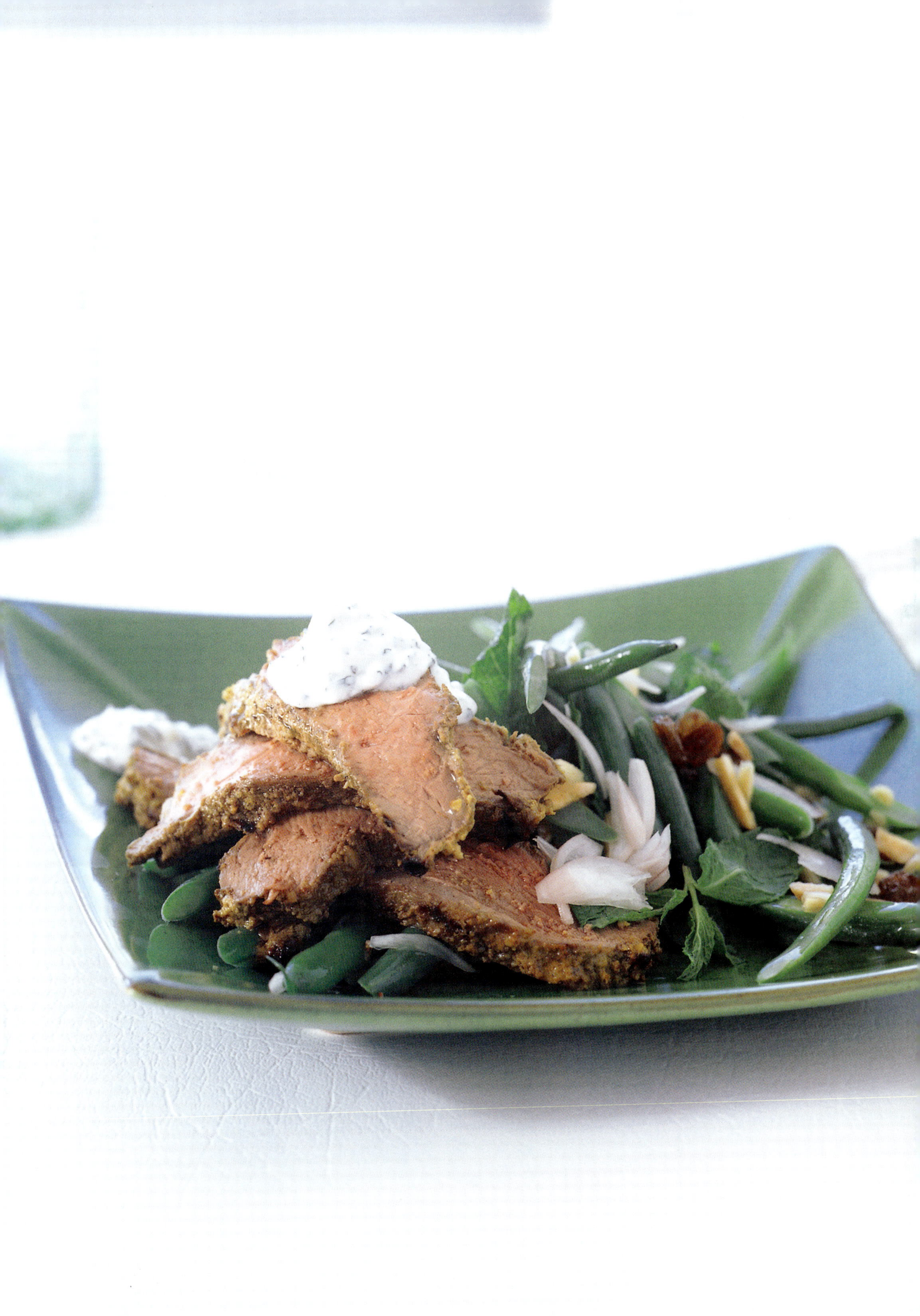

The Complete Book of Modern Asian

tuna skewers with soba

preparation time 20 minutes
cooking time 10 minutes serves 4

800g tuna steaks, diced into 2cm pieces
2 tablespoons olive oil
3 teaspoons wasabi paste
1 teaspoon ground coriander
⅓ cup finely chopped fresh coriander
300g dried soba noodles
1 medium carrot (120g), cut into matchsticks
4 green onions, sliced thickly
¼ cup firmly packed fresh coriander leaves
MIRIN DRESSING
¼ cup (60ml) mirin
2 tablespoons japanese soy sauce
1cm piece fresh ginger (5g), grated
1 teaspoon sesame oil
1 teaspoon fish sauce
1 teaspoon sugar

1 Combine tuna with oil, wasabi and ground coriander in large bowl. Thread tuna onto eight skewers; sprinkle with chopped coriander.
2 Cook noodles in large saucepan of boiling water, uncovered, until just tender; drain. Rinse under cold water; drain.
3 Meanwhile, place ingredients for mirin dressing in screw-top jar; shake well.
4 Combine noodles in large bowl with carrot, onion, coriander leaves and half of the dressing.
5 Cook skewers on heated oiled grill plate (or grill or barbecue), uncovered, until cooked as desired (do not overcook or tuna will dry out). Serve skewers on noodles, drizzled with remaining dressing.
per serving 22.5g total fat (6.2g saturated fat); 2847kJ (681 cal); 55g carbohydrate; 59.9g protein; 3.7g fibre

crisp five-spice salt pork belly

preparation time 15 minutes (plus refrigeration time)
cooking time 2 hours 30 minutes serves 6

1kg piece boned belly pork, skin on
1½ teaspoons fine sea salt
½ teaspoon five-spice powder
1 tablespoon peanut oil
¼ cup (60ml) light soy sauce
1 fresh small red thai chilli, chopped finely

1 Pat the pork rind dry with absorbent paper; score pork diagonally at 5mm intervals. Rub in combined salt, five-spice and oil. Place on metal rack over large shallow baking dish; cover, refrigerate 1 hour.
2 Preheat oven to 240°C/220°C fan-forced.
3 Roast pork, uncovered, about 1 hour or until rind begins to crisp.
4 Reduce oven temperature to 160°C/140°C fan-forced; roast pork a further 1 hour 30 minutes or until tender. Stand 15 minutes; slice thickly.
5 Serve pork with combined sauce and chilli.
per serving 34.6g total fat (11.6g saturated fat); 1914kJ (458 cal); 0.3g carbohydrate; 37.1g protein; 0g fibre

japanese-style duck with wombok and daikon salad

preparation time 45 minutes (plus standing time)
cooking time 1 hour 10 minutes serves 4

10 dried shiitake mushrooms
3 litres (12 cups) water
1.5 litres (6 cups) chicken stock
1 cup (250ml) cooking sake
1 cup (250ml) mirin
¼ cup (60ml) tamari
½ cup (125ml) japanese soy sauce
6 green onions, halved
3 cloves garlic, quartered
5cm piece fresh ginger (25g), unpeeled, chopped coarsely
½ cup (110g) firmly packed dark brown sugar
2kg duck
2 tablespoons teriyaki sauce
1 tablespoon japanese soy sauce, extra

WOMBOK AND DAIKON SALAD
2 small carrots (140g), cut into matchsticks
½ small daikon (200g), halved lengthways, sliced thinly
½ small wombok (350g), shredded finely
3 green onions, chopped coarsely
1 fresh long red chilli, sliced thinly
2 tablespoons white miso
1 tablespoon mirin
1 tablespoon cooking sake
1 tablespoon white sugar
¼ cup (60ml) rice vinegar
1 teaspoon soy sauce

1 Place mushrooms in small heatproof bowl, cover with boiling water, stand 20 minutes; drain. Discard stems; slice caps thickly.
2 Combine mushrooms, the water, stock, sake, mirin, tamari, soy sauce, onion, garlic, ginger and sugar in stock pot. Add duck; bring to a boil. Reduce heat, simmer, uncovered, about 1 hour or until duck is cooked through. Remove from heat; stand duck in cooking liquid about 2 hours or until cool. Remove duck from cooking liquid; stand on wire rack 2 hours (discard cooking liquid). Cut duck into quarters.
3 Make wombok and daikon salad.
4 Combine teriyaki and extra soy sauce in small bowl; brush over duck skin. Cook duck, skin-side down, on heated oiled grill plate (or grill or barbecue), 5 minutes. Turn duck skin-side up; brush with remaining teriyaki mixture. Cover; cook about 5 minutes or until duck is heated through. Serve duck with salad.
WOMBOK AND DAIKON SALAD
Place carrot, daikon, wombok, onion and chilli in medium bowl. Place miso, mirin, sake and sugar in small saucepan; stir over heat until sugar dissolves. Remove from heat; stir in vinegar and soy sauce. Add dressing to salad; toss gently to combine.
per serving 94.8g total fat (28.7g saturated fat); 5488kJ (1313 cal); 48.6g carbohydrate; 44.2g protein; 4.6g fibre

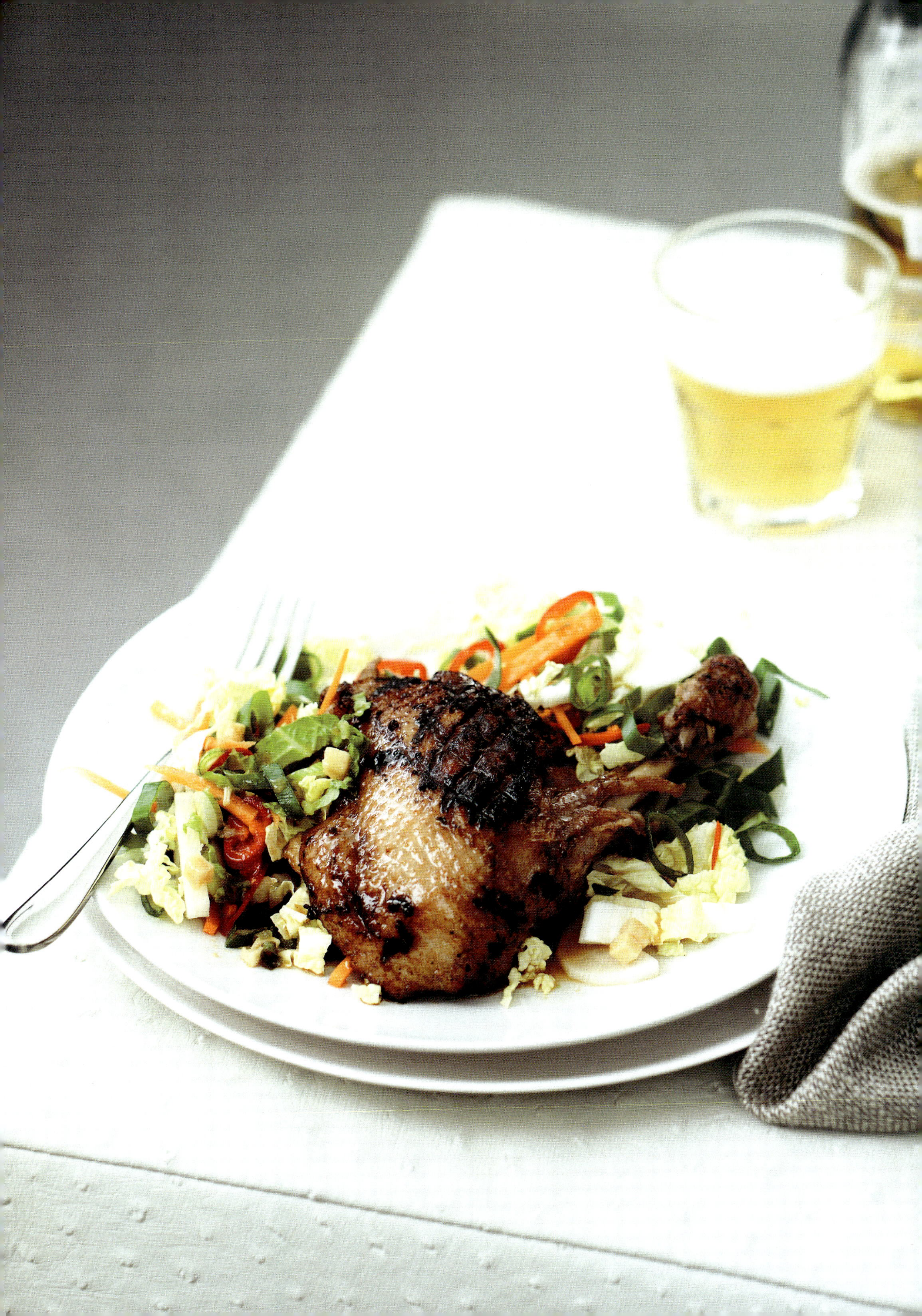

The Complete Book of Modern Asian

indochine grilled chicken salad

preparation time 25 minutes (plus refrigeration time)
cooking time 40 minutes   serves 4

4 x 200g chicken thigh cutlets
2 teaspoons five-spice powder
¼ cup (60ml) mirin
2 tablespoons chinese cooking wine
2 cloves garlic, crushed
125g rice vermicelli noodles
150g snow peas, sliced thinly
1 cup (80g) bean sprouts
2 green onions, sliced thinly
½ cup coarsely chopped fresh coriander
¼ cup loosely packed vietnamese mint leaves
2 medium carrots (240g), cut into matchsticks

LIME DRESSING
⅓ cup (80ml) lime juice
⅓ cup (80ml) mirin
2 cloves garlic, crushed
1 tablespoon grated palm sugar

1 Combine chicken with five-spice, mirin, wine and garlic in large bowl. Cover; refrigerate 3 hours or overnight.
2 Place ingredients for lime dressing in screw-top jar; shake well.
3 Cook chicken on heated oiled grill plate (or grill or barbecue), turning and brushing occasionally with marinade, about 40 minutes or until cooked.
4 Meanwhile, place noodles in large heatproof bowl, cover with boiling water; stand until just tender, drain. Rinse noodles under cold water; drain.
5 Place noodles and dressing in large bowl with remaining ingredients; toss gently to combine. Serve with chicken.
per serving 20.5g total fat (6.6g saturated fat); 1668kJ (399 cal); 17.2g carbohydrate; 26.9g protein; 4.2g fibre

fish with thai-style dressing

preparation time 15 minutes
cooking time 10 minutes   serves 4

100g snow pea sprouts, trimmed
1 cup loosely packed fresh mint leaves
½ cup loosely packed fresh coriander leaves
3 shallots (75g), sliced thinly
2 fresh long red chillies, sliced thinly
4 firm white fish fillets (800g)
⅓ cup (80ml) lime juice
2 tablespoons grated palm sugar
1 tablespoon fish sauce

1 Combine sprouts, mint, coriander, shallots and chilli in medium bowl.
2 Cook fish on heated oiled grill plate (or grill or barbecue) until cooked as desired.
3 Meanwhile, combine juice, sugar and sauce in small bowl.
4 Serve fish with salad drizzled with dressing.
per serving 1.6g total fat (0.3g saturated fat); 907kJ (217 cal); 13.0g carbohydrate; 36.8g protein; 2.6g fibre

lamb wrapped in banana leaf with thai salad

preparation time 50 minutes (plus refrigeration time)
cooking time 25 minutes   serves 4

1 cup coarsely chopped fresh coriander
2 coriander roots, chopped finely
10cm stick fresh lemon grass (20g), chopped finely
2 cloves garlic, crushed
1 teaspoon finely grated lime rind
2 tablespoons lime juice
1 fresh small red thai chilli, chopped finely
1 tablespoon grated palm sugar
2 tablespoons fish sauce
2 mini lamb roasts (700g)
2 large banana leaves
cooking-oil spray

THAI SALAD
2 medium carrots (240g), cut into matchsticks
150g snow peas, trimmed, sliced thinly
4 green onions, sliced thinly
½ cup coarsely chopped fresh coriander
½ cup coarsely chopped fresh mint
1 medium red capsicum (200g), sliced thinly
1 shallot (25g), sliced thinly

1 Combine chopped fresh coriander, coriander root, lemon grass, garlic, juice, rind, chilli, sugar and fish sauce in large bowl with lamb. Cover; refrigerate 3 hours or overnight.
2 Preheat oven to 180°C/160°C fan-forced.
3 Strain lamb through fine sieve over medium bowl; reserve marinade solids in strainer and marinade in separate bowl for thai salad. Cut each lamb roast in half horizontally.
4 Trim banana leaves into four 30cm squares. Using tongs, dip one square at a time into large saucepan of boiling water, remove immediately. Rinse under cold water; pat dry with absorbent paper. Banana leaf squares should be soft and pliable.
5 Using fingers, press lamb halves all over with marinade solids; place each half in the centre of one of the banana leaf squares. Fold banana leaf over lamb to enclose; secure each parcel with kitchen string.
6 Place lamb parcels, in single layer, in large shallow baking dish; spray parcels with cooking-oil spray. Roast, uncovered, about 30 minutes or until roast is cooked as desired.
7 Meanwhile, make thai salad. Serve lamb on opened banana leaf with salad.

THAI SALAD
Combine ingredients in large bowl. Place remaining reserved marinade in small saucepan; bring to a boil. Reduce heat, simmer, uncovered, 2 minutes. Cool marinade 10 minutes, pour over salad; toss gently to combine.

per serving 16.6g total fat (7.1g saturated fat); 1488kJ (356 cal); 11.1g carbohydrate; 40.5g protein; 4.9g fibre

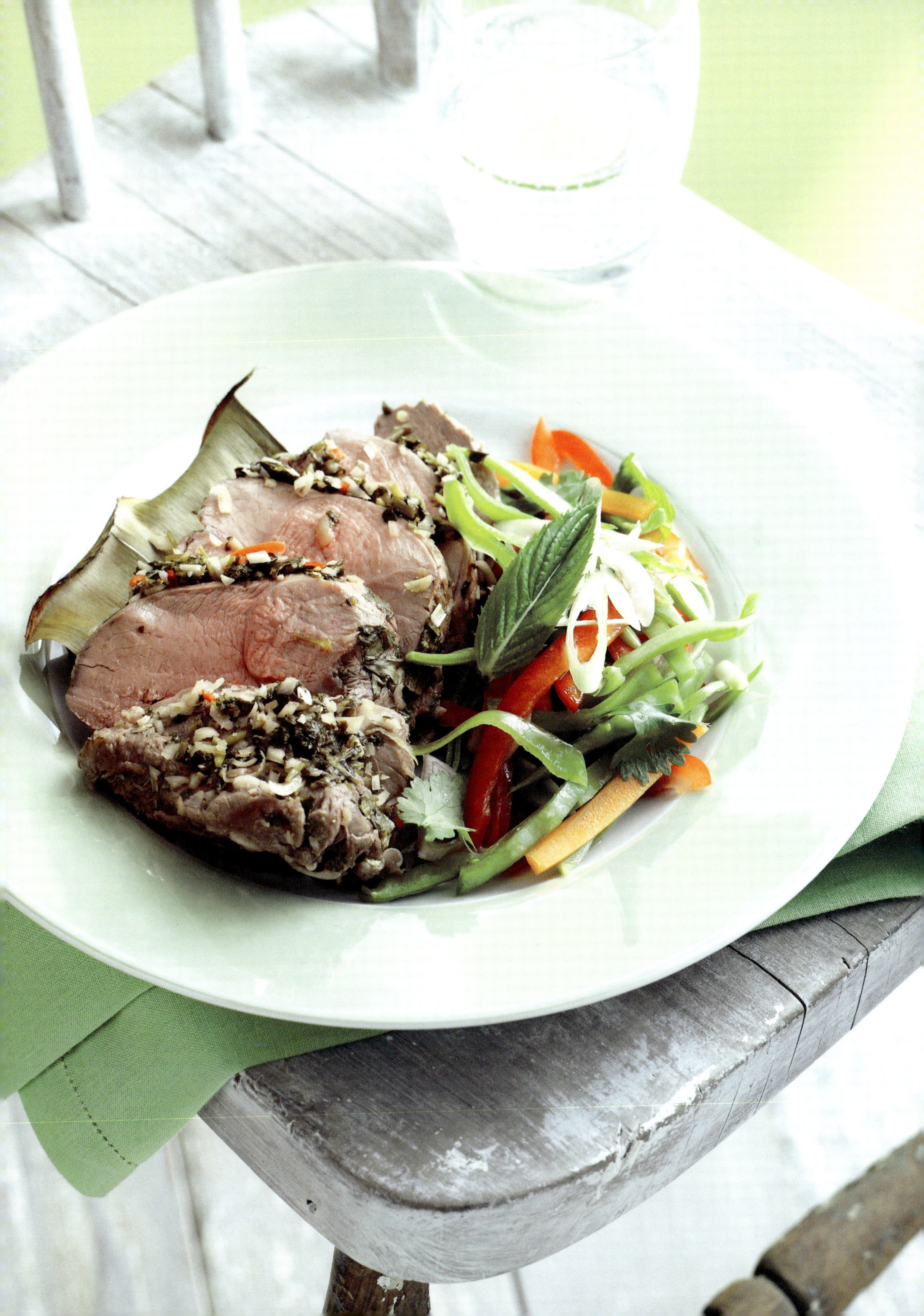

The Complete Book of Modern Asian

crisp-skinned thai chilli snapper

preparation time 15 minutes (plus refrigeration time)
cooking time 45 minutes   serves 6

1 whole snapper (1.2 kg)
4 cloves garlic, crushed
¼ cup chopped fresh lemon grass
¼ cup chopped fresh coriander
2 fresh small red thai chillies, chopped finely
2 tablespoons mild sweet chilli sauce
4cm piece fresh ginger (20g), grated finely
1 tablespoon thai red curry paste
2 tablespoons lime juice
2 tablespoons mild sweet chilli sauce, extra
½ cup firmly packed fresh coriander leaves, extra

1 Make four deep slits diagonally across both sides of fish; place fish in shallow non-metallic ovenproof dish.
2 Combine garlic, lemon grass, chopped coriander, chilli, chilli sauce, ginger, paste and juice in medium bowl. Pour over fish; cover, refrigerate 3 hours or overnight.
3 Preheat oven to 180°C/160°C fan-forced.
4 Cover dish with foil; bake about 35 minutes or until fish is almost tender.
5 Brush fish with extra chilli sauce then grill about 10 minutes or until skin is browned and crisp. Serve topped with coriander leaves.

per serving 2.9g total fat (0.7g saturated fat); 451kJ (108 cal); 3.5g carbohydrate; 16.1g protein; 1.6g fibre

soy duck breast with noodles

preparation time 30 minutes (plus refrigeration time)
cooking time 15 minutes   serves 6

6 duck breast fillets (950g)
½ cup (125ml) chinese rice wine
½ cup (125ml) light soy sauce
5cm piece fresh ginger (25g), grated
3 cloves garlic, crushed
1 tablespoon white sugar
2 fresh long red chillies, chopped
600g gai lan, chopped
450g thin fresh hokkien noodles

1 Score skin of duck breasts through to flesh.
2 Place duck in large bowl with combined wine, sauce, ginger, garlic, sugar and chilli. Cover; refrigerate 1 hour. Drain duck from marinade; reserve marinade.
3 Preheat oven to 240°C/220°C fan-forced.
4 Place duck breasts, skin-side up, on wire rack over shallow baking tray; roast about 15 minutes or until skin is crisp and duck is cooked as desired.
5 Meanwhile, boil, steam or microwave gai lan until just tender; drain.
6 Place reserved marinade in saucepan; bring to a boil. Reduce heat; simmer, uncovered, 1 minute.
7 Place noodles in heatproof bowl, cover with boiling water. Separate noodles with fork; drain.
8 Serve duck on noodles and gai lan; drizzle with hot marinade.

per serving 13.5g total fat (4.8g saturated fat); 1693kJ (405 cal); 23.4g carbohydrate; 39g protein; 6.3g fibre

calamari teppanyaki

preparation time 20 minutes
cooking time 10 minutes serves 4

1½ cups (300g) white medium-grain rice
3 cups (750ml) water
1 tablespoon peanut oil
1 fresh small red thai chilli, chopped finely
1 teaspoon finely grated lemon rind
1 clove garlic, crushed
1kg calamari rings
2 tablespoons drained pickled pink ginger, sliced thinly
6 green onions, sliced thickly
2 lebanese cucumbers (260g), seeded, chopped finely
3 fresh small red thai chillies, chopped finely, extra

LEMON SOY DIPPING SAUCE
¼ cup (60ml) rice vinegar
1 tablespoon sugar
1 tablespoon japanese soy sauce
1 teaspoon finely grated lemon rind

1 Make lemon soy dipping sauce.
2 Combine rice and the water in medium heavy-based saucepan, cover; bring to a boil, stirring occasionally. Reduce heat, simmer, covered tightly, about 10 minutes or until rice is cooked as desired. Remove from heat; stand, covered, 5 minutes.
3 Meanwhile, combine oil, chilli, rind and garlic in large bowl, add calamari; toss calamari to coat in mixture. Cook calamari on heated oiled flat plate (or grill or barbecue) until tender.
4 Divide rice and calamari among serving plates with ginger, onion, cucumber and extra chilli; serve with bowls of dipping sauce.

LEMON SOY DIPPING SAUCE
Stir vinegar, sugar and sauce in small saucepan over heat until sugar dissolves. Remove from heat; stir in rind.

per serving 8.1g total fat (1.9g saturated fat); 2240kJ (536 cal); 65.9g carbohydrate; 47.6g protein; 2g fibre

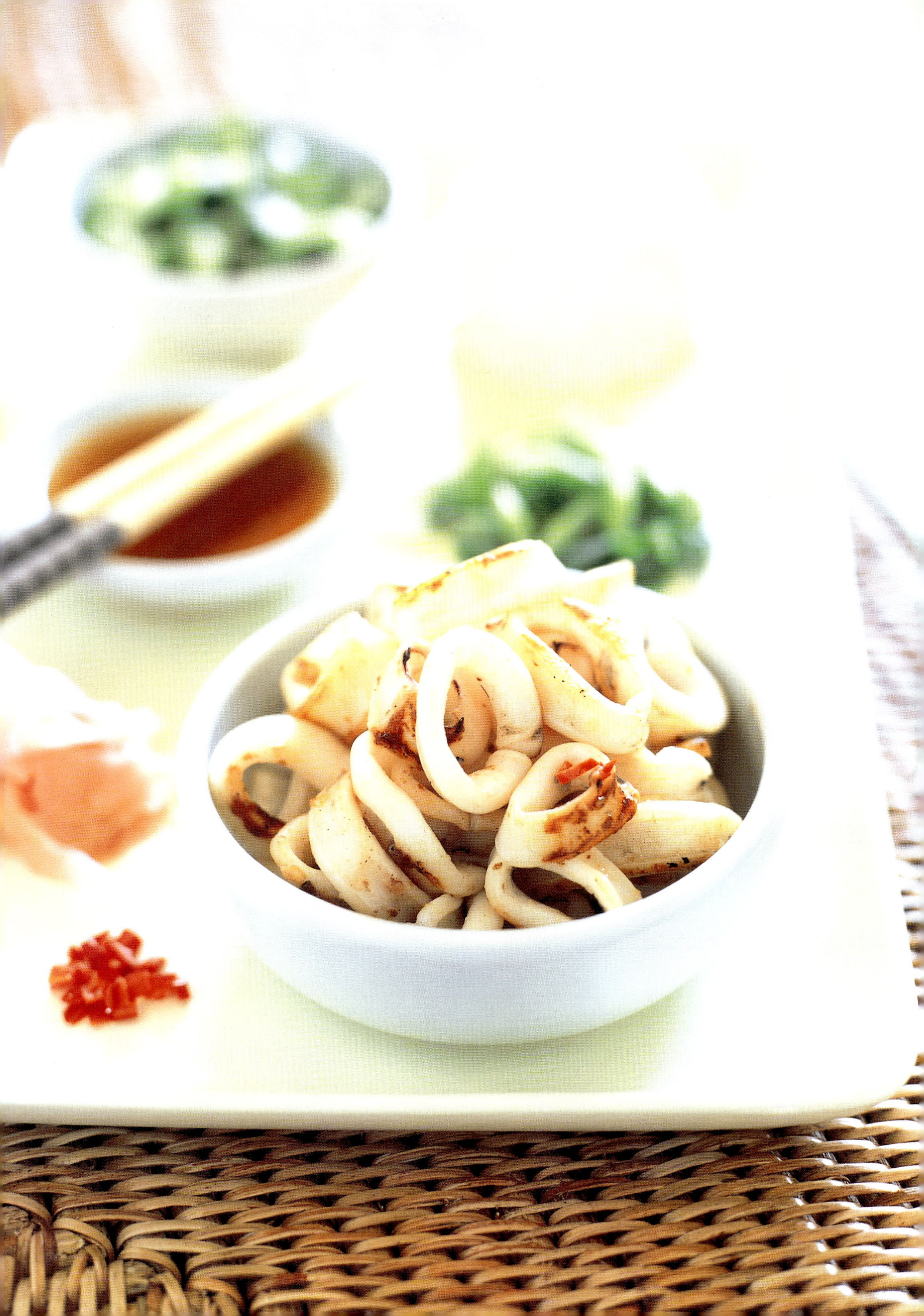

The Complete Book of Modern Asian

caramelised chicken cutlets

preparation time 20 minutes
cooking time 35 minutes serves 4

2 teaspoons vegetable oil
4 chicken thigh cutlets (800g), skin on
1 medium red onion (170g), sliced thinly
3 cloves garlic, sliced thinly
¼ cup (55g) brown sugar
1 tablespoon dark soy sauce
1 tablespoon fish sauce
⅓ cup coarsely chopped fresh coriander

1   Preheat oven to 200°C/180°C fan-forced.
2   Heat oil in large frying pan; cook chicken, both sides, until browned. Place chicken, in single layer, in baking dish. Roast chicken, uncovered, in oven, 25 minutes or until cooked through.
3   Meanwhile, heat same frying pan; cook onion and garlic, stirring, until onion softens. Add sugar and sauces; cook, stirring, 3 minutes. Return chicken to pan with coriander; turn chicken to coat in mixture.
per serving 22.4g total fat (6.9g saturated fat); 1538kJ (368 cal); 16.3g carbohydrate; 24.8g protein; 1g fibre

asian-spiced roasted pork belly

preparation time 10 minutes (plus refrigeration time)
cooking time 1 hour 25 minutes serves 6

1kg pork belly, skin on, boned
½ cup (125ml) chinese cooking wine
¼ cup (60ml) dark soy sauce
1 tablespoon tamarind concentrate
2 tablespoons honey
½ teaspoon sesame oil
4cm piece fresh ginger (20g), chopped finely
3 cloves garlic, crushed
2 teaspoons five-spice powder
1 star anise
1 dried long red chilli
1 teaspoon sichuan pepper
3 cups (750ml) water
900g baby buk choy, halved lengthways

1   Place pork in large saucepan of boiling water; return to a boil. Reduce heat, simmer, uncovered, about 40 minutes or until pork is cooked through; drain.
2   Meanwhile, combine wine, soy, tamarind, honey, oil, ginger, garlic, five-spice, star anise, chilli, pepper and the water in large bowl. Add pork, cover; refrigerate 3 hours or overnight.
3   Preheat oven to 220°C/200°C fan-forced.
4   Place pork, skin-side up, on wire rack in large shallow baking dish; reserve marinade. Pour enough water into baking dish to come halfway up side of dish. Roast pork, uncovered, about 30 minutes or until browned.
5   Meanwhile, strain marinade into small saucepan; bring to a boil. Boil, uncovered, about 20 minutes or until sauce reduces to about 1 cup. Boil, steam or microwave buk choy until just tender; drain.
6   Serve pork with sauce and buk choy and, if desired, steamed jasmine rice.
per serving 37.9g total fat (12.7g saturated fat); 2199kJ (526 cal); 10.5g carbohydrate; 32.6g protein; 2.4g fibre

asian star

chinese barbecued spareribs

preparation time 15 minutes (plus refrigeration time)
cooking time 1 hour   serves 4

Ask your butcher to cut pork spareribs "american-style" for this recipe. These will be slabs of 8 to 10 ribs, cut from the mid-loin, with almost all of the fat removed.

¾ cup (180ml) barbecue sauce
2 tablespoons dark soy sauce
1 tablespoon honey
¼ cup (60ml) orange juice
2 tablespoons brown sugar
1 clove garlic, crushed
2cm piece fresh ginger (10g), grated
2kg slabs american-style pork spareribs

1 Combine sauces, honey, juice, sugar, garlic and ginger in large shallow dish; add ribs, turn to coat in marinade. Cover; refrigerate 3 hours or overnight.
2 Preheat oven to 180°C/160°C fan-forced.
3 Brush ribs both sides with marinade; place, in single layer, in large shallow baking dish. Roast, covered, 45 minutes. Uncover; roast about 15 minutes or until ribs are browned. Serve with fried rice, if desired.
per serving 26.4g total fat (10.2g saturated fat); 2675kJ (640 cal); 35.2g carbohydrate; 64.7g protein; 0.8g fibre

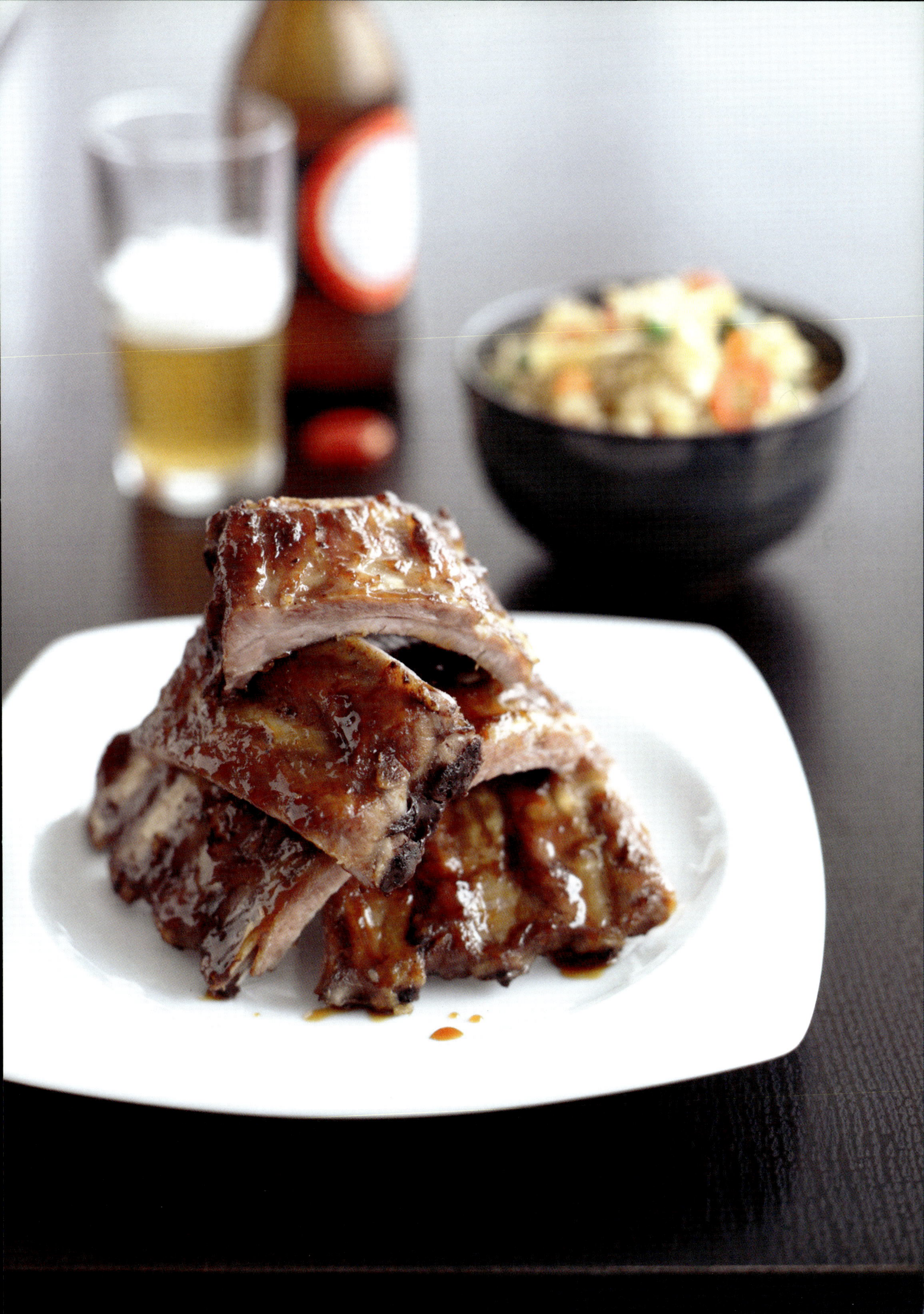

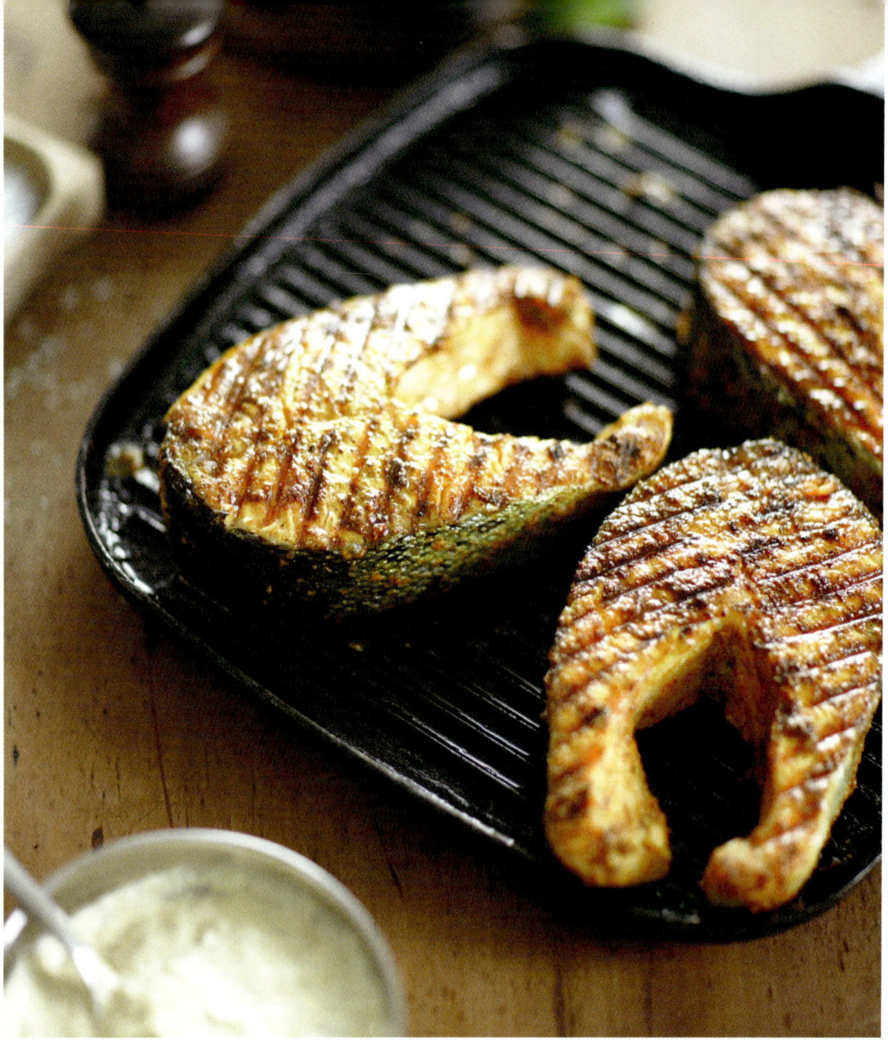

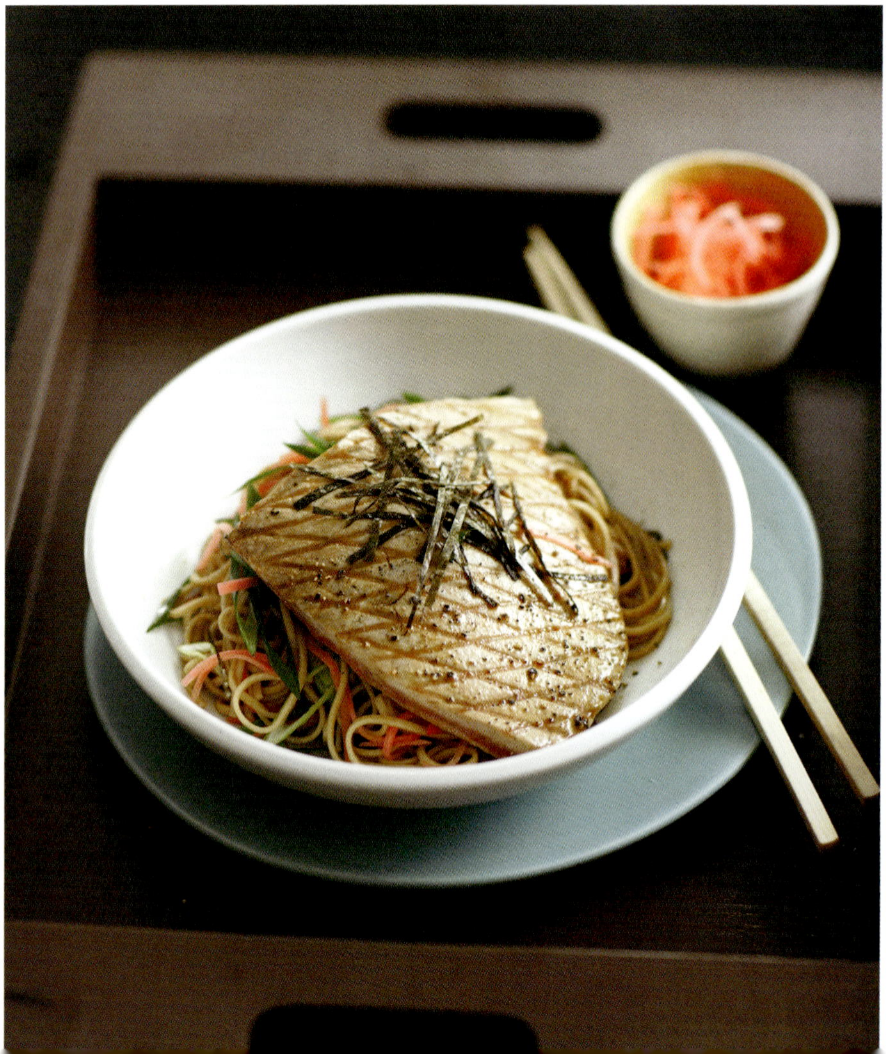

seared salmon kerala-style with lime pickle yogurt

preparation time 20 minutes (plus refrigeration time)
cooking time 15 minutes serves 4

2 teaspoons coriander seeds
1 teaspoon cumin seeds
2 cardamom pods, bruised
1 cinnamon stick
1 teaspoon ground turmeric
½ teaspoon chilli powder
2 tablespoons peanut oil
2 cloves garlic, crushed
4 x 265g salmon cutlets
100g baby spinach leaves

LIME PICKLE YOGURT
½ cup (140g) yogurt
2 tablespoons lime pickle, chopped finely

1 Dry-fry coriander, cumin, cardamom and cinnamon in small heated frying pan, stirring, over medium heat until fragrant. Stir in turmeric and chilli powder; remove from heat.
2 Crush spices, using mortar and pestle, until ground finely; transfer to large bowl. Stir in oil and garlic, add fish; turn fish to coat in marinade. Cover; refrigerate 30 minutes.
3 Meanwhile, combine ingredients for lime pickle yogurt in small bowl.
4 Cook fish on heated oiled grill plate (or grill or barbecue). Serve fish with spinach leaves and yogurt.
per serving 29.3g total fat (6.7g saturated fat); 2082kJ (498 cal); 3.9g carbohydrate; 54.1g protein; 1.1g fibre

grilled tuna with japanese chilled soba salad

preparation time 20 minutes (plus refrigeration time)
cooking time 10 minutes serves 4

250g soba noodles
¼ cup (70g) pickled pink ginger, sliced thinly
4 green onions, sliced thinly
4 x 175g tuna steaks
1 sheet toasted nori, shredded

SOY MIRIN DRESSING
¼ cup (60ml) light soy sauce
⅓ cup (80ml) mirin
1 tablespoon rice vinegar
2 tablespoons cooking sake
1 teaspoon sesame oil
1 teaspoon wasabi paste

1 Cook noodles in large saucepan of boiling water, uncovered, until tender; drain. Rinse under cold water, drain thoroughly.
2 Place ingredients for soy mirin dressing in screw-top jar; shake well.
3 Combine cold noodles, ginger and onion in large bowl, add three-quarters of the dressing; mix gently. Cover; refrigerate until chilled.
4 Cook tuna on heated oiled grill plate (or grill or barbecue) until just cooked (do not overcook or tuna will dry out).
5 Serve tuna drizzled with remaining dressing, topped with nori. Serve with soba salad.
per serving 11.9g total fat (4.3g saturated fat); 2207kJ (528 cal); 45.1g carbohydrate; 52.1g protein; 2.8g fibre

sri lankan spicy ribs with coconut pilaf

preparation time 20 minutes (plus marinating time)
cooking time 45 minutes serves 4

1.6kg american-style beef spareribs
¼ cup (60ml) peanut oil
¼ cup (60ml) white vinegar
1 teaspoon sambal oelek
1 teaspoon ground turmeric
4 cloves
½ teaspoon ground cardamom
3 cloves garlic, crushed
2cm piece fresh ginger (10g), grated
1 small brown onion (80g), chopped finely

COCONUT PILAF
40g butter
1 medium brown onion (150g), chopped coarsely
1 medium carrot (120g), chopped coarsely
2 cups (400g) basmati rice, washed, drained
1 litre (4 cups) chicken stock
¼ cup firmly packed fresh coriander leaves
¼ cup (10g) flaked coconut
¼ cup (40g) raisins

1 Using kitchen scissors, separate ribs into sections; place in large bowl with combined oil, vinegar, sambal, turmeric, cloves, cardamom, garlic, ginger and onion. Toss ribs to coat all over in marinade. Cover; refrigerate 3 hours or overnight.
2 Preheat oven to 220°C/200°C fan-forced.
3 Drain ribs; reserve marinade. Place ribs on wire rack over large shallow baking dish. Roast ribs, brushing frequently with reserved marinade, about 40 minutes or until browned and cooked through, turning once halfway through cooking time.
4 Meanwhile, make coconut pilaf.
5 Serve ribs on coconut pilaf.

COCONUT PILAF
Heat butter in medium saucepan; cook onion and carrot, stirring, until onion softens. Add rice; cook, stirring, 1 minute. Add stock; bring to a boil. Reduce heat; simmer, covered, about 20 minutes or until rice is just tender. Remove from heat; fluff rice with fork. Stir in coriander, coconut and raisins, cover; stand 5 minutes before serving.

per serving 30.2g total fat (11.9g saturated fat); 3240kJ (775 cal); 92.4g carbohydrate; 31.1g protein; 3.7g fibre

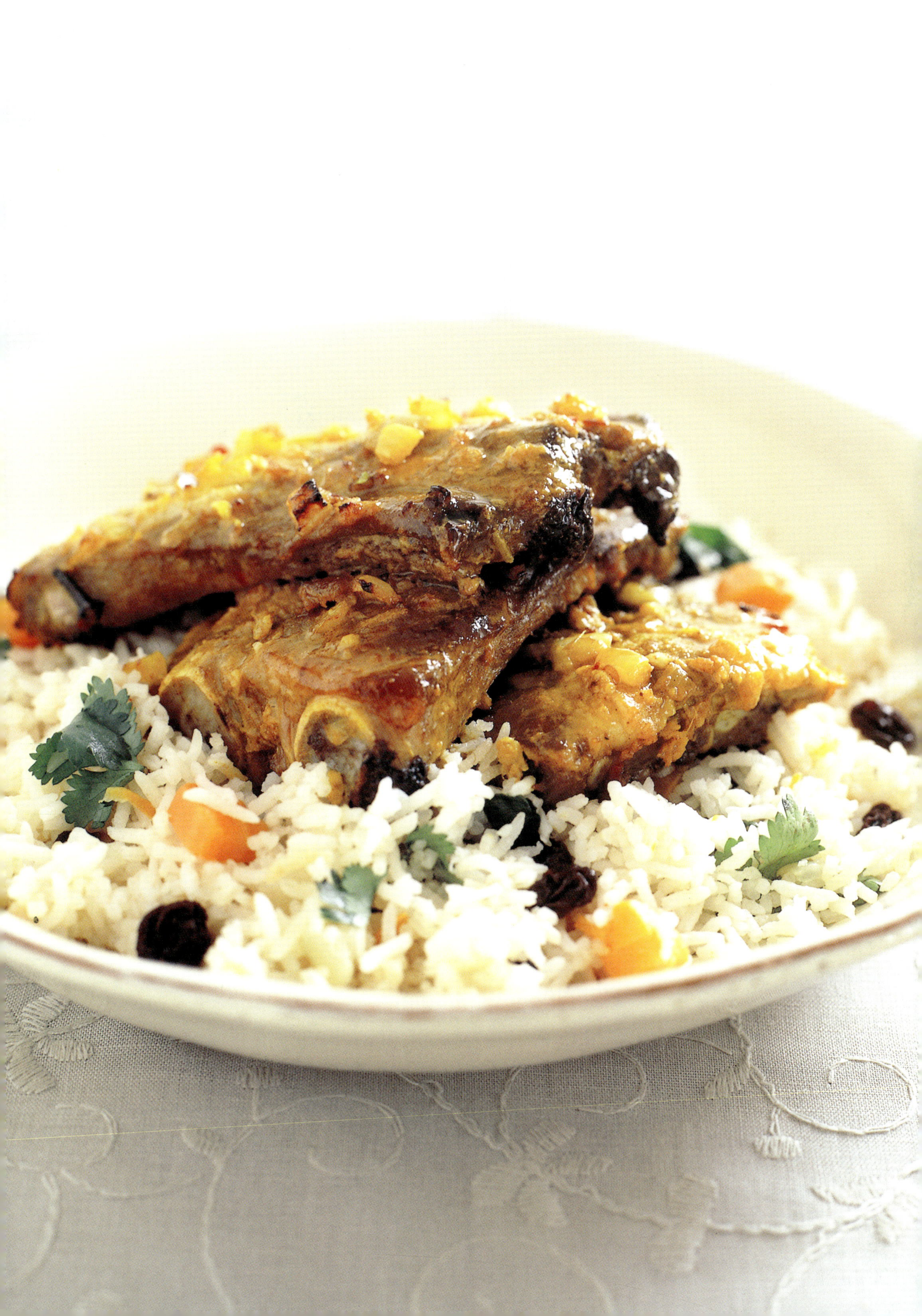

The Complete Book of Modern Asian

kaffir lime and lemon grass grilled trout

preparation time 20 minutes
cooking time 45 minutes serves 6

10cm stick fresh lemon grass (20g), chopped coarsely
4cm piece fresh ginger (20g), sliced thickly
2 cloves garlic, quartered
2 tablespoons peanut oil
1 tablespoon sweet chilli sauce
1 tablespoon lime juice
2 green onions, chopped finely
1 whole ocean trout (2.4kg)
1 lime, peeled, sliced thinly
10cm stick fresh lemon grass (20g), sliced diagonally
1 fresh kaffir lime leaf, shredded thinly
⅓ cup loosely packed fresh coriander leaves
1 lime, cut into wedges

1 Blend or process chopped lemon grass, ginger, garlic, oil, sauce and juice until smooth. Stir in onion.
2 Place long piece of baking paper on bench; place fish on paper. Fill cavity with lemon grass mixture.
3 Score fish three times both sides through thickest part of flesh, seal cuts with lime slices; sprinkle fish with sliced lemon grass and lime leaf. Fold paper over fish to completely enclose, then wrap fish tightly in foil.
4 Cook fish on heated oiled grill plate (or grill or barbecue) 25 minutes; turn, cook about 20 minutes or until cooked through.
5 Serve fish sprinkled with coriander; serve with lime wedges.

per serving 14.3g total fat (3g saturated fat); 1262kJ (302 cal); 1.2g carbohydrate; 41.4g protein; 0.7g fibre

beef teriyaki platter

preparation time 20 minutes
cooking time 10 minutes serves 4

3 x 200g sirloin steaks, trimmed
⅓ cup (80ml) teriyaki sauce
3cm piece fresh ginger (15g), grated finely
1 clove garlic, crushed
500g thick asparagus, trimmed
8 thick green onions, trimmed
1 teaspoon wasabi paste
¼ cup (60ml) japanese soy sauce

1 Combine steaks, teriyaki sauce, ginger and garlic in large bowl. Cover; refrigerate 3 hours or overnight.
2 Drain steaks; cook on heated oiled grill plate (or grill or barbecue) until cooked as desired. Transfer steaks to a warm plate; cover, stand 5 minutes.
3 Meanwhile, cook asparagus and onions on heated oiled grill plate (or grill or barbecue) until just tender.
4 Slice steaks thinly; place on warmed serving platter with asparagus and green onions. Serve with wasabi, soy sauce and steamed rice, if desired.

per serving 13.8g total fat (6.2g saturated fat); 1183kJ (283 cal); 3.2g carbohydrate; 35.4g protein; 1.9g fibre

tandoori lamb with dhal and pickled lemon

preparation time 1 hour (plus refrigeration time)
cooking time 2 hours serves 6

2 x 700g butterflied lamb shoulders
2 large eggplants (1kg), cut lengthways into eight wedges
2 large pieces naan

TANDOORI PASTE
2 teaspoons cumin seeds
2 teaspoons coriander seeds
1 teaspoon cardamom seeds
2 teaspoons garam masala
1 teaspoon salt
1 teaspoon cracked black pepper
3 cloves garlic, crushed
2cm piece fresh ginger (10g), chopped coarsely
1 fresh long red chilli, quartered
3 green onions, chopped coarsely
¼ cup (60ml) lemon juice
½ cup firmly packed fresh coriander leaves
1 cup (280g) yogurt

DHAL
20g butter
3 cloves garlic, crushed
1 large brown onion (200g), chopped finely
1 teaspoon ground cumin
1 teaspoon garam masala
4 curry leaves
1 cup (200g) yellow split peas
3 cups (750ml) water

PICKLED LEMON
1 tablespoon vegetable oil
2 teaspoons yellow mustard seeds
4 curry leaves
¼ cup (60ml) white wine vinegar
2 medium lemons (280g), chopped coarsely

1 Make tandoori paste; reserve 2 tablespoons in small bowl. Combine lamb with remaining paste in large bowl. Cover; refrigerate 1 hour.
2 Meanwhile, make dhal. Make pickled lemon.
3 Cook lamb on heated oiled grill plate (or grill or barbecue) about 20 minutes or until browned all over. Cover, cook a further 30 minutes or until cooked as desired. Cover lamb; stand 15 minutes then slice thickly.
4 Cook eggplant on same heated oiled grill plate (or grill or barbecue), brushing with reserved tandoori paste, about 10 minutes or until eggplant is tender. Cover; stand 10 minutes.
5 Toast naan both sides on heated oiled grill.
6 Serve lamb with eggplant, dhal, pickled lemon, naan and if desired, cucumber raita (see page 397).

TANDOORI PASTE
Dry-fry seeds in heated medium frying pan, stirring, until fragrant. Blend or process seeds with remaining ingredients until smooth.

DHAL
Heat butter in medium saucepan; cook garlic and onion, stirring, until onion softens. Add spices; cook, stirring, until fragrant. Add curry leaves, split peas and the water; bring to a boil. Reduce heat, simmer, uncovered, about 45 minutes or until split peas are tender.

PICKLED LEMON
Heat oil in medium frying pan; fry seeds, stirring, until they begin to pop. Add curry leaves, vinegar and lemon; cook until heated through. Drain; discard any excess liquid.

per serving 59.2g total fat (24.1g saturated fat); 5359kJ (1282 cal); 99.7g carbohydrate; 81.6g protein; 11.4g fibre

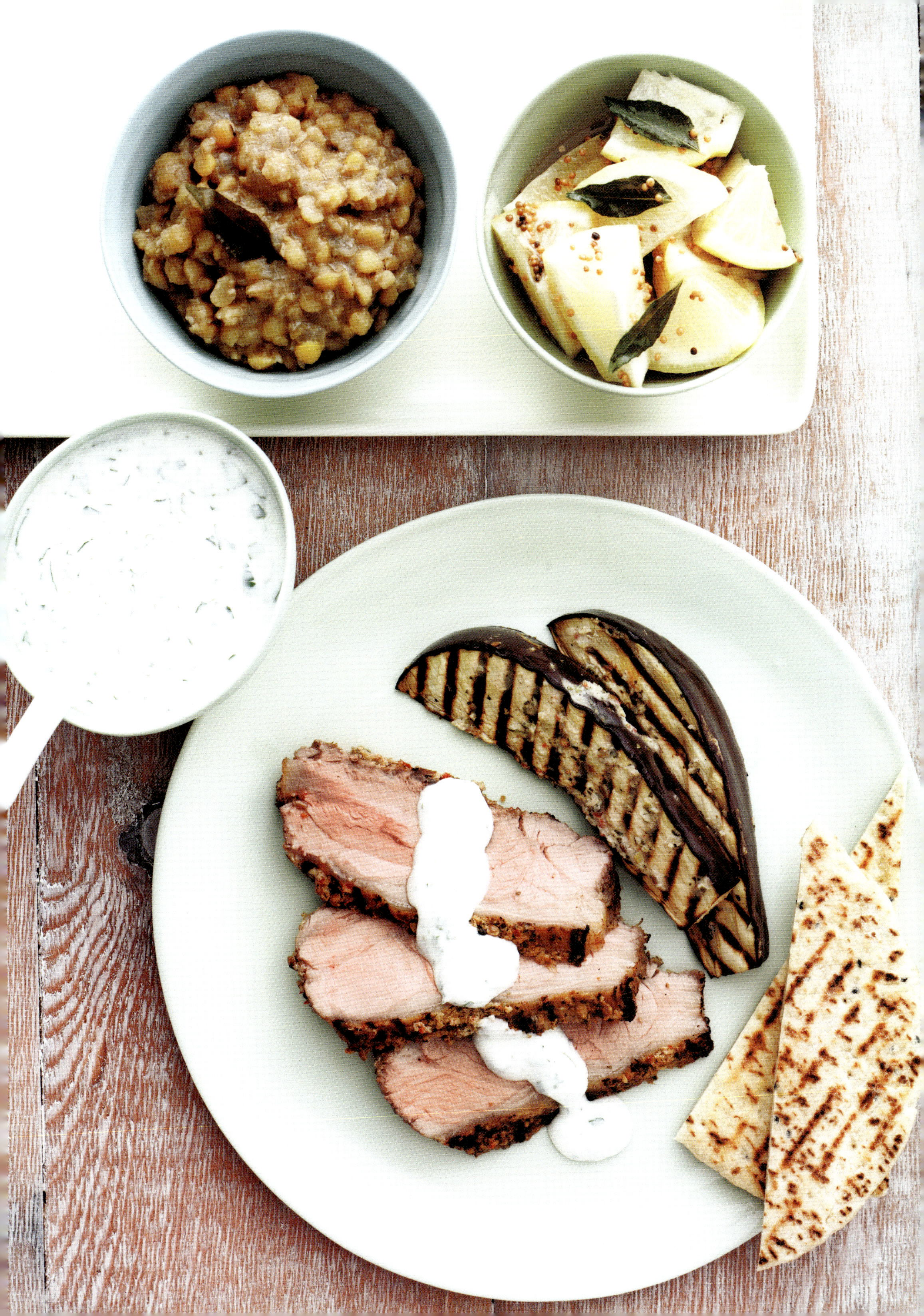

The Complete Book of Modern Asian

barbecued pork neck with five-spice star-anise glaze

preparation time 15 minutes (plus standing time)
cooking time 1 hour 20 minutes serves 6

1kg piece pork neck
1 clove garlic, sliced thinly
4cm piece ginger (20g), sliced thinly
2 x 100g packets baby asian greens

FIVE-SPICE STAR-ANISE GLAZE
1¼ cups (310ml) water
1 cup (220g) firmly packed brown sugar
3 fresh long red chillies, chopped finely
1 star anise
1 teaspoon five-spice powder
⅓ cup (80ml) light soy sauce
¼ cup (60ml) rice vinegar

1 Make five-spice star-anise glaze. Reserve 1 cup (250ml) of the glaze.
2 Make several shallow cuts in pork. Press garlic and ginger into cuts; brush ¼ cup (60ml) of the remaining glaze over pork.
3 Cook pork on heated oiled flat plate (or grill or barbecue), covered, over low heat, 30 minutes. Turn pork; cook, covered, 30 minutes. Increase heat to high; cook, uncovered, 5 minutes, turning and brushing with remaining glaze constantly. Remove pork from heat. Cover; stand 15 minutes, slice thickly.
4 Meanwhile, place reserved glaze in small saucepan; simmer about 5 minutes or until thickened slightly. Cool.
5 Combine greens with glaze in medium bowl; serve with pork.
FIVE-SPICE STAR-ANISE GLAZE
Combine the water and sugar in medium saucepan; simmer about 10 minutes or until glaze thickens slightly. Remove from heat; stir in remaining ingredients.
per serving 13.4g total fat (4.5g saturated fat); 1714kJ (410 cal); 36.4g carbohydrate; 36.5g protein; 0.6g fibre

indian spiced chicken with roasted eggplant

preparation time 25 minutes
cooking time 1 hour 20 minutes serves 6

1½ teaspoons coriander seeds
¾ teaspoon cumin seeds
1 teaspoon black peppercorns
1½ teaspoons sea salt flakes
½ teaspoon ground cinnamon
¾ teaspoon chilli powder
1 tablespoon plain flour
1 tablespoon olive oil
2kg whole chicken
1 lemon, halved
1 cup (250ml) chicken stock
2 large eggplants (1kg), halved, scored deeply
⅓ cup coarsely chopped fresh flat-leaf parsley

1 Preheat oven to 180°C/160°C fan-forced.
2 Using a mortar and pestle, crush coriander, cumin, peppercorns and salt until finely ground. Transfer to a small bowl, add cinnamon, chilli powder, flour and oil. Rub spice mixture evenly over chicken.
3 Squeeze lemon; reserve 1 tablespoon of the juice. Stuff lemon halves into cavity of chicken. Tie legs of chicken together; tuck wings under body. Place chicken on large rack in baking dish. Add stock to dish; cover tightly with foil. Bake 20 minutes.
4 Add eggplants, cut-side down, to same baking dish. Bake, uncovered, a further 1 hour.
5 Transfer chicken to serving dish; cover to keep warm. Carefully scoop eggplant flesh into a medium bowl. Add reserved lemon juice, parsley and salt and pepper to taste; stir well to combine.
6 Serve chicken with the warm eggplant mixture and extra lemon, if desired.
per serving 30.2g total fat (0.5g saturated fat); 1881kJ (450 cal); 6.2g carbohydrate; 36.8g protein; 4.4g fibre

thick roasted eggplant with spiced rice

preparation time 10 minutes
cooking time 30 minutes serves 4

3 medium eggplants (900g)
¼ cup (60ml) extra virgin olive oil
2 cloves garlic, sliced thinly
extra virgin olive oil, extra
1 tablespoon finely chopped fresh flat-leaf parsley
1 tablespoon finely chopped fresh mint

SPICED RICE
30g butter
1 medium brown onion (150g), chopped finely
1 clove garlic, crushed
3 cardamom pods, bruised
½ cinnamon stick
2 cups (400g) basmati rice
2 cups (500ml) vegetable stock
¼ cup (40g) toasted pine nuts, chopped coarsely

1 Preheat the oven to 220°C/200°C fan-forced.
2 Cut eggplants into 3cm slices crossways. Heat one-third of the oil in large heated frying pan; cook one-third of the eggplant until browned both sides. Transfer to large, shallow baking dish. Repeat with remaining oil and eggplant slices.
3 Sprinkle eggplant with garlic; bake about 20 minutes or until eggplant is tender.
4 Meanwhile, make spiced rice.
5 Drizzle eggplant with extra oil; top with parsley and mint. Serve with spiced rice.

SPICED RICE
Melt butter in medium saucepan; cook onion, garlic, cardamom and cinnamon, stirring, until onion softens. Add rice, stir to coat in butter mixture. Stir in stock; bring to a boil. Reduce heat, simmer, covered, about 15 minutes or until stock is absorbed. Remove from heat; stand, covered, 5 minutes. Stir in pine nuts.

per serving 37.7g total fat (8.1g saturated fat); 3164kJ (757 cal); 88.6g carbohydrate; 12.5g protein; 7.5g fibre

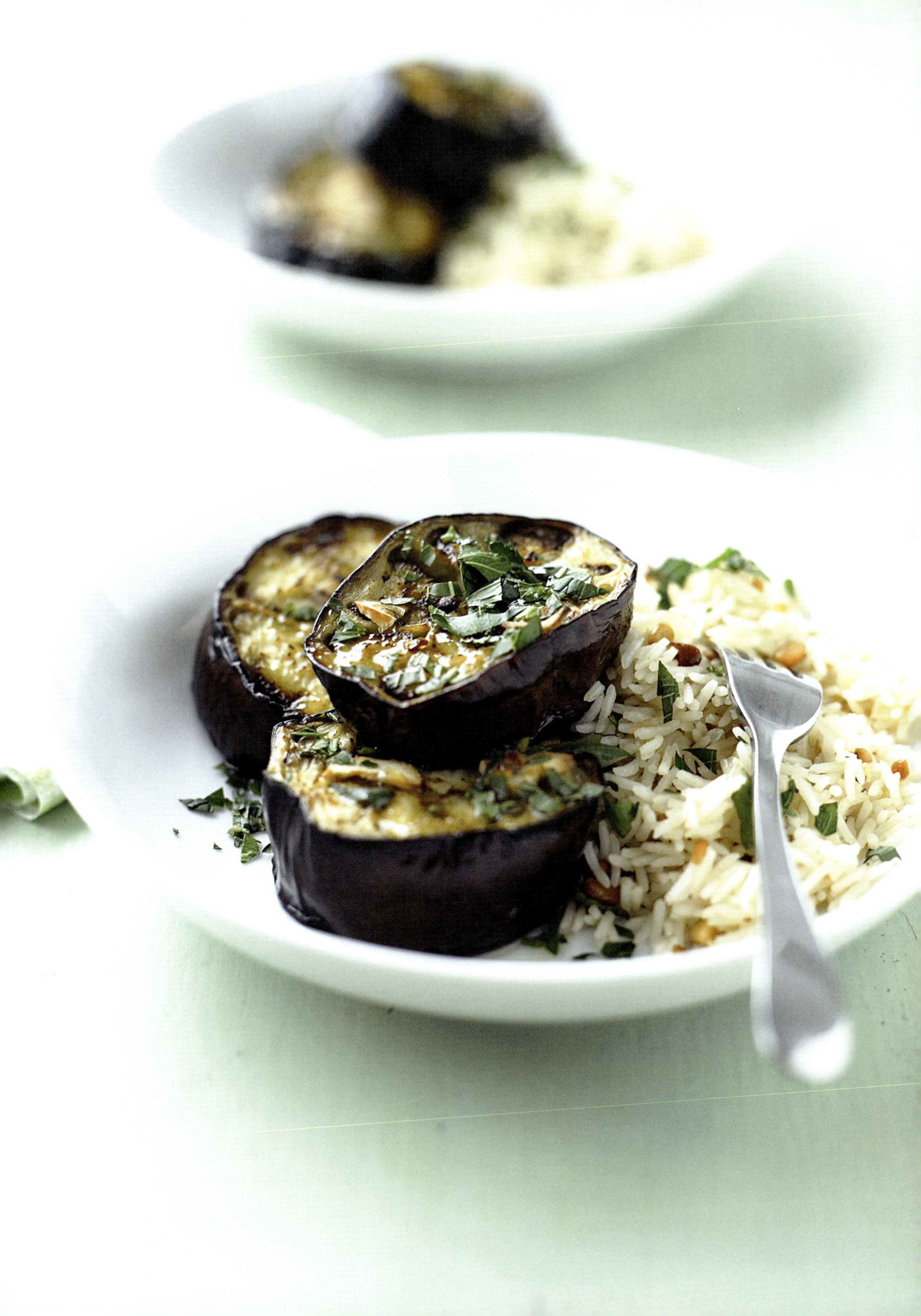

The Complete Book of Modern Asian

chicken tikka with cucumber-mint raita

preparation time 15 minutes
cooking time 10 minutes serves 4

1kg chicken breast fillets, trimmed
½ cup (150g) tikka paste
2 tablespoons yogurt
1 tablespoon lemon juice

CUCUMBER-MINT RAITA
¾ cup (200g) yogurt
1 lebanese cucumber (130g), peeled, seeded, chopped finely
2 tablespoons finely chopped fresh mint
1 teaspoon ground cumin

1 Combine chicken, paste, yogurt and juice in large bowl.
2 Cook chicken, in batches, on heated oiled grill plate (or grill or barbecue) until cooked through.
3 Meanwhile, combine ingredients for cucumber-mint raita in small bowl.
4 Serve chicken with raita.

per serving 27.6g total fat (6.8g saturated fat); 2161kJ (517 cal); 6.6g carbohydrate; 58.6g protein; 4.4g fibre

sichuan duck with watercress and snow pea salad

preparation time 20 minutes (plus refrigeration time)
cooking time 40 minutes serves 4

½ cup (125ml) chinese cooking wine
2 tablespoons light soy sauce
2 cloves garlic, crushed
4cm piece fresh ginger (20g), sliced thinly
1 teaspoon sesame oil
4 duck marylands (1.2kg)
2 teaspoons sichuan peppercorns
1 teaspoon sea salt
100g watercress, trimmed
150g snow peas, trimmed, sliced thinly
1 small red onion (100g), sliced thinly
½ cup loosely packed fresh coriander leaves
½ cup (70g) roasted unsalted peanuts, chopped coarsely
2 tablespoons lime juice
1 tablespoon peanut oil
1 clove garlic, crushed, extra

1 Combine wine, sauce, garlic, ginger and sesame oil in large bowl with duck. Cover; refrigerate 3 hours or overnight.
2 Drain duck; discard marinade. Dry-fry peppercorns in small frying pan until fragrant. Crush peppercorns and salt using mortar and pestle; press mixture onto duck skin.
3 Cook duck on heated oiled flat plate (or grill or barbecue), turning midway through cooking time, about 40 minutes or until cooked.
4 Meanwhile, combine remaining ingredients in large bowl; serve with duck.

per serving 92.9g total fat (25.6g saturated fat); 4314kJ (1032 cal); 6.5g carbohydrate; 35.1g protein; 4.1g fibre

spiced spatchcock with herb yogurt

preparation time 20 minutes
cooking time 20 minutes serves 4

4 x 500g spatchcocks
2 teaspoons ground cumin
1 teaspoon ground coriander
½ teaspoon hot paprika
½ teaspoon ground turmeric
¼ teaspoon ground cinnamon
1 teaspoon salt
½ teaspoon cracked black pepper
2 tablespoons olive oil
HERB YOGURT
½ teaspoon ground cumin
¼ teaspoon hot paprika
2cm piece fresh ginger (10g), grated
1 clove garlic, crushed
¼ cup loosely packed chopped fresh coriander
¼ cup loosely packed chopped fresh flat-leaf parsley
⅔ cup (190g) greek-style yogurt

1 Place spatchcocks on a board, cut down both sides of backbones with poultry shears or sharp knife; remove backbones. Rinse cavity of spatchcocks; pat dry.
2 Combine spices, salt, pepper and oil in small bowl. Rub spice mixture over spatchcocks
3 Cook on heated oiled grill plate (or grill or barbecue), covered, 10 minutes. Uncover, cook a further 10 minutes or until cooked through.
4 Meanwhile make herb yogurt.
5 Serve spatchcocks with herb yogurt, lemon wedges and couscous, if desired.
HERB YOGURT
Cook cumin and paprika in small frying pan, stirring, about 1 minute or until fragrant. Transfer to a bowl, stir in ginger, garlic, herbs and yogurt.
per serving 52g total fat (15.8g saturated fat); 2893kJ (692 cal); 4.9g carbohydrate; 52g protein; 1g fibre

teriyaki pork with pineapple

preparation time 20 minutes (plus refrigeration time)
cooking time 20 minutes serves 4

⅓ cup (80ml) mirin
¼ cup (60ml) japanese soy sauce
2 tablespoons cooking sake
2 teaspoons white sugar
5cm piece fresh ginger (25g), grated
2 cloves garlic, crushed
600g pork fillets
1 small pineapple (900g), sliced thinly
2 green onions, sliced thinly

1 Combine mirin, sauce, sake, sugar, ginger, garlic and pork in large bowl. Cover; refrigerate 3 hours or overnight.
2 Drain pork; reserve marinade. Cook pork on heated oiled grill plate (or grill or barbecue) until browned and cooked as desired. Cover; stand 10 minutes.
3 Cook pineapple on same grill plate about 2 minutes or until soft.
4 Bring reserved marinade to a boil in small saucepan; cook about 5 minutes or until sauce reduces by half.
5 Serve sliced pork with pineapple and onion; drizzle with sauce.
per serving 12.2g total fat (4.1g saturated fat); 1371kJ (328 cal); 13.3g carbohydrate; 34.1g protein; 3.0g fibre

Barbecues, Grills & Roasts

Poaching and steaming are pure and wholesome techniques adored by Asian cooks because they permit the natural flavour, colour and texture of ingredients to stand proud. From steamed gow gees to a whole poached fish, there are many possibilities for cooking this way, each with the bonus of minimal nutrient loss and little need for added fat.

chinese-spiced chicken *page 291*

poached flathead with green nam jim *page 288*

steamed & poached

ocean trout in baby buk choy parcels *page 300*

poached pork with chilli stone fruits *page 291*

poached flathead with green nam jim

preparation time 30 minutes
cooking time 10 minutes serves 4

8 flathead fillets (1kg)
1 litre (4 cups) water
1 tablespoon fish sauce
1 tablespoon lime juice

NAM JIM
2 cloves garlic, quartered
3 long green chillies, chopped coarsely
2 coriander roots
2 tablespoons fish sauce
2 tablespoons grated palm sugar
3 shallots (75g), chopped coarsely
⅓ cup (80ml) lime juice
1 tablespoon peanut oil

MIXED HERB SALAD
1½ cups loosely packed fresh mint leaves
1 cup loosely packed fresh coriander leaves
1 cup loosely packed fresh basil leaves, torn
1 medium red onion (170g), sliced thinly
2 lebanese cucumbers (260g), seeded, sliced thinly

1 Blend or process ingredients for nam jim until smooth.
2 Halve each fillet lengthways. Combine the water, sauce and juice in large frying pan; bring to a boil. Add fish; reduce heat, simmer, uncovered, about 5 minutes or until cooked as desired. Remove fish from pan with slotted spoon; cover to keep warm.
3 Meanwhile, combine ingredients for mixed herb salad in a medium bowl with a third of the nam jim.
4 Serve fish on salad; top with remaining nam jim.
per serving 7.6g total fat (1.9g saturated fat); 1501kJ (359 cal); 13.4g carbohydrate; 56.6g protein; 4.1g fibre

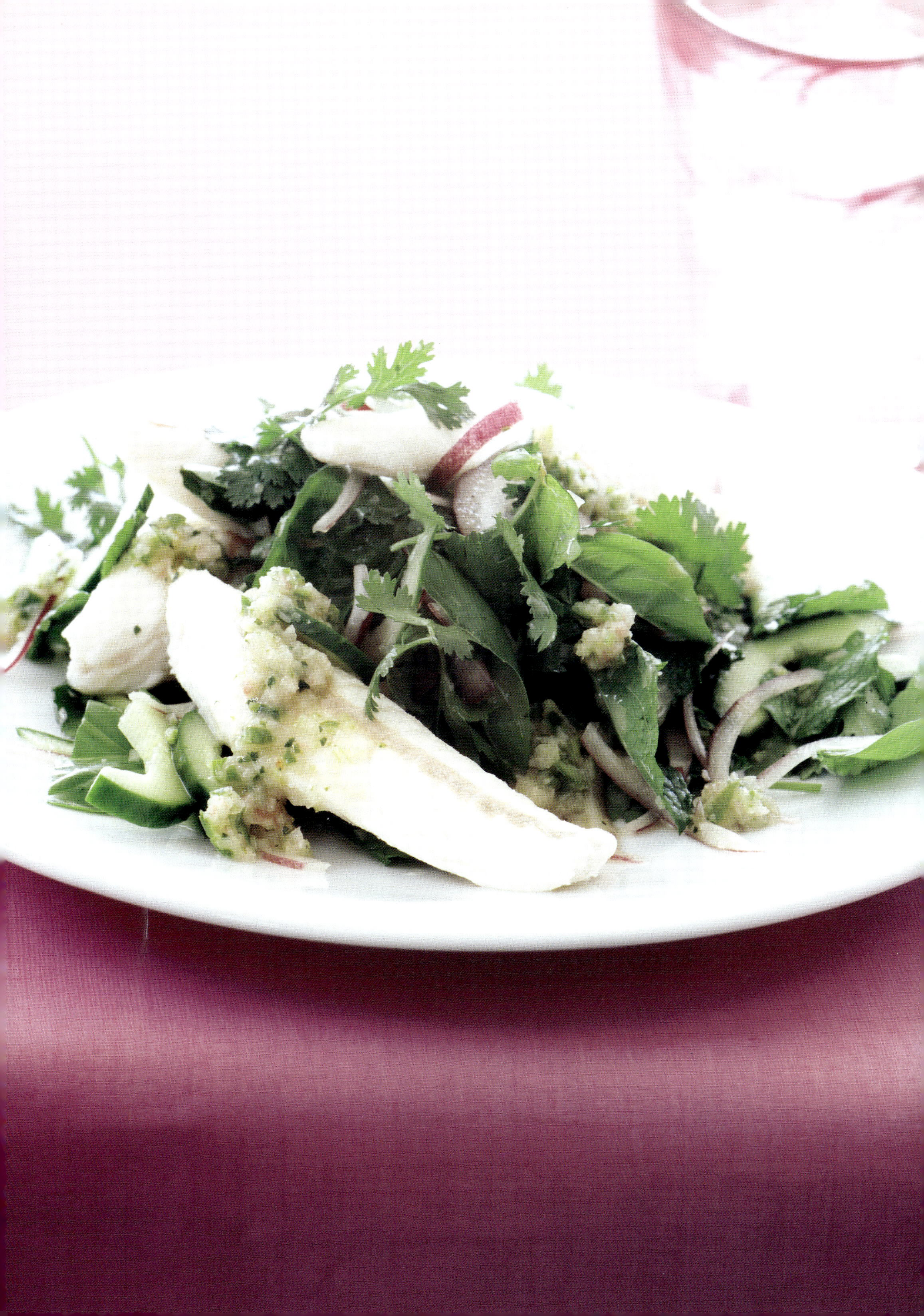

The Complete Book of Modern Asian

poached pork with chilli stone fruits

preparation time 15 minutes
cooking time 15 minutes serves 4

2 cups (500ml) water
1 cup (250ml) chinese cooking wine
½ cup (110g) sugar
2 cinnamon sticks
5 cloves
2 medium peaches (300g), stoned, quartered
4 medium plums (450g), stoned, quartered
2 medium nectarines (340g), stoned, quartered
4 medium apricots (200g), stoned, quartered
800g pork fillets, trimmed
1 fresh long red chilli, sliced thinly
1 long green chilli, sliced thinly

1 Stir the water, wine and sugar in large frying pan, constantly, without boiling, until sugar dissolves; bring to a boil. Add cinnamon, cloves and fruit; reduce heat, simmer, uncovered, about 5 minutes or until fruit is just tender. Using slotted spoon, transfer fruit to large bowl; cover to keep warm.
2 Return poaching liquid to a boil; add pork. Reduce heat, simmer, covered, about 10 minutes or until pork is cooked as desired. Cool pork in liquid 10 minutes then slice thickly. Discard poaching liquid.
3 Combine chillies with fruit; divide fruit and any fruit juices among serving bowls, top with pork.

per serving 4.9g total fat (1.6g saturated fat); 1885kJ (451 cal); 48.2g carbohydrate; 46.3g protein; 5.9g fibre

chinese-spiced chicken

preparation time 20 minutes
cooking time 20 minutes serves 4

1 tablespoon peanut oil
6 green onions, chopped finely
2cm piece fresh ginger (10g), grated
1 clove garlic, crushed
2 tablespoons soy sauce
2 tablespoons dry sherry
1 teaspoon toasted sesame seeds
700g chicken breast fillets
375g fresh thin egg noodles

BOUQUET GARNI
2 star anise
1 cinnamon stick, crushed
1 teaspoon fennel seeds
3 whole cloves

1 Heat oil in small saucepan; cook onion, ginger and garlic, stirring, 1 minute. Add soy sauce, sherry and seeds; simmer, stirring, 1 minute. Remove pan from heat; reserve.
2 Make bouquet garni. Place bouquet garni and chicken in large saucepan of boiling water; return to a boil. Reduce heat, simmer, stirring occasionally, about 10 minutes or until chicken is cooked through. Cool chicken in poaching liquid 10 minutes. Remove chicken from pan then slice thinly. Discard bouquet garni.
3 Return poaching liquid in pan to a boil; cook noodles, uncovered, until just tender. Drain noodles, reserving 2 tablespoons of the poaching liquid; stir liquid through noodles in large bowl. Divide noodles among serving bowls; top with chicken and onion mixture.
BOUQUET GARNI
Place ingredients in centre of 20cm muslin square; bring four corners together, tie together tightly with cotton kitchen string.

per serving 15.7g total fat (4g saturated fat); 2282kJ (546 cal); 49.7g carbohydrate; 47.2g protein; 2.4g fibre

white-cut chicken

preparation time 20 minutes (plus standing time)
cooking time 45 minutes serves 4

1.6kg whole chicken
2 litres (8 cups) water
¼ cup (60ml) light soy sauce
½ cup (125ml) dark soy sauce
1 cup (250ml) chinese cooking wine
½ cup (135g) coarsely chopped palm sugar
20cm piece fresh ginger (100g), sliced thinly
4 star anise
4 cloves garlic, sliced thinly
1 tablespoon sichuan peppercorns

SOY AND GREEN ONION DRESSING
¼ cup (60ml) dark soy sauce
¼ cup (60ml) rice vinegar
4 green onions, sliced thinly
2 teaspoons peanut oil
½ teaspoon sesame oil

1 Make soy and green onion dressing.
2 Place chicken, breast-side down with remaining ingredients in large saucepan; bring to a boil. Reduce heat; simmer, uncovered, 25 minutes. Turn chicken breast-side up; simmer, uncovered, 5 minutes. Remove pan from heat; turn chicken breast-side down, stand in poaching liquid 3 hours.
3 Remove chicken from pan; discard poaching liquid. Using cleaver, cut chicken in half through the centre of the breastbone and along one side of backbone; cut each half into eight pieces. Serve chicken drizzled with dressing; if desired, accompany with steamed jasmine rice and asian greens.
SOY AND GREEN ONION DRESSING
Whisk ingredients in small bowl.
per serving 26.2g total fat (8.7g saturated fat); 2621kJ (627 cal); 41.3g carbohydrate; 46.3g protein; 1.2g fibre

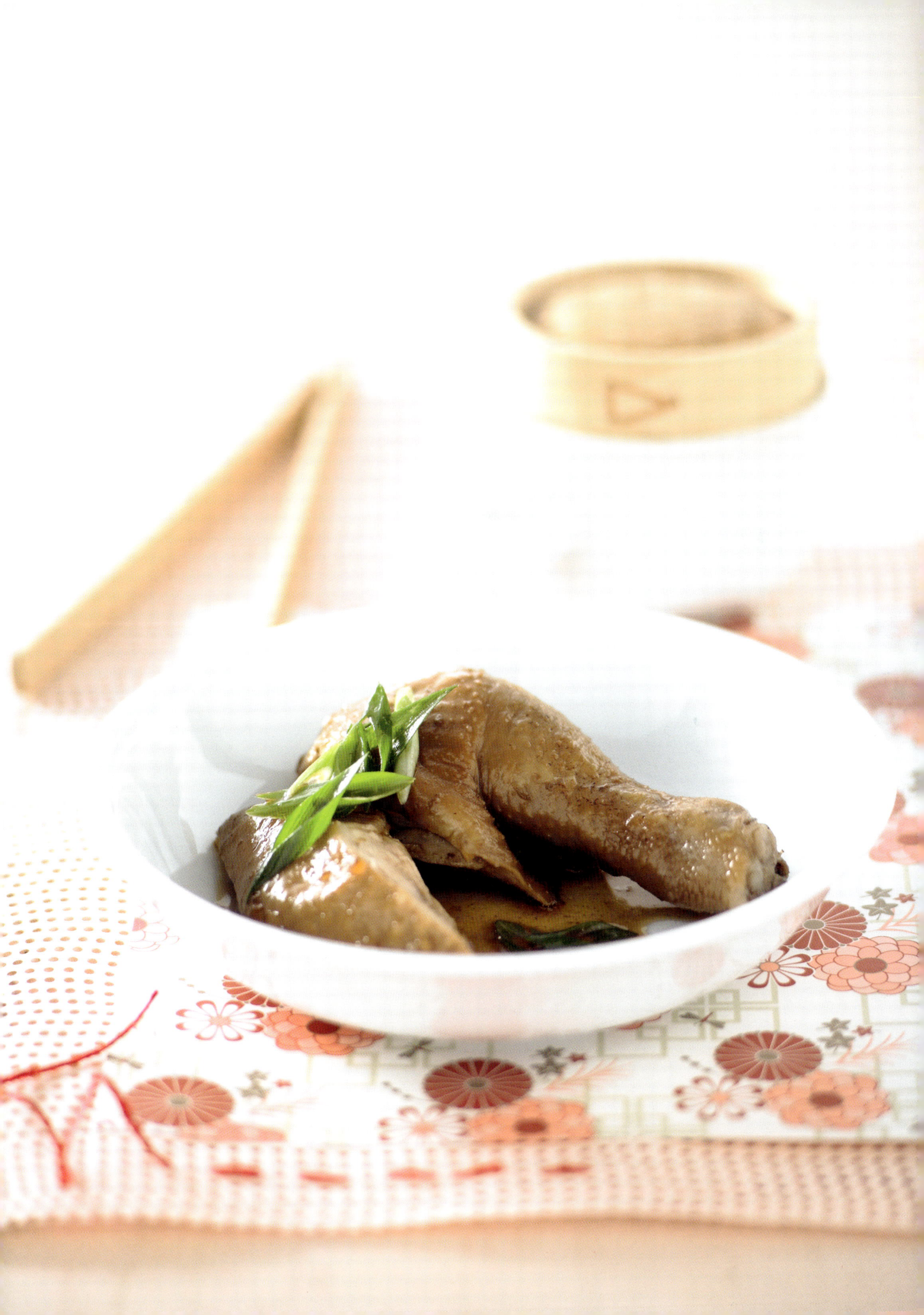

The Complete Book of Modern Asian

steamed fish with black bean and chilli sauce

preparation time 5 minutes
cooking time 8 minutes serves 4

500g gai lan, cut into 8cm lengths
4 x 180g bream fillets
2 tablespoons black bean sauce
1 tablespoon water
5cm piece fresh ginger (25g), sliced thinly
1 tablespoon peanut oil
2 fresh small red thai chillies, sliced thinly

1 Place gai lan stems on heatproof plate large enough to just fit inside bamboo steamer. Steam, covered, over wok of boiling water about 3 minutes.
2 Place leaves then fish on top of stems. Spread with combined sauce and water, sprinkle with ginger; steam, covered, about 5 minutes or until fish is just cooked through.
3 Meanwhile, place oil and chilli in small microwave-safe jug; cook on HIGH (100%) for 30 seconds until hot.
4 Serve fish on gai lan, drizzled with hot oil mixture.
per serving 14.2g total fat (4.1g saturated fat); 1283kJ (307 cal); 3.7g carbohydrate; 38.8g protein; 5.1g fibre

lemon grass and lime fish parcels

preparation time 10 minutes
cooking time 20 minutes serves 4

2 x 10cm sticks fresh lemon grass (40g)
½ cup coarsely chopped fresh coriander
1cm piece fresh ginger (5g), grated finely
3 cloves garlic, crushed
4 spring onions (100g), sliced thinly
2 fresh small red thai chillies, chopped finely
4 firm white fish fillets (800g)
1 lime, sliced thinly
1 tablespoon vegetable oil

1 Trim lemon grass; cut each piece in half lengthways.
2 Combine coriander, ginger, garlic, onion and chilli in small bowl.
3 Cut four sheets of foil, large enough to completely enclose fish. Place one lemon grass piece on each foil sheet; top with fish then coriander mixture and lime; drizzle with oil. Fold foil around fish to enclose completely.
4 Place parcels, in single layer, in large bamboo steamer; steam, covered, over wok of simmering water about 15 minutes or until fish is cooked through.
5 Remove fish from foil before serving; discard lemon grass.
per serving 9.1g total fat (2g saturated fat); 1078kJ (258 cal); 1.5g carbohydrate; 41.5g protein; 1.2g fibre

hainan chicken rice

preparation time 25 minutes
cooking time 1 hour 20 minutes serves 4

4 x 200g chicken breast fillets, skin-on
1 teaspoon chinese rice wine
2 teaspoons soy sauce
2cm piece fresh ginger (10g), sliced thinly
1 clove garlic, sliced thinly
2 green onions, chopped finely
2 litres (8 cups) water
1 teaspoon sesame oil
¼ teaspoon salt
1 cup (200g) jasmine rice
1 lebanese cucumber (130g), sliced thinly
1 green onion, sliced thinly

CHILLI GINGER SAMBAL
4 fresh small red thai chillies, chopped coarsely
1 clove garlic, chopped coarsely
2cm piece fresh ginger (10g), chopped coarsely
1 teaspoon sesame oil
1 teaspoon water
2 teaspoons lime juice

1 Rub chicken all over with combined rice wine and half the soy. Gently slide ginger, garlic and onion under chicken skin.
2 Bring the water to a boil in large saucepan; add chicken. Bring to a boil; reduce heat, simmer 3 minutes. Turn off heat; stand chicken in water 20 minutes.
3 Remove chicken from pan; remove and discard skin. Brush chicken all over with remaining soy, oil and salt.
4 Return cooking liquid to a boil; boil, uncovered, until reduced by a half.
5 Meanwhile, rinse rice thoroughly under cold running water. Place rice in large saucepan; add enough water to cover rice by 2cm. Cover pan; bring to a boil. Stir several times to prevent rice sticking. When boiling, remove lid and continue to boil until all the water has evaporated; do not stir. Cover; stand rice 20 minutes. Stir with fork; stand, covered, further 10 minutes.
6 Meanwhile, blend or process ingredients for chilli ginger sambal until just combined.
7 Cut chicken into pieces; serve with rice, cucumber and chilli ginger sambal. Accompany with a bowl of cooking liquid sprinkled with extra onion.
per serving 12.5g total fat (3.6g saturated fat); 1965kJ (470 cal); 41.1g carbohydrate; 46.7g protein; 1.4g fibre

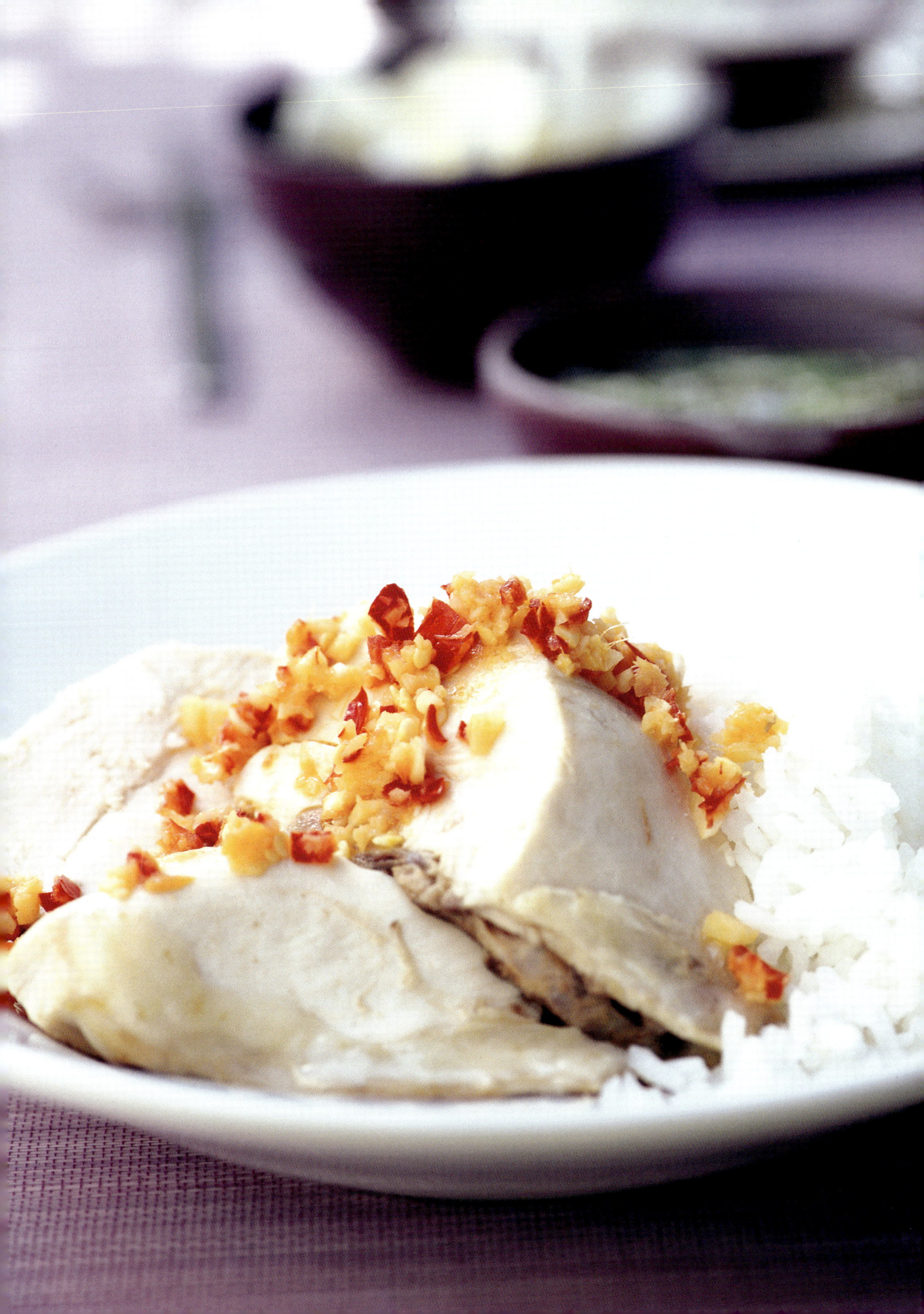

The Complete Book of Modern Asian

steamed fish with chilli and ginger

preparation time 10 minutes
cooking time 10 minutes serves 4

2 baby buk choy (300g), quartered
4 snapper cutlets (800g)
10cm piece fresh ginger (50g), cut into 4cm strips
2 green onions, cut into 4cm strips
¼ cup (60ml) light soy sauce
1 teaspoon sesame oil
1 fresh large red chilli, sliced thinly
1 cup loosely packed fresh coriander leaves

1 Place buk choy on large heatproof plate inside bamboo steamer; top with fish. Sprinkle ginger and onion over fish, then spoon over sauce and oil. Steam, covered, about 5 minutes or until fish is just cooked through.
2 Serve fish topped with chilli and coriander.
per serving 4.9g total fat (1.3g saturated fat); 823kJ (197 cal); 2.3g carbohydrate; 34.8g protein; 1.8g fibre

poached flathead with herb salad

preparation time 20 minutes
cooking time 10 minutes serves 1

3 cups (750ml) water
2 cloves garlic, crushed
5cm piece fresh ginger (25g), sliced thinly
2 flathead fillets (220g)
1 lime, cut into wedges

HERB SALAD
¼ cup loosely packed fresh mint leaves
¼ cup loosely packed fresh coriander leaves
¼ cup loosely packed fresh basil leaves, torn
½ small red onion (50g), sliced thinly
1 lebanese cucumber (130g), seeded, sliced thinly
1 tablespoon fresh lime juice
1cm piece fresh ginger (5g), grated

1 Place the water, garlic and ginger in medium frying pan; bring to a boil. Add fish; reduce heat, simmer, uncovered, about 5 minutes or until fish is cooked as desired. Remove fish with slotted spoon; discard liquid.
2 Meanwhile, combine ingredients for herb salad in medium bowl.
3 Serve fish with salad and lime wedges.
per serving 3g total fat (1g saturated fat); 1124kJ (269 cal); 8.3g carbohydrate; 49.6g protein; 6.6g fibre

ocean trout in baby buk choy parcels

preparation time 20 minutes (plus standing time)
cooking time 15 minutes serves 4

Wash the buk choy carefully. It's important to remove all the dirt hidden among the leaves without actually separating any of the leaves from the base, thus leaving each vegetable intact.

4 dried shiitake mushrooms
2 green onions, chopped finely
3cm piece fresh ginger (15g), grated
½ x 10cm stick fresh lemon grass (20g), chopped finely
2 cloves garlic, crushed
1 teaspoon sambal oelek
2 tablespoons soy sauce
4 ocean trout fillets (600g)
4 large baby bok choy (600g)
1½ cups (300g) jasmine rice

GINGER DRESSING
2cm piece fresh ginger (10g), grated
2 tablespoons rice wine vinegar
1 tablespoon vegetable oil
1 teaspoon sesame oil
2 tablespoons mirin
1 tablespoon soy sauce

1 Place mushrooms in small heatproof bowl, cover with boiling water, stand 20 minutes; drain. Discard stems; chop caps finely.
2 Meanwhile, place ingredients for ginger dressing in screw-top jar; shake well.
3 Combine mushroom, onion, ginger, lemon grass, garlic, sambal and sauce in small bowl; divide mushroom mixture among flesh side of fish fillets. Carefully insert one fillet, mushroom-side up, inside leaves of each buk choy; wrap leaves around fillet then tie parcels with kitchen string.
4 Place parcels in large steamer; steam, covered, over wok of boiling water about 10 minutes or until fish is cooked as desired.
5 Meanwhile, cook rice in large saucepan of boiling water, uncovered, until rice is just tender; drain.
6 Divide rice among plates; top with parcels, drizzle with dressing.

per serving 12.3g total fat (2.2g saturated fat); 2195kJ (525 cal); 64.6g carbohydrate; 37.1g protein; 3.6g fibre

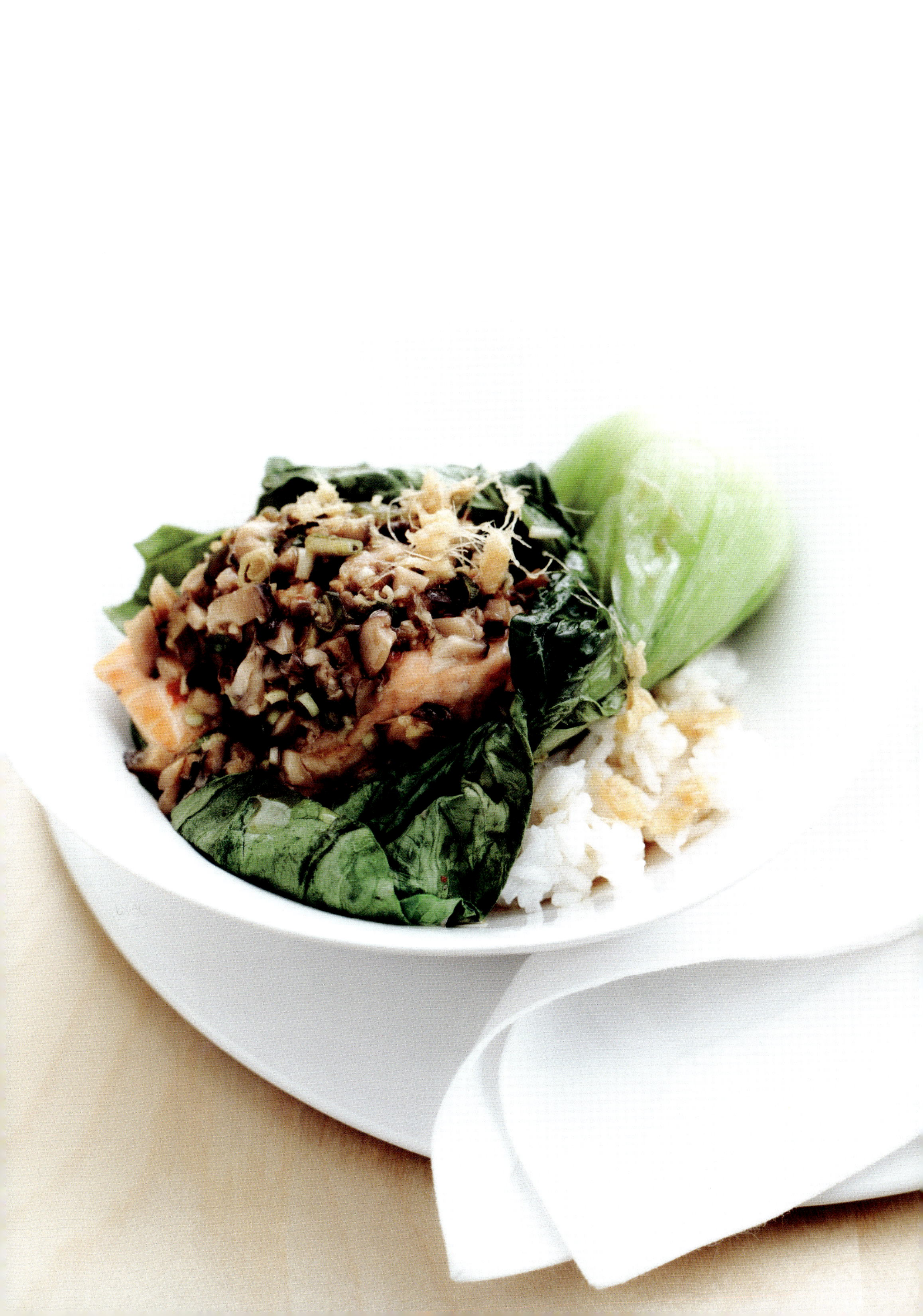

The Complete Book of Modern Asian

steamed mussels with saffron, chilli and coriander

preparation time 25 minutes
cooking time 10 minutes serves 6

¾ cup (180ml) dry white wine
¼ teaspoon saffron threads
1 tablespoon fish sauce
2 teaspoons finely grated lime rind
2kg medium black mussels
1 tablespoon peanut oil
5cm piece fresh ginger (25g), grated coarsely
2 cloves garlic, crushed
3 fresh small red thai chillies, sliced thinly
½ cup loosely packed fresh coriander leaves

1 Bring wine to a boil in small saucepan. Stir in saffron, sauce and rind; remove from heat. Stand 10 minutes.
2 Meanwhile, scrub mussels; remove beards.
3 Heat oil in large saucepan; cook ginger, garlic and chilli, stirring, until fragrant. Add wine mixture and mussels; bring to a boil. Reduce heat, simmer, covered, about 5 minutes or until mussels open (discard any that do not).
4 Spoon mussels and broth into serving bowls; sprinkle with coriander.
per serving 1.3g total fat (0.9g saturated fat); 451kJ (108 cal); 3.8g carbohydrate; 8.4g protein; 0.6g fibre

steamed snapper with cantonese vegetables

preparation time 20 minutes
cooking time 5 minutes serves 4

4 x 240g plate sized whole snapper
2 tablespoons soy sauce
2 tablespoons mirin
1 tablespoon honey
⅓ cup (80ml) orange juice
¼ cup (60ml) water
1 teaspoon five-spice powder
1 star anise
1 clove garlic, crushed
2cm piece fresh ginger (10g), cut into matchsticks
1 small carrot (70g), cut into matchsticks
3 green onions, sliced thinly
65g drained bamboo shoots, cut into matchsticks

1 Place fish, in single layer, in baking-paper-lined large bamboo steamer; steam, covered, over wok of simmering water about 15 minutes or until fish is cooked through.
2 Combine sauce, mirin, honey, juice, the water, five-spice, star anise and garlic in small saucepan; bring to a boil. Add ginger, carrot, onion and bamboo shoots; reduce heat, simmer, uncovered, about 5 minutes or until vegetables are tender and sauce thickens slightly.
3 Serve fish topped with vegetables and drizzled with sauce.
per serving 1.1g total fat (0.4g saturated fat); 477kJ (114 cal); 9.3g carbohydrate; 14.4g protein; 1.2g fibre

hot and sour fish steamed in banana leaves

preparation time 10 minutes (plus refrigeration time)
cooking time 20 minutes serves 4

4 medium whole bream (1kg)
1 large banana leaf
4 fresh small red thai chillies, sliced thinly
2 fresh kaffir lime leaves, shredded finely
2 green onions, sliced thinly
¼ cup loosely packed fresh coriander leaves
¼ cup loosely packed fresh thai basil leaves
2 x 10cm sticks fresh lemon grass (40g)

LIME AND SWEET CHILLI DRESSING
¼ cup (60ml) sweet chilli sauce
2 tablespoons fish sauce
2 tablespoons lime juice
2 tablespoons peanut oil
1 clove garlic, crushed
1cm piece fresh ginger (5g), grated finely

1 Place ingredients for lime and sweet chilli dressing in screw-top jar; shake well.
2 Score fish both sides through thickest part of flesh; place on large tray, drizzle with half of the dressing. Cover; refrigerate 1 hour.
3 Meanwhile, trim banana leaf into four 30cm squares. Using tongs, dip one square at a time into large saucepan of boiling water; remove immediately. Rinse under cold water; pat dry with absorbent paper.
4 Place leaves on work surface. Combine chilli, lime leaves, onion, coriander and basil in medium bowl. Halve lemon grass sticks lengthways, then halve crossways; you will have eight pieces.
5 Place two pieces of lemon grass on each leaf; place one fish on each. Top fish with equal amounts of the herb mixture. Fold opposite corners of the leaf to enclose centre part of fish; secure each parcel with kitchen string.
6 Place two parcels, in single layer, in large bamboo steamer; steam, covered, in two batches, over wok of simmering water about 15 minutes or until fish is cooked through. Unwrap fish; drizzle with remaining dressing.
per serving 16.4 total fat (4.1g saturated fat); 1150kJ (275 cal); 4.1g carbohydrate; 27.3g protein; 1.3g fibre

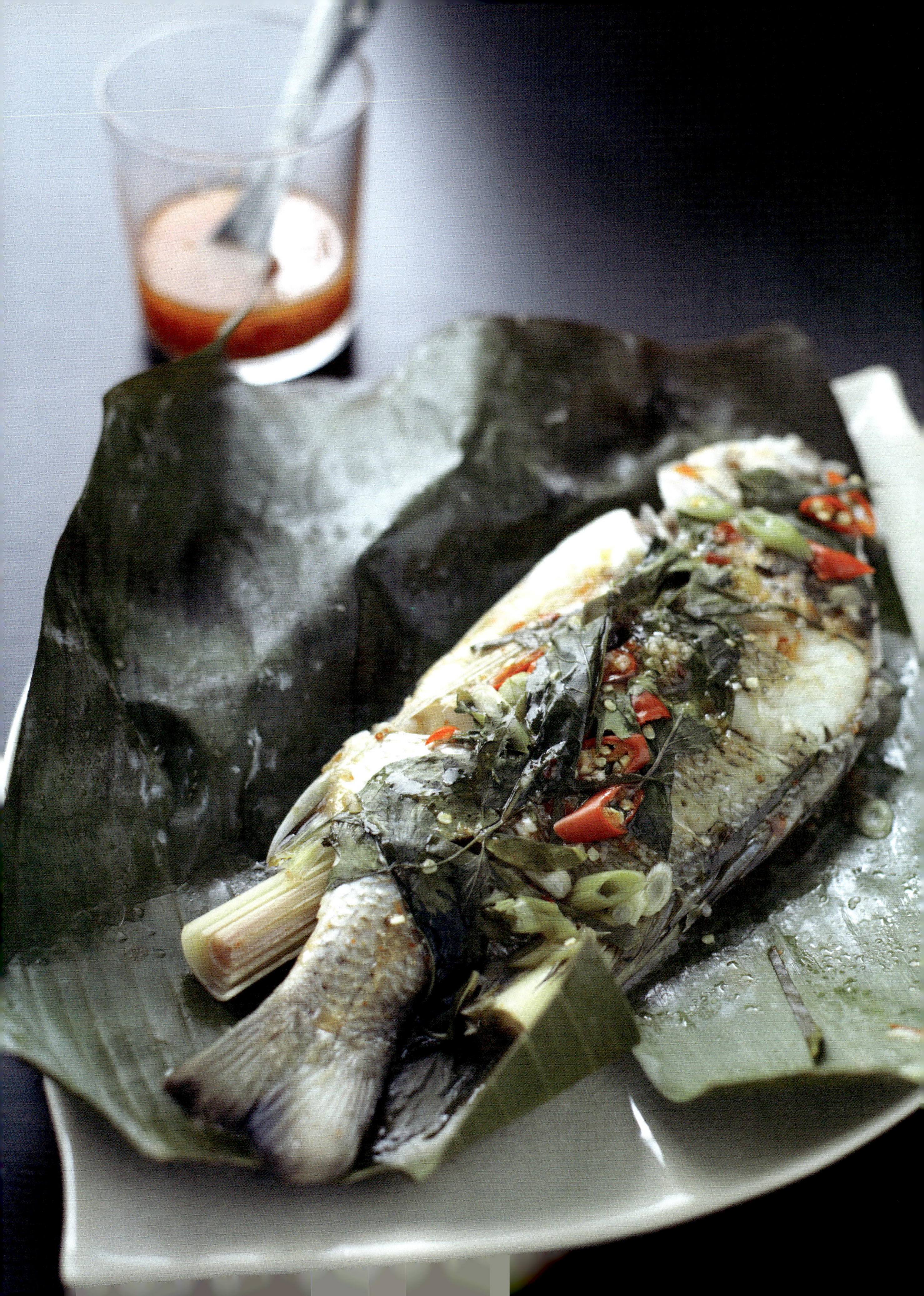

The Complete Book of Modern Asian

steamed scallops with asian flavours

preparation time 15 minutes
cooking time 15 minutes serves 4

1½ cups (300g) jasmine rice
3cm piece fresh ginger (15g)
20 scallops (800g), in half shell, roe removed
2 tablespoons thinly sliced fresh lemon grass
4 green onions, sliced thinly
1 tablespoon sesame oil
¼ cup (60ml) kecap manis
¼ cup (60ml) soy sauce

1 Cook rice in large saucepan of boiling water, uncovered, until just tender; drain.
2 Meanwhile, slice ginger thinly; cut slices into thin strips. Place scallops, in batches, in single layer in large bamboo steamer; top with ginger, lemon grass and onion. Steam, covered, over wok of simmering water about 5 minutes or until tender and cooked as desired.
3 Divide scallops among serving plates; top with combined remaining ingredients. Serve with rice, if desired.
per serving 5.5g total fat (0.9g saturated fat); 1517kJ (363 cal); 61.2g carbohydrate; 15.8g protein; 0.9g fibre

thai-style steamed chicken with noodles

preparation time 15 minutes (plus standing time)
cooking time 20 minutes serves 4

4 large silver beet leaves
4 single chicken breast fillets (680g)
2 fresh kaffir lime leaves, shredded finely
2 fresh small red thai chillies, sliced thinly
1 tablespoon finely chopped lemon grass
500g fresh rice noodles

SWEET CHILLI DRESSING
¼ cup (60ml) sweet chilli sauce
2 teaspoons fish sauce
1 tablespoon lime juice
1 clove garlic, crushed
2 tablespoons finely chopped fresh coriander

1 Drop silver beet into pan of boiling water, drain immediately, then dip into bowl of iced water until cold; drain well.
2 Place a chicken fillet on a silver beet leaf, sprinkle with lime leaves, chilli and lemon grass. Wrap silver beet around chicken to enclose.
3 Place chicken parcels in baking-paper-lined bamboo steamer; steam, covered, over wok of simmering water about 15 minutes or until cooked through.
4 Meanwhile, place noodles in large heatproof bowl, cover with hot water and stand for 5 minutes; drain.
5 Combine ingredients for sweet chilli dressing in small bowl; toss half of the dressing through noodles.
6 Serve sliced chicken with noodles and remaining sweet chilli dressing.
per serving 10.5g total fat (3g saturated fat); 1655kJ (396 cal); 31.6g carbohydrate; 40.9g protein; 4.4g fibre
TIPS If the silver beet leaves are small, use two per chicken breast. If kaffir lime leaves are unavailable, use 2 teaspoons of finely grated lime rind.

Some of the world's great comfort dishes originated in Asian kitchens. Clay-pot chicken, chickpea dhansak or slow-cooked ribs, necks and shanks are great-tasting because of their cooking treatment as much as their content. Some may take a while to simmer into readiness but the cook is off the hook as it bubbles away on its own – ideal for busy people.

clay-pot chicken *page 329*

hoisin-braised short ribs *page 321*

casseroles & one-pots

japanese seafood hotpot *page 310*

braised sweet ginger duck *page 318*

japanese seafood hotpot

preparation time 20 minutes (plus refrigeration time) cooking time 20 minutes serves 4

12 medium black mussels (300g)
12 uncooked medium king prawns (540g)
2 teaspoons cooking sake
1 tablespoon japanese soy sauce
2 teaspoons mirin
12 scallops without roe (300g)
400g firm white fish fillets, diced into 4cm pieces
1 tablespoon vegetable oil
2 cloves garlic, crushed
5cm piece fresh ginger (25g), chopped finely
3 cups (750ml) fish stock
1 cup (250ml) water
¼ cup (60ml) cooking sake, extra
¼ cup (60ml) japanese soy sauce, extra
1 teaspoon powdered dashi
1 small kumara (250g), halved lengthways, sliced thinly
250g spinach, chopped coarsely
2 green onions, chopped coarsely
270g dried udon noodles

1 Scrub mussels; remove beards. Shell and devein prawns, leaving tails intact.
2 Combine sake, soy and mirin in large bowl; add mussels, prawns, scallops and fish, toss seafood to coat in mixture.
3 Heat oil in large saucepan; cook garlic and ginger, stirring, until fragrant. Add stock, the water, extra sake, extra soy and dashi; bring to a boil. Add kumara; cook, uncovered, 2 minutes. Add undrained seafood; cook, covered, about 5 minutes or until mussels open (discard any that do not). Add spinach and onion; cook, uncovered, until spinach just wilts.
4 Meanwhile, cook noodles in large saucepan of boiling water, uncovered, until just tender; drain.
5 Divide noodles among bowls; top with seafood mixture.

per serving 7.8g total fat (1.3g saturated fat); 2307 kJ (552 cal); 57.3g carbohydrate; 56.8g protein; 4.5g fibre

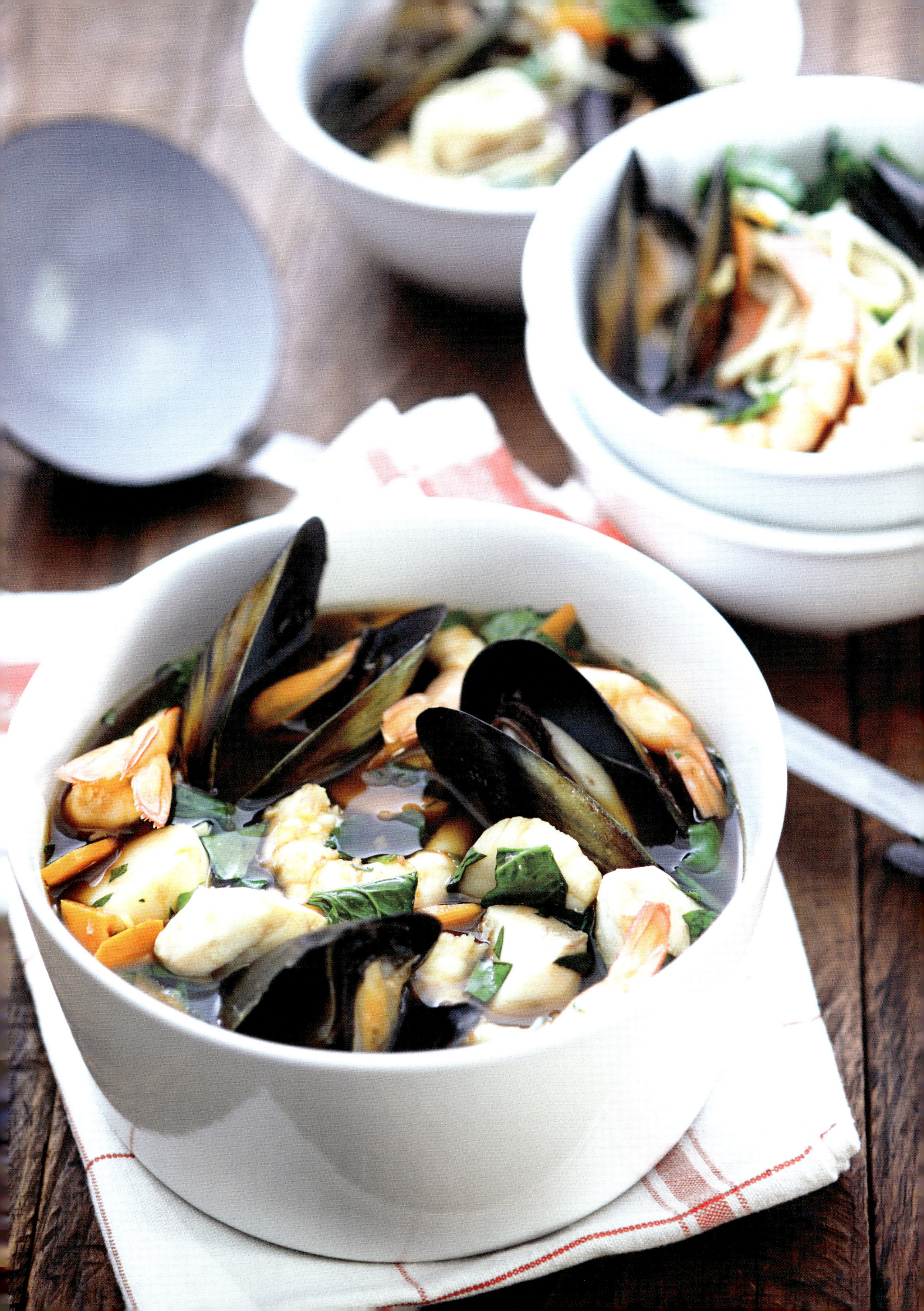

The Complete Book of Modern Asian

mixed vegetables in coconut milk

preparation time 25 minutes
cooking time 15 minutes serves 4

6 cloves garlic, quartered
3 fresh small red thai chillies, chopped coarsely
10cm stick fresh lemon grass (20g), chopped finely
1 tablespoon coarsely chopped pickled galangal
4cm piece fresh ginger (20g), chopped coarsely
20g piece fresh turmeric, chopped coarsely
2 cups (500ml) coconut milk
2 fresh kaffir lime leaves
4 medium zucchini (480g), chopped coarsely
6 yellow patty-pan squash (240g), chopped coarsely
200g cauliflower florets
100g baby corn, halved lengthways
2 tablespoons soy sauce
2 tablespoons lime juice
⅓ cup coarsely chopped thai basil
2 fresh kaffir lime leaves, shredded finely

1 Blend or process garlic, chilli, lemon grass, galangal, ginger and turmeric until mixture forms a paste.
2 Place half of the coconut milk in wok; bring to a boil. Add garlic paste; whisk over high heat until smooth. Reduce heat, add remaining coconut milk and whole lime leaves; simmer, stirring, until mixture thickens slightly.
3 Add zucchini, squash, cauliflower and corn; bring to a boil. Reduce heat, simmer, uncovered, about 5 minutes or until vegetables are just tender. Remove from heat; remove and discard whole lime leaves. Stir sauce, juice and basil into vegetable mixture; serve topped with shredded lime leaves.
per serving 27g total fat (22.8g saturated fat); 1467kJ (351 cal); 15.1g carbohydrate; 8.6g protein; 8.6g fibre

fish in spicy coconut cream

preparation time 20 minutes
cooking time 30 minutes serves 4

2 teaspoons peanut oil
2 cloves garlic, crushed
1cm piece fresh ginger (5g), grated finely
20g piece fresh turmeric, grated finely
2 fresh small red thai chillies, sliced thinly
1½ cups (375ml) fish stock
400ml can coconut cream
20g piece fresh galangal, halved
10cm stick fresh lemon grass (20g), cut into 2cm pieces
4 firm white fish fillets (800g)
2 tablespoons fish sauce
2 green onions, sliced thinly

1 Heat oil in wok; stir-fry garlic, ginger, turmeric and chilli until fragrant. Add stock, coconut cream, galangal and lemon grass; bring to a boil. Add fish; reduce heat, simmer, covered, about 8 minutes or until fish is cooked.
2 Using slotted spoon, remove fish carefully from sauce; place in serving bowl, cover to keep warm. Remove and discard galangal and lemon grass pieces from liquid. Bring liquid to a boil; boil 5 minutes. Remove from heat; stir in sauce and onion. Pour sauce over fish in bowl.
per serving 27.7g total fat (0.8g saturated fat); 915kJ (219 cal); 26.3g carbohydrate; 15.3g protein; 11.2g fibre

chicken donburi

preparation time 20 minutes (plus standing time)
cooking time 40 minutes   serves 4

4 dried shiitake mushrooms
½ teaspoon dashi powder
1 cup (250ml) boiling water
4 medium brown onions (600g), sliced thinly
1½ cups (300g) koshihikari rice
3 cups (750ml) cold water
¼ cup (60ml) japanese soy sauce
2 tablespoons mirin
1 teaspoon white sugar
600g chicken breast fillets, chopped coarsely
4 eggs, beaten lightly
2 green onions, sliced thinly

1 Place mushrooms in small heatproof bowl, cover with boiling water, stand 20 minutes; drain. Discard stems; slice caps thinly.
2 Meanwhile, combine dashi with the boiling water in small jug.
3 Cook brown onion in heated oiled large frying pan, stirring, about 10 minutes or until onion is browned lightly. Add half of the dashi mixture, reduce heat; simmer, stirring occasionally, about 10 minutes or until softened. Transfer to medium bowl.
4 Bring rice and the cold water to a boil in large saucepan, uncovered, stirring occasionally. Reduce heat to as low as possible; cover with a tight-fitting lid, cook rice 12 minutes. Do not remove lid or stir rice during cooking time. Remove from heat; stand, covered, 10 minutes.
5 Meanwhile, combine remaining dashi mixture with sauce, mirin and sugar in same frying pan; bring to a boil. Add chicken and mushroom; cook, covered, about 5 minutes or until chicken is cooked through.
6 Combine egg with cooked onion in bowl, pour over chicken mixture; cook, covered, over low heat, about 5 minutes or until egg just sets.
7 Divide rice among serving bowls; top with chicken mixture, sprinkle with green onion.

per serving 9.4g total fat (2.7g saturated fat) 2328kJ (557 cal) 67.9g carbohydrate 48.9g protein 2.9g fibre

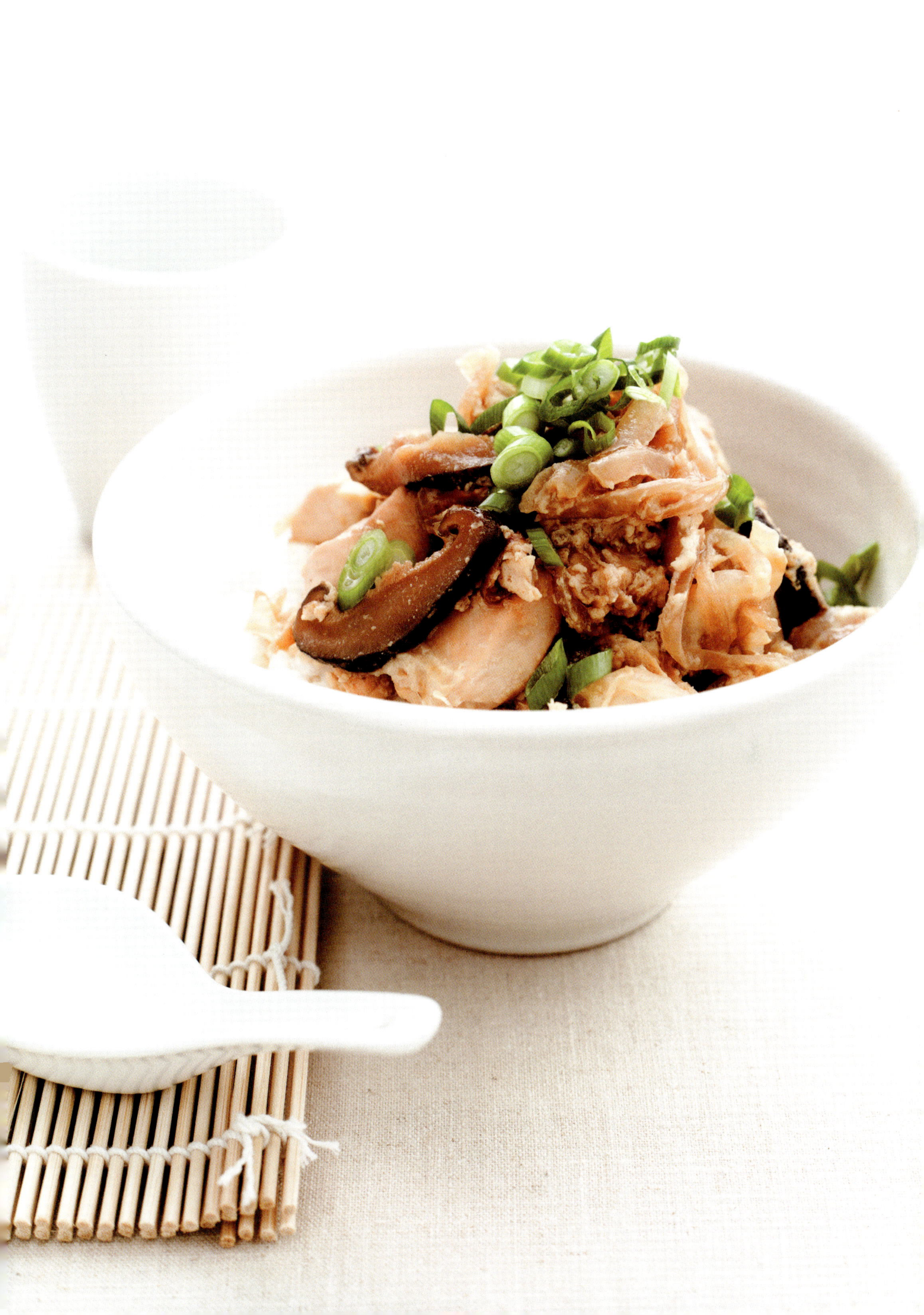

The Complete Book of Modern Asian

curried lamb shanks

preparation time 20 minutes
cooking time 2 hours 5 minutes serves 4

8 french-trimmed lamb shanks (1.5kg)
¼ cup (35g) plain flour
2 tablespoons peanut oil
1 medium brown onion (150g), chopped finely
2 cloves garlic, crushed
½ cup (150g) rogan josh curry paste
2 cups (500ml) water
400g can crushed tomatoes
1 teaspoon sugar
2 cups (500ml) beef stock
400g cauliflower, chopped coarsely
400g pumpkin, chopped coarsely
¾ cup (150g) red lentils
¼ cup coarsely chopped fresh coriander

1 Toss lamb in flour; shake away excess. Heat oil in large saucepan; cook lamb, in batches, until browned all over.
2 Cook onion and garlic in same pan, stirring, until onion softens. Add paste; cook, stirring, until fragrant. Return lamb to pan with the water, undrained tomatoes, sugar and stock; bring to a boil. Reduce heat, simmer, covered, 1½ hours.
3 Add cauliflower, pumpkin and lentils to curry; bring to a boil. Reduce heat, simmer, covered, 15 minutes or until cooked as desired. Remove from heat; stir in coriander.
4 Serve lamb shanks with warmed naan, if desired.
per serving 41.2g total fat (11.9g saturated fat); 3336kJ (798 cal); 39g carbohydrate; 61.1g protein; 14.3g fibre

beef do-piaza

preparation time 30 minutes
cooking time 2 hours serves 4

200g yogurt
¼ teaspoon saffron threads
¼ cup (60ml) vegetable oil
1kg chuck steak, cut into 2cm pieces
2 medium brown onions (300g), chopped finely
2 teaspoons ground cumin
2 teaspoons coriander seeds
1 teaspoon ground cardamom
1 teaspoon ground fenugreek
½ teaspoon ground turmeric
2 cloves garlic, crushed
2cm piece fresh ginger (10g), grated
2 long green chillies, sliced thinly
2 x 400g cans crushed tomatoes
1 cup (250ml) beef stock
2 tablespoons peanut oil
2 medium brown onions (300g), sliced thinly

1 Combine yogurt and saffron in small bowl. Set aside.
2 Heat vegetable oil in large flameproof casserole dish; cook beef, in batches, until browned all over.
3 Cook chopped onion in same dish, stirring, until soft. Add spices, garlic, ginger and chilli; cook, stirring, until fragrant. Add undrained tomatoes and stock; bring to a boil. Return beef to dish; simmer, covered, about 1½ hours or until beef is tender. Stir in yogurt mixture.
4 Meanwhile, heat peanut oil in large frying pan; cook sliced onion, stirring, until browned lightly. Sprinkle over curry to serve.
per serving 36.6g total fat (9.3g saturated fat); 2617kJ (626 cal); 14.8g carbohydrate; 57.5g protein; 4.7g fibre

asian star

braised sweet ginger duck

preparation time 20 minutes
cooking time 1 hour 50 minutes serves 4

2kg duck
3 cups (750ml) water
½ cup (125ml) chinese cooking wine
⅓ cup (80ml) light soy sauce
¼ cup (55g) firmly packed brown sugar
1 whole star anise
3 green onions, halved
3 cloves garlic, quartered
10cm piece fresh ginger (50g), unpeeled, chopped coarsely
2 teaspoons sea salt
1 teaspoon five-spice powder
800g baby buk choy, halved

1 Preheat oven to 180°C/160°C fan-forced.
2 Discard neck from duck, wash duck; pat dry with absorbent paper. Score duck in thickest parts of skin; cut duck in half through breastbone and along both sides of backbone, discard backbone. Tuck wings under duck.
3 Place duck, skin-side down, in medium shallow baking dish; add combined water, wine, soy, sugar, star anise, onion, garlic and ginger. Cover; cook in oven about 1 hour or until duck is cooked as desired.
4 Increase oven temperature to 220°C/200°C fan-forced. Remove duck from braising liquid; strain liquid through muslin-lined sieve into large saucepan. Place duck, skin-side up, on wire rack in same dish. Rub combined salt and five-spice all over duck; roast duck, uncovered, in oven about 30 minutes or until skin is crisp.
5 Skim fat from surface of braising liquid; bring to a boil. Reduce heat, simmer, uncovered, 10 minutes. Add buk choy; simmer, covered, about 5 minutes or until buk choy is just tender.
6 Cut duck halves into two pieces; divide buk choy, braising liquid and duck among plates. Serve with steamed jasmine rice, if desired.
per serving 105.7g total fat (31.7g saturated fat); 4974 kJ (1190 cal); 17.9g carbohydrate; 40.8g protein; 3.5g fibre

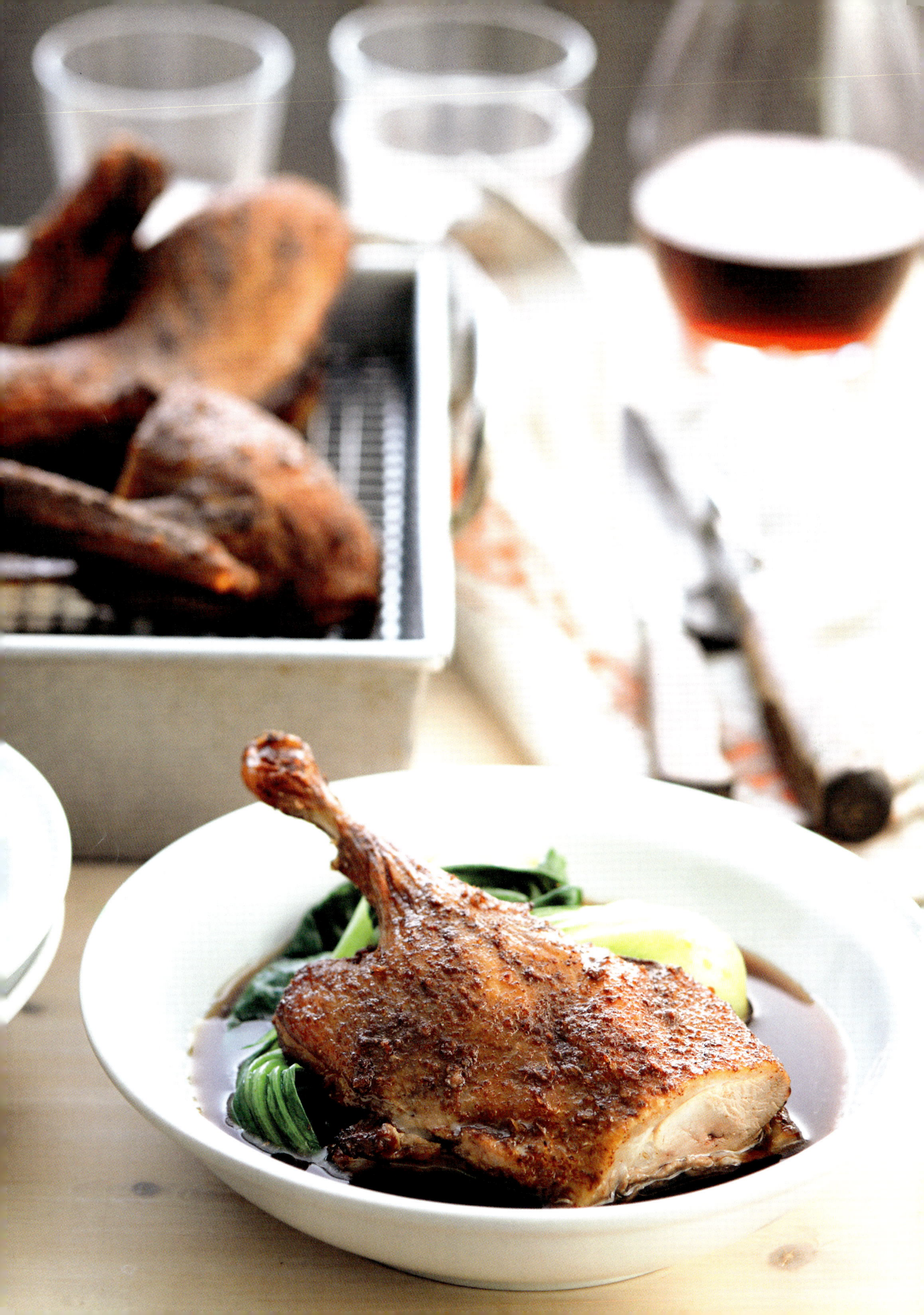

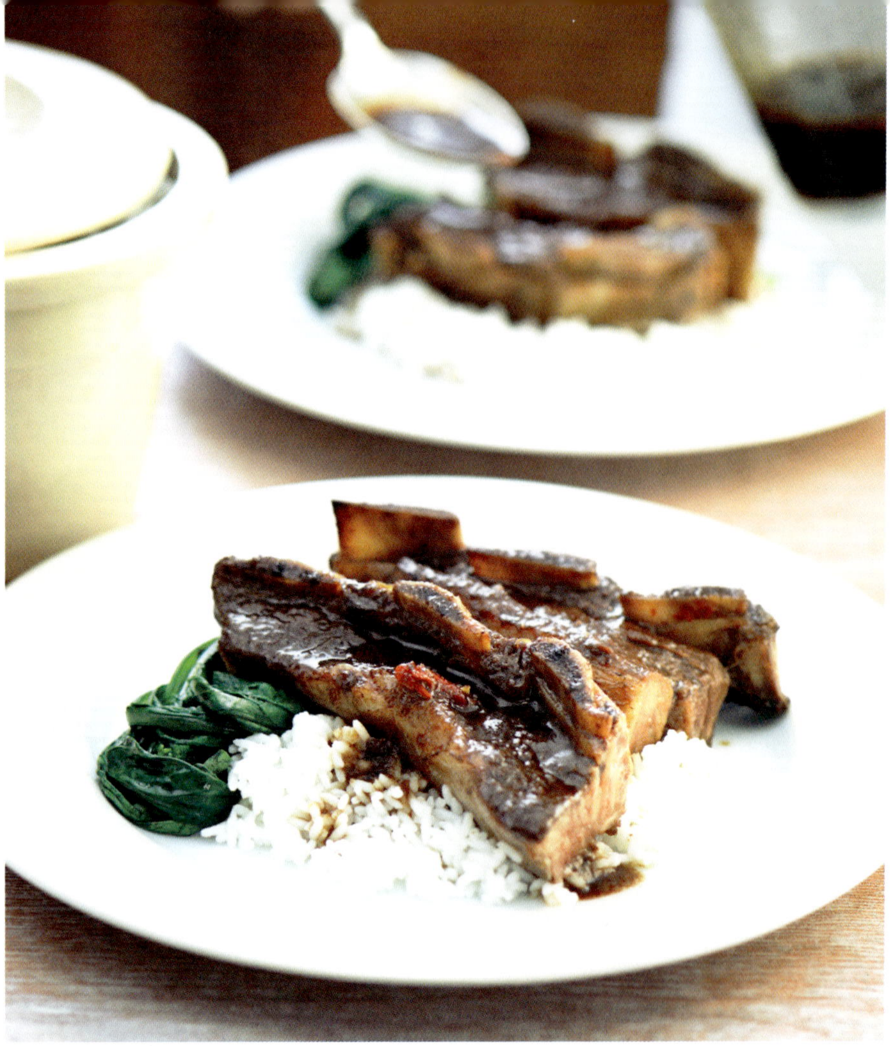

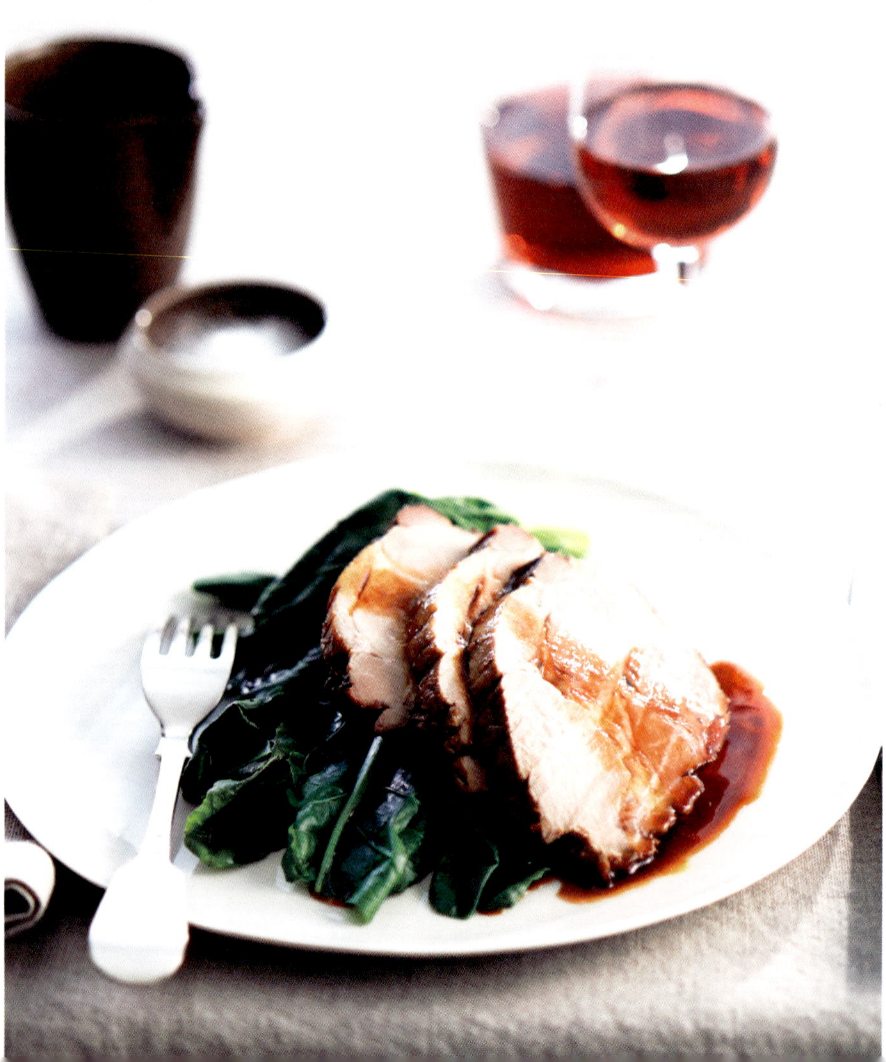

hoisin-braised short ribs

preparation time 10 minutes
cooking time 2 hours 45 minutes serves 4

2kg beef short ribs
½ cup (125ml) hoisin sauce
1 cup (250ml) beef stock
¼ cup (55g) firmly packed brown sugar
5cm piece fresh ginger (25g), grated
2 cloves garlic, crushed
2 star anise
½ cup (125ml) orange juice
5cm strip orange rind
1 fresh long red chilli, chopped coarsely

1 Preheat oven to 150°C/130°C fan-forced.
2 Combine ribs and remaining ingredients in large shallow baking dish. Cook, covered, 2 hours.
3 Turn ribs; cook, covered, about another 30 minutes or until ribs are tender. Remove ribs from dish; cover to keep warm.
4 Pour braising liquid into large jug; skim fat from surface. Place liquid in medium saucepan; bring to a boil. Reduce heat, simmer, uncovered, 10 minutes or until sauce thickens slightly.
5 Drizzle ribs with sauce; serve with steamed jasmine rice and choy sum, if desired.
per serving 27.6g total fat (11.7g saturated fat); 2780 kJ (665 cal); 29.6g carbohydrate; 75.5g protein; 4.2g fibre

asian-style braised pork neck

preparation time 10 minutes
cooking time 2 hours 30 minutes serves 4

1 tablespoon peanut oil
1kg piece pork neck
2 cinnamon sticks
2 star anise
½ cup (125ml) light soy sauce
½ cup (125ml) chinese rice wine
¼ cup (55g) firmly packed brown sugar
5cm piece fresh ginger (25g), sliced thinly
4 cloves garlic, quartered
1 medium brown onion (150g), chopped coarsely
1 cup (250ml) water

1 Preheat oven to 160°C/140°C fan-forced.
2 Heat oil in medium deep flameproof baking dish; cook pork, uncovered, until browned all over. Remove from heat.
3 Add combined spices, soy sauce, wine, sugar, ginger, garlic, onion and the water to baking dish; turn pork to coat in mixture. Cook, uncovered, in oven about 2 hours or until pork is tender, turning every 20 minutes.
4 Remove pork; cover to keep warm. Strain braising liquid through muslin-lined strainer over medium saucepan; bring to a boil. Reduce heat, simmer, uncovered, 5 minutes or until sauce thickens slighly.
5 Serve pork drizzled with sauce; accompany with steamed gai lan, if desired.
per serving 24.7g total fat (7.6g saturated fat); 2182kJ (522 cal); 17.2g carbohydrate; 55.4g protein; 1.3g fibre

vegetable dhansak

preparation time 40 minutes (plus standing time)
cooking time 1 hour 30 minutes serves 6

1 large eggplant (500g), chopped coarsely
500g pumpkin, chopped coarsely
2 medium tomatoes (300g), peeled,
   chopped coarsely
1 large brown onion (200g), sliced thinly
3 cups (750ml) water
420g can chickpeas, drained, rinsed
400g can brown lentils, drained, rinsed
1 tablespoon garam masala
2 cups (400g) basmati rice
2 teaspoons vegetable oil
2 medium brown onions (300g), sliced thinly, extra
¼ cup firmly packed fresh coriander leaves

MASALA PASTE
3 dried small red chillies
2 long green chillies
2cm piece fresh ginger (10g), quartered
3 cloves garlic, quartered
½ cup loosely packed fresh coriander leaves
2 tablespoons hot water

1 Blend or process ingredients for masala paste until mixture forms a smooth paste.
2 Place eggplant, pumpkin, tomato, onion and the water in large saucepan; bring to a boil. Reduce heat, simmer, covered, 15 minutes, stirring occasionally. Drain vegetable mixture through sieve over large bowl; reserve 1½ cups of the cooking liquid, discard remainder.
3 Combine half of the chickpeas, half of the lentils and half of the vegetable mixture in another large bowl; mash lightly.
4 Dry-fry garam masala and masala paste in same cleaned pan, stirring, until fragrant. Add mashed and whole chickpeas, lentils and vegetable mixtures and reserved cooking liquid to pan; bring to a boil. Reduce heat, simmer, uncovered, 20 minutes, stirring occasionally.
5 Meanwhile, cook rice in large saucepan of boiling water until tender; drain.
6 Heat oil in medium saucepan; cook extra onion, stirring, about 10 minutes or until browned lightly. Sprinkle onion over dhansak; serve with rice and lemon wedges, if desired.

per serving 3.7g fat (0.6 saturated fat); 1614kJ (386 cal); 74.4g carbohydrate; 13.4g protein; 8.9g fibre

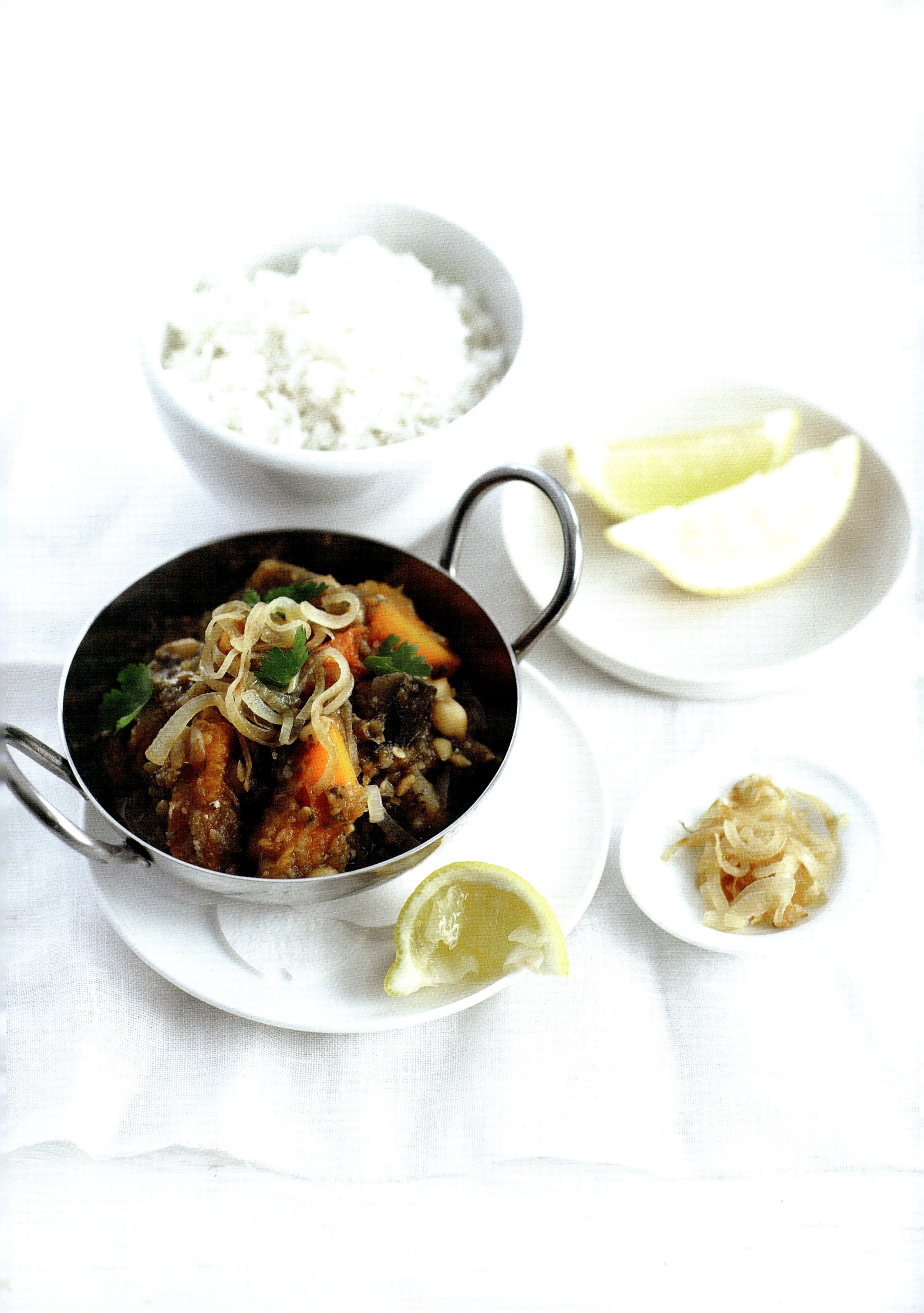

The Complete Book of Modern Asian

palak paneer

preparation time 10 minutes
cooking time 20 minutes   serves 6

1 tablespoon vegetable oil
1 teaspoon cumin seeds
1 teaspoon fenugreek seeds
2 teaspoons garam masala
1 large brown onion (200g), chopped finely
1 clove garlic, crushed
1 tablespoon lemon juice
500g spinach, trimmed, chopped coarsely
¾ cup (180ml) cream
2 x 100g packets paneer cheese, cut into 2cm pieces

1 Heat oil in large frying pan; cook spices, onion and garlic, stirring, until onion softens.
2 Add juice and half of the spinach; cook, stirring, until spinach wilts. Add remaining spinach; cook, stirring, until wilted.
3 Blend or process spinach mixture until smooth, return to pan; stir in cream. Add paneer; cook over low heat, uncovered, stirring occasionally, about 5 minutes or until heated through.

per serving 24.2g total fat (14.1g saturated fat); 1124kJ (269 cal); 3g carbohydrate; 9g protein; 3.4g fibre

braised oxtail in peanut sauce

preparation time 30 minutes
cooking time 3 hours 20 minutes   serves 4

2 oxtails (2kg), cut into 5cm pieces
2 tablespoons plain flour
2 tablespoons vegetable oil
1 large brown onion (200g), chopped coarsely
6 cloves garlic, crushed
1 tablespoon ground coriander
1 tablespoon ground cumin
2 star anise
2 fresh long red chillies, halved lengthways
1 litre (4 cups) beef stock
1 litre (4 cups) water
⅔ cup (200g) red curry paste (see page 249)
⅔ cup (90g) roasted unsalted peanuts, chopped coarsely
300g green beans, trimmed, chopped coarsely
2 green onions, sliced thinly

1 Coat oxtail in flour; shake off excess. Heat half the oil in large flameproof casserole dish; cook oxtail, in batches, until browned.
2 Heat remaining oil in same dish; cook onion and garlic, stirring, until onion softens. Add spices and chilli; cook, stirring, until fragrant. Return oxtail to dish with stock and the water; simmer, covered, 2 hours.
3 Strain beef over large bowl; reserve braising liquid, discard solids. Skim fat from braising liquid.
4 Cook curry paste in same cleaned dish, stirring, until fragrant. Add 4 cups of the reserved braising liquid; bring to a boil. Add oxtail; simmer, uncovered, 45 minutes or until oxtail is tender.
5 Add nuts and beans to dish; cook, uncovered, about 5 minutes or until beans are tender.
6 Serve curry sprinkled with green onion.

per serving 111.7g total fat (36.8g saturated fat); 5626kJ (1346 cal); 15.6g carbohydrate; 70g protein; 6.7g fibre

asian chicken pot au feu

preparation time 30 minutes
cooking time 1 hour 30 minutes serves 4

4 litres (16 cups) water
1.5kg chicken
2 cloves garlic, bruised
2 large carrots (360g), halved, quartered lengthways
10cm stick fresh lemon grass (20g), bruised
2 fresh kaffir lime leaves
2cm piece galangal (10g), sliced thinly
2 fresh long red chillies, halved lengthways
1 teaspoon sichuan peppercorns
½ teaspoon five-spice powder
¼ cup (60ml) mirin
½ cup (125ml) soy sauce
⅓ cup (80ml) kecap manis
350g broccolini, chopped coarsely

1 Bring the water to a boil in large deep saucepan. Add chicken, garlic, carrot, lemon grass, lime leaves, galangal, chilli, peppercorns, five-spice, mirin, sauce and kecap manis; return to a boil. Reduce heat, simmer, uncovered, 1 hour, occasionally skimming fat from surface.
2 Remove chicken; strain broth through muslin-lined sieve into large bowl. Reserve carrot; discard remaining solids. Cover chicken and carrot to keep warm.
3 Return all but 2 cups of the broth to same saucepan; bring to a boil. Cook broccolini in boiling broth, uncovered, until just tender; drain over large bowl. Reserve broth for another use.
4 Meanwhile, place the 2 cups of broth in small saucepan; bring to a boil. Boil rapidly, uncovered, until reduced to 1 cup.
5 Serve chicken with carrot, broccolini, reduced broth and, if desired, steamed jasmine rice.
per serving 28.6g total fat (8.8g saturated fat); 2082kJ (498 cal); 16.0g carbohydrate; 41.8g protein; 6.0g fibre

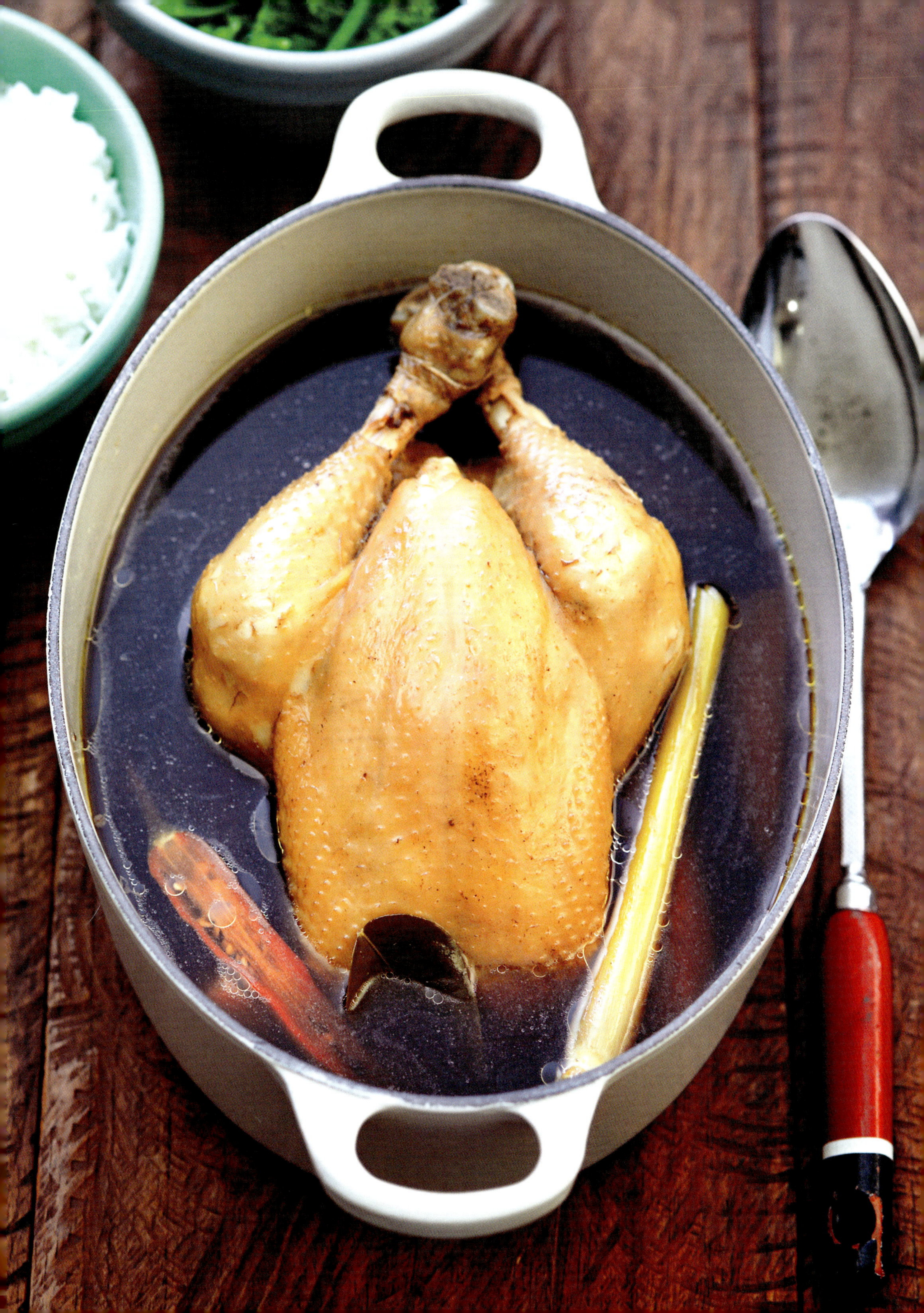

The Complete Book of Modern Asian

clay-pot chicken

preparation time 10 minutes (plus refrigeration time)
cooking time 1 hour serves 4

800g chicken thigh fillets, halved
4 cloves garlic, crushed
1 tablespoon fish sauce
1 tablespoon soy sauce
1 tablespoon hoisin sauce
2 tablespoons lime juice
10cm stick fresh lemon grass (20g), chopped finely
1 large brown onion (200g), quartered
1 fresh long red chilli, sliced thinly
½ cup (125ml) chicken stock
100g fresh shiitake mushrooms, halved
4 green onions, cut into 4cm pieces
½ small cabbage (600g), cut into 6cm squares

1 Combine chicken, garlic, sauces, juice and lemon grass in large bowl. Cover; refrigerate 3 hours or overnight.
2 Preheat oven to 180°C/160°C fan-forced.
3 Place chicken mixture in clay pot or 2.5-litre (10-cup) ovenproof dish with brown onion, chilli and stock; mix gently to combine. Cook, covered, in oven 45 minutes.
4 Add mushroom, green onion and cabbage to dish; cook, covered, stirring occasionally, a further 15 minutes or until chicken is cooked through.
per serving 15.3g total fat (4.5g saturated fat); 1530kJ (366 cal); 10.8g carbohydrate; 42.7g protein; 8.2g fibre

red emperor in thai-style coconut sauce

preparation time 20 minutes
cooking time 25 minutes serves 4

3¼ cups (800ml) coconut milk
4 fresh kaffir lime leaves, sliced thinly
2 fresh red thai chillies, sliced thinly
4cm piece fresh ginger (20g), chopped finely
1 tablespoon fish sauce
2 tablespoons lime juice
1 tablespoon finely chopped fresh coriander root
10cm stick fresh lemon grass (20g), chopped finely
1 tablespoon grated palm sugar
2 x 440g red emperor fillets, skinned
⅓ cup firmly packed fresh coriander leaves

1 Combine coconut milk, lime leaves, chilli, ginger, sauce, juice, coriander root, lemon grass and sugar in large frying pan; bring to a boil. Reduce heat, simmer, uncovered, 10 minutes.
2 Add fish to pan; simmer, covered, about 10 minutes or until fish is cooked through.
3 Remove pan from heat; stir in coriander leaves. Serve fish with coconut sauce and steamed jasmine rice, if desired.
per serving 46.4g total fat (37.9g saturated fat); 2776kJ (664 cal); 12.4g carbohydrate; 49.5g protein; 3.9g fibre

sweet and sour tamarind pork

preparation time 25 minutes
cooking time 50 minutes serves 4

2 tablespoons peanut oil
4 pork forequarter chops (1kg)
1 tablespoon chinese cooking wine
1 cup (250ml) chicken stock
⅓ cup (80ml) tamarind concentrate
¼ cup (60ml) light soy sauce
¼ cup (65g) grated palm sugar
1 medium red capsicum (200g), sliced thickly
1 medium green capsicum (200g), sliced thickly
1 medium red onion (170g), sliced thickly
3 green onions, sliced thickly

AROMATIC PASTE
4cm piece fresh galangal (20g), chopped finely
2 x 10cm sticks fresh lemon grass (40g), chopped finely
2 cloves garlic, quartered
2 shallots (50g), chopped coarsely
1 tablespoon sambal oelek

1 Preheat oven to 150°C/130°C fan-forced.
2 Blend or process ingredients for aromatic paste until mixture becomes a thick coarse puree.
3 Heat half of the oil in large deep flameproof baking dish; cook pork, in batches, until browned both sides.
4 Heat remaining oil in same dish; cook aromatic paste, stirring, until fragrant. Return pork to dish with wine, stock, tamarind, soy sauce, sugar, capsicums and red onion; bring to a boil. Cover; cook in oven 25 minutes, turning pork once halfway through cooking time.
5 Add green onion to dish; cook, covered, in oven about 10 minutes or until green onion is tender. Serve with steamed rice, if desired.

per serving 31.8g total fat (9.4g saturated fat); 2462 kJ (589 cal); 26.3g carbohydrate; 42.0g protein; 2.4g fibre

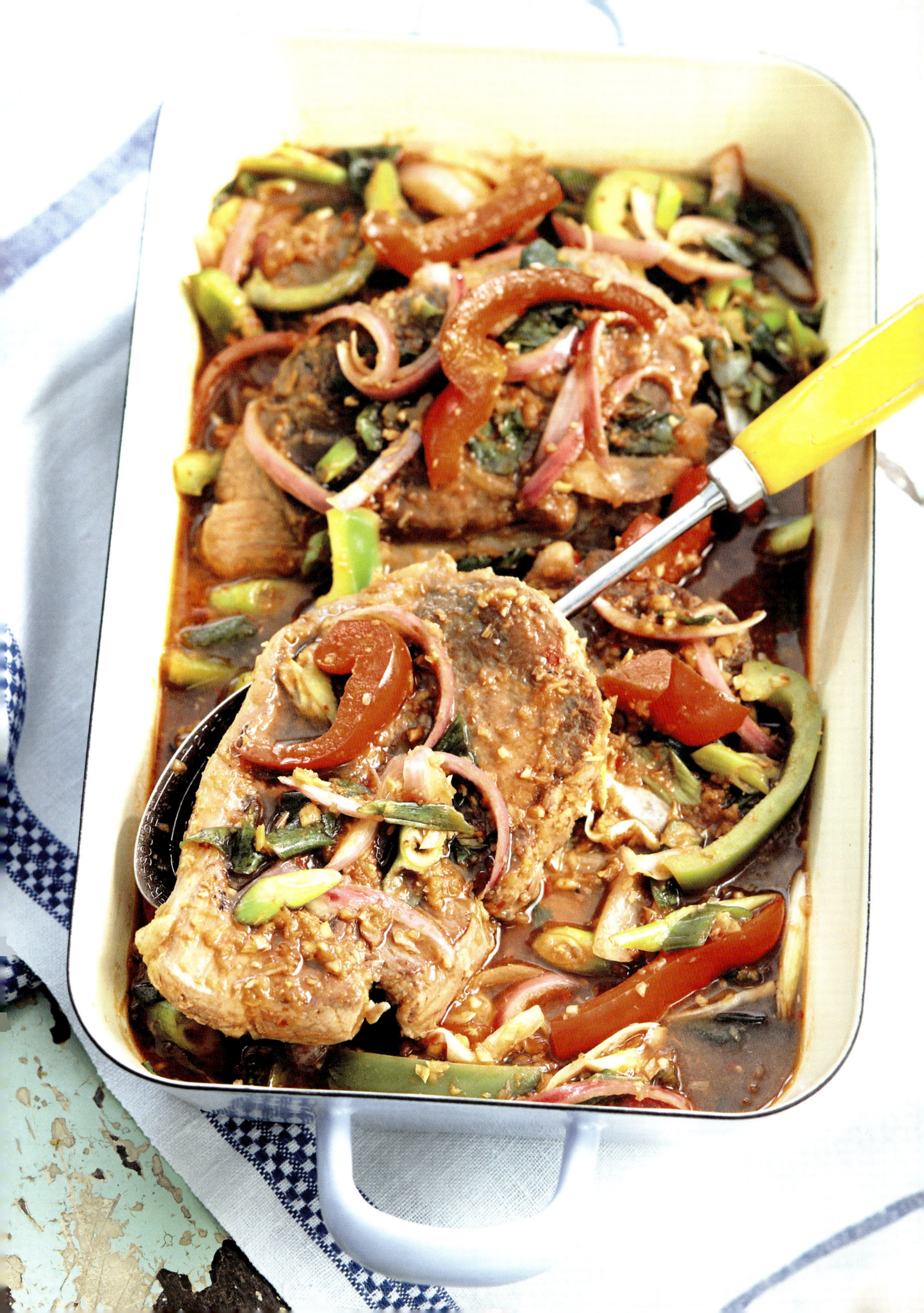

The Complete Book of Modern Asian

chilli marinated beef in spicy coconut sauce

preparation time 20 minutes (plus marinating time)
cooking time 2 hours serves 6

1.5kg beef chuck steak, chopped coarsely
40g ghee
2 medium red capsicums (400g), chopped finely
2 medium brown onions (300g), chopped finely
½ cup (125ml) beef stock
½ cup (125ml) coconut milk
1 cinnamon stick
5 dried curry leaves
⅓ cup chopped fresh coriander

MARINADE
⅓ cup (80ml) white vinegar
2 fresh small red thai chillies, sliced thinly
2 tablespoons tomato paste
1 tablespoon chopped fresh coriander
2 cloves garlic, crushed
3 cardamom pods, crushed
2 teaspoons cumin seeds
1 teaspoon ground turmeric

1 Combine ingredients for marinade in large bowl; add beef, mix well. Cover; refrigerate 3 hours or overnight.
2 Heat half of the ghee in large saucepan; cook beef mixture, in batches, stirring, until browned.
3 Heat remaining ghee in same pan; cook capsicum and onion, stirring, until onion is soft.
4 Return beef to pan; add stock, coconut milk, cinnamon and curry leaves. Simmer, covered, 1 hour, stirring occasionally.
5 Remove cover; simmer about 30 minutes or until beef is tender. Discard cinnamon stick; stir in coriander. Serve with steamed or boiled rice, if desired.

per serving 22.5g total fat (12.9g saturated fat); 1868kJ (447 cal); 6.8g carbohydrate; 53.2g protein; 2.2g fibre

keema with green chilli and tomato

preparation time 20 minutes
cooking time 45 minutes serves 4

2 tablespoons ghee
1 medium brown onion (150g), chopped finely
5cm piece fresh ginger (25g), grated
2 cloves garlic, crushed
3 long green chillies, chopped finely
2 teaspoons cumin seeds
2 teaspoons ground coriander
1 teaspoon ground turmeric
2 teaspoons garam masala
800g lamb mince
400g can diced tomatoes
2 large tomatoes (440g), chopped coarsely
⅓ cup (95g) yogurt
1 tablespoon lemon juice
1 cup (120g) frozen peas
2 tablespoons coarsely chopped fresh coriander

1 Heat ghee in large saucepan; cook onion, ginger, garlic and two-thirds of the chilli, stirring, until onion is soft. Add spices; cook, stirring, until fragrant. Add mince; cook, stirring, until mince changes colour.
2 Add undrained tomatoes and fresh tomato; cook, stirring occasionally, about 15 minutes or until mince is cooked through and sauce has thickened.
3 Add remaining chilli, yogurt, juice and peas; cook, uncovered, until peas are just tender. Serve curry sprinkled with coriander.

per serving 4.6g total fat (2.4g saturated fat); 364kJ (87 cal); 2.2g carbohydrate; 8.8g protein; 1.2g fibre

How did we ever survive before we discovered Asian noodle and rice dishes? Hokkien and rice noodles have grabbed shelf space alongside the various Italian pastas in our pantries. And the plain white rice we once ordered from the Chinese takeaway has evolved into main-courses like nasi goreng and biryani – fabulous rice dishes we now cook at home.

char kway teow *page 360*

balinese chilli lamb and fried noodles *page 347*

rice & noodles

fried noodles with garlic pork *page 363*

curried fried rice with pork and prawns *page 347*

mee krob

preparation time 35 minutes (plus standing time)
cooking time 20 minutes   serves 4

150g fresh firm silken tofu
vegetable oil, for deep-frying
125g rice vermicelli noodles
2 tablespoons peanut oil
2 eggs, beaten lightly
1 tablespoon water
2 cloves garlic, crushed
2 fresh small red thai chillies, chopped finely
1 small green thai chilli, chopped finely
2 tablespoons grated palm sugar
2 tablespoons fish sauce
2 tablespoons tomato sauce
1 tablespoon rice wine vinegar
200g pork mince
200g cooked small prawns, shelled, chopped coarsely
6 green onions, sliced thinly
¼ cup firmly packed fresh coriander leaves

1 Pat tofu all over with absorbent paper; cut into slices, then cut each slice into 1cm-wide matchsticks. Spread tofu, in single layer, on absorbent-paper-lined tray; cover with more absorbent paper, stand at least 20 minutes.
2 Meanwhile, heat vegetable oil in wok; deep-fry noodles quickly, in batches, until puffed. Drain on absorbent paper.
3 Using same heated oil, deep-fry drained tofu, in batches, until browned lightly. Drain on absorbent paper. Discard oil from wok.
4 Heat 2 teaspoons of the peanut oil in cleaned wok. Pour half of the combined egg and water into wok; cook over medium heat, tilting wok, until almost set. Remove omelette from wok; roll tightly, slice thinly. Heat 2 more teaspoons of the peanut oil in wok; repeat with remaining egg mixture.
5 Combine garlic, chillies, sugar, sauces and vinegar in small bowl; pour half of the chilli mixture into small jug, reserve.
6 Combine pork in bowl with remaining half of the chilli mixture. Heat remaining peanut oil in wok; stir-fry pork mixture about 5 minutes or until pork is cooked through. Add prawns; stir-fry 1 minute. Add tofu; stir-fry, tossing gently to combine.
7 Remove wok from heat; add reserved chilli mixture and half of the onion, toss to combine. Add noodles; toss gently to combine. Sprinkle with remaining onion, omelette strips and coriander.
per serving 20.7g total fat (4.5g saturated fat); 1509kJ (361 cal); 17.6g carbohydrate; 25.6g protein; 1.9g fibre

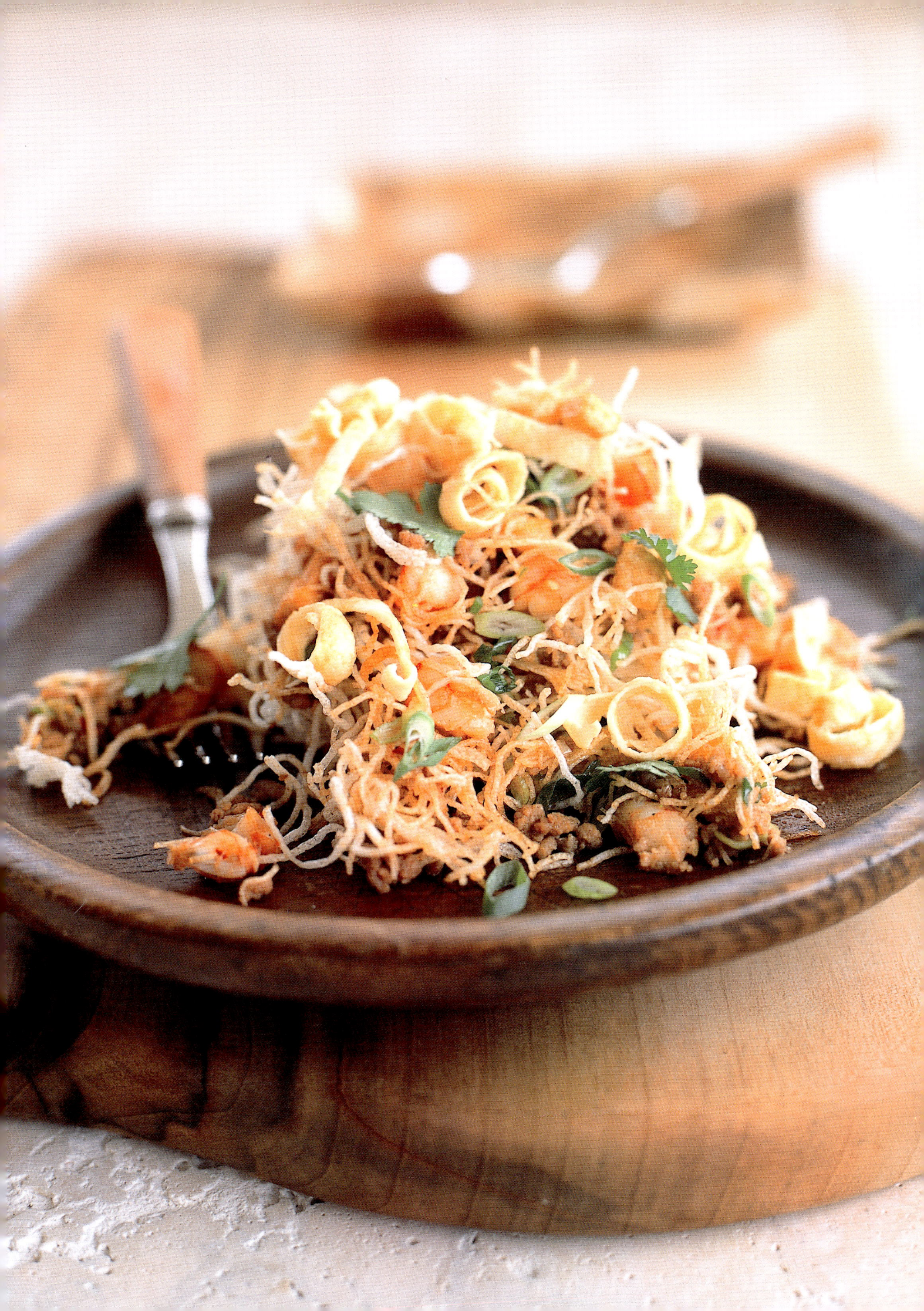

The Complete Book of Modern Asian

barbecued pork fried rice

preparation time 15 minutes
cooking time 25 minutes serves 8

3 cups (600g) long-grain rice
2 tablespoons peanut oil
2 tablespoons sesame oil
2 cloves garlic, crushed
3cm piece fresh ginger (15g), grated
1 litre (4 cups) chicken stock, warmed
1 large brown onion (200g), sliced thinly
2 trimmed sticks celery (200g), sliced thinly
1 large (180g) carrot, sliced thinly
6 green onions, sliced thickly
¼ cup (60ml) light soy sauce
500g chinese barbecue pork

1 Rinse rice in a strainer under cold water until water runs clear.
2 Heat half of the oils in medium saucepan; cook garlic and ginger until fragrant. Add rice; toss to coat. Add warmed stock; bring to a boil. Reduce heat to low; cook, covered tightly, 20 minutes or until rice is cooked.
3 Heat remaining oils in wok; stir-fry onion, celery and carrot until soft. Add white parts of green onions; stir-fry 1 minute. Add cooked rice and sauce; stir-fry until combined. Serve topped with sliced pork and green onions.
per serving 19.6g total fat (5.7g saturated fat); 2228kJ (533 cal); 65.7g carbohydrate; 21g protein; 4g fibre

hokkien mee with beef

preparation time 15 minutes
cooking time 15 minutes serves 4

300g hokkien noodles
1 tablespoon peanut oil
700g beef rump steak, sliced thinly
1 medium brown onion (150g), sliced thinly
3cm piece fresh ginger (15g), grated
2 cloves garlic, crushed
2 fresh small red thai chillies, sliced thinly
1 small red capsicum (150g), sliced thinly
1 small green capsicum (150g), sliced thinly
200g mushrooms, quartered
2 tablespoons hoisin sauce
1 tablespoon dark soy sauce

1 Place noodles in medium heatproof bowl, cover with boiling water; separate with fork, drain.
2 Heat half the oil in wok; stir-fry beef, in batches, until browned.
3 Heat remaining oil in wok; stir-fry onion until soft. Add ginger, garlic and chilli; stir-fry until fragrant. Add capsicums and mushrooms; stir-fry until tender.
4 Return beef to wok with noodles and sauces; stir-fry until hot.
per serving 17.4g total fat (6.2g saturated fat); 1927kJ (461 cal); 27.2g carbohydrate; 46.1g protein; 5.3g fibre

chicken and thai basil fried rice

preparation time 15 minutes
cooking time 10 minutes serves 4

¼ cup (60ml) peanut oil
1 medium brown onion (150g), chopped finely
3 cloves garlic, crushed
2 long green chillies, chopped finely
1 tablespoon brown sugar
500g chicken breast fillets, chopped coarsely
2 medium red capsicums (400g), sliced thinly
200g green beans, chopped coarsely
4 cups cooked jasmine rice
2 tablespoons fish sauce
2 tablespoons dark soy sauce
½ cup loosely packed thai basil leaves

1 Heat oil in wok; stir-fry onion, garlic and chilli until onion softens. Add sugar; stir-fry until dissolved. Add chicken; stir-fry until browned lightly. Add capsicum and beans; stir-fry until vegetables are just tender and chicken is cooked through.
2 Add rice and sauces; stir-fry, tossing gently until combined. Remove from heat; add basil, toss gently to combine.
per serving 19.7g total fat (4g saturated fat); 2445kJ (585 cal); 64g carbohydrate; 34.8g protein; 5g fibre
TIP You need to cook 1⅓ cups rice for this recipe.

vegetarian pad thai

preparation time 20 minutes (plus standing time)
cooking time 10 minutes serves 4

200g rice stick noodles
2 cloves garlic, quartered
2 tablespoons finely chopped preserved turnip
2 fresh small red thai chillies, chopped coarsely
¼ cup (60ml) peanut oil
2 eggs, beaten lightly
1 cup (90g) fried shallots
125g fried tofu, cut into small pieces
¼ cup (35g) coarsely chopped roasted unsalted peanuts
3 cups (240g) bean sprouts
6 green onions, sliced thinly
2 tablespoons soy sauce
1 tablespoon lime juice
2 tablespoons coarsely chopped fresh coriander

1 Place noodles in large heatproof bowl; cover with boiling water, stand until noodles just soften, drain.
2 Meanwhile, using mortar and pestle, crush garlic, turnip and chilli until mixture forms a paste.
3 Heat 2 teaspoons of the oil in wok. Pour egg into wok; cook over medium heat, tilting wok, until almost set. Remove omelette from wok; roll tightly, slice thinly.
4 Heat remaining oil in wok; stir-fry garlic paste and fried onion until fragrant. Add tofu; stir-fry 1 minute. Add half of the nuts, half of the sprouts and half of the green onion; stir-fry until sprouts are just wilted. Add noodles, sauce and juice; stir-fry, tossing gently until combined. Remove from heat; toss omelette strips, coriander and remaining nuts, sprouts and green onion through pad thai.
per serving 24.3g total fat (4.4g saturated fat); 1417kJ (339 cal); 15.2g carbohydrate; 13.4g protein; 4.3g fibre

Rice & Noodles

The Complete Book of Modern Asian

sweet soy fried noodles

preparation time 15 minutes
cooking time 15 minutes serves 4

1kg fresh wide rice noodles
2 teaspoons sesame oil
2 cloves garlic, crushed
2 fresh small red thai chillies, sliced thinly
600g chicken thigh fillets, chopped coarsely
250g baby buk choy, quartered lengthways
4 green onions, sliced thinly
2 tablespoons kecap manis
1 tablespoon oyster sauce
1 tablespoon fish sauce
1 tablespoon grated palm sugar
¼ cup coarsely chopped fresh coriander
1 tablespoon fried shallots

1 Place noodles in large heatproof bowl; cover with boiling water, separate noodles with fork, drain.
2 Heat oil in large wok; stir-fry garlic and chilli until fragrant. Add chicken; stir-fry until browned lightly. Add buk choy and green onion; stir-fry until onion softens and chicken is cooked through.
3 Add noodles, kecap manis, sauces and sugar to wok; stir-fry, tossing gently to combine. Remove from heat; add coriander, toss gently to combine. Sprinkle with fried shallots.

per serving 10g total fat (2.2g saturated fat); 2057kJ (492 cal); 59.9g carbohydrate; 38.3g protein; 2.7g fibre

crisp hot and sweet beef with noodles

preparation time 20 minutes (plus standing time)
cooking time 1 hour 45 minutes serves 4

750g piece beef corned silverside
1kg fresh wide rice noodles
¼ cup (60ml) peanut oil
3 cloves garlic, crushed
3 fresh small red thai chillies, sliced thinly
4 spring onions, sliced thinly
2 tablespoons fish sauce
¼ cup (65g) grated palm sugar
1 cup firmly packed fresh coriander leaves

1 Place beef in large saucepan, cover with cold water; bring to a boil, uncovered. Reduce heat, simmer, covered, 1 hour 30 minutes. Remove from pan, discard packaging; drain beef on rack over tray for 15 minutes.
2 Meanwhile, place noodles in large heatproof bowl; cover with boiling water, separate with fork, drain.
3 Trim excess fat from beef. Using two forks, shred beef finely. Heat oil in wok; stir-fry beef, in batches, until browned all over and crisp. Drain on absorbent paper.
4 Stir-fry garlic, chilli and onion in wok until onion softens. Add sauce and sugar; stir-fry until sugar dissolves. Return beef to wok with noodles; stir-fry gently until heated through. Remove from heat; stir through coriander.

per serving 23.8g total fat (6.4g saturated fat); 2905kJ (695 cal); 70.8g carbohydrate; 47.4g protein; 2.3g fibre

spiced vegetable biryani

preparation time 15 minutes
cooking time 30 minutes serves 4

1 tablespoon vegetable oil
1 clove garlic, crushed
1 medium brown onion (150g), sliced thinly
2 teaspoons garam masala
400g can diced tomatoes
1 medium potato (200g), cut into 1cm pieces
2 medium carrots (240g), chopped coarsely
½ cup (125ml) water
2 medium zucchini (240g), chopped coarsely
1 medium red capsicum (200g), sliced thinly
1 medium brown onion (150g), chopped finely
1½ cups (300g) basmati rice
8 cardamom pods, bruised
½ teaspoon chilli powder
¼ teaspoon ground turmeric
1½ cups (375ml) water, extra
¼ cup (40g) sultanas

1 Heat half of the oil in large saucepan; cook garlic and sliced onion, stirring, until onion softens. Add garam masala; cook, stirring, 1 minute. Stir in undrained tomatoes, potato, carrot and the water; bring to a boil. Reduce heat, simmer, covered, 10 minutes. Add zucchini and capsicum; simmer, covered, 10 minutes or until vegetables are tender.

2 Meanwhile, heat remaining oil in medium saucepan; cook chopped onion, stirring, until soft. Add rice and spices; cook, stirring, until fragrant. Stir in the extra water and sultanas; bring to a boil. Reduce heat, simmer, covered, about 15 minutes or until rice is just tender and water is absorbed.

3 Place half of the rice mixture in 2-litre (8-cup) serving dish; top with vegetable mixture then remaining rice mixture. Serve with yogurt, if desired.

per serving 5.7g total fat (0.7g saturated fat); 1802kJ (431 cal); 84.1g carbohydrate; 10g protein; 7.1g fibre

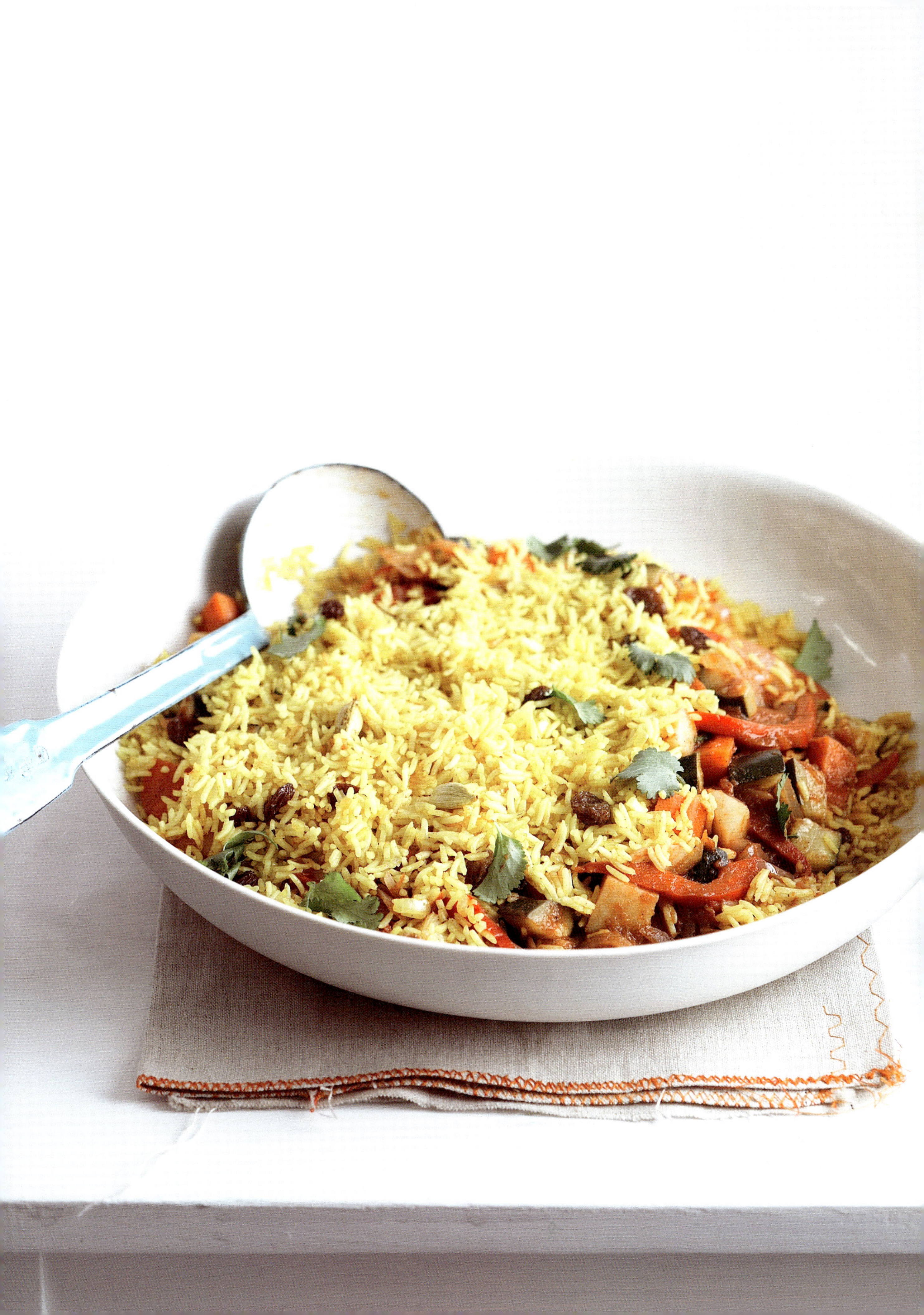

The Complete Book of Modern Asian

balinese chilli lamb and fried noodles

preparation time 15 minutes
cooking time 10 minutes serves 4

600g hokkien noodles
750g lamb backstraps, sliced thinly
1 tablespoon sambal oelek
1 tablespoon dark soy sauce
1 tablespoon fish sauce
2 cloves garlic, crushed
¼ cup (60ml) peanut oil
⅓ cup (55g) coarsely chopped brazil nuts
⅔ cup (160ml) beef stock
2 tablespoons oyster sauce
2 tablespoons lime juice
2 teaspoons brown sugar
150g sugar snap peas, trimmed
⅓ cup finely chopped fresh mint
2 fresh small red thai chillies, chopped finely

1 Place noodles in large heatproof bowl, cover with boiling water; separate with fork, drain.
2 Combine lamb, sambal oelek, sauces and garlic in large bowl.
3 Heat ½ teaspoon of the oil in wok; stir-fry nuts until browned lightly. Remove from wok.
4 Heat 2 tablespoons of remaining oil in wok; stir-fry lamb, in batches, until browned.
5 Heat remaining oil in wok; stir-fry noodles until browned lightly.
6 Add stock, oyster sauce, juice and sugar to wok; simmer about 3 minutes or until sauce thickens slightly.
7 Return lamb to wok with peas; stir-fry until hot. Serve noodles topped with lamb mixture and sprinkled with nuts, mint and chilli.

per serving 40.5g total fat (12.1g saturated fat); 3164kJ (757 cal); 45.4g carbohydrate; 50.2g protein; 5.4g fibre

curried fried rice with pork and prawns

preparation time 20 minutes
cooking time 25 minutes serves 4

1 tablespoon white sugar
2 tablespoons light soy sauce
800g pork leg steaks, sliced thinly
125g uncooked small prawns
2 tablespoons peanut oil
2 eggs, beaten lightly
1 teaspoon curry powder
2 cloves garlic, crushed
2 cups cold cooked white long-grain rice
4 green onions, sliced thinly
2 cups (240g) frozen peas and corn

1 Combine sugar and half the sauce in medium bowl with pork. Shell and devein prawns, leaving tails intact.
2 Heat 1 teaspoon of the oil in wok. Pour egg into wok; cook over medium heat, tilting wok, until almost set. Remove omelette from wok; roll tightly, slice thinly.
3 Heat 2 teaspoons of the remaining oil in wok; stir-fry pork, in batches, until cooked as desired.
4 Heat 1 teaspoon of remaining oil in wok; stir-fry prawns until just changed in colour. Remove from wok.
5 Heat remaining oil in wok; cook curry powder and garlic, stirring, until fragrant. Add rice, onion, pea and corn mixture and remaining sauce; stir-fry until vegetables are just tender.
6 Return pork, prawns and half of the omelette to wok; stir-fry until heated through. Sprinkle fried rice with remaining omelette.

per serving 18.1g total fat (4.3g saturated fat); 2337kJ (559 cal); 38g carbohydrate; 57.5g protein; 4.9g fibre
TIP You need to cook ⅔ cup rice for this recipe.

beef mee goreng

preparation time 10 minutes
cooking time 15 minutes serves 4

600g hokkien noodles
1 tablespoon peanut oil
3 eggs, beaten lightly
500g beef strips
2 cloves garlic, crushed
2cm piece fresh ginger (10g), grated
500g baby buk choy, chopped coarsely
4 green onions, sliced thinly
¼ cup coarsely chopped fresh coriander
2 tablespoons dried shrimp
¼ cup (60ml) kecap manis
2 teaspoons sambal oelek
¼ cup (60ml) beef stock
½ cup (75g) roasted unsalted peanuts, chopped coarsely

1 Place noodles in large heatproof bowl; cover with boiling water, separate with fork, drain.
2 Heat half of the oil in large wok. Pour half of the egg into wok; cook over medium heat, tilting wok, until almost set. Remove omelette from wok; roll tightly, slice thinly. Repeat with remaining egg.
3 Heat remaining oil in wok; stir-fry combined beef, garlic and ginger, in batches, until beef is browned all over and just cooked through.
4 Place buk choy in same wok; stir-fry until just wilted. Return beef to pan with noodles, onion, coriander, shrimp and combined kecap manis, sambal and stock; stir-fry until heated through. Serve topped with omelette and peanuts.
per serving 31.1g total fat (8.6g saturated fat); 3511kJ (840 cal); 82.4g carbohydrate; 53.5g protein; 6.6g fibre

beef kway teow

preparation time 10 minutes
cooking time 15 minutes serves 4

2 tablespoons peanut oil
500g beef strips
450g fresh wide rice noodles
3 cloves garlic, crushed
2cm piece fresh ginger (10g), grated
6 green onions, cut into 2cm pieces
1 small red capsicum (150g), sliced thinly
2 cups (160g) bean sprouts
¼ cup (75g) satay sauce
2 tablespoons fish sauce

1 Heat half of the oil in wok; stir-fry beef, in batches, until browned all over.
2 Place noodles in large heatproof bowl; cover with boiling water, separate with fork, drain.
3 Heat remaining oil in wok; stir-fry garlic and ginger until fragrant. Add onion and capsicum; stir-fry until vegetables are just soft. Return beef to wok with noodles, sprouts and sauces; stir-fry until hot.
per serving 21.8g total fat (6.2g saturated fat); 1935kJ (463 cal); 32.4g carbohydrate; 32.7g protein; 3.5g fibre

Rice & Noodles

The Complete Book of Modern Asian

chilli rice noodles with lamb and buk choy

preparation time 20 minutes
cooking time 15 minutes serves 4

400g fresh thin rice noodles
1 tablespoon peanut oil
500g lamb mince
3 cloves garlic, crushed
2 fresh small red thai chillies, chopped finely
400g buk choy, sliced thinly
2 tablespoons tamari
1 tablespoon fish sauce
2 tablespoons kecap manis
4 green onions, sliced thinly
1 cup firmly packed thai basil leaves
3 cups (240g) bean sprouts

1 Place noodles in medium heatproof bowl; cover with boiling water, separate with fork, drain.
2 Heat oil in wok; stir-fry mince until browned. Add garlic and chilli; stir-fry until fragrant. Add noodles, buk choy, tamari, sauce and kecap manis; stir-fry until buk choy just wilts.
3 Remove from heat; stir in onion, basil and sprouts. Serve topped with sliced chilli, if desired.
per serving 14.4g total fat (4.7g saturated fat); 1877kJ (449 cal); 44.5g carbohydrate; 34.3g protein; 5.3g fibre

sweet chilli plum noodles with chicken

preparation time 20 minutes (plus refrigeration time)
cooking time 20 minutes serves 4

¼ cup (60ml) sweet chilli sauce
2 tablespoons plum sauce
750g chicken thigh fillets, sliced thinly
450g hokkien noodles
227g can water chestnuts, rinsed, halved
8 green onions, sliced thickly
1 fresh long red chilli, sliced thinly
2 cloves garlic, crushed
300g buk choy, trimmed, chopped coarsely

1 Combine sauces with chicken in large bowl. Cover; refrigerate 1 hour.
2 Heat oiled wok; stir-fry chicken mixture, in batches, until browned.
3 Meanwhile, place noodles in medium heatproof bowl; cover with boiling water, separate with fork, drain.
4 Stir-fry chestnuts, onion, chilli and garlic in wok 2 minutes. Return chicken to wok with buk choy; stir-fry until chicken is cooked. Serve with noodles.
per serving 14.9g total fat (4.2g saturated fat); 2011kJ (481 cal); 43.1g carbohydrate; 41g protein; 5.4g fibre

asian star

pad thai

preparation time 20 minutes (plus standing time)
cooking time 10 minutes serves 4

40g tamarind pulp
½ cup (125ml) boiling water
2 tablespoons grated palm sugar
⅓ cup (80ml) sweet chilli sauce
⅓ cup (80ml) fish sauce
375g rice stick noodles
12 uncooked medium prawns (540g)
2 cloves garlic, crushed
2 tablespoons finely chopped preserved turnip
2 tablespoons dried shrimp
4cm piece fresh ginger (20g), grated finely
2 fresh small red thai chillies, chopped coarsely
1 tablespoon peanut oil
250g pork mince
3 eggs, beaten lightly
2 cups (160g) bean sprouts
4 green onions, sliced thinly
⅓ cup coarsely chopped fresh coriander
¼ cup (35g) coarsely chopped roasted unsalted peanuts
1 lime, quartered

1 Soak tamarind pulp in the boiling water 30 minutes. Pour tamarind into fine strainer over small bowl; push as much tamarind pulp through strainer as possible, scraping underside of strainer occasionally. Discard any tamarind solids left in strainer; reserve pulp liquid in bowl. Mix sugar and sauces into bowl with pulp liquid.
2 Meanwhile, place noodles in large heatproof bowl; cover with boiling water. Stand until just tender; drain.
3 Shell and devein prawns, leaving tails intact.
4 Blend or process garlic, turnip, shrimp, ginger and chilli until mixture forms a paste.
5 Heat oil in wok; stir-fry garlic paste until fragrant. Add pork; stir-fry until just cooked through. Add prawns; stir-fry 1 minute. Add egg; stir-fry until egg just sets. Add noodles, tamarind mixture, sprouts and half of the onion; stir-fry, tossing gently until combined. Remove from heat; add remaining green onion, coriander and nuts, toss gently until combined. Serve with lime wedges.
per serving 19.7g total fat (4.5g saturated fat); 2608kJ (624 cal); 65.6g carbohydrate; 42.6g protein; 5.4g fibre

Press the tamarind with the back of a spoon to extract as much of the pulp liquid as possible. Discard the solids left in the sieve.

Dice the preserved turnip as small as possible to make it easier to crush in the mortar and pestle when preparing the paste.

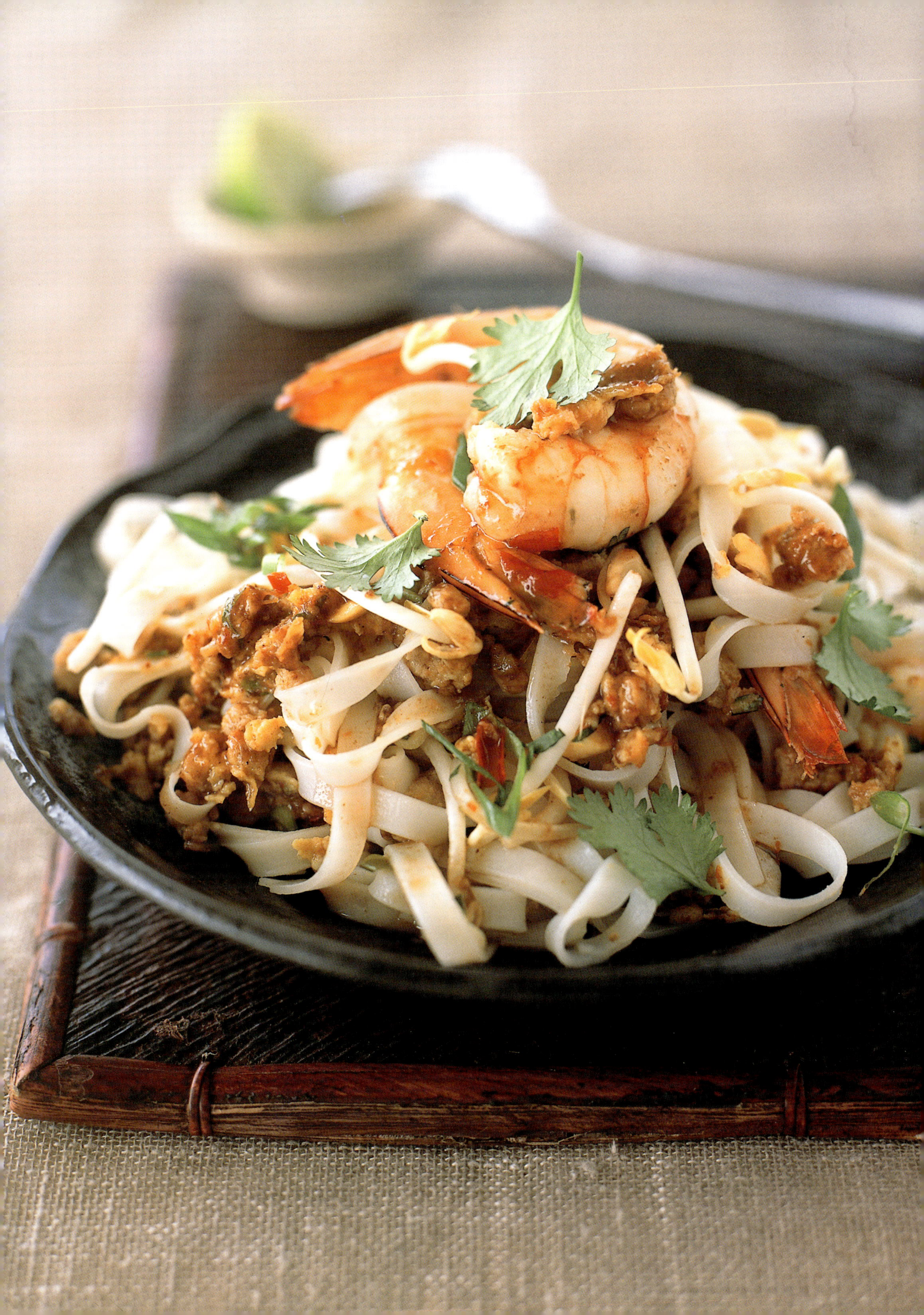

The Complete Book of Modern Asian

soy-fried noodles with tofu

preparation time 15 minutes
cooking time 20 minutes   serves 4

450g fresh wide rice noodles
1 tablespoon peanut oil
3 cloves garlic, sliced thinly
2 eggs, beaten lightly
280g gai lan, chopped coarsely
200g snake beans, cut into 5cm lengths
⅓ cup (80ml) kecap manis
2 tablespoons light soy sauce
½ teaspoon dried chilli flakes
350g packet fried tofu, cut into 2cm cubes
4 green onions, sliced thinly
¾ cup loosely packed thai basil leaves

1 Place noodles in large heatproof bowl, cover with boiling water; separate with fork, drain.
2 Heat oil in wok; stir-fry garlic until fragrant. Add egg; stir-fry until set. Add vegetables, sauces and chilli; stir-fry until vegetables are tender. Add noodles, tofu, onion and basil; stir-fry until hot.
per serving 18.2g total fat (4g saturated fat); 2036kJ (487 cal); 55.4g carbohydrate; 20.1g protein; 9.8g fibre
TIPS Known as "pad sieu" this traditional Thai dish is similar to the famous "pad thai", but uses kecap manis, a thick, sweet soy sauce, to give it its special flavour.

nasi goreng

preparation time 20 minutes
cooking time 20 minutes   serves 4

1 tablespoon peanut oil
2 eggs, beaten lightly
1 teaspoon sesame oil
1 medium brown onion (150g), sliced thinly
4 green onions, sliced thinly
1 clove garlic, crushed
5cm piece fresh ginger (25g), grated
2 cups (160g) shredded wombok
1 cup (80g) bean sprouts
3 cups cooked white long-grain rice
1 tablespoon sambal oelek
1 tablespoon kecap manis
1 lebanese cucumber (130g), sliced thinly
1 medium tomato (150g), sliced thinly

1 Heat 1 teaspoon of the peanut oil in large wok. Pour half of the egg into wok; cook over medium heat, tilting wok, until almost set. Remove omelette from wok; roll tightly, slice thinly. Repeat with another teaspoon of the peanut oil and remaining egg mixture.
2 Heat remaining peanut oil and sesame oil in wok; stir-fry onions, garlic and ginger until onion softens. Add wombok and sprouts; stir-fry over high heat until vegetables are just tender.
3 Add rice, omelette, sambal and kecap manis to wok; stir-fry until heated through.
4 Serve nasi goreng with cucumber and tomato.
per serving 8.9g total fat (1.8g saturated fat); 1292kJ (302 cal); 45.6g carbohydrate; 9.3g protein; 4.1g fibre
TIP You need to cook 1 cup rice for this recipe.

fried rice with prawns

preparation time 30 minutes (plus standing time)
cooking time 30 minutes serves 6

1 cup (200g) long-grain rice
10g dried shiitake mushrooms
400g can baby corn, drained
500g cooked king prawns, shelled
¼ cup (60ml) peanut oil
3 eggs, beaten lightly
1 medium brown onion (150g), chopped finely
2 cloves garlic, crushed
1 pork butterfly steak (160g), chopped finely
2 seafood sticks (65g), sliced thinly
1 medium green capsicum (200g), chopped finely
1 tablespoon red curry paste
2 tablespoons light soy sauce
1 tablespoon fish sauce
1 tablespoon finely chopped fresh coriander

1 Rinse rice under cold water, drain. Add rice to large saucepan of boiling water. Boil, uncovered, 10 minutes or until tender. Drain, rinse rice under cold water, drain.
2 Place mushrooms in bowl, cover with warm water, stand 20 minutes. Drain; discard stems, cut caps into thin slices. Cut corn into quarters. Cut prawns in half lengthways.
3 Heat 1 tablespoon of the oil in wok. Pour egg into wok; cook over medium heat, tilting wok, until almost set. Remove omelette from wok; roll tightly, slice thinly.
4 Heat remaining oil in wok; stir-fry onion and garlic until fragrant. Add pork, stir-fry until browned. Add prawns, seafood sticks, capsicum and paste; stir-fry 2 minutes. Add rice, sauces and coriander; stir-fry until hot. Serve rice topped with omelette slices.
per serving 15.5g total fat (3.3g saturated fat); 1530kJ (366 cal); 31.3g carbohydrate; 23.6g protein; 3g fibre

chicken, noodle and kaffir lime stir-fry

preparation time 15 minutes
cooking time 10 minutes serves 4

500g chicken thigh fillets, sliced thinly
¼ cup (60ml) vegetable oil
2 fresh small thai red chillies, sliced thinly
2 cloves garlic, crushed
4cm piece fresh ginger (20g), grated
8 green onions, sliced thickly
½ cup (125ml) chicken stock
2 tablespoons lime juice
¼ cup (60ml) oyster sauce
2 tablespoons caster sugar
5 fresh kaffir leaves, shredded
500g fresh wide rice noodles
1 cup loosely packed thai basil leaves
250g bean sprouts
¼ cup (25g) fried shallots

1 Heat half of the oil in wok; stir-fry chicken, in batches, until lightly browned.
2 Heat remaining oil in wok; add chilli, garlic, ginger and green onions; stir-fry until fragrant. Add stock, juice, oyster sauce, sugar, lime leaves and noodles; bring to a boil.
3 Return chicken to wok with basil and bean sprouts; stir-fry until hot. Serve sprinkled with fried shallots.
per serving 24.1g total fat (4.6g saturated fat); 2107kJ (504 cal); 40.8g carbohydrate; 29.4g protein; 3.7g fibre

Rice & Noodles

The Complete Book of Modern Asian

rice noodles with beef and black bean

preparation time 15 minutes
cooking time 15 minutes serves 4

250g dried rice stick noodles
1 tablespoon peanut oil
400g beef mince
1 medium brown onion (150g), sliced thinly
2 fresh small red thai chillies, sliced thinly
350g choy sum, chopped coarsely
150g sugar snap peas, trimmed
2 tablespoons black bean sauce
2 tablespoons kecap manis
⅓ cup (80ml) beef stock
4 green onions, sliced thinly

1 Place noodles in large heatproof bowl, cover with boiling water, stand for 5 minutes; drain.
2 Meanwhile, heat oil in wok; stir-fry beef, brown onion and chilli about 5 minutes or until beef is browned and cooked through. Add choy sum and peas; stir-fry until just tender.
3 Add noodles and combined sauce, kecap manis, stock and green onions; stir-fry until hot.
per serving 12.9g total fat (3.8g saturated fat); 1806kJ (432 cal); 48.2g carbohydrate; 28.1g protein; 4g fibre

crisp beef with egg noodles

preparation time 15 minutes
cooking time 15 minutes serves 4

2 tablespoons cornflour
½ teaspoon bicarbonate of soda
600g beef rump steak, cut into thin strips
⅔ cup (160ml) peanut oil
2 tablespoons sweet chilli sauce
¼ cup (60ml) kecap manis
1 tablespoon light soy sauce
2 teaspoons sesame oil
1 clove garlic, crushed
2 green onions, chopped finely
400g fresh thin egg noodles
200g shiitake mushrooms, quartered
½ small wombok (400g), shredded coarsely
300g baby buk choy, sliced thinly lengthways

1 Combine cornflour and soda in large bowl. Add beef; toss to coat all over, shaking off excess.
2 Heat one-third of the peanut oil in wok; stir-fry about one-third of the beef until crisp. Drain on absorbent paper, then cover to keep warm; repeat with remaining peanut oil and beef.
3 Combine sauces, sesame oil, garlic and onion in small bowl.
4 Place noodles in large heatproof bowl, cover with boiling water; separate with fork, drain.
5 Reheat same cleaned wok; stir-fry mushrooms about 2 minutes or until just tender. Add wombok and buk choy; stir-fry 1 minute. Add sauce mixture, noodles and beef; stir-fry until hot.
per serving 50.4g total fat (11.7g saturated fat); 3766kJ (901 cal); 61g carbohydrate; 47.8g protein; 7.1g fibre
TIP You can buy beef strips instead of a piece of rump to save time.

char kway teow

preparation time 20 minutes
cooking time 15 minutes serves 4

450g wide fresh rice noodles
250g uncooked small prawns
250g squid hoods
⅓ cup (80ml) peanut oil
250g firm white fish fillets, skinned, cut into 3cm pieces
2 cloves garlic, crushed
2 fresh small red thai chillies, chopped finely
4cm piece fresh ginger (20g), grated
2 eggs, beaten lightly
5 green onions, sliced thinly
2 cups (160g) bean sprouts
120g dried chinese sausage, sliced thinly
2 tablespoons dark soy sauce
1 tablespoon kecap manis
1 tablespoon light soy sauce

1 Place noodles in large heatproof bowl; cover with boiling water, separate with fork, drain.
2 Shell and devein prawns, leaving tails intact. Cut squid down centre to open out; score inside in diagonal pattern, then cut into 2cm-wide strips.
3 Heat 1 tablespoon of the oil in wok; stir-fry fish and squid, in batches, until browned lightly. Place in large bowl; cover to keep warm.
4 Heat another tablespoon of the oil in wok; stir-fry prawns, garlic, chilli and ginger until prawns just change colour. Add to bowl with fish and squid; cover to keep warm.
5 Heat remaining oil in wok; stir-fry egg, onion and sprouts until egg is just set. Slide egg mixture onto plate; cover to keep warm.
6 Stir-fry sausage in wok until crisp; drain. Return sausage to wok with seafood, egg mixture, sauces and noodles; stir-fry until hot.

per serving 29.9g total fat (6.9g saturated fat); 2291kJ (548 cal); 27g carbohydrate; 41.1g protein; 3.3g fibre

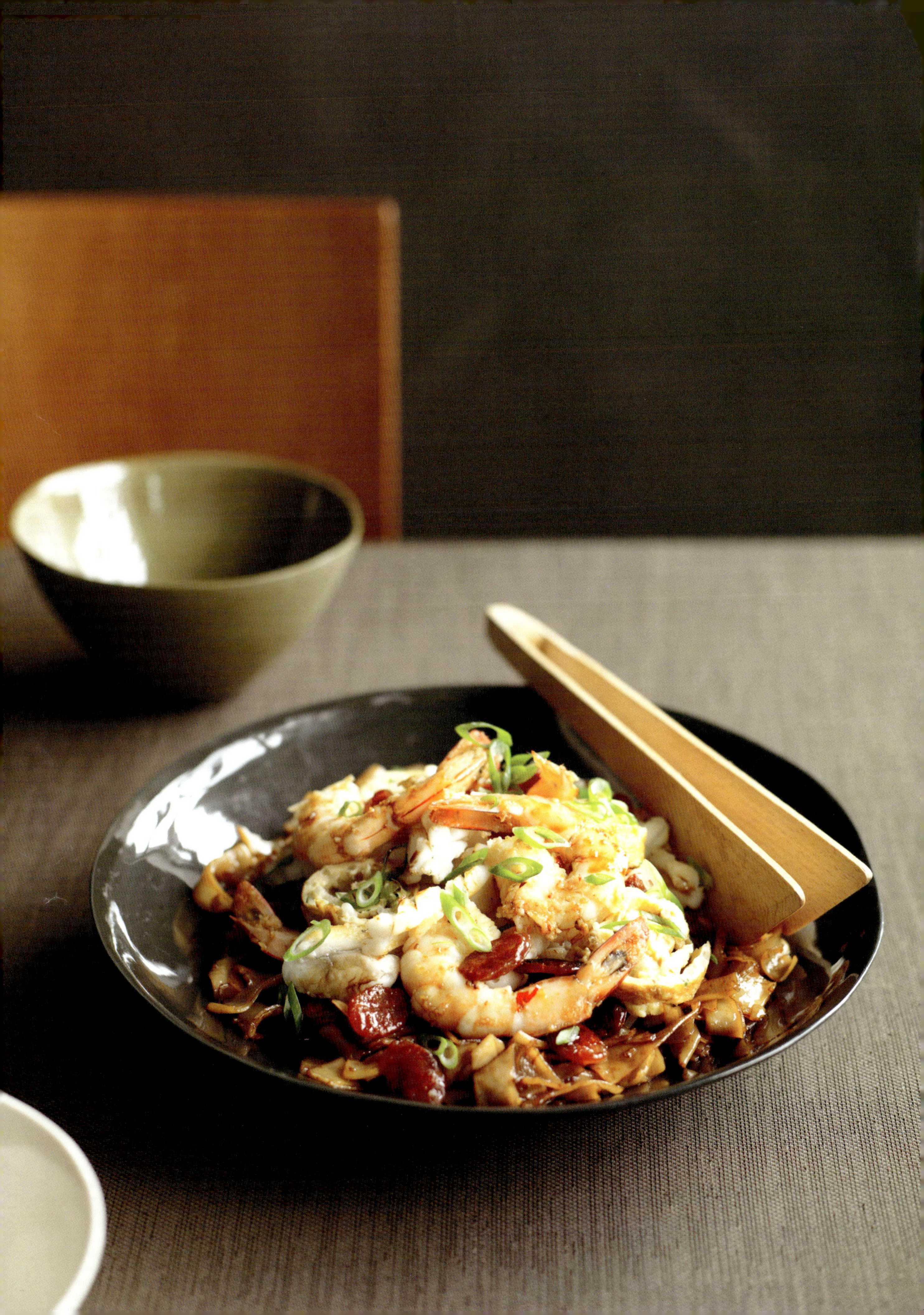

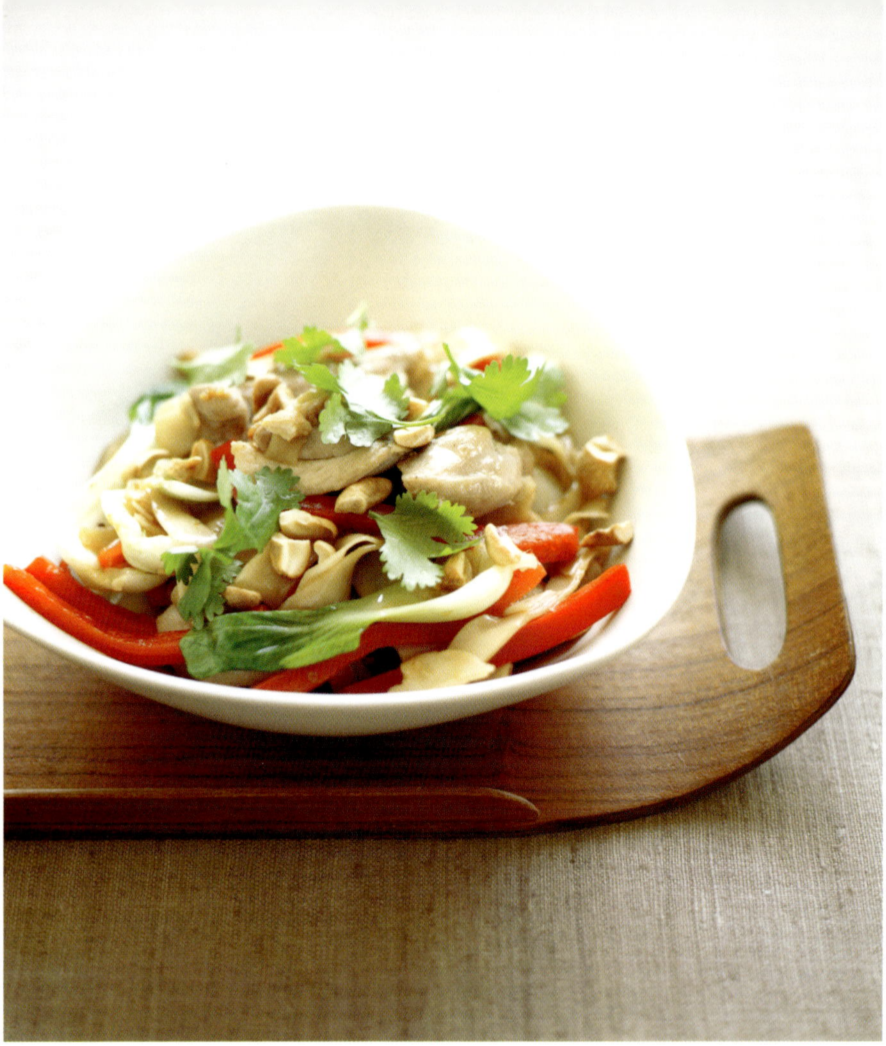

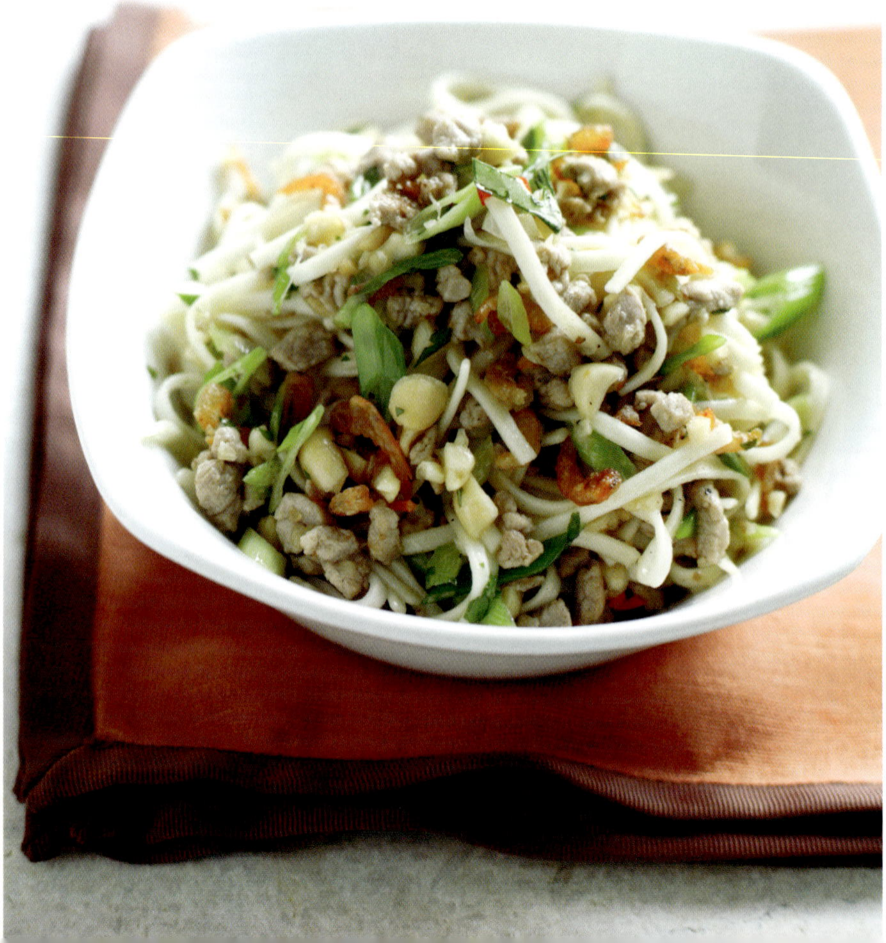

fried noodles with garlic pork

preparation time 15 minutes
cooking time 15 minutes serves 4

175g dried egg noodles
2 tablespoons peanut oil
2 cloves garlic, crushed
250g pork fillet, chopped finely
½ cup (70g) finely chopped peanuts
¼ cup (30g) dried shrimp
6 green onions, sliced thinly
2 tablespoons fish sauce
1 teaspoon grated palm sugar
1 fresh small red thai chilli, chopped finely
2 tablespoons lime juice
2 tablespoons finely chopped fresh coriander

1 Cook noodles in large saucepan of boiling water, uncovered, about 5 minutes or until tender; drain well.
2 Heat oil in wok; stir-fry garlic and pork until pork is browned.
3 Add peanuts, shrimp, onion, sauce, sugar, chilli and juice to wok; stir-fry 1 minute. Add noodles and coriander; stir-fry until hot.

per serving 23.1g total fat (4.7g saturated fat); 1885kJ (451 cal); 34.6g carbohydrate; 24.5g protein; 3.4g fibre

chicken mee goreng

preparation time 10 minutes
cooking time 15 minutes serves 4

450g wide fresh rice noodles
1 tablespoon peanut oil
600g chicken thigh fillets, sliced thinly
2 cloves garlic, crushed
1 medium red capsicum (200g), sliced thinly
500g baby buk choy, leaves separated
⅓ cup (80ml) oyster sauce
1 tablespoon light soy sauce
½ cup (75g) roasted unsalted cashews, chopped coarsely
¼ cup loosely packed fresh coriander leaves

1 Place noodles in large heatproof bowl; cover with boiling water, separate with fork, drain.
2 Heat half the oil in wok; cook chicken, in batches, until browned.
3 Heat remaining oil in wok; stir-fry garlic until fragrant. Add capsicum, buk choy and sauces; stir-fry until vegetables are tender.
4 Return chicken to wok with noodles; stir-fry until chicken is cooked. Remove from heat; sprinkle with nuts and coriander.

per serving 25.6g total fat (5.8g saturated fat); 2211kJ (529 cal); 35.8g carbohydrate; 36.6g protein; 4.2g fibre

beef chow mein

preparation time 30 minutes
cooking time 20 minutes serves 4

1 tablespoon vegetable oil
500g beef mince
1 medium brown onion (150g), chopped finely
2 cloves garlic, crushed
1 tablespoon curry powder
1 large carrot (180g), chopped finely
2 trimmed celery stalks (200g), sliced thinly
150g mushrooms, sliced thinly
1 cup (250ml) chicken stock
⅓ cup (80ml) oyster sauce
2 tablespoons dark soy sauce
440g thin fresh egg noodles
½ cup (60g) frozen peas
½ small wombok (350g), shredded coarsely

1 Heat oil in wok; stir-fry beef, onion and garlic until beef is browned. Add curry powder; stir-fry about 1 minute or until fragrant. Add carrot, celery and mushrooms; stir-fry until vegetables soften.
2 Add stock, sauces and noodles; stir-fry 2 minutes. Add peas and wombok; stir-fry until wombok just wilts.
per serving 15.7g total fat (4.6g saturated fat); 2571kJ (615 cal); 70.6g carbohydrate; 42.3g protein; 8.4g fibre

fried noodles with sausage and wombok

preparation time 25 minutes
cooking time 10 minutes serves 4

450g wide fresh rice noodles
2 teaspoons peanut oil
300g dried chinese sausages, sliced thickly
1 medium brown onion (150g), chopped coarsely
2 cloves garlic, crushed
100g shiitake mushrooms, chopped coarsely
1 small wombok (700g), chopped coarsely
¼ cup (60ml) chicken stock
¼ cup (95g) char siu sauce
2 tablespoons lime juice
½ cup loosely packed fresh coriander leaves
¼ cup loosely packed fresh mint leaves
⅓ cup (50g) coarsely chopped roasted unsalted cashews
1 fresh long red chilli, sliced thinly

1 Place noodles in large heatproof bowl, cover with boiling water, separate with fork; drain.
2 Heat oil in wok; stir-fry sausage, onion, garlic and mushrooms until sausage is browned and vegetables are tender.
3 Add wombok to wok; stir-fry until wombok wilts. Add stock, sauce, juice and noodles; stir-fry until hot. Remove from heat; sprinkle with coriander and mint. Serve with nuts and chilli.
per serving 28.4g total fat (7.8g saturated fat); 2161kJ (517 cal); 43.6g carbohydrate; 17.6g protein; 9.8g fibre

Rice & Noodles

The Complete Book of Modern Asian

singapore noodles

preparation time 30 minutes
cooking time 15 minutes serves 4

500g uncooked medium prawns
250g dried thin egg noodles
2 tablespoons peanut oil
4 eggs, beaten lightly
3 cloves garlic, crushed
4cm piece fresh ginger (20g), grated
1 medium white onion (150g), sliced thinly
2 tablespoons mild curry paste
230g can water chestnuts, drained, chopped coarsely
3 green onions, chopped coarsely
200g chinese barbecued pork, sliced
2 tablespoons light soy sauce
2 tablespoons oyster sauce

1 Shell and devein prawns.
2 Cook noodles in large saucepan of boiling water, uncovered, until just tender; drain.
3 Meanwhile, heat half of the oil in large wok. Pour half of the egg into wok; cook over medium heat, tilting wok, until almost set. Remove omelette from wok; roll tightly, slice thinly. Repeat with remaining egg.
4 Heat remaining oil in wok; stir-fry garlic and ginger 1 minute. Add white onion and paste; stir-fry 2 minutes or until fragrant.
5 Add chestnuts, green onion and pork; stir-fry 2 minutes or until chestnuts are browned lightly.
6 Add prawns; stir-fry until prawns are just changed in colour. Add noodles, combined sauces and omelette; stir-fry, tossing, until sauce thickens and noodles are heated through.
per serving 27.4g total fat (7.1g saturated fat); 2692kJ (644 cal); 55.3g carbohydrate; 40.6g protein; 6.3g fibre

balti biryani

preparation time 20 minutes (plus refrigeration time)
cooking time 1 hour 30 minutes serves 4

750g beef skirt steak, cut into 2cm cubes
¾ cup (225g) balti curry paste
2 cups (400g) basmati rice
8 cloves garlic, unpeeled
20g ghee
4 cardamom pods, bruised
4 cloves
1 cinnamon stick
3 green onions, sliced thinly
2 cups (500ml) beef stock
¾ cup (100g) toasted slivered almonds
¼ cup loosely packed fresh coriander leaves
2 fresh small red thai chillies, sliced thinly

1 Preheat oven to 180°C/160°C fan-forced.
2 Combine steak and curry paste in medium bowl, cover; refrigerate 1 hour.
3 Meanwhile, place rice in medium bowl, cover with water; stand 30 minutes. Drain rice in strainer; rinse under cold water, drain.
4 Place garlic in small baking dish; roast, uncovered, about 20 minutes or until softened.
5 Melt ghee in large saucepan; cook cardamom, cloves, cinnamon and onion, stirring, until fragrant. Add steak mixture; reduce heat, simmer, covered, stirring occasionally, about 45 minutes or until steak is tender.
6 Add rice with stock to pan; simmer, covered, stirring occasionally, about 15 minutes or until rice is just tender.
7 Peel garlic; chop finely. Add garlic, almonds and coriander to biryani, cover; stand 5 minutes. Sprinkle biryani with chilli; serve with raita and naan, if desired.
per serving 41.6g total fat (8.6g saturated fat); 4080kJ (976 cal); 86.2g carbohydrate; 59g protein; 10.1g fibre

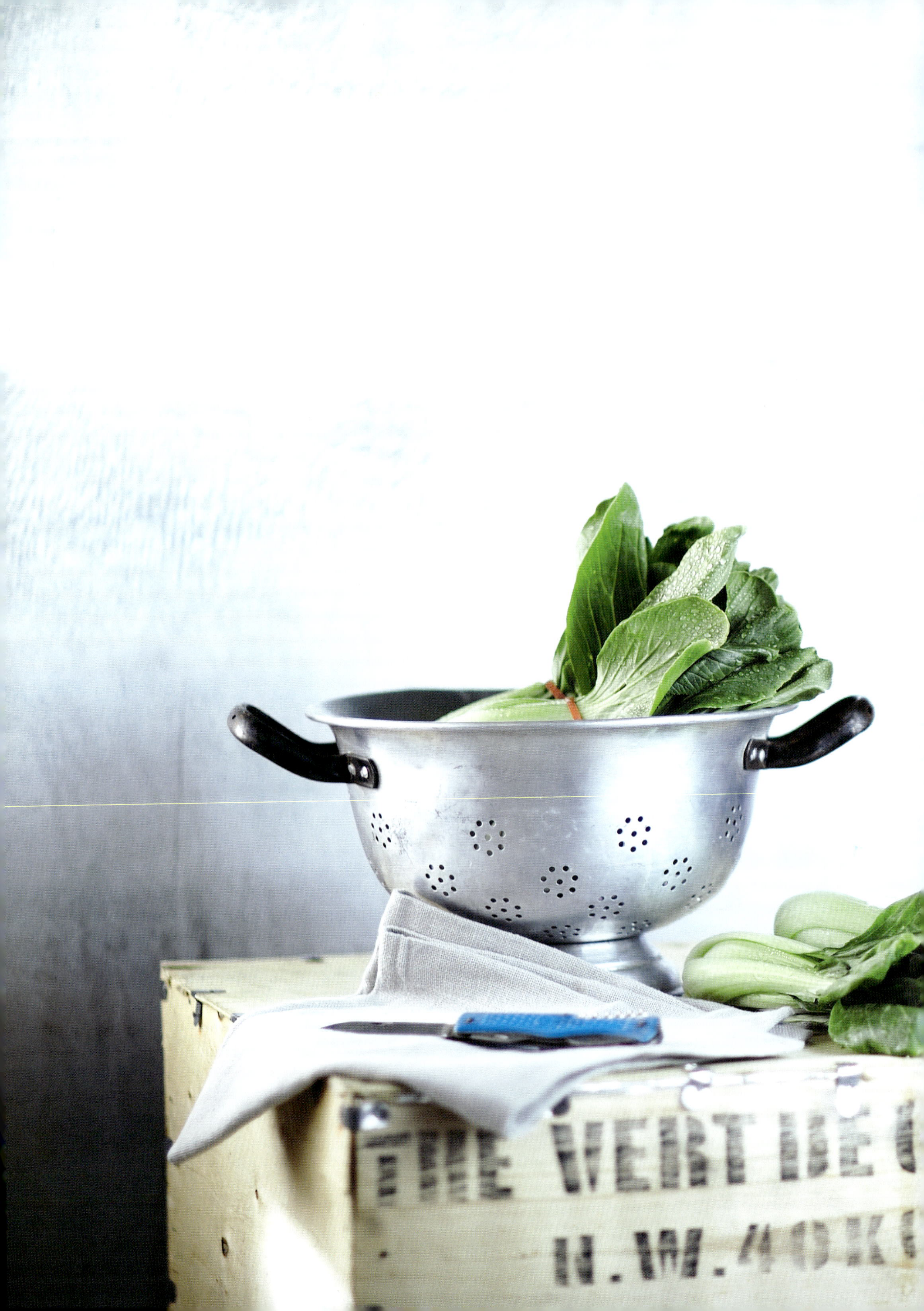

Sides

The rich depth of a curry or the robust heat of many stir-fries are actually enhanced when tempered by an accompanying plain bread, lentil or rice side dish. Straightforward to make, authentic Asian side dishes like dhal, chapati and pilao both help balance a meal and make it more complete, turning your choice of main into a weeknight feast.

spiced lentils *page 387*

chapati *page 379*

grains & legumes

roti *page 383*

naan *page 379*

parathas

preparation time 40 minutes (plus standing time)
cooking time 30 minutes makes 8

1 cup (150g) white plain flour
1 cup (160g) wholemeal plain flour
100g cold butter, chopped
½ cup (125ml) water
300g potatoes, peeled, chopped coarsely
1 tablespoon peanut oil
1 small brown onion (80g), chopped finely
1 clove garlic, crushed
½ teaspoon ground cumin
1 teaspoon coriander seeds, crushed
¼ teaspoon cayenne pepper
1 tablespoon finely chopped fresh coriander
vegetable oil, for shallow-frying

1 Process flours and butter until mixture resembles fine breadcrumbs; add the water, pulse until mixture forms a soft dough. Wrap dough in plastic wrap; stand 1 hour.
2 Meanwhile, boil, steam or microwave potato until tender; drain. Mash in medium bowl.
3 Heat peanut oil in small frying pan; cook onion and garlic, stirring, until onion softens. Add cumin, crushed coriander and cayenne; cook, stirring, until fragrant. Add onion mixture to potato with fresh coriander; mix to combine. Cool filling 10 minutes.
4 Divide dough into 16 pieces. Roll eight pieces on lightly floured surface to form 14cm rounds (use a 14cm plate as a guide). Spread half of the filling over four of the rounds, leaving 1cm border; brush borders with water. Cover with remaining rounds; press edges together to seal. Repeat process with remaining eight dough pieces and filling.
5 Heat vegetable oil in medium frying pan; cook parathas, one at a time, until browned lightly both sides. Drain on absorbent paper; cover to keep warm.
per paratha 16.2g total fat (6.9g saturated fat); 1150kJ (275 cal); 26.4g carbohydrate; 4.7g protein; 3.2g fibre

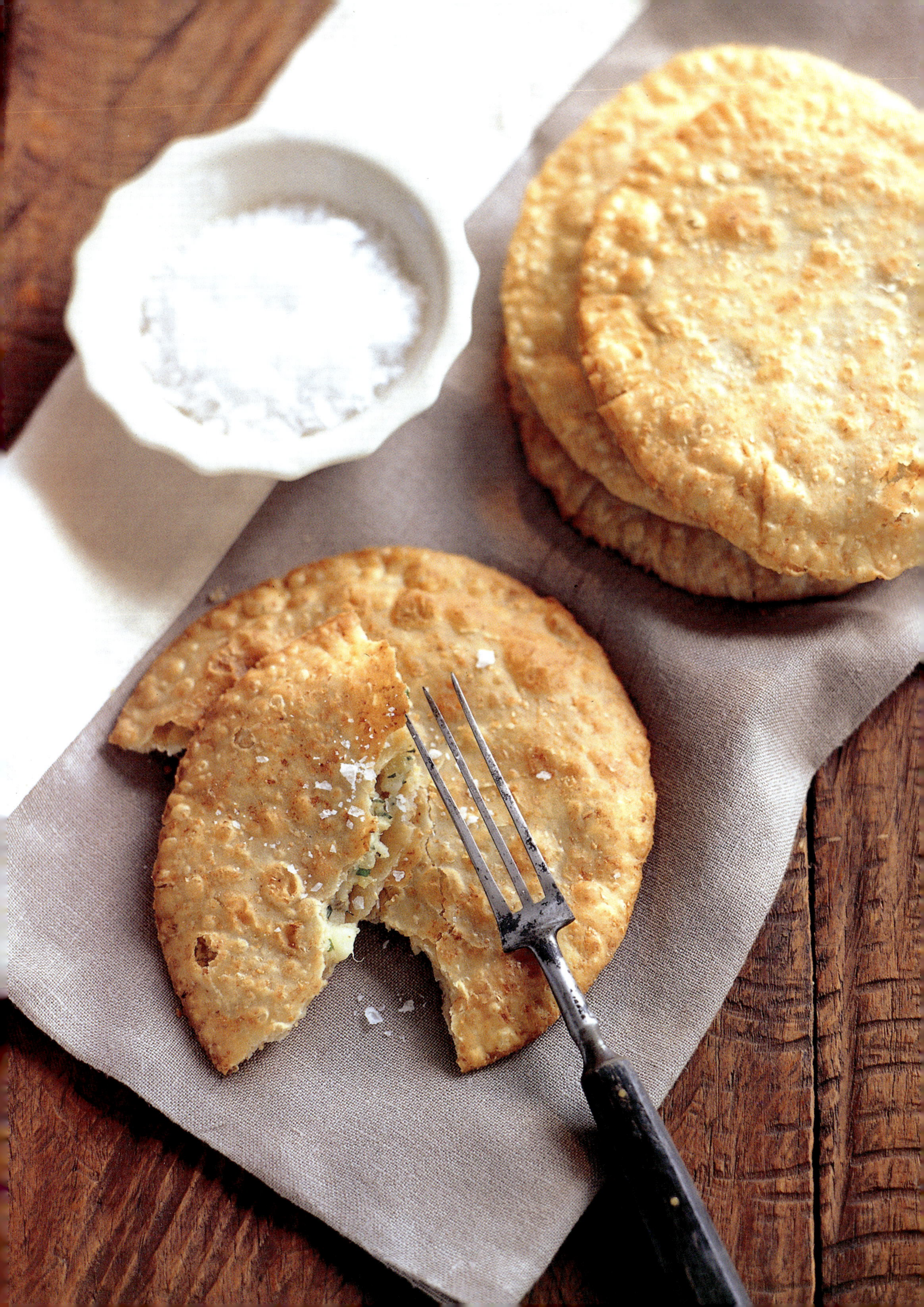

The Complete Book of Modern Asian

dhal and paneer vegetable curry

preparation time 25 minutes
cooking time 1 hour 15 minutes serves 4

2 tablespoons ghee
1 medium brown onion (150g), chopped finely
2 cloves garlic, crushed
2cm piece fresh ginger (10g), grated
2 teaspoons ground cumin
1 tablespoon ground coriander
1 teaspoon ground turmeric
2 teaspoons garam masala
2 cardamom pods, bruised
2 tablespoons mild curry paste
1 cup (200g) yellow split peas
810g can crushed tomatoes
2 cups (500ml) vegetable stock
2 cups (500ml) water
250g cabbage, chopped coarsely
2 medium carrots (240g), cut into 2cm pieces
½ cup (60g) frozen peas
2 x 100g packets paneer cheese, cut into 2cm pieces
⅓ cup loosely packed fresh coriander leaves

1 Heat ghee in large saucepan; cook onion, garlic and ginger, stirring, until onion softens. Add spices; cook, stirring, until fragrant. Add curry paste; cook, stirring, until fragrant.
2 Add split peas, undrained tomatoes, stock and the water; bring to a boil. Reduce heat; simmer, covered, 30 minutes, stirring occasionally. Uncover, add cabbage and carrot; cook, stirring occasionally, about 30 minutes or until split peas soften.
3 Add frozen peas and cheese; cook, uncovered, about 5 minutes or until cheese is heated through. Serve curry sprinkled with coriander.
per serving 20.1g total fat (10g saturated fat); 1923kJ (460 cal); 39.6g carbohydrate; 23.4g protein; 14.2g fibre
TIP You will need about a quarter of a small cabbage for this recipe.

tomato rice

preparation time 15 minutes
cooking time 30 minutes serves 4

2 tablespoons peanut oil
1 medium brown onion (150g), chopped finely
2 cloves garlic, crushed
3 medium tomatoes (450g), peeled, seeded, chopped finely
2 tablespoons tomato paste
4 cloves
2 cups (400g) white long-grain rice
3 cups (750ml) water

1 Heat oil in medium saucepan; cook onion, garlic, tomato, paste and cloves, uncovered, about 10 minutes or until mixture is thick and pulpy.
2 Stir in rice and the water; bring to a boil. Reduce heat; cook, covered tightly, over low heat, about 15 minutes or until water is absorbed. Remove from heat; stand, covered, 10 minutes. Fluff rice with fork. Serve sprinkled with coriander, and warmed chapati, if if desired.
per serving 9.8g total fat (1.8g saturated); 1973kJ (472 cal); 84.5g carbohydrate; 8.7g protein; 3.3g fibre

khitcherie

preparation time 15 minutes (plus standing time)
cooking time 20 minutes serves 6

1 cup (200g) yellow split peas
2 tablespoons ghee
1 medium brown onion (150g), chopped finely
2 cloves garlic, crushed
2 long green chillies, sliced thinly
3cm piece fresh ginger (15g), grated
½ teaspoon ground turmeric
1 teaspoon cumin seeds
½ teaspoon garam masala
1 teaspoon ground coriander
1 cinnamon stick
4 fresh curry leaves
1½ cups (300g) basmati rice, rinsed, drained
1 cup (150g) raisins
1 litre (4 cups) hot water
1 tablespoon lime juice
½ cup (75g) roasted unsalted cashews

1 Place split peas in small bowl, cover with cold water, stand 1 hour; drain.
2 Heat ghee in large deep frying pan; cook onion, garlic, chilli, ginger, spices and curry leaves, stirring, until onion softens.
3 Add split peas, rice, raisins and the hot water to pan; bring to a boil. Reduce heat, simmer, covered, about 15 minutes or until rice is tender.
4 Remove pan from heat, discard cinnamon stick, stir in juice; stand, covered, 5 minutes. Sprinkle khitcherie with nuts before serving.

per serving 13.2g total fat (5.1g saturated fat); 2073kJ (496 cal); 76.3g carbohydrate; 14.3g protein; 6.5g fibre

classic pulao

preparation time 10 minutes (plus standing time)
cooking time 20 minutes serves 4

1⅓ cups (265g) basmati rice, rinsed, drained
2½ cups (625ml) chicken stock
pinch saffron threads
50g butter
1 medium brown onion (150g), chopped finely
2 cloves garlic, crushed
1 cinnamon stick
6 cardamom pods
1 bay leaf
⅓ cup (55g) sultanas
½ cup (75g) roasted unsalted cashews

1 Place rice in medium bowl, cover with cold water; stand 20 minutes, drain.
2 Heat stock and saffron in small saucepan.
3 Meanwhile, melt butter in large saucepan; cook onion and garlic, stirring, until onion softens. Stir in cinnamon, cardamom and bay leaf; cook, stirring, 2 minutes.
4 Add rice; cook, stirring, 2 minutes. Add stock mixture and sultanas; simmer, covered, about 10 minutes or until rice is tender and liquid is absorbed.
5 Sprinkle pulao with nuts just before serving.

per serving 20.6g total fat (8.8g saturated fat); 2128kJ (509 cal); 68.7g carbohydrate; 10.5g protein; 3.0g fibre

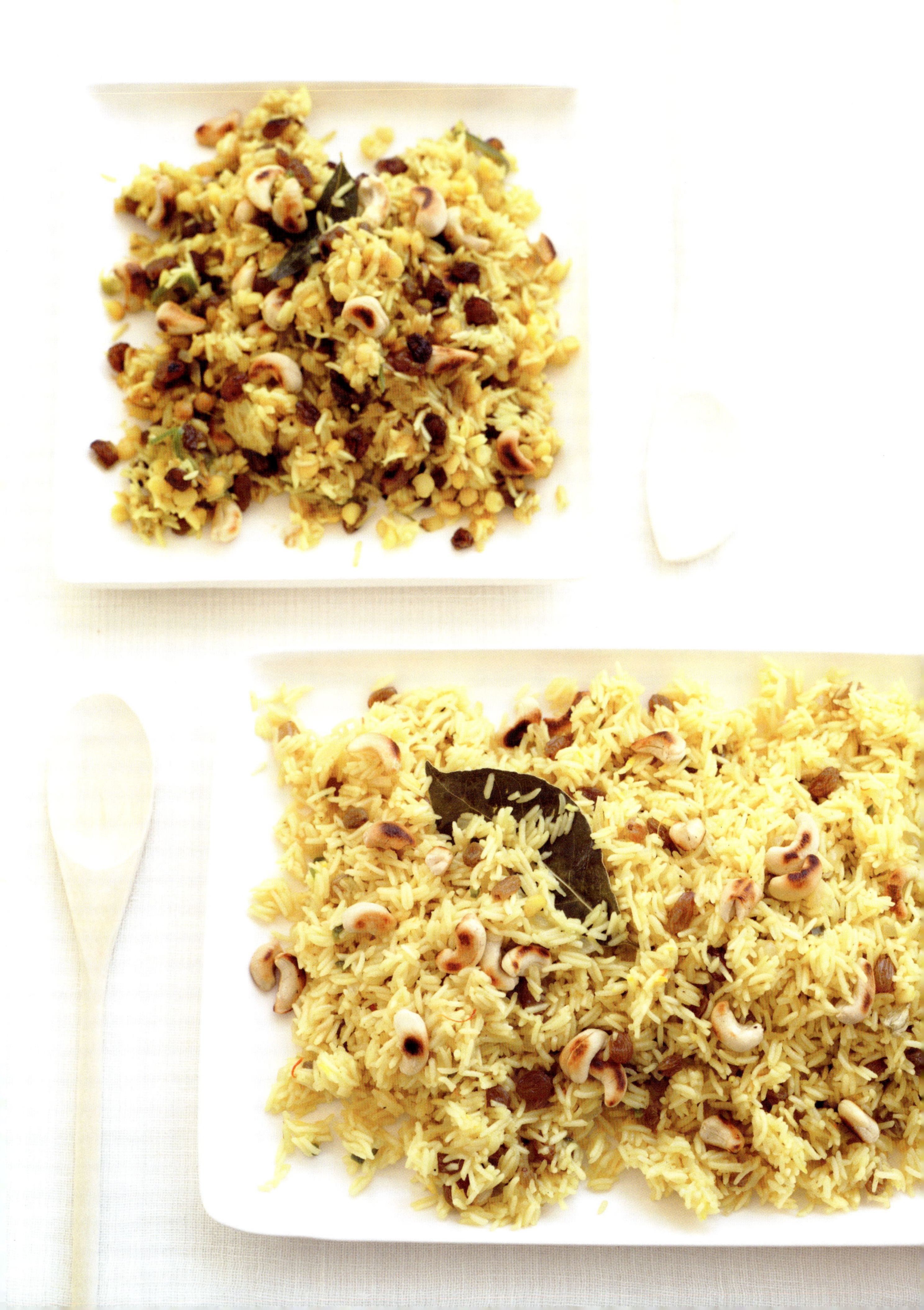

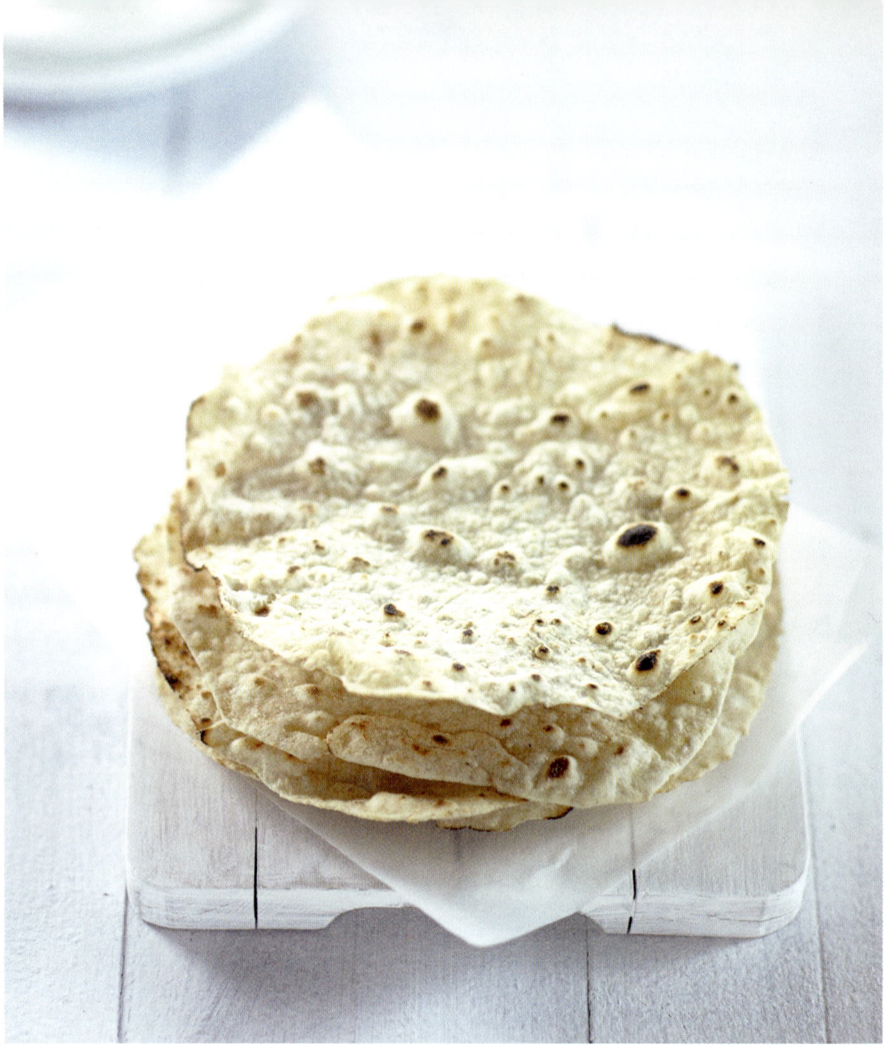

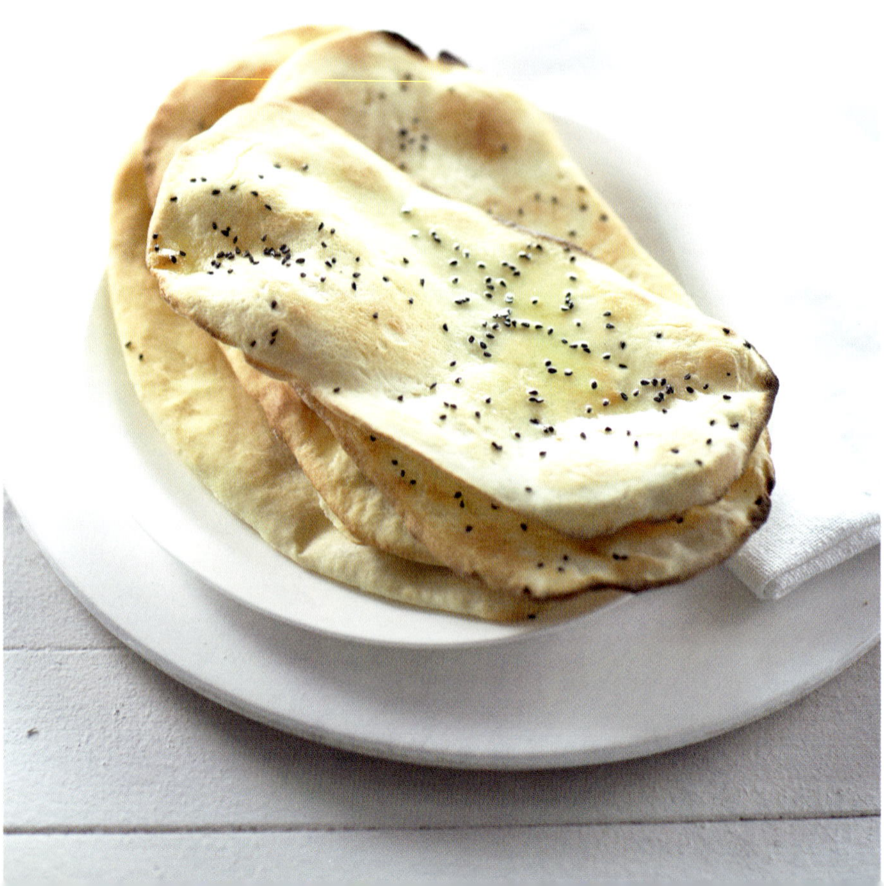

chapati

preparation time 35 minutes (plus standing time)
cooking time 20 minutes makes 14

1¼ cups (185g) white plain flour
1 cup (160g) wholemeal plain flour
1 teaspoon salt
1 tablespoon ghee
¾ cup (180ml) warm water, approximately

1 Sift 1 cup white flour, the wholemeal flour and salt into large bowl; rub in ghee. Add enough water to mix to a firm dough. Turn dough onto floured surface; knead 10 minutes, working in the remaining white flour.
2 Cover dough with cloth; stand 1 hour. Divide dough into 14 portions; roll portions on floured surface into 20cm rounds. Cover with cloth; stand 10 minutes before cooking.
3 Heat griddle or heavy-based frying pan until very hot; cook, one round at a time, about 30 seconds on first side or until round just begins to colour. Remove from pan. Place uncooked side of chapati directly over medium flame, checking frequently until chapati begins to blister. Repeat with remaining rounds. Wrap cooked chapati in a cloth to keep warm or serve while warm.
per chapati 1.8g total fat (1.0g saturated); 4.0kJ (98 cal); 16.6g carbohydrate; 2.8g protein; 1.8g fibre

naan

preparation time 20 minutes (plus standing time)
cooking time 15 minutes makes 6

⅔ cup (160ml) warm water
1 teaspoon dried yeast
1 teaspoon caster sugar
2 cups (300g) plain flour
1 teaspoon salt
2 tablespoons yogurt
4 tablespoon ghee, melted
2 teaspoons kalonji

1 Whisk the water, yeast and sugar in small bowl until yeast dissolves, cover; stand in warm place about 10 minutes or until mixture is frothy.
2 Sift flour and salt into large bowl, add yeast mixture, yogurt and half of the ghee; mix to a soft dough. Knead dough on floured surface about 5 minutes or until dough is smooth and elastic. Place dough in large greased bowl, cover; stand in warm place 1½ hours or until dough has doubled in size.
3 Turn dough onto floured surface; knead 5 minutes or until smooth. Divide dough into six pieces; roll each piece into an oval about 20cm long.
4 Preheat grill to very hot. Cover oven tray with foil; grease foil. Cook ovals, one at a time, under grill about 2 minutes each side or until puffed and just browned. Brush naan with a little of the remaining ghee, sprinkle with a little of the kalonji; grill further 30 seconds. Keep naan warm while cooking remainder.
per naan 12.4g total fat (7.9g saturated); 1204kJ (288 cal); 37.1g carbohydrate; 5.9g protein; 2.0g fibre

asian star

mixed dhal

preparation time 15 minutes
cooking time 1 hour 10 minutes serves 4

2 tablespoons ghee
1 medium brown onion (150g), chopped finely
2 cloves garlic, crushed
4cm piece fresh ginger (20g), grated
1½ tablespoons black mustard seeds
1 long green chilli, chopped finely
1 tablespoon ground cumin
1 tablespoon ground coriander
2 teaspoons ground turmeric
½ cup (100g) brown lentils
⅓ cup (65g) red lentils
⅓ cup (85g) yellow split peas
⅓ cup (85g) green split peas
400g can crushed tomatoes
2 cups (500ml) vegetable stock
1½ cups (375ml) water
140ml can coconut cream

1 Heat ghee in large saucepan; cook onion, garlic and ginger, stirring, until onion softens. Add seeds, chilli and spices; cook, stirring, until fragrant.
2 Add lentils and split peas to pan. Stir in undrained tomatoes, stock and the water; simmer, covered, stirring occasionally, about 1 hour or until lentils are tender.
3 Just before serving, add coconut cream; stir over low heat until curry is heated through.
per serving 18.4g total fat (12.5g saturated fat); 1898kJ (454 cal); 42.6g carbohydrate; 23.3g protein; 12.7g fibre

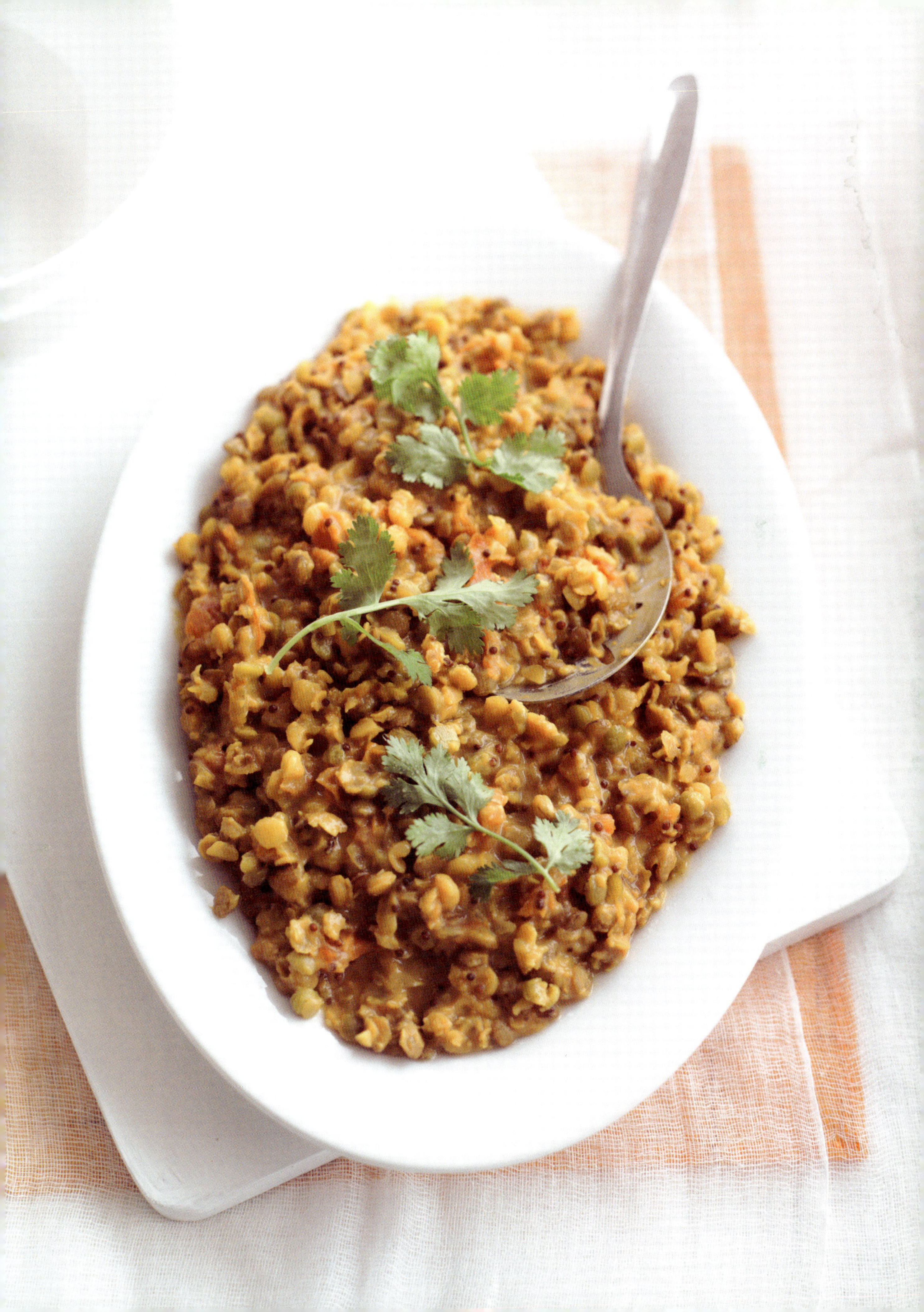

The Complete Book of Modern Asian

roti

preparation time 30 minutes (plus refrigeration time)
cooking time 30 minutes makes 16

1 cup (150g) white plain flour
1 cup (160g) wholemeal plain flour
1 teaspoon salt
1 teaspoon ground coriander
½ teaspoon ground turmeric
2 teaspoons cumin seeds
1 tablespoon vegetable oil
¾ cup (180ml) water, approximately
4 tablespoons ghee, approximately

1 Sift flours, salt and ground spices into large bowl. Make a well in centre of flour mixture; add seeds, oil and enough water to mix to a soft dough. Turn dough onto floured surface; knead 10 minutes. Wrap dough in plastic; refrigerate 30 minutes.
2 Divide dough into 16 portions; roll each portion on floured surface to 16cm round.
3 Heat heavy-based frying pan until very hot; add about 1 teaspoon of the ghee, quickly turn pan to coat base with ghee. Place one round into pan; cook about 1 minute or until round is puffed slightly and bubbles start to form. Turn; brown other side. Repeat with remaining ghee and rounds.
per roti 7.1g total fat (3.9g saturated); 531kJ (127 cal); 12.9g carbohydrate; 2.2g protein; 1.5g fibre

lentil and egg curry with lime pickle

preparation time 25 minutes
cooking time 50 minutes serves 4

3 cardamom pods, bruised
1 teaspoon cumin seeds
1 teaspoon fennel seeds
2 teaspoons coriander seeds
1 teaspoon ground turmeric
1 teaspoon vegetable oil
1 medium brown onion (150g), sliced thinly
2 cloves garlic, crushed
3cm piece fresh ginger (15g), grated
1 fresh small red thai chilli, chopped finely
1½ cups (300g) brown lentils
1 cup (250ml) light coconut cream
1¾ cups (430ml) water
1 tablespoon lime juice
1½ cups (300g) basmati rice
2 hard-boiled eggs, quartered
¼ cup (75g) lime pickle

1 Dry-fry spices in small frying pan, stirring, until fragrant. Using mortar and pestle, crush spices to a fine powder.
2 Heat oil in large deep frying pan; cook onion, garlic, ginger and chilli, stirring, until onion softens. Add spices; cook, stirring, 1 minute. Add lentils, coconut cream and the water; bring to a boil. Reduce heat, simmer, covered, stirring occasionally, about 35 minutes or until lentils are tender. Stir in juice.
3 Cook rice in medium saucepan of boiling water, uncovered, until just tender; drain.
4 Serve curry with rice; top with eggs and lime pickle.
per serving 12.2g fat (6.9g saturated fat); 2420kJ (579 cal); 90.8g carbohydrate; 27.7g protein; 12.3g fibre

steamed jasmine rice

preparation time 1 minute (plus standing time)
cooking time 12 minutes serves 4

2 cups (400g) jasmine rice
1 litre (4 cups) cold water

1 Combine rice and the water in large saucepan with a tight-fitting lid; bring to a boil, stirring occasionally.
2 Reduce heat as low as possible; cook rice, covered tightly, about 12 minutes or until all water is absorbed and rice is cooked as desired. Do not remove lid or stir rice during cooking time. Remove from heat; stand, covered, 10 minutes before serving.
per serving 0.5g total fat (0.1g saturated fat); 1480kJ (354 cal); 79.1g carbohydrate; 6.6g protein; 0.9g fibre

black rice

preparation time 2 minutes
cooking time 20 minutes serves 4

2 cups (400g) black rice

1 Rinse rice in strainer under cold water until water runs clear.
2 Place rice in large saucepan of boiling water; boil, uncovered, stirring occasionally, about 20 minutes or until rice is cooked as desired. Drain; stand, covered, 10 minutes before serving.
per serving 0.5g total fat (0.1g saturated fat); 1480kJ (354 cal); 79g carbohydrate; 6.6g protein; 0.8g fibre

glutinous rice

preparation time 10 minutes (plus standing time)
cooking time 40 minutes serves 4

2 cups (400g) glutinous rice

1 Rinse rice in strainer under cold water until water runs clear. Soak rice in large bowl of cold water overnight.
2 Drain rice. Line metal or bamboo steamer with muslin; place rice in steamer, cover tightly. Place steamer over large saucepan of boiling water, taking care that the bottom of the steamer does not touch the boiling water. Steam rice, tightly covered, about 40 minutes or until cooked as desired. Do not remove lid or stir rice during cooking time.
per serving 0.5g total fat (0.1g saturated fat); 1480kJ (354 cal); 79.1g carbohydrate; 6.6g protein; 0.6g fibre

From top: steamed jasmine rice; black rice; glutinous rice

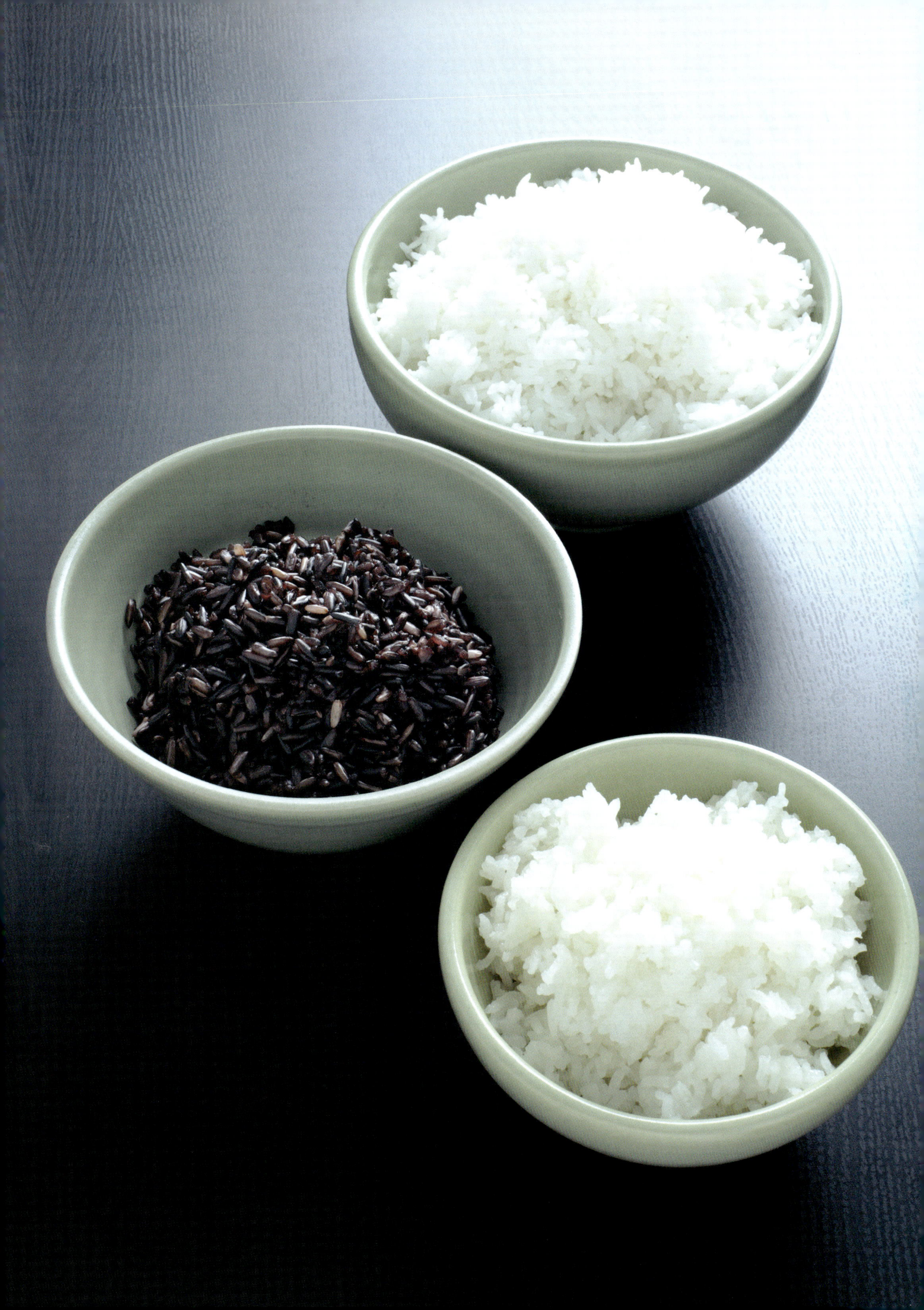

The Complete Book of Modern Asian

yellow coconut rice

preparation time 5 minutes (plus standing time)
cooking time 15 minutes serves 4

1¾ cups (350g) long-grain white rice
1¼ cups (310ml) water
400ml can coconut cream
½ teaspoon salt
1 teaspoon white sugar
½ teaspoon ground turmeric
pinch saffron threads

1 Soak rice in large bowl of cold water 30 minutes. Pour rice into strainer; rinse under cold water until water runs clear. Drain.
2 Place rice in large heavy-based saucepan with remaining ingredients; cover, bring to a boil, stirring occasionally. Reduce heat, simmer, covered, without stirring, about 15 minutes or until rice is tender. Remove from heat; stand, covered, 5 minutes.
per serving 21.1g total fat (18.2g saturated fat); 2186kJ (523 cal); 73.9g carbohydrate; 7.7g protein; 2.4g fibre

spiced lentils

preparation time 5 minutes
cooking time 15 minutes serves 4

1½ cups (300g) red lentils
50g butter
1 small brown onion (80g), chopped finely
1 clove garlic, crushed
½ teaspoon ground coriander
½ teaspoon ground cumin
¼ teaspoon ground turmeric
¼ teaspoon cayenne pepper
½ cup (125ml) chicken stock
2 tablespoons coarsely chopped fresh
    flat-leaf parsley

1 Cook lentils, uncovered, in large saucepan of boiling water until just tender; drain.
2 Meanwhile, melt half of the butter in large frying pan; cook onion, garlic and spices, stirring, until onion softens.
3 Add lentils, stock and remaining butter; cook, stirring, until hot. Stir parsley into lentils off the heat.
per serving 11.9g total fat (7g saturated fat); 1350kJ (323 cal); 29.6g carbohydrate; 18.9g protein; 10.8g fibre

coconut rice with capsicum and coriander

preparation time 15 minutes
cooking time 20 minutes serves 4

½ cup (40g) shredded coconut
2 tablespoons vegetable oil
2 teaspoons chilli oil
1 medium brown onion (150g), chopped coarsely
1 medium red capsicum (200g), chopped coarsely
3 cloves garlic, crushed
3cm piece fresh ginger (15g), grated
1½ cups (300g) calrose rice
1½ cups (375ml) chicken stock
1 cup (250ml) water
140ml can coconut milk
3 green onions, chopped coarsely
¼ cup coarsely chopped fresh coriander
¼ cup (60ml) lemon juice
¼ cup fresh coriander leaves

1 Dry-fry coconut in heated wok stirring constantly until browned lightly. Remove from wok.
2 Heat oils in wok; stir-fry brown onion, capsicum, garlic and ginger until onion softens.
3 Add rice; stir-fry 2 minutes. Add stock, the water and coconut milk; simmer, covered, about 20 minutes or until liquid is absorbed and rice is tender.
4 Remove from heat; stir in green onion, chopped coriander, juice and half the coconut. Sprinkle with remaining coconut and coriander leaves.

per serving 26.2g total fat (13.9g saturated fat); 2282kJ (546 cal); 66.4g carbohydrate; 9.0g protein; 4.5g fibre

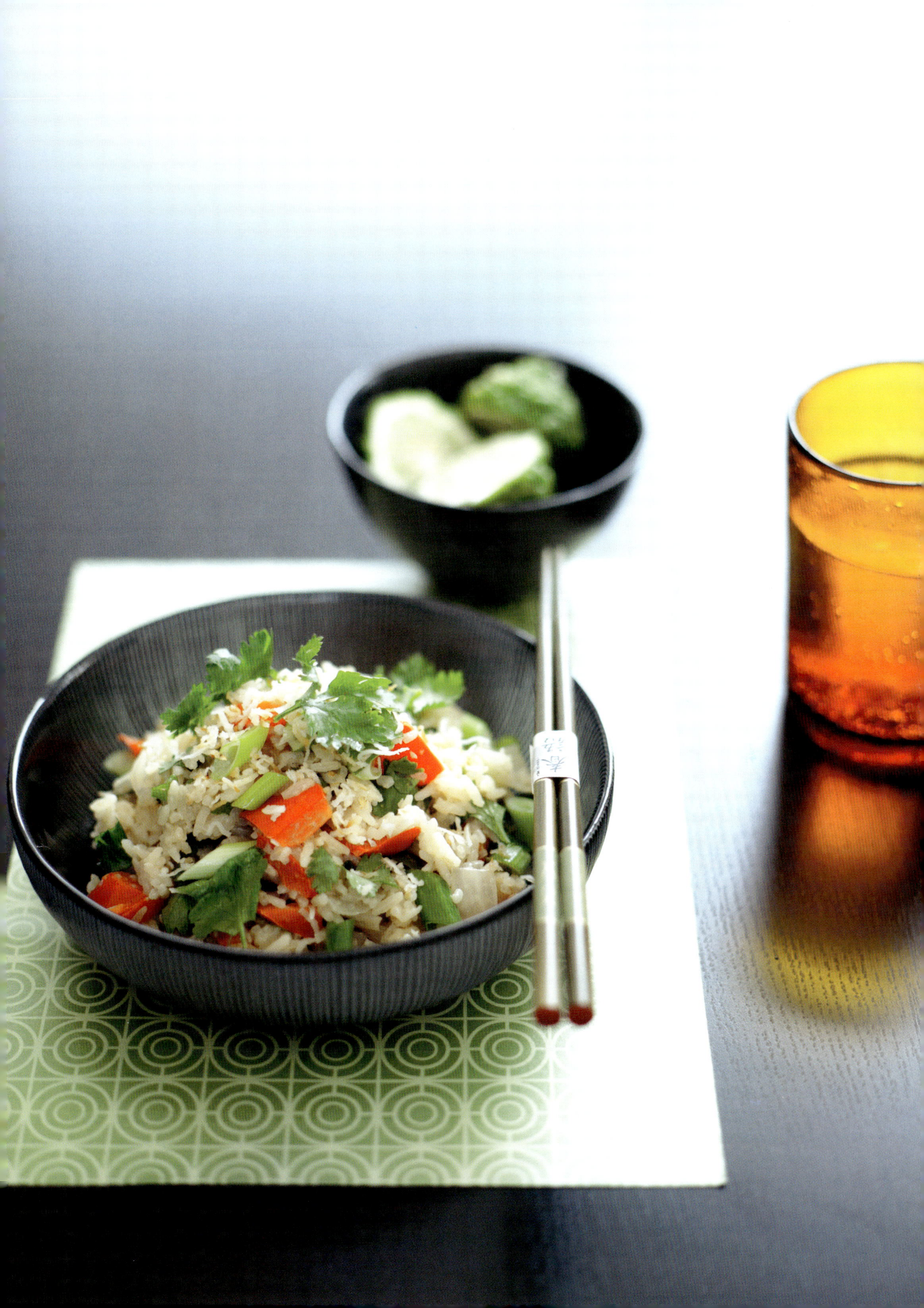

The Complete Book of Modern Asian

caramelised onion and red lentil dip

preparation time 10 minutes
cooking time 15 minutes makes 2½ cups

¾ cup (150g) red lentils
2 cups (500ml) boiling water
2 cloves garlic, quartered
1 medium potato (200g), chopped coarsely
¼ cup (60ml) olive oil
2 medium brown onions (300g), sliced thinly
½ teaspoon ground cumin
1 teaspoon ground coriander
¼ teaspoon sweet paprika
2 tablespoons lemon juice

1 Place lentils, the water, garlic and potato in medium saucepan; bring to a boil. Reduce heat, simmer, uncovered, about 15 minutes or until lentils soften, stirring occasionally.
2 Meanwhile, heat 2 tablespoons of the oil in medium frying pan; cook onion, stirring occasionally, 8 minutes or until caramelised. Remove 2 tablespoons of the onion from pan; reserve. Add spices to pan; cook, stirring, until fragrant. Remove from heat; stir in juice.
3 Blend or process lentil mixture and onion mixture with remaining oil until dip is smooth. Top with reserved onion; serve with toasted turkish bread or pitta crisps, if desired.
per tablespoon 1.9g total fat (0.3g saturated fat); 163kJ (39 cal); 3.4g carbohydrate; 1.5g protein; 1g fibre

curried red lentils with mushrooms and spinach

preparation time 15 minutes
cooking time 15 minutes serves 4

½ cup (100g) dried red lentils
1 tablespoon vegetable oil
½ teaspoon cumin seeds
1 small brown onion (80g), sliced thinly
1 clove garlic, crushed
2cm piece fresh ginger (10g), grated
1 small green chilli, sliced thinly
100g button mushrooms, halved
¾ cup (180ml) vegetable stock
¼ cup (60ml) water
½ teaspoon garam masala
125g baby spinach leaves

1 Preheat oven to 180°C/160°C fan-forced. Wash lentils well under running water.
2 Heat oil in wok; stir-fry seeds until fragrant. Add onion, garlic, ginger and chilli; stir-fry until onion is soft. Add mushrooms, stir-fry until browned lightly.
3 Add drained lentils, stock and water; bring to a boil. Reduce heat, simmer, uncovered, about 5 minutes or until lentils are tender.
4 Add garam masala and spinach; stir until spinach just wilts. Serve with warmed naan and yogurt, if desired.
per serving 5.5g total fat (0.8g saturated fat); 589kJ (141 cal); 11.6g carbohydrate; 8.6g protein; 5.4g fibre

It's said that Thai sweet chilli sauce is the new tomato sauce, and we have to agree. And raitas, sambals, chutneys and dipping sauces all have their place at our weeknight table. They bring added complexity and nuance to the taste of good food and can transform a steamed fish dish or a simple single stir-fried vegetable into a memorable tasty experience.

spicy dipping sauce *page 413*

sweet chilli dipping sauce *page 414*

chutneys, raitas & sauces

sweet and sour dipping sauce *page 413*

hoisin and peanut dipping sauce *page 414*

cucumber and pineapple sambal

preparation time 15 minutes
cooking time 2 minutes makes 3 cups

3 teaspoons shrimp paste
2 fresh small red thai chillies, chopped finely
1 tablespoon lime juice
1 tablespoon light soy sauce
1 teaspoon sugar
1 lebanese cucumber (130g), peeled, seeded, chopped coarsely
1 small pineapple (800g), chopped coarsely
6 green onions, sliced thinly

1 Cook paste in heated small saucepan until dry and crumbly. Combine paste and chilli in small bowl; grind with mortar and pestle. Stir in juice, sauce and sugar; mix well.
2 Combine cucumber, pineapple and onion in large bowl; stir in chilli mixture.

per tablespoon 0.1g total fat (0g saturated fat); 29kJ (7 cal); 1.3g carbohydrate; 0.3g protein; 0.3g fibre
TIP This goes well with pork, fish, prawns, chicken and duck.

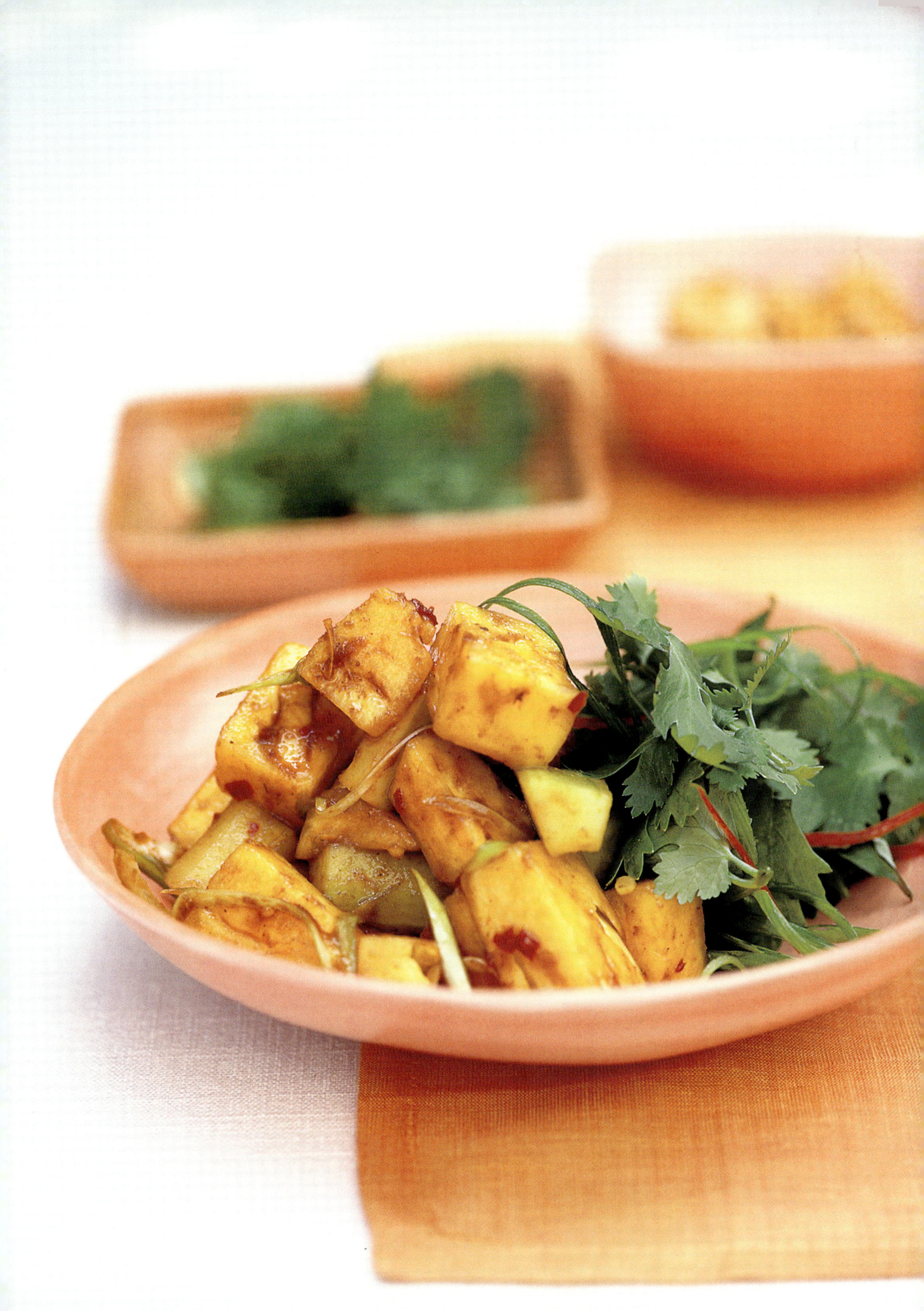

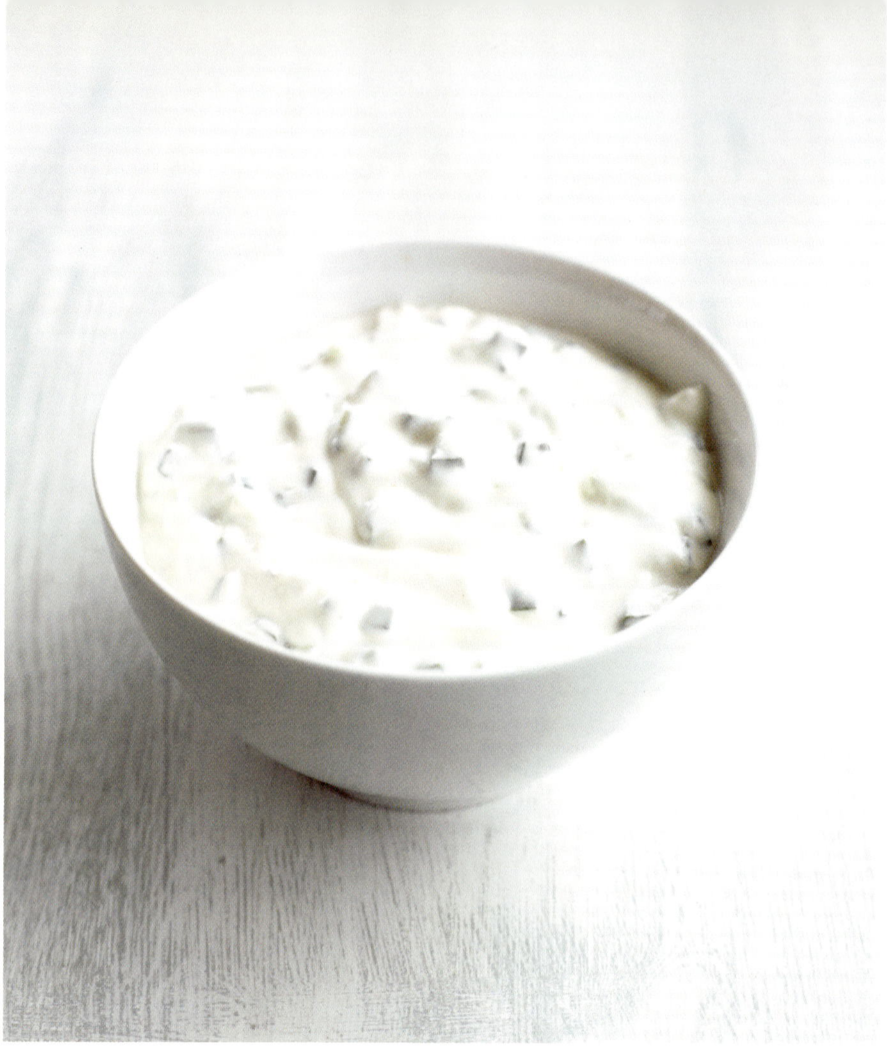

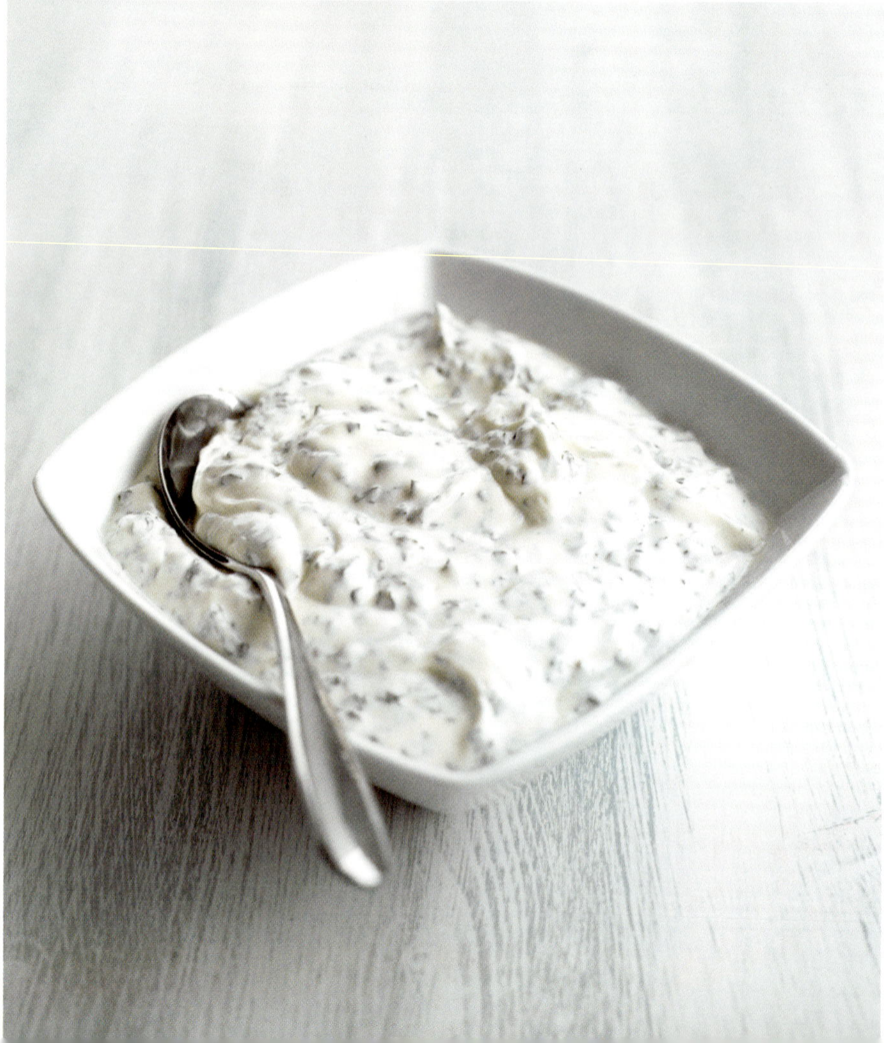

cucumber raita

preparation time 5 minutes
cooking time 2 minutes makes 2½ cups

2 teaspoons vegetable oil
¼ teaspoon black mustard seeds
¼ teaspoon cumin seeds
2 lebanese cucumbers (260g), seeded, chopped finely
500g yogurt

1 Heat oil in small frying pan; cook seeds, stirring, over low heat, 2 minutes or until seeds pop.
2 Combine seeds with remaining ingredients in medium bowl.
per tablespoon 0.9g total fat (0.4g saturated fat); 63kJ (15 cal); 0.9g carbohydrate; 0.8g protein; 0.1g fibre
TIP This goes well with fish, lamb, prawns and pork.

mint raita

preparation time 5 minutes
cooking time 2 minutes makes 2½ cups

2 teaspoons vegetable oil
¼ teaspoon black mustard seeds
¼ teaspoon ground cumin
1 cup finely chopped fresh mint
500g yogurt

1 Heat oil in small frying pan; cook spices, stirring, over low heat, 2 minutes or until seeds pop.
2 Combine spices with remaining ingredients in medium bowl.
per tablespoon 0.9g total fat (0.4g saturated fat); 63kJ (15 cal); 0.9g carbohydrate; 0.8g protein; 0.1g fibre
TIP This goes well with fish, lamb, pork and chicken.

ginger miso dressing

preparation time 10 minutes
cooking time 10 minutes makes ½ cup

¼ cup (60ml) rice vinegar
2 tablespoons white miso
1 tablespoon mirin
2 teaspoons caster sugar
2cm piece fresh ginger (10g), grated
1 clove garlic, crushed
1 teaspoon japanese soy sauce
1 teaspoon sesame oil
1 tablespoon water

1 Combine ingredients in small saucepan; stir, over low heat, until sugar dissolves.
2 Remove from heat; strain over small jug; discard solids.
per tablespoon 1.3g total fat (0.2g saturated fat); 125kJ (30 cal); 3.3g carbohydrate; 1.0g protein; 0.6g fibre
TIP *This goes well with prawns, chicken, fish, beef, stir-fried greens and pork.*

sesame soy dressing

preparation time 5 minutes
makes ½ cup

1 tablespoon toasted sesame seeds
1 tablespoon sesame oil
2 shallots (50g), chopped finely
1 tablespoon kecap manis
¼ cup (60ml) lime juice

1 Combine ingredients in small bowl.
per tablespoon 1.4g total fat (0.2g saturated fat); 63kJ (15 cal); 0.2g carbohydrate; 0.3g protein; 0.1g fibre
TIP *This goes well with chicken, beef and pork.*

Chutneys, Raitas & Sauces

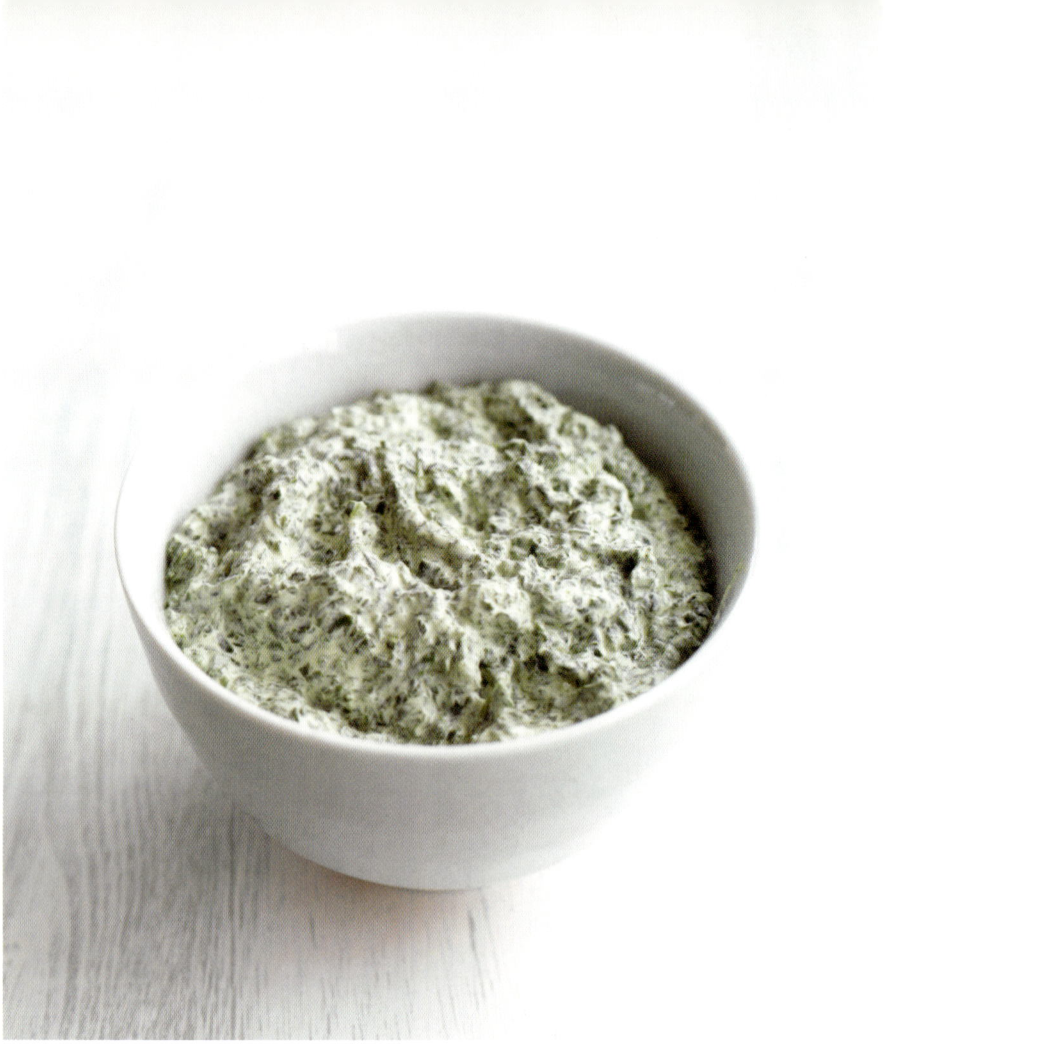

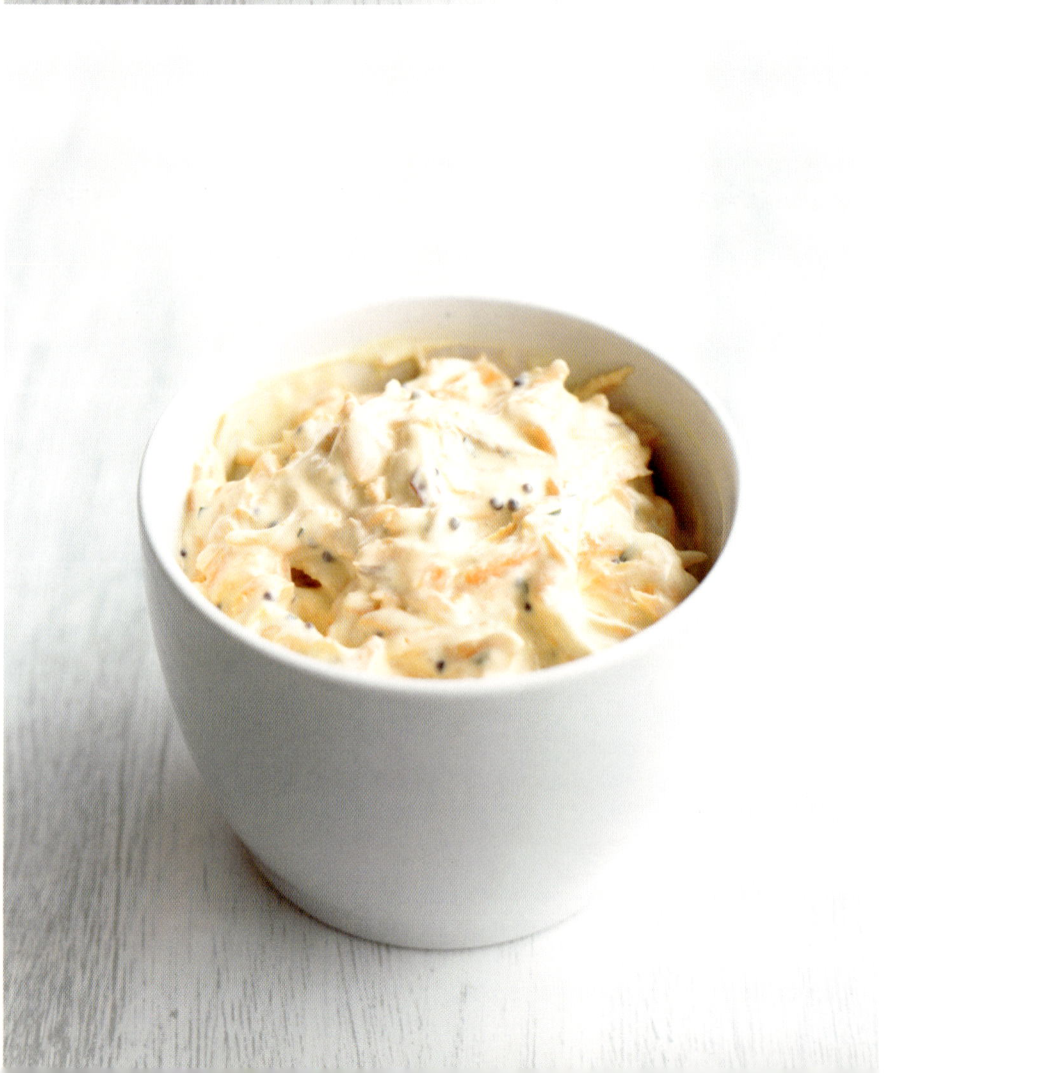

spinach raita

preparation time 5 minutes
cooking time 5 minutes makes 1½ cups

500g spinach
¾ cup (210g) yogurt
1 teaspoon lemon juice
½ teaspoon ground cumin
½ teaspoon caster sugar

1 Boil, steam or microwave spinach until just wilted; drain, squeeze out excess liquid.
2 Blend or process spinach with remaining ingredients until smooth.
per tablespoon 0.5g total fat (0.3g saturated fat); 59kJ (14 cal); 0.8g carbohydrate; 1.2g protein; 0.8g fibre
TIP This goes well with lamb, pork, beef, fish, prawns and chicken.

carrot raita

preparation time 5 minutes
cooking time 2 minutes makes 2 cups

2 teaspoons vegetable oil
5 fresh curry leaves, chopped finely
1 teaspoon black mustard seeds
1 dried small red chilli, chopped finely
2 medium carrots (240g), grated coarsely
250g yogurt

1 Heat oil in small frying pan; cook leaves and spices, stirring, over low heat, 2 minutes or until seeds pop.
2 Combine leaves and spices with remaining ingredients in medium bowl.
per tablespoon 1.1g total fat (0.5g saturated fat); 88kJ (21 cal); 1.5g carbohydrate; 1.1g protein; 0.3g fibre
TIP This goes well with lamb, pork, beef, fish and chicken.

date and tamarind chutney

preparation time 10 minutes
cooking time 45 minutes makes 2½ cups

2 cinnamon sticks
5 cardamom pods, bruised
2 teaspoons cloves
3½ cups (500g) seeded dried dates
1½ cups (375ml) white vinegar
½ cup (110g) firmly packed brown sugar
2 teaspoons coarse cooking salt
¼ cup (60ml) vegetable oil
2 tablespoons tamarind concentrate
2 teaspoons chilli powder

1 Place cinnamon, cardamom and cloves in centre of 20cm muslin square; tie tightly with kitchen string.
2 Combine muslin bag with remaining ingredients in large saucepan; bring to a boil, stirring constantly, then reduce heat.
3 Simmer, partially covered, stirring occasionally, about 40 minutes or until dates are soft. Remove and discard spice bag before using.
per tablespoon 1.9g total fat (0.2g saturated fat); 343kJ (82 cal); 15g carbohydrate; 0.4g protein; 1.7g fibre
TIP This goes well with pork, chicken, beef, lamb and duck.

eggplant chutney

preparation time 10 minutes (plus standing time)
cooking time 55 minutes makes 3 cups

1 medium eggplant (300g), peeled, chopped coarsely
¼ cup (70g) coarse cooking salt
1 medium brown onion (150g), chopped coarsely
2 medium tomatoes (300g), seeded, chopped coarsely
1 small green capsicum (150g), chopped coarsely
2 cloves garlic, crushed
½ cup (125ml) cider vinegar
½ cup (125ml) white vinegar
1 teaspoon chilli powder
1 teaspoon ground turmeric
½ cup (110g) firmly packed brown sugar

1 Place eggplant in colander, sprinkle with salt; stand 30 minutes. Rinse eggplant, pat dry.
2 Combine eggplant, onion, tomato, capsicum, garlic, vinegars, chilli and turmeric in large saucepan; simmer, uncovered, stirring occasionally, about 45 minutes or until vegetables are pulpy.
3 Stir in sugar; cook, stirring, over low heat, until sugar dissolves.
per tablespoon 0.0g total fat (0.0g saturated fat); 67kJ (16 cal); 3.5g carbohydrate; 0.3g protein; 0.3g fibre
TIP This goes well with pork, chicken, beef and lamb

Chutneys, Raitas & Sauces

asian star

green mango chutney

preparation time 25 minutes
(plus standing and cooling time)
cooking time 1 hour makes 8 cups

6 medium green mangoes (2kg), peeled, chopped coarsely
1 tablespoon coarse cooking salt
1¾ cups (385g) white sugar
2½ cups (625ml) brown vinegar
8cm piece fresh ginger (40g), grated
2 cloves garlic, crushed
¾ cup (110g) coarsely chopped dried dates
¾ cup (120g) coarsely chopped raisins
1 teaspoon chilli powder
1 teaspoon ground cinnamon
1 teaspoon ground cumin

1 Place mango and salt in large bowl. Barely cover with cold water, cover; stand overnight. Drain mango; discard water.
2 Stir sugar and vinegar in large saucepan over heat, without boiling, until sugar dissolves. Stir in mango and remaining ingredients; simmer, uncovered, stirring occasionally, 45 minutes or until mixture is thick. Pour into hot sterilised jars; seal.
per tablespoon 0g total fat (0g saturated); 188kJ (33 cal); 7.6g carbohydrate; 0.2g protein; 0.4g fibre
TIP This goes well with lamb, chicken, pork and beef.

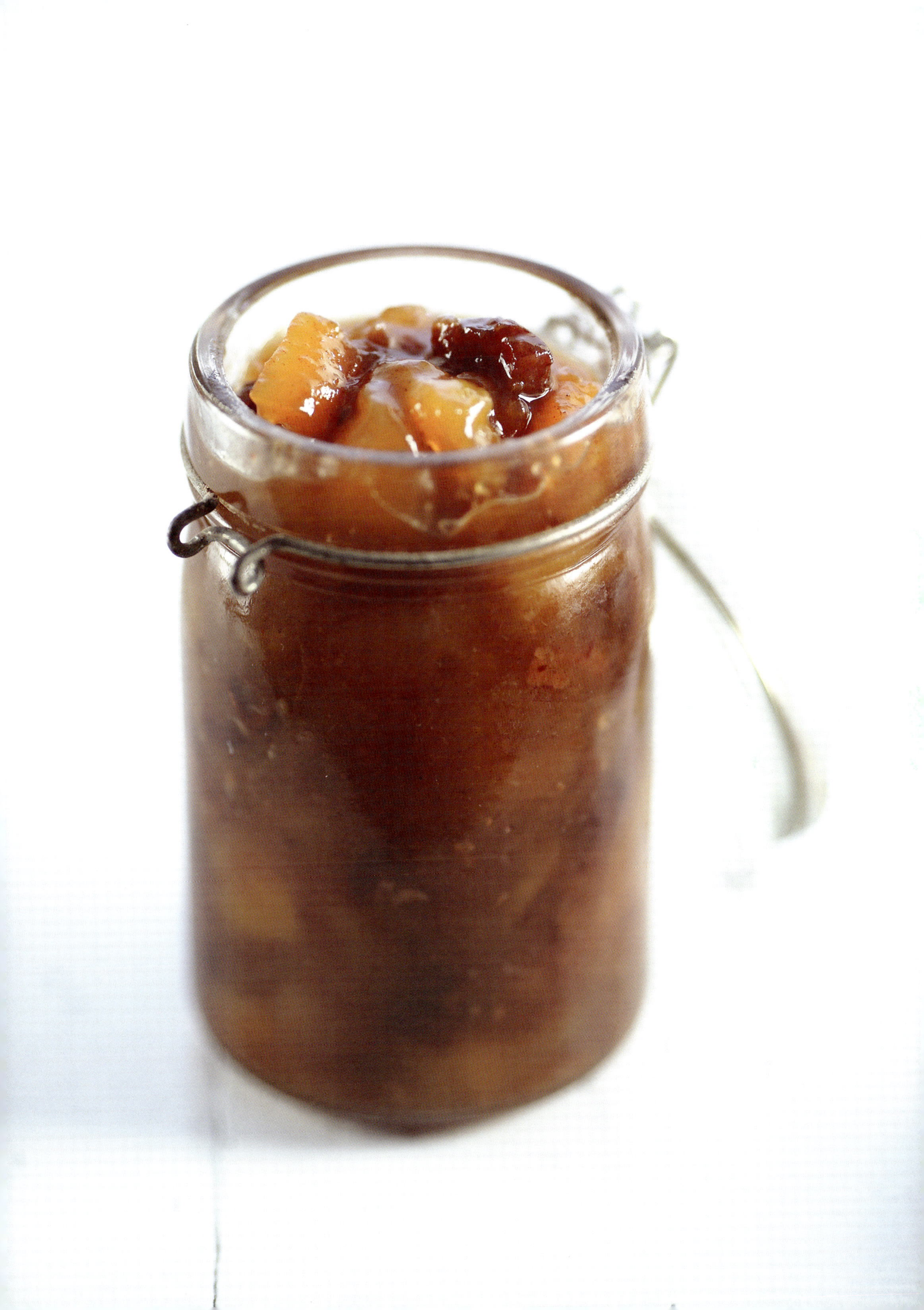

tomato kasaundi

preparation time 10 minutes
cooking time 50 minutes makes 3 cups

4 large tomatoes (880g), chopped coarsely
1 medium brown onion (150g), chopped coarsely
4 cloves garlic, chopped coarsely
3cm piece fresh ginger (15g), chopped finely
4 fresh small red thai chillies, chopped coarsely
2 teaspoons ground cumin
½ teaspoon ground turmeric
½ teaspoon chilli powder
¼ teaspoon ground clove
2 tablespoons vegetable oil
¼ cup (60ml) white vinegar
⅓ cup (75g) firmly packed brown sugar

1 Blend or process ingredients until smooth. Transfer mixture to large saucepan; cook, stirring, without boiling, until sugar is dissolved.
2 Simmer, uncovered, stirring occasionally, about 45 minutes or until kasaundi thickens slightly.
per tablespoon 1.6g total fat (0.2g saturated fat); 142kJ (34 cal); 4.1g carbohydrate; 0.5g protein; 0.6g fibre
TIP This goes well with pork, chicken and beef.

vietnamese carrot pickle

preparation time 10 minutes
makes 1½ cups

1 clove garlic, crushed
1 fresh long red chilli, chopped finely
¼ cup (60ml) lime juice
¼ cup (60ml) fish sauce
¼ cup (65g) grated palm sugar
½ cup (125ml) water
1 medium carrot (120g), grated coarsely

1 Combine ingredients in medium bowl.
per tablespoon 0g total fat (0g saturated fat); 79kJ (19 cal); 4.1g carbohydrate; 0.4g protein; 0.3g fibre
TIP This goes well with fish, crab, lobster, prawns, chicken and pork.

Chutneys, Raitas & Sauces

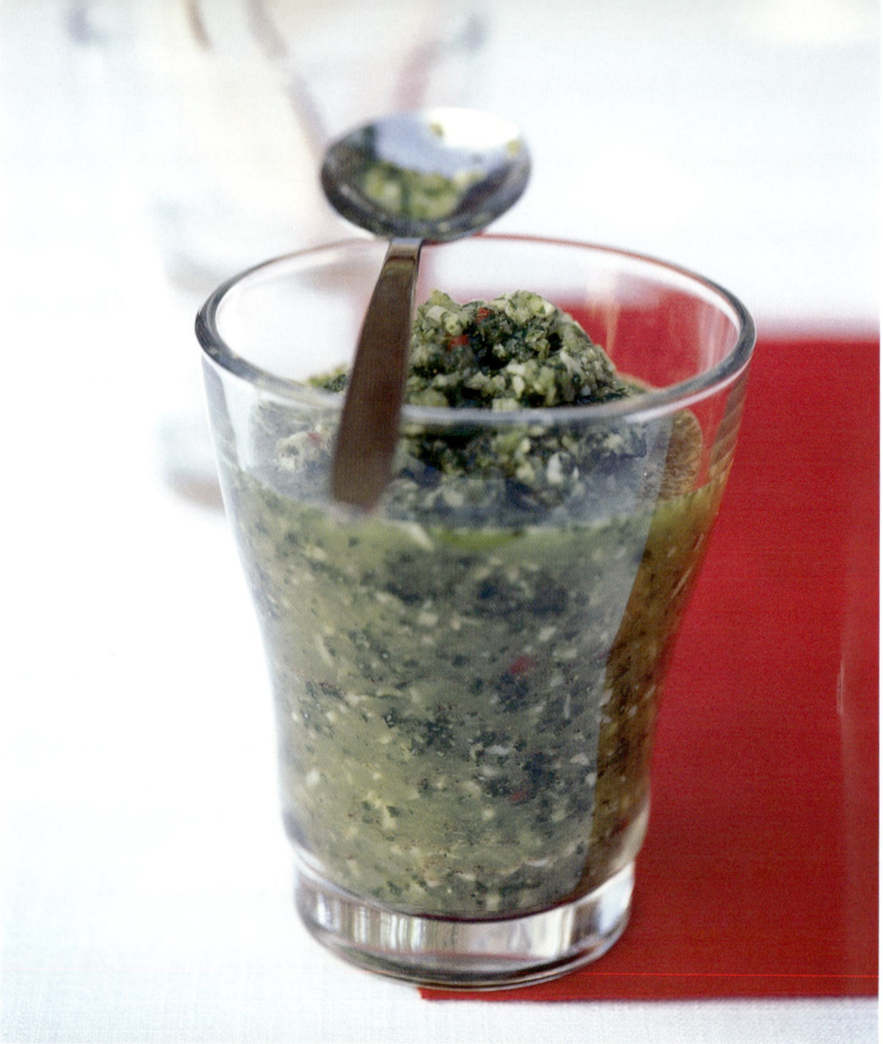

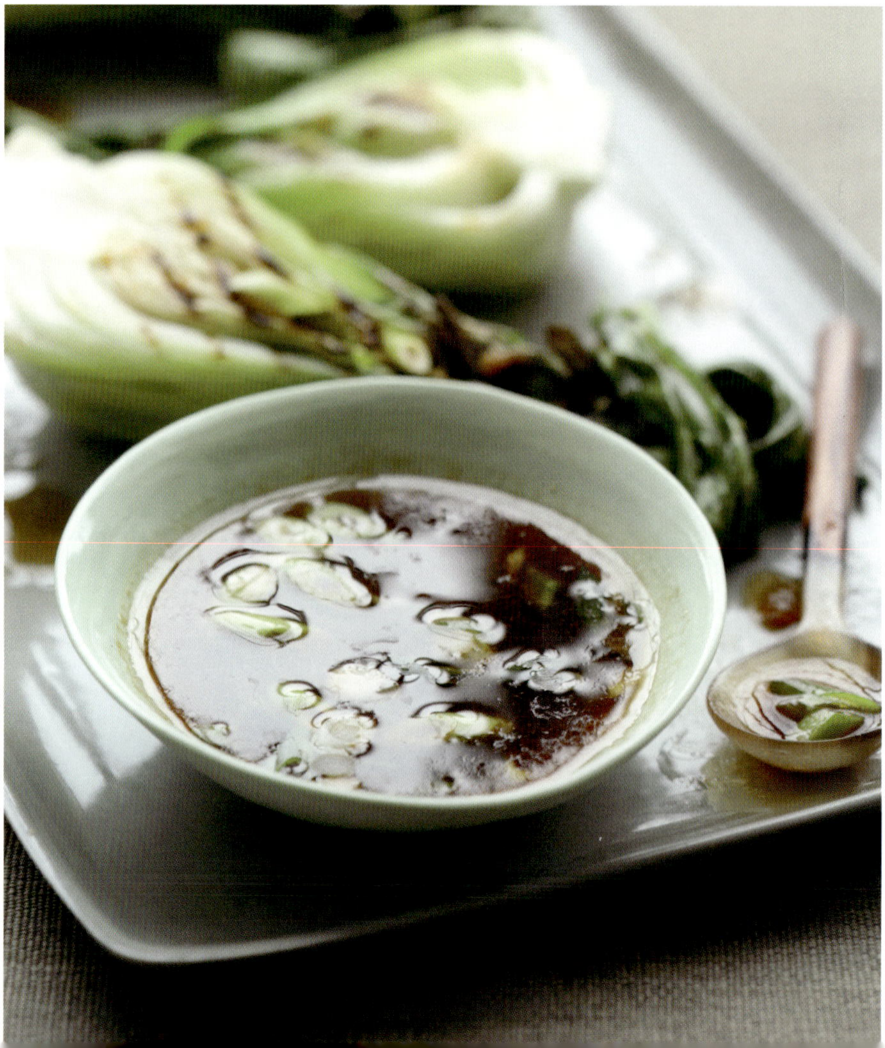

fresh coriander coconut chutney

preparation time 10 minutes
makes 1½ cups

⅓ cup (80ml) boiling water
⅓ cup (25g) shredded coconut
2 cups loosely packed fresh coriander
4 cloves garlic, chopped finely
1 small brown onion (80g), chopped finely
1½ teaspoons garam masala
¼ cup (60ml) lemon juice
2 tablespoons lime juice
1 fresh small red thai chilli, chopped finely

1 Pour the water over coconut in small heatproof bowl. Cover; stand about 5 minutes or until liquid is absorbed.
2 Blend or process coconut mixture, coriander, garlic, onion, garam masala and juices until well combined. Return mixture to bowl; stir in chilli.
per tablespoon 0.9g total fat (0.8g saturated fat); 63kJ (15 cal); 0.9g carbohydrate; 0.4g protein; 0.6g fibre
TIP *This goes well with fish, prawns, pork and chicken.*

rice wine and soy

preparation time 5 minutes
cooking time 10 minutes makes 1 cup

1 tablespoon peanut oil
2 teaspoons sesame oil
2 cloves garlic, crushed
5cm piece fresh ginger (25g), grated
1 green onion, sliced thinly
¼ cup (60ml) rice wine
2 tablespoons light soy sauce
2 teaspoons caster sugar
1 teaspoon cornflour
½ cup (125ml) water

1 Heat oils in wok; stir-fry garlic, ginger and onion until fragrant. Add wine, sauce and sugar; bring to a boil. Reduce heat, simmer, uncovered, 2 minutes.
2 Add blended cornflour and the water; cook, stirring, until mixture comes to a boil and thickens slightly.
per tablespoon 2.3g total fat (0.4g saturated fat); 134kJ (32 cal); 1.4g carbohydrate; 0.3g protein; 0.2g fibre
TIP *This goes well with fish, prawns, duck, chicken and pork.*

koshumbir

preparation time 10 minutes
makes 2 cups

1 small brown onion (80g), chopped finely
1 lebanese cucumber (130g), seeded, grated coarsely
1 small carrot (70g), grated coarsely
1 long green chilli, chopped finely
3cm piece fresh ginger (15g), grated
¼ cup (35g) crushed roasted unsalted peanuts
1 tablespoon lemon juice

1 Combine onion, cucumber, carrot, chilli, ginger and nuts in small bowl.
2 Just before serving, stir in juice.

per ¼ cup 2.1g total fat (0.2g saturated fat); 142kJ (34 cal); 1.7g carbohydrate; 1.4g protein; 1g fibre
TIP This goes well with chicken, fish and pork.

mango sambal

preparation time 10 minutes
cooking time 5 minutes makes 1½ cups

1 teaspoon shrimp paste
1 large mango (600g), peeled
1 fresh red thai chilli, chopped finely
1 teaspoon sugar
½ teaspoon light soy sauce

1 Cook paste in heated small saucepan until dry and crumbly.
2 Cut mango into 1cm cubes.
3 Combine paste and mango with remaining ingredients in medium bowl.

per tablespoon 0.1g total fat (0g saturated fat); 67kJ (16 cal); 3.2g carbohydrate; 0.3g protein; 0.4g fibre
TIP This goes well with pork, chicken and duck.

Chutneys, Raitas & Sauces

The Complete Book of Modern Asian

spicy dipping sauce

preparation time 10 minutes (plus standing time)
makes ⅓ cup

1 tablespoon rice vinegar
¼ cup (60ml) lime juice
1 clove garlic, crushed
1 tablespoon brown sugar
¼ cup (60ml) fish sauce
2 fresh small red thai chillies, sliced thinly
1 tablespoon finely chopped fresh coriander

1 Combine vinegar, juice, garlic, sugar and sauce in small jug; stand 15 minutes.
2 Strain sauce, discard garlic; stir in chilli and coriander.
per tablespoon 0.1g total fat (0.0g saturated fat); 105kJ (25 cal); 4.3g carbohydrate; 1.5g protein; 0.4g fibre
TIP This goes well with prawns, chicken, pork, beef and duck.

sweet and sour dipping sauce

preparation time 5 minutes
cooking time 5 minutes makes ½ cup

¼ cup (60ml) white vinegar
½ cup (110g) caster sugar
1½ tablespoons water
¼ lebanese cucumber (30g), seeded, chopped finely

1 Stir vinegar, sugar and the water in small saucepan until sugar is dissolved. Boil, uncovered, 3 minutes; cool.
2 Transfer mixture to serving bowl; stir in cucumber.
per tablespoon 0g total fat (0g saturated fat); 844kJ (202 cal); 49g carbohydrate; 0.1g protein; 0.1g fibre
TIP This goes well with prawns, chicken and pork.

hoisin and peanut dipping sauce

preparation time 5 minutes
cooking time 2 minutes makes ⅔ cup

2 teaspoons caster sugar
1 tablespoon rice vinegar
¼ cup (60ml) water
¼ cup (60ml) hoisin sauce
1 tablespoon crushed roasted peanuts

1 Stir sugar, vinegar and the water in small saucepan over medium heat until sugar dissolves.
2 Stir in sauce and nuts.

per tablespoon 1.1g total fat (0.2g saturated fat); 125kJ (30 cal); 4.1g carbohydrate; 0.5g protein; 1.0g fibre
TIP This goes well with stir-fried asian greens, chicken, pork and beef.

sweet chilli dipping sauce

preparation time 5 minutes
makes ⅓ cup

¼ cup (60ml) sweet chilli sauce
1 tablespoon lime juice
1 tablespoon fish sauce

1 Combine ingredients in small bowl.

per tablespoon 0.4g total fat (0.1g saturated fat); 88kJ (21 cal); 3.3g carbohydrate; 0.6g protein; 0.8g fibre
TIP This goes well with prawns, chicken, pork and beef.

Chutneys, Raitas & Sauces

Vegetables really come into their own in the hands of Asian cooks. Possibly because various religions and traditions place an emphasis on vegetarian eating, people living in the East have been inclined to come up with more ways to treat vegies than we meat-loving Westerners ever have – for which we are very, very thankful.

stir-fried asian greens in black bean sauce *page 426*

sichuan-style vegetables *page 418*

vegetables

grilled asian vegetables *page 426*

fried potatoes with black mustard seeds *page 421*

sichuan-style vegetables

preparation time 20 minutes
cooking time 25 minutes serves 4

2 large potatoes (600g), sliced thickly
8 baby eggplants (480g)
8 small zucchini (720g)
¼ cup (60ml) peanut oil
1 medium brown onion (150g), chopped coarsely
2 cloves garlic, crushed
100g green beans, trimmed, halved crossways
100g yellow beans, trimmed, halved crossways
¼ teaspoon sichuan peppercorns, crushed coarsely
¼ cup (60ml) vegetable stock
1 tablespoon red wine vinegar
1 tablespoon chilli bean sauce
1 tablespoon dark soy sauce
½ cup firmly packed thai basil leaves

1 Boil, steam or microwave potato until just tender; drain.
2 Meanwhile, using vegetable peeler, peel random strips of skin from eggplants and zucchini; discard skins. Halve each vegetable lengthways; cut halves into 3cm pieces.
3 Heat 1 tablespoon of oil in wok; stir-fry eggplant and zucchini, in batches, until browned lightly and just tender.
4 Heat 1 tablespoon of the remaining oil in wok; stir-fry potato, in batches, until browned and crisp.
5 Heat remaining oil in wok; stir-fry onion, garlic, beans and peppercorn until beans are just tender.
6 Return eggplant, zucchini and potato to wok with stock, vinegar and sauces; stir-fry until hot. Remove from heat; stir in basil.

per serving 15.1g total fat (2.5g saturated fat); 1262kJ (302 cal); 27.3g carbohydrate; 8.9g protein; 10.2g fibre

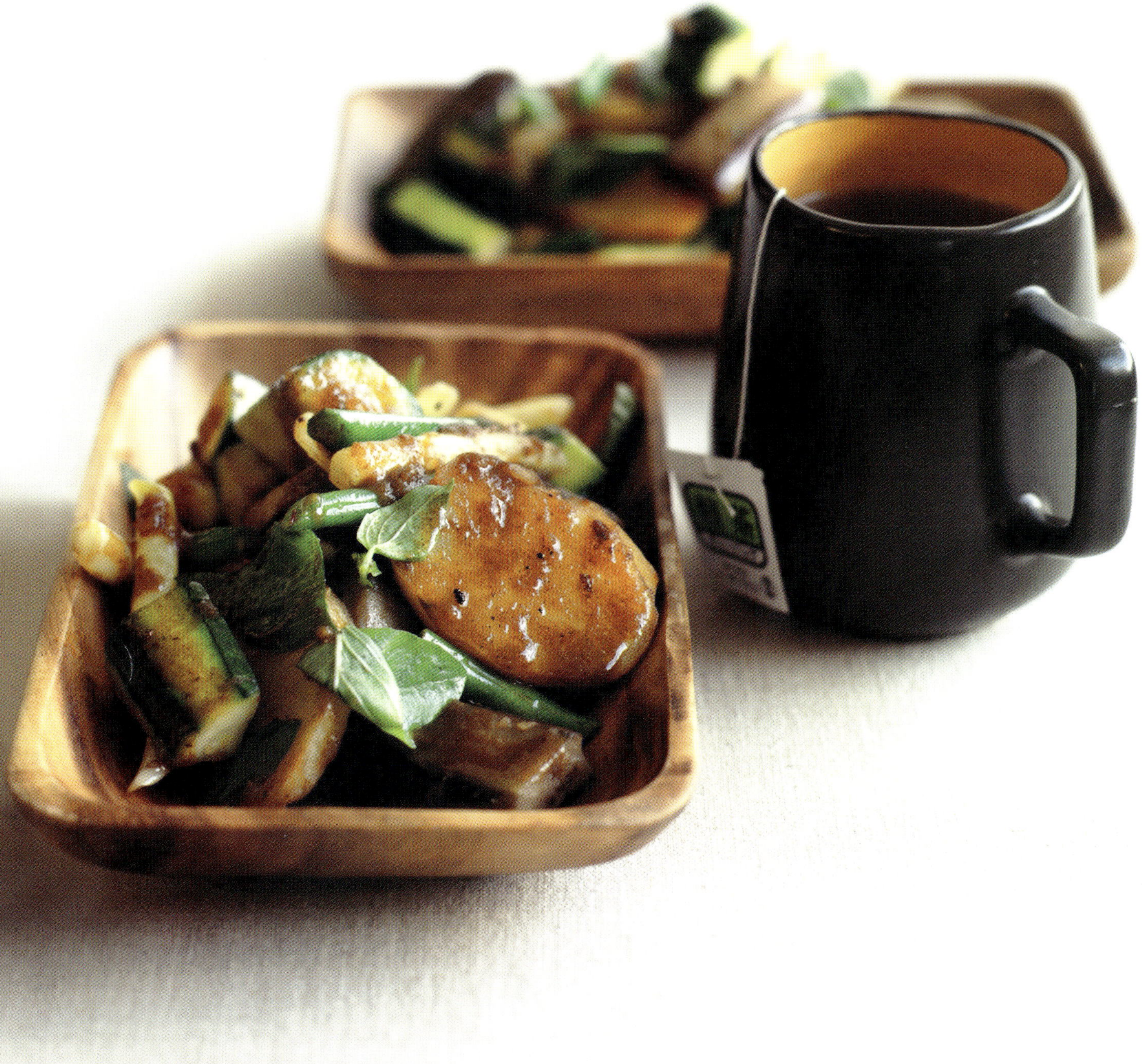

The Complete Book of Modern Asian

stir-fried vegetables with cracked black pepper

preparation time 10 minutes
cooking time 10 minutes serves 4

2 tablespoons peanut oil
2 cloves garlic, crushed
3 medium carrots (360g), sliced thinly
250g beans, halved
400g buk choy, chopped coarsely
1¼ cups (100g) bean sprouts
¼ cup (60ml) water
1 tablespoon fish sauce
1 tablespoon oyster sauce
1 teaspoon brown sugar
1 teaspoon cracked black peppercorns

1 Heat oil in wok; stir-fry garlic, carrot and beans until vegetables are just tender.
2 Add buk choy, sprouts and remaining ingredients; stir-fry until vegetables are just tender.
per serving 9.7g total fat (1.7g saturated fat); 648kJ (155 cal); 9.5g carbohydrate; 4.6g protein; 6.3g fibre

fried potatoes with black mustard seeds

preparation time 5 minutes
cooking time 25 minutes serves 4

1kg tiny new potatoes
2 tablespoons olive oil
1 tablespoon black mustard seeds
2 teaspoons sea salt flakes
1 teaspoon freshly ground black pepper
1 tablespoon coarsely chopped fresh flat-leaf parsley

1 Boil, steam or microwave potatoes until just tender; drain.
2 Heat oil in large frying pan; cook potatoes, stirring, until potatoes are browned lightly. Add mustard seeds, stirring, about 1 minute or until seeds pop.
3 Add remaining ingredients; toss gently to combine.
per serving 10g total fat (1.3g saturated fat); 1087kJ (260 cal); 33.3g carbohydrate; 6.5g protein; 5.2g fibre

aloo gobi

preparation time 15 minutes
cooking time 30 minutes serves 4

450g potatoes, peeled, chopped coarsely
20g ghee
1 tablespoon black mustard seeds
1 tablespoon cumin seeds
3 cloves garlic, crushed
½ teaspoon ground turmeric
½ teaspoon garam masala
1 large brown onion (200g), sliced thinly
2 medium tomatoes (380g), chopped coarsely
1kg cauliflower, chopped coarsely
1 cup (250ml) water
¼ cup loosely packed fresh coriander leaves

1 Boil, steam or microwave potato until just tender; drain.
2 Meanwhile, melt ghee in large saucepan; cook seeds, stirring, until they begin to pop. Add garlic, turmeric and garam masala; cook, stirring, until mixture is fragrant. Add onion; cook, stirring, until onion softens. Add tomato and cauliflower; cook, stirring, 1 minute.
3 Stir in the water; bring to a boil. Reduce heat, simmer, covered, 10 minutes. Stir in potato; simmer, covered, about 5 minutes or until vegetables are tender. Remove from heat; stir in coriander.
per serving 6.4g total fat (3.3g saturated fat); 878kJ (210 cal); 23.5g carbohydrate; 10.2g protein; 8.5g fibre

stir-fried cauliflower, choy sum and snake beans

preparation time 20 minutes
cooking time 10 minutes serves 4

1 tablespoon peanut oil
2 cloves garlic, crushed
1 teaspoon ground turmeric
1 teaspoon finely chopped coriander root and stem mixture
4 green onions, sliced thinly
500g cauliflower florets
¼ cup (60ml) water
200g snake beans, cut into 5cm pieces
200g choy sum, chopped coarsely
1 tablespoon lime juice
1 tablespoon soy sauce
1 tablespoon coarsely chopped fresh coriander

1 Heat oil in wok; stir-fry garlic, turmeric, coriander mixture and onion until onion just softens. Remove from wok; cover to keep warm.
2 Stir-fry cauliflower with the water in wok until cauliflower is almost tender. Add beans and choy sum; stir-fry until vegetables are just tender.
3 Add juice, sauce, chopped coriander and onion mixture; stir-fry until hot.
per serving 5.1g total fat (0.8g saturated fat); 401kJ (96 cal); 4.8g carbohydrate; 5.5g protein; 4.8g fibre

Vegetables

The Complete Book of Modern Asian

stir-fried gai lan with sesame

preparation time 10 minutes
cooking time 10 minutes serves 4

1kg gai lan, trimmed, chopped coarsely
1 tablespoon peanut oil
5 green onions, chopped coarsely
2 cloves garlic, crushed
2cm piece fresh ginger (10g), grated
2 tablespoons light soy sauce
2 tablespoons oyster sauce
1 tablespoon fish sauce
¼ cup (60ml) kecap manis
2 tablespoons sesame seeds

1 Boil, steam or microwave gai lan until just tender; drain.
2 Heat oil in wok; stir-fry onion, garlic and ginger until fragrant.
3 Add gai lan and sauces; stir until heated through. Drizzle with kecap manis; toss with sesame seeds.
per serving 8.4g total fat (1.3g saturated fat); 677kJ (162 cal); 7.2g carbohydrate; 9.8g protein; 10.5g fibre

stir-fried eggplant and tofu

preparation time 15 minutes (plus standing time)
cooking time 15 minutes serves 4

1 large eggplant (500g)
300g fresh firm silken tofu
1 medium brown onion (150g)
2 tablespoons peanut oil
1 clove garlic, crushed
2 fresh small red thai chillies, sliced thinly
1 tablespoon grated palm sugar
850g gai lan, chopped coarsely
2 tablespoons lime juice
⅓ cup (80ml) soy sauce
⅓ cup coarsely chopped fresh thai basil

1 Cut unpeeled eggplant in half lengthways; cut each half into thin slices. Place eggplant in colander, sprinkle with salt; stand 30 minutes.
2 Meanwhile, pat tofu all over with absorbent paper; cut into 2cm pieces. Spread tofu, in single layer, on absorbent-paper-lined tray; cover tofu with more absorbent paper, stand at least 10 minutes.
3 Cut onion in half, then cut each half into thin even-size wedges. Rinse eggplant under cold water; pat dry with absorbent paper.
4 Heat oil in wok; stir-fry onion, garlic and chilli until onion softens. Add sugar; stir-fry until dissolved. Add eggplant; stir-fry, 1 minute. Add gai lan; stir-fry until just wilted. Add tofu, juice and sauce; stir-fry, tossing gently, until combined. Remove from heat; toss basil through stir-fry.
per serving 15.3g total fat (2.4g saturated fat); 1241kJ (297 cal); 11.5g carbohydrate; 22.1g protein; 13.7g fibre

grilled asian vegetables

preparation time 10 minutes
cooking time 10 minutes   serves 4

400g baby buk choy, trimmed, halved lengthways
2 tablespoons peanut oil
175g broccolini, halved
100g snow peas, trimmed
200g baby corn, halved lengthways
2 tablespoons mirin
1 tablespoon vegetarian oyster sauce
1 tablespoon light soy sauce
1 clove garlic, crushed
1 teaspoon white sugar
½ teaspoon sesame oil

1 Boil, steam or microwave buk choy until wilted; drain. Brush with half of the peanut oil; cook on heated oiled grill plate (or grill or barbecue) until tender.
2 Combine broccolini, snow peas and corn in large bowl with remaining peanut oil. Cook vegetables, in batches, on same grill plate until tender.
3 Combine mirin, sauces, garlic, sugar and sesame oil in large bowl with vegetables.
per serving 10.7g total fat (1.8g saturated fat); 811kJ (194 cal); 13.4g carbohydrate; 6.5g protein; 6.1g fibre

stir-fried asian greens in black bean sauce

preparation time 10 minutes
cooking time 15 minutes   serves 4

1 tablespoon peanut oil
150g sugar snap peas, trimmed
400g gai lan, chopped coarsely
200g snake beans, trimmed, cut into 5cm lengths
2 cloves garlic, sliced thinly
1 fresh small red thai chilli, chopped finely
2 medium zucchini (240g), sliced thickly
2 tablespoons black bean sauce
1 tablespoon kecap manis
1 teaspoon sesame oil
⅓ cup (50g) toasted unsalted cashews, chopped coarsely

1 Heat peanut oil in wok; stir-fry peas, gai lan stems, snake beans, garlic, chilli and zucchini until stems are just tender.
2 Add sauces, sesame oil, gai lan leaves and nuts; stir-fry until leaves are just wilted.
3 Serve with steamed jasmine rice, if desired.
per serving 13.3g total fat (2.6g saturated fat); 2274kJ (544 cal); 89.5g carbohydrate; 15.4g protein; 8.8g fibre

Vegetables

asian star

steamed asian greens with char siu sauce

preparation time 5 minutes
cooking time 10 minutes serves 4

1 fresh long red chilli, sliced thinly
350g broccolini, trimmed
150g snow peas, trimmed
2 baby buk choy (300g), halved
2 tablespoons char siu sauce
2 teaspoons sesame oil
1 tablespoon peanut oil
1 tablespoon toasted sesame seeds

1 Layer chilli, broccolini, snow peas and buk choy in baking-paper-lined bamboo steamer. Steam, covered, over wok of simmering water about 5 minutes or until vegetables are just tender.
2 Combine vegetables, sauce and sesame oil in large bowl.
3 Heat peanut oil in small saucepan until hot. Pour hot oil over vegetable mixture; toss gently to combine. Serve sprinkled with seeds.
per serving 9.5g total fat (1.4g saturated fat); 635kJ (152 cal); 7g carbohydrate; 6.6g protein; 6.6g fibre

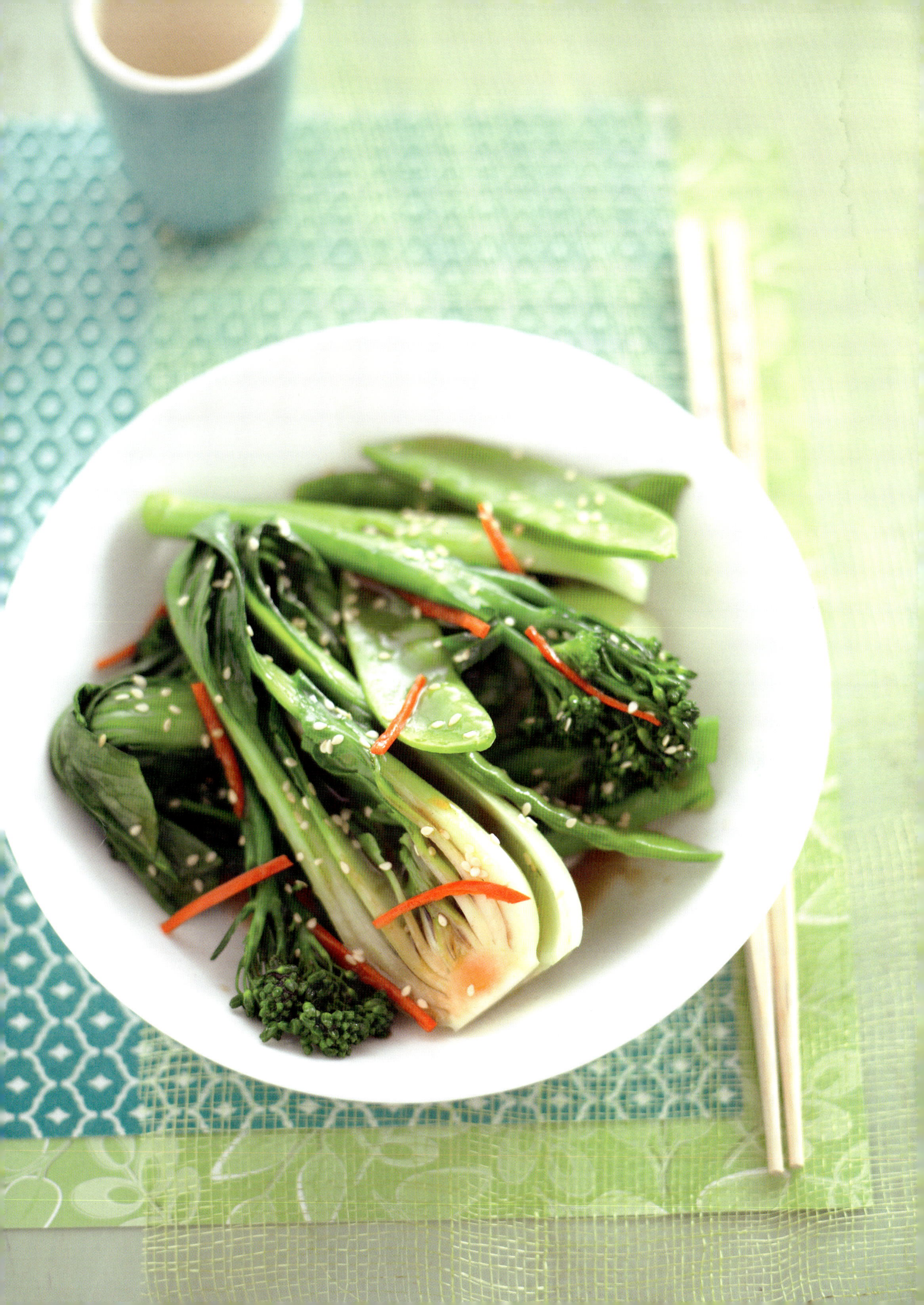

stir-fried sweet and sour vegetables

preparation time 20 minutes
cooking time 10 minutes serves 6

1 tablespoon peanut oil
2 cloves garlic, sliced thinly
2 fresh small red thai chillies, sliced thinly
500g fresh asparagus, cut into 5cm lengths
2 lebanese cucumbers (260g), seeded, sliced thickly
100g snow peas
250g broccoli, cut into florets
1 medium green capsicum (200g), chopped coarsely
2 tablespoons fish sauce
1½ tablespoons white vinegar
1 tablespoon brown sugar

1 Heat half of the oil in wok, stir-fry garlic and chilli until browned lightly; remove from wok.
2 Heat remaining oil in wok; stir-fry vegetables until just tender. Add combined sauce, vinegar and sugar; stir-fry 1 minute.
3 Serve vegetables sprinkled with garlic and chilli.
per serving 3.4g total fat (0.6g saturated fat); 368kJ (88 cal); 6.3g carbohydrate; 5.8g protein; 4.4g fibre

steamed buk choy with chilli oil

preparation time 5 minutes
cooking time 5 minutes serves 4

4 baby buk choy (600g)
1 tablespoon peanut oil
2 cloves garlic, crushed
2 tablespoons light soy sauce
2 teaspoons hot chilli sauce
2 green onions, sliced thinly
¼ cup firmly packed fresh coriander leaves
1 fresh red thai chilli, sliced thinly

1 Halve buk choy lengthways; place, cut-side up, in bamboo steamer. Drizzle buk choy with combined oil, garlic and sauces.
2 Steam buk choy, covered, over wok of simmering water about 5 minutes or until just tender.
3 Serve buk choy sprinkled with onion, coriander and chilli.
per serving 5.1g total fat (0.9g saturated fat); 318kJ (76 cal); 3.7g carbohydrate; 2.5g protein; 2.7g fibre

Vegetables

The Complete Book of Modern Asian

potato and onion bhaji

preparation time 15 minutes
cooking time 15 minutes serves 6

45g ghee
1 teaspoon brown mustard seeds
2 medium leeks (700g), sliced thinly
2 large brown onions (400g), sliced thinly
2 medium potatoes (400g), sliced thinly
1 medium carrot (120g), sliced thinly
2 cm piece fresh ginger (10g), grated
½ teaspoon cumin seeds
½ teaspoon ground turmeric
¼ teaspoon chilli powder
1 teaspoon garam masala
1 teaspoon salt

1 Heat ghee in large heavy-based frying pan; cook mustard seeds, stirring, 30 seconds.
2 Stir in leek, onion, potato, carrot, ginger, cumin seeds, turmeric and chilli powder; cook, stirring, 5 minutes.
3 Add garam masala and salt; cook, covered, over low heat about 10 minutes or until vegetables are tender.
per serving 8.3g total fat (4.9g saturated fat); 698kJ (167 cal); 16.4g carbohydrate; 4.4g protein; 4.9g fibre

sichuan eggplant, almond and wombok stir-fry

preparation time 15 minutes
cooking time 20 minutes serves 4

⅓ cup (55g) blanched almonds, halved
1 tablespoon peanut oil
1 medium brown onion (150g), chopped coarsely
2 cloves garlic, crushed
1 fresh small red thai chilli, chopped finely
12 baby eggplants (720g), sliced thickly
150g snake beans, trimmed, chopped coarsely
1 small wombok (700g), trimmed, chopped coarsely
2 teaspoons sichuan peppercorns, crushed coarsely
¼ cup (60ml) vegetable stock
2 tablespoons hoisin sauce
1 tablespoon dark soy sauce
1 tablespoon red wine vinegar
½ cup loosely packed thai basil leaves
1 fresh long red chilli, sliced thinly

1 Dry-fry nuts in heated wok until browned lightly; remove from wok.
2 Heat oil in wok; stir-fry onion, garlic and thai chilli until onion softens. Add eggplant and beans; stir-fry until tender. Add wombok; stir-fry until wilted.
3 Add pepper, stock, sauces and vinegar; stir-fry until hot. Remove from heat; stir in basil. Serve sprinkled with nuts and chilli.
per serving 13.6g total fat (1.4g saturated); 982kJ (235cal); 13.9g carbohydrate; 9.3g protein; 10.7g fibre

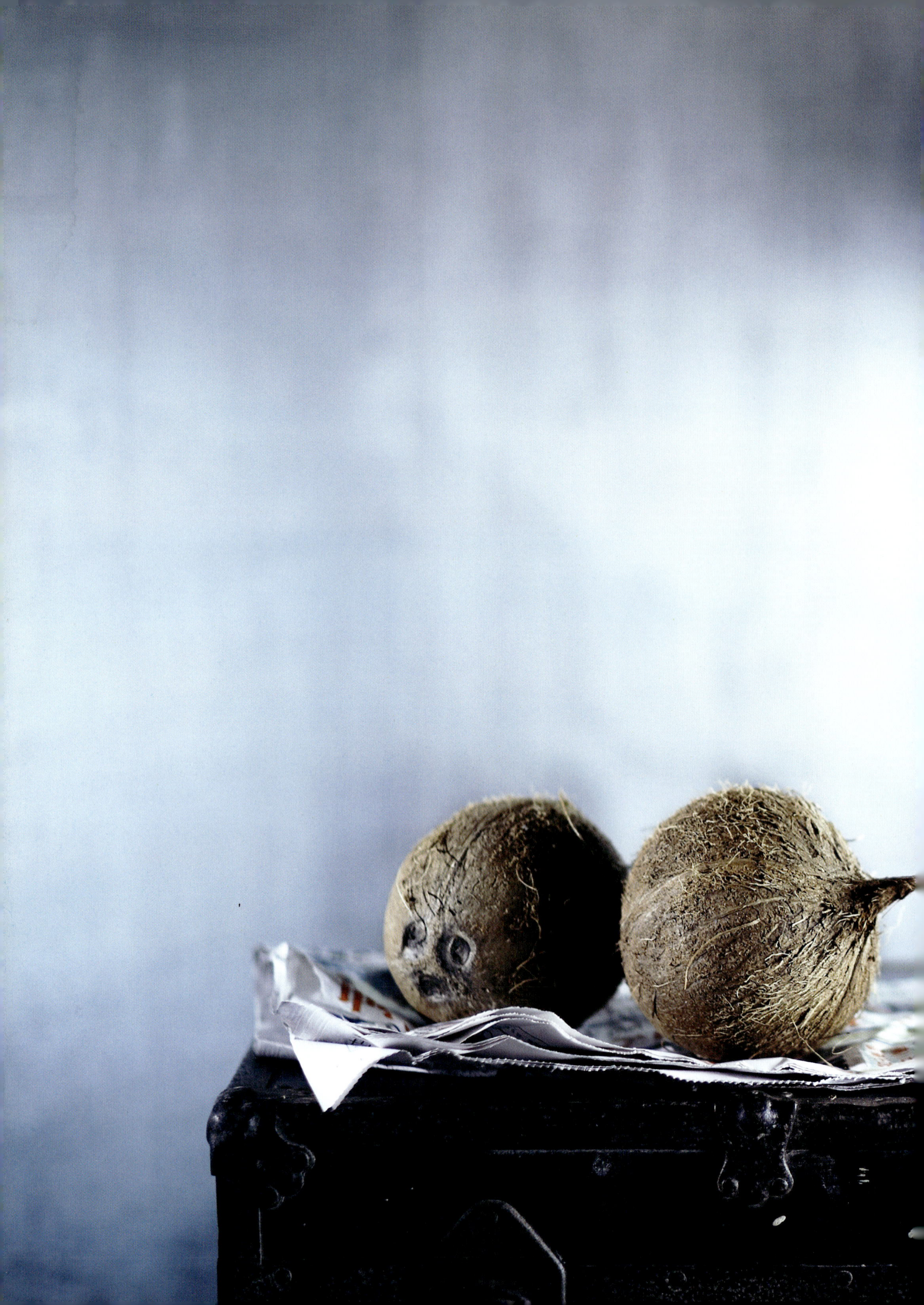

Desserts

The Complete Book of Modern Asian

Saving the best for last holds true when it comes to Asian desserts – as many possess the cooling natural sweetness of a tropical fruit, they signal a perfect end to a spicy meal. Many "typically" Asian desserts bear the fingerprint of a European past, especially those with a custard- or cake-like nature, becoming naturalised by the addition of local flavours and ingredients.

poached nashi in asian-spiced syrup *page 454*

asian fruit salad *page 442*

mango-passionfruit sorbet with grilled mango *page 445*   blood plums with honey and cardamom yogurt *page 441*

kaffir lime sorbet

preparation time 20 minutes
(plus cooling and freezing time)
cooking time 10 minutes serves 8

3 fresh kaffir lime leaves, chopped finely
1 cup (220g) caster sugar
2½ cups (625ml) water
¾ cup (180ml) lime juice
¼ teaspoon green food colouring
1 egg white

1 Stir lime leaves, sugar and the water in medium saucepan over high heat until sugar dissolves; bring to a boil. Reduce heat; simmer, uncovered, without stirring, 5 minutes. Transfer to large heatproof jug, cool to room temperature; stir in juice and food colouring.
2 Pour sorbet mixture into 14cm x 21cm loaf pan, cover tightly with foil; freeze 3 hours or overnight.
3 Process sorbet mixture with egg white until smooth. Return to pan, cover; freeze until firm.
per serving 0g total fat (0g saturated fat); 485kJ (116 cal); 27.8g carbohydrate; 0.6g protein; 0g fibre

lemon grass sorbet

preparation time 20 minutes
(plus cooling and freezing time)
cooking time 10 minutes serves 8

2 x 10cm sticks fresh lemon grass (40g), chopped finely
1 cup (220g) caster sugar
2½ cups (625ml) water
¾ cup (180ml) lemon juice
1 teaspoon yellow food colouring
1 egg white

1 Stir lemon grass, sugar and the water in medium saucepan over high heat until sugar dissolves; bring to a boil. Reduce heat; simmer, uncovered, without stirring, 5 minutes. Transfer to large heatproof jug, cool to room temperature; stir in juice and food colouring.
2 Pour sorbet mixture into 14cm x 21cm loaf pan, cover tightly with foil; freeze 3 hours or overnight.
3 Process sorbet mixture with egg white until smooth. Return to pan, cover; freeze until firm.
per serving 0g total fat (0g saturated fat); 489kJ (117 cal); 28.1g carbohydrate; 0.6g protein; 0g fibre

blood orange sorbet

preparation time 20 minutes
(plus cooling and freezing time)
cooking time 10 minutes serves 8

3 teaspoons finely grated blood orange rind
1 cup (220g) caster sugar
2½ cups (625ml) water
¾ cup (180ml) blood orange juice
1 egg white

1 Stir rind, sugar and the water in medium saucepan over high heat until sugar dissolves; bring to a boil. Reduce heat; simmer, uncovered, without stirring, 5 minutes. Transfer to large heatproof jug, cool to room temperature; stir in juice.
2 Pour sorbet mixture into 14cm x 21cm loaf pan, cover tightly with foil; freeze 3 hours or overnight.
3 Process sorbet mixture with egg white until smooth. Return to pan, cover; freeze until firm.
per serving 0g total fat (0g saturated fat); 510kJ (122 cal); 29.4g carbohydrate; 0.6g protein; 0.1g fibre

Clockwise from top left: kaffir lime sorbet; lemon grass sorbet; blood orange sorbet

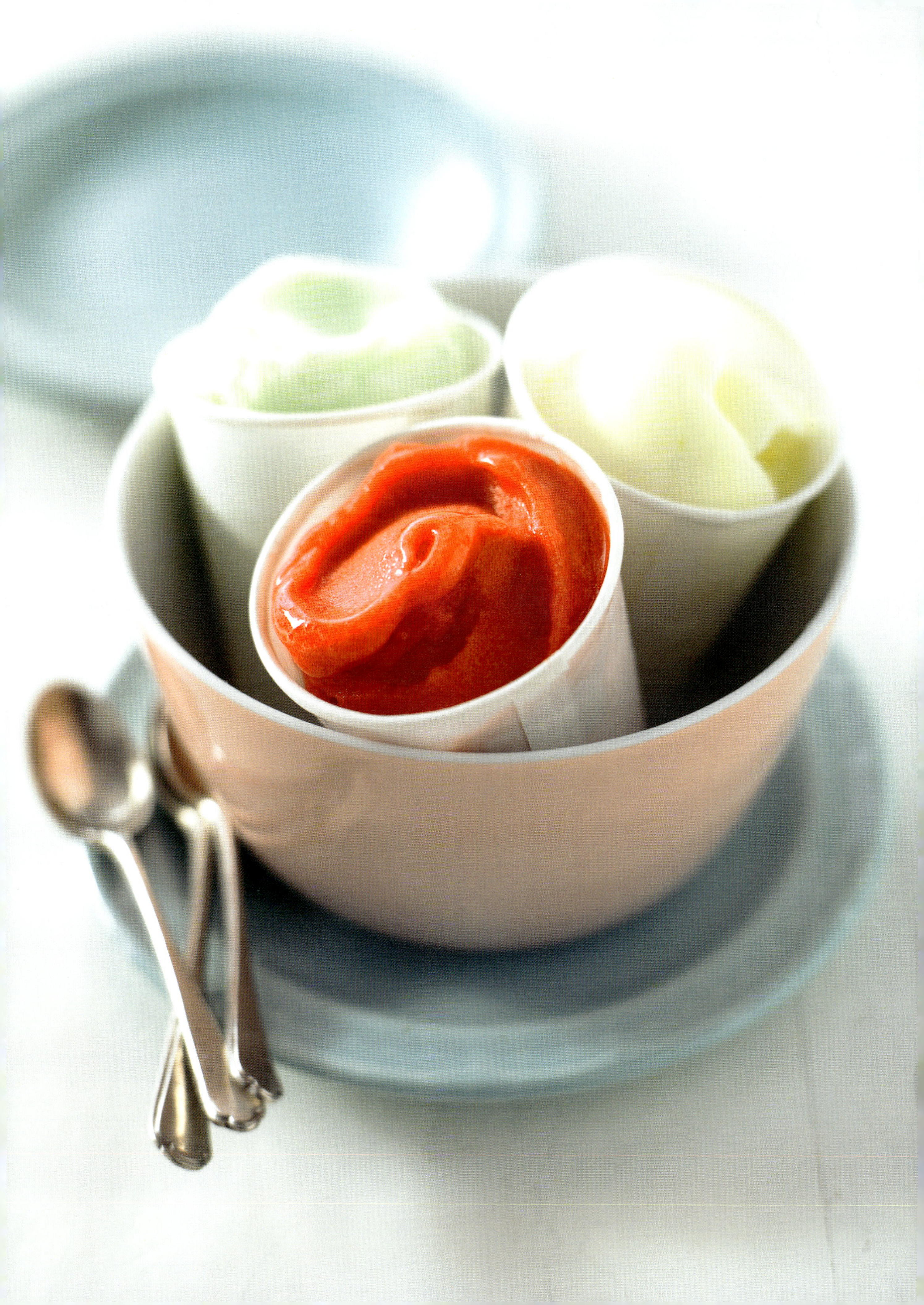

The Complete Book of Modern Asian

papaya with passionfruit and lime

preparation time 10 minutes
serves 4

3 small papaya (2 kg), cut into thick wedges
⅓ cup (80ml) fresh passionfruit pulp
2 tablespoons lime juice

1 Place papaya on serving plates.
2 Drizzle with passionfruit and juice.

per serving 0.4g total fat (0g saturated fat); 560kJ (134 cal); 25.1g carbohydrate; 2.1g protein; 10.7g fibre

blood plums with honey and cardamon yogurt

preparation time 5 minutes
serves 4

1 cup (280g) sheep milk yogurt
2 tablespoons honey
1 teaspoon ground cardamom
8 small blood plums (720g), quartered

1 Combine yogurt, honey and cardamom in small bowl.
2 Place plums on small serving plates; drizzle with yogurt mixture.

per serving 4.3g total fat (1.6g saturated fat); 690kJ (165 cal); 25.5g carbohydrate; 4.1g protein; 3.2g fibre

asian fruit salad

preparation time 20 minutes
(plus cooling and refrigeration time)
cooking time 15 minutes serves 8

1 litre (4 cups) water
1 cup (270g) grated palm sugar
1 vanilla bean
2cm piece fresh ginger (10g), chopped finely
3 star anise
1 tablespoon finely grated lime rind
⅓ cup (80ml) lime juice
½ cup coarsely chopped vietnamese mint
2 large mangoes (1.2kg), chopped coarsely
3 star fruit (450g), sliced thinly
2 large oranges (600g), segmented
1 large pineapple (2kg), chopped coarsely
1 medium papaya (1kg), chopped coarsely
½ cup (125ml) passionfruit pulp
12 rambutans (500g), halved
12 lychees (300g), halved

1 Stir the water and sugar in medium saucepan over high heat until sugar dissolves; bring to a boil. Reduce heat, simmer without stirring, uncovered, 5 minutes.
2 Split vanilla bean in half lengthways; scrape seeds into pan. Add pod, ginger and star anise; simmer, uncovered, about 10 minutes or until syrup thickens. Discard pod; cool to room temperature. Stir in rind, juice and mint.
3 Combine remaining ingredients in large bowl. Pour syrup over fruit; stir gently to combine. Refrigerate fruit salad, covered, until cold.
per serving 0.9g total fat (0g saturated fat); 1626kJ (389 cal); 82.8g carbohydrate; 5.2g protein; 12.4g fibre

tropical fruit salad with cardamom

preparation time 10 minutes (plus refrigeration time)
cooking time 20 minutes serves 4

2 cups (500ml) water
3 cardamom pods, bruised
4cm piece fresh ginger (20g), quartered
1 teaspoon finely grated lemon rind
1 tablespoon lemon juice
1 tablespoon lime juice
1 vanilla bean, split lengthways
½ medium rockmelon (850g), chopped coarsely
1 small papaya (600g), chopped coarsely
3 medium kiwi fruit (255g), sliced thickly
1 medium mango (430g), chopped coarsely
⅓ cup (80ml) passionfruit pulp

1 Place the water, cardamom, ginger, rind and juices into medium frying pan. Scrape vanilla seeds into pan then add pod; bring to a boil. Reduce heat, simmer, uncovered, without stirring, 20 minutes. Strain syrup into medium jug; discard spices and pod. Cool 10 minutes. Refrigerate, covered, until syrup is cold.
2 Just before serving, place syrup and remaining ingredients in large bowl; toss gently to combine.
per serving 0.6g total fat (0g saturated fat); 665kJ (159 cal); 30.2g carbohydrate; 3.3g protein; 9.6g fibre

Desserts

The Complete Book of Modern Asian

gulab jaman

preparation time 20 minutes (plus standing time)
cooking time 15 minutes makes 24

2 cups (440g) caster sugar
2 cups (500ml) water
8 cardamom pods, bruised
2 cinnamon sticks
3 star anise
1 teaspoon rosewater
½ cup (75g) self-raising flour
¼ cup (25g) full-cream milk powder
125g spreadable packaged cream cheese
24 raisins
vegetable oil, for deep-frying

1 Stir sugar, the water, cardamom, cinnamon and star anise in medium saucepan over heat, without boiling, until sugar dissolves; bring to a boil. Boil, uncovered, without stirring, 5 minutes. Remove from heat; stir in rosewater. Cool.
2 Place flour, milk powder and cheese in medium bowl; using a wooden spoon, mix to a soft dough. Turn onto floured surface; knead about 10 minutes or until smooth. Roll 1 rounded teaspoon of the dough around each raisin.
3 Heat oil in wok; deep-fry balls, in batches, until browned lightly. Add balls to rosewater syrup; stand gulab jaman 1 hour before serving.

per gulab jaman 2.5g total fat (1.4g saturated fat); 477kJ (144 cal); 21.4g carbohydrate; 1g protein; 0.1g fibre

mango-passionfruit sorbet with grilled mango

preparation time 30 minutes (plus freezing time)
cooking time 25 minutes serves 4

½ cup (125ml) passionfruit pulp
½ cup (110g) caster sugar
1 cup (250ml) water
1 large mango (600g), chopped coarsely
2 tablespoons lime juice
3 egg whites
4 small mangoes (1.2kg)
2 tablespoons brown sugar
1 lime, cut into 8 wedges

1 Strain passionfruit pulp over small jug; reserve seeds.
2 Stir caster sugar and the water in small saucepan over heat, without boiling, until sugar dissolves; bring to a boil. Reduce heat, simmer, uncovered, without stirring, about 10 minutes or until mixture thickens. Cool.
3 Blend or process chopped mango until smooth; transfer to small bowl. Stir in pulp, syrup and juice. Pour mixture into 14cm x 21cm loaf pan, cover with foil; freeze about 3 hours or until just firm.
4 Process sorbet with egg whites until almost smooth. Stir in 2 tablespoons reserved passionfruit seeds; discard remaining seeds. Return sorbet to pan, cover; freeze overnight.
5 Just before serving, slice cheeks from small mangoes; score each cheek in shallow criss-cross pattern. Sprinkle brown sugar over cheeks; cook under preheated grill until sugar caramelises. Serve sorbet with mango cheeks and lime wedges.

per serving 0.8g total fat (0g saturated fat); 1643kJ (393 cal); 80.1g carbohydrate; 6.9g protein; 9.4g fibre

grilled pineapple with coconut ice-cream

preparation time 15 minutes (plus freezing time)
cooking time 5 minutes serves 4

1 large pineapple (2kg), sliced thickly
1 tablespoon coconut-flavoured liqueur
2 tablespoons brown sugar
COCONUT ICE-CREAM
1 cup (75g) toasted shredded coconut
¼ cup (60ml) coconut-flavoured liqueur
1 litre vanilla ice-cream, softened

1 Make coconut ice-cream.
2 Combine pineapple, liqueur and sugar in large bowl.
3 Cook pineapple on heated greased grill plate (or grill or barbecue) until browned both sides.
4 Serve pineapple slices with coconut ice-cream.
COCONUT ICE-CREAM
Fold coconut and liqueur through slightly softened ice-cream, cover; freeze about 3 hours or overnight.
per serving 26g total fat (19.8g saturated fat); 2128kJ (509 cal); 49.4g carbohydrate; 7.7g protein; 7.3g fibre

coconut sago pudding with caramelised banana

preparation time 10 minutes
cooking time 25 minutes serves 4

5cm strip fresh lime rind
1 cup (200g) sago
½ cup (135g) firmly packed grated palm sugar
¼ cup (60ml) water
140ml can coconut cream
4 unpeeled sugar bananas (520g), halved lengthways
1 tablespoon grated palm sugar, extra
½ teaspoon finely grated lime rind

1 Place rind strip in large saucepan of cold water; bring to a boil. Discard rind; add sago. Reduce heat, simmer, uncovered, about 15 minutes or until sago is almost transparent. Drain; rinse under cold water, drain.
2 Meanwhile, stir sugar and the water in small saucepan over heat, without boiling, until sugar dissolves. Bring to a boil; boil, uncovered, without stirring, about 10 minutes or until toffee coloured. Remove from heat; stir in coconut cream. Cool 10 minutes.
3 Sprinkle cut side of banana with extra sugar. Place, cut-side down, on heated greased grill plate (or grill or barbecue). Cook about 5 minutes or until tender.
4 Combine sago in medium bowl with coconut mixture and grated rind. Divide among serving bowls; serve with banana, and extra lime rind, if desired.
per serving 7.5g total fat (6.4g saturated fat); 2065kJ (494 cal); 101.3g carbohydrate; 2.1g protein; 4.1g fibre
TIP This pudding is also great served topped with fresh mango slices if you want to forego the banana.

Desserts

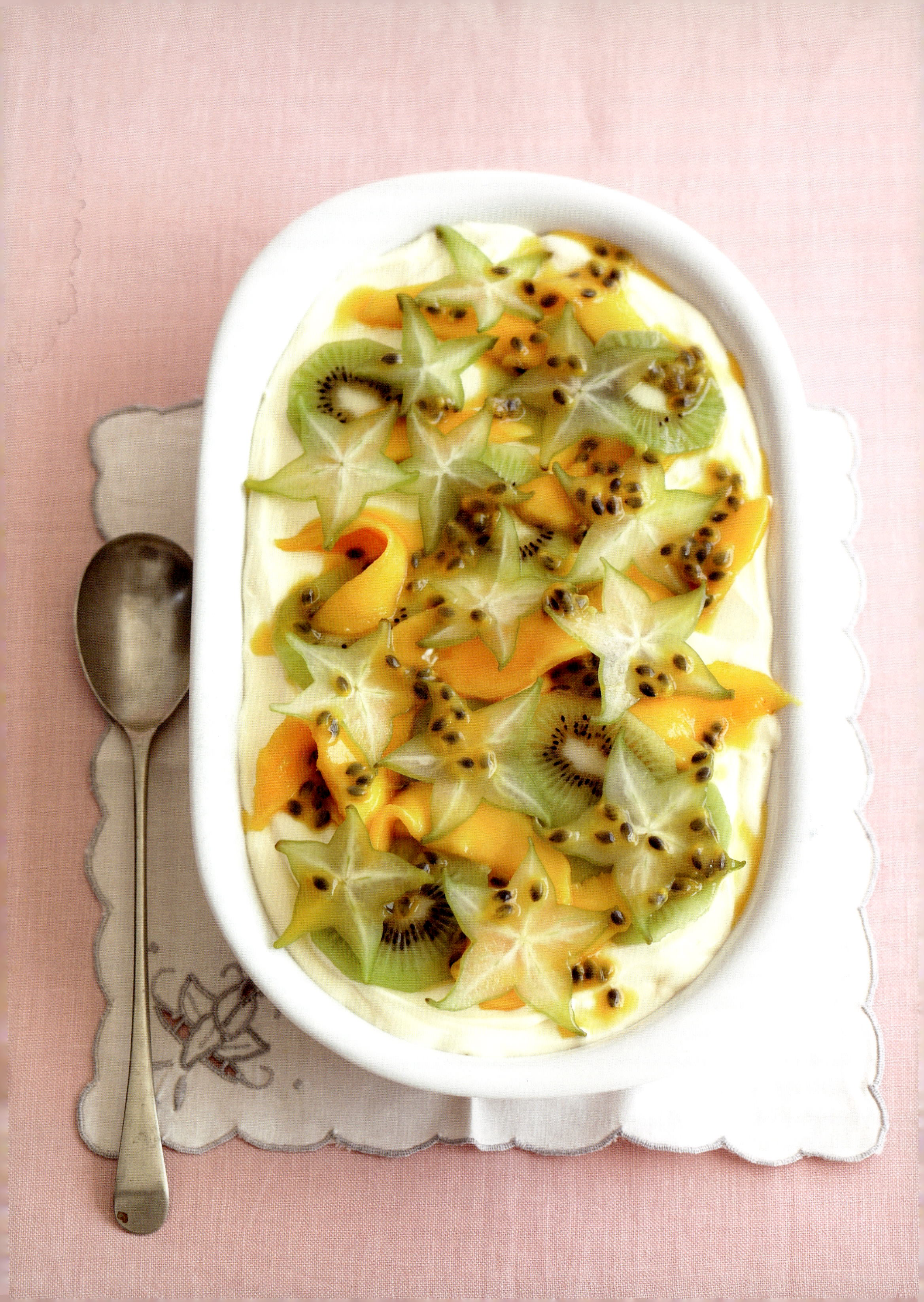

tropical fruit trifle

preparation time 25 minutes (plus refrigeration time)
cooking time 5 minutes   serves 6

85g packet mango jelly crystals
¼ cup (30g) custard powder
⅓ cup (75g) caster sugar
½ teaspoon vanilla extract
1½ cups (375ml) milk
⅓ cup (80ml) pineapple juice
⅓ cup (80ml) coconut-flavoured liqueur
6 savoiardi sponge fingers
⅔ cup (160ml) thickened cream
125g cream cheese, softened
1 medium kiwi fruit (85g), sliced
1 medium mango (430g), sliced
1 medium star fruit (160g), sliced
2 tablespoons passionfruit pulp

1 Make jelly according to directions on packet; pour into shallow container. Refrigerate 20 minutes or until jelly is almost set.
2 Blend custard powder, half the sugar, and extract with a little of the milk in small saucepan; stir in remaining milk. Stir over heat until mixture boils and thickens. Cover custard surface with plastic wrap; cool.
3 Combine juice and liqueur in small bowl. Soak sponge fingers, one at a time, in juice mixture; place over base of shallow 2-litre (8-cup) serving dish. Pour jelly over sponge fingers, cover; refrigerate 15 minutes or until jelly is set.
4 Stir half the cream into custard; pour over jelly.
5 Beat cream cheese with remaining cream and sugar in small bowl with electric mixer until smooth. Spread over custard, top with fruit and pulp. Refrigerate 3 hours or overnight.

per serving 20.1g total fat (12.7g saturated fat); 2027kJ (485 cal); 58.9g carbohydrate; 7.5g protein; 2.9g fibre

sweet lime mangoes

preparation time 5 minutes
cooking time 8 minutes serves 4

4 small mangoes (1.2kg)
1 tablespoon grated lime rind
1 tablespoon lime juice
1 tablespoon finely grated palm sugar
½ cup (140g) yogurt

1 Slice cheeks from mangoes; score each in shallow criss-cross pattern. Combine rind and juice in small bowl; drizzle over each cheek, sprinkle with sugar.
2 Cook mango cheeks under preheated grill until sugar caramelises; serve with yogurt.

per serving 1.7g total fat (0.7g saturated fat); 798kJ (191 cal); 35.8g carbohydrate; 4.1g protein; 4.1g fibre

tropical fruit skewers with coconut dressing

preparation time 30 minutes
cooking time 5 minutes serves 4

2 medium bananas (400g)
½ medium pineapple (625g)
2 large starfruit (320g)
1 large mango (600g), chopped coarsely

COCONUT DRESSING
⅓ cup (80ml) coconut-flavoured liqueur
¼ cup (60ml) light coconut milk
1 tablespoon grated palm sugar
1cm piece fresh ginger (5g), grated

1 Place ingredients for coconut dressing in screw-top jar; shake well.
2 Cut each unpeeled banana into eight pieces. Cut unpeeled pineapple into eight slices; cut slices in half. Cut each starfruit into eight slices.
3 Thread fruit onto skewers, alternating varieties. Cook skewers on grill plate (or grill or barbecue), brushing with a little of the dressing, until browned lightly. Serve drizzled with remaining dressing.

per serving 2.4g total fat (1.6g saturated fat); 1321kJ (316 cal); 53.6g carbohydrate; 3.6g protein; 6.9g fibre

Desserts

The Complete Book of Modern Asian

almond and rosewater jelly

preparation time 20 minutes
(plus standing and refrigeration time)
cooking time 15 minutes serves 4

3 cups (750ml) milk
1½ cups (240g) blanched almonds
⅓ cup (75g) caster sugar
3½ teaspoons gelatine
1 teaspoon rosewater
2 passionfruits
1 medium mango (430g), chopped coarsely
1 starfruit (160g), sliced thinly
565g can lychees, rinsed, drained

1 Grease 8cm x 26cm bar cake pan.
2 Blend milk, nuts and sugar until mixture forms a smooth puree. Transfer to medium saucepan; heat until hot but not boiling. Remove from heat; stand 1 hour.
3 Pour mixture into large jug; strain through muslin-lined sieve into same cleaned pan; discard solids. Sprinkle gelatine over mixture; stir over heat, without boiling, until dissolved. Remove from heat, stir in rosewater; pour mixture into cake pan. Cover; refrigerate 3 hours or overnight.
4 Scoop pulp from passionfruit into medium bowl with remaining fruit; toss to combine.
5 Turn jelly onto chopping board, cut into 24 cubes. Serve jelly with fruit.
per serving 41.2g total fat (6.9g saturated fat); 2955kJ (707 cal); 56.1g carbohydrate; 23g protein; 11.2g fibre

pistachio, honey and cardamom kulfi

preparation time 10 minutes
(plus cooling and freezing time)
cooking time 15 minutes serves 4

2 x 375ml cans evaporated milk
¾ cup (180ml) cream
3 cardamom pods, bruised
2 tablespoons honey
⅓ cup (45g) finely chopped roasted pistachios
2 tablespoons coarsely chopped roasted pistachios

1 Combine milk, cream and cardamom in large heavy-based saucepan; bring to a boil. Reduce heat, simmer, uncovered, stirring occasionally, about 10 minutes or until reduced to about 3 cups. Stir in honey, remove from heat; cool 15 minutes.
2 Strain mixture into large bowl; discard cardamom. Divide kulfi mixture among four ¾-cup (180ml) moulds; sprinkle with finely chopped nuts. Cover with foil; freeze 3 hours or overnight.
3 Turn kulfi onto serving plates; sprinkle with coarsely chopped nuts to serve.
per serving 45.1g total fat (25.6g saturated fat); 2621kJ (627 cal); 36.3g carbohydrate; 19.3g protein; 1.7g fibre

coconut custards with papaya

preparation time 25 minutes
cooking time 15 minutes serves 4

½ cup (135g) grated palm sugar
⅓ cup (80ml) water
3 eggs
⅔ cup (160ml) coconut cream
2 tablespoons milk
1 teaspoon vanilla extract
1 large red papaya (580g)
2 teaspoons grated lime rind
1 tablespoon lime juice
1 tablespoon grated palm sugar, extra

1 Place sugar and the water in small saucepan; cook over low heat until sugar is dissolved.
2 Whisk eggs, coconut cream and milk until combined, but not frothy. Gradually whisk hot sugar syrup into egg mixture, then stir in extract. Strain custard into heatproof jug.
3 Pour custard into four ⅔-cup (160ml) heatproof dishes. Place dishes in bamboo steamer, cover dishes with a sheet of baking paper; place lid on steamer; gently steam about 15 minutes or until just set.
4 Meanwhile, peel and seed papaya; cut into quarters. Combine papaya in medium bowl with rind, juice and extra sugar.
5 Cool custards 5 minutes; serve with papaya mixture.
per serving 13.5g total fat (9.1g saturated fat); 1492kJ (357 cal); 54.4g carbohydrate; 7.3g protein; 3.0g fibre
TIPS The custards can be made several hours ahead and served cold, if desired. Store custards, covered, in refrigerator.

poached nashi in asian-spiced syrup

preparation time 5 minutes
cooking time 40 minutes serves 6

6 medium nashi (1.2kg)
2 cups (440g) sugar
1 litre (4 cups) water
1 vanilla bean
2 cinnamon sticks
2 star anise
2 cardamom pods, bruised

1 Peel nashi, leaving stems intact.
2 Stir sugar with the water in large saucepan over heat, without boiling, until sugar dissolves.
3 Split vanilla bean in half lengthways; scrape seeds directly into sugar syrup. Add nashi to syrup with cinnamon, star anise and cardamom; bring to a boil. Reduce heat; simmer, covered, about 20 minutes or until nashi are just tender, turning occasionally. Remove from heat; cool in syrup.
4 Remove nashi from syrup. Strain syrup over medium jug; discard solids and all but 2 cups of the syrup.
5 Bring reserved syrup to a boil in small saucepan. Reduce heat, simmer, uncovered, about 15 minutes or until syrup reduces by half. Remove from heat; cool. Divide nashi among serving bowls; drizzle with syrup. Serve with yogurt, if desired.
per serving 0.2g total fat (0g saturated fat); 1639kJ (392 cal); 94g carbohydrate; 0.7g protein; 2.9g fibre

Desserts

The Complete Book of Modern Asian

grilled nashi with rosewater syrup

preparation time 10 minutes
cooking time 15 minutes serves 4

¾ cup (165g) caster sugar
2 cups (500ml) water
2½ teaspoons rosewater
4 medium nashi (1kg), halved
1 tablespoon honey
1 tablespoon grated jaggery

1 Combine caster sugar, the water and rosewater in medium saucepan; stir over heat, without boiling, until sugar dissolves. Add nashi; simmer, uncovered, about 10 minutes or until nashi is just tender.
2 Drain nashi over large heatproof bowl. Reserve syrup; cover to keep warm. Place nashi on oven tray. Drizzle with honey; sprinkle with jaggery.
3 Grill nashi until sugar dissolves and nashi is browned lightly. Serve warm or cold with warm rosewater syrup.
per serving 0.2g total fat (0g saturated fat); 1333kJ (319 cal); 75g carbohydrate; 0.9g protein; 4.7g fibre

little lime syrup cakes

preparation time 20 minutes
cooking time 30 minutes makes 6

125g butter, chopped
½ cup (110g) caster sugar
2 teaspoons grated lime rind
2 eggs
1 cup (150g) self-raising flour
½ cup (125ml) buttermilk

LIME SYRUP
½ cup (110g) caster sugar
⅓ cup (80ml) lime juice
2 tablespoons water
1 teaspoon grated lime rind

1 Preheat oven to 180°C/160°C fan-forced. Grease a six-hole mini fluted tube pan or texas (¾-cup/180ml) muffin pan.
2 Beat butter, sugar and rind in small bowl with electric mixer until light and fluffy. Add eggs, one at a time, beating until just combined between additions. Transfer mixture to medium bowl; stir in sifted flour and buttermilk.
3 Divide mixture among pan holes, smooth tops. Bake about 25 minutes.
4 Meanwhile, make lime syrup.
5 Stand cakes 5 minutes before turning onto wire rack over a tray. Pour hot lime syrup evenly over hot cakes. Serve warm or cooled with whipped cream and extra grated lime rind, if desired.
LIME SYRUP
Stir sugar, juice and the water in small saucepan over low heat until sugar dissolves. Bring to a boil; remove from heat. Strain into medium heatproof jug. Stir in rind.
per cake 19.6g total fat (12.1g saturated fat); 1781kJ (426 cal); 55.9g carbohydrate; 5.8g protein; 1g fibre

asian star

coconut rice pudding with mango

preparation time 15 minutes
serves 4

300ml thickened cream
½ cup (125ml) coconut cream
½ cup (80g) icing sugar
2¼ cups cooked medium-grain white rice
1 large mango (600g), chopped coarsely
½ cup (25g) toasted flaked coconut

1 Beat cream, coconut cream and sugar in small bowl with electric mixer until soft peaks form.
2 Place rice in large bowl; fold in cream mixture. Cover; refrigerate while preparing mango.
3 Blend or process three-quarters of the mango until smooth; slice remaining mango into thin strips.
4 Divide rice mixture and mango puree, in alternate layers, among four 1-cup (250ml) glasses; top with mango strips and coconut.
per serving 38.8g total fat (27.6g saturated fat); 2596kJ (621 cal); 61.1g carbohydrate; 5.6g protein; 3.7g fibre
TIP You will need to cook about ¾ cup of medium-grain rice for this recipe.

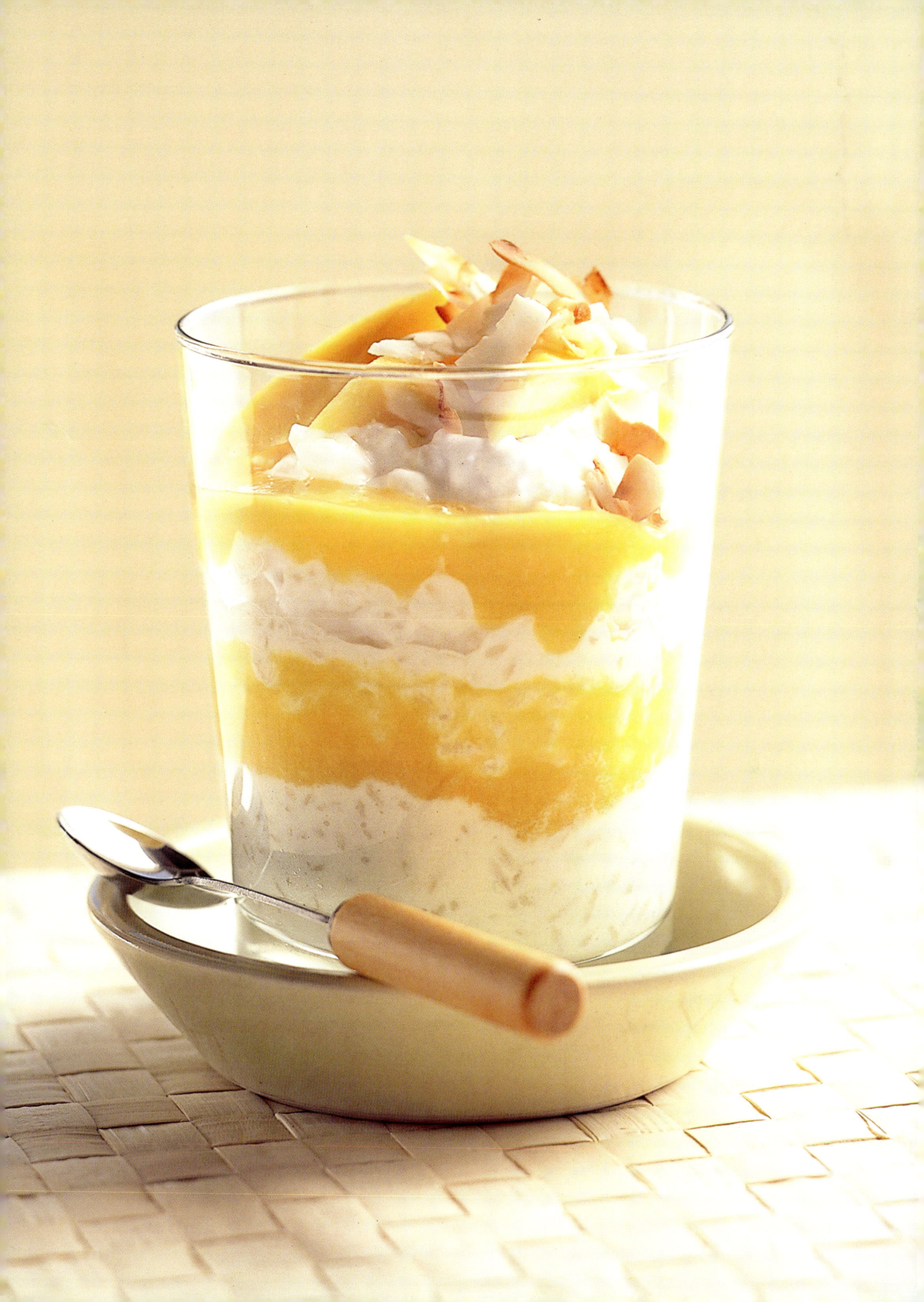

The Complete Book of Modern Asian

kiwi fruit, lychee and lime salad

preparation time 5 minutes
serves 4

3 kiwi fruits (255g), cut into wedges
8 fresh lychees (200g)
¼ cup loosely packed fresh mint leaves
¼ cup (60ml) lime juice

1. Combine ingredients in large bowl.
2. Serve with lime wedges, if desired.

per serving 0.2g total fat (0g saturated fat); 234kJ (56 cal); 11.1g carbohydrate; 1.3g protein; 2.3g fibre

lychees with passionfruit

preparation time 5 minutes
serves 4

You need about 6 passionfruit for this recipe.

1kg fresh lychees
½ cup (140g) yogurt
½ cup (125ml) fresh passionfruit pulp

1. Blend or process half of the lychees with the yogurt until smooth; stir in half of the passionfruit.
2. Place remaining lychees in serving bowls; top with lychee mixture and remaining passionfruit.

per serving 1.5g total fat (0.7g saturated fat); 761kJ (182 cal); 33.8g carbohydrate; 4.6g protein; 6.8g fibre

ginger and lime crème brûlée

preparation time 20 mins (plus refrigeration time)
cooking time 30 mins serves 6

2 eggs
4 egg yolks
¼ cup (55g) caster sugar
600ml thickened cream
1 tablespoon grated lime rind
1 tablespoon grated fresh ginger
2 tablespoons finely grated palm sugar

1 Preheat oven to 160°C/140°C fan-forced.
2 Whisk eggs, egg yolks and caster sugar in medium heatproof bowl.
3 Combine cream, rind and ginger in medium saucepan; bring to a boil. Gradually whisk hot cream mixture into egg mixture. Place bowl over medium saucepan of simmering water; do not allow water to touch base of bowl. Whisk over heat about 10 minutes or until mixture thickens slightly and coats the back of a spoon.
4 Divide custard among six ¾-cup (180ml) ovenproof dishes. Place dishes in large baking dish. Pour enough boiling water into baking dish to come halfway up side of dishes; bake about 15 minutes or until custard just sets. Remove dishes from water; cool to room temperature. Cover; refrigerate 3 hours or overnight.
5 Just before serving, sprinkle each custard evenly with 1 heaped teaspoon of palm sugar. Place under preheated hot grill until sugar caramelises. Serve immediately.
per serving 42.7g total fat (26.1g saturated fat); 1973kJ (472 cal); 16.7g carbohydrate; 6.5g protein; 0.1g fibre

banana lumpia with brown sugar syrup and coconut ice-cream

preparation time 20 minutes (plus freezing time)
cooking time 15 minutes makes 12

1 cup (250ml) water
¼ cup (55g) brown sugar
¼ cup (55g) caster sugar
1 vanilla bean, split lengthways
2 star anise
2 tablespoons white sugar
2 teaspoons ground cinnamon
1 tablespoon cornflour
1 tablespoon water, extra
3 small ripe bananas (390g)
12 x 12.5cm-square spring roll wrappers
vegetable oil, for deep-frying
¾ cup (35g) toasted flaked coconut

COCONUT ICE-CREAM
1 cup (75g) toasted shredded coconut
¼ cup (60ml) coconut-flavoured liqueur
1 litre vanilla ice-cream, softened

1 Make coconut ice-cream.
2 Stir the water, brown sugar, caster sugar, vanilla bean and star anise in small saucepan over heat, without boiling, until sugar dissolves. Bring to a boil; boil, uncovered, without stirring, about 15 minutes or until syrup thickens. Remove and discard solids.
3 Meanwhile, combine white sugar and cinnamon in small bowl. Blend cornflour with the extra water in another small bowl.
4 Quarter each banana lengthways. Centre 1 piece of banana on each wrapper then sprinkle each with about ½ teaspoon cinnamon sugar. Fold wrapper over banana ends then roll wrapper to enclose filling. Brush edges with cornflour mixture to seal.
5 Heat oil in wok; deep-fry lumpia, in batches, until golden brown and crisp. Drain on absorbent paper. Sprinkle with combined remaining cinnamon sugar and coconut, drizzle with syrup; serve with ice cream.
COCONUT ICE-CREAM
Fold coconut and liqueur through slightly softened ice-cream, cover; freeze about 3 hours or overnight.
per lumpia and ⅓ cup ice-cream 9.9g total fat (6.9g saturated fat); 882kJ (211 cal); 24.8g carbohydrate; 2.4g protein; 1.5g fibre

Desserts

The Complete Book of Modern Asian

passionfruit and coconut crème brûlée

preparation time 15 minutes (plus refrigeration time)
cooking time 50 minutes   serves 4

1 egg
2 egg yolks
2 tablespoons caster sugar
¼ cup (60ml) passionfruit pulp
280ml can coconut cream
½ cup (125ml) cream
1 tablespoon brown sugar

1 Preheat oven to 180°C/160°C fan-forced.
2 Combine egg, egg yolks, caster sugar and passionfruit in medium heatproof bowl.
3 Combine coconut cream and cream in small saucepan; bring to a boil. Gradually whisk hot cream mixture into egg mixture. Place bowl over medium saucepan of simmering water; stir over heat about 10 minutes or until custard thickens slightly.
4 Divide custard among four deep ½-cup (125ml) heatproof dishes. Place dishes in large baking dish; pour enough boiling water into baking dish to come halfway up sides of dishes. Bake, uncovered, about 30 minutes or until custards set. Remove custards from water; cool. Cover; refrigerate 3 hours or overnight.
5 Preheat grill. Place custards in shallow flameproof dish filled with ice cubes. Sprinkle each custard with 1 teaspoon brown sugar; using finger, gently smooth sugar over the surface of each custard. Place baking dish under grill until tops of crème brûlée caramelise.
per serving   30.3g total fat (21.6g saturated fat); 1526kJ (365 cal); 16.7g carbohydrate; 5.7g protein; 3.3g fibre
TIP Use ice in the baking dish to help keep the custard cold while grilling the sugar topping. You need three passionfruits for this recipe.

green tea ice-cream with asian fruit salsa

preparation time 15 minutes
(plus refrigeration and freezing time)
cooking time 10 minutes   serves 4

2 tablespoons green tea powder
2 tablespoons boiling water
1 tablespoon caster sugar
1 vanilla bean
1 cup (250ml) milk
2 egg yolks
¼ cup (55g) caster sugar, extra
300ml thickened cream, whipped
10 fresh lychees (250g), chopped finely
2 medium kiwifruits (170g), chopped finely
½ small papaya (325g), chopped finely
1 tablespoon finely chopped fresh mint

1 Combine tea, the water and sugar in small bowl; stand 10 minutes.
2 Split vanilla bean lengthways; scrape out seeds. Combine pod, seeds and milk in small saucepan; bring to a boil. Stir in tea mixture; stand 5 minutes.
3 Meanwhile, whisk egg yolks and extra sugar in small bowl until creamy; gradually whisk into hot milk mixture. Stir over low heat, without boiling, until mixture thickens slightly.
4 Strain mixture into medium heatproof bowl; discard pod. Cover surface of custard with plastic wrap; cool. Refrigerate about 1 hour or until cold.
5 Fold whipped cream into cold custard. Pour mixture into ice-cream maker; churn according to manufacturer's instructions (or place custard in shallow container, cover with foil; freeze until almost firm). Place ice-cream in large bowl, chop coarsely then beat with electric mixer until smooth. Cover; freeze until firm. Repeat process twice more.
6 Combine fruit and mint in small bowl. Serve ice-cream with salsa.
per serving   33.5g total fat (20.9g saturated fat); 2123kJ (508 cal); 43.7g carbohydrate; 6.9g protein; 3.3g fibre

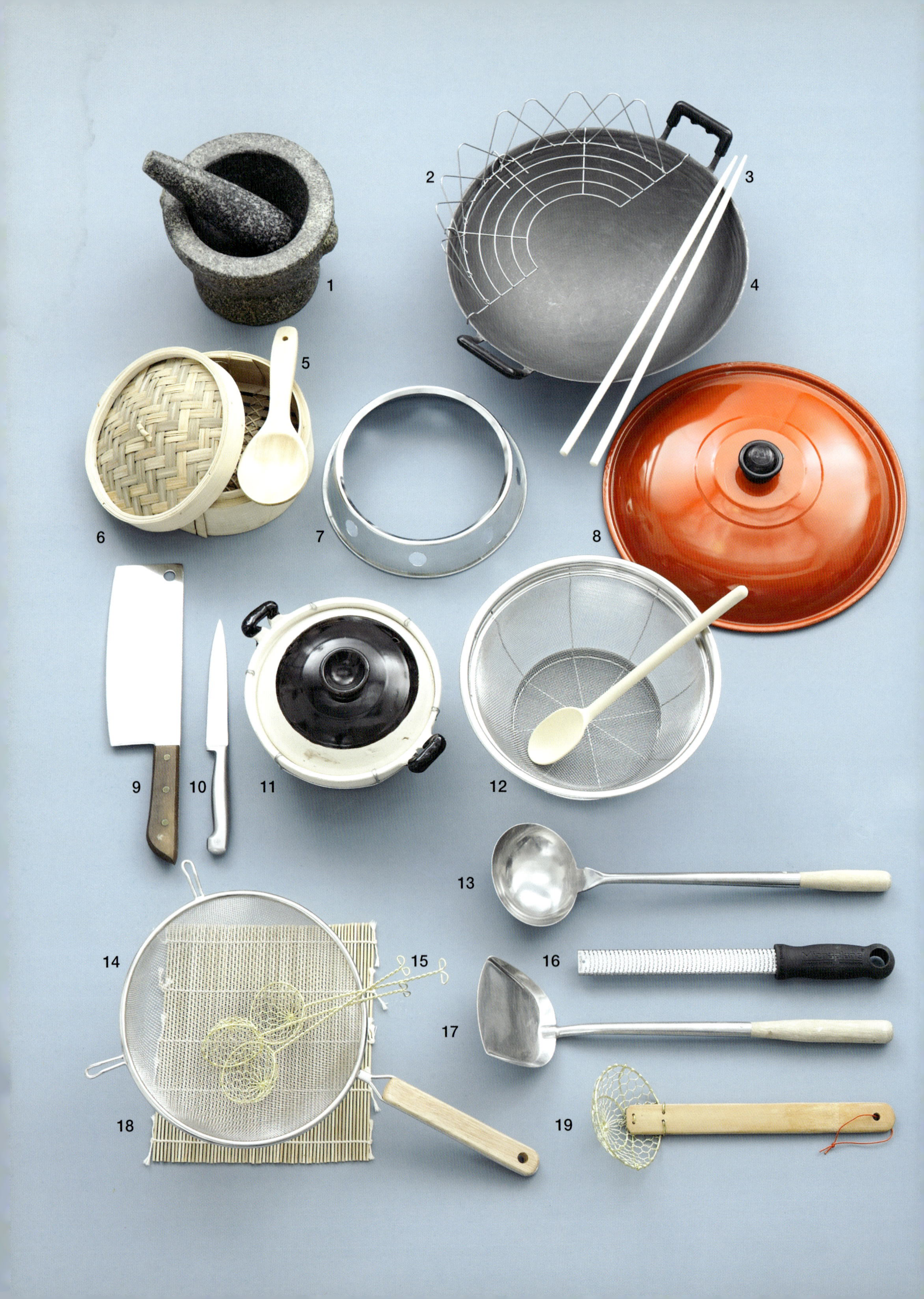
1
2
3
4
5
6
7
8
9
10
11
12
13
14
15
16
17
18
19

1 MORTAR AND PESTLE The mortar (bowl) and pestle (bat) grind and pulverize herbs and spices.

2 TEMPURA RACK Sits on the rim of a wok to drain deep-fried foods, such as tempura.

3 BAMBOO COOKING CHOPSTICKS Shaped like regular chopsticks but longer in length; great for stirring noodles in hot water.

4 WOK Traditional pressed-steel woks are the most common and inexpensive woks available.

5 RICE PADDLE Used to separate grains of rice during cooking, making sushi rice or to scoop rice out of a steamer.

6 BAMBOO STEAMER BASKET Bamboo steaming baskets and lids come in various sizes.

7 WOK RING Holds rounded-bottom woks in place during cooking.

8 HIGH-DOMED WOK LID Should fit inside rim of wok and be high enough to cover a whole chicken.

9 CLEAVER Multi-purpose Asian-style knife; used for chopping through bones and fine shredding meat or vegetables.

10 SHARP FILLETING KNIFE Used to fillet fish; shape of blade allows knife to cut fish away from skeleton. Must be kept sharp to ensure perfect cut.

11 CLAY POT Also known as a 'sand pot'; usually soaked in water about 30 minutes before cooking to release steam during cooking process.

12 COLANDER Available in plastic, metal and ceramic; used to drain liquids from rice or noodles.

13 WOK LADLE Used to add stocks to the wok as needed, as well as to serve soups and sauces.

14 SIEVE Also referred to as a strainer; made with perforated holes or wire mesh.

15 SMALL STRAINER Lifts small foods, such as wontons, from hot oil or hot water in wok.

16 MICROPLANE GRATER Comes in various degrees of fineness/coarseness; grates food cleanly due to its super-sharp blades.

17 WOK CHAN Designed to fit curve of wok; used to keep food moving constantly during stir-fry cooking.

18 BAMBOO MAT Large or small mat made from bamboo sticks tied together with cotton string; essential to use when preparing rolled sushi.

19 TEMPURA STRAINER/SPIDER Lifts large pieces of food, such as tempura, from hot oil or water in wok. Long wooden handle protects hot liquid burning skin.

Cooking equipment

The Complete Book of Modern Asian

rice serving spoon

hot rice
table container

tea cup &
tea strainer

individual side or
dipping bowl

condiment dish

Tableware

Glossary

ALLSPICE Also known as pimento or Jamaican pepper, allspice is so-named because it tastes like a combination of nutmeg, cumin, clove and cinnamon. It is available whole (a pea-sized dark-brown berry) or ground, and used in both sweet and savoury dishes. Available from most supermarkets and specialty spice stores.

ALMONDS Flat, pointy-tipped nuts having a pitted brown shell enclosing a creamy white kernel which is covered by a brown skin; there are two types, sweet and bitter, with the former being the most readily available and most used in cooking.

blanched Brown skins removed.

flaked Paper-thin slices.

slivered Small pieces cut lengthways.

BABY SPINACH LEAVES See *spinach*.

BAMBOO SHOOTS Tender, pale yellow, edible first-growth of the bamboo plant; add crunch and fibre as well as a certain distinctive sweetness to a dish. Available fresh in Asian greengrocers, in season, but usually purchased canned; these must be drained and rinsed before use. There are many different types and sizes of bamboo shoots but the largest is most commonly canned, sliced and used in stir-fries.

BANANA LEAVES Used to line steamers and cook food "en papillote" (enclosed, wrapped); sold in bundles in Asian food shops, greengrocers and supermarkets. Leaves are cut, on both sides of the centre stem, into the required size pieces then immersed in hot water or held over a flame until pliable enough to wrap around or fold over food; they are secured with kitchen string, toothpicks or bamboo skewers before barbecuing or steaming.

BAY LEAVES Aromatic leaves from the bay tree available fresh or dried; used to add a strong, slightly peppery flavour to soups, stocks and casseroles.

BEAN SPROUTS Also called bean shoots; tender new growths of assorted beans and seeds germinated for consumption as sprouts. The most readily available are mung bean, soybean, alfalfa and snow pea sprouts. Sprout mixtures or tendrils are also available.

BEANS

snake long (about 40cm), thin, round, fresh green beans, Asian in origin, with a taste similar to green or french beans. Used most frequently in stir-fries, they are also known as yard-long beans because of their (pre-metric) length.

soy the most nutritious of all legumes; only recently embraced by the West but a staple in Asia for centuries. High in protein and low in carbohydrates, and the source of products such as tofu, soy milk, soy sauce, tamari and miso. Sometimes sold fresh as edamame; also available dried and canned.

BEEF

chuck steak Inexpensive cut from the neck and shoulder area; good minced and slow-cooked.

eye-fillet Tenderloin, fillet; fine texture, most expensive and extremely tender.

minced Also known as ground beef.

oxtail A flavourful cut originally from the ox but these days more likely to be from any beef cattle; requires long, slow cooking so it is perfect for curries.

round steak Boneless cut from the tender muscle running from rump to ankle; used for stir-fries, minute steaks and schnitzel.

BEETROOT Also known as red beets; firm, round root vegetable. Can be grated or finely chopped; boiled or steamed then diced or sliced; or roasted then mashed.

BETEL LEAVES See Essential Ingredients, page 8.

BICARBONATE OF SODA Also known as baking soda; a mild alkali used as a leavening agent in baking. Many cooks use "bicarb" to help soften soaking pulses or assist cooking vegetables retain their green colour.

BREADCRUMBS

japanese Also called panko; available in two kinds: larger pieces and fine crumbs; have a lighter texture than Western-style breadcrumbs. Available from Asian food shops and some supermarkets, and unless you make rather coarse breadcrumbs from stale white bread that's either quite stale or gently toasted, nothing is an adequate substitution.

packaged Prepared fine-textured but crunchy white breadcrumbs; good for coating or crumbing foods that are to be fried.

stale Crumbs made by grating, blending or processing 1- or 2-day-old bread.

BROCCOLINI A cross between broccoli and Chinese kale; long asparagus-like stems with a long loose floret, both completely edible. Resembles broccoli in look but is milder and sweeter in taste.

BRUISE A cooking term to describe the slight crushing given to aromatic ingredients (lemon grass, cardamom pods) with the flat side of a heavy knife or cleaver to release flavour and aroma.

BUK CHOY See Essential Ingredients, page 8 and 9.

BUTTER This book uses salted butter unless stated otherwise; 125g is equal to 1 stick (4 ounces) in other recipes.

BUTTER LETTUCE Small, round, loosely formed heads with a sweet flavour; soft, buttery-textured leaves range from pale green on the outer leaves to pale yellow-green inner leaves.

BUTTERMILK In spite of its name, buttermilk is actually low in fat, varying between 0.6 per cent and 2.0 per cent per 100 ml. Originally the term given to the slightly sour liquid left after butter was churned from cream, today it is intentionally made from no-fat or low-fat milk to which specific bacterial cultures have been added during the manufacturing process. It is readily available from the dairy department in supermarkets. Because it is low in fat, it's a good substitute for dairy products such as cream or sour cream in some baking and salad dressings.

CANDLENUT A hard nut, used to thicken curries in Malaysia and Indonesia. Almonds, brazil nuts or macadamias can be substituted.

CAPSICUM Also known as pepper or bell pepper. Native to Central and South America; found in red, green, yellow, orange or purplish-black varieties. Seeds and membranes should be discarded before use.

CARAWAY SEEDS The small, half-moon-shaped dried seed from a member of the parsley family; adds a sharp anise flavour when used in both sweet and savoury dishes. Used widely, in such different foods as rye bread, harissa and the classic Hungarian fresh cheese, liptauer.

CARDAMOM A spice native to India and used extensively in its cuisine; can be purchased in pod, seed or ground form. Has a distinctive aromatic, sweetly rich flavour and is one of the world's most expensive spices. Used to flavour curries, rice dishes, sweet desserts and cakes.

CASHEWS Plump, kidney-shaped, golden-brown nuts having a distinctive sweet, buttery flavour and containing about 48 per cent fat. Because of this high fat content, they should be kept, sealed tightly, under refrigeration to avoid becoming rancid. We use roasted unsalted cashews in this book, available from health-food stores and most supermarkets; as with most nuts intended to be eaten as snacks, roasting cashews brings out their intense nutty flavour.

CAYENNE PEPPER Also known as cayenne; a thin-fleshed, long, extremely hot, dried red chilli, usually purchased ground.

CHAPATI A popular unleavened Indian bread, similar in appearance to pitta, chapati accompany saucy curries, often serving as cutlery to scoop up the food. Made from whole-wheat flour, salt and water, and dry-fried on a "tawa" (a cast-iron griddle). Available from Indian food shops and on the bread shelf in most supermarkets.

CHEESE

cream Commonly known as philadelphia or philly; a soft cow-milk cheese with a fat content ranging from 14 per cent to 33 per cent.

paneer A simple, delicate fresh cheese used as a major source of protein in the Indian diet; substitute it with ricotta.

CHICKEN

breast fillet Breast halved, skinned and boned.

drumstick Leg with skin and bone intact.

drumette Small fleshy part of the wing between shoulder and elbow, trimmed to resemble a drumstick.

maryland Leg and thigh still connected in a single piece; bones and skin intact.

tenderloin Thin strip of meat lying just under the breast, good for stir-frying.

thigh Skin and bone intact.

thigh cutlet Thigh with skin and centre bone intact; sometimes found skinned with bone intact.

thigh fillet Thigh with skin and centre bone removed; makes flavoursome mince.

wing The whole wing, bone and skin intact.

CHICKPEAS Also called garbanzos, hummus or channa; an irregularly round, sandy-coloured legume used extensively in Mediterranean, Indian and Hispanic cooking. Firm texture even after cooking, a floury mouth-feel and robust nutty flavour; available canned or dried (the latter need several hours reconstituting in cold water before being used).

CHILLI Always use rubber gloves when seeding and chopping fresh chillies as they can burn your skin. We use unseeded chillies in our recipes because the seeds contain the heat; use fewer chillies rather than seeding the lot.

flakes Also sold as crushed chilli; dehydrated deep-red extremely fine slices and whole seeds; good in cooking or for sprinkling over a dish.

green Any unripened chilli; also some particular varieties that are ripe when green, such as jalapeño, habanero, poblano or serrano.

hot sauce We use a hot Chinese variety made from bird's-eye chillies, salt and vinegar. Use sparingly, increasing the quantity to suit your taste.

long red Available fresh and dried; a generic term used for any moderately hot, long, thin chilli (about 6cm to 8cm long).

paste Every Asian cuisine has its own chilli paste, and each is different from the next: Vietnamese chilli paste is quite hot; Indonesian sambal oelek (chilli with ginger, oil and garlic) has medium heat; or, for more sweetness than fire, mild sweet thai chilli sauce, made with vinegar and sugar.

powder The Asian variety is the hottest, made from dried ground thai chillies; can be used instead of fresh chillies in the proportion of ½ teaspoon chilli powder to 1 medium chopped fresh red chilli.

red thai Also known as "scuds"; tiny, very hot and bright red in colour.

sauce, sweet See sauces.

CHINESE BARBECUED DUCK
See duck.

CHINESE BARBECUED PORK
See pork.

CHINESE COOKING WINE Also known as hao hsing or chinese rice wine; made from fermented rice, wheat, sugar and salt with a 13.5 per cent alcohol content. Inexpensive and found in Asian food shops; if you can't find it, replace with mirin or sherry.

CHOY SUM See Essential Ingredients, page 8.

CINNAMON Available both in pieces (called sticks or quills) and ground into powder; one of the world's most common spices, used universally as a sweet, fragrant flavouring for both sweet and savoury foods. The dried inner bark of the shoots of the Sri Lankan native cinnamon tree; much of what is sold as the real thing is in fact cassia, Chinese cinnamon, from the bark of the cassia tree. Less expensive to process than true cinnamon, it is often blended with Sri Lankan cinnamon to produce the type of "cinnamon" most commonly found in supermarkets.

CLOVES Dried flower buds of a tropical tree; can be used whole or in ground form. They have a strong scent and taste so should be used sparingly.

COCONUT

cream Obtained commercially from the first pressing of the coconut flesh alone, without the addition of water; the second pressing (less rich) is sold as coconut milk. Available in cans and cartons at most supermarkets.

desiccated Concentrated, dried, unsweetened and finely shredded coconut flesh.

flaked Dried flaked coconut flesh.

milk Not the liquid found inside the fruit, which is called coconut water, but the diluted liquid from the second pressing of the white flesh of a mature coconut (the first pressing produces coconut cream). Available in cans and cartons at most supermarkets.

shredded Unsweetened thin strips of dried coconut flesh.

COCONUT-FLAVOURED LIQUEUR We use Malibu.

CORIANDER Also known as cilantro, pak chee or chinese parsley; bright-green-leafed herb having both pungent aroma and taste. Used as an ingredient in a wide variety of cuisines from Mexican to South East Asian. Often stirred into or sprinkled over a dish just before serving for maximum impact as, like other leafy herbs, its characteristics diminish with cooking. Both the stems and roots of coriander are used in Thai cooking: wash well before chopping. Coriander seeds are dried and sold either whole or ground, and neither form tastes remotely like the fresh leaf but rather like an acrid combination of sage and caraway. Seeds and ground are both used in garam masala, mixed spice, Indian and Thai curry pastes and sauces, sausages, and some breads and desserts.

CORNFLOUR Also called cornstarch. Available made from corn or wheat (wheaten cornflour, gluten-free, gives a lighter texture in cakes); used as a thickening agent in cooking.

COS LETTUCE Also known as romaine lettuce; the traditional caesar salad lettuce. Long, with leaves ranging from dark green on the outside to almost white near the core; the leaves have a stiff centre rib that gives a slight cupping effect to the leaf on either side.

CUMIN Also known as zeera or comino; resembling caraway in size, cumin is the dried seed of a plant related to the parsley family. Its spicy, almost curry-like flavour is essential to the traditional foods of Mexico, India, North Africa and the Middle East. Available dried as seeds or ground. Black cumin seeds are smaller than standard cumin, and dark brown rather than true black; they are mistakenly confused with kalonji.

CURRANTS Dried tiny, almost black raisins so-named from the grape type native to Corinth, Greece; most often used in jams, jellies and sauces (the best-known of which is the English cumberland sauce). These are not the same as fresh currants, which are the fruit of a plant in the gooseberry family.

CURRY LEAVES Available fresh and dried; buy fresh leaves at Indian food shops. Used to give extra flavour and depth to curries.

CURRY PASTES Make your own with the recipes found in this book or purchase the ready-made pastes found, in various strengths and flavours, on supermarket shelves.

green Hottest of the traditional Thai pastes; particularly good in chicken and vegetable curries, and a great addition to stir-fry and noodle dishes.

korma A classic north Indian sauce with a rich yet delicate coconut flavour and hints of garlic, ginger and coriander.

massaman Rich, spicy flavour reminiscent of Middle Eastern cooking; favoured by southern Thai cooks for use in hot and sour stew-like curries and satay sauces.

panang Based on the curries of Penang, an island off the north-west coast of Malaysia, close to the Thai border. A complex, sweet and milder variation of red curry paste; good with seafood and for adding to soups and salad dressings.

red Probably the most popular Thai curry paste; a hot blend of different flavours that complements the richness of pork, duck and seafood. Also works well stirred into marinades and sauces.

rogan josh A paste of medium heat, from the Kashmir region of India, made from fresh chillies or paprika, tomato and spices, especially cardamom. It sometimes has beetroot added to make it a dark red.

tikka In Indian cooking, the word "masala" loosely translates as paste and the word "tikka" means a bite-sized piece of meat, poultry or fish, or sometimes a cutlet. Tikka paste is any maker's choice of spices and oils, mixed into a mild paste, frequently coloured red. Used for marinating or brushing over meat, seafood or poultry, before or during cooking instead of as an ingredient.

vindaloo A Goan combination of vinegar, tomatoes, pepper and other spices that exemplifies the Portuguese influence on this part of India's west coast.

yellow One of the mildest thai pastes; similar in appearance to Indian curries as they both include yellow chilli and fresh turmeric. Good blended with coconut in vegetable, rice and noodle dishes.

CURRY POWDER A blend of ground spices used for making Indian and some South East Asian dishes. Consists of some of the following spices: dried chilli, cinnamon, coriander, cumin, fennel, fenugreek, mace, cardamom and turmeric. Available in mild or hot varieties.

CUSTARD POWDER Instant mixture used to make pouring custard; similar to North American instant pudding mixes.

DAIKON See Essential Ingredients, page 8.

DASHI The basic fish and seaweed stock that accounts for the distinctive flavour of many Japanese dishes, such as soups and various casseroles. Made from dried bonito (a type of tuna) flakes and kombu (kelp); instant dashi (dashi-no-moto) is available as powder, granules and liquid concentrate from Asian food shops.

DATES Fruit of the date palm tree, eaten fresh or dried, on their own or in prepared dishes. About 4cm to 6cm in length, oval and plump, thin-skinned, with a honey-sweet flavour and sticky texture.

DRIED CHINESE SAUSAGE Also known as lap cheong; highly spiced, bright red, thin pork sausages. The meat is preserved by the high spice content and can be kept at room temperature.

DUCK We use whole ducks in some recipes; available from specialty chicken shops, open-air markets and some supermarkets.

chinese barbecued Traditionally cooked in special ovens in China; dipped into and brushed during roasting with a sticky sweet coating made from soy sauce, sherry, ginger, five-spice, star anise and hoisin sauce. Available from Asian food shops as well as dedicated chinese barbecued meat shops.

maryland See *chicken*.

EGG If a recipe calls for raw or barely cooked eggs, exercise caution if there is a salmanella problem in your area.

EGGPLANT Also known as aubergine; often thought of as a vegetable but actually a fruit and belongs to the same family as the tomato, chilli and potato. Ranging in size from tiny to very large and in colour from pale green to deep purple. Can be purchased char-grilled, packed in oil, in jars.

pea Tiny, about the size of peas; sometimes known by their thai name, "makeua puang". Sold in clusters of 10 to 15 eggplants, similar to vine-ripened cherry tomatoes; very bitter in flavour, a quality suited to balance rich, sweet coconut-sauced thai curries. They can be found in Asian greengrocers and food shops, fresh or pickled.

thai Found in a variety of different sizes and colours, from a long, thin, purplish-green one to a hard, round, golf-ball size having a white-streaked pale-green skin. This last looks like a small unripe tomato and is the most popular eggplant used in thai and vietnamese curries and stir-fries.

FENNEL Also known as finocchio or anise; a crunchy green vegetable slightly resembling celery that's eaten raw in salads; fried as an accompaniment; or used as an ingredient in pasta sauces, soups and sauce. Also sometimes the name given to the dried seeds of the plant which have a stronger licorice flavour.

FENUGREEK Hard, dried seed usually sold ground as an astringent spice powder. Good with seafood and in chutneys, fenugreek helps mask unpleasant odours.

FIVE-SPICE POWDER Although the ingredients vary from country to country, five-spice is usually a fragrant mixture of ground cinnamon, cloves, star anise, sichuan pepper and fennel seeds. Used in Chinese and other Asian cooking; available from most supermarkets or Asian food shops. Also called chinese five-spice.

FLOUR

besan Also known as chickpea flour or gram; made from ground chickpeas so is gluten-free and high in protein. Used in Indian cooking to make dumplings, noodles and chapati; for a batter coating for deep-frying; and as a sauce thickener.

plain Also known as all-purpose; unbleached wheat flour is the best for baking: the gluten content ensures a strong dough, which produces a light result. Also used as a thickening agent in sauces and gravies.

self-raising All-purpose plain or wholemeal flour with baking powder and salt added; can be made at home with plain or wholemeal flour sifted with baking powder in the proportion of 1 cup flour to 2 teaspoons baking powder.

GAI LAN See Essential Ingredients, page 9.

GALANGAL See Essential Ingredients, page 9.

GARAM MASALA Literally meaning blended spices in its northern Indian place of origin; based on varying proportions of cardamom, cinnamon, cloves, coriander, fennel and cumin, roasted and ground together. Black pepper and chilli can be added for a hotter version.

GELATINE We use powdered gelatine in the recipes in this book; it's also available in sheet form known as leaf gelatine. A thickening agent made from either collagen, a protein found in animal connective tissue and bones, or certain algae (agar-agar). Two teaspoons of powdered gelatine (7g or one sachet) is roughly equivalent to four gelatine leaves. Professionals use leaf gelatine because it generally results in a smoother, clearer consistency; it is also commonly used throughout Europe. The two types are interchangable but leaf gelatine gives a much clearer mixture than powdered gelatine; it's perfect in dishes where appearance really counts.

GHEE Clarified butter; with the milk solids removed, this fat has a high smoking point so can be heated to a high temperature without burning. Used as a cooking medium in most Indian recipes.

GINGER

fresh Also known as green or root ginger; the thick gnarled root of a tropical plant. Can be kept, peeled, covered with dry sherry in a jar and refrigerated, or frozen in an airtight container.

ground Also known as powdered ginger; used as a flavouring in cakes, pies and puddings but cannot be substituted for fresh ginger.

pickled Pink or red coloured; available, packaged, from Asian food shops. Pickled paper-thin shavings of ginger in a mixture of vinegar, sugar and natural colouring; most used in Japanese cooking.

KAFFIR LIME Also known as magrood, leech lime or jeruk purut. The wrinkled, bumpy-skinned green fruit of a small citrus tree originally grown in South Africa and South East Asia. As a rule, only the rind or leaves are used.

KAFFIR LIME LEAVES See Essential Ingredients, page 8 and 9.

KALONJI Also known as nigella or black onion seeds. Tiny, angular seeds, black on the outside and creamy within, with a sharp nutty flavour that can be enhanced by frying briefly in a dry hot pan before use. Typically sprinkled over Turkish bread immediately after baking or as an important spice in Indian cooking, kalonji can be found in most Asian and Middle Eastern food shops. Often erroneously called black cumin seeds.

KUMARA The polynesian name of an orange-fleshed sweet potato often confused with yam; good baked, boiled, mashed or fried similarly to other potatoes.

LAMB

backstrap Also known as eye of loin; the larger fillet from a row of loin chops or cutlets. Tender, best cooked rapidly: barbecued or pan-fried.

chump Cut from just above the hind legs to the mid-loin section; can be used as a piece for roasting or cut into chops.

cutlet Small, tender rib chop; sometimes sold french-trimmed, with all the fat and gristle at the narrow end of the bone removed.

diced Cubed lean meat.

fillets Fine texture, most expensive and extremely tender.

leg Cut from the hindquarter; can be boned, butterflied, rolled and tied, or cut into dice.

minced Ground lamb.

rolled shoulder Boneless section of the forequarter, rolled and secured with string or netting.

shank Forequarter leg; sometimes sold as drumsticks or frenched shanks if the gristle and narrow end of the bone are discarded and the remaining meat trimmed.

shoulder Large, tasty piece having much connective tissue so is best pot-roasted or braised. Makes the best mince.

LEBANESE CUCUMBER Short, slender and thin-skinned. Probably the most popular variety because of its tender, edible skin, tiny, yielding seeds, and sweet, fresh and flavoursome taste.

LEMON GRASS See Essential Ingredients, page 10.

LENTILS (red, brown, yellow) Dried pulses often identified by and named after their colour. Eaten by cultures all over the world, most famously perhaps in the dhals of India, lentils have a high food value. French green lentils are a local cousin to the famous (and very expensive) French lentils du puy, green-blue, tiny lentils with a nutty, earthy flavour and a hardy nature that allows them to be rapidly cooked without disintegrating.

LYCHEES A small fruit from China with a hard shell and sweet, juicy flesh. The white flesh has a gelatinous texture and musky, perfumed taste. Discard the rough skin and seed before using in salads or as a dessert fruit. Also available canned in a sugar syrup.

MANGO, GREEN Sour and crunchy, green mangoes are just immature fruit that can be eaten in salads, curries and stir-fries. They will keep, wrapped in plastic, in the refrigerator up to two weeks. Available from most greengrocers.

MIRIN A Japanese champagne-coloured cooking wine, made of glutinous rice and alcohol. It is used expressly for cooking and should not be confused with sake. A seasoned sweet mirin, manjo mirin, made of water, rice, corn syrup and alcohol, is used in various Japanese dipping sauces.

MISO Fermented soybean paste. There are many types of miso, each with its own aroma, flavour, colour and texture; it can be kept, airtight, for up to a year in the fridge. Generally, the darker the miso, the saltier the taste and denser the texture. Salt-reduced miso is available. Buy in tubs or plastic packs.

MIZUNA Japanese in origin; the frizzy green salad leaves have a delicate mustard flavour.

MUSHROOMS

dried black fungus Also known as dried cloud ear or wood ear, is popular in Asian cooking. Sold dried, it's black on one side and pale grey on the other. Needs to be soaked before use. Swells to about five times its dried size when rehydrated.

enoki Also known as enokitake; grown and bought in clumps, these delicately-flavoured mushrooms have small cream caps on long thin stalks. Available from Asian food shops and most supermarkets.

oyster Also known as abalone; grey-white mushrooms shaped like a fan. Prized for their smooth texture and subtle, oyster-like flavour.

shiitake When fresh are also known as chinese black, forest or golden oak mushrooms; although cultivated, have the earthiness and taste of wild mushrooms. Are large and meaty; often used as a substitute for meat in some Asian vegetarian dishes. When dried, they are known as donko or dried chinese mushrooms; rehydrate before use.

swiss brown Also known as roman or cremini. Light to dark brown mushrooms with full-bodied flavour; suited for use in casseroles or being stuffed and baked.

MUSTARD SEEDS

black Also known as brown mustard seeds; more pungent than the white variety; used frequently in curries.

white Also known as yellow mustard seeds; used ground for mustard powder and in most prepared mustards.

NAAN The rather thick, leavened bread associated with the tandoori dishes of northern India, where it is baked pressed against the inside wall of a heated tandoor (clay oven). Now available prepared by commercial bakeries and sold in most supermarkets.

NASHI A member if the pear family but resembling an apple with its pale-yellow-green, tennis-ball-sized appearance; more commonly known as the Asian pear to much of the world. The nashi is different from other pears in that it is crisp, juicy and ready to eat as soon as it is picked and for several months thereafter, unlike its European cousins. These very qualities are more apple- than pear-like, which probably accounts for the widespread misconception that the nashi is a cross between an apple and a pear. Its distinctive texture and mildly sweet taste make it perfect for use raw in salads, or as part of a cheese platter.

NOODLES

bean thread (wun sen) Made from mung bean paste; also known as cellophane or glass noodles because they are transparent when cooked. White in colour (not off-white like rice vermicelli), very delicate and fine; available dried.

fried Crispy egg noodles that have been deep-fried then packaged for sale on supermarket shelves.

hokkien See Essential Ingredients, page 9.

rice See Essential Ingredients, page 10 and 13.

rice stick Also known as sen lek, ho fun or kway teow; especially popular South East Asian dried rice noodles. They come in different widths (thin used in soups, wide in stir-fries), but all should be soaked in hot water to soften. The traditional noodle used in pad thai which, before soaking, measures about 5mm in width.

rice vermicelli Also known as sen mee, mei fun or bee hoon. Used throughout Asia in spring rolls and cold salads; similar to bean threads, only longer and made with rice flour instead of mung bean starch. Before using, soak the dried noodles in hot water until softened, boil them briefly then rinse with hot water. Vermicelli can also be deep-fried until crunchy and then used in Chinese chicken salad, or as a garnish or bed for sauces.

singapore Pre-cooked wheat noodles best described as a thinner version of hokkien; sold, packaged, in the refrigerated section of supermarkets.

soba See Essential Ingredients, page 11.

udon Available fresh and dried, these broad, white, Japanese wheat noodles are similar to the ones in home-made chicken noodle soup.

NORI See Essential Ingredients, page 10 and 11.

OIL

cooking spray We use a cholesterol-free cooking spray made from canola oil.

peanut Pressed from ground peanuts; the most commonly used oil in Asian cooking because of its high smoke point (capacity to handle high heat without burning).

sesame Made from roasted, crushed, white sesame seeds; a flavouring rather than a cooking medium.

vegetable Any number of oils sourced from plant rather than animal fats.

ONION

flakes Packaged (usually in 55g packets) chopped and dehydrated white onion pieces; used more often for garnish than as an ingredient.

fried onion/shallot Served as a condiment on Asian tables to be sprinkled over just-cooked food. Found in cellophane bags or jars at all Asian grocery shops; once opened, they will keep for months if stored tightly seeled. Make your own by frying thinly sliced peeled shallots or baby onions until golden brown and crisp.

green Also known as scallion or (incorrectly) shallot; an immature onion picked before the bulb has formed, having a long, bright-green edible stalk.

purple shallots Also known as Asian shallots; related to the onion but resembling garlic (they grow in bulbs of multiple cloves). Thin-layered and intensely flavoured, they are used in cooking throughout South East Asia.

shallots Also called french shallots, golden shallots or eschalots. Small, elongated, brown-skinned members of the onion family; they grow in tight clusters similar to garlic.

spring Crisp, narrow green-leafed tops and a round sweet white bulb larger than green onions.

PAPRIKA Ground dried sweet red capsicum (bell pepper); there are many grades and types available, including sweet, hot, mild and smoked.

POMELO Similar to grapefruit but sweeter, somewhat more conical in shape and slightly larger, about the size of a small coconut. The firm rind peels away easily and neatly, like a mandarin, and the segments are easy to separate.

POPPY SEEDS Small, dried, bluish-grey seeds of the poppy plant, with a crunchy texture and a nutty flavour. Can be purchased whole or ground in most supermarkets.

PORK

belly Fatty cut sold in rashers or in a piece, with or without rind or bone.

butterfly Skinless, boneless mid-loin chop, split in half and flattened.

chinese barbecued pork Roasted pork fillet with a sweet, sticky coating. Available from Asian food shops or specialty stores.

fillet Skinless, boneless eye-fillet cut from the loin.

minced Ground lean pork.

neck Sometimes called pork scotch, boneless cut from the forelion.

shoulder Joint sold with bone in or out.

PRESERVED TURNIP Also known as hua chai po or cu cai muoi, or dried radish because of its similarity to daikon. Sold packaged whole or sliced, it is very salty and must be rinsed and dried before use.

QUAIL Small, delicate-flavoured game birds ranging in weight from 250g to 300g; also known as partridge.

RAMBUTANS Related to the lychee; also know as hairy lychees as they are similar in appearance with the additional feature of long red tendrils.

RICE

basmati A white, fragrant long-grained rice; the grains fluff up beautifully when cooked. It should be washed several times before cooking.

calrose A medium-grain rice that is extremely versatile; can substituted for short- or long-grain rices if necessary.

jasmine Also known as thai jasmine, it is a long-grained white rice recognised around the world as having a perfumed aromatic quality; moist in texture, it clings together after cooking. Sometimes substituted for basmati rice.

koshihikari Small, round-grain white rice. If unavailable, substitute with a short-grain rice such as arborio and cook using the absorption method.

ROSEWATER Extract made from crushed rose petals, called gulab in India; used for its aromatic quality in many sweetmeats and desserts.

SAFFRON Stigma of a member of the crocus family, available ground or in strands; imparts a yellow-orange colour to food once infused. The quality can vary greatly; the best is the most expensive spice in the world.

SAKE Japan's favourite wine, made from fermented rice, is used for marinating, cooking and as part of dipping sauces. If sake is unavailable, dry sherry, vermouth or brandy can be substituted. If drinking sake, stand it first in a container in hot water for 20 minutes to warm it through.

SAGO A grain often used in puddings and desserts; similar to tapioca but sourced from a variety of palm, while tapioca is from the root of the cassava plant.

SAMBAL OELEK Also ulek or olek; Indonesian in origin, this is a salty paste made from ground chillies and vinegar.

SASHIMI A Japanese method of slicing raw fish. When purchasing fish for sashimi, it has a firm texture and a pleasant (but not 'fishy') sea-smell.

SAUCE

black bean An Asian cooking sauce made from salted and fermented soybeans, spices and wheat flour; used most often in stir-fries.

char siu Also known as chinese barbecue sauce; a paste-like ingredient that is dark-red-brown in colour and possesses a sharp sweet and spicy flavour. Made with fermented soybeans, honey and various spices, char siu can be diluted and used as a marinade or brushed directly onto grilling meat.

fish Called naam pla on the label if Thai-made, nuoc naam if Vietnamese; the two are almost identical. Made from pulverised salted fermented fish (most often anchovies); has a pungent smell and strong taste. Available in varying degrees of intensity, so use according to your taste.

hoisin A thick, sweet and spicy Chinese barbecue sauce made from salted fermented soybeans, onions and garlic; used as a marinade or baste, or to accent stir-fries and barbecued or roasted foods. From Asian food shops and supermarkets.

kecap manis A dark, thick sweet soy sauce used in most South East Asian cuisines. Depending on the manufacturer, the sauces's sweetness is derived from the addition of either molasses or palm sugar when brewed. Use as a condiment, dipping sauce, ingredient or marinade.

oyster Asian in origin, this thick, richly flavoured brown sauce is made from oysters and their brine, cooked with salt and soy sauce, and thickened with starches. Use as a condiment. Vegetarian oyster sauce, made from water, mushroom extract, soy beans, salt, sugar and starch, is available from most Asian food shops.

plum A thick, sweet and sour dipping sauce made from plums, vinegar, sugar, chillies and spices.

sweet chilli Comparatively mild, fairly sticky and runny bottled sauce made from red chillies, sugar, garlic and white wine vinegar; mostly used as a condiment.

teriyaki Either home-made or commercially bottled, this Japanese sauce, made from soy sauce, mirin, sugar, ginger and other spices, imparts a distinctive glaze when brushed over grilled meat or poultry.

SAVOIARDI SPONGE FINGERS Also known as savoy biscuits, lady's fingers or sponge fingers; Italian-style crisp fingers made from sponge cake mixture.

SAVOY CABBAGE Large, heavy head with crinkled dark-green outer leaves; a fairly mild tasting cabbage.

SEAFOOD

blue-eye Also known as deep sea trevalla or trevally and blue-eye cod; thick, moist white-fleshed fish.

bream (yellowfin) Also known as silver or black bream, seabream or surf bream; soft, moist white flesh. Substitute with snapper or ocean perch.

calamari A mollusc, a type of squid; substitute with baby octopus.

clams Also known as vongole; we use a small ridge-shelled variety of this bivalve mollusc.

crab meat Flesh of fresh crabs; frozen flesh is also available. Use canned if neither is available.

dried shrimp Also known as goong hang, salted sun-dried prawns ranging in size from not much larger than a rice seed to big ones measuring about 1cm in length. They are sold packaged, shelled as a rule, in Asian grocery stores.

fish fillet Use your favourite firm-fleshed white fish fillet.

flathead Many varieties, most commonly dusky flathead, which is also the largest. Mostly fished from river mouths and estuaries; substitute with whiting or your favourite white fish.

lobster (rock lobster) Also known as cray, spiny lobster, eastern, southern or western lobster. Substitute with balmain or moreton bay bugs.

mud crab Also known as mangrove crab, green or black. Native to the tropical regions of the Bay of Bengal and the Pacific and Indian oceans. Substitute with scampi, lobster or balmain bugs.

mussels Should be bought from a fish market where there is reliably fresh fish; they must be tightly closed when bought, indicating they are alive. Before cooking, scrub the shells with a strong brush and remove the beards; discard any shells that do not open after cooking. Varieties include black and green-lip.

ocean trout A farmed fish with pink, soft flesh. It is from the same family as the atlantic salmon; one can be substituted for the other.

octopus Are usually tenderised before you buy them; both octopus and squid require either long slow cooking (usually for the large molluscs) or quick cooking over high heat (usually for the small molluscs) – anything in between will make the octopus tough and rubbery.

oysters Available in many varieties, including pacific, bay/blacklip, and Sydney or New Zealand rock oyster.

prawns Also known as shrimp. Varieties include, school, king, royal red, Sydney harbour, tiger. Can be bought uncooked (green) or cooked, with or without shells.

salmon Red-pink firm flesh with few bones; moist delicate flavour.

scallops A bivalve mollusc with fluted shell valve; we use scallops that have the coral (roe) attached.

squid Also known as calamari; a type of mollusc. Buy squid hoods to make preparation and cooking faster.

tuna Reddish, firm flesh; slightly dry. Many varieties available including bluefin, yellowfin, skipjack or albacore; substitute with swordfish.

white fish Means non-oily fish. This category includes bream, flathead, whiting, snapper, dhufish, redfish and ling.

SESAME SEEDS Black and white are the most common of this small oval seed, however there are also red and brown varieties. A good source of calcium, the seeds are used in cuisines the world over as an ingredient and as a condiment. To roast, spread the seeds in a heavy-base frying pan; roast briefly over low heat.

SHRIMP PASTE Also known as kapi, trasi and blanchan; a strong-scented, very firm preserved paste made of salted dried shrimp. Used sparingly as a pungent flavouring in many South East Asian soups, sauces and rice dishes. It should be chopped or sliced thinly then wrapped in foil and roasted before use.

SICHUAN PEPPERCORNS See Essential Ingredients, page 10.

SILVER BEET Also known as swiss chard and incorrectly, spinach; has fleshy stalks and large leaves.

SNOW PEAS Also called mange tout; a variety of garden pea, eaten pod and all (though you may need to trim the ends). Used in stir-fries or eaten raw in salads. Snow pea sprouts are available from supermarkets or greengrocers and are usually eaten raw in salads or sandwiches.

SOY SAUCE Also known as sieu; made from fermented soybeans. Several variations are available in supermarkets and Asian food shops; we use japanese soy sauce unless indicated otherwise.

dark Deep brown, almost black in colour; rich, with a thicker consistency than other types. Pungent but not particularly salty, it is good for marinating.

Glossary

japanese An all-purpose low-sodium soy sauce made with more wheat content than its Chinese counterparts; fermented in barrels and aged. Possibly the best table soy and the one to choose if you only want one variety.

light Fairly thin in consistency and, while paler than the others, the saltiest tasting; used in dishes in which the natural colour of the ingredients is to be maintained. Not to be confused with salt-reduced or low-sodium soy sauces.

SPATCHCOCK A small chicken (poussin), no more than 6 weeks old, weighing a maximum of 500g. Also, a cooking term to describe splitting a small chicken open, then flattening and grilling.

SPINACH Also known as english spinach and incorrectly, silver beet. Baby spinach leaves are best eaten raw in salads; the larger leaves should be added last to soups, stews and stir-fries, and should be cooked until barely wilted.

SUGAR

brown An extremely soft, fine granulated sugar retaining molasses for its characteristic colour and flavour.

caster Also known as superfine or finely granulated table sugar. The fine crystals dissolve easily so it is perfect for cakes, meringues and desserts.

jaggery Also known as gur; a moulded sugar lump made from either distilled sugarcane or palm juice. Available from Asian speciality shops; substitute dark brown sugar.

palm See Essential Ingredients, page 10.

white Unless otherwise specified we use coarse, granulated table sugar, also known as crystal sugar.

yellow rock Also known as lump sugar or rock candy; is a solidified mixture of honey, refined and unrefined sugar. Traditionally used in braised 'red-cooked' dishes, soups, sweet soups and beverages. Available from Asian food shops.

STAR ANISE See Essential Ingredients, page 11.

TAMARI Similar to but thicker than japanese soy sauce; very dark in colour with a distinctively mellow flavour. Good used as a dipping sauce or for basting.

TAMARIND See Essential Ingredients, page 11 and 12.

TAPIOCA Made from the root of the cassava plant. *See also sago.*

TAT SOI See Essential Ingredients, page 11 and 13.

THAI BASIL See Essential Ingredients, page 10 and 12.

TOFU See also Essential Ingredients, page 12.

firm Made by compressing bean curd to remove most of the water. Good used in stir-fries as it can be tossed without disintegrating. Can also be flavoured, preserved in rice wine or brine.

fried puffs Packaged pieces of deep-fried soft bean curd; the surface is brown and crunchy and the inside almost totally dried out. Add to soups and stir-fries at the last minute so they don't soak up too much liquid.

soft Delicate texture; does not hold its shape when overhandled. Can also be used as a dairy substitute in ice-cream or cheesecakes.

TREACLE Thick, dark syrup not unlike molasses.

TURMERIC See Essential Ingredients, page 12 and 13.

VANILLA

bean Dried, long, thin pod from a tropical golden orchid grown in central and South America and Tahiti; the minuscule black seeds inside the bean are used to impart a luscious vanilla flavour in baking and desserts. Place a whole bean in a jar of sugar to make the vanilla sugar often called for in recipes; a bean can be used three or four times before losing its flavour.

extract Obtained from vanilla beans infused in water; a non-alcoholic version of essence.

VIETNAMESE MINT See Essential Ingredients, page 12.

VINEGAR

cider Made from fermented apples.

malt Made from fermented malt and beech shavings.

rice A colourless vinegar made from fermented rice and flavoured with sugar and salt. Also known as seasoned rice vinegar; sherry can be substituted.

white Made from spirit of cane sugar.

white wine Made from white wine.

WASABI (PASTE) See Essential Ingredients, page 11 and 13.

WATER CHESTNUTS See Essential Ingredients, page 12 and 13.

WOMBOK See Essential Ingredients, page 13.

WRAPPERS

gyoza Are thin pastry rounds made from wheat flour that the Japanese use to wrap around fillings for dumplings and pot stickers. If unavailable, substitute gow gee wrappers.

spring roll Also called egg roll wrappers; they come in various sizes and can be purchased fresh or frozen. Made from a delicate wheat-based pastry, they can be used for making gow gee and samosas as well as spring rolls.

wonton Also known as wonton skins; made of flour, eggs, and water, they come in varying thicknesses. Sold packaged in large amounts and found in the refrigerated section of Asian grocery stores; gow gee, egg or spring roll pastry sheets can be substituted.

YOGURT We use plain full-cream yogurt in our recipes unless specifically noted otherwise.

ZUCCHINI Also known as courgette; small, pale- or dark-green, yellow or white vegetable belonging to the squash family. Harvested when young, its edible flowers can be stuffed and deep-fried or oven-baked.

Index

A

allspice 470
almond and rosewater jelly 453
almonds 470
aloo gobi 422
apple salad, chinese pork and 151
asian broth, vegetable dumplings in 110
asian broth with crisp pork belly 118
asian chicken pot au feu 326
asian fruit salad 442
asian greens
    black bean sauce, stir-fried in 426
    buk choy 8
    chilli beef and vegetables with noodles 201
    chilli rice noodles with lamb and buk choy 351
    choy sum 8
    crispy fish with 161
    dipping sauce for, 414
    gai lan 9
    grilled asian vegetables 426
    ocean trout in baby buk choy parcels 300
    peanut chilli beef with choy sum 181
    ravioli with 117
    spicy citrus prawn and tat soi salad 147
    steamed buk choy with chilli oil 430
    steamed, with char siu sauce 428
    stir-fried cauliflower, choy sum and snake beans 422
    stir-fried gai lan with sesame 425
    stir-fried sweet and sour vegetables 430
    stir-fried vegetables with cracked black pepper 421
    tat soi 11
    twice cooked chicken with 158

asian-spiced roasted pork belly 267
asian-style braised pork neck 321
asparagus
    beef teriyaki platter 275
    stir-fried sweet and sour vegetables 430

B

balinese chilli lamb and fried noodles 347
balti biryani 367
bamboo cooking chopsticks 467
bamboo mat 467
bamboo shoots 470
    steamed snapper with cantonese vegetables 303
    udon noodle soup 109
bamboo steamer basket 467
banana
    caramelised, coconut sago pudding with 446
    lumpia with brown sugar syrup and coconut ice-cream 462
    tropical fruit skewers with coconut dressing 450
banana leaves 470
    hot and sour fish steamed in 304
    lamb wrapped in, with thai salad 260
bang bang chicken salad 143
basil see thai basil
bay leaves 470
bean sprouts 470
beans 470
beef 470
    asian beef and rice noodle soup 113
    beef and rice noodle salad 75

(*beef* continued)
    beef with green papaya, chilli and coriander salad 155
    beef with oyster sauce 186
    braised oxtail in peanut sauce 325
    char-grilled beef and noodle salad 152
    chilli beef and vegetables with noodles 201
    chilli beef in spicy coconut sauce 333
    chilli beef stir-fry 170
    chow mein 364
    chutney for, 402, 404
    crisp beef with egg noodles 359
    crisp hot and sweet beef with noodles 343
    crying tiger 76
    curry, aromatic vietnamese 227
    curry, dry, with onions and peanuts 211
    curry, massaman 228
    curry, panang 243
    curry puffs 26
    do-piaza 317
    dipping sauce for, 413, 414
    dressing for, 398
    ginger beef stir-fry 173
    ginger teriyaki beef 193
    hoisin-braised short ribs 321
    hokkien mee with beef 339
    honey and five-spice beef with broccolini 189
    indian rice pilaf with spiced beef 186
    kasaundi for, 406
    kway teow 348
    mee goreng 348
    peanut chilli beef with choy sum 181
    peppercorn beef 197
    pho bo 106
    raita for, 401

Index

(*beef* continued)
    rice noodles with beef and black bean 359
    sri lankan spicy ribs with coconut pilaf 272
    sukiyaki 169
    teriyaki platter 275
    thai beef salad 136
    twice-fried sichuan beef 190
    xacutti 247
beetroot 470
beetroot dip 21
bengali mushroom and lamb with mango chutney yogurt 223
besan flour 473
betel leaves 8
    green mango salad on 25
bhaji, potato and onion 433
bicarbonate of soda 470
biryani, balti 367
biryani, spiced vegetable 344
black bean sauce 475
    mongolian lamb stir-fry 165
    rice noodles with beef and 359
    steamed fish with black bean and chilli sauce 295
    stir-fried asian greens in 426
    stir-fried lamb in 170
black rice 384
blood orange sorbet 438
blood plums with honey and cardamom yogurt 441
bouquet garni 291
breadcrumbs 470
broccoli
    chilli chicken with broccoli and cashews 194
    ginger teriaki beef 193
    stir-fried sweet and sour vegetables 430

broccolini 470
    grilled asian vegetables 426
    honey and five-spice beef with 189
    orange-flavoured octopus and 197
    steamed asian vegetables with char siu sauce 428
    sweet and sour duck with broccolini 173
    thai-style sticky pork on 67
bruising 470
    cardamom pods 228
buk choy 8 *see also* asian greens
    chilli beef and vegetables with noodles 201
    chilli beef stir-fry 170
    chilli rice noodles with lamb and 351
    ocean trout in baby buk choy parcels 300
    steamed asian vegetables with char siu sauce 428
    steamed buk choy with chilli oil 430
    sweet soy fried noodles 343
butter 470
butter lettuce 470
buttermilk 470

C

calamari 476
    teppanyaki 264
candlenut 470
cantonese lobster 201
cantonese vegetables, steamed snapper with 303
capsicum 470
    capsicum, chilli and hoisin chicken 174
    coconut rice with capsicum and coriander 388
    hokkien mee with beef 339

(*capsicum* continued)
    hot and sour prawn vermicelli salad 131
    seafood and vegetable tempura 205
    sesame omelette and crisp mixed vegetable salad 128
    spiced vegetable biryani 344
    thai pickle 60
    wok-seared mushroom omelettes 161
caramelised chicken cutlets 267
caramelised onion and red lentil dip 391
caraway seeds 470
cardamom 471
    blood plums with honey and cardamom yogurt 441
    bruising 228
    gulab jaman 445
    pistachio, honey and cardamom kulfi 453
    tropical fruit salad with cardamom 442
carrot
    chinese wonton soup 90
    dhal and paneer vegetable curry 375
    gado gado 155
    pho bo 106
    raita 401
    steamed snapper with cantonese vegetables 303
    vietnamese carrot pickle 406
cashews 471
    chilli chicken with broccoli and 194
cauliflower
    aloo gobi 422
    cauliflower and green pea curry 247
    cauliflower, pea and paneer balti 215
    gado gado 155

(cauliflower continued)
    mixed vegetables in coconut milk 313
    stir-fried cauliflower, choy sum and snake beans 422
cayenne pepper 471
chan, wok 467
chapati 379, 471
char kway teow 360
char siu dressing 158
char siu sauce 475
    steamed asian greens with 428
cheese
    cream 471
    paneer see paneer
chengdu chicken 181
chiang mai pork and eggplant 189
chicken 471
    asian chicken pot au feu 326
    bang bang chicken salad 143
    capsicum, chilli and hoisin chicken 174
    caramelised chicken cutlets 267
    chengdu chicken 181
    chicken and galangal soup 113
    chicken and thai basil fried rice 340
    chicken and thai basil stir-fry 169
    chicken in citrus wakame broth 105
    chicken, noodle and kaffir lime stir-fry 356
    chicken with red nam jim 177
    chilli chicken with broccoli and cashews 194
    chinese-spiced chicken 291
    chutney for, 402, 404, 409
    clay-pot chicken 329
    coconut, chicken and kaffir lime soup 105
    coconut chicken salad in crisp wonton cups 49

(chicken continued)
    coconut chicken vietnamese summer rolls 50
    combination long soup 101
    curry, green 223
    curry kapitan 224
    curry, korma 236
    curry, panang 231
    curry, red 215
    dipping sauce for, 413, 414
    donburi 314
    dressing for, 398
    hainan chicken rice 296
    indian spiced chicken with roasted eggplant 279
    indochine grilled chicken salad 259
    kasaundi for, 406
    korma 236
    koshumbir for, 410
    laksa 94
    larb with thai pickle 60
    lemon grass chicken with chilli dipping sauce 80
    malaysian chicken noodle soup 101
    mee goreng 363
    mixed mushrooms and chicken with crispy noodles 185
    money bags 34
    pho 93
    pickle for, 406
    raita for, 397, 401
    sambal for, 394, 410
    sauce for, 409
    spiced spatchcock with herb yogurt 284
    stuffed chicken wings 54
    sweet chilli plum noodles with chicken 351
    tandoori chicken, spinach and mint salad with spiced yogurt 147

(chicken continued)
    thai chicken and lychee salad 135
    thai-style steamed chicken with noodles 307
    tikka with cucumber-mint raita 283
    twice cooked chicken with asian greens 158
    udon noodle soup 109
    vietnamese chicken salad 144
    vietnamese chicken spring rolls 42
    white-cut chicken 292
    yakitori with sesame dipping sauce 75
chickpeas 471
    masala dosa with mint rasam 212
    vegetable dhanksak 322
chilli 471
chilli beef and vegetables with noodles 201
chilli beef in spicy coconut sauce 333
chilli beef stir-fry 170
chilli chicken with broccoli and cashews 194
chilli crab laksa 98
chilli dipping sauce 80
chilli flakes 471
chilli ginger sambal 296
chilli lime dressing 135, 202
chilli paste 471
chilli plum dressing 127
chilli powder 471
chilli salt squid 87
chilli sauce 471
chilli sesame dressing 128
chilli stone fruits, poached pork with 291
chinese barbecued spareribs 268
chinese cooking wine 471
chinese pork and apple salad 151
chinese-spiced chicken 291
chinese wonton soup 90

Index

chopstick rests 468
chopsticks 468
chopsticks, bamboo cooking 467
chow mein, beef 364
choy sum 8 see also asian greens
    peanut chilli beef with 181
    stir-fried cauliflower, snake beans and 422
    twice cooked chicken with asian greens 158
chutney
    date and tamarind 402
    eggplant 402
    fresh coriander coconut chutney 409
    green mango 404
    mango chutney yogurt 223
cinnamon 471
clay pot 467
clay-pot chicken 329
cleaver 467
cloves 471
coconut 471
    banana lumpia with brown sugar syrup and coconut ice-cream 462
    chilli beef in spicy coconut sauce 333
    coconut, chicken and kaffir lime soup 105
    coconut chicken salad in crisp wonton cups 49
    coconut chicken vietnamese summer rolls 50
    coconut custards with papaya 454
    coconut rice pudding with mango 458
    coconut rice with capsicum and coriander 388
    coconut sago pudding with caramelised banana 446
    cream 471

(*coconut* continued)
    curries see curry
    desiccated 471
    fish in spicy coconut cream 313
    flaked 471
    fresh coriander coconut chutney 409
    grilled pineapple with coconut ice-cream 446
    ice-cream 446, 462
    lime and coconut prawns 41
    milk 471
    mixed vegetables in coconut milk 313
    passionfruit and coconut crème brûlée 465
    red emperor in thai-style coconut sauce 329
    shredded 471
    sri lankan spicy ribs with coconut pilaf 272
    tropical fruit skewers with coconut dressing 450
    yellow coconut rice 387
coconut-flavoured liqueur 471
colander 467
combination long soup 101
condiment bowl 468
condiment dish 469
cooking oil spray 475
coriander 472
    beef with green papaya, chilli and coriander salad 155
    coconut rice with capsicum and coriander 388
    fish curry with coriander and snake beans 211
    fresh coriander coconut chutney 409
    herb salad 68, 288, 299
    paste 25

(*coriander* continued)
    steamed mussels with saffron, chilli and coriander 303
cornflour 472
cos lettuce 472
crab
    chilli crab laksa 98
    crab fried rice in omelette 84
    mud crab 476
    pickle for, 406
    singapore chilli crab 182
    spicy seafood soup 97
    thai crab and mango salad 79
crème brûlée
    ginger and lime 462
    passionfruit and coconut 465
crying tiger 76
cucumber
    dipping sauce 22
    gado gado 155
    herb salad 288, 299
    lebanese 474
    nasi goreng 355
    raita 64, 397
    raita, cucumber-mint 283
    sambal, cucumber and pineapple 394
    sashimi stacks 49
    stir-fried sweet and sour vegetables 430
    sushi salad 140
    thai beef salad 136
    thai pickle 60
    tuna and cucumber mini maki 33
cumin 472
currants 472
curried fried rice with pork and prawns 347
curry 472
    balti biryani 367

(*curry* continued)
    balti, cauliflower, pea and
       paneer 215
    beef, aromatic vietnamese 227
    beef massaman 228
    beef panang 243
    beef, xacutti 247
    bengali mushroom and lamb with
       mango chutney yogurt 223
    cauliflower and green pea 247
    cauliflower, pea and paneer
       balti 215
    chicken green 223
    chicken, kapitan 224
    chicken korma 236
    chicken panang 231
    chicken red 215
    chicken tikka 283
    dhal and paneer vegetable 375
    dry beef, with onions and
       peanuts 211
    duck jungle 208
    fish ball and eggplant red 235
    fish, malaysian 232
    fish, with coriander and snake
       beans 211
    green, chicken 223
    green paste 249, 472
    kapitan 224
    korma, chicken 236
    korma, lamb 219
    korma paste 472
    korma, spinach and mushroom 235
    lamb, bengali, with mango chutney
       yogurt 223
    lamb korma 219
    lamb madras 243
    lamb rendang 239
    lamb, rogan josh 231
    lamb shanks 317
    lentil and egg, with lime pickle 383

(*curry* continued)
    lentil soup, curry and lime 97
    lentils with mushrooms and
       spinach 391
    madras lamb 243
    malaysian fish 232
    masala dosa with mint rasam 212
    massaman beef 228
    massaman paste 248, 472
    massaman, tofu and
       thai eggplant 244
    panang beef 243
    panang chicken 231
    panang paste 249, 472
    panang pork 220
    pork panang, with pickled snake
       beans 220
    pork, sour 244
    pork, tamarind and citrus 239
    pork vindaloo 240
    pork, with eggplant 227
    red, chicken 215
    red, fish ball and eggplant 235
    red paste 249, 472
    rogan josh 231, 472
    seafood and thai eggplant
       yellow 216
    spinach and mushroom korma 235
    sri lankan fried pork 219
    tikka, chicken 283
    tikka paste 472
    tofu and thai eggplant
       massaman 244
    vegetable yellow 240
    vindaloo paste 472
    vindaloo, pork 240
    xacutti 247
    yellow paste 248, 472
    yellow, seafood and thai
       eggplant 216
    yellow, vegetable 240

curry leaves 472
curry pastes 472
    green 249, 472
    korma 472
    massaman 248, 472
    panang 249, 472
    red 249, 472
    tikka 472
    vindaloo 472
    yellow 248, 472
curry powder 472
curry puffs 26
custard powder 472

D

daikon 8
    japanese-style duck with
       wombok and daikon salad 256
    japanese-style tuna with
       chilli-daikon 63
    mixed sashimi 79
    soba and daikon salad 151
    sushi salad 140
dashi 472
date and tamarind chutney 402
dates 472
dhal 276
    curry, dhal and paneer
       vegetable 375
    mixed 380
    tandoori lamb with dhal and
       pickled lemon 276
dhanksak, vegetable 322
dipping sauce *see* sauces
donburi, chicken 314
dressings *see also* sauces
    char siu 158
    chilli lime 135, 202
    chilli plum 127

Index

(*dressings* continued)
    chilli sesame 128
    coconut 450
    ginger 300
    hot and sour 152
    lime and chilli 75, 79, 304
    lime and ginger 127
    mirin 151
    mirin and wasabi 140
    palm sugar 83
    sesame 63, 128
    sesame and peanut 143
    soy and green onion 292
    sweet chilli 143, 307
    sweet-sour 71, 124
    thai-style 139, 259
    vietnamese 144
dried chinese sausage 472
    fried noodles with sausage and wombok 364
duck 472
    braised sweet ginger duck 318
    chinese barbecued 472
    chutney for, 402
    crisp duck with mandarin, chilli and mint 198
    crisp duck with tamarind soy sauce 177
    crispy-fried duck and mango salad 131
    duck and mushroom soup 109
    japanese-style duck with wombok and daikon salad 256
    jungle curry 208
    peking duck 72
    sambal for, 394, 410
    sauce for, 409
    sichuan duck with watercress and snow pea salad 283
    soy duck breast with noodles 263

(*duck* continued)
    sweet and sour duck with broccolini 173
    tamarind duck stir-fry 194
    thai-style duck salad 139
dumplings, prawn 45
dumplings, vegetable, in asian broth 110

E

egg 472
    crab fried rice in omelette 84
    eggplant egg foo yung 193
    lentil and egg curry with lime pickle 383
    sesame omelette and crisp mixed vegetable salad 128
    sukiyaki 169
    udon noodle soup 109
    wok-seared mushroom omelettes 161
egg noodles *see noodles*
eggplant 472
    chutney 402
    eggplant egg foo yung 193
    chiang mai pork and eggplant 189
    fish ball and eggplant red curry 235
    indian spiced chicken with roasted eggplant 279
    pea 473
    pork curry with eggplant 227
    seafood and thai eggplant yellow curry 216
    sichuan eggplant, almond and wombok stir-fry 433
    sichuan-style vegetables 418
    stir-fried eggplant and tofu 425
    tandoori lamb with dhal and pickled lemon 276

(*eggplant* continued)
    thai 473
    thick roasted eggplant with spiced rice 280
    tofu and thai eggplant massaman curry 244

F

fennel 473
fenugreek 473
filleting knife, sharp 467
fish *see also seafood*
    cakes 54
    char kway teow 360
    chutney for, 409
    crisp fish salad with chilli lime dressing 135
    crisp-skinned thai chilli snapper 263
    crispy fish with asian greens 161
    curry, fish ball and eggplant red 235
    curry, malaysian 232
    curry with coriander and snake beans 211
    dressing for, 398
    fish in spicy coconut cream 313
    fish with thai-style dressing 259
    hot and sour fish steamed in banana leaves 304
    japanese seafood hotpot 310
    kaffir lime and lemon grass grilled trout 275
    koshumbir for, 410
    lemon grass and lime fish parcels 295
    masala fish 162
    mixed sashimi 79
    ocean trout in baby buk choy parcels 300
    pickle for, 406

483

(fish continued)
   poached flathead with green nam jim 288
   poached flathead with herb salad 299
   raita for, 397, 401
   red emperor in thai-style coconut sauce 329
   sambal for, 394
   sashimi stacks 49
   sauce for, 409
   seafood and thai eggplant yellow curry 216
   seafood and vegetable tempura 205
   seafood wontons with sesame dressing 63
   seared salmon kerala-style with lime pickle yogurt 271
   spicy seafood soup 97
   steamed fish with black bean and chilli sauce 295
   steamed fish with chilli and ginger 299
   steamed snapper with cantonese vegetables 303
   sushi salad 140
   thai-style seafood and rice vermicelli salad 139
   tuna see tuna
fish cakes 54
fish sauce 475
five-spice 473
   barbecued pork neck with five-spice star-anise glaze 279
   crisp five-spice salt pork belly 255
   five-spice pork and nashi salad with chilli plum dressing 127
   honey and five-spice beef with broccolini 189

flathead 476
   poached, with green nam jim 288
   poached, with herb salad 299
fried rice see rice
fruit salad, asian 442
fruit salad with cardamom, tropical 442

G

gado gado 155
gai lan 9 *see also asian greens*
   crispy fish with asian greens 161
   stir-fried asian greens in black bean sauce 426
   stir-fried with sesame 425
galangal 9
   aromatic paste 330
   galangal and chicken soup 113
garam masala 473
garlic and chilli quail, baked 21
garlic chive and pork-wrapped prawns 38
garlic pork, fried noodles with 363
gelatine 473
ghee 473
ginger 473
   braised sweet ginger duck 318
   chilli ginger sambal 296
   chilli, lime and ginger octopus salad 148
   dressing 300
   ginger and lime crème brûlée 462
   ginger beef stir-fry 173
   ginger miso dressing 398
   ginger teriyaki beef 193
   lime and ginger dressing 127
   pickled 473
   pork, ginger and mint larb 67
   steamed fish with chilli and ginger 299

glutinous rice 384
gow gees, vegetable, with miso dipping sauce 46
green chilli 471
green curry 472
   chicken 223
   paste 249
green onion 475
   beef teriyaki platter 275
   nasi goreng 355
   soy and green onion dressing 292
   steamed snapper with cantonese vegetables 303
green tea ice-cream with asian fruit salsa 465
gulab jaman 445
gyoza with soy vinegar sauce 41
gyoza wrappers 477

H

hainan chicken rice 296
herb salad 68, 288, 299
hoisin sauce 475
   asian broth with crisp pork belly 118
   capsicum, chilli and hoisin chicken 174
   hoisin and peanut dipping sauce 414
   hoisin-braised short ribs 321
   hokkien mee with beef 339
   twice-cooked pork 165
hokkien noodles 9 *see also noodles*
   beef mee goreng 339
   hokkien mee with beef 339
honey and cardamom yogurt, blood plums with 441
honey and five-spice beef with broccolini 189
honey, pistachio and cardamom kulfi 453

Index

hot and sour fish steamed in banana leaves 304
hot and sour prawn vermicelli salad 131
hotpot, japanese seafood 310

I

ice-cream, coconut 446, 462
ice-cream, green tea 465
indian rice pilaf with spiced beef 186

J

japanese breadcrumbs 470
japanese seafood hotpot 310
japanese soy sauce 477
japanese-style duck with wombok and daikon salad 256
japanese-style tuna with chilli-daikon 63
jasmine rice 384
jungle curry, duck 208

K

kaffir lime 473
    chicken, noodle and kaffir lime stir-fry 356
    coconut, chicken and kaffir lime soup 105
    kaffir lime and lemon grass grilled trout 275
    leaves 9
    sorbet 438
    sticky pork with 25
kalonji 473
kasaundi, tomato 406
kecap manis 476
keema with green chilli and tomato 333
khitcherie 376

kiwi fruit
    kiwi fruit, lychee and lime salad 461
    tropical fruit salad with cardamom 442
    tropical fruit trifle 449
korma 472
    chicken 236
    lamb 219
    spinach and mushroom 235
koshumbir 410
kulfi, pistachio, honey and cardamom 453
kumara 473
    japanese seafood hotpot 310
    seafood and vegetable tempura 205
kung pao prawns 178
kway teow, beef 348

L

laksa
    chicken 94
    chilli crab 98
    paste 114
    vegetable 114
lamb 473
    balinese chilli lamb and fried noodles 347
    bengali mushroom and lamb with mango chutney yogurt 223
    chilli rice noodles with lamb and buk choy 351
    chutney for, 402, 404
    crisp twice-fried lamb with thai basil 178
    curried lamb shanks 317
    curry, korma 219
    curry, madras 243

(*lamb* continued)
    curry, rendang 239
    curry, rogan josh 231
    keema with green chilli and tomato 333
    korma 219
    lamb wrapped in banana leaf with thai salad 260
    lemon grass lamb with vietnamese vermicelli salad 124
    mongolian lamb stir-fry 165
    raan with spiced yogurt 252
    raita for, 397, 401
    rendang 239
    rogan josh 231
    samosas with tamarind sauce 30
    stir-fried lamb in black bean sauce 170
    tandoori lamb with dhal and pickled lemon 276
larb, chicken, with thai pickle 60
larb, pork, ginger and mint 67
lebanese cucumber see cucumber
lemon grass 10
    aromatic paste 330
    kaffir lime and lemon grass grilled trout 275
    lemon grass and lime fish parcels 295
    lemon grass chicken with chilli dipping sauce 80
    lemon grass lamb with vietnamese vermicelli salad 124
    mussels with basil and lemon grass 84
    sorbet 438
lemon pepper dipping sauce 68
lemon, pickled, tandoori lamb with dhal and 276
lemon soy dipping sauce 264

lentils 474
    caramelised onion and red lentil dip 391
    curried red lentils with mushrooms and spinach 391
    curry and lime lentil soup 97
    lentil and egg curry with lime pickle 383
    mixed dhal 380
    spiced 387
    vegetable dhanksak 322
lime
    chilli, lime and ginger octopus salad 148
    crisp fish salad with chilli lime dressing 135
    curry and lime lentil soup 97
    ginger and lime crème brûlée 462
    kiwi fruit, lychee and lime salad 461
    lemon grass and lime fish parcels 295
    lentil and egg curry with lime pickle 383
    lime and chilli dressing 75, 79, 304
    lime and coconut prawns 41
    lime and ginger dressing 127
    little lime syrup cakes 457
    mini scallop and lime kebabs 45
    papaya with passionfruit and lime 441
    pork, lime and peanut salad 143
    salt and pepper tofu with chilli lime dressing 202
    seared salmon kerala-style with lime pickle yogurt 271
    sweet lime mangoes 450
    tamarind and citrus pork curry 239
lobster 476
    cantonese 201
    pickle for, 406

lychees 474
    almond and rosewater jelly 453
    asian fruit salad 442
    green tea ice-cream with asian fruit salsa 465
    kiwi fruit, lychee and lime salad 461
    lychees with passionfruit 461
    thai chicken and lychee salad 135

M

madras lamb curry 243
malaysian chicken noodle soup 101
malaysian fish curry 232
mandarin, chilli and mint, crisp duck with 198
mango
    almond and rosewater jelly 453
    asian fruit salad 442
    bengali mushroom and lamb with mango chutney yogurt 223
    coconut rice pudding with mango 458
    crispy-fried duck and mango salad 131
    green 474
    green mango and seared tuna salad 127
    green mango chutney 404
    green mango salad on betel leaves 25
    mango-passionfruit sorbet with grilled mango 445
    sambal 410
    sweet lime mangoes 450
    thai crab and mango salad 79
    thai-style duck salad 139
    tropical fruit salad with cardamom 442

(*mango* continued)
    tropical fruit skewers with coconut dressing 450
    tropical fruit trifle 449
masala dosa with mint rasam 212
masala fish 162
masala paste 322
massaman curry 472
    beef 228
    paste 248
    tofu and thai eggplant 244
mee goreng, beef 348
mee goreng, chicken 363
mee krob 336
microplane greater 467
mint
    crisp duck with mandarin, chilli and mint 198
    cucumber-mint raita 283
    herb salad 68, 288, 299
    pork, ginger and mint larb 67
    raita 397
    rasam 212
    vietnamese 12
mirin 474
    dressing 151
    japanese-style duck with wombok and daikon salad 256
    mirin and wasabi dressing 140
    sukiyaki 169
miso 474
    dipping sauce 46
    ginger miso dressing 398
    vegetable gow gees with miso dipping sauce 46
    wombok and daikon salad 256
mizuna 474
    chilli, lime and ginger octopus salad 148
money bags 34
mongolian lamb stir-fry 165

mortar and pestle 467
mushrooms 474
    bengali mushroom and lamb with mango chutney yogurt 223
    chicken donburi 314
    combination long soup 101
    curried red lentils with mushrooms and spinach 391
    dried black fungus 474
    duck and mushroom soup 109
    enoki 474
    mixed mushrooms and chicken with crispy noodles 185
    oyster 474
    shitake 474
    spinach and mushroom korma 235
    sukiyaki 169
    swiss brown 474
    udon noodle soup 109
    vegetable dumplings in asian broth 110
    wok-seared mushroom omelettes 161
mussels 476
    japanese seafood hotpot 310
    mussels with asian flavours 162
    mussels with basil and lemon grass 84
    seafood and thai eggplant yellow curry 216
    spicy seafood soup 97
    steamed mussels with saffron, chilli and coriander 303
mustard seeds
    aloo gobi 422
    black 474
    carrot raita 401
    cucumber raita 397
    fried potatoes with 421
    mint raita 397
    white 474

N

naan 379, 474
nam jim 288
    chicken with red 177
    poached flathead with green 288
nashi 474
    five-spice pork and nashi salad with chilli plum dressing 127
    grilled, in rosewater syrup 457
    poached, in asian-spiced syrup 454
nasi goreng 355
noodles 474
    asian beef and rice noodle soup 113
    balinese chilli lamb and fried noodles 347
    bang bang chicken salad 143
    barbecued pork and crunchy noodle salad 71
    bean thread 474
    beef and rice noodle salad 75
    beef chow mein 364
    beef kway teow 348
    beef mee goreng 348
    char-grilled beef and noodle salad 152
    char kway teow 360
    chicken laksa 94
    chicken mee goreng 363
    chicken, noodle and kaffir lime stir-fry 356
    chicken pho 93
    chilli beef and vegetables with noodles 201
    chilli beef stir-fry 170
    chilli crab laksa 98
    chilli rice noodles with lamb and buk choy 351
    combination long soup 101

(*noodles* continued)
    crisp beef with egg noodles 359
    crisp hot and sweet beef with noodles 343
    fried 474
    fried noodles with garlic pork 363
    fried noodles with sausage and wombok 364
    grilled tuna wtih japanese chilled soba salad 271
    hokkien mee with beef 339
    hokkien noodles 9
    hot and sour prawn vermicelli salad 131
    indochine grilled chicken salad 259
    japanese seafood hotpot 310
    lemon grass lamb with vietnamese vermicelli salad 124
    malaysian chicken noodle soup 101
    mee goreng, beef 348
    mee goreng, chicken 363
    mee krob 336
    mixed mushrooms and chicken with crispy noodles 185
    pad thai 352
    pad thai, vegetarian 340
    pho bo 106
    prawn soup 93
    rice noodles 10
    rice noodles with beef and black bean 359
    rice stick 474
    rice vermicelli 474
    singapore noodles 367
    soba and daikon salad 151
    soba noodles 11
    soy duck breast with noodles 263
    soy-fried noodles with tofu 355
    sukiyaki 169

(*noodles* continued)
   sweet chilli plum noodles with chicken 351
   sweet soy fried noodles 343
   thai-style seafood and rice vermicelli salad 139
   thai-style steamed chicken with noodles 307
   tuna skewers with soba 255
   udon 474
   udon noodle soup 109
   vegetarian pad thai 340
nori 10
   tuna and cucumber mini maki 33

O

ocean trout in baby buk choy parcels 300
octopus 476
   chilli, lime and ginger octopus salad 148
   orange-flavoured octopus and broccolini 197
oil 475
omelette
   crab fried rice in omelette 84
   sesame omelette and crisp mixed vegetable salad 128
   wok-seared mushroom omelettes 161
onion 475
   beef do-piaza 317
   caramelised onion and red lentil dip 391
   chicken donburi 314
   dry beef curry with onions and peanuts 211
   onion and spinach pakoras with cucumber raita 64

(*onion* continued)
   pho bo 106
   potato and onion bhaji 433
   sichuan-style vegetables 418
   soy and green onion dressing 292
   spiced vegetable biryani 344
   tomato and onion raita 18
orange
   asian fruit salad 442
   blood orange sorbet 438
   orange-flavoured octopus and broccolini 197
oxtail, braised, in peanut sauce 325
oyster sauce 475
   beef with 186
oysters 476
   thai-style 36

P

pad thai 352
pad thai, vegetarian 340
palak paneer 325
palm sugar 10
palm sugar dressing 83
panang curry 472
   beef 243
   chicken 231
   paste 249
   pork 220
pancakes for peking duck 72
paneer 471
   cauliflower, pea and paneer balti 215
   dhal and paneer vegetable curry 375
   palak paneer 325
papaya
   asian fruit salad 442
   beef with green papaya, chilli and coriander salad 155
   coconut custards with papaya 454

(*papaya* continued)
   green tea ice-cream with asian fruit salsa 465
   papaya with passionfruit and lime 441
   pickled green papaya salad 83
   tropical fruit salad with cardamom 442
paprika 475
parathas 372
passionfruit
   almond and rosewater jelly 453
   asian fruit salad 442
   lychees with 461
   mango-passionfruit sorbet with grilled mango 445
   papaya with passionfruit and lime 441
   passionfruit and coconut crème brûlée 465
   tropical fruit salad with cardamom 442
   tropical fruit trifle 449
pea
   cauliflower and green pea curry 247
   cauliflower, pea and paneer balti 215
   curried fried rice with pork and prawns 347
   dhal and paneer vegetable curry 375
   keema with green chilli and tomato 333
   khitcherie 376
   snow peas *see* snow peas
peanut
   braised oxtail in peanut sauce 325
   crisp potato and peanut cakes 18
   dipping sauce 34, 41
   dry beef curry with onions and peanuts 211
   hoisin and peanut dipping sauce 414

(*peanut* continued)
    peanut and hoisin sauce 72
    peanut chilli beef with choy sum 181
    pork, lime and peanut salad 143
    sauce 155
    sesame and peanut dressing 143
    sweet chilli peanut sauce 54
peanut oil 475
peking duck 72
peppercorn beef 197
pho bo 106
pho, chicken 93
pickled ginger 473
pickled green papaya salad 83
pickled lemon 276
pickled snake beans 220
pilaf, coconut, sri lankan spicy ribs with 272
pineapple
    asian fruit salad 442
    cucumber and pineapple sambal 394
    grilled pineapple with coconut ice-cream 446
    pickled green papaya salad 83
    sticky-glazed pork with pineapple 29
    tamarind honey prawns with pineapple 185
    teriyaki pork with pineapple 284
    tropical fruit skewers with coconut dressing 450
pistachio, honey and cardamom kulfi 453
plain flour 473
plum sauce 476
    chilli plum dressing 127
    sweet chilli plum noodles with chicken 351
pomelo 475

pomelo salad 87
poppy seeds 475
pork 475
    asian broth with crisp pork belly 118
    asian-spiced roasted pork belly 267
    asian-style braised pork neck 321
    barbecued pork and crunchy noodle salad 71
    barbecued pork fried rice 339
    barbecued pork neck with five-spice star-anise glaze 279
    chiang mai pork and eggplant 189
    chinese barbecued spareribs 268
    chinese pork and apple salad 151
    chinese wonton soup 90
    chutney for, 402, 404, 409
    combination long soup 101
    crisp five-spice salt pork belly 255
    crisp pork belly with wombok salad 132
    curried fried rice with pork and prawns 347
    curry, panang, with pickled snake beans 220
    curry, sour 244
    curry, sri lankan 219
    curry, tamarind and citrus 239
    curry, vindaloo 240
    curry with eggplant 227
    dipping sauce for, 413, 414
    dressing for, 398
    five-spice pork and nashi salad with chilli plum dressing 127
    fried noodles with garlic pork 363
    fried rice with prawns 356
    gyoza with soy vinegar sauce 41
    kasaundi for, 406
    koshumbir for, 410
    mee krob 336
    pad thai 352

(*pork* continued)
    pickle for, 406
    poached pork with chilli stone fruits 291
    pork and garlic chive-wrapped prawns 38
    pork and prawn vietnamese summer rolls 50
    pork, ginger and mint larb 67
    pork, lime and peanut salad 143
    pork with sticky asian glaze 166
    raita for, 397, 401
    sambal for, 394, 410
    sang choy bow 83
    sauce for, 409
    singapore noodles 367
    sticky-glazed pork with pineapple 29
    sticky pork with kaffir lime leaves 25
    sweet and sour tamarind pork 330
    teriyaki pork with pineapple 284
    thai-style sticky pork on broccolini 67
    twice-cooked pork 165
    vindaloo 240
potato
    aloo gobi 422
    crisp potato and peanut cakes 18
    curry puffs 26
    fried potatoes with black mustard seeds 421
    gado gado 155
    masala dosa with mint rasam 212
    parathas 372
    potato and onion bhaji 433
    sichuan-style vegetables 418
    spiced vegetable biryani 344
prawns 476
    char kway teow 360
    chutney for, 409
    combination long soup 101

(prawns continued)
   curried fried rice with pork and prawns 347
   deep-fried prawn balls 53
   dipping sauce for, 413, 414
   dressing for, 398
   fried rice with prawns 356
   hot and sour prawn vermicelli salad 131
   japanese seafood hotpot 310
   kung pao prawns 178
   lime and coconut prawns 41
   mee krob 336
   pickle for, 406
   pork and garlic chive-wrapped prawns 38
   pork and prawn vietnamese summer rolls 50
   prawn dumplings 45
   prawn sambal 202
   prawn soup 93
   raita for, 397, 401
   sambal for, 394
   sauce for, 409
   seafood and thai eggplant yellow curry 216
   seafood and vegetable tempura 205
   singapore noodles 367
   spicy butterflied prawns on crisp wontons 29
   spicy citrus prawn and tat soi salad 147
   tamarind honey prawns with pineapple 185
   thai spring rolls 22
   thai-style seafood and rice vermicelli salad 139
   tom yum goong 102
pulao, classic 376

Q

quail 475
   baked garlic and chilli quail 21
   deep-fried spicy quail 71
   salt and pepper quail with lemon pepper dipping sauce 68

R

raan with spiced yogurt 252
raita
   carrot 401
   cucumber 64, 397
   cucumber-mint 283
   mint 397
   spinach 401
   tomato and onion 18
rambutan 475
   asian fruit salad 442
ravioli with asian greens 117
red thai chilli 471
red curry 472
   chicken 215
   fish ball and eggplant 235
   paste 249
red emperor in thai-style coconut sauce 329
rendang, lamb 239
ribs
   chinese barbecued spareribs 268
   hoisin-braised short ribs 321
   sri lankan spicy ribs with coconut pilaf 272
rice 475
   balti biryani 367
   barbecued pork fried rice 339
   basmati 475
   black rice 384

(rice continued)
   calrose 475
   chicken and thai basil fried rice 340
   coconut rice pudding with mango 458
   coconut rice with capsicum and coriander 388
   crab fried rice in omelette 84
   curried fried rice with pork and prawns 347
   fried rice with prawns 356
   glutinous rice 384
   hainan chicken rice 296
   indian rice pilaf with spiced beef 186
   jasmine 475
   jasmine rice, steamed 384
   khitcherie 376
   koshihikari 475
   nasi goreng 355
   pulao, classic 376
   spiced vegetable biryani 344
   sri lankan spicy ribs with coconut pilaf 272
   thick roasted eggplant with spiced rice 280
   tomato rice 375
   yellow coconut rice 387
rice noodles see noodles
rice paddle 467
rice serving spoon 469
rice table container 469
rice wine and soy sauce 409
rogan josh 231, 472
rosewater 475
   almond and rosewater jelly 453
   grilled nashi in rosewater syrup 457
   gulab jaman 445
roti 383

S

saffron 475
    beef do-piaza 317
    classic pulao 376
    steamed mussels with saffron, chilli and coriander 303
sago 475
    coconut sago pudding with caramelised banana 446
sake 475
salads
    bang bang chicken 143
    barbecued pork and crunchy noodle 71
    beef and rice noodle 75
    char-grilled beef and noodle 152
    chilli, lime and ginger octopus 148
    chinese pork and apple 151
    coconut chicken, in crisp wonton cups 49
    crisp fish salad with chilli lime dressing 135
    crisp mixed vegetable 128
    crispy-fried duck and mango 131
    five-spice pork and nashi 127
    gado gado 155
    green mango and seared tuna 127
    green mango salad on betel leaves 25
    green papaya, chilli and coriander 155
    herb 68, 288, 299
    hot and sour prawn vermicelli 131
    indochine grilled chicken 259
    japanese chilled soba 271
    mixed herb 288
    pickled green papaya 83
    pomelo 87
    pork, lime and peanut 143

(*salads* continued)
    sesame tofu 128
    soba and daikon 151
    spicy citrus prawn and tat soi 147
    sushi 140
    tandoori chicken, spinach and mint 147
    thai 260
    thai beef 136
    thai chicken and lychee 135
    thai crab and mango 79
    thai-style duck 139
    thai-style seafood and rice vermicelli 139
    vietnamese chicken 144
    vietnamese vermicelli 124
    watercress and snow pea 283
    wombok 132
    wombok and daikon 256
salmon 476
    mixed sashimi 79
    sashimi stacks 49
    seared salmon kerala-style with lime pickle yogurt 271
    sushi salad 140
    thai-style seafood and rice vermicelli salad 139
salt and lemon-pepper squid 53
sambal
    chilli ginger 296
    cucumber and pineapple 394
    mango 410
    oelek 475
    prawn 202
samosas with tamarind sauce 30
sang choy bow 83
sashimi 475
    mixed sashimi 79
    sashimi stacks 49

sauces 475 *see also dressings*
    chilli dipping sauce 80
    cucumber dipping sauce 22
    ginger miso dressing 398
    hoisin and peanut dipping sauce 414
    lemon pepper dipping sauce 68
    lemon soy dipping sauce 264
    miso dipping sauce 46
    peanut dipping sauce 34
    peanut sauce 155
    rice wine and soy sauce 409
    sesame dipping sauce 75
    sesame soy dressing 398
    soy vinegar 41
    spicy dipping sauce 413
    sweet and sour dipping sauce 413
    sweet chilli dipping sauce 414
    sweet chilli peanut sauce 54
    tamarind soy 177
savoiardi sponge fingers 476
savoy cabbage 476
scallops 476
    japanese seafood hotpot 310
    mini scallop and lime kebabs 45
    steamed, with asian flavours 307
seafood 476 *see also fish*
    calamari teppanyaki 264
    cantonese lobster 201
    char kway teow 360
    chilli, lime and ginger octopus salad 148
    crab *see crab*
    japanese seafood hotpot 310
    mini scallop and lime kebabs 45
    mussels *see mussels*
    orange-flavoured octopus and broccolini 197
    prawns *see prawns*

(seafood continued)
    seafood and thai eggplant
        yellow curry 216
    seafood and vegetable tempura 205
    seafood wontons with sesame
        dressing 63
    spicy seafood soup 97
    steamed scallops with asian
        flavours 307
    thai-style seafood and rice
        vermicelli salad 139
seaweed
    chicken in citrus wakame broth 105
    nori 10
    sushi salad 140
    tuna and cucumber mini maki 33
self-raising flour 473
sesame and peanut dressing 143
sesame dipping sauce 75
sesame dressing 63, 128
sesame oil 475
sesame omelette and crisp mixed
    vegetable salad 128
sesame seeds 476
sesame soy dressing 398
sesame tofu salad 128
shallots 475
shrimp, dried 476
shrimp paste 476
sichuan beef, twice-fried 190
sichuan duck with watercress and
    snow pea salad 283
sichuan eggplant, almond and
    wombok stir-fry 433
sichuan peppercorns 10
sichuan-style vegetables 418
sieve 467
silver beet 476
singapore chilli crab 182
singapore noodles 367

snake beans 470
    aromatic vietnamese beef curry 227
    bang bang chicken salad 143
    beeg panang curry 243
    fish curry with coriander and 211
    pickled, panang pork curry
        with 220
    stir-fried asian greens in
        black bean sauce 426
    stir-fried cauliflower, choy sum
        and 422
snow peas 476
    chilli beef and vegetables with
        noodles 201
    gado gado 155
    green mango salad on
        betel leaves 25
    grilled asian vegetables 426
    indochine grilled chicken
        salad 259
    ravioli with asian greens 117
    sichuan duck with watercress and
        snow pea salad 283
    steamed asian vegetables with
        char siu sauce 428
    stir-fried sweet and sour
        vegetables 430
    thai-style duck salad 139
    thai-style seafood and rice
        vermicelli salad 139
    twice cooked chicken with
        asian greens 158
soba noodles 11 *see also noodles*
    grilled tuna wtih japanese chilled
        soba salad 271
    soba and daikon salad 151
    tuna skewers with soba 255
sorbet
    blood orange 438
    kaffir lime 438

(*sorbet* continued)
    lemon grass 438
    mango-passionfruit, with grilled
        mango 445
soup
    asian beef and rice noodle 113
    asian broth with crisp pork belly 118
    chicken and galangal 113
    chicken in citrus wakame broth 105
    chicken laksa 94
    chicken pho 93
    chilli crab laksa 98
    chinese wonton 90
    coconut, chicken and kaffir lime 105
    combination long soup 101
    curry and lime lentil 97
    duck and mushroom 109
    malaysian chicken noodle 101
    pho bo 106
    prawn 93
    spicy seafood 97
    tom yum goong 102
    udon noodle 109
    vegetable dumplings in
        asian broth 110
    vegetable laksa 114
soup bowls and spoons 468
sour pork curry 244
soy beans 470
soy sauce 476
soy vinegar sauce 41
spareribs, chinese barbecued 268
spatchcock 477
    spiced spatchcock with
        herb yogurt 284
spinach 477
    chengdu chicken 181
    curried red lentils with mushrooms
        and spinach 391
    japanese seafood hotpot 310

Index

(*spinach* continued)
    onion and spinach pakoras with cucumber raita 64
    raita 401
    spinach and mushroom korma 235
    tandoori chicken, spinach and mint salad with spiced yogurt 147
split peas
    dhal and paneer vegetable curry 375
    khitcherie 376
    mixed dhal 380
spring onion 475
spring rolls
    thai 22
    vietnamese chicken 42
    wrappers 477
squid
    calamari 476
    calamari teppanyaki 264
    char kway teow 360
    chilli salt squid 87
    salt and lemon-pepper squid 53
    seafood and thai eggplant yellow curry 216
    spicy seafood soup 97
sri lankan fried pork curry 219
sri lankan spicy ribs with coconut pilaf 272
star anise 11
    barbecued pork neck with five-spice star-anise glaze 279
    gulab jaman 445
star fruit
    almond and rosewater jelly 453
    asian fruit salad 442
    tropical fruit skewers with coconut dressing 450
    tropical fruit trifle 449
stir-fried cauliflower, choy sum and snake beans 422

stir-fried eggplant and tofu 425
stir-fried gai lan with sesame 425
stir-fried lamb in black bean sauce 170
stir-fried sweet and sour vegetables 430
stir-fried vegetables with cracked black pepper 421
stone fruits, poached pork with chilli 291
strainer, small 467
strainer, tempura 467
sugar 477
sukiyaki 169
summer rolls, vietnamese
    coconut chicken 50
    pork and prawn 50
sushi
    rice 33
    salad 140
    tuna and cucumber mini maki 33
    vinegar 33
sweet and sour dipping sauce 413
sweet and sour duck with broccolini 173
sweet and sour tamarind pork 330
sweet and sour vegetables, stir-fried 430
sweet chilli dipping sauce 414
sweet chilli dressing 143, 307
sweet chilli peanut sauce 54
sweet chilli plum noodles with chicken 351
sweet chilli sauce 476
sweet-sour dressing 71, 124

T

tamari 477
tamarind 11, 352
    asian-spiced roasted pork belly 267

(*tamarind* continued)
    crisp duck with tamarind soy sauce 177
    crying tiger 76
    date and tamarind chutney 402
    pad thai 352
    samosas with tamarind sauce 30
    sauce 30
    sweet and sour tamarind pork 330
    tamarind and citrus pork curry 239
    tamarind duck stir-fry 194
    tamarind honey prawns with pineapple 185
tandoori chicken, spinach and mint salad with spiced yogurt 147
tandoori lamb with dhal and pickled lemon 276
tapioca 477
tat soi 11
    bang bang chicken salad 143
    spicy citrus prawn and tat soi salad 147
tea cup and strainer 469
tempura rack 467
tempura, seafood and vegetable 205
tempura strainer/spider 467
teriyaki sauce 476
    beef teriyaki platter 275
    ginger teriyaki beef 193
    spicy teriyaki tuna 37
    teriyaki pork with pineapple 284
thai basil 12
    chicken and thai basil fried rice 340
    chicken and thai basil stir-fry 169
    crisp twice-fried lamb with thai basil 178
    herb salad 288, 299
    mussels with basil and lemon grass 84

thai beef salad 136
thai chicken and lychee salad 135
thai dressing 139
thai eggplant see eggplant
thai pickle, chicken larb with 60
thai salad 260
thai spring rolls 22
thai-style duck salad 139
thai-style oysters 36
thai-style steamed chicken with
   noodles 307
tofu 12, 477
   curry, tofu and thai eggplant
      massaman 244
   mee krob 336
   salt and pepper tofu with
      chilli lime dressing 202
   sesame tofu salad 128
   soy-fried noodles with tofu 355
   stir-fried eggplant and tofu 425
tom yum goong 102
tomato
   aloo gobi 422
   chilli beef and vegetables with
      noodles 201
   dhal and paneer vegetable
      curry 375
   kasaundi 406
   keema with green chilli and 333
   nasi goreng 355
   rice 375
   thai beef salad 136
   tomato and onion raita 18
treacle 477
tropical fruit salad with cardamom 442
tropical fruit skewers with coconut
   dressing 450
tropical fruit trifle 449
trout, kaffir lime and lemon grass
   grilled 275

trout, ocean, in baby buk choy
   parcels 300
tuna 476
   green mango and seared tuna
      salad 127
   grilled tuna wtih japanese chilled
      soba salad 271
   japanese-style tuna with
      chilli-daikon 63
   mixed sashimi 79
   spicy teriyaki tuna 37
   tuna and cucumber mini maki 33
   tuna skewers with soba 255
turmeric 12
turnip, preserved 475
   pad thai 352
   vegetarian pad thai 340

U

udon 474 *see also noodles*
   japanese seafood hotpot 310
   sukiyaki 169
   udon noodle soup 109

V

vanilla bean 477
vanilla extract 477
veal, dressing for, 398
vegetable biryani, spiced 344
vegetable dhanksak 322
vegetable dumplings in asian
   broth 110
vegetable gow gees with miso
   dipping sauce 46
vegetable laksa 114
vegetable oil 475
vegetable yellow curry 240

vegetables
   cantonese, steamed snapper
      with 303
   coconut milk, in 313
   grilled asian 426
   sichuan-style 418
   spiced vegetable biryani 344
   stir-fried sweet and sour 430
   stir-fried with cracked black
      pepper 421
vegetarian pad thai 340
vermicelli see noodles
vietnamese beef curry, aromatic 227
vietnamese carrot pickle 406
vietnamese chicken salad 144
vietnamese chicken spring rolls 42
vietnamese dressing 144
vietnamese mint 12 *see also mint*
vietnamese summer rolls
   coconut chicken 50
   pork and prawn 50
vindaloo 472
   pork 240
vinegar 477
   soy vinegar sauce 41
   sushi vinegar 33

W

wakame broth, chicken in citrus 105
wasabi 13
   mirin and wasabi dressing 140
water chestnuts 13
watercress and snow pea salad,
   sichuan duck with 283
wok 467
wok chan 467
wok ladle 467
wok lid, high-domed 467
wok ring 467

wombok 13
　　crisp pork belly with wombok
　　　　salad 132
　　fried noodles with sausage and
　　　　wombok 364
　　green mango salad on
　　　　betel leaves 25
　　japanese-style duck with wombok
　　　　and daikon salad 256
　　ravioli with asian greens 117
　　sichuan eggplant, almond and
　　　　wombok stir-fry 433
wonton
　　chinese wonton soup 90
　　coconut chicken salad in crisp
　　　　wonton cups 49
　　money bags 34
　　ravioli with asian greens 117
　　seafood wontons with sesame
　　　　dressing 63
　　spicy butterflied prawns on
　　　　crisp wontons 29
　　vegetable dumplings in asian
　　　　broth 110
　　wrappers 477

X
xacutti 247

Y
yakitori, chicken, with sesame
　　dipping sauce 75
yellow coconut rice 387
yellow curry 472
　　paste 248
　　seafood and thai eggplant 216
　　vegetable 240

yogurt 477
　　herb 284
　　honey and cardamom 441
　　lime pickle 271
　　lychees with passionfruit 461
　　mango chutney 223
　　raita see raita
　　spiced 147, 252

Z
zucchini 477
　　mixed vegetables in coconut
　　　　milk 313
　　seafood and vegetable tempura
　　　　205
　　sichuan-style vegetables 418
　　spiced vegetable biryani 344
　　stir-fried asian greens in black bean
　　　　sauce 426

Conversion chart

MEASURING EQUIPMENT
The difference between one country's measuring cups and another's is within a 2 or 3 teaspoon range. Metric measures in Australia: 1 cup holds (approximately) 250ml, 1 tablespoon holds 20ml and 1 teaspoon holds 5ml. North America, NZ and the UK use 15ml tablespoons.

HOW TO MEASURE
The most accurate way of measuring dry ingredients is to weigh them. When using graduated metric measuring cups, shake dry ingredients loosely into the appropriate cup. Do not tap the cup on a bench or tightly pack the ingredients unless directed to do so. Level top of measuring cups and spoons with a knife. When measuring liquids, place a clear glass or plastic jug with metric markings on a flat surface to check accuracy at eye level.
We use large eggs having an average weight of 60g.

OVEN TEMPERATURES
These oven temperatures are only a guide for conventional ovens. For fan-forced ovens, check the manufacturer's manual.

	°C (CELSIUS)	°F (FAHRENHEIT)	GAS MARK
Very slow	120	250	½
Slow	150	275-300	1-2
Moderately slow	160	325	3
Moderate	180	350-375	4-5
Moderately hot	200	400	6
Hot	220	425-450	7-8
Very hot	240	475	9

DRY MEASURES

METRIC	IMPERIAL
15g	½oz
30g	1oz
60g	2oz
90g	3oz
125g	4oz (¼lb)
155g	5oz
185g	6oz
220g	7oz
250g	8oz (½lb)
280g	9oz
315g	10oz
345g	11oz
375g	12oz (¾lb)
410g	13oz
440g	14oz
470g	15oz
500g	16oz (1lb)
750g	24oz (1½lb)
1kg	32oz (2lb)

LIQUID MEASURES

METRIC	IMPERIAL
30ml	1 fluid oz
60ml	2 fluid oz
100ml	3 fluid oz
125ml	4 fluid oz
150ml	5 fluid oz (¼ pint/1 gill)
190ml	6 fluid oz
250ml	8 fluid oz
300ml	10 fluid oz (½ pint)
500ml	16 fluid oz
600ml	20 fluid oz (1 pint)
1000ml (1 litre)	1¾ pints

LENGTH MEASURES

METRIC	IMPERIAL
3mm	⅛in
6mm	¼in
1cm	½in
2cm	¾in
2.5cm	1in
5cm	2in
6cm	2½in
8cm	3in
10cm	4in
13cm	5in
15cm	6in
18cm	7in
20cm	8in
23cm	9in
25cm	10in
28cm	11in
30cm	12in (1ft)